PC Techniques

C/C++ Power Tools®

PC Techniques C/C++ Power Tools®

HAX, Techniques, and Hidden Knowledge

Jeff Duntemann
Keith Weiskamp

BANTAM BOOKS
NEW YORK • TORONTO • LONDON • SYDNEY • AUCKLAND

PC Techniques C/C++ Power Tools®
A Bantam Book / November 1992

Designed and produced by The Coriolis Group.

ISBN 0-553-37126-6

Published simultaneously in the United States and Canada.

Bantam Books are published by Bantam Books, a division of Bantam Doubleday Dell Publishing Group, Inc. Its trademark, consisting of the words "Bantam Books" and the portrayal of a rooster, is Registered in U.S. Patent and Trademark Office and in other countries. Marca Registrada, Bantam Books, 666 Fifth Avenue, New York, New York 10103.

PRINTED IN THE UNITED STATES OF AMERICA

0 9 8 7 6 5 4 3 2 1

Contents

Introduction

Some ideas turn up because you have gaps in your knowledge. The idea for this book came up, ultimately, because there were holes in my magazine.

Back in 1988, I was in charge of a programmer's magazine called *TURBO TECHNIX*, published by Borland International. The magazine was well-received and garnered a lot of goodwill for the company. It died when the advertising equation consistently came up on the wrong side of zero. That was later. In mid-1988 we were redesigning the layout for the November/December issue. It was full of holes.

You see, it's no mean feat to take 160 pages, lay out articles, ads, tables of contents, and get everything to fit exactly, with no bulges, no gaps, and nothing left on the light table. You either spend a lot of time snipping text and squeezing photos and drawings, or you learn to live with holes. Our art director did not like holes, and I didn't like all that snipping and fitting. There isn't a lot of fat to trim in an article about linked lists. It's not as though we were *Soap Opera Digest*. If you snip, most of the time, you lose content.

So I had an idea to create small, variable-sized articles designed specifically to fill holes, have people write them in every size from a single page down to a handful of lines, and keep a drawerful of them around at all times. That way, if a hole of any given size turned up while we were assembling an issue, we'd always have something to drop into it.

In a fit of inspiration, I wrote a couple and called them HAX. The art director loved them. We began accumulating them for the eventual construction of the November/December issue. Then, in September, while the issue was being put together, HAX and all, Borland decided it had fished long enough for nonexistent advertising revenue and decided to cut bait.

It took me a year, but I put another magazine together, this time in partnership with author Keith Weiskamp. When the first issue of *PC TECHNIQUES* appeared in March of 1990, the HAX were there, but there was a significant difference. They weren't just hole fillers. They were a major feature of the magazine. And when the magazine hit the streets, people went absolutely nuts over them.

As near as I can tell, there are large topics that should be books, smaller topics that should be magazine articles, and even smaller topics that should be . . . well . . . HAX. Those smaller topics simply weren't being covered in the other magazines. In just a handful of issues, our HAX had evolved to a body of knowledge that just wasn't available anywhere else. Other magazines either didn't mind holes or snipped them out entirely. In short order, we had hundreds of HAX, either in print or waiting to be printed, with more coming in all the time. From there it was no great leap of imagination to propose a collection of our tips, tricks, and "hidden knowledge"—programming arcana dredged from the depths of the PC and not generally known—to be made into a full-length book.

Some of the material in the book has been reprinted from the pages of *PC TECHNIQUES*, including a lot of HAX and short articles from early issues that are no longer available. We thought it was important that latecomers still be able to access this information and have it on their shelves when the need might arise. But a great many of these HAX are appearing here for the first time.

Before wrapping up, I want to call attention to a few of the many people who helped bring this project to reality. Keith and I shepherded it along—*especially* Keith—and our names are on the cover, but the measure of teamwork that went into the book's creation was seriously awesome. Martin Waldron did all of the tech edits on the new material; with his able hands he helped smooth out the seams between the hundred-and-fifty odd "moving parts" that came together. Without his help and fine editorial craftsmanship, there would be no book. Robin Watkins handled editorial and production management (no small task when well over a hundred individual styles are at work). Jean Davis Taft at Bantam helped us produce a first-rate book. Brad Grannis, assisted by Barbara Nicholson, did much of the layouts and illustrations. Lenity Himburg created the index. Additional thanks go to Robin for handling the paperwork involved in letting a hundred authors know that they were being published, and paying them. Finally, we would like to thank Steve Guty, our fantastic editor at Bantam, and the many talented writers who contributed their best for this book.

We hope to produce additional books like this in the future. Lord knows, there's no shortage of material. What would you like to see? Drop me a note and let me know. And if you liked what you saw here, why not tune in to *PC TECHNIQUES*? We publish practical how-it-works and how-to-do-it material every other month, like clockwork. See the coupon at the back of this book for details.

And whatever else you do, keep hacking!

Jeff Duntemann KG7JF
Scottsdale, Arizona
September 1992

1

Identifying and Accessing the Hardware

Sometimes we, as programmers, forget that there was hardware before there was software, especially given the university community's attitude toward portability: the notion that hardware is "unclean" and should be suppressed beneath as many insulating layers of "virtual machine" as can be done before performance grinds to a glacial halt.

What a joke.

Rather than build layers over all machines to make them all look alike (and in doing so end up with a least common denominator that does none of them justice), we should choose one hardware platform, learn everything possible about it, and create software that makes the most of it.

To do this, you have to understand how the hardware works, and create software that identifies what hardware is installed in a given system. That done, we have to tread a thin line between taking control of the hardware in dangerous ways or ways that dilute the value of working standards—and making the machine work as quickly and as effectively as possible.

In this first chapter our authors explain how to identify installed hardware, and how to access it directly. (This, along with odd tips on hardware quirks encountered along the way.) The judgment required to use information like this safely and effectively—well, you pick it up as you go. One of my favorite enhancements brought to the PC world by the much-maligned "clone" machines is the front-panel reset switch. To err is human. To reboot—finally—is easy.

Locating Disk Drives

■ Deborah L. Cooper

Here's a useful utility to help you search for all drives attached to a PC.

Several years ago, I wrote a file-finding program in assembly language. Although many similar programs were readily available at the time (and still are), I was doing it for the pure fun of it just as an exercise in recursive programming.

But just recently, I was thinking of modifying this program to have it automatically search all disk drives attached to the computer system for the specified file or files. The routine I came up with is shown in Listing 1.1. The file DRIVES.ASM is a demonstration program that displays the message "Valid drive: #" as it methodically and quickly seeks out all disk drives attached to the system.

The method used to accomplish this feat is simple. You begin by saving the currently logged drive so that you can restore it after testing. The test itself is a loop through possible drive letters beginning with A. Using Function 0EH, Select New Drive, you set the current drive to the next drive letter in the sequence. To determine if this drive exists, you call Function 19H, the Get Default Drive function. If the system has been set to a legitimate default drive, registers DL and AL will be equal on return from the DOS call, indicating that the drive does in fact exist.

By looping through drive letters you can test for all valid drives between the values 1 (A:) to 26 (Z:). Note that if your system contains gaps between drive specifiers (that is, if you have a drive F: but no drive D: or E:) this program will *not* find drives after the first gap it encounters.

CODE DESCRIPTION

Overview

The listing provided is used to search for all the drives attached to a PC.

Listing Available

Listing	*Description*	*Used with*
DRIVES.ASM	Assembly languge listing that performs the drives search operation.	------

How to Compile/Assemble

DRIVES.ASM can be assembled with any TASM-compatible assembler and turned into a .COM program by using either EXE2BIN or TLINK'S It option.

■ LISTING 1.1 DRIVES.ASM

```
;DRIVES.ASM
;(c) 1991 by Deborah L. Cooper
```

```
codesg  segment
        assume  cs:codesg
        org     100h            ;make this a COM program
start:  jmp     start_2         ;skip over data area

org_drive       db      0       ;current drive code
got_drive       db      0dh,0ah,'Valid drive: ','$' ;output msg

;Get and save the current drive so we can restore it later on
start_2:
        mov     ah,19h          ;get default drive code
        int     21h             ;call dos
        mov     org_drive,al    ;save it (0=A, 1=B, ... )
;Now go through 1-26 possible drive codes and display the
;message when we find a valid disk drive
select: mov     ah,0eh          ;select drive function
        mov     dl,0            ;start with Drive A
        int     21h             ;call dos
;Use function 19h to see if drive actually exists
select_2:
        mov     ah,19h          ;get default disk drive
        int     21h             ;call dos
        cmp     dl,al           ;is it a valid drive?
        je      got_one         ;yes, show the message!
next_drive:
        inc     dl              ;no, prepare to test next one
        cmp     dl,27d          ;maximum 26 possible!
        jae     all_done        ;go if done now
        mov     ah,0eh          ;select drive function
        int     21h             ;call dos
        jmp     select_2        ;and go back to test it
got_one:
        push    dx              ;save our drive number
        mov     dx,offset got_drive ;point DX to message
        mov     ah,09h          ;display string function
        int     21h             ;call dos
;Show the message with drive letter
        pop     dx              ;recover test drive code
        push    dx              ;save on stack for a minute
        xchg    al,dl           ;put drive code in AL for printing
        add     al,41h          ;convert to ASCII letter
        mov     ah,0eh          ;display byte function
        int     10h             ;call bios
        pop     dx              ;recover our drive number
        jmp     next_drive      ;and go back
;Now restore our original drive and exit
all_done:
        mov     ah,0eh          ;select drive function
        mov     dl,org_drive    ;original drive code
        int     21h             ;call dos
        mov     ah,4ch          ;terminate program function
        int     21h             ;call dos
codesg  ends
        end     start           ;end of demo!
```

Simple CPU Detection

■ Nicholas Wilt

Here's a useful trick for detecting a PC's CPU.

Detecting the exact CPU model from software is complicated and error-prone. This is because many CPU detection routines insist on minute detail: Am I running on an 8088, they ask, or a NEC V20? Is it an 80386SX or an 80386DX? The problem is a difficult one, and it is only going to get more so as the family of Intel and Intel-compatible processors grows.

Fortunately, you don't always have to know the exact model of CPU you are running on. From a software standpoint, you really need only classify it as pre-286, 80286, or 80386. If you're running on a pre-286 machine, you're in for no fun at all—no extended instructions, no 32-bit registers. If you're running on a 286 or better, you can use an extended instruction set, including **PUSH** immediate, **INS** (input string), and **OUTS** (output string). If you're running on a 386 or better, you can use 32-bit registers and a still more extended instruction set (including **SET** on condition). You can write the most highly optimized code by taking advantage of the facilities available in silicon.

Listing 1.2 shows a brief assembler function that returns the CPU type. If the computer has a pre-286 CPU (including the 8086, 8088, V20, and V30), the function returns 0. If the CPU is an 80286, it returns 1. If the CPU is a 386-class machine, it returns 2. Listing 1.3 is the C test program, and Listing 1.4 is the simple batch file used to create the test program. The batch file makes certain assumptions about your directory structure; check it before you try it.

The function takes no arguments, so adapting it to run with various programming languages and calling conventions should be simple. Just change the **.MODEL** directive at the beginning of the assembler file to reflect the other compiler's memory model.

CODE DESCRIPTION

Overview

The C and ASM listings provided are written to detect the class of CPU running on a PC—8086, 80286, or 80386.

Listings Available

Listing	*Description*	*Used with*
CPUTEST.C	C test program that uses the assembly language processor detect function.	CPUTYPE.ASM
CPUTYPE.ASM	Contains the low-level function **cputype** that determines the class of processor available.	------
MAKECPU.BAT	Batch file to assemble, compile, and link the above source files with Borland C++.	------

How to Compile/Assemble

Use the batch file or assemble and compile the source files separately with Borland C++ and TASM. If you use the batch file, you may need to modify it to support your directory configuration.

■ LISTING 1.2 CPUTYPE.ASM

```
.MODEL LARGE,C
.386
.CODE
; cputype: function returns 0 if 8088 family
;         1 if 80286 family
;         2 if 80386 or better
; No arguments.
; Returns value in AX.
        PUBLIC cputype

cputype PROC
xor     dx,dx                   ; Assume 8086 for now
push    dx                      ; flags <- 0
popf                            ;
pushf                           ; Get flags back
pop     ax                      ;
and     ax,0f000h               ; If the top 4 bits are set,
cmp     ax,0f000h               ;
je      quitcputype             ; return.  It's an 8086.
inc     dx                      ; It's at least an 80286.
push    0F000h                  ; flags <- 0F000h
popf                            ;
pushf                           ; Get flags back
pop     ax                      ;
and     ax,0F000h               ; If the top 4 bits aren't set,
jz      quitcputype             ; it's an 80286
inc     dx                      ; Otherwise it's a 386 or better
quitcputype:
xchg    ax,dx                   ; Return value in AX
ret                             ; Return
cputype ENDP

END
```

■ LISTING 1.3 CPUTEST.C

```
/*cputest.c: Tests the cputype() function.  Prints message
 * telling the results.
 */

#include <stdio.h>
int cputype(void);
```

```
main()
{
  printf("cputype detects an ");
  switch (cputype()) {
    case 0:
      printf("8086.  I sympathize.\n");
      break;
    case 1:
      printf("80286.  You\'re getting there!\n");
      break;
    case 2:
      printf("80386.  You\'re cookin\'!");
      break;
  }
}
```

■ LISTING 1.4 MAKECPU.BAT

```
tcc  -I\TC\INCLUDE -ml -v -c cputest.c
tasm /mx/zi cputype.asm
tlink /v/c/map \tc\lib\c0l test cputype,cputest.exe,,\tc\lib\emu \tc\lib\cl
\tc\lib\mathl
```

An I/O Port Class in C++

■ Kevin Dean

Here's a useful header file you can include with your C++ programs to use objects for I/O port access.

Unlike Turbo C's **inport()** and **outport()** functions, Turbo Pascal's **Port** and **PortW** arrays are an intuitive way to address hardware ports. Although the following two lines of code are functionally the same

```
outportb(0x3F8, data);  /* Turbo C */
Port[$3F8] := Data;     { Turbo Pascal }
```

(they both transmit a byte from COM1), the latter is closer to the notion that ports are objects that can be read and written in much the same way as memory.

The key word here is *objects*, and with Turbo C++ we can encapsulate the **inportb()** and **outportb()** functions in a class with even more functionality than Turbo Pascal's **Port** and **PortW** arrays (see Listing 1.5).

TIP: The **const** modifier for a class member function means that the function does not modify any member of the class. Any attempt to modify the **_addr** member in a **const** function or to call a non-**const** function for a **const** object would generate a compiler error or warning.

Because some ports are used as bit masks (e.g., the modem control register of a COM port controls interrupts and certain line signals), the operators **|=**, **&=**, and **^=** have all been defined to simplify bit manipulation. Also, many devices use an array of ports instead of just one port and have one port defined as the base (e.g., 0x3F8 for COM1). The operator **[](int index)** defined in the **bytePort** class simplifies access to port arrays by accessing the port at **_addr+index**. For example,

```
char data;
bytePort com1(0x3F8);      // Base port of COM1
com1 = data;               // Transmit byte
com1[4] |= 0x08;           // Turn on interrupts
data = com1;               // Receive byte
```

This declares a port object for COM1, transmits a byte of data, turns on interrupts through the modem control register (at offset 4 or address 0x3F8 + 4 = 0x3FC), and receives a byte of data.

To simulate Turbo Pascal's **PortW** array, copy the **bytePort** class definition, rename it to **wordPort**, and replace all instances of the type **byte** with the type **word**.

CODE DESCRIPTION

Overview

The header file provided can be used to support C++ I/O port classes. Use this header file with any C++ program that needs to read or write data to an I/O port.

Listing Available

Listing	*Description*	*Used with*
PORTS.H	A C++ header file that contains class definitions for accessing I/O ports.	------

How to Compile/Assemble

Include PORTS.H in a C++ program by using the **#include** directive.

■ LISTING 1.5 PORTS.H

```
// Get prototypes for inport and outport functions.
#include <dos.h>

typedef unsigned char byte;
typedef unsigned short word;

// Byte port.
class bytePort {
  word _addr;    // Port address

  public:

  // Constructors and destructor
```

```
bytePort(word addr) : _addr(addr) { }
bytePort(const bytePort &p) : _addr(p._addr) { }
bytePort() { }
~bytePort() { }

// Set port address
void addr(word addr) {
_addr = addr;
}

// Get port address
word addr() const {
return _addr;
}

// Read byte value from port
operator byte() const {
return inportb(_addr);
}

// Write byte value to port
bytePort& operator=(byte value) const {
outportb(_addr, value);
return *this;
}

// Set bits at port
bytePort& operator|=(byte value) const {
outportb(_addr, inportb(_addr) | value);
return *this;
}

// Mask bits at port
bytePort& operator&=(byte value) const {
outportb(_addr, inportb(_addr) & value);
return *this;
}

// Toggle bits at port
bytePort& operator^=(byte value) const {
outportb(_addr, inportb(_addr) ^ value);
return *this;
}

// Copy value from one port to another
bytePort& operator=(const bytePort& p) const {
outportb(_addr, inportb(p._addr));
return *this;
}

// Treat port as base of an array of ports
bytePort operator[](int index) const {
return _addr + index;
}
};
```

Mylex 386 Motherboards and Bus Mice

■ Jeff Duntemann

Here's a hardware hax for setting up a Mylex 386 motherboard.

To beef up performance on their MX-series 386 motherboards, Mylex jumpered the AT bus DRAM refresh signal so as to remove it from the bus by default. Theoretically this shouldn't matter, since all 32-bit DRAM is on a separate, proprietary bus socket unrelated to the standard AT bus.

Unfortunately, there are AT bus cards that *do* require the DRAM refresh signal, even though they don't contain any DRAM. Most common of these are the bus-mouse interface boards sold by Microsoft, Logitech, and other companies as an alternative to serial-port mice. The bus-mouse driver software will not load without the DRAM refresh signal on the bus. The resulting error message complains of a missing interrupt jumper, but in fact what has happened is that the interrupting *signal*—the DRAM refresh signal—is missing, as though the interrupt selection jumper block had been removed entirely from the mouse controller board.

The solution to the problem is to pull the shorting block from the Mylex motherboard jumper J4. With the block removed from J4, the DRAM refresh signal is returned to the AT bus, and the mouse interface board will work normally. The price to be paid is in performance: On my motherboard, the Landmark CPU Speed Test reported 41.0 before the J4 block was pulled, and 37.8 after. If you don't need a bus mouse—or some other peripheral that depends on the DRAM refresh signal—you can retain those few extra performance points.

Certainly, if you encounter an add-in board that refuses to work in a Mylex MX motherboard, try pulling the J4 shorting block before doing anything else—like panicking.

Who's on Second? Identifying the Second Video Adapter

■ Bob Falk

Making use of the second screen in a dual monitor environment is a neat trick—but first you have to find it!

Few things are more frustrating than purchasing a program that failed to take advantage of the little extras on your computer. You knew the program should benefit from the megabytes of EMS memory and the coprocessor you installed—at no small expense—but alas, the program refused to tap into the extra power available to it.

Likewise, you want the software that you produce to take advantage of everything available to it. When software started taking advantage of extra memory, users began buying extra memory. When 80386-specific software became more available, sales of 80386-based machines increased. There is one hardware add-on that is rarely recognized or used by software today—a second video adapter. Perhaps that great new idea of yours will make dual display systems as indispensable as hard disks.

Types of Video

Before you can take advantage of a second video display, you must find out if one is present. You'll now learn how to detect and identify the video systems installed in IBM PCs and compatibles. The most common video adapter types are listed in Table 1.1. They are the ones you should be able to detect from within your programs.

Videos in Combination

You can't just stick any combination of two video adapters into a computer and expect them to coexist peacefully. Even among the allowable combinations of video adapters, you must still be careful to avoid video modes that cause the two adapters to fight over the same video memory addresses.

Figure 1.1 illustrates the allowable combinations of the common video adapters. A general rule of thumb is that the two video subsystems must be opposites. If one is color compatible, the other must be monochrome compatible, and vice versa. This is to avoid video memory conflicts arising from two adapters attempting to share the same memory addresses.

Downward Compatibility

Downward compatibility was an important concern as each new video adapter was introduced. New video adapters, while adding new capabilities, were expected to retain support for the features of their predecessors. This downward compatibility requirement results in some well-known problems, such as flaky cursor emulation. But, it also helps make it easier to determine which adapter type is installed.

TIP: For more information about how to work with cursor emulation, see "What Cursor?" in Chapter 4.

■ TABLE 1.1 Types of video adapters

Adapter	Label
Monochrome Display Adapter	(MDA)
Color Graphics Adapter	(CGA)
Enhanced Graphics Adapter	(EGA)
Multi-Color Graphics Array	(MCGA)
Video Graphics Array	(VGA)
Hercules Graphics Card	(HGC)
Hercules Graphics Card Plus	(HGC+)
Hercules InColor Card	(InColor)
IBM 8514/A adapter	(8514/A)
IBM Professional Graphics Controller	(PGA)
Indigenous Display Controller	(6300 CGA)

	MDA	MGA	EGA	PGA	MCGA	VGA	8514/A	HGC	HGC+	InColor	6300CGA
MDA		XXX	XXX	XXX	XXX	XXX	XXX				XXX
CGA	XXX		XXX					XXX	XXX	XXX	
EGA	XXX	XXX			XXX			XXX	XXX	XXX	XXX
PGA	XXX					XXX		XXX	XXX	XXX	
MCGA	XXX		XXX			XXX	XXX	XXX	XXX	XXX	
VGA	XXX			XXX	XXX		XXX	XXX	XXX	XXX	
8514/A	XXX				XXX	XXX		XXX	XXX	XXX	
HGC		XXX	XXX	XXX	XXX	XXX	XXX				XXX
HGC+		XXX	XXX	XXX	XXX	XXX	XXX				XXX
InColor		XXX	XXX	XXX	XXX	XXX	XXX				XXX
6300 CGA	XXX		XXX					XXX	XXX	XXX	

■ **FIGURE 1.1 The allowable combinations of adapters**

Another consequence of downward compatibility is the I/O ports used by the various video adapters. MDA-compatible adapters use ports 3B0h-3BFh, EGA-compatible adapters use 3C0h–3CFh, and CGAs use 3D0–3DFh. By using different I/O ports, these adapters do not conflict with one another. We will make use of this property in our adapter detection routines.

The essential approach in identifying the type of video adapter(s) in use is to start at the top and work your way down in a process of elimination. Begin by trying a function only available with the newer generation of video systems. The BIOS video services will respond in a predictable manner if that function is not available. If the newer video services aren't available, step down to the next level until you encounter success with a known function. This route starts with VGA-type systems and moves to EGA, CGA, and then MDA.

To ensure accuracy you must be prepared to handle some special exceptions that require a little extra work. The trick is in knowing when to trust the information returned by the BIOS, and when to double check for yourself. Detecting the installed video hardware at first seems very complicated. It is an example of an algorithm that can be easily described using a flowchart as shown in Figure 1.2. The following information describes the implementation in more detail.

Function 1Ah as a Starting Place

When BIOS Int 10h, Function 1Ah, Subfunction 00h—Get Display Combination Code (DCC) is called, the return value tells us whether this function is supported. This function is supported on PS/2 machines and machines with VGA-type adapters installed. If function 01Ah is supported, the DCC value returned in BX actually tells us which adapters and monitors are available in the system. BL contains the DCC for the active display, and BH contains the DCC for the inactive display. The values in BL and BH are interpreted as shown in Table 1.2.

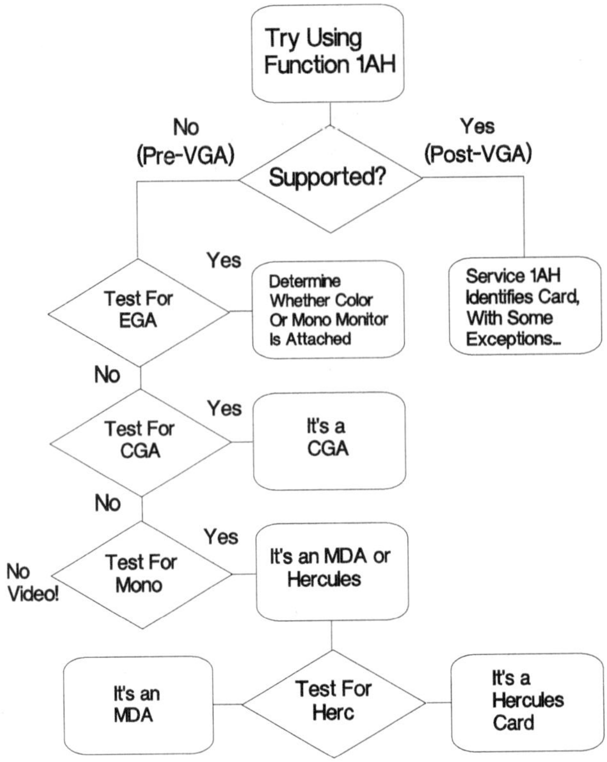

■ **FIGURE 1.2 The process of detecting the installed video hardware**

■ **TABLE 1.2 Return values from a successful function 1Ah call**

Value	Description
00h	Not installed
01h	MDA with monochrome display
02h	CGA with color display
03h	(reserved)
04h	EGA with hi-res (EGA) color (or gray-scale) display
05h	EGA with monochrome display
06h	hi-res (VGA) color (or gray-scale) display
07h	VGA with (VGA) monochrome display
08h	VGA with hi-res (VGA) color (or gray-scale) display
09h	(reserved)
0Ah	MCGA with hi-res (EGA) color (or gray-scale) display
0Bh	MCGA with (VGA) monochrome display
0Ch	MCGA with hi-res (VGA) color (or gray-scale) display
FFh	Unknown

Unfortunately, you can't always trust the information contained in the DCC. If the computer is a PS/2 model 30, the DCC may be incomplete. You can identify a PS/2 model 30 by checking the Machine ID byte at F000:FFFEh. A model 30 (or 25) will contain 0FAh at that memory location. There are two specific problems with the DCC on the PS/2 Model 30:

1. If the active video adapter is an MCGA, the inactive video adapter could be an EGA, but the DCC will not indicate it. So on a PS/2 model 30 with an MCGA as the active adapter, you must explicitly check for the presence of an EGA as the inactive adapter.
2. If the active video adapter is a VGA, then the inactive video adapter could be an MCGA; but again the DCC will fail to mention it. To be sure that both video systems are identified, you will need to check for the presence of an MCGA.

If the machine is not a PS/2 and neither a VGA nor MCGA is installed, AL will not contain the value 1Ah. In this case, you will need to explicitly check for an EGA, CGA, and MDA.

TIP: To get a closer look at how you can explicitly check for an EGA, CGA, or MDA hardware examine the **CheckPS2BIOS** routine in VIDEOID.ASM. (See listings diskette.)

You can tell if an MCGA is installed by checking for the presence of the 6845 CRTC (Cathode Ray Tube Controller) at port 3D4h. This same port is used by CGA adapters as well, but, because this check is performed only under the special case involving the PS/2 model 30, you will already know that the adapter is not a CGA (the DCC would have been correct if a CGA were present). Therefore the presence of the CRTC at port 3D4h can only indicate an MCGA. The type of display attached to the MCGA will be the opposite of the one attached to the VGA (active) adapter. In other words, if the active display is monochrome, the inactive will be color, and vice versa.

8514/A

IBM's 8514/A is gaining in popularity among PS/2 users and provides greater capabilities than the VGA. However, it is designed for IBM's MCA-bus machines and will not work in clones with an ISA or EISA architecture.

If either adapter is identified as a VGA, you should check to see if it is actually an 8514/A. Checking for the presence of an 8514/A is done by attempting to modify the Error Term Register at I/O port 92E8h. First, reset the 8514/A hardware by sending the value 9000h to port 42E8h. Next, reenable sync between the pixel chip and the CRT chip by sending the value 5000h to the same port. Finally, save the contents of the Error Term Register at port 92E8h, and try to change its contents (being sure to restore the original contents). If you are able to change the register contents, an 8514/A is installed. To see how this is done, see the **Check8514A** routine in VIDEOID.ASM. (See listings diskette.)

EGA Check

You can check for an EGA using Int 10h, Function 12h, Subfunction 10h—Get Configuration Information. Because this function is also available with the VGA, be sure to use this method only after you know that a VGA is not present (i.e., after trying function 1Ah). If an EGA is not installed, the Get Configuration Information function will return with BL still containing 10h. You will then have to explicitly check for an MDA or CGA.

If an EGA is installed, the display type is returned in BH (0 = color, 1 = monochrome). The EGA dip switch settings are returned in CL. The dip switch settings will vary depending on whether the EGA is set up as the primary or secondary display adapter. The bitmap for the value in CL is interpreted in Table 1.3.

Dividing the decimal value returned in CL by 2 provides the following translation values:

0 = Low-res (CGA) color display
1 = Hi-res (EGA) color (or gray-scale) display
2 = Monochrome display
3 = Low-res (CGA) color display
4 = Hi-res (EGA) color (or gray-scale) display
5 = Monochrome display

Of course, if the DIP switches are not correctly set, the information will be inaccurate. If an EGA is present and is the active adapter, you will still want to check for the presence of

■ TABLE 1.3 DIP switch settings for the EGA

If the EGA is the primary adapter:

SW4	SW3	SW2	SW1	Display type	Decimal value
0	1	1	0	CGA	6
0	1	1	1	CGA	7
1	0	0	0	EGA	8
1	0	0	1	EGA	9
1	0	1	0	MDA	10
1	0	1	1	MDA	11

If the EGA is the secondary adapter:

SW4	SW3	SW2	SW1	Display type	Decimal value
0	0	0	0	CGA	0
0	0	0	1	CGA	1
0	0	1	0	EGA	2
0	0	1	1	EGA	3
0	1	0	0	MDA	4
0	1	0	1	MDA	5

DIP switch settings: (1 = off, 0 = on)

a second (inactive) adapter. If the EGA display is color, you should check for an MDA; if the EGA display is monochrome, you should check for a CGA.

Is It CGA or MDA?

Checking for either an MDA or CGA is done by looking for the 6845 CRTC at the appropriate I/O port. For an MDA use port 3B4h. For a CGA use port 3D4h, same as the MCGA. Send the value 0Fh to the specified I/O port, telling the CRTC that you intend to access the Cursor Location Low Register (register 0Fh). Use the next higher I/O port to access the register (3B5h on MDAs, 3D5h on CGAs). First, save the value currently in that register, then try to change it. If you are able to change the value, the CRTC is present at that port address. Be sure to restore the register to the original value when you are done.

TIP: Adapters such as the Hercules Color card (*not to be confused with the InColor card*) will be identified as a CGA.

Telling Hercules from MDA

The BIOS will not differentiate between an ordinary MDA and a monochrome Hercules adapter. If you determine that an MDA adapter is installed, you should establish whether it is a Hercules card, and which one. Hercules cards can be distinguished from ordinary MDA adapters by the Vertical Sync bit (bit 7) of the CRT Status Byte (see Figure 1.3). The CRT Status Register is located at I/O port 3BAh. This bit changes on Hercules cards but does not change on ordinary MDA adapters.

TIP: To see how the Vertical Sync bit (bit 7) of the CRT Status Byte is used, see the **Check4MDAorHerc** routine in VIDEOID.ASM. (See Listings Diskette.)

Once you have determined that the adapter is a Hercules card, determining which Hercules card is a snap. If bits 4–6 in the CRT Status Register are clear (0), it's a plain old HGC card. If bit 4 is set (1) then it's an HGC Plus. If bits 4 and 6 are set, it's an InColor card.

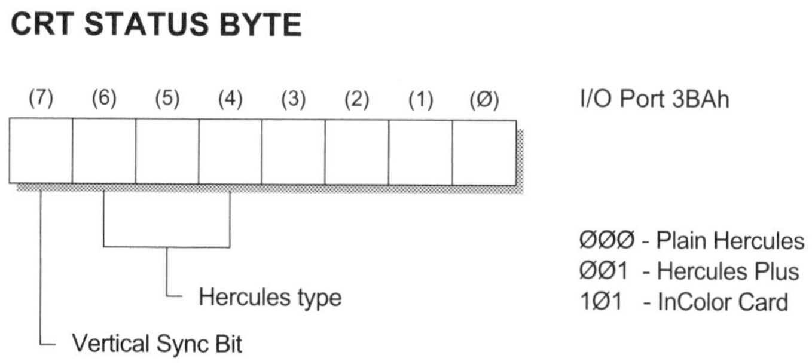

■ **FIGURE 1.3 Hercules detection**

Some Special Cases—The Olivetti Maneuver

Another adapter, once produced by Olivetti, is a modified CGA that came standard in the AT&T 6300, Xerox 6060, and some Compaq portables. For some reason, it was called the Indigenous *Display Controller Board*. The Olivetti-modified CGA allows a program to write directly to the screen without regard for the vertical retrace "snow" problem of a regular CGA.

This modified CGA was also available with a *Display Enhancement Board*. If you determine that a CGA adapter is installed, you may want to consider the possibility that it is actually an Olivetti-modified CGA (found in the AT&T 6300, Xerox 6060, and some Compaq portables). If the word "OLIVETTI" is present at ROM address FC05:0000, then you will also want to consider the possibility that a Display Enhancement Board is installed.

With the Olivetti-modified CGAs, bit 5 of the CRT Status Register at port 3DAh will always be set (see Figure 1.4). If bit 4 is set, then it's connected to a monochrome display; otherwise it's connected to a color display. To determine if a Display Enhancement Board is installed, use bits 6 and 7 of the CRT Status Register. These bits will normally be set when the Olivetti CGA is present, but will be clear when the Display Enhancement Board is installed.

Now, Which One Is Active?

At this point you have identified the adapter/monitor combinations installed in the machine. The only detail left is to determine which video system is the currently active one. That's the easy part. Find the current video mode using Int 10h, Function 0Fh—Get Video Mode. If the current video mode is a color mode, the color system must be the active system; if it's a monochrome mode then the monochrome system must be the active system. Of course, if you have determined that only one video subsystem is present, then it must be the active one.

Not a Finite Science

Unfortunately, detecting the installed video hardware is not a finite science. There will always be exceptions based on new adapters introduced in the future, vendor-specific extensions, etc. One example is the Compaq SLT/286 laptop, which can use its built-in LCD screen, or it can be connected to an external display. The internal screen is always

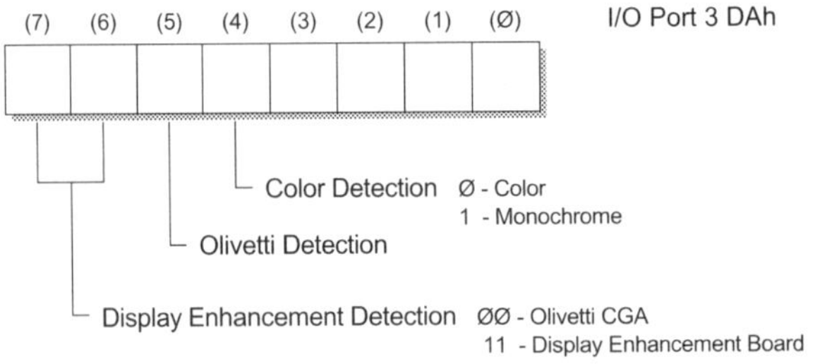

■ **FIGURE 1.4 Olivetti detection**

gray-scale, but the external display could be monochrome or color. Compaq provides an extension to the video BIOS that allows you to determine whether the internal or external display is in use and, if external, what type of display it is. (By the way, this is done through Interrupt 10h, function BFh, subfunction 03h.)

As you've undoubtedly noticed, it's extremely difficult to cover every possible combination of video subsystems. However, being able to identify the vast majority of common (and not so common) adapter/monitor combinations will promote customer confidence in your products. That's what makes all this effort worthwhile.

About the Listings

The assembly language routines in VIDEOID.ASM (included on disk) will detect and identify both video adapters and monitors. It can be assembled using OPTASM, TASM, or MASM, and is designed to be interfaced in Large memory model; but you can change this to suit your needs. Listings 1.6 and 1.7 contain the code for the C header files. Listing 1.8 contains the source code for VIDEOID.C, a C module which uses the assembly language routines. Listing 1.9 provides a small sample program that demonstrates the use of the VIDEOID routines. Listing VIDSTUFF.INC (included on disk) is the assembly language include file used with VIDEOID.ASM.

CODE DESCRIPTION

Overview

The listings provided can be used to detect which video adapters are installed in your PC. To run the demo program, VIDDEMO.C, you'll need to compile the C programs, assemble the assembly language listing, and link the two together.

Listings Available

Listing	*Description*	*Used with*
VIDEOID.H	Header file that defines the structures used to detect adapter and monitor types.	VIDEO.C VIDDEMO.C
VIDEO.H	Header file that defines the function prototypes for the video detection functions.	VIDEO.C VIDDEMO.C
VIDEO.C	Main source file that contains video detection functions.	------
VIDDEMO.C	Sample program that demonstrates how some of the video functions work.	------
VIDEOID.ASM	The library of low-level video detection functions (included on disk).	VIDEO.C
VIDSTUFF.INC	Include file used with VIDEOID.ASM.	VIDEOID.ASM

How to Compile/Assemble

- The VIDEO.C and VIDDEMO.C files can be compiled with Borland C++. Make sure the header files VIDEOID.H and VIDEO.H can be located by the compiler.
- VIDEOID.ASM can be assembled using OPTASM, TASM, or MASM. It is designed to be interfaced in Large Memory Model, but you can change this to suit your needs.

Note: If you want to add additional detection features, you'll need to add the detection code to VIDEOID.ASM. You'll also need to update VIDSTUFF.INC and VIDEOID.H.

Tip: When using Borland C++ for these files, make sure that "treat enums as int" is turned *off*.

■ LISTING 1.6 VIDEOID.H

```
/*VideoID.H*/
/*Implemented in VIDEOID.ASM*/

typedef enum  {NotInstalled,   /* only when 1 adapter in system */
                 MDA,          /* Monochrome Display Adapter */
                 CGA,          /* Color Graphics Adapter */
                 EGA,          /* Enhanced Graphics Adapter */
                 PGA,          /* Professional Graphics Controller */
                 MCGA,         /* Multi-Color Graphics Array */
                 VGA,          /* Video Graphics Array */
                 A8514,        /* 8514/A Adapter (IBM) */
                 HGC,          /* Hercules Graphics Card */
                 HGCPlus,      /* Hercules Graphics Card Plus */
                 InColor,      /* Hercules InColor Card */
                 ATTCGA,       /* AT&T 6300 modified CGA */
                 ATTEnhCGA,    /* AT&T 6300 CGA with Enh. Board */
                 VidUnknown    /*  (just in case) */
                } AdapterType;
    typedef enum  {
               MTNone,         /* only when 1 adapter in system */
               MDADisplay,     /* Monochrome Only */
               CGADisplay,     /* Low-Res Color */
               EGAColorDisplay,/* Hi-Res Color or Gray-Scale */
               VGAMonoDisplay, /* Monochrome Only */
               VGAColorDisplay /* Hi-Res Color or Gray-Scale */
               } MonitorType;

typedef enum  {ColorMode,MonoMode} VideoModeType;

void IdentifyVideo(void);
  /* Initializes VideoRecord */

typedef struct _VideoSystemType {
                       AdapterType Adapter1;
                       MonitorType Monitor1;
                       AdapterType Adapter2;
                       MonitorType Monitor2;
                       } VideoSystemType;

extern VideoSystemType VideoRecord;

extern char IsOlivetti;
extern char IsCompaq;
```

■ LISTING 1.7 VIDEO.H

```
/*video.h*/
AdapterType GetAdapterType(char Current);
  /* Returns the primary (current) or secondary adapter type */

MonitorType GetMonitorType(char Current);
  /* Returns the primary (current) or secondary adapter type */

void UpdateVideo(void);
  /* Reinitializes the video adapter/monitor record.  Primarily   */
  /* useful on dual monitor systems.  When the current adapter/   */
  /* monitor may have been changed, you should call this routine  */
  /* to ensure that the video record is current.  If your program */
  /* is a TSR you should call this routine each time your program */
  /* is popped up.  Anytime you shell to DOS or EXEC another      */
  /* program you should call this routine upon return.            */

VideoModeType CurrentVideoMode(void);
  /* Returns the current video mode (color or mono) */
  /* Useful when initializing color variables */

void VideoInit(void);
  /* Initializes video functions and data structures */
  /* Should be called first before accessing other functions */
```

■ LISTING 1.8 VIDEO.C

```
/*video.c*/
#include <string.h>
#include <dos.h>
#include <stdlib.h>
#include "videoid.h"
#include "video.h"

char far *OlivettiSig;
/* Used to check for Olivetti BIOS, used in AT&T 6300 and Xerox 6060 */

char far *CompaqSig;
/* Used to check for Compaq signature */

AdapterType GetAdapterType(char Current)
{
  /* Returns the primary (current) or secondary adapter type */

 if (Current)
    return VideoRecord.Adapter1;
  else
    return VideoRecord.Adapter2;
}
/* Function GetAdapterType */

MonitorType GetMonitorType( char Current )
{
```

```
  /* Returns the primary (current) or secondary adapter type */

  if ( Current )
    return VideoRecord.Monitor1;
  else
    return VideoRecord.Monitor2;
};   /* Function GetMonitorType */

VideoModeType CurrentVideoMode(void)
{
  /* Returns the current video mode (color or mono) */
  /* Useful when initializing color variables */

      if ((VideoRecord.Monitor1 == MDADisplay) || (VideoRecord.Monitor1 ==
VGAMonoDisplay))
      return MonoMode;
    else
      return ColorMode;
};   /* Function CurrentVideoMode */

void VideoInit(void)
  /*Initializes Video Detection Routines*/
{
  OlivettiSig = MK_FP(0xFC05,0x0000);
  CompaqSig = MK_FP(0xFFFE,0x000A);
  IsOlivetti = strncmp(OlivettiSig, "OLIVETTI", 8);
  IsCompaq   = strncmp(CompaqSig , "COMPAQ", 6);

  IdentifyVideo();
}
```

■ LISTING 1.9 VIDDEMO.C

```
/*VidDemo.c*/
/* Demonstrates VideoID Unit  */
/* By Bob Falk                */

#define TRUE 1
#define FALSE 0

#include "videoid.h"
#include "video.h"
#include <conio.h>
#include <stdio.h>
#include <string.h>

char * AdapterArray[] =
            {"Not Installed",
             "MDA",
             "CGA",
             "EGA",
             "PGA",
             "MCGA",
             "VGA",
             "8514/A Adapter (IBM)",
```

```
                "HGC",
                "HGC Plus",
                "Hercules InColor",
                "AT&T 6300 CGA",
                "AT&T 6300 CGA (enhanced)",
                "Unknown"};

char* MonitorArray[] =
          { "Not Installed",
            "Monochrome",
            "Low-Resolution Color",
            "Hi-Res Color or Gray-Scale",
            "Monochrome",
            "Hi-Res Color or Gray-Scale"
          };

#define GreenOnBlack  0x02
#define YellowOnBlack  0x0E

#define  Dim  0x07
#define  Intense 0x0A

char  ClrNorm,  ClrHi;

void InitAttributes(void)
  /* Initializes the color attributes */
{
  if (CurrentVideoMode == ColorMode)
  {
    ClrNorm = GreenOnBlack;
    ClrHi   = YellowOnBlack;
  }
  else
  {   /* MonoMode */
    ClrNorm = Dim;
    ClrHi   = Intense;
  };
  textattr(ClrNorm);
};   /* InitAttributes */

void OpeningMessage(void)
  /* Displays the title message */
{
  clrscr();
  printf( "\n\nVidDemo:  Identifies the installed video subsystems.\n" );
};   /* Procedure OpeningMessage */

void ShowVideoSystem(void)
  /* Displays the installed video system */
{
int temp;
char buf[32];
  /* Display the primary adapter/monitor combination: */
  cprintf( "Active (current) Video Subsystem:\r\n" );

  cprintf("  Adapter    " );
```

```
    textattr(ClrHi);
    temp = GetAdapterType(TRUE);
    strcpy(buf,AdapterArray[temp]);
    cprintf( "%s\r\n", AdapterArray[temp]);
    textattr(ClrNorm);
    cprintf( "  Monitor  " );
    textattr(ClrHi);
    temp = GetMonitorType(TRUE);
    strcpy(buf,MonitorArray[temp]);
    cprintf( " %s\r\n", MonitorArray[temp]);
    textattr(ClrNorm);

    /* Display the secondary adapter/monitor combination: */
    cprintf( "Inactive (non-current) Video Subsystem:\r\n" );

    cprintf("  Adapter   " );
    textattr(ClrHi);
    cprintf( "%s\r\n", AdapterArray[ GetAdapterType(FALSE) ] );
    textattr(ClrNorm);
    cprintf( "  Monitor  " );
    textattr(ClrHi);
    cprintf( " %s\r\n", MonitorArray[ GetMonitorType(FALSE) ] );
    textattr(ClrNorm);
  };   /* Procedure ShowVideoSystem */

  void main(void)
  {
    VideoInit();
    InitAttributes();
    OpeningMessage();
    ShowVideoSystem();
  }
  /* eof VidDemo.C */
```

Build Your Own Breakout Switch

■ Nicholas Temple III

Learn how to create a handy breakout switch for your PC.

Here's a simple hardware add-in for any debugger that can trap on the 80x86-family Non-Maskable Interrupt (NMI). It is a breakout switch that triggers the NMI, and allows you to break out of endless loops that would otherwise force you to reboot the machine. Best of all, it can be made for less than $5.

When a program under test goes into an endless loop, a debugger such as Turbo Debugger can usually regain control when you press Ctrl-C. But when interrupts are disabled, your only hope is the "three-finger salute"; that is, Ctrl-Alt-Del to reboot.

With a breakout switch, you have another option. The NMI is basically an interrupt that cannot be disabled. If you tell your debugger to watch for the NMI (see your debugger documentation for the details of doing this) you simply need to press the breakout switch—and, magically, you're back in the debugger!

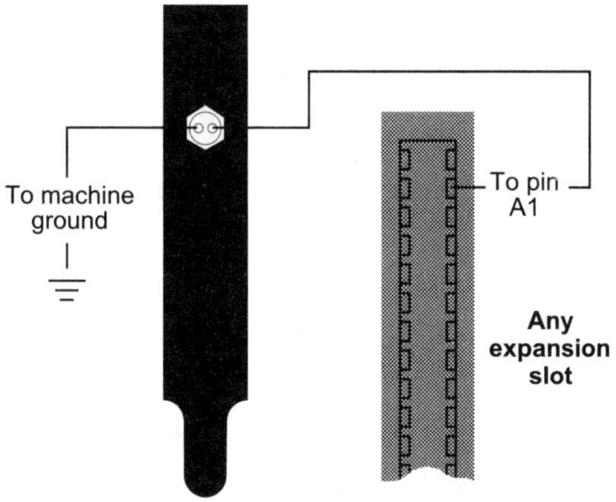

■ **FIGURE 1.5 Breakout switch connection**

Making the switch assembly is simple. (And do this with power to the machine turned *off.*) Take one of those "blank" expansion slot brackets that cover vacant expansion slot access holes in the back panel. Drill a 1/4" hole in the center of the bracket about 2" down from the top. Mount a normally open momentary-contact SPST switch in the hole. (Radio Shack part #275-1547 will work fine.) Solder a length of wire to each of the switch's two contacts. One wire goes to the computer's electrical ground. The other (and this is the tricky part) must make contact with pin A1 on the expansion bus, which is the electrical input to the 80x86-family NMI line. (See Figure 1.5.) The best way is to remove the nearest card from its slot (power off!), slip the wire down into the slot immediately in front of pin A1, and then slowly reinsert the card so that the wire is wedged between the leaf spring in the card connector and the card's gold contact strip for pin A1.

TIP: Remember that the breakout button is there. If you're *not* in the debugger and you press it (say, if you're working in a compiler environment or some other application), the machine may reboot or go berserk. Or it may not. Keep in mind that this sort of modification may void machine and/or expansion-card warranties.

Switching between Monitors without MODE

■ Donna Campanella

Switching between a monochrome and color display yourself can bring a nice side effect.

My system at home has a Super VGA display. For quite some time, I was interested in attaching a second monitor because I thought it would be helpful to display a piece of text or directory listing, etc., on the alternate monitor for reference. Since I frequently use Turbo products, I wanted to take advantage of their dual monitor mode. The Turbo documentation merely states that you must have the "appropriate hardware." Since I found that less than helpful, I did some investigation on my own. After determining what I needed, I bought and installed a monochrome card and monitor and made it work. Except for one minor detail.

All the discussions I have seen regarding dual monitor systems use DOS's MODE.COM to switch between monochrome and color. This is done by executing MODE MONO or MODE CO80—which works fine, except that the screen you are switching *to* is cleared (the screen is not cleared on the monitor you are switching *from*). It turns out that when the mode is changed with INT 10h Function 00h, the screen is cleared. For VGA, EGA, and PC convertibles, it is possible to avoid clearing the screen by calling the function with the high bit in AL set.

So, I came up with SWITCH.C (Listing 1.10) as a replacement for MODE.COM. SWITCH leaves the color screen intact; however, the monochrome display is cleared when switching *to* it. If you are simply switching between color mode and monochrome mode on a single-monitor color system, SWITCH will not clear the screen, just change the mode. The program also checks the currently active display (as indicated by the 2-byte word at hex 410—see Figure 1.6) and switches to the alternate display without having to specify CO80 or MONO as you would have to with DOS's MODE.COM.

CODE DESCRIPTION

Overview

The listing provided is used to switch between monitors (EGA/VGA and monochorme) without clearing the screen.

Listing Available

Listing	*Description*	*Used with*
SWITCH.C	C program that switches monitors by using the video interrupt 010h and the current video mode status data stored at 0x410h.	------

How to Compile/Assemble

SWITCH.C should be compiled with Borland C++. It is designed to be executed as a stand-alone program.

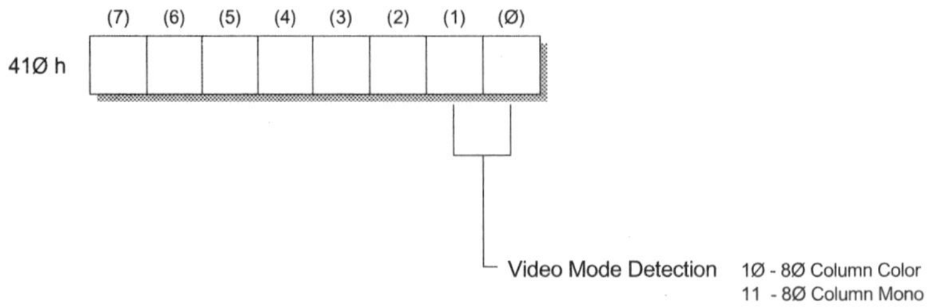

■ **FIGURE 1.6 Checking the current video mode**

■ LISTING 1.10 SWITCH.C

```
/*  SWITCH.C
     by Donna Campanella
    Program to switch between Monochrome mode and EGA/VGA Color Mode
    for computers with both a color and monochrome video adapter and
    dual monitors.  Detects the currently active display and switches
    to the alternate one.  Does not clear the screen when switching
    to color mode as DOS's MODE.COM does.
*/

#include <dos.h>

#define MONO_MODE          0x30
#define MONO               7
#define COLOR              3
#define VIDEO              0x10
#define SET_VIDEO_MODE     0x00
#define SET_CURSOR         0x02
#define CURSOR_COL         0
#define SCREEN_ROW         0x18
#define VIDEO_PAGE         0
#define CURRENT_MODE_ADDR  0x410

/*   CURRENT_MODE_ADDR:  The two-byte word at 410h as defined in
     Norton's Programmer's Guide to the IBM PC.
     Word that holds the equipment list that is reported
     by equipment-list service interrupt 11h)
     Initial video mode:   7  6  5  4  3  2  1  0
                                               x  x
     where: 10 ==> 80 column color
            11 ==> 80 column monochrome
     Set/clear bit to switch modes.                              */

void main(void)
{
    union REGS regs;
    int new_mode;
    unsigned char video_mode;
    int far *vid_mode_ptr;

    /* Get current active display */
    vid_mode_ptr = (int far *) CURRENT_MODE_ADDR;
    video_mode = *(vid_mode_ptr);

    /* Test current mode and switch to alternate mode */
    if ((video_mode & MONO_MODE) == MONO_MODE)
    {
        /* clear bit to set color mode */
        video_mode &= 0xEF;
        new_mode = COLOR;
        }
    else
    {
        /* set bit to set monochrome mode */
```

```
        video_mode |= 0x10;
        new_mode = MONO;
      }

    /* Enable the display by updating the "equipment list"  */
    *vid_mode_ptr = video_mode;

    /* Switch mode, setting high bit in AL (OR mode with    */
    /* hex 80)  to avoid clearing the EGA/VGA screen.       */
    regs.h.al = (char) (new_mode | 0x80);
    regs.h.ah = SET_VIDEO_MODE;
    int86(VIDEO, &regs, &regs);

    /* Set cursor to bottom of screen */
    regs.h.ah = SET_CURSOR;
    regs.h.dh = SCREEN_ROW;
    regs.h.bh = VIDEO_PAGE;
    regs.h.dl = CURSOR_COL;
    int86(VIDEO, &regs, &regs);
}
```

Programming the AT Real-Time Clock

■ Jim Mischel

Master the black art of programming the real-time clock.

A few years back, one of my high-flying friends mortgaged his life and bought a Ferrari. It was one fine-looking automobile, and faster than anything I'd ever driven. We'd take it out on the back roads and run it up to 130 mph. Around town, he still couldn't get to places much faster than I and my VW Rabbit could. In fact, many times it took him longer—because he simply had to drive at the *speed limit*. So, after about a year, he sold the Ferrari and bought something more sensible. The reason: What good is a Ferrari if it never gets out of second gear?

Our goal now is to explore the Real-Time Clock (RTC) chip in the AT-compatible (and later) PCs. What do Ferraris have to do with RTC chips? When you see what the chip can do, compared with how DOS and the BIOS actually "drive" it, you may conclude that this chip, like my friend's Ferrari, never gets out of second gear. Stick with me, and we'll explore some of the *higher* gears.

Peeking under the Hood

Inside every AT-compatible computer is a Motorola MC146818 Real-Time Clock (RTC) chip or one of its functional equivalents. (The earlier PC/XT class of machines lacked this feature.) The RTC chip provides a real-time clock, and 14 bytes of clock, calendar, and control registers, along with 50 bytes of general-purpose RAM. The onboard memory is backed up by a battery that allows the information to be retained when the system is shut down. In addition, the chip is capable of generating a hardware interrupt at a program-specified frequency or time.

In the AT, the primary function of the RTC is to retain time, date, and system setup information when the system is shut down. At power-on, the BIOS power on self-test (POST) code verifies the system setup information and sets the system clock from the RTC's date and time. The chip is then completely ignored unless specifically activated by an application program.

What's It Good for?

The standard AT BIOS provides interrupts and functions that use the RTC's features. With BIOS interrupt 15H, there are functions 83H (Set/Cancel Wait Interval) and 86H (Wait). There is also interrupt 1AH (time-of-day service). These functions use the RTC chip for real-time control capabilities; capabilities that were not totally present in the PC/XT BIOS. Table 1.4 summarizes the time-related RTC functions.

INT 1AH, the BIOS time-of-day service, is available in both the PC/XT BIOS and the AT BIOS. In the PC/XT, however, only functions 0 and 1 are present. These functions respectively read and set the System Time Counter; i.e., the number of system clock "ticks" since midnight. (The system clock ticks approximately 18.2 times per second, or once every 54.9 milliseconds.) These functions provide a simpler and more accurate method of timing operations than the MS-DOS clock function (INT 21H, function 2DH).

The AT BIOS adds six new functions to INT 1AH, as shown in Table 1.4. Functions 2 through 5 read and set the RTC time and date. They are of little real use to applications programs. The only program that should attempt to set the RTC time or date is the SETUP program in ROM, or a similar program provided with your system software. Reading the clock should'nt be necessary unless you disable interrupts for an extended period and want to reset the DOS system clock.

■ TABLE 1.4 Time-related BIOS functions

INT 15h (System Services)
  Function 83h (Set/Cancel Wait Interval)
    Subfunction 0 (Set Interval)
    Subfunction 1 (Cancel Interval)
  Function 86h (Wait)

INT 1Ah (Time-of-Day Service)
  Function 00h (Read System Timer Time Counter) †
  Function 01h (Set System Timer Time Counter) †
  Function 02h (Read Real Time Clock Time)
  Function 03h (Set Real Time Clock Time)
  Function 04h (Read Real Time Clock Date)
  Function 05h (Set Real Time Clock Date)
  Function 06h (Set Real Time Clock Alarm)
  Function 07h (Reset Real Time Clock Alarm)

†Also avail able on the PC/XT

Functions 6 and 7, the alarm set/reset functions, provide a way to interrupt a process at a specific time of day. Just as with a normal alarm clock, you set the alarm and then go about your business. When the specified time comes, the alarm interrupts you, prompting you to do whatever should be done at this time. (I'll discuss how you program the alarm in just a bit.)

Table 1.5 shows data areas used in BIOS RTC support.

Egg Timers and Traffic Lights

The BIOS INT 15H repertoire includes two "wait" functions that perform related but subtly different tasks. Function 83H, subfunction 0, sets a wait interval and allows processing to continue. When the wait interval expires, the function logic sets a flag at a user-specified memory location. Think of function 83H as an hourglass egg timer; all it tells you is whether or not the time period is over, not how much time has elapsed or how much time is left—and you have to look at it to find out. You can stop an egg timer at any moment by turning it on its side. Function 83H has a "turned-on-side" mode: subfunction 1, which resets (upsets?) the timer.

Function 86H, on the other hand, suspends processing until the specified time period has elapsed. Think of function 86H as a traffic signal that you control, but with a catch: This red light can't be run.

Unfortunately, the designers of the AT BIOS decided that functions 83H and 86H should share data areas. As a result, you cannot use these functions concurrently. The rationale behind this design decision escapes me, as I can think of several situations in which concurrent use of these functions would be beneficial, if not downright necessary. However, since these functions do share data areas, remember: You can't boil eggs while waiting for the light to turn green.

How Does It Work?

The BIOS support for reading and setting the real-time clock is relatively straightforward. For INT 1AH functions 2 through 5, the BIOS simply accesses the CMOS RAM and

■ TABLE 1.5 RAM data area for the RTC

0040:006C	4 bytes	System Timer Tick Counter †
0040:0070	1 byte	24-hour rollover flag †
0040:0098	4 bytes	Far pointer to user wait flag
0040:009C	4 bytes	Wait count
0040:00A0	1 byte	Wait active flag
	Bit 7	= 1 Wait time elapsed
	Bits 6–1	= Reserved
	Bit 0	= 1 Wait active

† The System Timer Tick Counter and 24-hour rollover flag are used by the System Timer ISR (INT 8) on both the XT and AT.

returns the status of the operation. There is really not much to it. The Wait and Alarm functions, on the other hand, require a little background.

I mentioned earlier that the MC146818 is capable of generating a hardware interrupt. It is through this interrupt (INT 70H for IRQ line 8) and the Real-Time Clock Interrupt Servicing Routine (ISR) that the Wait and Alarm functions are processed.

Using the BIOS Functions

RTCBIOS.C and RTCBIOS.H are available on the listings diskette with this book but are not printed here because of space limitations. They illustrate the use of the RTC functions and provide the timer functions **Wait()**, **SetWait()**, and **CancelWait()**. They also include the Real-Time Clock functions **GetRTCtime()**, **SetRTCtime()**, **GetRTCdate()**, **SetRTCdate()**, **SetAlarm()** and **ClearAlarm()**. If compiled with the **#define** for TESTING removed, the resulting object file can be linked with other programs or included in a library. This program works correctly under all Turbo C++ memory models. The only problem I had was with TC++ failing to emit an external declaration in TINY model. This problem was fixed as shown in **AlarmInterrupt()**.

The first part of the test program simply sets a wait interval, prompts for a key, and then reports whether the key was pressed before or after the wait interval expired. It then waits one second before prompting for the next key. Pressing [Esc] will continue to the next part of the program.

The only function here that warrants discussion is **SetWait()**. The calling program must supply a wait interval and the address of a byte that will have its high bit set when the wait interval expires. This variable must be declared using the **volatile** keyword, and should be cleared by the program before calling **SetWait()**.

Sounding the Alarm

Although more involved than the first part, the second part of the test program is still quite simple. It reads and displays the current date and time and then sets an alarm to sound 30 seconds after the current time. If you wish to exit the program before the alarm sounds, simply press any key.

The AT BIOS configures the RTC to store time and date information in binary-coded decimal (BCD) format. To more easily manipulate these values in C, the functions that access the RTC time and date fields accept and return binary, rather than BCD values. The functions themselves handle the conversions.

SetAlarm() requires that you supply it with the address of the interrupt service routine that will process the alarm interrupt. When the alarm time is reached, the BIOS invokes INT 4AH to process the alarm. As with most interrupt routines, this function should be small and fast and it must *not* use DOS calls. You must save the current alarm interrupt vector (INT 4AH) using **getvect()** before calling **SetAlarm()** and you must restore it using **setvect()** before exiting the program. Failure to save and restore this vector can lead to some very strange behavior: typically, a system crash at a seemingly random time.

The AT functions are lacking in several areas. Not being able to use **Wait()** and **SetWait()** concurrently is the biggest drawback. The ability to query the alarm time or set more than one alarm would also be useful. These capabilities and more are all possible, but to get the RTC chip out of "second gear," we must put the pedal to the metal and program at the hardware level.

CMOS RAM

The AT CMOS RAM is divided into three areas: the clock/calendar bytes, the control registers, and general-purpose RAM. Table 1.6 shows the CMOS RAM locations and describes what each is used for. As you can see, there are 33 bytes—more than half of the total—of "reserved memory" in three areas. These locations are not currently defined by the AT BIOS and may be used to store data that will be retained after power is shut down. Access to the CMOS RAM is through ports 70H (CMOS control/address) and 71H (CMOS data).

■ TABLE 1.6 CMOS RAM data descriptions

Real time clock data

Offset	Size	Description
00	1 Byte	Current second in BCD
01	1 Byte	Alarm second in BCD
02	1 Byte	Current minute in BCD
03	1 Byte	Alarm minute in BCD
04	1 Byte	Current hour in BCD
05	1 Byte	Alarm hour in BCD
06	1 Byte	Current day of week in BCD
07	1 Byte	Current day in BCD
08	1 Byte	Current month in BCD
09	1 Byte	Current year in BCD

Status registers (See Table 1.7)

Offset	Size	Description
0A	1 Byte	Status Register A
0B	1 Byte	Status Register B
0C	1 Byte	Status Register C
0D	1 Byte	Status Register D

Configuration data

Offset	Size	Description
0E	1 Byte	Diagnostic Status
	Bit 1	= 1 Clock lost power
	Bit 6	= 1 CMOS checksum is bad
	Bit 5	= 1 invalid configuration information found at POST
	Bit 4	= 1 Memory size compare error at POST
	Bit 3	= 1 Fixed disk or adapter failed initialization
	Bit 2	= 1 CMOS time invalid
	Bits 1-0	= Reserved

■ **TABLE 1.6 CMOS RAM data descriptions *(continued)***

Offset	Size	Description
0F	1 byte	Reason for shutdown
	00	= Power on or reset
	01	= Memory size pass
	02	= Memory test pass
	03	= Memory test fail
	04	= POST end: boot system
	05	= JMP doubleword pointer with EOI
	06	= Protected tests pass
	07	= Protected tests fail
	08	= Memory size fail
	09	= INT 15h Block Move
	0A	= JMP doubleword pointer without EOI
10	1 Byte	Diskette Drive Types
	Bits 7–4	= Diskette drive 0 type
	0000b	= No drive
	0001b	= 360K drive
	0010b	= 1.2 MB drive
	0011b	= 720K drive
	0100b	= 1.44 MB drive
	Bits 3–0	= Diskette drive 1 type
11	1 Byte	Reserved
12	1 Byte	Fixed Disk Drive Types (0 = no drive)
	Bits 7–4	= Fixed Disk drive 0 type
	Bits 3–0	= Fixed Disk drive 1 type

Note: These drive types do not necessarily correspond with the values stored at locations 19h and 1Ah.

Offset	Size	Description
13	1 Byte	Reserved
14	1 Byte	Equipment installed
	Bits 7–6	= # of diskette drives
	00b	= 1 Diskette drive
	01b	= 2 diskette drives
	Bits 5–4	= Primary display
	00b	= Reserved
	01b	= 40x25 color
	10b	= 80x25 color
	11b	= 80x25 monochrome
	Bits 3–2	= Reserved
	Bit 1	= 1 Math coprocessor installed
	Bit 0	= 1 Diskette drive installed

■ **TABLE 1.6 CMOS RAM data descriptions *(continued)***

Offset	Size	Description
15	1 Byte	Base memory in 1K, low byte
16	1 Byte	Base memory in 1K, high byte
17	1 Byte	Expansion mem. size,low byte
18	1 Byte	Expansion mem. size,high byte
19	1 Byte	Fixed disk drive 0 type
1A	1 Byte	Fixed disk drive 1 type
1B–2D	19 Bytes	Reserved
2E	1 Byte	Config. information checksum—high byte
2F	1 Byte	Config. information checksum—low byte
30	1 Byte	Actual expansion memory size—low byte
31	1 Byte	Actual expansion memory size—high byte
32	1 Byte	Century in BCD
33	1 Byte	Information flag
	Bit 7	= 1 128 KByte expanded memory is present
	Bit 6	= 1 Setup flag (?)
	Bits 5–0	= Reserved
34–3F	12 Bytes	Reserved

The four status registers (A through D), located appropriately at CMOS locations 0AH through 0DH, define the chip's operating parameters and provide information about interrupts and the state of the RTC. See Table 1.7 for information on the particulars of each status register.

With very few restrictions, all CMOS RAM locations may be directly accessed by an application program. Locations 11H, 13H, and 1BH through 2DH are used in calculating the CMOS checksum that the BIOS stores at locations 2FH and 2EH. If a program changes these bytes it must also recalculate the checksum and store the new value. Changing these bytes without replacing the checksum results in a "CMOS Checksum Error" at boot, forcing you to run Setup before you can access the hard disk. The reserved memory at locations 34H through 3FH is not used in checksum calculations and may therefore be changed with apparent impunity. I say "apparent" only because individual hardware or BIOS manufacturers may use the reserved CMOS RAM locations for extended system setup information.

■ **TABLE 1.7 Status registers**

Status Register A
CMOS RAM Location 0AH—Read/Write except UIP

b7	b6	b5	b4	b3	b2	b1	b0
UIP	DV2	DV1	DV0	RS3	RS2	RS1	RS0

■ **TABLE 1.7 Status registers *(continued)***

Bit 7 (UIP)	Update In Progress flag. Read-only. When set, an update cycle is in progress and the time, calendar and alarm bytes cannot be accessed. When clear, at least 244us are available for accessing TCA.
Bits 6–4	Divider bits that define the RTC operating frequency. In the AT, the operating frequency is 32.768 kHz and the value of these bits is "010." Changing this value will cause the chip to not operate correctly.
Bits 3–0	Rate Selection bits that define the periodic interrupt rate. Periodic interrupt rates are shown in Table 1.8

Status Register B
CMOS RAM Location 0BH—Read/Write

b7	b6	b5	b4	b3	b2	b1	b0
SET	PIE	AIE	UIE	SQWE	DM	24/12	DSE

Bit 7 (SET)	When set to 1, any update cycle in progress is aborted and a program may initialize the TCA bytes without an update occurring. Setting this bit clears UIE (Bit 4). Clearing this flag allows the update cycle to continue.
Bit 6 (PIE)	Periodic Interrupt Enable. When set, the periodic interrupt will occur at the frequency specified by the Rate Selection bits in Status Register A.
Bit 5 (AIE)	Alarm Interrupt Enable. When set, the alarm interrupt will be asserted once for each second that the current time matches the alarm time.
Bit 4 (UIE)	Update-ended Interrupt Enable. When set, the update-ended interrupt will be asserted once each second after the end of the update cycle. This bit is cleared when the SET bit goes high and is not reset when SET is cleared.
Bit 3 (SQWE)	Square Wave Enable. When set, enables a square wave output on the SQW pin at the frequency specified by the Rate Selection bits in Status Register A. The SQW pin is not connected to anything in the AT.
Bit 2 (DM)	Data Mode. Indicates whether TCA bytes are in binary or BCD format. "1" indicates binary data and "0" indicates BCD. This bit should not be changed from the BIOS setting of "0."

■ **TABLE 1.7 Status registers *(continued)***

Bit 1 (24/12)	Controls format of the hours bytes. "1" indicates 24-hour format (i.e. "military time") and "0" indicates 12-hour format. This bit should not be changed from the BIOS setting of "1."
Bit 0 (DSE)	Daylight Savings Enable. When set, two special updates will occur. On the last Sunday in April the time will increment from 01:59:59 to 03:00:00 and on the last Sunday in October the time will change from 01:59:59 to 01:00:00. When set to "0," these updates will not occur.

Status Register C
CMOS RAM Location 0CH—Read Only

b7	b6	b5	b4	b3	b2	b1	b0
IRQF	PF	AF	UF	0	0	0	0

Bit 7 (IRQF)	Interrupt Request Flag. When set, one of the interrupts enabled by the bits in Status Register B has occurred.
Bit 6 (PF)	Periodic interrupt Flag. When set, the periodic interrupt has occurred.
Bit 5 (AF)	Alarm interrupt Flag. When set, the alarm interrupt has occurred.
Bit 4 (UF)	Update-ended interrupt Flag. When set, the update-ended interrupt has occurred. Note: PF, AF, and UF are set regardless of the state of the corresponding "enable" bits in Status Register B. IRQF will be set only if the interrupt flag and its corresponding enable bit are set. These 4 flags are cleared each time Status Register C is read.
Bits 3-0	Reserved. Always read as "0."

Status Register D
CMOS RAM Location 0D—Read Only

b7	b6	b5	b4	b3	b2	b1	b0
VRT	0	0	0	0	0	0	0

Bit 7 (VRT)	Valid RAM and Time. Indicates the condition of the CMOS RAM. When set, power is connected. When clear, the RTC has lost power and the time and date information are invalid.

The Update Cycle

Once each second, for 1948 µs, the Time, Calendar, and Alarm (TCA) bytes are electrically switched to the RTC chip's internal update logic in order to be advanced by one second and to check for an alarm condition. At completion, the RTC sets the UF bit in Status Register C to indicate that an update cycle has completed. An interrupt will not be asserted unless UIE in Status Register B is also set.

During the update cycle, the TCA bytes are unavailable to the outside world and the result of any attempted access to them is unpredictable. The trick is knowing when the TCA bytes are available. Enter UIP—the Update In Progress flag (bit 7 of status register A). At 244 µs before the start of an update cycle (and before switching the TCA bytes to the internal update logic), the RTC logic sets the UIP flag in Status Register A. The flag is then reset at the completion of the update cycle (2228 µs later). *The UIP flag is set whenever the TCA bytes are unavailable.* In addition, when the UIP flag is cleared, the program is *guaranteed* at least 244 µs (1464 machine cycles at 6-MHz) to perform an access—plenty of time, even with subroutine call overhead.

To prevent an update from occurring while you are setting the time or date, it is possible to halt the update cycle by setting bit 7 (the SET bit) in Status Register B. Once the program has initialized the TCA bytes, the SET bit is cleared and the update cycle continues.

Hardware Interrupts

The RTC is capable of generating three different types of interrupts. The Periodic interrupt can be programmed to occur at frequencies ranging from 2 Hz to 8.192 kHz. The Update-Ended interrupt, if enabled, will occur once each second, after the update cycle has completed. And the Alarm interrupt can be programmed to occur at any specified time.

Status Register B defines which events within the RTC can generate an interrupt, but the AT's second Programmable Interrupt Controller (PIC) determines whether or not the RTC can interrupt the processor. For RTC-generated interrupts to be recognized, bit 0 of the PIC's mask register (port A1H) must be set to 0. Before this interrupt is enabled, you must have a working INT 70H ISR installed and the RTC should be programmed to function as you require.

All three interrupts (Periodic, Alarm, and Update-Ended) are asserted on Interrupt Request Line 8, and cause the INT 70H ISR to be executed. It is the ISR's responsibility to identify which interrupts have occurred and to execute the proper servicing routine. Determining which interrupts have occurred is a simple matter of reading Status Register C and "ANDing" with Status Register B. Bits that remain set reflect which events caused the hardware interrupt.

Setting the UIE bit in Status Register B enables the once-per-second Update Ended interrupt that occurs at the end of the update cycle. The ISR that processes this interrupt must complete within one second.

One use of this interrupt is to keep the current RTC time in RAM so an application doesn't have to wait for an update cycle before reading CMOS RAM. Each time the update-ended interrupt occurs, the ISR reads the RTC time and date and stores it in memory. Any program that requires the time can then read it directly from memory rather than going to CMOS RAM and possibly having to wait for an entire update cycle.

Periodically Speaking

The RTC can be programmed to generate a periodic interrupt at several different rates, as shown in Table 1.8. When the PIE bit is set in Status Register B, the RTC will generate an interrupt at the frequency defined by the RS bits in Status Register A. The ISR that processes this interrupt must complete before the next periodic interrupt occurs.

Accessing the TCA bytes during a periodic interrupt ISR is a no-no and, at higher interrupt frequencies, can cause strange behavior due to interrupts occurring while you are waiting for an update cycle to complete.

The most versatile of the RTC interrupts is the Alarm interrupt. For normal usage, you program the RTC to generate an interrupt once per day at the hour, minute, and second specified by the alarm time in CMOS RAM. There are, however, several "don't care" conditions in the chip design, which give you greater control.

Setting any of the alarm bytes to FFH creates a "don't care" condition for that particular byte, which means it will match *any* value. For example, an alarm time of FF:00:00 will generate an interrupt once each hour, on the hour. Similarly, FF:FF:00 generates an interrupt once each minute, and FF:FF:FF causes an interrupt to occur once each second.

Odd combinations of "don't care" conditions can create some strange and possibly quite useful interrupt frequencies. For example, an alarm time of FF:00:FF will generate an interrupt once each second during the first minute of each hour, and 00:FF:00 will generate an interrupt once each minute for the first hour of the day.

■ TABLE 1.8 Periodic interrupt rates available

RS Bits 3 2 1 0	Periodic Rate	Ticks/ Second
0 0 0 0	None	None
0 0 0 1	3.90625 ms	256
0 0 1 0	7.8125 ms	128
0 0 1 1	122.070 µs	8,192
0 1 0 0	244.141 µs	4,096
0 1 0 1	488.281 µs	2,048
0 1 1 0	976.562 µs	1,024†
0 1 1 1	1.93125 ms	512
1 0 0 0	3.90625 ms	256
1 0 0 1	7.8125 ms	128
1 0 1 0	15.625 ms	64
1 0 1 1	31.25 ms	32
1 1 0 0	62.50 ms	16
1 1 0 1	125 ms	8
1 1 1 0	250 ms	4
1 1 1 1	500 ms	2

†default

Using the RTC Functions

RTC.H (Listing 1.11) contains function prototypes and defined constants used in accessing the functions and RTCHDW.C (Listing 1.12) contains the functions that access the RTC. CMOS.C (Listing 1.13) is a small program that dumps the contents of CMOS RAM to the screen and adds 1 to the value at location 1BH. The program recalculates the CMOS checksum and then exits. If you turn your computer off, reboot and run the program again, you will see that the value you stored at location 1BH is still there. TIMERTST.C (Listing 1.14) sets up a simple clock and a 4096 ticks-per-second counter that displays the number of ticks once each second. Pressing any key will exit the program.

Timing Considerations

Using the precision Zen timer from Michael Abrash's excellent book, *Zen of Assembly Language*, I timed the **NewRTCint()** routine. On my 10-MHz Kaypro AT, the routine takes approximately 110 μs, or about 1100 machine cycles, to execute when all of the interrupt routines are called. Using this information, we can calculate the maximum supportable interrupt rate for a given 80286 processor by dividing the clock rate by 1100. For example, a 12-MHz 80286 can support a maximum interrupt frequency of 10.909 kHz (12,000,000 / 1,100).

Be aware, however, that this is the *absolute maximum* supportable frequency. To paraphrase the auto ads, your actual rate may vary. Why? Because this calculation does not take into account other work that the processor will probably be doing. It assumes that the processor is doing nothing but servicing the RTC interrupts.

NewRTCint() could be sped up a great deal by replacing the calls to **ReadCMOS()** with in-line assembly language code. The two calls to **ReadCMOS()** take a total of approximately 54 μs—almost one-half of the total execution time. Further speed gains can be realized by replacing the two calls to **outportb()** with in-line assembly language.

Other Considerations

You'll notice that much of the code for **NewRTCint()** deals with storing the caller's context and preventing stack overflow. This is required because the RTC will sometimes generate a periodic interrupt asynchronously—while the alarm interrupt is being processed. Without this stack check logic, **NewRTCint()**—which is not reentrant—and the asynchronous interrupt will cause a system to crash. The only other way to handle this potential problem is to keep interrupts off for the duration of the routine—possibly losing other interrupts in the process.

RTCHDW.C *must* be compiled with standard stack frames enabled (the -k switch with Borland C++). If you compile without standard stack frames, the **NewRTCint()** routine will not exit properly. If, for some reason, you want to compile without standard stack frames, replace the pop bp instruction in **NewRTCint()** (right before the iret instruction) with a line that reads:

```
asm mov bp,[word ptr cs:bp+6]
```

As with any device, it is possible that another program will be using the RTC when your program wants to use it. The easiest way to check for a potential conflict is to examine bit 0 of the second PIC's mask register (port 0xA1). If this bit is 0, some other program may be using the RTC chip. If the PIC mask bit is reset, examining the interrupt-enable flags in the RTC's Status Register B will determine which (if any) of the RTC interrupts are permitted. If none of the interrupt enable flags is set, RTC interrupts are not being processed and your program can take control of the RTC without causing any problems.

Let It Rip

Like my friends former Ferrari, the RTC chip has many gears that never get used when the standard BIOS and DOS drive it. *Unlike* my friend, if you decide to take some of the "higher gear" RTC functions for a ride in one of your time-dependent applications (see Table 1.8), you won't attract the attention of the county mounties, but you may have the Real-Time of your life!

CODE DESCRIPTION

Overview

Two programs are presented here in the listings. TIMERTST is a program which sets up a single clock and outputs to the screen. CMOS dumps the contents of the CMOS RAM to the screen and stores a value in the non-volatile memory area.

Listings Available

Listing	*Description*	*Used with*
RTC.H	Prototypes and constants for accessing functions in RTCHDW.C.	RTCHDW.C
RTCHDW.C	Functions which control the AT-Real Time Clock functions.	CMOS.C
TIMERTST.C	Example program which uses RTCHDW.C and RTC.H.	------
CMOS.C	Example program which uses RTCHDW.C and RTC.H.	------

How to Compile/Assemble

The listing can be compiled and linked with any C/C++ compiler which supports inline assembly language.

■ LISTING 1.11 RTC.H

```
/* RTC.H - Symbols and function prototypes for RTCHDW.C */

#define PIC1data 0x20                  /* PIC 1 data register */
#define PIC1ctrl 0x21               /* PIC 1 control register */
```

```
#define PIC2data 0xa0                        /* PIC 2 data register */
#define PIC2ctrl 0xa1                     /* PIC 2 control register */
#define EOI  0x20                        /* "End of Interrupt" value */
#define ALARMINT 0x4A                 /* User Alarm Interrupt number */
#define RTCINT 0x70                                /* RTC interrupt */
#define CMOS_Control 0x70                   /* CMOS RAM control port */
#define CMOS_Data 0x71                         /* CMOS RAM data port */
#define SRA 0x0a                              /* Status Register A */
#define SRB 0x0b                              /* Status Register B */
#define SRC 0x0c                              /* Status Register C */
#define SRD 0x0d                              /* Status Register D */

/* Status Register A flag masks */
#define UIP 0x80                              /* Update in Progress */

/* Status Register B flag masks */
#define SET     0x80                            /* Halt update flag */
#define PIE     0x40                   /* Periodic Interrupt Enable */
#define AIE     0x20                      /* Alarm Interrupt Enable */
#define UIE     0x10               /* Update-ended Interrupt Enable */
#define SQWE    0x08                          /* Square Wave Enable */
#define DM      0x04                                   /* Data Mode */
#define AMPM    0x02                                /* 24/12 Switch */
#define DSE     0x01                     /* Daylight Savings Enable */

/* Status Register C flag masks */
#define IRQF    0x80                           /* Interrupt Request */
#define PF      0x40                          /* Periodic Interrupt */
#define AF      0x20                             /* Alarm Interrupt */
#define UF      0x10                      /* Update-ended Interrupt */

/* Status Register D flag masks */
#define VRT     0x80                              /* Valid RAM & Time */

/* Time structure used by SetAlarmInt */
struct RTCTIME {
    unsigned int Hour;
    unsigned int Min;
    unsigned int Sec;
    unsigned int Daylight;
};

int ReadCMOS (int Addr);
void WriteCMOS (int Loc, int Data);
void NewCMOSChecksum (void);
int SetPeriodicInt (int Freq, void far (*isr)());
int SetUpdateInt (void far (*isr)());
int SetAlarmInt (struct RTCTIME *Time, void far (*isr)());
void EnableRTCint (int Which);
void DisableRTCint (int Which);
void ResetRTCint (int Which);
void TimerOn (void);
void TimerOff (void);
```

■ LISTING 1.12 RTCHDW.C

```
#pragma inline
#pragma option -1                    /* generate 286 instructions */
/* RTCHDW.C - AT Real-Time Clock control functions
 * Author Jim Mischel.  Last update 03/22/92 */
#include <stdio.h>
#include <dos.h>
#include "rtc.h"

/* Loop until "Update in Progress" bit is clear */
static void WaitForUpdate (void) {
    while (ReadCMOS (SRA) & UIP)
    ;
}

/* Read Value from CMOS RAM */
int ReadCMOS (int Addr) {
    int ch;
    asm pushf                              /* save interrupt flag */
    disable ();
    if (Addr < SRA) WaitForUpdate ();
    outportb (CMOS_Control, Addr);
    ch = inportb (CMOS_Data);
    asm popf                            /* restore interrupt flag */
    return ch;
} /* ReadCMOS */

/* Write Value to CMOS RAM */
void WriteCMOS (int Addr, int Value) {
    asm pushf                              /* save interrupt flag */
    disable ();
    if (Addr < SRA) WaitForUpdate ();
    outportb (CMOS_Control, Addr);
    outportb (CMOS_Data, Value);
    asm popf                            /* restore interrupt flag */
} /* WriteCMOS */

/* Compute and store new CMOS checksum */
void NewCMOSChecksum (void) {
    int Loc, CheckSum = 0;
    for (Loc = 0x10; Loc < 0x2E; Loc++)
    CheckSum += ReadCMOS (Loc);
    WriteCMOS (0x2E, (CheckSum >> 8));
    WriteCMOS (0x2F, (CheckSum & 0xFF));
}

/* ISR pointers initially point to DummyIsr in case an
 * interrupt is enabled for which no ISR has been installed. */
static void far DummyIsr (void) {
}

static void far (*PeriodicIsr) (void) = DummyIsr;
static void far (*UpdateIsr) (void) = DummyIsr;
```

```
static void far (*AlarmIsr) (void) = DummyIsr;

/* Setup periodic interrupt frequency and ISR */
int SetPeriodicInt (int Freq, void far (*isr)()) {
    if (ReadCMOS (SRB) & PIE)
    return 1;                   /* can't set - already enabled */
    if (isr != NULL) PeriodicIsr = isr;
    /* set new periodic rate */
    WriteCMOS (SRA, (ReadCMOS (SRA) & 0xf0) | (Freq & 0x0f));
    return 0;
}

/* Setup update-ended ISR */
int SetUpdateInt (void far (*isr)()) {
    if (ReadCMOS (SRB) & UIE)
    return 1;                   /* can't set - already enabled */
    if (isr != NULL) UpdateIsr = isr;
    return 0;
}

/* Convert binary value (0-99) to BCD */
static int BinToBCD (int Bin) {
    return ((Bin / 10) << 4) + (Bin % 10);
}

/* Setup alarm time and ISR */
int SetAlarmInt (struct RTCTIME *Time, void far (*isr)()) {
    unsigned char srb;
    if (ReadCMOS (SRB) & AIE)
       return 1;                /* already set, exit with error */
    if (isr != NULL) AlarmIsr = isr;
    srb = ReadCMOS (SRB);
    WriteCMOS (SRB, srb | 0x80);            /* turn on SET bit */
    WriteCMOS (0x05, (Time->Hour < 0xc0) ?                  BinToBCD (Time-
>Hour) : Time->Hour);
    WriteCMOS (0x03, (Time->Min < 0xc0) ?              BinToBCD (Time->Min) :
Time->Min);
    WriteCMOS (0x01, (Time->Sec < 0xc0) ?              BinToBCD (Time->Sec) :
Time->Sec);
    WriteCMOS (SRB, srb);                   /* restore SET bit */
    return 0;
}

/* Enable individual RTC interrupts */
void EnableRTCint (int Which) {
    WriteCMOS (SRB, (ReadCMOS (SRB) | (Which & (UF | PF | AF))));
}

/* Disable individual RTC interrupts */
void DisableRTCint (int Which) {
    WriteCMOS (SRB, (ReadCMOS (SRB) &          ~(Which & (UF | PF | AF))));
}

/* Reset individual RTC interrupts and ISRs */
```

```
void ResetRTCint (int Which) {
    DisableRTCint (Which);
    if (Which & PIE) {
     PeriodicIsr = DummyIsr;
     /* reset rate to 1024 ticks/sec */
     WriteCMOS (SRA, (ReadCMOS (SRA) & 0xf0) | 6);
    }
    if (Which & UIE) UpdateIsr = DummyIsr;
    if (Which & AIE) AlarmIsr = DummyIsr;
}

static void far NewRTCint (void);               /* ISR Prototype */
static void interrupt (*OldRTCint) () = NULL;   /* Old RTC ISR */

/* Pointer to new RTC ISR */
static void interrupt (*RTCintPtr) () =
 (void interrupt *)NewRTCint;

/* Enable the RTC interrupt */
void TimerOn (void) {
    disable ();
    if (OldRTCint == NULL) {          /* save old RTC int vector */
      OldRTCint = getvect (RTCINT);
      setvect (RTCINT, RTCintPtr);
    }
    ReadCMOS (SRC);           /* clear pending RTC interrupts... */
    /* ...and enable RTC interrupt */
    outportb (PIC2ctrl, inportb (PIC2ctrl) & 0xfe);
    enable ();
}

/* Disable RTC hardware interrupt */
void TimerOff (void) {
    disable ();
  /* disable RTC interrupt */
    outportb (PIC2ctrl, inportb (PIC2ctrl) | 1);
    setvect (RTCINT, OldRTCint);               /* reset RTC ISR */
    OldRTCint = NULL;
    enable ();
}

/* New INT 70H ISR.  Because the state of the stack is unknown
 * when this function is entered, we must create a new stack
 * before doing any processing.  As a result there can be no
 * automatic (i.e. stack) variables defined within this function. */
/* Define stack size and number of stacks */
#define StackSize 128
#define Stacks 3
#define SaveRecordSize 8
static char NewStack[StackSize*Stacks];

static unsigned char IntFlags;

static void far NewRTCint (void) {
```

```
  /* save caller's context and setup new stack */
    asm xchg bp,[word ptr cs:SaveArea]  /* get next stack area */
    asm cmp bp,Offset EndSaveArea                /* last stack? */
    asm jc Around                                   /* nope, OK */
    asm jmp StackError                      /* Stack overflow! */
Around:
    asm mov [word ptr cs:bp+2],sp                 /* save stack */
    asm mov [word ptr cs:bp+4],ss
    asm mov sp,[word ptr cs:SaveArea]       /* get and save... */
    asm mov [word ptr cs:bp+6],sp            /* ...original BP */
    asm mov sp,[word ptr cs:bp]             /* Setup new SP... */
    asm add bp,SaveRecordSize             /* ...and point to... */
    asm mov [word ptr cs:SaveArea],bp      /* ...next save area */
    asm mov bp,DGROUP
    asm mov ss,bp                     /* SS = local data segment */
    asm pusha                       /* save general registers... */
    asm push es                   /* ...and segment registers... */
    asm push ds                               /* ...on new stack */
    asm mov ds,bp                                    /* ds = ss */

  /* Determine which interrupts occurred */
    IntFlags = ReadCMOS (SRC) & ReadCMOS (SRB);
    enable ();                              /* interrupts OK now */
  /* call appropriate interrupt routines */
    if (IntFlags & PF) (*PeriodicIsr) ();
    if (IntFlags & UF) (*UpdateIsr) ();
    if (IntFlags & AF) (*AlarmIsr) ();
    outportb (PIC2data, EOI);   /* Reset interrupt controllers */
    outportb (PIC1data, EOI);

  /* restore caller's context and return */
    disable ();
    asm pop ds                 /* restore segment registers... */
    asm pop es
    asm popa                       /* ...and general registers */
    asm mov bp,[word ptr cs:SaveArea]            /* Restore... */
    asm sub bp,SaveRecordSize         /* ...save area pointer, */
    asm mov [word ptr cs:SaveArea],bp
    asm mov ss,[word ptr cs:bp+4]                /* ...stack,... */
    asm mov sp,[word ptr cs:bp+2]
    asm pop bp                                     /* ...and BP */
    asm iret

/*
 * Stack overflow handler.
 * Display an error message and hang the system.
 */
StackError:
    asm mov ax,cs
    asm mov ds,ax
    asm mov dx,offset OverflowMessage
    asm mov ah,9
    asm int 21h
DeadLoop:                                  /* system hangs here */
```

```
    asm jmp short DeadLoop
      /*** Local data ***/
    asm OverflowMessage = $
    asm db 13,10,7,'RTC Stack overflow'
    asm db 13,10,'System Halted$'
    asm SaveArea = $
    asm dw Offset SaveArea+2
    asm dw Offset DGROUP:NewStack + (Stacks * StackSize)
    asm dw 3 dup (?)
    asm dw Offset DGROUP:NewStack + ((Stacks-1) * StackSize)
    asm dw 3 dup (?)
    asm dw Offset DGROUP:NewStack + ((Stacks-2) * StackSize)
    asm dw 3 dup (?)
    asm EndSaveArea = $
}
```

■ LISTING 1.13 CMOS.C

```
/* CMOS.C -- test CMOS RAM functions of RTCHDW.C
 *
 * Sample MAKE file:
 *
 * .c.obj:
 *    bcc -c $<
 *
 * cmos.exe: cmos.obj rtchdw.obj
 *    bcc cmos.obj rtchdw.obj
 */
#include <stdio.h>
#include "rtc.h"

void main (void) {
  int x,y,Loc,Data;

  printf ("\n%33s\n\n   ", "CMOS RAM Dump");
  for (x = 0; x < 0x10; x++)
    printf (" %2X", x);
  puts ("\n----------------------------------------------------");
  for (x = 0; x < 4; x++) {
    printf ("%X ", x);
    for (y = 0; y < 0x10; y++) {
      Loc = (x << 4) + y;
      Data = ReadCMOS (Loc);
      printf (" %02X", Data);
    }
    printf ("\n");
  }
  WriteCMOS (0x1B, ReadCMOS (0x1B) + 1);
  NewCMOSChecksum ();
  printf ("\nNew value at location 1B = %02X\n", ReadCMOS (0x1B));
}
```

■ LISTING 1.14 TIMERTST.C

```
/* TIMERTST.C
 * Example program using RTCHDW functions.
 *
 * Sample MAKE file:
 *
 * .c.obj:
 *     bcc -c $<
 *
 * timertst.exe: timertst.obj rtchdw.obj
 *     bcc timertst.obj rtchdw.obj
 */
#include <stdio.h>
#include <bios.h>
#include "rtc.h"

static volatile unsigned long TickCount = 0;
static volatile int SecCount = 0;
static volatile unsigned int MinCount = 0;
static volatile int Tick = 0;

/* Periodic ISR simply increments tick counter */
void far MyPeriodicISR (void) {
    TickCount++;
}

/* Update ISR increments second count and
 * sets the tick flag */
void far MyUpdateISR (void) {
    SecCount++;
    Tick = 1;
}

/* Alarm ISR increments minute count, clears second
 * count and sets the tick flag. */
void far MyAlarmISR (void) {
    MinCount++;
    SecCount = 0;
    Tick = 1;
}

/* Enable a 4.096 KHz timer, the update interrupt
 * and a once-per-minute alarm ISR.
 * Each second, display the elapsed time and the
 * total number of timer ticks. */
void main (void) {
    struct RTCTIME Time = {0xff, 0xff, 0, 0};

    SetAlarmInt (&Time, MyAlarmISR);
    SetUpdateInt (MyUpdateISR);
```

```
    SetPeriodicInt (4, MyPeriodicISR);
    EnableRTCint (PIE+UIE+AIE);
    TimerOn ();
    do {                                /* do until key pressed */
        if (Tick) {
            Tick = 0;
            printf ("%02d:%02d  Tick count = %ld\n",
                    MinCount, SecCount, TickCount);
        }
    } while (!bioskey (1));
    TimerOff ();
    ResetRTCint (PIE+UIE+AIE);
    bioskey (0);                        /* read keyboard buffer */
}
```

Stamped Metal Diskette Drive Frames

■ Jeff Duntemann

The quality of the manufacture of hardware is important, even with floppy drives.

Don't buy a diskette drive with a stamped metal frame.

One reason drive prices have come down a lot is that some manufacturers have been cutting back on formerly sacrosanct assumptions about disk drives. One of those is that disk drives need a diecast frame to work reliably. Because some manufacturers now choose to ignore that dictum doesn't mean it's no longer true.

You can tell a diecast frame by its silver color. Stamped metal frames will be golden and slightly iridescent due to the antirust coating on the stamped steel. A diecast frame looks like it was poured from a mold. Different parts will be different thicknesses; there will be metal posts for screws to screw into, things like that. Stamped metal, by contrast, looks like a piece of sheet metal bent and formed into shape, and it is of uniform thickness throughout.

Reading and writing to a diskette is a high-precision business. It needs to be done on a foundation that is *absolutely* rigid; flexing in the frame can make a diskette written one day unreadable the next. Building a diskette drive on a stamped frame is like building a cathedral on a sandhill—such drives are trash.

Examine a drive before you buy it. If you're buying a configured system, pull the case and check out the drive frames. If you're buying by mail, buy only name-brand drives like Teac. Beware of no-names or odd names like Copal, which is one stamped frame drive that I've encountered and had trouble with (and a 1.2MB model, yet!).

2

The Keyboard and Keyboard Input

Sometimes you just get it right the first time. As much as people hype the use of the mouse, or trackballs, or (most recently) pen-based computing, I remain unconvinced. The humble keyboard has been with us for a very long time, first as a musical entry device and only in the last hundred years for character data entry. We don't play the piano with a stylus; we play it with ten practiced fingers. I'd say that until we get into serious general voice recognition (which is still a distance off) there will be nothing like the keyboard to take information from our minds into our machines.

This isn't to say that keyboards have not done some serious evolving in our own time, nor that there's no room for further improvement. In the early formative years of the PC, IBM was rearranging the keyboard for every new model of machine they released. Many keyboards were giant steps backward; the original IBM PCjr "Chicklet" keyboard comes to mind, and (far worse) that mainframe-soiled abomination that pulled the function keys from where my left hand could easily reach them, up to the top of the keyboard where nothing belongs but pencils.

The PC keyboard hides a whole country siloful of tricks and subtlety. There's a lot of tortuous handshaking between the BIOS in memory and the keyboard on its cable, as George Seaton explains in "The Story of an 'O'." Off the top of your head, can you explain what the SysReq key does and why it's special? If not (and even I had to peek to remind myself) you'll find Michael Covington's explanation most intriguing. Do you know how to alter the keyboard repeat rate? Hint: It's done differently for the XT keyboard than for the microprocessor-controlled AT keyboard. But we'll lay it out for you both ways.

And hey, how do you identify a keyboard with F11 and F12? Even I failed to get that one right—but we'll tell you in this chapter.

Speeding Up Your AT's Keyboard

■ Marty Franz

Make your keyboard repeat keystrokes machine-gun fast with a little BIOS work.

You've got the latest 486, a 33-MHz clock, and 16 megs of RAM. Your VGA can display data with no wait states. You've even sprayed the bottom of your mouse with Pam. You can't get any faster than that, right?

Wrong. Your *keyboard* is still slowing you down.

If you're not convinced, go into DOS and hold down the spacebar. You'll first wait what seems like an eternity and then the cursor will slowly plod across the screen. That's because your keyboard's default rate for repeating characters is agonizingly slow. You pay this penalty when you move the cursor around in your favorite programming editor or scroll through a page of text in your word processor. Even with all your fast hardware, you're still keyboard-bound.

Luckily, you can remedy this situation. If you own an AT, PS/2, or even a lowly PCjr, you can set the rate at which keys repeat. KEYSPEED, the program presented in this article, will show you how.

TIP: For more information on how the key repeat delay can be set for PC/XT class machines see "Changing the Key Repeat Delay on the PC/XT" later in this chapter.

First, let's clarify what we're talking about. The PC's keyboard is what's called *typematic*. This means that when you hold down a key for longer than the duration of a keypress, it will repeat that keycode until released. The delay the keyboard waits before it starts sending repeated keycodes is called the *typematic delay*. It is measured in milliseconds (ms), with a fairly long 500 ms being the default. You can cut this in half to 250 ms or lengthen it to 750 or even a glacial 1000 ms (1 second).

Once the keyboard starts repeating, it sends characters at a rate called the *typematic rate*. Normally, this is 10 characters/second for an AT, and 10.9 characters for a PS/2. You can speed this up to 30 characters/second, or slow it down to 2 characters/second.

Cranking up the typematic rate and shortening the typematic delay will speed up your keyboard, especially when you're zipping the cursor around the screen a lot during editing.

Setting the Typematic Rate and Delay

To set the keyboard's typematic rate and delay, use the same BIOS service used to read the keyboard, interrupt 0x16. This time, however, you use service 0x0305. Unlike many other BIOS services, *both* AH and AL must be set for this service. The settings of the registers are detailed below:

```
Interrupt 0x16
AH = 0x03 Set typematic rate and delay
```

```
AL = 0x05BH = typematic delay (Table 2.1)
BL = typematic rate (Table 2.2)
```

Register BH holds the typematic delay. The delays allowed are summarized in Table 2.1. (All times are in milliseconds.) Any other value in BH is considered "reserved for future use."

The typematic rate is set through a code in BL. The legal code values are shown in Table 2.2, along with their equivalent rate of key repeats per second. Once again, anything other than one of the values shown in the table is considered "reserved for future use."

The KEYSPEED Program

The program KEYSPEED.C, Listing 2.1, sets the typematic rate and delay from the DOS command line. The command line parameters are the decimal values of the codes shown above. For example, calling KEYSPEED 0 0 sets the keyboard to the fastest it can go, and KEYSPEED 31 3 sets it to the slowest. After it sets the key speed, KEYSPEED displays a message telling what the new settings are.

The **inregs** and **outregs** register structures are used in the program to hold the PC register contents before and after the BIOS call.

TIP: The KEYSPEED program can be easily changed to compile with any C/C++ compiler that can make BIOS calls by changing the code that accesses **inregs** and **outregs**.

The string arrays **rates** and **delays** are used to hold the values of the settings as shown in the tables above. If you want to expand KEYSPEED beyond a strictly demo program, you could use the strings in these arrays to compare with the command line arguments. This would let your user type KEYSPEED 30.0 250 instead of KEYSPEED 0 0, which is a little friendlier.

The only restriction on using KEYSPEED is that it can't be run on a traditional PC or XT. That's because the BIOS ROMs in these machines don't support this service. On true-blue IBM PCs or XTs, KEYSPEED at least does no harm. On oddball no-name clone machines, however, you're on your own.

Besides using KEYSPEED to speed up your own machine, you can use the BIOS service described here when you develop your own software. Here's a suggestion: Offer your users the ability to set their typing speed preferences in a spreadsheet or word-

■ TABLE 2.1 Typematic delay

Code in BH	Delay
0x00	250 ms
0x01	500 ms (default)
0x02	750 ms
0x03	1000 ms

■ TABLE 2.2 Repeat codes and typematic rates

Code in BL	Rpts/Sec	Code in BL	Rpts/Sec
0x00	30.0	0x10	7.5
0x01	26.7	0x11	6.7
0x02	24.0	0x12	6.0
0x03	21.8	0x13	5.5
0x04	20.0	0x14	5.0
0x05	18.5	0x15	4.6
0x06	17.1	0x16	4.3
0x07	16.0	0x17	4.0
0x08	15.0	0x18	3.7
0x09	13.3	0x19	3.3
0x0a	12.0	0x1a	3.0
0x0b	10.9	0x1b	2.7
0x0c	10.0	0x1c	2.5
0x0d	9.2	0x1d	2.3
0x0e	8.6	0x1e	2.1
0x0f	8.0	0x1f	2.0

processing program. This way, lightning typists will not be held back by a least-common-denominator typematic rate, and their productivity will increase accordingly.

CODE DESCRIPTION

Overview

The listing provided is used to change the typematic rate and delay of the keyboard. To run the program, compile with Borland C++ and link as a stand-alone .EXE file.

Listing Available

Listing	*Description*	*Used with*
KEYSPEED.C	Csource file that changes the keyboard typematic rate and delay by using the BIOS keyboard interrupt 016h.	------

How to Compile/Assemble

KEYSPEED.C can be compiled and linked with any C/C++ compiler.

■ LISTING 2.1 KEYSPEED.C

```
/*
KEYSPEED.C:     Set the typematic rate and delay on the keyboard
module type:    .EXE (small model)  */

#include <stdio.h>
```

```
#include <stdlib.h>
#include <bios.h>
#define KEYBOARD 0x16         /* keyboard interrupt */
#define SET_RATES 0x0305      /* services to set rate and delay */

char *rates[32] =
{
"30.0", "26.7", "24.0", "21.8", "20.0", "18.5", "17.1",
"16.0", "15.0", "13.3", "12.0", "10.9", "10.0",  "9.2",
"8.6",  "8.0",  "7.5",  "6.7",  "6.0",  "5.5",  "5.0",
"4.6",  "4.3",  "4.0",  "3.7",  "3.3",  "3.0",  "2.7",
"2.5",  "2.3",  "2.1",  "2.0"
};

char *delays[4] =
 {
     "250", "500", "750", "1000"
 };

 void main(int argc, char *argv[])
 {
     int temp;
     union REGS inregs, outregs;

     if (argc != 3)
     {
         printf("Usage: %s <rate> <delay>\n", argv[0]);
         puts("Sets keyboard typematic rate and delay.");
         puts("Use 0 0 for fastest, 31 3 for slowest.");
         exit(1);
     }
     inregs.x.ax = SET_RATES;
     temp = atoi(argv[1]);
     inregs.h.bl = (temp < 0x20) ? temp : 0x1f;
     temp = atoi(argv[2]);
     inregs.h.bh = (temp < 0x04) ? temp : 0x03;
     printf("Rate: %s characters/second\nDelay: %s milliseconds\n",
       rates[inregs.h.bl], delays[inregs.h.bh]);
     int86(KEYBOARD, &inregs, &outregs);
     exit(0);
 }
```

A Use for the SysReq Key

■ Michael Covington

Here's how you can make the SysReq key a dedicated TSR hot key.

Whats the SysReq key for? IBM designed it for calling up memory-resident utilities, but nobody ever uses it for that—or for anything else!

The memory-resident program given in Listing 2.2 remedies this neglect. It sends a form-feed character to the printer whenever SysReq is pressed. You can change the program to make SysReq do a wide variety of other things.

SysReq stands for "system request." You'll find a SysReq key on all ATs and PS/2s, as well as on some late-model XTs, but not on the original PC. You'll also find SysReq on IBM mainframes, and there, it's the key you press when you want to talk to the communication system rather than your program—sort of like putting your modem in command mode. Likewise, the microcomputer SysReq key is designed for calling up a routine unrelated to the program that's running.

When SysReq is pressed, the system performs an interrupt 15H with 8500H in the AX register as shown in Figure 2.1. When the key is released, the same interrupt occurs again, but AX contains 8501H. These are not the regular keyboard interrupts; they are generated only by SysReq. Their effect depends entirely on software. By default, BIOS catches them and does nothing, returning immediately to the program that was running. But you can install your own service routines to make SysReq do anything you fancy.

The SysReq Program

Take a look at Listing 2.2. The heart of the program is the **PROC** called **ISR**, which will be called whenever interrupt 15H is invoked. But interrupt 15H has many uses—ranging from cassette I/O to extended memory access—so **ISR** must first check that AX contains 8500H. If so, it prints a form feed, then exits (using **IRET**); otherwise, it jumps to the original INT 15H service routine provided by BIOS or other software.

Crucially, **ISR** accesses the printer through BIOS services, not through DOS. The reason is that DOS isn't reentrant; things can go wrong if a DOS interrupt is called while another DOS interrupt is executing, as it would be if the user pressed SysReq during disk access. There are ways to untangle some of these conflicts if necessary, but in this case it isn't worth the effort.

To work, **ISR** must reside in memory all the time, and the CPU must be told that it is the service routine for INT 15H. The program as a whole, therefore, doesn't *execute* **ISR**, but rather *installs* it.

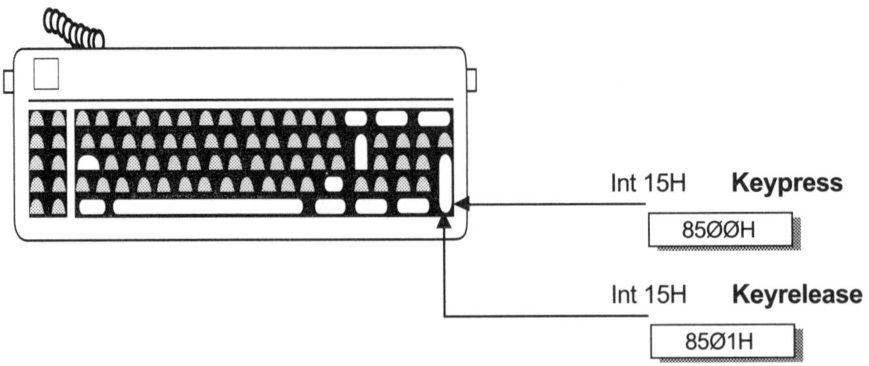

■ **FIGURE 2.1 The SysReq interrupts**

The whole program, when properly assembled and linked, is called SYSREQFF.COM. Because it's a .COM file, it's loaded into memory as a block of contiguous bytes at offset 100H in the current code segment. The first instruction jumps right past **ISR**, landing on the label **INSTALL**. The code there saves the address of the pre-existing INT 15H service routine, then installs **ISR** as the new service routine for that interrupt (see Figure 2.2).

Next, to save memory, the program discards its copy of the DOS environment space. (That's the block of data you see if you type **SET** with no parameters.) This is done by looking at offset 2CH in the program segment prefix to find the segment address of the environment block, then passing that address to DOS service 49H (deallocate memory).

This is an optional step; most TSR utilities don't do it. But it does save a couple of hundred bytes of memory that would otherwise be part of the permanently resident program. An interesting side effect of discarding the environment block is that programs that map your memory-resident utilities can no longer tell the name of this program. But they can still tell it's there and can report its size.

Finally, the program ends by calling DOS service 31H, the Terminate and Stay Resident (TSR) function. The DX register tells DOS how much of SYSREQFF is supposed to stay resident—in this case, not all of it—only the part extending from address 0 to the end of **ISR**.

The value in DX is the amount of memory space in paragraphs, where a paragraph is 16 bytes. It's computed at assembly time and includes the program segment prefix at addresses 0 to 0FFH. If I'd been more clever, I could have made **ISR** relocate itself to avoid wasting this space, but the code would have looked rather obscure.

Adding Additional Features

To make SysReq do other things, put your own routine in place of **PROC ISR**. Remember not to call any DOS services within the procedure unless you've mastered the arcane art of memory-resident DOS programming.

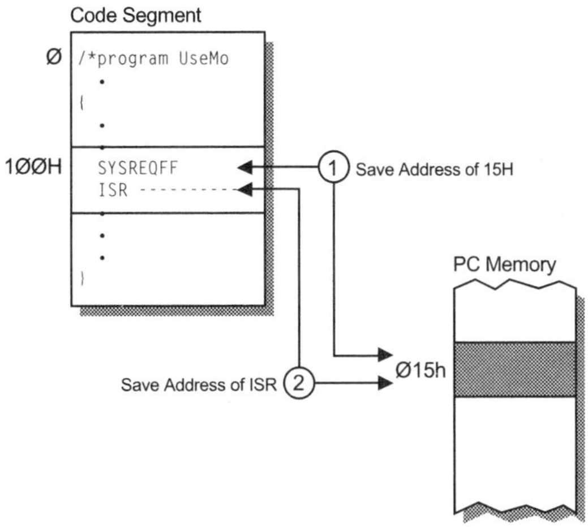

■ **FIGURE 2.2 Installing the SYSREQ program**

For greater versatility, you can let the user type other keys while holding down SysReq. To do this, clear the keyboard buffer when SysReq is pressed. A second or two later, when SysReq is released, read the characters that were typed and go your merry way.

CODE DESCRIPTION

Overview

The listing provided is used to assign a simple TSR to the SysReq key. The TSR sends a formfeed to the printer when the SysReq key is pressed.

Listing Available

Listing	*Description*	*Used with*
SYSREQFF.ASM	ASM source file that shows how to use the SysReq key.	------

How to Compile/Assemble

SYSREQFF.ASM should be assembled with TASM and linked with TLINK. The executable file produced should be a .COM.

■ LISTING 2.2 SYSREQFF.ASM

```
; SYSREQFF - Michael A. Covington
; Makes the Sys Req key formfeed the printer.
; Has no effect on computers without a Sys Req key.
; Assemble this file with the following commands:
;    C> TASM SYSREQFF.ASM SYSREQFF.OBJ
;    C> TLINK SYSREQFF.OBJ /T
; The /T is important - you're creating a .COM file.
FORMFEED        EQU  0CH
CR              EQU  0DH
LF              EQU  0AH
;; Code segment ------------------------
                .MODEL TINY
                .CODE
                ORG  100H
MAIN            PROC FAR
                JMP  INSTALL     ; don't execute it, install it!
;; Data area used by interrupt service routine --------
OLD_ISR         DD   0       ; to hold address of pre-existing
                             ; service routine for this interrupt
;; Interrupt service routine -----------------
ISR             PROC FAR
                STI                         ; re-enable interrupts
                CMP  AX,8500H               ; Sys Req pressed?
                JE   PRINT_FF              ; yes, print a formfeed
                JMP  CS:OLD_ISR   ; no, use pre-existing routine
PRINT_FF:       MOV  AL,FORMFEED
                MOV  AH,0                       ; print char in AL
                MOV  DX,0                               ; on LPT1:
                INT  17H                      ; using BIOS service
```

```
                IRET                            ; all done
BAIL_OUT:       JMP   CS:OLD_ISR
ISR             ENDP
END_OF_ISR      EQU   $-MAIN+100H         ; where resident code ends
                                          ; (Assembler does not know
                                          ; about loading and has to
                                          ; be reminded of 100h org)
;; Instructions to install the interrupt service routine ---
INSTALL:        ;;  Copy the current INT 15H vector into OLD_ISR
                MOV   BX,OFFSET OLD_ISR          ; where to store it
                MOV   AX,0
                MOV   ES,AX                    ; it's in segment 0000
                MOV   AX,ES:[0054H]       ; first word at 0000:0054
                MOV   [BX],AX
                MOV   AX,ES:[0056H]      ; second word at 0000:0056
                MOV   [BX+2],AX
                ;; Ask DOS to install new routine
                MOV   AH,25H          ; install new service routine
                MOV   AL,15H                   ; for interrupt 15H
                MOV   DX,OFFSET ISR       ; here's what to install
                INT   21H
                ;; Display message
                MOV   AH,09H             ; DOS call: display string
                MOV   DX,OFFSET MESSAGE              ; what to print
                INT   21H
                ;; Deallocate this program's copy of environment
                ;             (Optional. Doing this saves memory,
                ;            but it prevents MAP and its kin from
                ;              showing the name of this program.)
                MOV   AX,CS:[002CH]          ; PSP:002C contains the
                MOV   ES,AX              ; segment address of the env
                MOV   AH,49H    ; DOS call: free a block of memory
                INT   21H
                ;; Compute number of paragraphs of memory needed
                MOV   DX,(OFFSET END_OF_ISR+15)/16
                ;; Terminate and stay resident
                MOV   AH,31H     ; DOS call: Term & Stay Resident
                MOV   AL,0                           ; return code
                INT   21H            ; (DX contains memory request)
MESSAGE DB 'SysReq key will advance paper in printer.',CR,LF,'$'
MAIN            ENDP
                END   MAIN
CODE            ENDS
```

Getting Rid of the NumLock Nuisance

■ Dan Illowsky

Here's a trick to easily turn off the NumLock key.

When IBM released the first PC/AT computer, it came with a new "enhanced" keyboard that contained dedicated cursor control keys—in addition to the combination cursor control/number entry keys of the older model keyboards. Unfortunately for those of us who got used to using the old cursor keys, and for those who prefer using them, the new keyboards boot in the NumLock state. Thus the cursor control keys are initially inactive.

It's annoying trying to remember to toggle the NumLock state before using the keys for cursor movement. What we need is a program that can be invoked in AUTOEXEC.BAT to turn off the NumLock state automatically when the computer boots. To do this, all the program has to do is clear bit 5 of the byte at location 0:0417. Here is a procedure to create such a program using the standard DEBUG facility that comes with DOS:

```
>debug
-n nonum.com
-e cs:100 31 c0 8e d8 80 26 17 04 df cd 20
-r cx
CX 0000
:b
-w
-q
```

The **n** command names the program to be saved—NONUM.COM. The **e** command enters the actual values for the 11-byte program into memory. The **r cx** command causes the value of the CX register and the **:** prompt to be displayed. Typing **b** in response to the **:** prompt changes the value in CX to 0Bh (11 decimal), which is the number of bytes to write to disk. The **w** command causes the 11 bytes to be written to the file NONUM.COM. Finally, the **q** command quits the debug session and returns you to the DOS prompt.

For those of you who prefer real honest-to-God assembler files for this sort of thing, the source code looks like this:

```
xor   ax,ax                  ;Use data segment 0
mov   ds,ax                  ;
mov   bx,0417h               ;Point to byte 417 hex
and   byte ptr [bx],0dfh     ;Clear bit 5 at 0:417
int   20h                    ;Exit back to DOS
```

The Caps Lock Corrector

■ David Gerrold

Make your Caps Lock key behave properly with this useful program.

IBM got it wrong and everybody else followed because it was a "standard." How many times have you heard that?

From a touch typist's point of view, IBM's worst mistake is the behavior of the Caps Lock key, which acts like the shift-lock key on a typewriter. (Remember typewriters?) When you press the Caps Lock key, it toggles the seventh bit in the byte at address 0040:0017h. When that bit is on, every key typed will be an uppercase character—and the

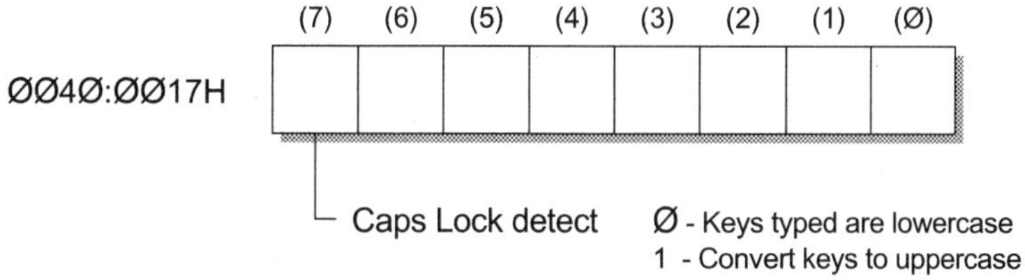

■ **FIGURE 2.3 The Caps Lock detect**

behavior of the shift keys will be reversed (see Figure 2.3); every shifted character typed will be lowercase. And how useful is that?

Touch typists expect to get an uppercase character and an automatic release of the Caps Lock whenever they hit a shift key. Instead, they get the exact opposite—a lowercase character. They not only have to go back and correct their mistake, they still have to hit the Caps Lock key to toggle the Caps Lock function off.

If you've done any serious typing at all on a computer, you've probably run into this problem.

Listing 2.3 presents a short demonstration program in C, showing how to make the Caps Lock key work like the shift lock key on a typewriter. Instead of the built-in C **getchar()** function, use **ReadChar()** to get a character from the keyboard.

ReadChar() first calls the normal **getch()** function, which does not echo characters back to the screen when they are entered. The routine checks the key state byte at 0040:0017h. If either shift key has been pressed, the first or second bit will be on. ANDing the key state byte will give you either a 1 or a 2. If a shift key has been pressed, the routine uppercases the character—that's what you want, that's why you pressed the shift key—and then turns off bit 7, the Caps Lock bit. And that's it. The demo program will let you enter text until you hit the Enter key.

If you use this **ReadChar()** function, instead of the built-in **getchar()** function, all your programs will automatically have a built-in Caps Lock corrector.

CODE DESCRIPTION

Overview

The listing provided shows how the Caps Lock key can be programmed to work like the shift lock key on a typewriter.

Listing Available

Listing	*Description*	*Used with*
CAPSLOCK.C	C source file that checks the state of the Caps Lock key at address 0040:0017h to determine how typed in characters should be handled.	------

How to Compile/Assemble

CAPSLOCK.C should be compiled with Borland C++ or with Turbo C++.

■ **LISTING 2.3 CAPSLOCK.C**

```
/*capslock.c*/
#include <dos.h>
#include <conio.h>
#include <ctype.h>

char Ch;

char ReadChar(void)

{
char  LocalCh;
char far *KeyStateBytePtr;

   KeyStateBytePtr = MK_FP(0x40,0x17);

   LocalCh = getch();
   if ((*KeyStateBytePtr & 0x03) > 0)    /* If either shift then*/
   {
     LocalCh = toupper(LocalCh);          /* upcase ch */
     *KeyStateBytePtr = (*KeyStateBytePtr & 0xBF);  /* Turn off CapsLock */
   }
     return LocalCh;                    /* Return char */
}

void main(void)                      /* Test program */
{
   while (Ch != 0x0D)                      /*Wait for carriage return*/
   {
     Ch = ReadChar();
     putch(Ch);
   }
}
```

Using the F11 and F12 Keys

■ Jeff Duntemann and George Seaton

Use a BIOS memory location to test whether an extended keyboard is available.

The newer 101/102-key keyboards have 12 function keys rather than the traditional ten. All well and good, but in this game, if you can't tell who's got the dominos, you can't play with 'em.

The newer 101-key keyboard, with its two extra function keys, requires extensions to the ROM BIOS keyboard services—both Int 09H and Int 16H. If you plug the newer keyboard into an older PC with an older ROM BIOS, you'll quickly discover that it does not work especially well. The BIOS extensions for the new keyboard parallel and duplicate existing services, but only the newer versions recognize the extra keys. (In fact, only the

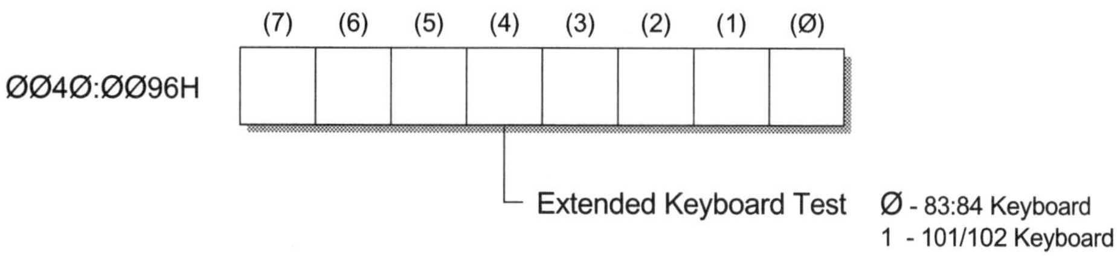

■ **FIGURE 2.4 Testing for extended keyboard**

newer services recognize some key combinations from the old keyboard—combinations that the older BIOS threw away!) The BIOS extensions also include logic for maintaining new, keyboard-related BIOS data words, at 0040:0096h and 0040:0097h.

Listing 2.4 shows a function, **IsNewKey()**, that returns 1 if the newer type keyboard is present, and 0 otherwise. This version uses one of the new ROM BIOS locations. The test location is 0040:0096h, and our keyboard flag is bit 4. If this bit is set, there is a 101/102-key keyboard attached and you can use the F11 and F12 key combinations. If the bit is reset, you can assume that the old 83/84-key keyboard is still in use (see Figure 2.4).

CODE DESCRIPTION

Overview

The listing provided defines a function, IsNewKey(), for determining if a PC has an extended keyboard available.

Listing Available

Listing	*Description*	*Used with*
NEWKEY.C	C source file that checks the address 0040:0096h to determine if an extended keyboard is available.	------

How to Compile/Assemble

NEWKEY.C should be compiled with Borland C++ or with Turbo C++.

■ **LISTING 2.4 NEWKEY.C**

```
/*NewKey.c*/

/* IsNewKey: A function for determining whether
   a 101/102-key keyboard is attached to the
   user's system */

#include <dos.h>

char IsNewKey(void)
{
```

```
int far *buffptr;

  buffptr = MK_FP(0x0040,0x0096);
  return ((*buffptr & 0x10) == 0x10);
}
```

Keyboard Buffer Stuffer

■ Shawn D. Wolf

Give your C programs a talent for touch typing using functions that manipulate the BIOS keyboard buffer.

There are plenty of touch-typing tutor programs around—programs that teach you how to type. While developing a menu program, I came up with the inverse situation: I needed to teach the program how to type. Here's why:

For each menu selection, my menu program would create an *ad hoc* batch file, with all the commands for invoking the selected application. I wanted the menu program to terminate and then automatically invoke the batch file. The batch file itself would recall the menu program after the selected application finished. This approach was preferable to invoking a secondary COMMAND.COM, since terminating the main program would leave all memory available to the selected application.

The Life-After-Death Problem

How could I get the main program to call a batch file *after* terminating? The answer lay in teaching it to type! More precisely, by having it stuff the keyboard buffer with the batch filename and a carriage return *just before* terminating. DOS would then think the batch filename had been typed in from the keyboard.

There are other potential uses for keyboard buffer stuffing: for example, a TSR (Terminate and Stay Resident) program that controls other application programs unattended; or a keyboard macro processor that expands simple keystrokes into lengthy command strings.

Whatever the application, all you need is an understanding of the BIOS keyboard buffer layout and operation, and a few good C functions for manipulating the buffer contents. Hopefully, the following paragraphs will fill the bill.

The One-Way Street

When dealing with the keyboard and input through its buffer, both DOS and the BIOS provide services for accessing the waiting keypresses in the buffer. However, this access is a one-way street: from keyboard to application. You can only *read* information from the buffer: i.e., get the next keypress from the buffer, find out if there is a keypress waiting in the buffer, get the keyboard status (Caps Lock, Num Lock, etc.), or get a string from the buffer.

The way keypresses *usually* get into the buffer is through the processing of a keyboard interrupt—something that only occurs when you press or release a key. Normally, this interrupt processing is invisible to the other services and to the user; you press a key, "a miracle occurs," and the keypress codes are available in the buffer.

For the purposes of this discussion, the "miracle part" can be summarized as follows (see Figure 2.5):

1. Pressing a key interrupts the PC processor (INT 09H).
2. The keyboard interrupt servicing routine (ISR) asks the keyboard for the identity of the key.
3. The keyboard responds with a code number ("scan code") that uniquely identifies the pressed key.
4. The ISR then creates a two-byte entry for insertion into the BIOS keyboard buffer in lower memory. The exact entry depends on the key's identity, and other factors such as whether one of the shift keys (Shift, Ctrl, or Alt) is being held down, or whether a "toggle" like Caps Lock is currently active.
5. Based on these considerations, the ISR inserts the appropriate two bytes into the keyboard buffer and adjusts the buffer pointers.

TIP: For more information on how the keyboard interrupts process keypresses into characters see "The Story of 'O'" later in this chapter.

An application that is expecting keyboard input uses a DOS (INT 21H) or BIOS (INT 16H) "read keyboard" service to retrieve the keypress codes from the buffer.

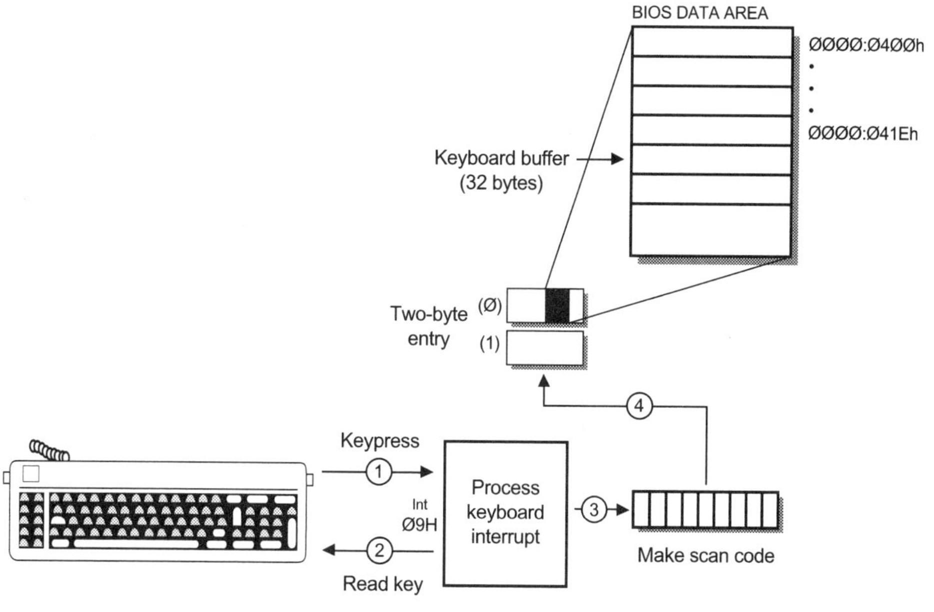

■ **FIGURE 2.5 Processing a keypress**

For the normal QWERTY (typewriter) keys, the first buffer byte is the corresponding ASCII code for the key; the second byte is the key's scan code. In most situations, this scan code is ignored when the buffer is accessed for ASCII characters.

When a special key is pressed (for example, a function key or cursor movement key), or when a key is shifted using the Alt key, the first byte placed in the buffer is usually a zero. This indicates that there is no ASCII code associated with the key. The second byte is the key's extended code. For unshifted function and cursor key's, the extended code is the same as the scan code. For shifted keypresses, a different, unique code number appears in the second byte. This allows applications to discriminate between the various shifted and unshifted combinations for the special keys.

Table 2.3 is a listing of the extended codes for the special keys found on all PC/XT/AT and later keyboards. Let's take a close look at how the keyboard buffer works; perhaps we can perform our own miracle and duplicate a portion of the keyboard interrupts function.

■ TABLE 2.3 Extended keyboard codes (hex)

Code	Keypress
0F	Shift Tab
10–19	Alt Q, W, E, R, T, Y, U, I, O, P
1E–26	Alt A, S, D, F, G, H, J, K, L
2C–32	Alt Z, X, C, V, B, N, M
3B–44	F1 through F10
47	Home
48	Cursor Up
49	Page Up
4B	Cursor Left
4D	Cursor Right
4F	End
50	Cursor Down
51	Page Down
52	Insert
53	Delete
54–5D	Shift F1 through F10
5E–67	Ctrl F1 through F10
68–71	Alt F1 through F10
72	Ctrl Print Screen
73	Ctrl Cursor Left
74	Ctrl Cursor Right
75	Ctrl End
76	Ctrl Page Down
77	Control Home
78–83	Alt 1, 2, 3, 4, 5, 6, 7, 8, 9, 0, -, = (keyboard top)
84	Ctrl Page Up

Buffer Biography

The keyboard buffer is located in low memory within the BIOS data area that begins at address 0000:0400h. The buffer itself begins at 0000:041Eh and is 32 bytes long. The buffer is a FIFO (first in, first out) type. The first keypress placed into the buffer will be the first one taken out when an application retrieves its keyboard input.

The buffer also operates as a *circular list*, meaning that no particular memory address is the beginning of the data in the buffer. Instead, there are two pointers that keep track of the "head" and the "tail" of the data.

By convention, the buffer is "empty" when the head pointer and tail pointer refer to the same buffer position. When a key is pressed, two bytes are placed in the buffer, starting at the offset in the tail pointer. The tail pointer is then incremented by two, to point to the next *free* buffer position. When the highest memory position (0000:043Dh) in the buffer is filled, the tail pointer "wraps around" to the lowest buffer position (0000:041Eh).

Since the definition for an *empty* buffer requires that the head and tail pointer be equal, the tail pointer cannot "catch up" with (become equal to) the head pointer while receiving new keypresses into the buffer. In practice this means that the buffer can hold only 15 keypress codes, even though there is room for 16 two-byte entries. After adding a sixteenth keypress, incrementing the tail pointer would make it equal to the head pointer, defining the buffer as "empty," which it plainly is not.

Assuming no keypresses are removed and the head pointer remains stationary, the buffer becomes "full" with the *fifteenth* keypress. The system will reject further keyboard input. When this happens, you get those annoying beeps that let you know you've typed too far ahead of the receiving application.

The head and tail pointers are located in memory right below the buffer, at addresses 0000:041Ah and 0000:041Ch, respectively. These are not true pointers, but are actually integers (two bytes long). They reflect offsets from the beginning of the BIOS data area (0000:0400h). This means that the values placed into the head and tail pointers *must* be offsets in the range of 1Eh to 3Ch. (Placing a value out of that range into one of the pointers would probably put the BIOS into hyperspace; certainly *not* something we would encourage!)

When an application retrieves a keypress from the buffer, the BIOS logic increments the head pointer by two. Here too, wraparound occurs after the highest buffer position is accessed. As the application takes more keypresses out of the buffer, the head pointer can catch up with the tail pointer. If it does, the buffer is once again empty.

Programs sometimes "clear" the buffer by setting the tail pointer and the head pointer to the same value. The value must be an even number so that wraparound does not occur in the middle of keypress byte pairs. To be safe, the clear operation can simply set the tail pointer equal to the current head pointer, or vice versa.

Buffer Maps

Figure 2.6 shows keyboard buffer maps for different states of "fullness." The leftmost map represents an empty buffer. Both the head and the tail pointers refer to the same buffer position.

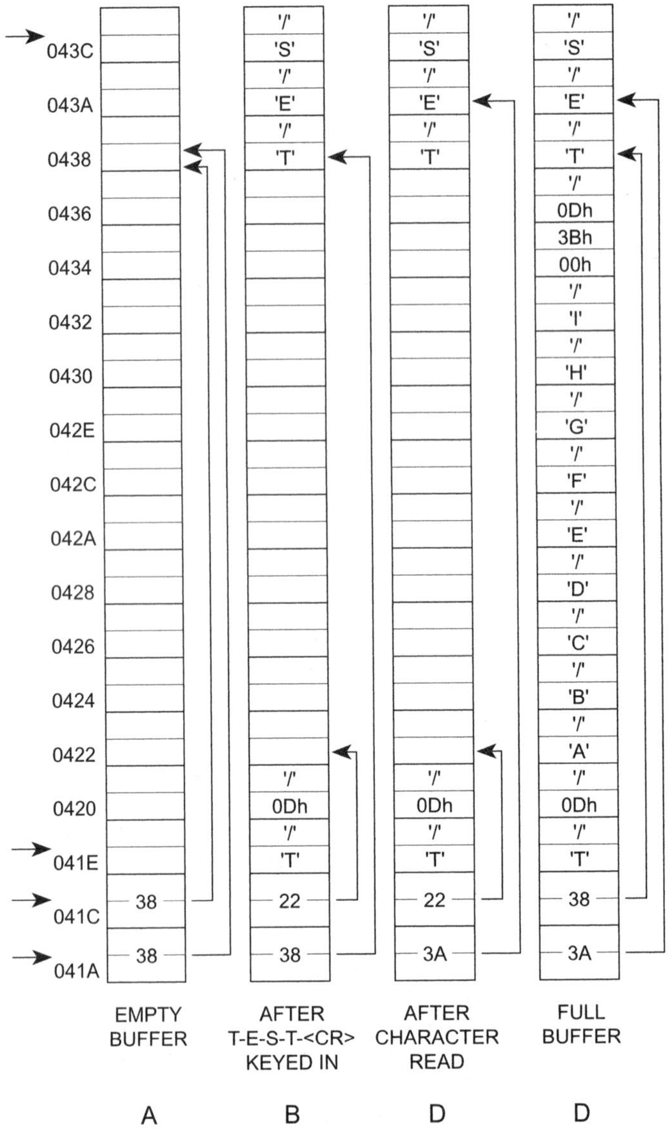

■ **FIGURE 2.6 Placing a keystroke into the buffer**

The next map shows the buffer after the keys "T," "E," "S," "T," and Enter have been pressed. The head pointer remains unchanged, but the tail pointer has incremented by ten, and has wrapped around to point to the buffer position following the last keypress entry. (These memory maps use dummy "/" characters to represent the key-scan codes that normally follow the ASCII bytes in the buffer.)

The next map depicts the same buffer after an application reads one keypress from the buffer. The application retrieved the first "T," and the BIOS logic incremented the head pointer by two. Notice that the "T" character code that was read remains in the buffer, but is ignored. The system will overwrite it when the tail pointer passes it again.

The final map diagram shows a full buffer. The letters "A" through "I" have been entered, along with F1 and Enter keystrokes. Notice that the tail pointer cannot be incremented again since it would equal the head pointer. The F1 keypress in the buffer has a first byte of 00H and a second byte of 3BH, the scan code for the F1 key.

The Buffer Stuffing Functions

Now that we have a good understanding of how the keyboard buffer operates, we can create a function that "stuffs" a program-generated keypress into the buffer. Listing 2.5 includes just such a function: **put_char_in_buff()**. Programs pass two parameters to the function, the first being the keypress to be inserted. The second parameter is a flag to let the function know whether the keypress parameter is for a normal or special key. (To handle an entire string of keypresses, we can use this basic function to create a **put_string_in_buff()** function, which also appears in Listing 2.5.)

Before we place a keypress into the buffer, we must make sure that the buffer isn't already full. The algorithm for calculating how many *more* keypresses (not bytes) the buffer will hold is

```
ROOM IN BUFFER = (15 - [(TAIL - HEAD) / 2]) modulus 16
```

This calculation takes into account that the head pointer can be greater than the tail pointer, due to wraparound. The **key_buff_space()** function in Listing 2.5 calculates and returns the available keypress spaces for our program. (The **clear_key_buff()** function in the listing shows how to arbitrarily clear the buffer, making sure we have space!)

After determining there is enough room, we are ready to insert our keypress. As we have seen, we must place two bytes into the buffer. The first byte goes into the buffer position specified by the current tail pointer. We then increment the tail pointer by one, and store the second byte in the same manner. We increment the tail pointer again, to point to the next free location. This time, however, we check to see if the tail is pointing past the end of buffer memory. If so, we point it to the start of the buffer memory, thus performing the wraparound.

When calling our function, the parameters we pass to it depend on the type of keypress we are sending. If it's a normal key (i.e., QWERTY type), we send the ASCII value of the key in the first parameter and a zero (**FALSE**) in the second. If it's a special key (function or cursor movement key), we send the key's extended code in the first parameter and a one (**TRUE**) in the second.

The contents of the two bytes placed into the buffer by the function depend on the state of the second passed parameter. For a normal key (second parameter is **FALSE**), we place the first parameter (ASCII code) into the first byte, and a dummy scan code into the second byte. If this is a special key (second parameter is **TRUE**), we place a zero into the first byte, and the first parameter (extended code) into the second byte.

Remember that the keyboard buffer has a size limit. If you are stuffing characters into the buffer, and they are not being read and removed while you are doing this, you will fill the buffer after 15 insertions.

Also remember to terminate your keystroke sequences with a carriage return (0DH) when entering a program or batch filename for DOS invocation. If you do not, it will be as if you typed in the keys but never pressed Enter.

You Are Not Alone

One more important point: Keep in mind that you are not the only source of keypresses for the keyboard buffer. The keyboard ISR is constantly waiting for the keyboard to signal that it has a keypress available. Once this happens, the keyboard interrupt instantly grabs the keypress and stuffs it into the buffer. This *could* happen while our function is in the middle of placing a string there—catching us in the act of adjusting the pointers. The result could be disastrous for applications waiting for *our* simulated keypresses.

To insure that this does not happen, we have to turn off the hardware interrupts during the period when characters from the keyboard might interfere with what we're trying to do. To turn off interrupts, we use the **disable()** function. To turn them back on we use the **enable()** function. (Those are the library function names for Borland's Turbo C; for Microsoft C use **_disable()** and **_enable()**.)

You must decide in your own program when you cannot afford to have stray keypresses coming in from the keyboard. It may be during a string insertion into the buffer, or could even be between string insertions. For the demonstration program in Listing 2.5, we disable interrupts so that a single string cannot be interrupted (i.e., within **put_string_in_buff()**), and when clearing the buffer, as in **clear_key_buff()**.

A Practical Demonstration

Listing 2.5 is a demonstration program that uses our buffer insertion functions to write a string and two separate characters into the keyboard buffer and then return to DOS. What we simulate here is typing **DIR<Enter>** (to request a directory listing), followed by a program-generated [F3] keystroke, to do it one more time. The inserted keystrokes are then read by COMMAND.COM (the part of DOS that is running when you see the DOS prompt), which executes them. You should see two consecutive "DIR" listings after running the KEYBUFF.EXE program.

You could also try replacing the "DIR" string with the name of a batch file. That should clearly demonstrate the utility of these buffer-stuffer functions.

CODE DESCRIPTION

Overview

The listing provided defines functions for writing a string to the keyboard buffer.

Listing Available

Listing	*Description*	*Used with*
KEYBUFF.C	C source file that writes strings to the keyboard buffer.	------

How to Compile/Assemble

KEYBUFF.C should be compiled with Borland C++ or with Turbo C++. Do not compile the listing in "ANSI source" mode because an 80x86-specific far keyword is used.

To compile the listing with Microsoft C, follow the directions provided in the file.

Note: The executable program should be run from the DOS prompt.

■ LISTING 2.5 KEYBUFF.C

```
/* REMEMBER:
   This source uses the 80x86-specific (non-ANSI) "far"
   keyword (supported by both Turbo C/C++ and Microsoft C
   in their "native" modes).  DO NOT compile the source in
   an "ANSI source" mode.

   ALSO: Do not run the .EXE from the Borland IDE. (It will
   "type" into the IDE windows!)  Shell out to DOS and run
   it from the DOS prompt. */

/* --- function prototypes --- */
void clear_key_buff(void);
int key_buff_space(void);
int put_char_in_buff(unsigned char bchar,int extend);
int put_string_in_buff(char *str_ptr);

#include <dos.h>

/* --- global pointers --- */
/* keyboard buffer head: */
static int far *bufferhead = (int far *) 0x41A;
/* keyboard buffer tail: */
static int far *buffertail = (int far *) 0x41C;
/* keyboard buffer: */
static char far *keybuffer = (char far *) 0x41E;

/* --- start of code --- */
/* This listing for Turbo C. For Microsoft C, change disable() to
   _disable() and enable() to _enable(). */

main ()
   {
   clear_key_buff();
   put_string_in_buff("DIR\x0D");
   /* Now let's put an 'F3' to repeat last command. */
   put_char_in_buff('\x3D',1);     /* Put 'F3' into buffer. */
   put_char_in_buff('\x0D',0);     /* Put 'RETURN' into buffer. */
   return 0;
   }

void clear_key_buff(void)
   /* clears the keyboard buffer by setting the tail = head */
```

```
   {
   disable();     /* turn off the normal keyboard interrupt */
   *buffertail = *bufferhead;
   enable();                /* restore the normal interrupts */
   }

int key_buff_space(void)
   /* Returns the number of free keypress spaces in the buffer.
      (not bytes.) Returns 15 if buffer is empty, 0 if full. */
   {
   return (15 - ((*buffertail - *bufferhead) / 2)) % 16;
   }

int put_char_in_buff(unsigned char bchar,int extend)
   /* Places passed character into keyboard buffer. If extend is
      true, treats keypress as extended and places it into
      second byte.  Otherwise, places it into first byte. */
   {
   unsigned char first_byte,second_byte;

   if (!key_buff_space())      /* Is the keyboard buffer full? */
      return 0;                /* If so, return error. */

   if (extend)                 /* Is this an extended keypress? */
      {                        /* Yes, it is extended. */
      first_byte = 0;          /* Zero goes in first byte. */
      second_byte = bchar;     /* Passed char goes into second. */
      }
   else                              /* No, it is not extended. */
      {
      first_byte = bchar;  /* Passed char goes into first byte. */
      second_byte = '/';   /* Dummy scan code goes into second. */
      }

   /* Place first byte: */
   *(keybuffer + (*buffertail - 0x1E)) = first_byte;
   /* Increment the tail - no need to check for wrap: */
   ++(*buffertail);

   /* Place 2nd byte: */
   *(keybuffer + (*buffertail - 0x1E)) = second_byte;
   if (++(*buffertail) > 0x3D) /* Increment tail - check for wrap. */
      *buffertail = 0x1E;      /* If wrap, set tail to
                                  lowest buffer memory. */

   return 1;
   }

int put_string_in_buff(char *string_ptr)
   /* Takes passed string and places it into keyboard buffer.
      Returns true on success, false on failure. */
   {
   int rval;
```

```
rval = 1;
disable();                     /* Don't interrupt this string. */
while (*string_ptr)            /* Loop thru each char in string.  */
   /* Put char into buffer: */
   if (!put_char_in_buff(*string_ptr++,0))
      {              /* We're assuming it's a normal keypress.  */
      rval = 0;      /* If placement not successful, exit loop. */
      break;
      }

enable();                            /* Restore interrupts. */

return rval;                         /* Return success status. */
}
```

The Story of "O"

■ George Seaton

The intimate account of the travels of a single keystroke from your fingertips to the BIOS keyboard buffer.

When you press a key on your PC keyboard—the letter "O," for example—you initiate a sequence of BIOS, DOS, and program operations that ultimately lead to your keyboard character appearing on the screen and becoming part, perhaps, of your next best-seller. While perhaps not as interesting as a Jackie Collins book, *this* intimate story of "O" strips the veil away from PC keyboard operations, exposing the secrets of scan codes and entries in the keyboard buffer.

We Interrupt This Novel

Pressing down on the "O" key causes the keyboard to generate an interrupt in the PC. Releasing the key also generates an interrupt. Most PCs use IRQ1 (Interrupt Request Line #1) for keyboard interrupts. The interrupt processor for the CPU responds to the keyboard interrupt by transferring control to the INT 09H Interrupt Servicing Routine (ISR), using a far pointer located at 0000:0024H in memory. (The ISR pointer for "INT nn" resides at the address that is four times the interrupt number "nn." The ROM BIOS logic fills in the address of its built-in INT 09H ISR during system startup.)

The INT 09H ISR has much to do. First, it must determine which key you pressed or released. It does so by executing an **IN** instruction for the keyboard port; usually port number 60H. The keyboard responds by sending back a "scan code" that uniquely identifies the key. For a "key make" (pressing down), the identifying key code bytes are in the range 01H to 7FH (high-order bits reset). For the "key break" (release), the high-order bit for the key code bytes are set.

On the original 83-key PC keyboard, the "make" scan code consisted of a single byte in the range 1 to 83 (53H). The AT keyboard added the SysRq key, rearranged the scan codes, and extended the one-byte scan codes to 84 (54H). Life was simpler then.

New Keys on the Block

With the arrival of the 101/102-key keyboard, both life and scan codes got more complex. Rather than simply add another 18 single-byte scan codes, the keyboard designers decided to get clever. First, they recognized that the new keyboards had *two* of some "shift" and cursor keys: two Alt keys, two page-up keys, two delete keys, and so on. For each new duplicate key, the keyboard now generates *two* scan code bytes. The first byte, 0E0H or 0E1H, says "Hey, I'm a new duplicate key." The second scan code byte is the same one-byte code used for the original key on the 83/84-key keyboard. (They went a little overboard with the new Pause and Print Screen keys—these produce *three- and four-byte* scan codes!)

After receiving the scan code byte(s) from the keyboard controller, the ROM BIOS INT 09H logic must decide what to do with the key data. The new 101/102 key keyboards required an entirely new BIOS since the old PC/XT/AT BIOS choked on the scan codes for the newly added keys.

The INT 09H ISR can usually ignore most key *break* interrupts, since it took action on the preceding "make." The Alt, Ctrl, and Shift keys are exceptions; releasing one of these keys changes a "shifted state," so some action is necessary. (More on this in just a bit.)

The Well-Stuffed Buffer

For the normal QWERTY typewriter keys—those having equivalent ASCII character codes—the INT 09H logic usually sticks two bytes into the BIOS keyboard buffer. Table 2.4 lists the BIOS addresses for the buffer and its pointers. The first buffer byte is the ASCII code for the key character; the second is the key's scan code. Most applications that expect ASCII input from the user can simply ignore the second byte.

TIP: To learn more about the techniques of working with the BIOS keyboard buffer, see "Buffer Stuffing Functions" earlier in this chapter.

For the letter, number, and punctuation keys, the inserted ASCII code depends on the current Shift state (and the Caps Lock state, for letters). These states tell the logic whether to use the upper or lowercase ASCII code for letters, or whether to use the shifted or unshifted character code for the number/punctuation keys. Similarly, the Shift and NumLock states control the codes used for keys on the original numeric keypad: the ASCII code or a cursor control code.

■ TABLE 2.4 The BIOS keyboard buffer address

Address	Description
041Ah	(Two bytes) Pointer to the keyboard buffer head
041Ch	(Two bytes) Pointer to the keyboard buffer tail
041Eh	(32 bytes) Keyboard buffer, sized for 16 keystrokes
0480h	(Two bytes) Pointer to the keyboard buffer start offset
0482h	(Two bytes) Pointer to the keyboard buffer end offset

Some Ctrl-shifted QWERTY keys also have valid ASCII equivalents: the familiar nonprinting control codes like Tab, Backspace, Form Feed, and so on. For these, the same procedure applies: the first buffer byte is the ASCII code; the second is the key's scan code.

Breaking All the Rules

So far, it's all pretty logical and straightforward. It becomes interesting when we examine the INT 09H logic for keys that *do not* have equivalent ASCII codes. These include the Alt-shifted QWERTY keys (and some Ctrl-shifted ones), the function keys, and the cursor control keys. ("Alt-shifted" and "Ctrl-shifted" mean using the Alt and Ctrl keys *like* the Shift key; you hold one of these down while pressing a regular key.)

The *general* rule is: For Alt-shifted QWERTY keys and for *unshifted* function and cursor key's, the INT 09H ISR puts a zero in the first keyboard buffer byte and puts the key's scan code in the second buffer byte. There are some glaring exceptions to this general rule. For example, the Alt-shifted *number* keys on the QWERTY keyboard—but *not* the punctuation keys—use "scan code plus 76H" for the second byte. The new F11 and F12 function keys use "scan code plus 2EH" for the unshifted key. Also, some Alt-shifted keys get 0F0H (rather than 00H) in the *first* byte. Interesting, right?

Another general rule is that the Ctrl- and Alt-shifted function and cursor movement keys use the zero-byte/other-byte scheme. In these cases, the second byte is a unique number, derived from a numbering scheme that was (it appears) based on the designer's shoe size.

The new duplicate keys provide their own glaring exceptions. For example, the BIOS INT 09H logic puts 0E0H (not zero) in the first buffer byte for the duplicate keys on the new cursor control keypads—but only for the normal, Shift, and Ctrl keys; the Alt-shifted keys (infuriatingly!) use zero.

Toggling Under the Shifts

The shift keys themselves (Shift, Ctrl, and Alt) do not result in any entries in the BIOS keyboard buffer; nor do the "toggle" keys, Caps Lock, NumLock, and Scroll Lock. For these, the INT 09H ISR sets or resets status bits that it maintains in four words in the BIOS data area. (See Table 2.5.) These status bits indicate whether a shift or toggle key is currently pressed and whether a toggle state is currently active. (If you hold down more than one shift key, the order or precedence is Alt:Ctrl:Shift.) Note that the Insert keys get both a "pressed" flag and a state toggle (not always accurate), *and* they generate a keyboard buffer entry.

Table 2.6 is a valiant attempt to get it all down in black-and-white. It is at least correct for an AST Premium/286 of 1988 vintage, with a Northgate Omnikey Ultra keyboard. The Alt-shifted numbers for the numeric keypad are a bit of a SWAG since most BIOSes insist on giving you "^G" when you press **[Alt-7]**. You can use **DEBUG** to poke around in the BIOS keyboard buffer to see what gets stuffed for *your* particular PC/keyboard combination. Hint: Preset DS to 0040h. Press some key combination a few times (backspace if it produces characters on the screen), and then enter "D1E L20." This will show you the keyboard buffer.

■ TABLE 2.5 Bit maps of BIOS keyboard states

At Byte address 0040:0017h:

Bit 7 = Insert mode locked
Bit 6 = CapsLock state locked
Bit 5 = NumLock state locked
Bit 4 = ScrollLock state locked
Bit 3 = Alt pressed
Bit 2 = Ctrl pressed
Bit 1 = Left Shift pressed
Bit 0 = Right Shift pressed

At Byte address 0040:0018h:

Bit 7 = Insert pressed
Bit 6 = CapsLock pressed
Bit 5 = NumLock pressed
Bit 4 = ScrollLock pressed
Bit 3 = Pause state locked
Bit 2 = SysRq pressed
Bit 1 = Left Alt pressed
Bit 0 = Left Ctrl pressed

At Byte address 0040:0096h:

Bit 7 = Read ID in progress †
Bit 6 = Last character was first ID character †
Bit 5 = Force NumLock if read ID and KBX †
Bit 4 = 101/102-key keyboard attached
Bit 3 = Right Alt pressed
Bit 2 = Right Ctrl pressed
Bit 1 = Last code was 0E0h
Bit 0 = Last code was 0E1h
† = Internal BIOS flags

At Byte address 0040:0097h:

Bit 7 = Keyboard transmit error
Bit 6 = Mode Indicator update
Bit 5 = Resend receive flag
Bit 4 = ACK received
Bit 3 = Reserved (must be reset)
Bit 2 = Keyboard CapsLock LED state
Bit 1 = Keyboard NumLock LED state
Bit 0 = Keyboard ScrollLock LED state

■ TABLE 2.6 Scan codes/key buffer entries

Key Cap	"Make" Scan Codes	Scan and ASCII Codes Put in Buffer Normal	+[Shft]	+[Ctrl]	+[Alt]
FUNCTION KEYS (Top Row)					
[ESC]	01	1B 01	1B 01	00 AF	F0 01†
[F1]	3B	00 3B	00 54	00 5E	00 68
[F2]	3C	00 3C	00 55	00 5F	00 69
[F3]	3D	00 3D	00 56	00 60	00 6A
[F4]	3E	00 3E	00 57	00 61	00 6B
[F5]	3F	00 3F	00 58	00 62	00 6C
[F6]	40	00 40	00 59	00 63	00 6D
[F7]	41	00 41	00 5A	00 64	00 6E
[F8]	42	00 42	00 5B	00 65	00 6F
[F9]	43	00 43	00 5C	00 66	00 70
[F10]	44	00 44	00 5D	00 67	00 71
[F11]	57	00 85	00 87	00 89	00 8B
[F12]	58	00 86	00 88	00 8A	00 8C
[Print Screen]	E02A E037	37 2A	(INT 5)	00 72	00 AD?
[Scroll Lock]	46	———(Refer to Table 2.5)———			
[Pause]/[Break]	E11D 45	———(Refer to Table 2.5)———			
1ST QWERTY ROW					
[']/[~]	29	60 29	7E 29	00 B3	F0 29†
[1]/[!]	02	31 02	21 02	00 B9	00 78
[2]/[@]	03	32 03	40 03	00 03	00 79
[3]/[#]	04	33 04	23 04	00 BB	00 7A
[4]/[$]	05	34 05	24 05	00 BC	00 7B
[5]/[%]	06	35 06	25 06	00 BD	00 7C
[6]/[^]	07	36 07	5E 07	1E 07	00 7D
[7]/[&]	08	37 08	26 08	00 BF	00 7E
[8]/[*]	09	38 09	2A 09	00 C0	00 7F
[9]/[(]	0A	39 0A	28 0A	00 C1	00 80
[0]/[)]	0B	30 0B	29 0B	00 B8	00 81
[-]/[_]	0C	2D 0C	5F 0C	1F 0C	00 82
[_]/[+]	0D	3D 0D	2B 0D	00 B1	00 83
[Bksp]	0E	08 0E	08 0E	7F 0E	F0 0E†

† The new INT 16H read service (AH=10h) converts the 0F0H byte to 00H.

■ TABLE 2.6 Scan codes/key buffer entries *(continued)*

Key Cap	"Make" Scan Codes	Scan and ASCII Codes Put in Buffer Normal	+[Shft]	+[Ctrl]	+[Alt]
2ND QWERTY ROW					
[Tab]	0F	09 0F	00 0F	00 94	00 A5
[Q]	10	71 10	51 10	11 10	00 10
[W]	11	77 11	57 11	17 11	00 11
[E]	12	65 12	45 12	05 12	00 12
[R]	13	72 13	52 13	12 13	00 13
[T]	14	74 14	54 14	14 14	00 14
[Y]	15	79 15	59 15	19 15	00 15
[U]	16	75 16	55 16	15 16	00 16
[I]	17	69 17	49 17	09 17	00 17
[O]	18	6F 18	4F 18	0F 18	00 18
[P]	19	70 19	50 19	10 19	00 19
[[]/[{]	1A	5B 1A	7B 1A	1B 1A	F0 1A†
[]]/[}]	1B	5D 1B	7D 1B	1D 1B	F0 1B†
[\]/[|]	2B	5C 2B	7C 2B	1C 2B	F0 2B†
3RD QWERTY ROW					
[Caps Lock]	3A	———	(Refer to Table 2.5)	———	
[A]	1E	61 1E	41 1E	01 1E	00 1E
[S]	1F	73 1F	53 1F	13 1F	00 1F
[D]	20	64 20	44 20	04 20	00 20
[F]	21	66 21	46 21	06 21	00 21
[G]	22	67 22	47 22	07 22	00 22
[H]	23	68 23	48 23	08 23	00 23
[J]	24	6A 24	4A 24	0A 24	00 24
[K]	25	6B 25	4B 25	0B 25	00 25
[L]	26	6C 26	4C 26	0C 26	00 26
[;]/[:]	27	3B 27	3A 27	00 98	F0 27†
[']/["]	28	27 28	22 28	00 99	F0 28†
[Enter]	1C	0D 1C	0D 1C	0A 1C	F0 1C†

† The new INT 16H read service (AH=10h) converts the 0F0H byte to 00H.

Key Cap	"Make" Scan Codes	Normal	+[Shft]	+[Ctrl]	+[Alt]
4TH QWERTY ROW					
[ShiftLeft]	2A	———	(Refer to Table 2.5)	———	
[Z]	2C	7A 2C	5A 2C	1A 2C	00 2C
[X]	2D	78 2D	58 2D	18 2D	00 2D

■ **TABLE 2.6 Scan codes/key buffer entries *(continued)***

Key Cap	"Make" Scan Codes	Scan and ASCII Codes Put in Buffer Normal	+[Shft]	+[Ctrl]	+[Alt]
[C]	2E	63 2E	43 2E	03 2E	00 2E
[V]	2F	76 2F	56 2F	16 2F	00 2F
[B]	30	62 30	42 30	02 30	00 30
[N]	31	6E 31	4E 31	0E 31	00 31
[M]	32	6D 32	4D 32	0D 32	00 32
[,]/[<]	33	2C 33	3C 33	00 B4	00 33
[.]/[>]	34	2E 34	3E 34	00 BE	00 34
[/]/[?]	35	2F 35	3F 35	00 B5	00 35
[ShiftRight]	36	————(Refer to Table 2.5)————			
BOTTOM ROW					
[Ctrl]-Left	1D	————(Refer to Table 2.5)————			
[Alt]-Left	38	————(Refer to Table 2.5)————			
[Space]	39	20 39	20 39	20 39	20 39
[Alt]-Right	E038	————(Refer to Table 2.5)————			
[Ctrl]-Right	E01D	————(Refer to Table 2.5)————			
NUMERIC KEYPAD					
[Num Lock]	45	————(Refer to Table 2.5)————			
[</>]	E035	2F E0	2F E0	00 95	00 A4
[<*>]	37	2A 37	2A 37	00 96	F0 37††
[Min]	4A	2D 4A	2D 4A	00 8E	F0 4A††
[Home]/[7]	47	00 47	37 47	00 77	00 97 ?
[Up]/[8]	48	00 48	38 48	00 8D	00 98 ?
[Pg Up]/[9]	49	00 49	39 49	00 84	00 99 ?
[Left]/[4]	4B	00 4B	34 4B	00 73	00 9B ?
[Ctr]/[5]	4C	F0 4C††	35 4C	00 8F	00 9C ?
[Right]/[6]	4D	00 4D	36 4D	00 74	00 9D ?
[Pls]	4E	2B 4E	2B 4E	00 90	F0 4E††
[End]/[1]	4F	00 4F	31 4F	00 75	00 9F ?
[Down]/[2]	50	00 50	32 50	00 91	00 A0 ?
[Pg Dn]/[3]	51	00 51	33 51	00 76	00 A1 ?
[Ins]/[0]*	52	00 52	30 52	00 92	00 A2
[Del]/[.]	53	00 53	2E 53	00 93	00 A3
[<Enter>]	E01C	0D E0	0D E0	0A E0	00 A6

* Refer also to Table 2.5

†† Returned "as is" by the new INT 16H read service (AH=10h).

■ **TABLE 2.6 Scan codes/key buffer entries *(continued)***

Key Cap	"Make" Scan Codes	Scan and ASCII Codes Put in Buffer Normal	+[Shft]	+[Ctrl]	+[Alt]
SEPARATE CURSOR CONTROL KEYS					
[Insert]	E052	E0 52	E0 52	E0 92	00 A2
[Home]	E047	E0 47	E0 47	E0 77	00 97
[Page Up]	E049	E0 49	E0 49	E0 84	00 99
[Delete]	E053	E0 53	E0 53	E0 93	00 A3
[End]	E04F	E0 4F	E0 4F	E0 75	00 9F
[Page Down]	E051	E0 51	E0 51	E0 76	00 A1
[Up Arrow]	E048	E0 48	E0 48	E0 8D	00 98
[Left Arrow]	E04B	E0 4B	E0 4B	E0 73	00 9B
[Down Arrow]	E050	E0 50	E0 50	E0 91	00 A0
[Right Arrow]	E04D	E0 4D	E0 4D	E0 74	00 9D

■ **TABLE 2.7 Int 16H services**

Setting	Description
AH = 0:	Keyboard Read (Remove character if ready; wait if no character ready)
AH = 1:	Keystroke Status (Return Zero Flag = 1 if no character is ready; return ZF = 0 AND character if ready, but do not remove character from buffer)
AH = 2:	Get Shift Status (Return AL = contents of 0040H:0017H)
AH = 3:	Set Typematic Rate and Delay - AL = 05 - BL = 00H (30.0 cps) through 1FH (2.0 cps) - BH = 00H (250 ms) through 03H (1000 ms)
AH = 5:	Write to Keyboard Buffer - CL = ASCII code
AH = 10:	Extended Keyboard Read (101/102 key keyboards)
AH = 11:	Extended Keystroke Status (101/102 key keyboards)
AH = 12:	Get Extended Shift Status (101/102 key keyboards) Bits in returned AL are: Bit 7 = SysReq pressed (from 0040:0018, bit 02) Bit 6 = CapsLock pressed (from 0040:0018, bit 06) Bit 5 = NumLock pressed (from 0040:0018, bit 05) Bit 4 = ScrollLock pressed (from 0040:0018, bit 04)

■ **TABLE 2.7 Int 16H services *(continued)***

Setting	Description
AH = 12:	Bit 3 = Right Alt pressed (from 0040:0096, bit 03) Bit 2 = Right Ctrl pressed (from 0040:0096, bit 02) Bit 1 = Left Alt pressed (from 0040:0018, bit 01) Bit 0 = Left Ctrl pressed (from 0040:0018, bit 00)

Note : The "extended" services became necessary with the introduction of the 101/102 key keyboards. The "regular" services ignore (throw away) key codes returned by the additional keys on the newer keyboards.

Get Your O's Outta Here

The INT 09H ISR logic can get your "O" as far as the keyboard buffer. It's up to your word processor to retrieve it and do something with it. The ultimate tool for getting data out of the BIOS keyboard buffer is INT 16H; the keyboard *software* interrupt. Basically, all applications that receive user input from the keyboard (or from keyboard buffer stuffers) must periodically invoke INT 16H to pull the oldest key codes out of the buffer and adjust the buffer pointers. Otherwise, it's beep-beep time as you type madly away and fill up the buffer.

INT 16H provides a number of services for application programs. The byte value in the AH register determines just what service to perform for the calling program (see Table 2.7 for a summary of these services). The most important services are, of course, the "Keyboard Reads," since they take keystroke characters *out* of the buffer. You can learn more about the details of INT 16H from Peter Norton's *Programmer's Guide to the IBM PC and PS/2,* or any similar book.

And in the End

To complete our story of "O," a programming loop in the word processor program might call INT 16H to pluck that well-rounded beauty from the keyboard buffer, display it on the screen, and add it to the file buffer for your steamy masterpiece.

Changing the Key Repeat Delay on the PC/XT

■ Donald G. Costello

Learn how to speed up your keyboard by changing the key repeat delay.

The AT class machine has a BIOS interrupt call that can be used to increase the repeat rate. This interrupt doesn't exist for the PC or XT. Listing 2.6 will increase the typematic rate on any DOS machine—PC, XT, or AT.

KEYFAST gives you control over both the typematic delay and the character repeat rate. The program installs itself as a TSR. Both the clock interrupt and the keyboard interrupt routines are intercepted. The keyboard intercept, **Intercept09h**, checks each keyboard interrupt first to determine if it is a "make" or "break" keypress and then to determine if it is a new key or a repeat key. If it is a new key then the **IDelay** (typematic delay) value is placed in the delay count buffer and the repeat processes is turned off. If it is a repeat key then the repeat key delay is placed in the delay count. If no character was retrieved from the keyboard (this signals a break) then the repeat is turned off before an exit is made.

The clock intercept, **Intercept08h**, has control over all the delays. If nothing is pending, an exit is taken through the usual clock routine. If a delay has just ended, then the current repeat character is repeated by placing it in the keyboard buffer maintained by the BIOS.

The initial delay, **IDelay**, has been set at 7 clock ticks, which is around 1/3 second. The repeat key delay, **RDelay**, is set to 1, which gives a repeat rate of about 18 characters per second. This repeat rate is about 80% faster than the default rate of the PC or the XT. If you want to experiment with other delay times or rates simply change **IDelay** and/or **RDelay** and reassemble and relink the program.

The following steps are necessary to regenerate the program:

```
masm    KEYFAST;
link    KEYFAST;
exe2bin KEYFAST KEYFAST.COM
```

CODE DESCRIPTION

Overview

The listing provided is an installable TSR program that speeds up the key repeat delay on any keyboard.

Listing Available

Listing	*Description*	*Used with*
KEYFAST.ASM	ASM source file that changes the key repeat delay by intercepting both the BIOS and clock interrupts.	------

How to Compile/Assemble

KEYFAST.ASM should be assembled with MASM. The actual steps for building the TSR program are:

```
masm    KEYFAST;
link         KEYFAST;
exe2bin KEYFAST KEYFAST.COM
```

■ LISTING 2.6 KEYFAST.ASM

```
IDelay  =       7               ; Initial delay (clock ticks).
RDelay  =       1               ; Repeat key delay (clock ticks).
CSeg            segment
```

```
                org 100h
assume cs:CSeg,ds:nothing,es:nothing
Install:;>>>>>>>>>>>> Installation <<<<<<<<<<<<<<<<<<<<<<<<<<
        xor     ax,ax
        mov     es,ax                  ; Set to start of vectors.
        lds     ax,dword ptr es:[4*08h]; Get vector for clock.
        cmp     ax,offset Intercept08h; Check if already set up.
        je      SI60                   ; Exit to DOS if already there.
        cli                            ; Turn off the interrupts.
        mov     cs:OldVec,ax           ; Save the old vector.
        mov     cs:OldVec+2,ds
        mov     word ptr es:[4*08h],offset Intercept08h
        mov     es:[4*08h+2],cs
        lds     ax,dword ptr es:[4*09h]; Get vector for keyboard.
        mov     cs:OldVec+4,ax         ; Save the old vector.
        mov     cs:OldVec+6,ds
        mov     word ptr es:[4*09h],offset Intercept09h
        mov     es:[4*09h+2],cs
        mov     dx,offset Exit08h+32; Save this many bytes.
        int     27h                    ; Terminate and Stay Resident.
SI60:   int     20h                    ; Exit to DOS.
; >>>>>>>>>>>>>>>>>>>>>> Data Storage <<<<<<<<<<<<<<<<<<<<<<<<
BIOSD           dw      40h            ; BIOS_Data segment.
RepeatCNT       db      0              ; Repeat count.
RepeatChar      dw      0              ; Repeat character here.
OldVec          dw      0,0,0,0        ; Old Timer & Keyboard vectors.
Intercept09h:;>> Intercept Keyboard Routine <<<<<<<<<<<<<<<<
        push    ds                     ; Save registers.
        push    bx
        mov     ds,cs:BIOSD            ; Set DS to BIOS data segment.
        mov     cs:RepeatCNT,0         ; Stop Repeat for now.
        mov     bx,ds:[1ch]            ; Pick up tail (at 40h:1ch).
        pushf                          ; Dummy up an interrupt.
        call    dword ptr cs:OldVec+4; Go to regular routine.
        cmp     bx,ds:[1ch]            ; Did tail Change?
        jne     NewKey                 ; Yes, a new key to consider.
        mov     cs:RepeatChar,0        ; So won't match anything.
        jmp     short Exit09h          ; Exit with repeat off.
NewKey: mov     bx,[bx]                ; Pick up key typed.
        or      bh,bh                  ; Zero scan code indicates Alt
        jz      Exit09h                ; created keys which are skipped.
        cmp     bx,cs:RepeatChar       ; Present repeat key?
        mov     cs:RepeatChar,bx       ; Store as repeat key.
        mov     cs:RepeatCnt,IDelay    ; Assume initial delay.
        jne     Exit09h                ; A new key.
        mov     cs:RepeatCnt,RDelay    ; Change to Repeat delay.
Exit09h:pop     bx                     ; Restore registers.
        pop     ds
        iret
Intercept08h:;>>> Intercept Timer Interrupt <<<<<<<<<<<<<<<<
        dec     cs:RepeatCNT           ; Time to repeat?
        jg      Exit08h                ; Not time to repeat.
        mov     cs:RepeatCNT,0         ; Reset for next time.
        jl      Exit08h                ; Not repeating.
```

```
I08h00: push    ds                  ; Repeat the character.
        push    bx
        mov     ds,cs:BIOSD         ; Segment of buffer.
        mov     bx,ds:[1ch]         ; Get tail (at 40h:1ch).
        add     bx,2                ; Bump pointer.
        cmp     bx,ds:[82h]         ; Check buffer end (at 40h:82h).
        jne     I08h1               ; Not at end of buffer.
        mov     bx,ds:[80h]         ; Buffer start (at 40h:80h).
I08h1:  cmp     bx,ds:[1ah]         ; Check head (at 40h:1ah).
        je      I08h50              ; Exit if buffer is full.
        push    cs:RepeatChar       ; Pick up character to repeat.
        xchg    ds:[1ch],bx         ; Update tail.
        pop     word ptr [bx]       ; Put character in buffer.
        mov     cs:RepeatCNT,RDelay ; Set repeat delay count.
I08h50: pop     bx                  ; Restore registers.
        pop     ds
Exit08h:jmp     dword ptr cs:OldVec ; Go to regular routine.
CSeg    ends
        end     Install
```

Safer Buffer-Stuffing Through BIOS

■ Ben Myers

Here's a trick for safely stuffing keys in the keyboard buffer.

After several attempts, IBM finally got it *right.* Many revisions of the PC BIOS actually support keyboard stuffing via a BIOS call. According to published IBM specifications, any AT BIOS dated 11/15/85 or later, PC XT dated 1/10/86 or later, the PC XT 286, and all PS/2 products support the Keyboard Write (AH=05h) BIOS call to interrupt 16h, with the scan code in DH and the ASCII character code in DL. (My ancient and original *IBM PS/2 and PC BIOS Interface Technical Reference* contains this information.) Any popular and fairly recent BIOS (AMI, Phoenix, Award, Compaq, and so on) will support the same call.

Buffer stuffing via a BIOS call is more portable than stuffing to memory directly, which is why IBM saw the light and did it via BIOS calls. This method is more portable because it doesn't depend on an absolute memory address for the keyboard buffer itself, which is sometimes relocated elsewhere in memory by keyboard enhancement utilities. The function **BIOSstuff()** in Listing 2.7 illustrates this function.

CODE DESCRIPTION

Overview

The listing provided defines a function, **BIOSstuff()**, for stuffing a character in the keyboard buffer.

Listing Available

Listing	*Description*	*Used with*
BIOSSTF.C	C source file that includes a function for stuffing a character in the keyboard buffer by using a BIOS call.	------

How to Compile/Assemble

BIOSSTF.C can be compiled and linked with any C/C++ compiler. When using the **BIOSstuff()** function with a program, make sure you include the header file DOS.H.

■ LISTING 2.7 BIOSSTF.C

```
int BIOSstuff(char scan, char ch)
/*returns zero for success, one for failure*/
{
union REGS r;
      r.h.ah = 0x05;
      r.h.ch = scan;
      r.h.cl = ch;
      int86(0x16,&r,&r);
      return r.h.al;
}
```

3

Working with Disk Files

If you think about programming for a while, you may come to the conclusion (as I often do) that disk files are the reason we do this stuff. Disk files are "safe homes" for data—all our work eventually ends up in a file somewhere, no matter what sort of work it is that we do. So it pays to have a handle on some of the tricks that can be played with disk files.

DOS is the troll under the bridge that handles data transfers into files at our command, and as trolls go it's pretty good. DOS allows us to treat an executable program file as a data file and store configuration in it, as Bryan Flamig explains in this chapter. DOS can redirect output from files to the screen, from the screen to files, or from one file to another, through its redirection facility—and Hugh Myers explains how to tell when this is happening and when it isn't, from inside a program.

Mastering Turbo Debugger author Tom Swan lays out a neat trick that you can use with TDREMOTE: Clone a directory tree with all its files from one machine to another through Turbo Debugger's remote serial link.

This chapter also contains the grand prize winner HAX from our first HAX contest: Jeff Roberts' trick of reserving extra space in a file before you actually *use* that space. Jeff's method prevents DOS from allocating that space to some other file, leaving you high, dry, and empty when you need sectors for critical data.

A lot of these techniques took me by surprise, as much of an old-timer as I consider myself. You'll probably be surprised, too.

Configuring .EXE Files

■ Bryan Flamig

Add custom configuration data to your .EXE files by using a simple C program.

Some products have a configuration program that allows you to reconfigure such options as colors, menus, and so on. Many of these configuration programs store the options permanently in the .EXE file of the application itself. Have you ever wondered how this is done? How do the configuration programs know where the option data is stored?

The solution is this: Simply store a constant marker string just before the configuration option data in the application program. This string will become part of the application's .EXE file. Then, at configuration time, have your configuration program open the .EXE file and search for this marker. If the configuration program finds the marker, then it has found the data, too. The program can then read this data, modify it, and put it back.

The C program COUNT.C (Listing 3.1) uses this trick. In fact, it's a program that modifies itself. You've probably heard of self-modifying programs before, but this one is a little different. Rather than modifying the copy of itself that's running, it modifies the .EXE file from which it came. The modification involves incrementing a counter each time the program is run. Thus, the program can count how many times it has been executed. It even prints a message to this effect.

Of course, the secret of this trick is to use a good marker string. Remember that .EXE files contain binary data, which means any string of byte values is possible. If you really want to be safe, you can search for all occurrences of the marker. If you find more than one, then you know some set of opcodes or other data stored in your program happens to look just like the marker string. In such a case, it's not safe to update the file, because you don't know which occurrence is the right one. The marker used in the COUNT.C program, "%(@#@)" seems to work really well.

This trick also depends on the marker string and option data remaining together when the source file is compiled and linked. The way to ensure this is to package the marker and data into a structure, as COUNT.C does. A structure is *never* broken up across module boundaries.

TIP: Although this example is develeped in C, you should easily be able to configure .EXE files produced by other languages in much the same way. Remember that before you use the program to modify an .EXE file, you should make a backup copy of the .EXE file.

CODE DESCRIPTION

Overview

The listing provided is used to read and then attach custom configuration information to an .EXE file. As an example, the program actually modifies a copy of itself.

Listing Available

Listing	*Description*	*Used with*
COUNT.C	C source file that opens its corresponding .EXE file, searches for a marker string, and increments a stored counter if the marker string is found.	------

How to Compile/Assemble

COUNT.C can be compiled with most C compilers.

Note: The program can easily be modified to add other configuration information to other .EXE files. To do this, change the string assigned to **cdat** at the start of the program and modify the **fopen()** function so that a different file is opened.

■ LISTING 3.1 COUNT.C

```
/* Example of an .EXE modifying program. This program works on
/* itself by incrementing counter every time it's executed.    */

#include <stdio.h>
#include <string.h>

typedef struct { char marker[7]; int counter; } config_data;
config_data cdat = { "%(@#@)", 0 };

long find_data(FILE *f, char *marker)
/* Returns the location of the data, or returns -1 */
{
  long nf = 0;
  int ns = 0;

  while(!feof(f)) {
     nf++;
     /* if characters don't match, reset search string */
     if (marker[ns++] != fgetc(f)) ns = 0;
     /* if we have match at end, return location */
     if (marker[ns] == 0) return nf-strlen(marker);
  }
  return -1L;
}

/* The self-modifying program */
int main(int argc, char *argv[])
{
  FILE *f;
  long data_locn;

  f = fopen(argv[0], "r+b"); /* open up self for update */
  data_locn = find_data(f, cdat.marker);
  if (data_locn == -1)
     fprintf(stderr, "Oops! Can't find the data!\n");
  else {
```

```
        fseek(f, data_locn, 0); /* read data */
          fread(&cdat, sizeof(cdat), 1, f);
        cdat.counter++;          /* increment counter */
        printf("Program has executed %d times\n", cdat.counter);
        fseek(f, data_locn, 0); /* store data */
        fwrite(&cdat, sizeof(cdat), 1, f);
    }
    fclose(f);
    return 0;
}
```

Using setvbuf() to Accelerate File I/O

■ Tom Campbell

*Use the **setvbuf()** function to alter the size of the file I/O buffer.*

One of the most poorly documented functions in the ANSI C library, **setvbuf()**, is also one of the most useful. This function lets you alter the size of the file I/O buffer. In FCOPY.C (Listing 3.2), **setvbuf()** is used in a function named **fcopy()** to copy one file to another. Using **setvbuf()** to adjust the buffer size on some systems can reduce the I/O time to 50% or more. Thus, you can copy a 498,501-byte file in 12 seconds, versus 23 seconds without changing the buffer size.

A Closer Look

Here is the function prototype for **setvbuf()**:

```
int setvbuf(FILE *stream, char *buf, int mode, size_t size);
```

The parameter **stream** is an open file, **buf** is a block of memory **size** chars wide, and **mode** is one of the following constants:

```
_IOFBF - Full buffering
_IOLBF - Line buffering
_IONBF - No buffering
```

Notice that options are available for different I/O buffering configurations. Unfortunately, most C reference books are vague about the differences between full buffering and line buffering. With a fully buffered file, data is not actually written to disk until the buffer is completely full. Likewise, when data is read from a fully buffered file, the input function attempts to completely fill the buffer. With a line-buffered file, input operations still attempt to fill the entire buffer. On the other hand, when you write to a line-buffered file, the buffer will be flushed whenever a new line character is received. Unbuffered files bypass the buffer altogether, reading and writing directly to the file.

TIP: For optimum speed, consider using the **_IOFBF** mode for full buffering and then copy all files in binary mode, even your text files. The **_IONBF** mode is the safest of the three modes because no delay is used in getting data to the disk, but it'll cost you. In my tests, it took *120 seconds* to copy a 500KB file, versus 12 seconds for fully buffered copies—a tenfold difference.

In ANSI C, the constant **BUFSIZ** is defined to express the size of the default system buffer. In Borland C++, **BUFSIZ** is set to 512 bytes.

Rules to Live By

The **setvbuf()** function requires a little more care than most functions. When using it, you *must* remember to follow these rules:

1. Always include the proper prototypes (**#include <stdio.h>).**
2. The buffer should be a global or static quantity; it can't disappear when it goes out of scope, as would an auto variable. If your buffer goes out of scope, it will disappear completely, guaranteeing disaster on a system without memory protection—your next I/O would write over critical space on the stack.
3. The file you associate with a buffer must be opened *before* calling **setvbuf()**.
4. Call **setvbuf()** immediately after **fopen()** and before any other I/O is done on the file—this also ensures that Rule #3 is followed.
5. *Never* touch the buffer yourself. When you use **setvbuf()**, you are giving the C compiler's run time system a workspace to use as it sees fit. Don't violate this trust by reading or writing to or from this buffer. Simply pretend it no longer exists.

In Listing 3.2 the buffer is allocated dynamically. This gives you the biggest possible buffer and the most efficient use of memory. The accompanying example also decreases the likelihood of the call failing because it keeps trying to allocate a buffer with succeedingly smaller sizes (down to 1K) if a request fails for lack of memory.

One easily overlooked aspect of **setvbuf()** is that the buffer has a maximum size, and it is also implementation dependent. In other words, you don't want to allocate too large a buffer. In my case the maximum buffer size available is 32,767, since I compiled using Borland C++ and that's BC++'s limit.

An Example

The example program, FCOPY.C (Listing 3.2) provides a function named **fcopy()** and driver code to copy a file from the command line. The syntax for the driver program is

```
fcopy  file1  file2
```

This command copies *file1* to *file2*.

The **fcopy()** function is fairly complete, and you can easily plug it into your own program. It contains full error checking code and allocates its buffer intelligently, trying for the maximum size and, failing that, attempting to allocate smaller and smaller buffers until a minimum acceptable buffer size is reached. (After that point, the program fails.) If your program operates on other files you might consider making the file buffer **NewBuffer** global, so that **setvbuf()** can be used on those files as well. Better still, pass a pointer to it and avoid the use of the global.

TIP: The program contains the following two lines of special debugging code that you may want to remove at some point:

```
fprintf(stderr, "\nSystem buffer is: %u bytes.", BUFSIZ);
fprintf(stderr, "\nCustom buffer is: %u bytes.", BufSize);
```

This code lets you compare the size of the custom buffer to the size of the system buffer.

CODE DESCRIPTION

Overview

The listing provided shows how to increase I/O performance by using the ANSI C **setvbuf()** function.

Listing Available

Listing	*Description*	*Used with*
FCOPY.C	C source file that allocates a large copy buffer dynamically using **setvbuf()**. The program copies a file and prints a message to compare the size of the system buffer to the size of the dynamically allocated buffer.	------

How to Compile/Assemble

FCOPY.C can be compiled with most C compilers.

Note: To run the program type in:

FCOPY file1 file2

The copy buffer is assigned a maximum of 32767 bytes. If less memory is available, FCOPY will request a smaller amount.

You can take out the **fcopy()** function and insert it into your own programs unchanged. This function does not support wildcard characters for filenames.

■ LISTING 3.2 FCOPY.C

```
/*  FCOPY.C    */
#include <stdio.h>
#include <stdlib.h>
/* Prototypes */
void Quit(char *msg, int errlev);
```

```
void fcopy(char *Source, char *Dest);

void main(int argc, char *argv[])
{
   /* Check for correct number of arguments */
   if (argc != 3)
         Quit("Usage: fcopy file1 file2", 1);
   /* Copy 1st file named on command line to 2nd. */
   fcopy(argv[1], argv[2]);
}

void fcopy(char *Source, char *Dest)
/* Copy file Source to Dest.  If Dest exists,  it's written over
   without warning.

   This function is a standalone file copy routine showing how
   to use setvbuf() to improve file I/O. */
{
   static char *NewBuffer; /* Pointer to a copy buffer. */
   unsigned int copied;    /* Keeps track of bytes copied. */
   FILE *InFile;           /* File to be copied. */
   FILE *NewFile;          /* File to be created. */
   int BufSize = 32767;    /* Maximum size of copy buffer. This
                              figure is implementation-dependent;
                              see your manual or stdlib.h for
                              your compiler's maximum. */

   /* Open the file to be copied with read-only access in binary
      mode. */
   InFile = fopen(Source, "rb");
   if (InFile == NULL)
     Quit("Unable to open source file", 1);

   /* Create a buffer BufSize bytes or less in size. */
   while ((NewBuffer=(char *)malloc(BufSize))==NULL) {
     /* If BufSize bytes aren't available, try allocating 1000 bytes
        less. */
     BufSize -= 1000;
     /* If BufSize drops below 0, it's hopeless. */
     if (BufSize < 0)
       Quit("Unable to allocate memory. Quitting.", 1);
   }

   /* The call to setvbuf replaces the system buffer with NewBuffer.
      _IOFBF means read until the NewBuffer is completely filled. */
   if (setvbuf(InFile, NewBuffer, _IOFBF, BufSize != 0))
     Quit("setvbuf() failed.", 1);

   fprintf(stderr, "\nSystem buffer is: %u bytes.", BUFSIZ);
   fprintf(stderr, "\nCustom buffer is: %u bytes.", BufSize);

   /* Read a bufferful of bytes into NewBuffer. */
   copied = fread((void *)NewBuffer, sizeof(char), BufSize, InFile);

   /* Create output file only if source file is at least 1 byte. */
   if (copied > 0) {
```

```
    NewFile = fopen(Dest, "wb");
    if (NewFile == NULL)
      Quit("Unable to open output file", 1);
  }

  while (copied != 0) {
    /* Write the previous to the destination file. */
    fwrite((void *)NewBuffer, sizeof(char), copied, NewFile);
    /* If the file is bigger than NewBuffer, keep reading until the
       file has been completely copied. */
    copied=fread((void *)NewBuffer, sizeof(char), BufSize, InFile);
  }

  /* Deallocate buffer. */
  free((void *)NewBuffer);

} /* fcopy() */

void Quit(char *msg, int errlev)
/* Displays msg, then exits to the operating system with an error
   code of errlev. */
{
  printf("\n%s\n", msg);  /* Display the message. */
  exit(errlev);           /* Exit to OS w/error code. */
}
```

Cloning the Beaten Path

■ Tom Swan

Use the Turbo Debugger Remote File utility along with this utility to easily clone directories.

Copying a nest of nested directories to my portable with TDRF (the Turbo Debugger Remote File utility) is too much work. First, I have to issue TDRF or DOS commands on the remote machine to recreate every subdirectory. Then, I have to transfer files from my development system, one path at a time.

After fussing with those steps, I decided to write a program, CLONE.CPP, to clone an entire directory tree from one PC to another. (See Listing 3.3.) The program works by creating and running a batch file of TDRF commands. To use CLONE, connect two computers' COM ports with an RS-232 serial cable, and start TDRF's partner utility TDREMOTE on the remote machine. Then, back at the source, change to any directory and run CLONE to copy all files and subdirectories from there to the remote's current drive. Or, type commands such as CLONE D:\PAS\SECRETS and CLONE C:\ to clone other paths.

Requirements

CLONE's batch-file commands require TDRF.EXE, which must be in a directory on the source computer's default path. The remote needs only TDREMOTE.EXE.

TIP: If you have trouble getting the two utilities to communicate, you may need to buy or make a null modem RS-232 cable with pins 2-3, 3-2, and 7-7 connected. Other pin assignments may also work. To get more help, type **TDRF -h** and **TDREMOTE -h** for instructions about selecting COM ports and adjusting transfer speeds with command-line options.

Once the computers are talking to each other, use **w** to save the new defaults. For example, to configure TDRF for COM2: (-rp2) at 115K baud (-rs3), enter:

```
TDRF -rp2 -rs3 -w
```

Use similar options to configure TDREMOTE.

How CLONE Works

CLONE creates and runs a DOS batch file, a technique that you may find useful for other projects. The program begins by calling **getcwd()** from DIR.H to set **originalPath** to the current working directory name. Because CLONE changes paths, it needs this string to get back to the original directory later.

Next, if you entered a path on the command line, CLONE calls **chdir()** to change to the path provided. Otherwise, it starts in the current directory. The variable **err** intercepts errors associated with the changing of directories, in which case the program displays brief instructions. To see these instructions, enter CLONE ?, or specify any other invalid directory name.

If CLONE detects no errors, it creates a new batch file and calls **readDirectory()**. That function then calls **preparePath()** to create TDRF batch file commands for cloning the current path.

Getting the Current Directory Name

The **preparePath()** function uses a string pointer (**p**) to hold its place in the path string. Because path names returned from **getcwd()** include the drive specifier, **p** is initialized to two bytes after the beginning of the string. Inside the inner **while** loop, the program calls **strchr()** to locate the next backslash in the string, replacing that character with 0. Because C strings are terminated by a NULL (ASCII 0), this is an easy way to extract the front portion of a string—in this case, to form the commands needed to make nested directory paths.

After **preparePath()** writes TDRF commands to batch file **bf**, **readDirectory()** continues by calling **findfirst()**. Using the "*.*" string causes all filenames from the current directory to be read.

The **if** statement rejects pseudo-directory aliases ('.' and "..") and inspects the file attribute's directory bit. If that bit is set, CLONE calls **chdir()** to change to the directory. The program then calls **readDirectory()** recursively to process files on this new level.

When done, the **chdir('..')** backs up a level, undoing the previous **chdir()**. At the loop's bottom, **findnext()** reads the next filename, or returns a nonzero value, ending **readDirectory()**.

About Recursion

If you don't understand recursion, **readDirectory()**'s operation may seem like hocus pocus. But recursion is not magic; it's just a buzzword for the way functions in C can call themselves.

CLONE uses recursion to "walk" through a directory tree, starting from the current path. Because the steps for processing filenames in one directory are the same as the steps for processing filenames in any other, instead of adding "housekeeping" to track each new path, **readDirectory()** simply calls itself over and over until it has visited all branches of the tree.

Like the endless feedback that howls if you talk into a microphone held close to the speaker, **readDirectory()**'s recursive "echoes" go on and on until something stops the music. That something happens when **findnext()** returns a nonzero value, indicating that no more subdirectories are to be found on this level. The recursion then "unwinds" (as if you played a tape of the echoes in reverse), causing the previous instances to continue where they left off until the program locates every directory, no matter how deeply nested.

Calling Batch Files

The result of all this is C:\CLONE@@@.BAT, a batch file of TDRF commands that will clone a pack of nested paths. To run the batch file, CLONE calls **execl()**, using **getenv("COMSPEC")** to find the DOS shell's location and name, usually COMMAND.COM. This allows CLONE to run on systems that use a different shell or that install a copy of COMMAND.COM onto a RAM drive. After **execl()** returns, CLONE erases the batch file and calls **chdir()** to return to the original path, saved earlier when the program began.

If necessary, you can change the **batchFile** string to use another drive, directory, and filename. Just be sure to use a unique filename with the extension .BAT.

CLONE Tidbits

Here are some important points to keep in mind when running CLONE:

- Typing **CLONE** \ clones the current drive's subdirectories onto the remote, but doesn't copy any root files. This is a safety feature to prevent you from overwriting the remote's AUTOEXEC.BAT and CONFIG.SYS files. Use the commands TDRF c \ and TDRF t *.* to copy root files.
- Before cloning paths, CLONE deletes existing files (but not subdirectories) in cloned directories on the remote. If you don't want CLONE to do this, delete the second **fprintf()** function call in **preparePath()**.
- You may see the TDRF errors "Can't make directory on remote," "No matching files," and "No matching files on remote." Ignore these messages, which TDRF displays when it tries to remake existing directories and to copy and delete empty ones—harmless actions all.
- After cloning, directory dates and times may not be identical on the two computers. However, all files in those directories will have the correct dates and times.

- CLONE ignores drive letters; therefore, if you make C: the current drive on the remote system and enter CLONE D:\STUFF at the source, CLONE will transfer files and subdirectories from D:\STUFF to C:\STUFF on the remote.

CODE DESCRIPTION

Overview

The listing provided is used to copy directories and files from one computer to another. The program works in conjunction with the Turbo Debugger Remote File (TDRF) utility.

Listing Available

Listing	*Description*	*Used with*
CLONE.CPP	C source file that creates and runs a batch file of TDRF commands to clone a set of subdirectories.	------

How to Compile/Assemble

CLONE.C should be compiled with Borland C++ or Turbo C++.

Note: To run the program you'll need the Turbo Debugger Remote File utility, TDRF.EXE, available on the source computer and its companion program TDREMOTE.EXE available on the remote computer.

■ LISTING 3.3 CLONE.CPP

```
/* CLONE.C—Clone Directories with TDRF, by Tom Swan */
#include <stdio.h>
#include <stdlib.h>
#include <process.h>
#include <dir.h>
#include <dos.h>
#include <string.h>
#define PATHLEN 65

const char *batchFile = "c:\\clone@@@.bat";
char originalPath[PATHLEN];
FILE *bf;         // Batch file

void readDirectory(void);
void preparePath(void);

main(int argc, char *argv[])
{
   int err = 0;

   if (getcwd(originalPath, PATHLEN) != NULL) {
      if (argc > 1) err = chdir(*++argv);
      if (!err) {
         if ((bf = fopen(batchFile, "wt")) == NULL) {
            fprintf(stderr, "Error creating batch file\n");
```

```
            return(1);
         }
         readDirectory();     // Write commands to batch file
         fclose(bf);          // Close batch file before running
         execl(getenv("COMSPEC"), argv[0], "/C", batchFile, NULL);
         remove(batchFile);  // Erase the batch file
         chdir(originalPath);
      } else {
         puts("Clone Directories with TDRF, by Tom Swan");
         puts("Syntax: CLONE [-?] [pathName]");
      }
   }
   return(0);   // End program, no errors
}

// Walk through all paths from current directory
void readDirectory()
{
   int done;
   struct ffblk sr;

   preparePath();
   done = findfirst("*.*", &sr, FA_DIREC);
   while (!done) {
      if ((sr.ff_name[0] != '.') &&
          (sr.ff_attrib & FA_DIREC)) {
         chdir(sr.ff_name);    // Change to next level
         readDirectory();      // Process files there
         chdir("..");          // Return to previous level
      }
      done = findnext(&sr);
   }
} // readDirectory

// Write TDRF commands to batch file bf
void preparePath()
{
   char *p;                  // Next backslash position
   char fExpand[PATHLEN];   // Full current path name
   char *plainPath;          // Path without drive info

   plainPath = getcwd(fExpand, PATHLEN) + 2;
   if (strcmp(plainPath, "\\") != 0) {
      p = plainPath;  // Initialize search for backslashes
      while ((p = strchr(++p, '\\')) != NULL) {
         *p = 0;       // Cut off string at backslash
         fprintf(bf, "tdrf md %s\n", plainPath);
         *p = '\\';    // Replace backslash
      }
      fprintf(bf, "tdrf md %s\n", plainPath);
      fprintf(bf, "tdrf del %s%s\n", plainPath, "\\*.*");
      fprintf(bf, "tdrf t %s%s%s\n", plainPath, "\\*.* ",
              plainPath);
   }
} // preparePath
```

Flushing File Buffers

■ Kevin Weeks

Here's a technique you can use to make sure your files are properly flushed in all versions of DOS.

It doesn't seem to be common knowledge, but the DOS file buffers (**BUFFERS=xx** in your CONFIG.SYS file) are not write-through buffers. In other words, when you issue the DOS write command (Int 21H, Function 40H) the data is simply written to the DOS buffer(s). The data is not necessarily written to disk until the buffer is needed for another read or write, or when the file is closed. If a user turns the PC off after a session instead of exiting from a program (which forces DOS to close the files) the data in the buffer will be lost.

If you can guarantee that your program runs only under DOS versions 3.3 and later, you can issue a Commit File call (Int 21H, Function 68H), which will flush the buffers. Unfortunately, Microsoft was a bit late introducing this function—and there are *many* copies of DOS 3.2 and earlier out there. Here's another option that works on DOS versions 2.0 and up.

As mentioned earlier, DOS will flush buffers when the file is closed. If you close the file after every write, then the buffers will be flushed. Unfortunately, you then have to reopen the file. However, ever since DOS 2.0, the Duplicate Handle function (Int 21H, Function 46H) has been available. If you clone the original file handle and then close the duplicate handle, the buffers are flushed but the original file handle isn't closed! You don't need to reopen the file and swallow the consequent overhead—the original file handle is still valid and can be freely read from and written to.

The function **flush()** (Listing 3.4) is meant to be called by a C program. The function is passed the handle of an open file that has just been written to. The **flush()** function creates a duplicate handle and then closes it. Voila! The buffer has been emptied! And the file need not be reopened. Here is an example of how you can perform a write operation in your C programs:

```
/* check for error */
if (write(handle,buffer,num_bytes) != ERROR)
    if (flush(handle) != 0)
    return ERROR;
```

Unless your users can hit the Big Red Switch in that brief moment between the call to **write()** and the call to **flush()** (unlikely!), your files will be safe.

CODE DESCRIPTION

Overview

The listing provided is used to flush opened DOS files by using the Duplicate Handle function (Int 21h, Function 46h).

Listing Available

Listing	*Description*	*Used with*
FLUSH.ASM	ASM source file that defines the function **flush()**. This function is used in C programs to properly flush an opened file in all versions of DOS (including DOS 3.3 and earlier).	------

How to Compile/Assemble

FLUSH.ASM can be assembled with any TASM-compatible assembler and linked to any C program using the following prototype:

```
int flush(int handle);
```

■ LISTING 3.4 FLUSH.ASM

```
;   int     flush(int handle);
.model small
.code
    public  _flush
_flush proc
    push    bp
    mov     bp,sp
    push    bx
    mov     bx,[bp + 4]             ; Get file handle
    mov     ax,4500h                ; DOS Dup Handle function
    int     21h                     ; Call DOS-returns with
                                    ;   new handle in ax
    jc      flush_out               ; Jump if error
    mov     bx,ax                   ; Move new handle to bx
    mov     ax,3e00h                ; DOS Close function
    int     21h                     ; Call DOS
    jc      flush_out               ; Jump if error
    mov     ax,0                    ; Clear ax
    jmp     short flush_out         ; Exit
flush_out:
    pop     bx
    pop     bp
    ret
_flush endp
end
```

Safe File Pointers in C++

■ Bruce Eckel

Here's a clever way to process files using a C++ class.

Opening a file always requires the same tedious code to check to see that the file opening operation was successful. You must also remember to close the file. Why not encapsulate that code in a class, use the constructor to open the file and check for success, and use the destructor to automatically close the file? The C++ header file, FILE.HPP (Listing 3.5), shows how this can be done in a clever way.

Recall that the main reason for creating a **class** is to make an existing type safer. The class **fileptr** contains only a **FILE***, the pointer traditionally used with the ANSI C file I/O library functions. By putting **FILE*** in a class, however, you can insure that proper initialization will always take place, in this case by attempting to open the file and exiting with an error message if it fails. In addition, the destructor will automatically close the file when the object goes out of scope.

Now the question arises: Do we have to create a special member function for each ANSI C file I/O library function, and for any other function that takes a **FILE*** as an argument? This seems too complicated to make such a class worthwhile. Fortunately, there's a very simple solution:

```
operator FILE*() { return filep; }
```

This is an overloaded operator that performs automatic type conversion. You should be familiar with the concept in C that when the compiler encounters a variable of one type used in a place where another type is expected, the compiler will attempt to perform an automatic type conversion. (And in C, at least, the compiler will often perform the conversion even when it's questionable.) Consider this code:

```
void foo(float);
int i;
foo(i);
```

The function **foo** expects a **float** as an argument but is given an **int**. The compiler knows how to convert an **int** to a **float**, and it does so automatically.

In C++, if the compiler sees a variable of a user-defined type used where it expects some other type, it will check to see if there's some way to convert the type it has to the type it needs. If so, it will call that conversion function and quietly perform the conversion. Since we have created an automatic type conversion operator that produces a **FILE*** from a **fileptr**, we can, for example, code this:

```
fileptr f("myfile", "w"); //create a file and open it for writing

fprintf(f, "hello"); //output string to the file
```

You can thus use this new **fileptr** type everywhere you previously used a **FILE***. The difference is that initialization and cleanup are taken care of for you.

TIP: When you create an operator to do automatic type conversion, the syntax is simpler than with normal operator overloading—the return value is implied by the name of the operator, so you do not specify it. You should also be aware that too much automatic type conversion can cause problems, especially when dealing with numerous derived classes.

CODE DESCRIPTION

Overview

The listing provided is used to automate the process of opening and closing files.

Listing Available

Listing	*Description*	*Used with*
FILE.HPP	C++ header file that defines a class for opening and closing files.	------

How to Compile/Assemble

FILE.HPP can be included in a C++ program by using the directive:

```
#include "FILE.HPP"
```

■ LISTING 3.5 FILE.HPP

```
// FILE.HPP : encapsulation of FILE* for ease and safety
#ifndef FILE_HPP_
#define FILE_HPP_
#include <stdio.h>
#include <stdlib.h>

class fileptr {
  FILE* filep;
public:
  fileptr(char * name, char * mode = "r") {
    filep = fopen(name, mode);
    if(!filep) {
      fprintf(stderr, "cannot open %s\n", name);
      exit(1);
    }
  }
  ~fileptr() { fclose(filep); }
  // automatic type conversion operator, so you can
  // use a fileptr everywhere you use a FILE*:
  operator FILE*() { return filep; }
};

#endif FILE_HPP_
```

Calculating True Directory Size

■ Howard Rosenberg

Find out the real size of your directories with this simple C utility.

Whenever you display a directory using DIR in later versions of DOS and its replacements, the next-to-last line contains the size of the directory. However, the sum of the sizes of the files in the directory will not equal the directory's size. In the instance below, for example, the directory size (12,288) is 4640 bytes more than the sum of the file's sizes:

```
Directory of  e:\adirctry\*.*
.            <DIR>       1-11-91  10:00
..           <DIR>       1-11-91  10:00
filea.exe        5904    1-11-91  10:00
fileb.exe        1744    6-05-89   0:37
      12,288 bytes in 4 file(s)
     147,456 bytes free
```

Is there an error in the DIR routine? No. The difference occurs because DOS allocates disk space for files in clusters; even a "1 byte" file occupies a whole cluster.

A complicating factor is that "cluster size" varies with the drive type and even among partitions in a drive. For example, my Plus Hardcard II is partitioned into two drives, one with a cluster size of 2048, and another with a cluster size of 4096. Thus, to arrive at DOS's directory size, you must

1. Find the cluster size for the drive the directory is on.
2. Determine how many clusters each file in the directory occupies.
3. Sum the number of clusters occupied by all the files in the directory.
4. Multiply the total by the cluster size.

The SHOWDIR program (Listing 3.6) demonstrates how to do it. As Figure 3.1 demonstrates, this program also shows the cluster size, the number of clusters each file occupies, the "clusterized" size of each file, the sum of all the file's actual sizes, and the total number of clusters the directory's files occupy.

```
C:\MAGIC>showdir
The files in the current directory are ...

SHOWDIR.EXE         11740        3
CHAP03B.DOC         45332       12
CHAP08.DOC          34596        9
PRDNOTES.DOC         3526        1
NORMAL.STY           2048        1
CHAP02A.DOC         67768       17
CHAP01.DOC          79043       20
CHAP02B.DOC         49442       13
CHAP03A.DOC         54710       14
CHAP06A.DOC         64946       16
CHAP06B.DOC         50510       13
DIXA.DOC             6656        2
CHAP07A.DOC         65036       16
CHAP07B.DOC         33026        9

Totals            568379       146
Total Size On Disk = 598016

C:\MAGIC>
```

■ **FIGURE 3.1 Displaying directory information with SHOWDIR**

CODE DESCRIPTION

Overview

The listing provided is used to display the true size of a directory including cluster size, number of clusters for each file, "clusterized" size of each file, the sum of all file sizes, and total number of clusters the files occupy.

Listing Available

Listing	*Description*	*Used with*
SHOWDIR.C	C source file that determines the directory size information by examining the clusters in each file in a directory.	------

How to Compile/Assemble

SHOWDIR.C can be compiled with most C compilers.

■ LISTING 3.6 SHOWDIR.C

```
#include <direct.h>
#include <dos.h>
#include <stdio.h>
void listfile(struct ffblk *filedata);
long BytesPerCluster(int drive);
unsigned int clusterSize;

struct ffblk filedata;
long numClusters = 0;
int disk; /* drive A=1, B-2,... */

void main(void)
{
long total= 0 ;
  disk = _getdrive();
  clusterSize = BytesPerCluster(disk);
  if (findfirst("*.*", &filedata, FA_ARCH) == 0)
  {
      printf("The files in the current directory are ...\n\n");
      listfile(&filedata);
      total += filedata.ff_fsize;
      while (findnext(&filedata) == 0) {
         listfile(&filedata);
         total += filedata.ff_fsize;
      }
      printf("\n%-14s %8ld %8ld\n",
            "Totals ", total, numClusters);
      printf("Total Size On Disk = %ld\n ", numClusters * clusterSize );
  }
  else perror("findfirst error");
}
```

```
void listfile(struct ffblk *filedata)
{
        printf("%-14s %8ld %8ld\n",
              (filedata->ff_name), (filedata->ff_fsize),
              ((filedata->ff_fsize / clusterSize)+1 ));
        numClusters += (filedata->ff_fsize / clusterSize)+1;
}

long BytesPerCluster(int drive)
{
union REGS regs;
struct SREGS sregs;

  regs.h.ah = 0x1C;
  regs.h.dl = drive;
  if (intdosx(&regs, &regs, &sregs) != -1)
    return (long) regs.h.al  * regs.x.cx ;
}
```

Testing for Path Existence

■ Christopher Nelson

Here's a quick method for determining if a specific directory exists on your computer.

It is sometimes desirable to determine if a directory exists without actually trying to go there or creating a file on the disk. A convenient way to do this is to test for the presence of the NUL device in the specified directory. Because of the way DOS handles NUL, NUL exists in every valid directory. Therefore, testing for the presence of NUL will fail only for a non-existent directory. Listing 3.7 shows a short Borland C program which implements this test.

CODE DESCRIPTION

Overview

The listing provided is used to determine if a specific directory exists.

Listing Available

Listing	*Description*	*Used with*
TESTPATH.C	C source file that tests for the existence of a directory by testing for the presence of the NUL device in the directory.	------

How to Compile/Assemble

TESTPATH.C can be compiled and linked with any C/C++ compiler.

■ LISTING 3.7 TESTPATH.C

```
#include <stdio.h>
#include <string.h>

void main(void)
{
FILE *fp;

char path[80];
char buf[90];
int len;

     printf("Directory to test: ");
     gets(path);

     strcpy(buf,path);
     strcat(buf,"\\NUL");
     fp = fopen(buf,"wb");
     if (fp == NULL)
        printf("%s doesn't exist\n",path);
     else
     {
         printf("%s exists\n",path);
         fclose(fp);
     }
}
```

Grab Disk Space When You Need It

■ Jeff Roberts

Grab a chunk of disk space by using a DOS trick to allocate a file of a specific size.

Protecting a user against common problems such as running out of disk space is the sign of any well-written program. Generally, programs will employ DOS service 36H to ensure that these low disk space errors never arise. That is, they get the amount of free disk space (with 36H) and see if it's more than they'll need. However, in certain situations, this method doesn't go far enough.

Consider, for example, a network environment. You begin downloading a very large report file describing how to climb the corporate ladder by discrediting your boss. Your communication package quickly checks the available space on the file server, and says, in effect, "Go ahead, there's plenty of space here!"

Meanwhile, elsewhere on the network, one of your underlings (who has already downloaded the same file) is creating a huge Excel spreadsheet containing information he thinks will discredit you. By saving it to the file server, he uses up all the remaining disk space, thereby aborting your file transfer. You never get to read the report file, and he gets promoted instead of you. "Could this have been avoided?"

It can indeed! By allocating all the disk space you'll require before you begin filling it, you can be sure that you'll never run out of space during a critical task. Unfortunately, writing out filler bytes to create such a file would require a prohibitive amount of disk-writing time. However, using two strange features of DOS, you can set a file to any length almost instantly. No writing of data is involved, and the only changes made to the disk are in the directory and FATs.

The first strange feature is the ability to seek to *any* position in a file—even positions that don't yet exist! The second strange feature is a quirk of the write file function: by positioning the file pointer to some position in a file, and then writing zero bytes to the file, you truncate the file at that position—regardless of the file pointer's position. For example, if you have opened a ten-megabyte file and you seek to byte 128, then writing zero bytes will truncate the file at position 128.

Similarly, if you open a new and totally empty file, seek to the ten-megabyte mark, and then write zero bytes, a ten-megabyte file is immediately created. Note that the file isn't initialized with anything. This trick only updates the directory information. (Writing one byte at the ten-megabyte mark will also create a ten-megabyte file—but you still have the overhead of writing that one byte.)

Listing 3.8 contains a short assembly routine that will set a file to any valid size. You can make the same system calls from most high-level languages or you can set up the assembly code as a C callable function.

CODE DESCRIPTION

Overview

The listing provided is used to allocating disk space by creating a dummy file and setting its length using a DOS programming trick.

Listing Available

Listing	*Description*	*Used with*
GRAB.ASM	ASM source file that sets a specific file handle to a specified size by using the DOS functions 42h—seek to a position in the file, and 40h—write to the file. The trick involves writing 0 bytes to a file after the file pointer has been set at the desired file size.	------

How to Compile/Assemble

GRAB.ASM can be assembled with MASM or TASM.

■ LISTING 3.8 GRAB.ASM

```
ideal
proc setfile   far
; DX:AX contains the size to set to.  BX contains the file
; handle to set. All registers are returned unchanged-only
; the flags are modified. If an error occurs, the carry flag
; will be set.  Possible errors are "invalid handle" and
```

```
; "insufficient disk space."  The file size will be unchanged
; on error. If successful, file pointer is positioned at the
; end of the file (EOF=TRUE).
        push cx
        push dx
        push ax
        mov  cx,dx
        mov  dx,ax
        mov  ax,04200h
        int  021h       ;Move to the correct position
        jc   @@err1
        mov  ah,040h
        xor  cx,cx
        int  021h       ;Set the file size
        jc   @@err1
        mov  ax,04202h
        mov  dx,cx
        int  021h       ;Get the actual size to see
                        ;if everything was written
        jc   @@err1
        pop  cx
        cmp  ax,cx      ;Check the low  word
        je   @@cont
        mov  ax,cx
        stc             ;Set error condition
        jmp  @@err2
@@cont:
        pop  cx
        or   dx,cx      ;Check the high word (and clear
                        ;the carry flag)
jz   @@done
        mov  dx,cx
        stc             ;Set the error condition
        db   0b9h       ;Jump to @@done without emptying prefetch
                        ;(trashes CX)
@@err1:
        pop  ax
@@err2:
        pop  dx
@@done:
        pop  cx
        retf
endp set_file
```

The Nature of a Filename

■ Philip J. Erdelsky

Learn how to use "forbidden" characters in DOS filenames.

What's in a DOS filename? According to my DOS manual, it can contain from one to eight characters, excluding ASCII characters lower than 20H (the ASCII "control" characters) and a number of punctuation marks, mostly those reserved for other purposes. In another place, it says that small letters are capitalized. A DOS file extension is supposed to operate by the same rules, except that it contains at most three characters. The rules for directory names are the same.

I read manuals, but I don't trust them completely, especially when I suspect that they're not telling me everything. I've seen DIR listings with some pretty unusual stuff in them. I started experimenting with filenames (as submitted directly to DOS through the **_creat** function) and found quite a few anomalies.

Blanks *are* permitted in filenames and extensions. The rules applying to blanks are apparently as follows:

1. If a name or extension isn't at least eight or three characters long, respectively, it's padded with blanks at the end. This rule is well known.
2. Interior blanks are permitted in filenames and extensions. This rule is not so well known. It makes it possible to create files and directories that cannot be accessed by standard DOS commands like TYPE and CHDIR, which treat blanks as command-line argument separators.
3. A filename cannot begin with a blank.
4. An extension cannot begin with a blank unless it is entirely blank.

Extended characters 80H–FFH are permitted; and capitalization isn't limited to small letters. It also applies to æ, which capitalizes to æ, and a number of accented small letters in the extended character set.

TIP: For more information regarding capitalization of the extended character set, see "DOS Code Pages" in Chapter 4.

I ended up writing the simple test program shown in Listing 3.9, which tries every character from 00H to FFH in a filename and determines which ones are acceptable, and what DOS changes them to when it capitalizes them. It puts the results into a C array called

```
filename_character[].
```

Then **filename_character[c]** is 0 if c is an unacceptable character, or the "capitalization" of c if it is acceptable.

I tried this with several DOS versions. Versions 3.10, 3.20, and 3.30 produce exactly the same output. Versions 2.00 and 2.10 (remember them?) are a little different. They automatically strip the parity bit from each character, so they don't recognize the extended character set at all. They also accept (.).&X&, probably changing it to (.), and they don't accept interior blanks.

CODE DESCRIPTION

Overview

The listing provided is used to display all of the possible characters that can be used in a filename.

Listing Available

Listing	*Description*	*Used with*
NAMETEST.C	C source file that tries characters from 00H to FFh to see if they can be used in a filename. The acceptable characters are returned in an array.	------

How to Compile/Assemble

NAMETEST.C can be compiled and linked with any C/C++ compiler.

■ LISTING 3.9 NAMETEST.C

```
#include <stdio.h>
#include <dir.h>
#include <dos.h>
#include <io.h>

void main()
{
  unsigned n;
  printf("unsigned char filename_character[256] = \n{\n");
  for (n=0; n<256; n++)
  {
    static char name[] = "(?).&X&";
    int h;
    name[1] = n;
    h = _creat(name, 0);
    if (h<0) printf("  0");
    else
    {
      struct ffblk f;
      unsigned c;
      _close(h);
      findfirst("(?).&X&", &f, 0);
      c = f.ff_name[1]&0xFF;
      printf(c=='\\' || c=='\'' ? "  '\\%c'" : ' '<=c && c<='~' ?
        "  '%c'" : "  %d", c);
      unlink(name);
    }
    if (n!=255) putchar(',');
    putchar('\n');
  }
  printf("};\n");
}
```

Detecting I/O Redirection in C++

■ Hugh Myers

Learn how to use I/O redirection to make your C++ programs much more flexible.

A program should get as much information as possible from the current context, rather than depending on outside help. A small but useful example of such self-knowledge is I/O redirection. The program should know where its output is going! This makes the difference between forcing a prompt for the next screen versus no prompt if your output is going to a file or a printer.

The technique is short and sweet, and I've taken advantage of the inline assembly feature of Borland C++. The method is to compare **stdin** with **stdout**, and if they are not equal then you'll know redirection is in place.

The only complication is that **stdin** and **stdout** are not quite the standard library **stdin** and **stdout**. In this instance they are the literal file handle table entries. The entries are written into the program's PSP at load time. Given this fact and the commonly available **_psp** variable (supported by both Borland's and Microsoft's compilers), it only takes 12 instructions to find, load, and compare the two handles.

To start, DS is pointed to the PSP. Then ES:BX is loaded with the address of the handle table, which is at offset 34H from the start of the PSP. At this point, ES:[BX] holds **stdin** and ES:[BX+1] holds **stdout**, allowing us to get them into AX, compare them, and get out. Listing 3.10 displays a hex dump of the first page of the user's graphics BIOS, with "Continue" prompts if output is going to the screen, and without prompts if output is redirected.

CODE DESCRIPTION

Overview

The listing provided is used to easily redirect output to different devices. The program also demonstrates the inline assembly feature of Borland C++.

Listing Available

Listing	*Description*	*Used with*
VIDINFO.CPP	C++source file that uses I/O redirection to print a hex dump of the graphics BIOS to either the screen or another device.	------

How to Compile/Assemble

VIDINFO.CPP should be compiled with Borland C++ or Turbo C++.

■ **LISTING 3.10 VIDINFO.CPP**

```
#pragma option -k-  // Disable stack from if not needed
#pragma option -O   // Eliminate redundant jumps (to self etc.)
```

```
#include <stdio.h>
#include <stdlib.h>
#include <dos.h>
#include <conio.h>
#include <string.h>
#define ERROR -1
typedef unsigned int uint;
typedef unsigned char uchar;

int    redirected();
uint   get_key();
char   *dump(uint offset,uint segment);
void   next_page();

main()
{
    int redirection = redirected(), i, j;
    if(!redirection) clrscr();
    printf("____________________________________________________\n");
    printf("_ Video Information      Bios Dump C000-C0FF _\n");
    printf("____________________________________________________\n");
    for(i = j = 0;i < 20;i++,j += 8)
      printf("_ %s _\n",dump(0xc000,uint(j)));
    if(!redirection) next_page();
    for(;j < 256;j += 8)
      printf("_ %s _\n",dump(0xc000,uint(j)));
    printf("____________________________________________________\n");
    if(!redirection) {
      printf(" Press any key to continue... ");
      get_key(); clrscr();
    }
}

void next_page()
{
    printf("____________________________________________________\n");
    printf(" Press any key to continue... ");
    get_key(); clrscr();
    printf("____________________________________________________\n");
}

char *dump(uint offset,uint segment)
{
    int    i;
    uchar far *ptr = (uchar far *)MK_FP(offset,segment);
    static char string[80];
    uchar   c;
    char    trailer[40], temp[40];

    sprintf(string,"%04X:%04X ",offset,segment);
    trailer[0] = temp[0] = 0;
    for(i = 0;i < 8;i++) {
      c = *ptr++;
```

```
        sprintf(temp,"%02x ",c);
        strcat(string,temp);
        if(c < ' ' || c > 126)
            temp[0] = '.';
        else temp[0] = c;
        temp[1] = 0;
        strcat(trailer,temp);
    }
    strcat(string,trailer);
    return string;
}

uint get_key()
{
    asm {
        xor  ah,ah
        int  0x16
    }
    return _AX;
}
int redirected()
{
    asm {
    push ds
    mov  ax,_psp         // Get segment of PSP
    mov  ds,ax           // Put it in DS
    xor  bx,bx           // Zero out BX
    les  bx,[bx + 0x34]  // at DS:BX to ES and BX
    mov  al,es:[bx]      // stdin normally = 1(i.e. CON)
    mov  ah,es:[bx + 1]  // stdout normally = 1(i.e. CON)
    pop  ds
    cmp  al,ah           // Compare the two handles
    mov  ax,1            // Return 1 if not equal
    jne  EXIT
    xor  ax,ax           // Clear to 0 AX if equal
    }
EXIT:
    return _AX;
}
```

Switching between Logical Drives

■ Kevin Dean

Learn how to bypass DOS and write your own code to change disk drives.

Single-diskette PCs have the inherent problem that drive A and drive B are shared by the same physical drive. When MS-DOS changes the drive allocation, the message, “Insert diskette for drive X: and strike any key when ready,” is displayed, which usually disrupts the beautiful screen layout you spent hours designing.

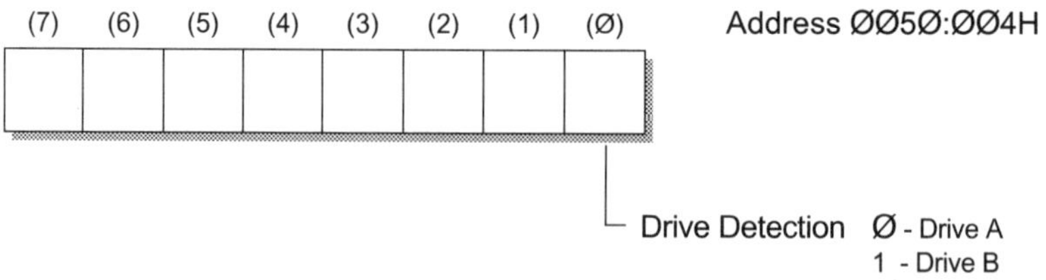

■ **FIGURE 3.2 Accessing the active drive**

With DOS 3.20 and later, you can also attach more than one drive letter to a block device. For example, if you had a high-density drive and wanted to access it as low density, you could do so by loading the DRIVER.SYS device driver in your CONFIG.SYS file. Once loaded, you could treat your high-density drive as a low-density drive through the drive letter assigned by DRIVER.SYS. The message when you switch from the high to the low-density drive is the same.

In my never-ending quest for the perfect user interface, I wrote routines (Listing 3.11) that bypass the DOS message by determining the current logical drive, prompting the user, and changing the drive.

As Figure 3.2 shows, the address of the byte that contains the active drive letter for drives A or B is at 0050:0004H. The value is 0 for drive A and 1 for drive B, but is converted to the drive letter itself by the **get_logical_drive()** function. For DOS versions 3.20 and greater, the logical drive is determined by function 44H (IOCTL) service 0EH (get logical drive).

The **get_logical_drive()** function returns the current drive letter attached to the block device, or 0 if an error occurs. If an error occurs, **_doserrno** is set.

The **set_logical_drive()** function sets the logical drive to the drive letter passed to it. On success, it returns the drive letter previously attached to the block device. If an error occurs, it returns 0 and sets **_doserrno**. Note: this function does not actually change the *active* drive; use **setdisk()** for that.

These functions are transparent to the SUBST command. Any drive assigned using the SUBST command will be recognized and **set_logical_drive()** will function accordingly. These functions do not, however, recognize drives reassigned using the ASSIGN command. They will still prompt for a change of diskette even though one of the drives attached to the block device is currently reassigned by ASSIGN.

These routines will not work with some RAM disks and other block device drivers and return **EINVFNC** (invalid function number) in **_doserrno**. This problem is a failing of the device driver, not this code.

Code Description

Overview

The listing provided is used to access and select logical drives.

Listing Available

Listing	*Description*	*Used with*
DOSDISK.C	C source file that defines two functions for accessing logical drives—**get_logical_drive()** and **set_logical_drive()**.	------

How to Compile/Assemble

DOSDISK.C should be compiled with Borland C++ or Turbo C++.

■ LISTING 3.11 DOSDISK.C

```
/* DOSDISK.C */

#include <ctype.h>
#include <dir.h>
#include <dos.h>
#include <errno.h>
#include <stdio.h>

#define DOS_DATA_SEG  0x0050

/***/
/* Returns drive currently attached to block device
   defined by 'drive'. */
char get_logical_drive(char drive)
{
char cur_drive;        /* Current drive attached to block device. */
union REGS regs;       /* Registers for interrupt calls. */

/* Default to current drive. */
drive = drive ? toupper(drive) : (getdisk() + 'A');

/* Check for valid drive letter. */
if (!isalpha(drive))
  {
  cur_drive = 0;
  _doserrno = EINVDRV;
  }
else
  /* Check for DOS version 3.20 or above. */
  if (_osmajor > 3 || _osmajor == 3 && _osminor >= 20)
    {
    /* IOCTL request 0x0E (get logical drive). */
    regs.x.ax = 0x440E;

    /* Drive number (1 = A, 2 = B, etc) is in BL. */
    regs.h.bl = drive - ('A' - 1);
    intdos(&regs, &regs);
    if (regs.x.cflag)
      /* Carry flag set, error in _doserrno. */
      cur_drive = 0;
```

```
      else
        /* Return code of 0 in AL means only one drive attached
           to block device. */
        cur_drive = regs.h.al == 0 ? drive : regs.h.al + ('A' - 1);
      }
    else
      /* For lower versions of DOS, only drives
         A and B are interchangeable. */
      if (drive == 'A' || drive == 'B')
        {
        int86(0x11, &regs, &regs);

        /* Bit 0 in AX is 1 if diskette drives are present. */
        if (regs.x.ax & 0x0001)
          if (((regs.x.ax & 0xC0) >> 6) == 0)
            /* Only one diskette installed. */
            cur_drive = drive == 'A' || drive == 'B'
            ? peekb(DOS_DATA_SEG, 0x0004) + 'A' : drive;
          else
            /* More than one diskette installed. */
            cur_drive = drive;
        else
          /* No diskette drive. */
          {
          cur_drive = 0;
          _doserrno = EINVDRV;
          }
        }
      else
        cur_drive = drive;

return (cur_drive);
}

/***/
/* Attaches logical drive to block device
   if not already attached. */
char set_logical_drive(char drive)
{
char cur_drive;     /* Current drive attached to block device. */
union REGS regs;    /* Registers for interrupt calls. */

/* Default to current drive. */
drive = drive ? toupper(drive) : (getdisk() + 'A');

if ((cur_drive = get_logical_drive(drive = toupper(drive)))
   != 0 && cur_drive != drive)
  {
  /* REPLACE THIS WITH WHATEVER YOU WANT TO PROMPT FOR CHANGE. */
  printf("Insert disk for drive %c: and press RETURN", drive);
  getchar();

  /* Check for DOS version 3.20 or above. */
  if (_osmajor > 3 || _osmajor == 3 && _osminor >= 20)
    {
    /* IOCTL request 0x0F (set logical drive). */
```

```
      regs.x.ax = 0x440F;

      /* Drive number (1 = A, 2 = B, etc) is in BL. */
      regs.h.bl = drive - ('A' - 1);

      intdos(&regs, &regs);

      if (regs.x.cflag)
        /* Carry flag set, error in _doserrno. */
        drive = 0;
      }
    else
      /* For lower versions of DOS, only drives A and B
         are interchangeable. */
      if (drive == 'A' || drive == 'B')
        pokeb(DOS_DATA_SEG, 0x0004, drive - 'A');
    }

  return (cur_drive);
  }
```

A Directory Description Utility

■ Kim T. Hastings

Here's a useful utility for reporting important size information about your directories.

DIRGT is a utility used to determine the directory structure of your DOS-formatted drives. (See Listing 3.12.) It will display the total kilobytes used in the default directory including the subdirectories. One parameter can be passed on the command line to determine the number of subdirectory levels to be displayed in the output report. This report is displayed using STDOUT so that it may be redirected with standard DOS commands.

```
Usage  :  DIRGT [LEVELS]
```

where **LEVELS** is the number of sublevels to include in the report, up to 99.

Examples

```
C:\>DIRGT 2
```

lists the total kilobytes used on drive C: and a breakdown of the total kilobytes used for the first and second level subdirectories of the root.

```
C:\WINDOWS>DIRGT 99 > WIN.RPT
```

lists the total kilobytes used in the windows directory and a breakdown of the total kilobytes used for up to 99 levels of subdirectories under C:\WINDOWS and redirects the output to a file called WIN.RPT.

How It Works

The program starts off by calling **getfatd**, a DOS-specific routine which returns information about the File Allocation Table (FAT) of the current drive. Information provided by this function includes the number of bytes per sector, the number of sectors per cluster, and the number of clusters on the drive. Multiplying these values together gives the total number of bytes on the drive.

The program then calls **scan_dirs**, which calls **get_bytes** to find the total number of bytes used by the directory and its subdirectories. Then, based on the number of levels specified in the command line, **scan_dirs** calls itself recursively to report on the individual subdirectories.

get_bytes adds up the bytes in the current directory, then proceeds to look for subdirectories. The pseudo directory entries '.' and '..' are skipped. If any real directories are encountered, **get_bytes** in turn calls itself recursively to sum all the branches available in that particular directory tree. **get_bytes** returns the total number of bytes used in all subdirectories of a given path.

Both **get_bytes** and **scan_dirs** make use of **findfirst** and **findnext** to process files and subdirectories.

CODE DESCRIPTION

Overview

The listing provided is used to determine the directory structure of your DOS formatted drives.

Listing Available

Listing	*Description*	*Used with*
DIRGT.CPP	C++ source file that displays various directory information including the total kilobytes used, and a breakdown of the sizes of selected subdirectories.	------

How to Compile/Assemble

DIRGT.CPP should be compiled with Borland C++ or Turbo C++.

■ LISTING 3.12 DIRGT.CPP

```
/*  DIRGT.CPP
Directory Grand Total Utility
By: Kim T. Hastings
*/

#include <dir.h>
#include <dos.h>
#include <stdio.h>
#include <stdlib.h>

long total_disk;                // Total Disk Space
```

```
long get_bytes (void)          // Get bytes for current directory
{
struct ffblk ffblk;
long   total_bytes = 0;

int done = findfirst ("*.*", &ffblk, 0xff);     // Loop through files
while (!done)
  {
  total_bytes += ffblk.ff_fsize;
  done = findnext (&ffblk);
  }
done = findfirst ("*.*", &ffblk, FA_DIREC);     // Loop through directories
while (!done)
  {
  if (ffblk.ff_name[0] != '.' && ffblk.ff_attrib == FA_DIREC)
     {
     chdir (ffblk.ff_name);
     total_bytes += get_bytes();
     chdir ("\.\.");
     }
  done = findnext (&ffblk);
  }
return (total_bytes);
}

void scan_dirs (int max_level)  //------ Loop through subdirectories
{
char   path[MAXPATH];
struct ffblk ffblk;
static level = 0;

long bytes = get_bytes();
printf ("%-50s%10.1f KBytes  %4.1f\% \n",getcwd (path,MAXPATH-1),
         bytes / 1024.0, (float) bytes / total_disk * 100);
int done = findfirst ("*.*", &ffblk, FA_DIREC);
while (!done)
  {
  if (ffblk.ff_name[0]!='.' && ffblk.ff_attrib==FA_DIREC && level<max_level)
     {
     level++;
     chdir (ffblk.ff_name);
     scan_dirs (max_level);
     if (level– == 1) putchar ('\n');
     chdir ("\.\.");
     }
  done = findnext (&ffblk);
  }
}

void main (int argc, char * argv[])
{
struct fatinfo diskinfo;              //  Calculate total disk space
getfatd(&diskinfo);
total_disk = (long) diskinfo.fi_sclus * diskinfo.fi_nclus *
    diskinfo.fi_bysec;
```

```
if (argc > 0)
  scan_dirs (atoi(argv[1]));
else
  scan_dirs(0);
}
```

Deleting Subdirectories Along with Files

■ Russell Preston

Here's a useful utility for deleting files and subdirectories.

It's a real pain to delete files from subdirectories, especially when the directories are nested more than one or two deep. Not only do you have to delete the files, but you have to climb up out of the subdirectory before you can remove it, too. Here's a program which recursively uses **findfirst** and **findnext** to delete all specified files in the current directory and will pursue them into subdirectories. (See Listing 3.13.)

What Happens

In ZAP.CPP, **main** uses the **MAXFILE**, **MAXPATH**, **MAXDRIVE**, and **MAXDIR** macros from DIR.H to build up a path and filename mask with **fnsplit** and **fnmerge**. If no mask is given on the command line, "*.*" is assumed. **file_name** is then used by **del_files** to delete files with matching names in the current directory. **del_files** then recurses into all available subdirectories matching and deleting files. If "*.*" is the file mask, then all subdirectories recursed into will also be removed.

Because of the relentless nature of the program, the user is prompted before deletion begins.

CODE DESCRIPTION

Overview

The listing provided is used to delete selected files in a directory including subdirectories.

Listing Available

Listing	*Description*	*Used with*
ZAP.CPP	C++ source file that uses recursion to step through a directory and delete files—including subdirectories.	------

How to Compile/Assemble

ZAP.CPP can be compiled with Borland C++ or Turbo C++.

■ LISTING 3.13 ZAP.CPP

```
\ Program    : ZAP.CPP                                                  \
/                                                                       /
```

```
\ Programmer: Russell Preston                                        \
/                                                                    /
\ Function  : ZAP deletes the specified files.  If the file spec.    \
/             is "*.*" then the subdirectories are also removed.     /
\                                                                    \
/ Switches  : A /U switch will unconditionally override the user     /
\             confirmation of the deletion process.                  \
/-----------------------------------*/
#include <conio.h>
#include <ctype.h>
#include <dir.h>
#include <dos.h>
#include <io.h>
#include <direct.h>
#include <stdio.h>
#include <string.h>
#include <stat.h>

char file_name[MAXFILE + MAXEXT - 1];

void del_files(void)
  {
  struct ffblk ffblk;
  int    done;
  char   cur_path[MAXPATH];

                        //Find and delete files in the current directory.
  done = findfirst(file_name, &ffblk, 0xff ^ FA_DIREC);
  while (!done)
    {
    if (strlen(getcwd(cur_path, MAXPATH)) > 3)  strcat(cur_path, "\\");
       printf("Deletingùùù %s%s\n", cur_path, ffblk.ff_name);
       chmod(ffblk.ff_name, S_IWRITE);
          remove(ffblk.ff_name);
          done = findnext(&ffblk);
     }                        //Change the current path to a subdirectory
                              //and recurse into it to delete its files.
  done = findfirst("*.*", &ffblk, 0xff);
  while (!done)
    {
    if (ffblk.ff_attrib == FA_DIREC && ffblk.ff_name[0] != '.')
      {
        chdir(ffblk.ff_name);
        del_files();
        chdir("\.\.");
      if(!strcmp(file_name, "*.*"))  rmdir(ffblk.ff_name);
      }
    done = findnext(&ffblk);
    }
  }

void main(int argc, char *argv[])
  {
  int  prompt_flag = 1;
  char path[MAXPATH] = "";
```

```
  char drive[MAXDRIVE];
  char dir[MAXDIR];
  char file[MAXFILE] = "*";
  char ext[MAXEXT] = ".*";

  if (argc > 1)
    {
    for (int idx=1; idx<argc; idx++)            //Parse command line switches
      {
      if (!stricmp(argv[idx], "/U"))
        prompt_flag = 0;
      else if (!strchr(argv[idx], '/'))
        strncpy(path, argv[idx], MAXPATH);
      }
    int flag = fnsplit(path, drive, dir, file, ext);
    if(flag & DRIVE)   _chdrive(toupper(drive[0]) - 64);
    if(flag & DIRECTORY)
      {                                         //Strip backslash
      if (strlen(dir) > 1) dir[strlen(dir) - 1] = NULL;
      chdir(dir);
      }
    if (!chdir(file))        strcpy(file, "*");   //Test filename for a
    if(!(flag & FILENAME))   strcpy(file, "*");   //directory.
    if(!(flag & EXTENSION)) strcpy(ext, ".*");
    }
  fnmerge(file_name, "", "", file, ext);
  if (prompt_flag)
    {
    if (strlen(getcwd(path, MAXPATH)) > 3) strcat(path, "\\");
    printf("All files specified by %s%s and all of its\n"
           "subdirectories will be deleted!  Are you sure (Y/N)?",
           path, file_name);
    if (toupper(getche()) == 'Y')
      {
      printf("\n");
      del_files();
      }
    }
  else
    del_files();
  }
```

Reading Fixed-Length Records

■ Alan Ray Nielsen

Pick fields cleanly from exported fixed-length database records with scanfix.

Getting user input in C can be as simple as calling **scanf** or **gets**. If you need a more robust user interface, you can choose from a plethora of library routines that use windows, pop-up and pull-down menus, and elaborate data-entry forms.

Likewise, reading data from a data file can be as simple as calling **fscanf** or **fgets** (the file versions of **scanf** and **gets**). An intermediate level of file I/O involves the use of C structures to read and write data. This approach typically involves using functions like **fread**, **fwrite**, and **fseek**. More demanding file and data management needs can be solved by using third-party file-management libraries.

It might seem at first glance that the above sources cover all types of file input. However, there is still a common form of data input that is not handled well with any of the above methods: reading sequential, fixed-length record ASCII files.

Fixed-Length Record ASCII Files

This type of file is characterized by a series of new-line ('\n') terminated, fixed-length records. Each record is further divided into a number of fixed-length fields. This type of file can originate in a number of ways. For example, C's own **fprintf** can create them. They may also get created as data is exported from spreadsheets or database management systems for use in other applications.

If you use **fgets** alone to read the data, then you must parse through the resultant data string and pick out the various fields individually. This can be messy. **fscanf** works with only the best-behaved data. And **fread** is no better than **fgets**.

What, then, is to be done? In the spirit of C programming, allow me to present **scanfix**, which was written to accomplish this specific task. **scanfix** uses a **sscanf**-like syntax (**sscanf** is the string version of **scanf**) to pick apart various fields from a fixed-length string. The string, in all likelihood, will be read using **fgets**.

By necessity, **scanfix** uses a variable number of arguments. Therefore, we'll need to examine the techniques for accessing a variable number of arguments first.

Three Problems to Solve

When C calls a function, the arguments to that function are placed on the program's stack. Figure 3.3 shows how C puts arguments on the stack for the following function call:

```
sample(arg1, arg2, arg3);
```

In C the stack grows down from high memory to low memory. Figure 3.3 shows that the arguments are placed on the stack in reverse order from how they appear in the function call. This makes it easier for the compiler to access them in the order listed. After the function's arguments are placed on the stack, the return address is also placed there.

With this understanding of how arguments are placed on the stack, three problems become apparent: First, how do you determine the address of the first argument on the stack? Second, how do you access subsequent arguments from the stack? And finally, how do you know how many arguments are there and when the arguments end? C itself provides solutions to the first two problems. The last problem must be handled by your program logic.

C provides three macros that help solve the first two problems: **va_start**, **va_arg**, and **va_end**. It also provides a couple of other declarations that help in the process.

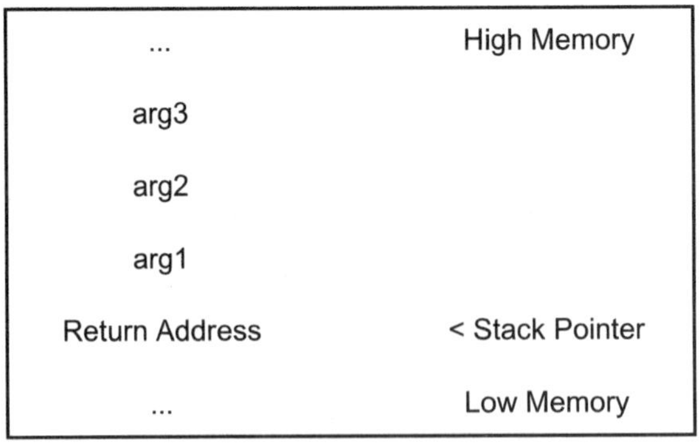

■ **FIGURE 3.3 The stack after calling sample**

There are actually two versions of the above macros: a UNIX and an ANSI version. The UNIX version was introduced with UNIX System V. Later, the ANSI C committee introduced its own slightly different version. This article discusses both versions and points out their similarities and differences. Your compiler may offer one or the other.

Accessing the Arguments

Listing 3.14 incorporates both macro versions, selected via conditional compilation. Notice that the listing includes a number of **#if** statements. Looking at the code between the **#if** and **#endif** statements will help you to see the differences. By changing the word **ANSI** to **UNIX** in line 4 of the code, you can compile either the ANSI version (default) or the UNIX version.

The following discussion uses Listing 3.14 as a reference to explain the process of creating a function that uses a variable number of arguments. Each step will clearly indicate which elements apply to the ANSI or UNIX versions. Referenced line numbers are for Listing 3.14 starting with the first **#include** statement.

First, you must include the header file **stdarg.h** (ANSI, line 6) or **varargs.h** (UNIX, line 8). These header files contain the definitions for **va_start**, **va_arg**, **va_end,** and other necessary declarations.

Second, you must indicate in your function declaration that the function takes a variable number of arguments. This is done in the ANSI version by including the ellipses ". . ." as the last argument in your function declaration (line 15). The UNIX version requires that you include the placeholder **va_alist** (declared in **varargs.h**; line 17).

Third, (for UNIX only) you must place the declaration **va_dcl** (also declared in **varargs.h**) as the last item in your function declaration (line 19). Notice that there is no semicolon after this statement.

Fourth, declare a variable of type **va_list** (defined in **stdarg.h** or **varargs.h**) in your program (both ANSI and UNIX, line 41). Within the scope of **scanfix** and this article, this variable is called **argp**. It serves as the means whereby C passes back the various arguments to the caller.

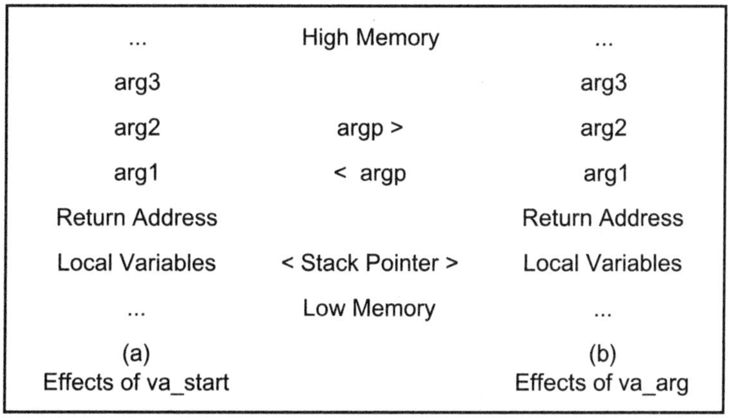

■ **FIGURE 3.4 Modifying argp**

Fifth, call the macro **va_start** to initialize the pointer (**argp**) declared above (ANSI, line 44; UNIX, line 46). This call points **argp** to the first argument in the list of variable arguments. Figure 3.4(a) shows the effects of calling **va_start** on **argp**. For this call, the syntax of the ANSI and UNIX versions is slightly different.

The prototype for the ANSI version follows:

```
void va_start(va_list,<prev_arg>)
```

In actual code **va_list** is **argp** as defined above. The **<prev_arg>** parameter is the name of the argument prior to the ellipses ("...") in the function declaration. The preceding variable *must not* be a register variable. The prototype for the UNIX version is simpler:

```
void va_start(va_list)
```

Again, **argp** is the **va_list** field.

Sixth, call the macro **va_arg** as needed to retrieve subsequent fields from the variable list (both ANSI and UNIX; lines 111, 116, 121, 128, 145, and 150). Calling **va_arg** simply returns what **argp** is currently pointing to and then increments **argp** to point to the next argument. The prototype for this function follows:

```
<type> va_arg(va_list, <type>)
```

The **<type>** field represents the type of field to expect (**char ***, **int**, and so on). This field tells the compiler the size of the argument being accessed. Again, **va_list** is simply the **argp** parameter. Figure 3.4 shows the effects of calling **va_arg** after a call to **va_start**.

Seventh, as your function ends, call **va_end** to reset the argument pointer (**argp**; ANSI and UNIX, line 163). In DOS this call simply resets **argp** to NULL. In other operating systems it may do other things. It should be included for maximum compatibility and portability.

Knowing When to Say When

The last problem to be solved is knowing when the function's arguments run out. This must be handled by our program's logic. There are (at least) three simple ways to handle this.

First, you may choose a predefined value that signals the end of the argument list. Every time the function is called, then, this value must be the last argument in the function call. For example, if you have a function that adds a variable number of integers you might use -1 (or another value) as a signal that the list of integers has been exhausted.

Second, you may include as one of your fixed arguments a counter indicating how many variable arguments are to follow. In this case you would simply read that argument and use it in a loop to retrieve the remaining arguments.

Third, you may "encode" one of your fixed arguments with the information necessary to know when to stop. This is the method **scanfix** uses. For example, **scanfix** knows when to stop looking for arguments when it runs out of fields to convert.

Presenting Scanfix

The **scanfix** function is very much like **sscanf**. In fact, almost everything you know about **sscanf** (or **scanf**) applies directly to **scanfix**. Both functions read fields from a character string and convert the values found into C variables. A series of format specifiers serves as the blueprint for converting the fields. The function prototype for **scanfix** follows:

```
int scanfix(char *buffer,char *format,...);
```

where **buffer** is a pointer to the character string being scanned, **format** is a pointer to a string of format specifiers, and the ellipses (". . .") represent the variable number of arguments (fields) to be assigned.

The only difference between **scanfix** and **sscanf** is the format string. The format string for **sscanf** is made up of three significant components: whitespace characters, non-whitespace characters (except '%'), and format specifiers that begin with the percent sign ('%'). When **sscanf** encounters whitespace in the format string it scans and skips all whitespace characters in its buffer until it encounters a non-whitespace character. When a non-whitespace character (except '%') is found in the format string, **sscanf** expects that character to be the next character found in the buffer. If the indicated character is not found, **sscanf** terminates. As mentioned above, the format specifiers are introduced with the percent sign and serve as a blueprint for the conversion of the field.

By contrast, **scanfix**'s format string consists of a single significant component: format specifiers. Like those for **sscanf**, they begin with a percent sign. The form of **scanfix**'s format specifiers follows and must be strictly adhered to:

```
%[*][-]width[h|l]type
```

The items in braces ([]) are optional. The percent sign signals the beginning of a format specifier. The asterisk ('*') is optional. If included, it tells **scanfix** that some number of characters from **buffer** are to be scanned but not assigned to any field. The number of characters to skip in this way is indicated by the **width** field.

The optional hyphen ('-') is borrowed from **printf**, with modifications. For string and character fields it causes **scanfix** to ignore leading whitespace in the input field. This guarantees that the first character in the receiving field will not be a whitespace character. This is especially useful if you're reading a right- or an irregularly-justified character string.

The **width** parameter is a positive integer. It is the number of characters to be read from the buffer to make up the indicated field.

The *h* and *l* fields are optional and mutually exclusive. They are used as modifiers to the next field, **type**. The *h* modifier forces the receiving integer to be interpreted as a short integer. The *l* modifier forces the receiving integer to be interpreted as a long integer. The *l* modifier also forces a receiving **float** to be interpreted as a *long float* or **double**. If these modifiers are not used as described above, they are ignored.

The **type** parameter specifies the type of the receiving field. In its present form, **scanfix** recognizes four types: c, d, f, and s. They are identical to their **sscanf** counterparts.

Type c is used to "convert" the incoming characters into the receiving character buffer. The optional hyphen ('-') will cause leading whitespace to be ignored. Therefore, the actual number of characters copied may be less than the indicated width. The receiving field is *not* null-terminated.

Type d is used to convert the incoming characters into an integer. As indicated above, it may be modified by prefixing it with *h* or *l* to force the integer to be assigned either as a **short** or **long** integer, respectively.

Type f is used to convert the incoming characters into a floating-point number (**float**). If the receiving field is a **double**, the f must be preceded with the l modifier.

Type s is treated exactly as is type c with one exception: Type s will null-terminate the receiving string. Therefore, you must make sure that the receiving string is at least **width**+1 characters in length.

By definition, the **type** field is required. However, when the asterisk ('*') is included in the format specifier, all fields after the width are in fact discarded.

Unlike **sscanf**, **scanfix** ignores all characters between format specifiers. Therefore, spaces can be safely placed between specifiers to increase their readability.

Like **sscanf**, **scanfix** returns the number of fields converted. If an error is encountered before converting the first field, **scanfix** returns **EOF**.

Using scanfix

The comments given in Listing 3.14 should be sufficient to understand the operation of **scanfix**. So now let's look at it in action.

Listing 3.15 shows a sample program, **scantest**, that calls **scanfix**. This program reads in a short data file of fictitious students (STUDENTS.DAT), prints the fields from each record, sums the age and GPA fields, and then prints out some summary statistics about the file. Figure 3.5 shows the format and contents for STUDENTS.DAT. It also shows a column template that is not part of the file.

There are a few things to note about using **scanfix**. First, Listing 3.15 (line 14) shows how to declare **scanfix** in the calling function. Second, **scantest** (Listing 3.15) uses **fgets** to actually read the string from the file. Since **scanfix** only works on a fixed-length string, **fgets** is probably the best way to read the string. Notice also how **scantest** checks the length of the string before continuing (line 26). Third, even though the data in STUDENTS.DAT is poorly aligned, **scanfix** has no problem aligning it correctly—which is an important part of its reason for being. (See Figure 3.6.)

```
          File Format
   Position          Description
     1 - 25          Name
    26 - 26          Sex
    27 - 29          Age
    30 - 32          GPA
    33 - 33          New line ('\n')
---------------------------------------

          File Contents
--+--1--+--2--+--3-
Wren, Robin              F 203.5
Clayton, Jason           M 243.7
          Graham, AllisonF 214.0
   Henderson, L. Don     M23 2.9
Huish, Craig J.          M 282.7
Larsen, Tammy            F1013.9
    Madsen, Steven J.    M 233.7
Roberts, Roberta R.      F 543.0
Smith, J. Thomas III     M 223.5
```

■ **FIGURE 3.5 The file STUDENTS.DAT**

```
Name                     Sex Age GPA

Wren, Robin               F   20 3.5
Clayton, Jason            M   24 3.7
Graham, Allison           F   21 4.0
Henderson, L. Don         M   23 2.9
Huish, Craig J.           M   28 2.7
Larsen, Tammy             F   32 3.9
Madsen, Steven J.         M   23 3.7
Roberts, Roberta R.       F   54 3.0
Smith, J. Thomas III      M   22 3.5

Number of records =   9
Average age       =  35.1
Average gpa       =   3.4
```

■ **FIGURE 3.6 Results from SCANTEST**

CODE DESCRIPTION

Overview

The listings provided are used to scan fixed-length ASCII strings and break out various fields according to specified format flags.

Listing Available

Listing	*Description*	*Used with*
SCANFIX.C	C source file that defines the main scanning function named **scanfix()**.	------

SCANTEST.C	Sample program that uses the **scanfix()** function to process a simple data file of records.	------

How to Compile/Assemble

SCANFIX.C and SCANTEST.C should be compiled with Borland C++ or Turbo C++.

■ LISTING 3.14 SCANFIX.C

```
/*  scanfix.c - scan a fixed-length ASCII string and break
 *  out various fields according to the format specifiers supplied. */
#include <stdio.h>
#include <stdlib.h>
#include <ctype.h>
#include <string.h>
#define ANSI
#ifdef ANSI
#include <stdarg.h>
#else
#include <varargs.h>
#endif
#define FALSE 0
#define TRUE !FALSE

#ifdef ANSI
int scanfix(char *string, char *control, ...)
#else
int scanfix(string, control, va_alist)
char *string, *control;
va_dcl
#endif
{
    char    *csPtr;              /* control string pointer */
    char    *sPtr;               /* string pointer */
    char    *cPtr;               /* ptr for type s and c */
    char    *sNextPtr;           /* next string pointer */
    char    *nonWhite;           /* ptr to non-white space */
    char    c;                   /* temporary character */
    char    cTemp;               /* another temp character */
    char    type;                /* type of field */
    char    longFlag;            /* convert to long? */
    char    shortFlag;           /* convert to short? */
    char    skipFlag;            /* skip field? */
    char    leftJust;            /* left justify field? */
    int     nFields = 0;         /* number of fields */
    int     length;              /* length of field */
    short   *hPtr, shortValue;   /* use to convert shorts */
    int     *iPtr, intValue;     /* use to convert ints */
    long    *lPtr, longValue;    /* use to convert longs */
    float   *fPtr, floatValue;   /* use to convert floats */
    double  *dPtr, doubleValue;  /* use to convert doubles */
    va_list argp;                /* argument pointer */

#ifdef ANSI
```

```
    va_start(argp, control);
#else
    va_start(argp);              /* init argument pointer */
#endif

    sPtr = string;
    csPtr = control;
    /* process format specifiers in the control string */
    while (*csPtr != '\0') {
       /* find next field % identifier */
       if (*(csPtr++) != '%')
          continue;
       /* determine if current field is to be skipped */
       skipFlag = FALSE;
       if (*csPtr == '*') {
          skipFlag = TRUE;
          csPtr++;
       }
       /* determine if field is to be left-justified */
       leftJust = FALSE;
       if (*csPtr == '-') {
          leftJust = TRUE;
          csPtr++;
       }
       /* determine field length */
       length = 0;
       while (isdigit(c = *(csPtr++)))
          length = length * 10 + c - '0';
       if (length == 0)
          break;
       /* skip the field if necessary */
       if (skipFlag) {
          sPtr += length;
          continue;
       }
       /* determine field type */
       longFlag = FALSE;
       shortFlag = FALSE;
       if (c == 'l') {                /* test for long */
          longFlag = TRUE;
          c = *(csPtr++);
       }
       else if (c == 'h') {           /* test for short */
          shortFlag = TRUE;
          c = *(csPtr++);
       }
       type = c;

       /* check for valid type */
       if (strchr("dscf", type) == NULL)
          break;
       /* save first char of next field and */
       /* replace it with \0               */
       sNextPtr = sPtr + length;
       cTemp = *sNextPtr;
       *sNextPtr = '\0';
```

```
    switch (type) {
      case 'd':
        if (longFlag) {
          lPtr = va_arg(argp, long *);
          longValue = atol(sPtr);
          *lPtr = longValue;
        }
        else if (shortFlag) {
          hPtr = va_arg(argp, short *);
          shortValue = (short) atoi(sPtr);
          *hPtr = shortValue;
        }
        else {
          iPtr = va_arg(argp, int *);
          intValue = atoi(sPtr);
          *iPtr = intValue;
        }
        break;
      case 's':
      case 'c':
        cPtr = va_arg(argp, char *);
        nonWhite = cPtr-1;
        if (leftJust)
        /* skip white space */
          while (isspace(*sPtr) && *sPtr != '\0')
          sPtr++;
        while(*sPtr != '\0') {
        *cPtr = *(sPtr++);
        if (!isspace(*cPtr)) nonWhite = cPtr;
        cPtr++;
        } /* while(*sPtr != '\0') */
        if (type == 's')    /* null for string */
        *(++nonWhite) = '\0';
        break;
      case 'f':
        if (longFlag) {
          dPtr = va_arg(argp, double *);
          doubleValue = atof(sPtr);
        *dPtr = doubleValue;
        }
        else {
          fPtr = va_arg(argp, float *);
          floatValue = atof(sPtr);
          *fPtr = floatValue;
        }
        break;
  } /* end switch */
  nFields++;
  /* restore first character of next field */
  *sNextPtr = cTemp;
  sPtr = sNextPtr;
} /* end while */
va_end(argp);

if (nFields == 0)
  return(EOF);
```

```
        else
           return(nFields);
}
```

■ LISTING 3.15 SCANTEST.C

```
#include <stdio.h>
#include <stdlib.h>
#include <string.h>

#define FALSE 0
#define TRUE !FALSE
#define RECORDSIZE 33

main()
{
    FILE    *inFile;
    char    name[26], sex, buf[RECORDSIZE + 1];
    int     age = 0, totAge = 0, totRecs = 0, length;
    double  gpa;
    float   totGPA = 0.0;
    int scanfix(char *, char *, ...);

    /* open the input data file */
    inFile = fopen("students.dat", "rt");
    if (inFile == NULL) {
       fprintf(stderr, "Cannot open input file\n");
       exit(1);
    }

    /* process each record */
    printf("Name                        Sex Age GPA\n\n");
    while (fgets(buf, RECORDSIZE + 1, inFile) != NULL) {
       if ((length = strlen(buf)) != RECORDSIZE) {
          printf("Invalid record length (%d)\n", length);
          exit(1);
       }
       scanfix(buf, "%-25s %1c %3d %3lf",
          name, &sex, &age, &gpa);
       printf("%-25s %c  %3d %3.1f\n",
          name, sex, age, gpa);

       totRecs++;
       totAge += age;
       totGPA += gpa;
    }

    fclose(inFile);
    printf("\nNumber of records = %3d\n", totRecs);
    printf("Average age       = %5.1f\n",
       (float) totAge / totRecs);
    printf("Average gpa       = %5.1f\n", totGPA / totRecs);
}
```

4

Text Video Programming

There's a lot of life left in the text video arena, all this GUI hype notwithstanding. Your machine doesn't boot up into graphics mode, and even Borland's renowned Turbo Debugger works only in text mode. Besides, even if you consider yourself a graphics specialist, you're going to be stubbing your toes on text mode mechanisms and conventions everywhere you go in the PC world.

For example, if your graphics program returns to DOS and leaves the text cursor in some weird shape (or missing altogether) you're not going to make any points with your user. Bob Falk can help you out here, with his very detailed explanation of how the hardware text cursor works and how to manipulate it gracefully and hardware-independently.

Furthermore, there are whole markets where text mode is the dominant mode and always will be. XT_class machines and the slower 286 machines (some would say all 286 machines) simply don't have the guts to do graphics effectively. Some of these markets are overseas, where they use whole different keyboard layouts and text_mode character sets. Do you have any notion how to deal with issues like these? Tab Julius can get you started in his discussion of DOS code pages in this chapter.

Whatever your preferences in display technology, text mode is necessary background information, and it's important. Don't neglect the basics. Ignorance of any area in programming will come back to bite you when you least expect it.

What Cursor? Hardware-Independent Cursor Handling Routines

■ Bob Falk

Use some helpful low-level programming tricks to control the text mode cursor in your applications.

Don't you just hate it when a program exits without restoring the cursor to its familiar shape? Why is it seemingly so difficult for software to behave itself when handling the cursor? You should be able to write one function that will shape the cursor the way you want it, regardless of the particular video hardware installed. Well, you can!

To control the cursor correctly, we'll use the video identification routines (VideoID) presented in Chapter 1 (see Listing 1.6) to tell us what kind of video adapter we are working with. We'll be building on the VideoID module to add cursor control.

Cursor Emulation

You'll encounter several limitations involved with simple cursor handling. First, a character box can have 8, 9, 14, or 16 scan lines, depending on both the hardware and the current video mode. Adding to these limitations is *cursor emulation*. When IBM introduced the EGA, they wanted to provide downward compatibility with the CGA. Cursor emulation means that you can specify values for the cursor's starting and ending scan lines just as you would for a CGA, and they will be converted into the corresponding values for the EGA with its higher resolution (more scan lines per character block).

This approach makes sense, but someone goofed during the implementation. On the EGA, cursor emulation works by adding 5 to all scan line values greater than 4. This algorithm becomes useless when the character matrix is not 14 scan lines high. To make matters worse, cursor emulation has carried over as well to the MCGA and VGA (and hence to the 8514/A). For the record, cursor emulation is enabled by default in video modes 0–3.

The bottom line is that if we want complete control over the cursor, we don't want to rely on BIOS emulation. We need a way to directly turn cursor emulation off. However, many programs will expect cursor emulation to be turned on. To be "well behaved," our programs need to turn cursor emulation back on when they quit and return to DOS. If we are writing TSRs, we turn the cursor emulation off when we pop up, and turn emulation back on when control is returned to the underlying application. To do this we'll create two C functions:

```
void far EmulationOFF(void);
  /* Disables cursor emulation and sets a normal size cursor */
  /* Should be called in TSRs when they pop up */
void far EmulationON(void);
  /* Enables cursor emulation and sets a normal size cursor */
  /* Should be called in TSRs before returning control to */
  /* the underlying program */
```

Our Own Cursor Shapes

Since there are so many low-level details that can get in our way (and encourage us to compromise), let's use a top-down approach. We want a function that is easy to use and to modify. One technique, which will be easy to expand later, is to pass an enumerated type to the function controlling the cursor.

So what cursor shapes do we want for our programs? The obvious choices are no cursor at all (invisible), and a block cursor that fills an entire character matrix. We can't forget the default (normal) two scan line cursor and a cursor that fills the bottom or top half of the character block. We'll round out our choices with a cursor that fills the bottom, middle, and top third of the character block. These eight cursor types are shown in Figure 4.1.

The following enumerated typedef is defined in VIDCURSR.H (Listing 4.1) to help define the eight cursor types:

```
typedef enum {
             CursorHidden,
             CursorNormal,
             CursorBtmHalf,
             CursorBtmThird,
             CursorMiddle,
             CursorTopThird,
             CursorTopHalf,
             CursorBlock
             } CursorShape;
```

Next, we need a function to set the cursor size. Also, we need a function to get the cursor type:

```
void far SetCursorShape( CursorShape  Cursor );
  /* Sets the cursor to the specified shape */

CursorShape  GetCursorShape(void);
  /* Returns the current cursor shape */
```

We're going to implement some of our functions as assembly language routines to keep them small and fast. (See the listings diskette included with this book.) They are marked as **far** in their prototypes. There are two reasons why this compiler directive is used. First, a quick glance at the code tells us that far calls are used and therefore the code can be

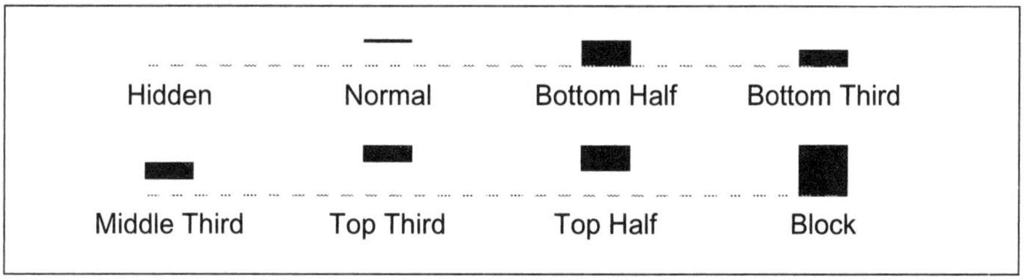

■ **FIGURE 4.1 The eight cursor types**

implemented somewhere else. Second, and more important, is that if we later decide to pull the definitions out of the header, we won't encounter a nasty system crash just because we forgot that the assembly language routines are set up with far returns.

Because we want cursor emulation to be turned off when our program starts, **EmulationOFF()** is called when our program initializes itself. We also need to be certain that emulation will be turned back on when our program ends. So we need **EmulationON()** to be called automatically as part of the program's chain of exit routines. Borland C++ provides us with a mechanism to do this with the **atexit()** function:

```
atexit(CursorCleanUp);
```

To implement the **GetCursorShape()** function, we'll use a variable of type **CursorShape** called **CurrentCursor**. Since the actual cursor handling routines are going to be implemented in assembly language, we'll let the assembly language routines keep **CurrentCursor** updated. The **GetCursorShape()** function simply returns the current value stored in **CurrentCursor**. This technique is better than interfacing the **CurrentCursor** variable because we can make changes without affecting programs that use the **GetCursorShape()** return value. The function is coded as:

```
CursorShape   GetCursorShape(void)
{
    return CurrentCursor;
};
```

Now that we have the "high-level" code work completed, we can take a closer look at the actual cursor control routines. As with the video identification routines, there are times when it just doesn't pay to trust the BIOS. And, there are some special exceptions you need to be aware of when it comes to some clone machines.

We will not be programming the CRTC registers directly to specify the cursor shape, for portability reasons. Instead, we will be using Video BIOS Interrupt 10h, Function 1h—Set Cursor Size. To use this function, place the top (starting) cursor scan line in register CH, the bottom (ending) cursor scan line in register CL, the function number (1) in AH, and call Int 10h (see Figure 4.2).

We need to address a few compatibility problems before we can make our routines reliable. First, the number of scan lines in a character block varies among adapters and even some video modes. Since we intend to disable cursor emulation on the adapters that provide it, we will have to develop our own cursor emulation. It will have to be smart enough to handle character blocks that are 8, 9, 14, or 16 scan lines high.

You should also keep in mind that turning off cursor emulation happens differently on the VGA and 8514/A than on the EGA and MCGA.

Invisible Cursor

Most programmers rely on a well-known "magic number." When you specify a value of 20h for the starting scan line, the cursor disappears on the MDA, CGA, and VGA. It also

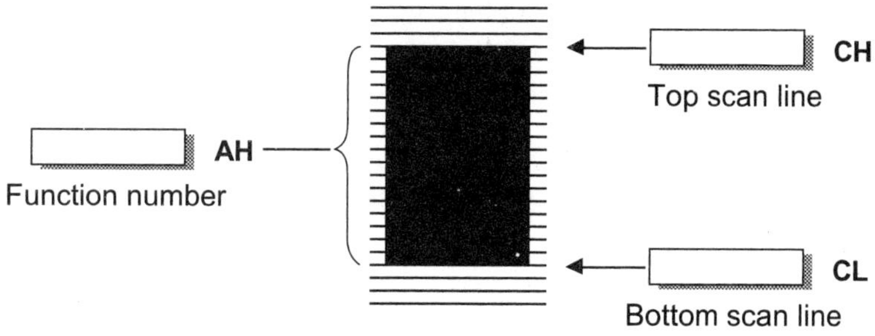

■ **FIGURE 4.2 Using the Set Cursor Size function**

works on the EGA by virtue of the fact that 20h is greater than the total height of the character matrix.

Unfortunately, some clone MDA cards don't recognize this trick. To hide the cursor on these machines you will have to specify a value greater than the total character matrix for *both* the starting and ending scan line values. Fortunately, this can be done by specifying 20h for both values. This still satisfies the compatible adapters, and works great on the not-so-compatible clones, too. **CursorOff** (in Listing 4.3) sets both the starting and ending scan lines for the cursor to 20H by means of BIOS interrupt 10h, Function 1.

TIP: A word of warning is in order for another common technique used to make the cursor invisible. Some programmers hide the cursor by moving it off the displayable area of the screen. There are two problems with this trick. On some machines, the BIOS will try to help you out by moving the cursor back onto the screen (how thoughtful). That's the good news. The bad news is that that trick will often hang machines such as the AT&T 6300.

Table-Driven Means Extendable

Earlier I mentioned that the code should be easy to use, and easy to change. One of the best ways to ensure that we can change the code is to use a table-driven approach. We'll set up a list of tables containing the proper scan lines for various adapters and character matrix heights, and use the tables to determine the actual shape of the cursor. That way, if you want to add more options later, you can because the code doesn't care what the values are; it uses whatever values are provided in the tables.

In VIDCURSR.ASM, **SetCursorShape** starts by taking its argument off the stack. If the argument is zero, it simply calls **CursorOff** to hide the cursor. Otherwise, it uses the current monitor type to look up the correct beginning and ending scan line values for each of the predefined cursor types. This is done by means of a jump table calculated in **GtbxJumpTable** where the values for each of the monitors supported are mapped (EGA and PGA to EGA, MCGA, VGA and 8514/A to VGA, and so on). **CursorSize** then uses these scan line values to call BIOS Int 10h, function 1 to set the cursor size.

EmulationOn and **EmulationOff** call **EnableEmulation** and **DisableEmulation** respectively, where the correct action to turn emulation on and off for each monitor and mode is taken. For example, MDA, CGA, Olivetti CGA, and Hercules don't do emulation because they are the ones being emulated. PGA, EGA, MCGA adapters have emulation controlled by the info byte at 0040:0087h. Emulation control on the VGA is achieved via BIOS function calls (Int 12h, subfunction 34h).

Listing 4.2 is CURSDEMO.C, a short example program that demonstrates the various cursors we have defined. It calls **SetCursorShape** to illustrate each of the available cursors.

To make CURSDEMO.EXE, compile CURSDEMO.C, VIDCURSR.ASM, along with the listings from Chapter 1—VIDEO.C and VIDEOID.ASM. The code should be compiled in large model. Finally, remember to link the files. This program shows how taking cursor control into your own hands can help customize your programs without leaving the user saying, "Now, where's the cursor?"

CODE DESCRIPTION

Overview

The listing provided is used to control the text mode cursor with different video adapters. Functions are provided for hiding the cursor and displaying the cursor using different formats (scan lines).

Listing Available

Listing	*Description*	*Used with*
VIDCURSR.H	C header file that defines the structures and function prototypes for the cursor control functions.	CURSDEMO.C
CURSDEMO.C	Demonstration program that shows how the low-level cursor control functions are used.	------
VIDCURSR.ASM	Assembly language code for the low-level cursor control routines. (See listings diskette.)	------

How to Compile/Assemble

In addition to VIDCURSR.H, CURSDEMO.C, and VIDCURSR.ASM, you will need VIDEO.H, VIDEOID.H, VIDEO.C, VIDSTUFF.INC, and VIDEOIS.ASM from Chapter 1. These files can be compiled and assembled with any C/C++ compiler and TASM-compatible assembler. *You must use the Large memory model for this code to work properly.*

■ LISTING 4.1 VIDCURSR.H

```
/*VidCursr.H*/
/*Interface to C and Assembly modules*/

typedef enum {
            CursorHidden,
            CursorNormal,
            CursorBtmHalf,
            CursorBtmThird,
```

```
              CursorMiddle,
              CursorTopThird,
              CursorTopHalf,
              CursorBlock
              } CursorShape;

void far EmulationOFF(void);
  /* Disables cursor emulation and sets a normal size cursor */
  /* Should be called in TSRs when they pop up */

void far EmulationON(void);
  /* Enables cursor emulation and sets a normal size cursor */
  /* Should be called in TSRs before returning control to */
  /* the underlying program. */

void SetCursorShape(CursorShape  Cursor);
  /* Sets the cursor to the specified shape */

CursorShape far GetCursorShape(void);
  /* Returns the current cursor shape */

extern char CurrentCursor;
```

■ LISTING 4.2 CURSDEMO.C

```
/* CursDemo.C*/

/* Demonstrates Cursor handling routines    */
/* By Bob Falk                              */

#include <dos.h>
#include <conio.h>
#include <stdlib.h>
#include "videoid.h"
#include "video.h"
#include "vidcursr.h"

#define  GreenOnBlack  0x02
#define  YellowOnBlack 0x0E

#define  Dim  0x07
#define  Intense 0x0A

#define  PauseTime 2000

char  ClrNorm, ClrHi;

void InitAttributes(void)
  /* Initializes the color attributes */
{
  if (CurrentVideoMode == ColorMode)
  {
    ClrNorm = GreenOnBlack;
    ClrHi   = YellowOnBlack;
  }
```

```
  else
  {   /* MonoMode */
    ClrNorm = Dim;
    ClrHi   = Intense;
  };
  textattr(ClrNorm);
}   /* Procedure InitAttributes */

void OpeningMessage(void)
  /* Displays the title message */
{
  clrscr();
  cprintf( "\r\nCursDemo:  Demonstrates Cursor Handling Routines.\r\n\r\n" );
}
   /* Procedure OpeningMessage */

void CursorInit(void)
{
    EmulationOFF();
    atexit(EmulationON);
}
void main(void)
{
  VideoInit();
  CursorInit();
  InitAttributes();
  OpeningMessage();

  SetCursorShape( CursorHidden );
  cprintf( "CursorHidden ..." );
  delay( PauseTime );
  cprintf("\r\n");

  SetCursorShape( CursorNormal );
  cprintf( "CursorNormal ..." );
  delay( PauseTime );
  cprintf("\r\n");

  SetCursorShape( CursorBtmHalf );
  cprintf( "CursorBtmHalf ..." );
  delay( PauseTime );
  cprintf("\r\n");

  SetCursorShape( CursorBtmThird );
  cprintf( "CursorBtmThird ..." );
  delay( PauseTime );
  cprintf("\r\n");

  SetCursorShape( CursorMiddle );
  cprintf( "CursorMiddle ..." );
  delay( PauseTime );
  cprintf("\r\n");

  SetCursorShape( CursorTopThird );
```

```
    cprintf( "CursorTopThird ..." );
    delay( PauseTime );
    cprintf("\r\n");

    SetCursorShape( CursorTopHalf );
    cprintf( "CursorTopHalf ..." );
    delay( PauseTime );
    cprintf("\r\n");

    SetCursorShape( CursorBlock );
    cprintf( "CursorBlock ..." );
    delay( PauseTime );
    cprintf("\r\n");

    cprintf("\r\n");
}
/* eof CursDemo.C */
```

43 (Not 50!) Lines on the VGA

■ Michael Covington

Use a simple BIOS call to extend the power of text mode VGA.

You probably know that the EGA has a 43-line mode and the VGA has a 50-line mode. But the VGA's 43-line mode and its EGA-like screen font (complete with slashed zeros) are well-kept secrets. They shouldn't be; both can enhance legibility on VGA screens.

The VGA has an EGA emulation mode in which its video scan pattern, in text modes only, is 640 x 350 instead of the usual 640 x 480. In this mode, it uses EGA fonts and displays 25 or 43 lines of text. (It also has a 640 x 200 CGA emulation mode, but you don't want to see it!)

Once the video scan pattern is set to 640 x 350, it remains so until explicitly changed; resetting the video mode doesn't affect the scan pattern. All VGA graphics modes, however, remain available and work properly.

Listing 4.3 is a sample C program that illustrates this aspect of VGA video text. To get 43 lines on the screen, first turn the VGA into an EGA as shown in the **set350()** function. Selecting the small (8 x 8-pixel) screen font via BIOS function 11h, subfunction 12h as shown in **Font8x8()** will give you 43 lines of video text.

TIP: My documentation says that if this BIOS call is made any time except immediately after a video mode set, the results will be "unpredictable"—hence the extra mode 3 reset.

BIOS manages to keep track of the number of lines and has no trouble writing on the screen, but DOS has a tendency to sometimes think there are still only 25 lines. To get back to 25 lines, just reset the video mode. Remember also (as courteous programming requires) to change back to normal VGA 640 x 480 scanning before exiting your application, as shown in **set480()**.

CODE DESCRIPTION

Overview

The listing provided is used to configure a VGA in text mode display with 43 lines of text.

Listing Available

Listing	*Description*	*Used with*
LINES43.C	C source file that configures a VGA display in 43 text lines by using the BIOS video call 11h, function 12h.	------

How to Compile/Assemble

LINES43.C should be compiled with Borland C++ or with Turbo C++.

■ LISTING 4.3 LINES43.C

```
#include <dos.h>
#include <conio.h>
#include <stdio.h>
#include <string.h>

#define ESC 0x1b

void printscreen(void)
{
int i;
    for (i=50;i>0;i--)
        printf("\n%d",i);
}

void set350(void)
{
union REGS r;
      r.x.ax = 0x03;   //reset video mode #3
      int86(0x10, &r,&r);
      r.x.ax = 0x1201;
      r.x.bx = 0x30;
      int86(0x10, &r, &r);
}

void Font8x8(void)
{
union REGS r;
      r.x.ax = 0x03;
      int86(0x10, &r, &r);
      r.x.ax = 0x1112;
      r.h.bl = 0x0;
      int86(0x10,&r,&r);
}
```

```
void Reset480(void)
{
union REGS r;
      r.x.ax = 0x03;   //reset video mode #3
      int86(0x10,&r,&r);
      r.x.ax = 0x1202;
      r.x.bx = 0x0030;
      int86(0x10,&r,&r);
}

void main(void)
{
        Font8x8();
        printscreen();
        getch();
        set350();
        Font8x8();
        printscreen();
        getch();
        Reset480();
        printscreen();
        getch();
}
```

Using Code Pages to Internationalize DOS Programs

■ Tab Julius

Internationalizing your applications can be easy—if you let DOS do the work for you.

The advent of DOS version 3.30 brought an important new set of features: Code Page and Country Information (CP/CI). Although available in a limited form in prior versions, it was only with 3.30 that CP/CI became "complete." Most American programmers are not very familiar with CP/CI because there has been little call for it until recently. With the onset of a global market economy (the European Community, for example), and the simple recognition by American software companies that there is a market outside our borders, it is becoming more and more necessary for programmers to internationalize their products. This means that programs can be translated and modified (then marketed and sold) in different countries and languages without being recompiled, and in different source versions. Code Pages are the first step in this internationalizing process.

CP/CI comprises a two-part set of tools and resources with which character sets for other languages can be used (the "CP" or Code Page part) and by which information about the current country environment can be retrieved or manipulated (the "CI" or Country Information part).

Code Pages

When the EGA architecture was introduced, it brought with it an ability to load more than one character set into memory and then switch between the sets. A character set is referred to as a code page, so called (supposedly) because each character is a "code point." What programmers take for granted as the sacred ASCII table is officially Code Page 437. DOS provides a number of ASCII tables, actually, such as Code Page 850 (the multinational set), Code Page 865 (Nordic set), and others. A code page is merely a character map set that is referred to when characters are drawn on the screen.

Because ASCII characters are defined by just seven bits (values 0–127) and PCs use a full byte (0–255) for characters, the high 128 characters can be implementation-defined. Character #243 may be defined one way in one code page (the "less-than-or-equal-to symbol" in code page 437) and look different under another (the "3/4" symbol in code page 850). Fortunately, all the ASCII characters remain the same in all these sets; only the upper 128 change. Values above 128 contain characters specific to a language or class of languages. Keeping the lower 128 the same also maintains compatibility with CGA and mono systems. On those systems, you can remap the upper 128 only. Since they don't have the same abilities as the EGA, a different utility, GRAFTABL, is used to provide switchable code page functionality (see Listing 4.4).

Setting Up the System for Code Page Switching

In your CONFIG.SYS file, you can reserve space for video code page character sets via the DEVICE command:

```
DEVICE = DISPLAY.SYS CON=(EGA,437,2)
```

With this command you reserve space for the number of code pages you want to switch among (two in this case). Then, in your AUTOEXEC.BAT file (or at the command line if you prefer) you need to specifically load those code pages into memory, otherwise known as "preparing" the code page. The MODE command is used for this purpose. It is also necessary to run a memory-resident program called NLSFUNC to tie the National Language Support Functions together:

```
MODE CON CP PREPARE=((437 850) EGA.CPI)
NLSFUNC  COUNTRY.SYS
```

The MODE command tells the system to install video code pages 437 and 850 and to use EGA.CPI as the code page font file. Although for the purposes of this discussion I am referring to video code pages (for the CON: device), there are equivalent MODE commands for the PRN and LPT devices. Each of these system setup functions are part of DOS versions 3.30 and greater. With all this in place, you now have switchable CP/CI ability in your system.

All systems have queryable CP/CI ability, regardless of whether code pages were set up in the system. This is good news for programmers. It means that you can issue calls to get current country information and use it in your programs without actually worrying if CP/CI was explicitly set up in the system. To change code pages or countries from within your program, however, requires that CP/CI functions be set up already.

The program listing CODEPAGE.C (Listing 4.5) is included as a set of routines that you may find useful when working in the CP/CI world. It requires a single call by the application to **CP_Init()** that will load the info buffer initially and set up a pointer to the sort routine. After setting new countries or code pages, you will most likely want to follow it with a call to reload the info buffer (macro **CP_Update_Info()**). One simple way to test for installation is to try to set the codepage value to its current value. This is demonstrated in the program listing as the **CP_Test_Installed** macro.

Country Information

The Country number is important because it denotes which country conventions are subscribed to, such as how dates are formatted and how periods and commas are used in numeric entry. The COUNTRY command is executed in the CONFIG.SYS file, and governs the kind of information returned by calls to retrieve Country Information (CI). The country numbers tend to follow the international dial codes, which is why the United States gets the 001 number.

Access to country information permits your program to accommodate the conventions of the country in which it is running, and to properly sort and uppercase characters. CP_INFO_STRUCT in the program listing shows the structure of information returned by a call to the DOS Get Extended Country Information interrupt (called by **CP_Load_Special_Info()**). Explanations for some of the info returned is shown in Table 4.1.

It is necessary in an internationalized program to query this table and present data according to the country conventions, as well as to accept data in that form. For example, 5,342.90 in the United States is 5.342,90 in Norway and Spain. This problem is compounded by U.S. compilers, which assume U.S. format for numeric entry. Thus, before converting a string to a numeric value, your program will need to replace the symbols of the current country with the U.S. equivalent. Likewise, on displaying a numeric value, you can't simply print out the number. Instead, you need to convert it to a string and then replace the U.S. values with ones appropriate to the country. Also, you will want to keep these alternative characters in mind when building lists of allowable input characters.

Sorting International Text

Another important area is sorting and uppercasing. With plain old A–Z words, sorting is accomplished by comparing the relative positions of the letters in the ASCII table for whichever is higher or lower, since their relationship to each other in the table matches their relationship in alphabetic sorting. Once we introduce code pages with letters outside the A-Z range (in the upper 128 characters) this becomes a problem: If sorted traditionally, all the extended language characters would sort to the end of the list.

To get around this problem, DOS provides a sorting table appropriate to the current country and code page. By accessing this table, equivalent values for each letter can be

■ **TABLE 4.1 Country information**

Date Format Code

0 (USA) = M-D-Y
1 (Europe) = D-M-Y
2 (Japan) = Y-M-D

Currency Code

Bit 0 zero - Currency format precedes value
Bit 0 set - Currency format follows value

Bit 1 zero - No space between value and symbol
Bit 1 set - One space between value and symbol

Bit 2 zero - Symbol and decimal are separate
Bit 2 set - Symbol replaces decimal

Hour24 Indicator

0 = 12 hour clock
1 = 24 hour clock

located. Thus, an accented "O" in code page 850 (ASCII 224 in that table) is "normalized" to a regular "O" (ASCII 79) and should be sorted in that order. The program listing shows the function **CP_SortXlate_Token()** which returns a sort-ready version of the token passed down.

Another problem is uppercasing. No longer can you simply subtract 32 from a character to get the uppercase equivalent, because the upper characters aren't organized as conveniently. Again, however, DOS provides a routine to return the uppercase equivalent of a given character that takes into account CP/CI conventions. The example functions **toupper()** and **strupr()** replace the normal compiler calls with code-page-aware functions.

There is also a table to return an equivalent letter valid for filenames; but to the best of my knowledge, this table is the same as the uppercasing table.

Consequences of Code Pages

Your application may not care what code page it is running under, but it is important to know that symbols which exist in one code page may not be present in another, so if your application uses such symbols, it'll look very strange in a different code page. For example, code page 850 replaces some of the DOS box-drawing characters and math symbols with accented characters used in other languages. You'll also want to know the code page if you're in a graphical environment and you need to display graphic fonts from a symbol set based on the ASCII character.

When a program is internationalized, all text strings can be placed in separate resource files (which would permit translation without requiring compilation). The application could then have more than one resource file, using the one that best matches the current code page.

CGAs: Turning the Tables

CGA systems are more of a problem, since they can't remap the lower 128 characters. GRAFTABL is a way to enable code page switching on a device that doesn't really support it. When GRAFTABL is run, it maps a character set into conventional memory and sets interrupt vector 0x1F to point to it. CGAs can utilize the interrupt 0x1F pointer to an upper 128 set. If the character set is changed (via GRAFTABL), the pointer itself remains the same, but a new set of characters is mapped in. This is substantially slower than the EGA system, which has the code pages "prepared" in advance and simply changes the pointer to point from one to another, but it is certainly better than nothing.

The big problem with GRAFTABL, however, is that (1) you need a way to find out if it's there and (2) you need to find out at what value it's set. For this, we need to resort to undocumented DOS calls. To see if it's there, you can query the multiplex interrupt (see function **CP_Test_Graftabl_Installed()**), but to see what its "code page" value is a touch trickier. The function **CP_Graftabl_Setting()** demonstrates how to do this. This code example differs in a couple of ways from the information in the book *Undocumented DOS* from Addison-Wesley (ISBN 0-201-57064-5). The block uses **DS:BX** to receive the table pointer instead of **DS:DX** (which is incorrect); and the book doesn't go so far as to explain how to retrieve the code page number. In my example, a call is made through the multiplex interrupt to return what seems to be a far pointer to the character table loaded in memory. Adding 400h to the pointer gives the address of the location where the "code page" value is kept (as a word).

The program listing has a conditional define for GRAFTABL, so that it will return the code page number or GRAFTABL number (if present). It's more transparent for programming purposes, but not exactly "pure." To make up for the lack of pureness, I have included a global variable called **CP_Graftable_Active** that gets set if GRAFTABL is detected in the system. This enables your program to distinguish between true code paging and simulated paging.

Changing Country Information

At the DOS prompt level you can use the CHCP command to change code pages for all devices. DOS doesn't offer a command-line way of changing the Country value short of editing the CONFIG.SYS file and rebooting. Although I haven't yet figured out how to switch the GRAFTABL page from within a program, it is very easy to change the normal code page or country information from within programs. The program listing shows how to do this in routines **CP_Set_Code_Page()** and **CP_Set_Country_Num()**.

When setting countries, DOS requires a compatible code page to be set as well, which it will try to do for you. You can run into problems if the call to change the country sets the code page to a value which is not "prepared" in your system. In the example, the code page test will render code page detection false. In addition to testing if the call was successful, you may want to call **CP_Test_Installed()** to see if the current code page is supported (by trying to switch to the new code page). This traps the situation where the CP value changes without being valid.

At any rate, I hope this takes a level of mystery out of CP/CI.

References

Undocumented DOS. Andrew Schulman, *et al.* Addison-Wesley Publishing. ISBN 0-201-57064-5

CODE DESCRIPTION

Overview

The listing provided is used to access DOS's Code Page and Country Information (CP/CI) to internationalize programs.

Listing Available

Listing	*Description*	*Used with*
CODEPAGE.H	C header file that defines the structures and function prototypes for the CP/CI functions.	CODEPAGE.C
CODEPAGE.C	Source file that defines the functions to access the CP/CI features.	------

How to Compile/Assemble

CODEPAGE.C can be compiled and linked with any C/C++ compiler.

■ LISTING 4.4 CODEPAGE.H

```
#define TRUE 1
#define FALSE 0
#define DEFAULT_CTRY -1          // Selects default Country code
#define DEFAULT_CP   -1          // Selects default CP
#define INIT_CP_SORT "$INIT_CP_SORT$"     // Tells sort routine to initialize

int      CP_Active_CP(void);
int      CP_Default_CP(void);
int      CP_Set_Code_Page(int New_CP);
int      CP_Set_Country_Num(int New_Ctry);
int      CP_Load_Special_Info(int which_ctry, int which_cp);
int      toupper(int one_char);
char     *strupr(char *token);
void far *CP_Get_Table_Ptr(int which_table);
char     *CP_SortXlate_Token(char *token);
int      CP_Country_Number(void);
int      CP_Code_Page_Number(void);
char     *CP_Thous_Sep(void);
char     *CP_Decimal_Sep(void);
char     *CP_Date_Sep(void);
char     *CP_Time_Sep(void);
```

```
char     *CP_Datalist_Sep(void);
void     CP_Init(void);

#define CP_Update_Info()   CP_Load_Special_Info(DEFAULT_CTRY,DEFAULT_CP);

#define CP_Get_CharXlate_Ptr()   CP_Get_Table_Ptr(2)  // The 2,4,6's are the
#define CP_Get_FileXlate_Ptr()   CP_Get_Table_Ptr(4)  // dos request codes
#define CP_Get_SortXlate_Ptr()   CP_Get_Table_Ptr(6)  // under int-21 #65/2

#define CP_Test_Installed()      CP_Set_Code_Page(CP_Active_CP()) // Test rtn

struct CP_INFO_STRUCT    far *CP_Info;            // Buffer of country info
int  (far *CP_ToUpper)(void);                     // Ptr to upcase map rtn
extern int  CP_Installed;                         // Perm INSTALLED flag

int CP_Graftabl_Setting(void);
```

■ LISTING 4.5 CODEPAGE.C

```
#include <dos.h>              // For interrupt calls
#include <stdio.h>
#include <string.h>
#include "codepage.h"

#define SUPPORT_GRAFTABL

#ifdef SUPPORT_GRAFTABL
#define MK_FP(seg,ofs)((void far*) (((unsigned long) (seg) << 16 /
                | (unsigned) (ofs)))
#endif

#pragma pack(1)
static struct   CP_INFO_STRUCT
{
   unsigned char  ID;                     // Info ID byte
   unsigned int   buffer_length;          // Length of buffer
   unsigned int   country_id;             // Country ID number
   unsigned int   cp_number;              // CodePage number
   unsigned int   date_format_code;       // Format code for date
   char           currency[5];            // ASCIIZ Currency symbol
   char           thous_sep[2];           // ASCIIZ Thousands style
   char           dec_sep[2];             // ASCIIZ Decimal style
   char           date_sep[2];            // ASCIIZ Date separator
   char           time_sep[2];            // ASCIIZ Time separator
   unsigned char  currency_code;          // Symbol placement guide
   unsigned char  currency_places;        // # of decimal places
   unsigned char  hour24_indicator;       // 24-hour clock indicator
   void far      *Upcase_Mapper;          // Ptr to uppercase mapping
   char           datalist_sep[2];        // Datalist separator
   char           reserved[10];           // Reserved to DOS
} CP_Info_Buffer; /* struct  cp info */
#pragma pack()
```

```
#pragma pack(1)
struct   CP_PTR_INFO_STRUCT
{
   unsigned char  ID;                       // Info ID byte
   void far      *table_ptr;                // Ptr to requested table
}; /* struct  cp ptrinfobuffer */
#pragma pack()

extern int CP_Installed;                    // Global installed flag
int CP_Installed;

#ifdef SUPPORT_GRAFTABL
extern int CP_Graftabl_Active;              // Global Graftabl flag
int CP_Graftabl_Active;
#endif

#pragma check_stack(off)

int CP_Active_CP(void)
/* Gets active code page, returning CP number, or 0 if failure */
{
   union REGS  dosregs;                        // Set of DOS registers

#ifdef SUPPORT_GRAFTABL
   if (!CP_Graftabl_Active)
   {
#endif
      dosregs.h.ah =0x66;                      // Get/Set CP function
      dosregs.h.al =0x01;                      // 'Get' CP subfunction
      int86(0x21,&dosregs,&dosregs);           // Call the function
      if (dosregs.x.cflag != 0)                // If not successful,
         return(FALSE);                        // return 0
      else
         return( (int)dosregs.x.bx )           // else return the value
      ;
#ifdef SUPPORT_GRAFTABL
   }
   else
      return( (int)CP_Graftabl_Setting() )
   ;
#endif
}  /* cp active cp */

int CP_Default_CP(void)
/* Gets default code page, returning CP number, or 0 if failure */
{
   union REGS  dosregs;                        // Set of DOS registers

#ifdef SUPPORT_GRAFTABL
   if (!CP_Graftabl_Active)
   {
#endif
      dosregs.h.ah =0x66;                      // Get/Set CP function
      dosregs.h.al =0x01;                      // 'Get' CP subfunction
```

```
        int86(0x21,&dosregs,&dosregs);          // Call the function
        if (dosregs.x.cflag != 0)               // If not successful,
            return(FALSE);                      // return 0
        else
           return( (int)dosregs.x.dx )          // else return the value
        ;
#ifdef SUPPORT_GRAFTABL
    }
    else
       return( (int)CP_Graftabl_Setting() )
    ;
#endif
}  /* cp default cp */


int CP_Set_Code_Page(int New_CP)
/* Sets new active code page, returning true if set, false if not */
{
   union REGS  dosregs;                         // Set of DOS registers
   int         status;                          // Status of call

#ifdef SUPPORT_GRAFTABL
   if (CP_Graftabl_Active)
       return(FALSE);
   else
   {
#endif
       dosregs.h.ah =0x66;                      // Get/Set CP function
       dosregs.h.al =0x02;                      // 'Set' CP subfunction
       dosregs.x.bx =New_CP;                    // Declare new CP num
       int86(0x21,&dosregs,&dosregs);           // Call the function
       if (dosregs.x.cflag !=0)                 // If not success,
           status =FALSE;                       // return FALSE
       else
           status =TRUE                         // else return true
       ;
       return(status);
#ifdef SUPPORT_GRAFTABL
   }
#endif
} /* cp set code page */

int CP_Set_Country_Num(int new_ctry)
/* Sets new country number, returning true if set, false if not */
{
   union REGS  dosregs;                     // Set of DOS registers
   int         status;                      // Status of call

   dosregs.h.ah =0x38;                      // Get/Set country
   dosregs.h.al =(unsigned char) new_ctry;  // Put new country here
   if (new_ctry > 0xff)                     // Unless it's over 255
   {
      dosregs.h.al =0xff;                   // Then AL goes to $FF
      dosregs.x.bx =new_ctry;               // and BX gets country num
```

```
   }
   dosregs.x.dx =0xffff;                   // 'Set' subfunction
   int86(0x21,&dosregs,&dosregs);          // Call the function
   if (dosregs.x.cflag !=0)                // If not successful,
      status =FALSE;                       // return FALSE
   else
      status =TRUE                         // else return TRUE
   ;
   return(status);
} /* cp set country num */

int CP_Load_Special_Info(int which_ctry, int which_cp)
/* Loads info buffer for a specific country & cp, returns true
   for success or false if not
*/
{
   union  REGS   dosregs;                  // Set of DOS registers
   struct SREGS  segregs;                  // Set of segment registers

   segread(&segregs);                      // Save current segregs
   dosregs.h.ah =0x65;                     // Get extended ctry info
   dosregs.h.al =0x01;                     // Get general info
   dosregs.x.bx =which_cp;                 // Use active code page
   dosregs.x.dx =which_ctry;               // Use active country code
                                           // Declare size of buffer:
   dosregs.x.cx =sizeof(struct CP_INFO_STRUCT);

   segregs.es   =FP_SEG(CP_Info);          // ES has info buffer seg
   dosregs.x.di =FP_OFF(CP_Info);          // DI has info buffer off

   int86x(0x21,&dosregs,&dosregs,&segregs);

   if (dosregs.x.cflag !=0)                // If not successful,
      return(FALSE);                       // return FALSE
   else
      return(TRUE)
   ;
}  /* cp load special info */

int toupper(int one_char)
/* Performs uppercase remapping, utilizing the codepage remapping
   function, and replaces the C-language toupper */

/* Note:  This takes advantage of the fact that MSC51 returns AX if nothing
   else is returned (AL holds the translated character value).  In Turbo C,
   where the regs structure is mapped to the actual registers, you'd want
   to assign AL to some variable and return that. */
{
   union REGS  dosregs;                    // Set of DOS registers

                                           // Is it lowercase?
if ( (one_char >=*"a") & (one_char <=*"z") )
   {
      return(one_char - *" ");             // If so, bop it upward
```

```
   }
   else
   {
      dosregs.h.al=one_char;            // Call to upper for top 128
      return((*CP_ToUpper)());          // And return it
   }
} /* toupper */

char *strupr(char *token)
/* Performs uppercase remapping of a token, using our redefined
   toupper function to make use of code page uppercase conversion.
*/
{
   static char temp_str[80];              // Translate 80 chars
   int         str_len;                   // Length of string
   int         x;                         // Temp variable

   strcpy(temp_str,token);                // Make temp copy of token
   str_len =strlen(temp_str);             // Find its length
   for (x =0; x < str_len; x++)           // Go thru it one by one
      temp_str[x] =toupper(temp_str[x])   // And make it uppercase
   ;
   return(temp_str);                      // Then send it back
} /* strupr */

void far *CP_Get_Table_Ptr(int which_table)
/* Called by macros */
{
   union  REGS   dosregs;                // Set of DOS registers
   struct SREGS  segregs;                // Set of segment regs
   struct CP_PTR_INFO_STRUCT CP_Ptr_Info;  // Table ptr info buffer
   char *table_ptr;

   segread(&segregs);                    // Save current segregs
   dosregs.h.ah =0x65;                   // Subfunction code
   dosregs.h.al =which_table;            // Must specify table in AL
   dosregs.x.bx =DEFAULT_CP;             // Specify the CP to use
   dosregs.x.dx =DEFAULT_CTRY;           // Specify country to use
   dosregs.x.cx =sizeof(struct CP_PTR_INFO_STRUCT);   // Buffer size

    table_ptr=(char *) &CP_Ptr_Info.ID;
    segregs.es   =FP_SEG(table_ptr);
    dosregs.x.di =FP_OFF(table_ptr);
   int86x(0x21,&dosregs,&dosregs,&segregs);

   if (dosregs.x.cflag !=0)              // If not successful,
      return(FALSE)                      // return FALSE
   ;

    table_ptr =CP_Ptr_Info.table_ptr;
    table_ptr +=2;
    return((void *) table_ptr);
} /* cp get table ptr */
```

```
char *CP_SortXlate_Token(char *token)
{
   static char far *sort_table_ptr;         // Translation table ptr
   static char temp_str[80];                // Translate to 80 chars
   unsigned char   char_ord;                // Ord of compared char
   int            str_len;                  // Length of string
   int            x;                        // Temp variable

   if (!strcmp(token,INIT_CP_SORT))             // If called to init,
   {                                            // then call routine
      sort_table_ptr =CP_Get_SortXlate_Ptr();   // to return the ptr
      return;                                   // to the sort
                                                // translation table
   }

   strcpy(temp_str,token);                 // Make temp copy of token
   str_len =strlen(temp_str);              // Find its length
   for (x =0; x < str_len; x++)            // Go thru it one by one
   {
      char_ord =(int) temp_str[x];              // Find it's ord
      temp_str[x] =*(sort_table_ptr+char_ord);  // and get equivalent
   }
   return(temp_str);                            // Then send it back
} /* cp sortXlate token */

/* This next group of routines simply passes back information
   derived from the info buffer.  */

int CP_Country_Number(void)
{
   return(CP_Info->country_id);
} /* cp country number */

int CP_Code_Page_Number(void)
{
#ifdef SUPPORT_GRAFTABL
   if (!CP_Graftabl_Active)
#endif
      return(CP_Info->cp_number);
#ifdef SUPPORT_GRAFTABL
   else
      return(CP_Graftabl_Setting())
   ;
#endif
} /* cp code page number */

char *CP_Thous_Sep(void)
{
   return(CP_Info->thous_sep);
} /* cp thous sep */

char *CP_Decimal_Sep(void)
{
   return(CP_Info->dec_sep);
} /* cp decimal sep */
```

```
char *CP_Date_Sep(void)
{
   return(CP_Info->date_sep);
} /* cp date sep */

char *CP_Time_Sep(void)
{
   return(CP_Info->time_sep);
} /* cp time sep */

char *CP_Datalist_Sep(void)
{
   return(CP_Info->datalist_sep);
} /* cp datalist sep */

int CP_Date_Format_Code(void)
{
   return(CP_Info->date_format_code);
} /* cp date format code */

int CP_24_Hour_Code(void)
{
   return(CP_Info->hour24_indicator);
} /* cp 24 hour code */

#ifdef SUPPORT_GRAFTABL
int CP_Test_Graftabl_Installed(void)
{
   union REGS  dosregs;                      // Set of DOS registers

   dosregs.x.ax =0xB000;                     // 2F Multiplex B000
   int86(0x2F,&dosregs,&dosregs);            // tests for Graftabl
   if (dosregs.h.al == 0xff)                 // presence
       return(TRUE);
   else
       return(FALSE)
   ;
} /* cp test graftabl installed */
#endif

#ifdef SUPPORT_GRAFTABL
int CP_Graftabl_Setting(void)
{
   union   REGS  dosregs;
   struct  SREGS segregs;

#pragma pack(1)
   struct  GRAFTABL_BUFFER_REC               // Start of buffer
                                             // to be filled by
   {                                         // multiplex info call
      unsigned int Offset;
      unsigned int Segment;
   } buf_record;
#pragma pack()
```

```
   void *graftabl_buf_ptr;                    // Ptr to the buffer
   int  *graftabl_value_ptr;                  // Ptr to the value

   segread(&segregs);

   graftabl_buf_ptr =&buf_record.Offset;      // Point to the buffer

   dosregs.x.ax =0xB001;                      // Set up the function
   segregs.ds   =FP_SEG(graftabl_buf_ptr);    // Load the Seg & Off
   dosregs.x.bx =FP_OFF(graftabl_buf_ptr);
   int86x(0x2F,&dosregs,&dosregs,&segregs);   // Call the function

   graftabl_value_ptr =MK_FP(buf_record.Segment,
                             buf_record.Offset+0x400);

   return(*graftabl_value_ptr);           // Extract value at 0x400
} /* cp graftabl setting */               // after the table start
#endif

void CP_Init(void)
// Initializes the code page subsystem
{
   int result;

   CP_Installed =CP_Test_Installed();      // See if CP's are active
#ifdef SUPPORT_GRAFTABL
                                          // See if graftabl here
   CP_Graftabl_Active  =CP_Test_Graftabl_Installed();
#endif

   CP_Info =&CP_Info_Buffer;           // Use address of the buffer
   result =CP_Update_Info();           // Load info buff for this CP
   if (result)
   {
      CP_ToUpper =CP_Info->Upcase_Mapper;       // Address of mapper
      CP_SortXlate_Token(INIT_CP_SORT);         // Init sort xlator
   }
   return;
} /* cp init */
```

5

Graphics Programming

Long ago (before our machines were a shadow of what they are today) a physicist friend of mine said quite firmly that "Graphics are what computers are *for*."

Strong statement for 1979—strong, and prophetic. Graphics may not be entirely what computers are for, but more and more, graphics are how computers do what they do. This chapter speaks to PC graphics other than platforms like Windows. Windows will ultimately become the defining PC graphics toolkit, but that may not happen for another few years, until Windows NT (or whatever it will come to be called) pulls 32-bit computing together under one OS standard.

Until then, you might as well do your homework, and understand how graphics works apart from a specific operating platform. Keith Weiskamp and Loren Heiny do a fine job explaining the innards of your garden-variety paint program in this chapter, providing in the bargain a tool-oriented framework for adding power to your suite of graphics programming techniques.

Marv Luse, founder of the Autumn Hill Software graphics house, shares some of his secrets for screen typography and graphics dithering for image colors and shades.

And Michael Abrash, who has become something of the patron of fast, PC-specific graphics, presents a scheme for smooth graphics animation by VGA page-flipping—a technique he described in *PC TECHNIQUES* before it appeared anywhere else in the industry. The quality of Michael's code will astonish you. Read it closely. You can't help but learn a *lot*.

Graphics Drawing Tools in C

■ Keith Weiskamp and Loren Heiny

Learn how to develop and use interactive drawing tools that work with the mouse.

If you're driven to be an artist and the only tools you have are a spray can and a magic marker, you might end up in the last car on a New York subway heading for the Bronx. Unfortunately, subway art is a dangerous occupation for a C programmer (even more dangerous than debugging dangling pointers). So, let's get street smart and build our own drawing tools that we can use to engage in some "safe graffiti."

We'll use the built-in Borland Graphics Interface (BGI) as our backdrop. The drawing tools we'll present use the mouse and work in VGA or EGA mode. Because the tools are interactive, you'll be able to easily create basic shapes and figures without having to explicitly specify the screen coordinates of the shapes to be drawn.

Interactive Drawing

If you've ever tried to write a sophisticated graphics application, you know that the user interaction component ends up being the one you suffer over the most. What's the problem? It's much more natural for someone to whip out a spray can and leave their message "Kilroy Lives," than it is to type a command that says, "Put my message in red spray paint at screen location 100,50."

We can, however, make the user's job a little easier by incorporating an input device (such as the mouse) for drawing graphics. But, by itself, the BGI does not include interactive drawing routines. We must, then, build routines around the BGI drawing functions in order to draw figures with the mouse.

The Interactive Graphics Package

Our interactive drawing package includes five functions that extend from line drawing to spray can effects. The source file that contains these functions—DRAW.C, and its header file, DRAW.H—are shown in Listings 5.3 and 5.4. Listings 5.1 and 5.2 contain the source file for the mouse support functions. Listing 5.5 presents a sample drawing program that uses all of the drawing tools.

Getting the Canvas Ready

Each of the interactive drawing functions follows several conventions. The routines assume that you'll be using the mouse tools presented in Listings 5.1 and 5.2. In addition, the drawing functions restrict their output to a predefined window. Therefore, whenever one of the drawing functions is called, the current viewport is set to the drawing window, and clipping is enabled. When the function exits, the viewport is set back to the full screen. The boundaries of the drawing window must be initialized in the application program by setting the four global variables **wl**, **wt**, **wr**, and **wb** to the left, top, right, and bottom corners of the drawing window desired.

Two other global variables must be set to initialize the drawing parameters that are used by the drawing routines. These variables must be set to the appropriate macro constants defined in graphics.h. For example, **globallinestyle** can take values of **DASHED_LINE**, **SOLID_LINE**, and so on. Take a close look at the sample drawing program presented in Listing 5.5, and you'll see how these variables are set.

Creating the Pencil

The **pencil()** function is probably the simplest drawing function. Briefly, **pencil()** is used to draw freehand figures. As you'll see in the upcoming sections, **pencil()** is like all the other interactive drawing tools in draw.c, in that it does not require any parameters and does not return a value.

With **pencil()**, you can draw a continuous curve as long as the left mouse button is pressed. Whenever the mouse button is released, the drawing stops. To resume drawing, you simply hold down the left button again. To exit the function, you click the left mouse button outside the drawing window. Presumably, this will be to select another drawing function. This is the technique we have used in our painting program, PAINT.C (shown in Listing 5.5) to access the pencil tool.

The function begins by setting the current viewport to the drawing window and resetting the drawing color as shown here.

```
setviewport(wl,wt,wr,wb,1);
setcolor(globaldrawingcolor);
```

The drawing color must be reset to **globaldrawcolor** because it may have been changed by another function in the application program.

The core of **pencil()** consists of three **while** loops and a handful of other statements. The outer **while** loop is an infinite loop that ensures that the two inner **while** loops are continually executed. The only way out of the infinite loop and the function **pencil()** is by executing the **return** statement after the topmost inner **while** loop.

The first inner **while** loop is actually the empty loop as shown:

```
while (!buttonstatus(PRESSED,LEFT_BUTTON)) ;
```

It continually calls **buttonstatus()** until the left mouse button is pressed, at which time **buttonstatus()** returns a nonzero value and the loop terminates. As long as the specified button, in this case the left button, is not pressed, **buttonstatus()** will return zero.

Once the left button is pressed, the mouse coordinates are retrieved by a call to **getmousecoords()**. These coordinates are checked against the drawing viewport to see if the user has clicked outside the drawing window. If so, the viewport is reset to the full screen and **pencil()** is terminated.

The **return** statement in **pencil()** provides the only exit. All the other interactive drawing routines are exited in a similar manner. If the left mouse button is clicked while the cursor is inside the drawing viewport, **pencil()** continues to the next **while** loop, where the drawing action is performed.

Freehand curves are drawn by connecting lines from the mouse's previous position to its current position. Therefore, as the mouse moves, the line grows. To avoid unnecessary screen writing, however, **pencil()** only draws lines if the mouse has been moved. All these statements are included in the bottommost **while** loop.

Now take a close look at the last **while** loop, along with a couple of preliminary statements. The first two lines save the current location of the mouse in **oldx** and **oldy** so that later the function can test whether the mouse has moved. Next, the BGI's **moveto()** function sets the current position to the mouse's current position. Later, we'll use a series of calls to **lineto()** to draw the freehand curve, starting from this point.

Note that the coordinates passed to **moveto()** are adjusted by the left and top boundaries of the drawing viewport. This must be done because **moveto()** uses coordinates that are relative to the current viewport, the drawing window, and because the mouse coordinates, x and y, are always given in full-screen coordinates.

Once the preliminary work has been taken care of, the bottom **while** loop is entered. It draws the connected line segments that make up the freehand curve. Note that the Boolean expression in the lower **while** loop continues until the left mouse button is released, at which time **buttonstatus()** returns a nonzero value. When this occurs, the drawing stops and the function climbs back to the topmost **while** loop, which waits for the next press of the left button.

If the mouse button is still pressed, the current mouse coordinates are retrieved by the function **getmousecoords()**. If these coordinates are different than the last occurrence (those saved in **oldx** and **oldy**), then a line is drawn from the previous mouse location to its current position using **lineto()**. The calls to **mousestatus()** surround **lineto()** to prevent the mouse cursor from interfering with the screen. Once these statements have been executed, the values in **oldx** and **oldy** are updated to the current location of the mouse.

Erasing Mistakes

Now that you've learned how to draw figures, take a look at how you can remove them. For this, we'll use a function called **erase()**, which is designed to erase small portions of the screen. Images are erased by setting a rectangular region under the cursor to the background color. By holding down the left mouse button and moving the mouse around, you can erase any area of the drawing window that you'd like.

The **erase()** function is similar to **pencil()** except that it draws small bars filled with the background color to the screen, rather than a series of lines. To generate these small erasing blocks, the fill style is set to **SOLID_FILL** and the fill and drawing colors are set to the background color.

The function draws these small solid-filled bars wherever the mouse cursor is located while the mouse button is pressed. Actually, as with **pencil()**, **erase()** does not erase the current location of the screen if the mouse has not been moved. This avoids unnecessary screen writes. The pixel dimensions of the eraser bar are specified by **ERASERSIZE**, which is a macro constant defined at the top of DRAW.H. You might try making the eraser size a variable so that the user could interactively change the size of the eraser.

A Simple Spray Can

The function **spraycan()** provides a simple spray-painting effect by randomly setting pixels within a rectangular region to the current drawing color. While the left mouse button is pressed, the spray painting action will occur as shown in Figure 5.1. To temporarily stop the spray painting, you release the left mouse button; and to exit the spray painting function, you move the mouse cursor outside the drawing viewport and click the left button.

The spray painting effect is produced by two **for** loops contained within the **while** loop that tests for the mouse button release. Each of the **for** loops is responsible for plotting eight pixels in a rectangular region around the mouse cursor. The first **for** loop plots pixels away from the mouse cursor, while the second **for** loop plots pixels closer.

Note that the particular pixel that is painted by each iteration of the **for** loops is randomly selected using the C function **random()**. This distributes the pixels evenly. The size of the spray region is partly determined by the macro constant **SPRAYSIZE**, declared in DRAW.H. However, the other integer values in the two **for** loops affect the distribution and location of the spray painting as well. You may want to experiment with other spray patterns.

Notice that **spraycan()** does not test to see if the mouse has been moved before drawing on the screen. This allows you to keep the mouse in one location and fill that region with painted pixels to the desired level. If the mouse is held in the same location long enough, the rectangular region becomes completely filled.

Drawing Lines

The function **drawlines()** is used to draw line segments. It lets you draw a single line by pointing to where the line is to begin, pressing and holding down the left mouse button, and then dragging the mouse cursor to the line's end point. When the button is released, the line is frozen. However, while the button is pressed, **drawlines()** continues to draw the line from the initial location of the mouse where the button was pressed to the mouse's current screen position.

So, as the mouse cusor is moved around the screen, the line will shrink and stretch as needed. This procedure for drawing lines is shown in Figure 5.2. This type of line is called a *rubber-banding* line because the line segment appears to be flexible like a rubber band. Anyway, to draw more lines, you just repeat this simple line-drawing process.

As you might expect, **drawlines()** is similar to the previously discussed functions. The first thing **drawlines()** does is set the viewport and drawing parameters. The line style and drawing color must be reset to the proper global variables because we'll be using them when we draw our lines. Note that the line width is restricted to **NORM_WIDTH**. This is done to simplify the code. You may want to modify DRAW.C so that the line width is a variable like **globallinestyle** and **globaldrawcolor**.

An important aspect of **draw-lines()** is the rubber-banding line effect. The technique uses the exclusive "ORing" feature provided by the BGI **setwritemode()** function to allow us to draw and move a line around the screen without permanently affecting what it overwrites. Once the exclusive OR mode is set, lines can be erased from the screen by

■ **FIGURE 5.1 Using the Spray Can tool**

writing over them with another line. The exclusive OR feature is turned on after the left button is pressed by the line:

```
setwritemode(XOR_PUT);
```

After this point, all lines are drawn by exclusive ORing them to the screen. Sometimes you will see the effects of the exclusive ORing as the line changes color as it crosses over other figures on the screen.

When you press the left mouse button while the cursor is inside the drawing window, the exclusive ORing mode is set as described earlier and the first line is drawn, although at this time it is merely a point. While the mouse button is pressed, the code proceeds into the lower **while** loop in **drawlines()**.

Within this loop, you can see that the line drawing is performed by the two calls to the **line()** function. Since the exclusive ORing mode is on, the first line erases the old line and the second line draws the line at the new position. Notice that the first coordinate pair in each call to **line()** corresponds to the position on the screen where the user first pressed the mouse button. This point does not change. The end point of the line that does change is the one that you drag around the screen with the mouse. These two lines create the rubber-banding effect.

When the left mouse button is released, the bottom **while** loop terminates and the code proceeds to redraw the line using the following statements:

```
setwritemode(COPY_PUT);
mousestatus(HIDE_MOUSE);
line(x1-wl,y1-wt,x2-wl,y2-wt);
mousestatus(SHOW_MOUSE);
```

The line is redrawn with **setwritemode()** taken out of the exclusive OR mode, so that the line is drawn in its proper color. Remember that a figure exclusively ORed with an object on the screen may change its color. This also explains why the **setwritemode()** function must be included within the outer **while** loop rather than at the top of **drawlines()**—to set it back to the exclusive OR mode.

Drawing Circles

For the finale, we'll create an interactive function to draw a circle, **drawcircle()**. A circle is drawn by first marking its center by pressing the left mouse button and then dragging the mouse to the left or to the right to set the circle's size.

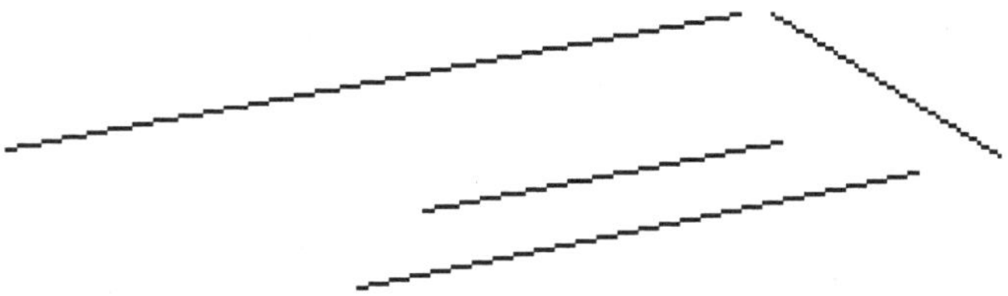

■ **FIGURE 5.2 Drawing lines with the Line Drawing tool**

The circle function is a sticky wicket. Why? The BGI doesn't provide the capability to draw circles using an exclusive OR. (Remember that we used the exclusive ORing technique to draw rubber-banding lines.) We'll use **getimage()** and **putimage()** to help us create the rubber-banding effect needed to draw circles. This is done by saving the screen image where the circle is to be drawn, so that later we can remove it from the screen by copying back to the screen with **putimage()**. In effect, we are doing nothing more than popping-up a window with the figure inside it. Let's begin by taking a closer look at **drawcircle()**.

The first thing you'll notice about **drawcircle()** is that it is much longer and probably more intimidating than any of the prior functions. However, taken in pieces, the function is actually similar to those discussed earlier. First, notice that **drawcircle()** is built around three **while** loops as in **pencil()**.

Now look at what makes **drawcircle()** unique. If you trace through the code, you'll discover several differences right from the start. One of the first statements, in fact, is a call to **malloc()**, which allocates memory space for two pointers **covered1** and **covered2**, which we'll use in our calls to **getimage()** when producing the rubber-banding effect.

Since there is the possibility that the figure we want to draw encompasses the whole drawing window, we must allocate enough space to save the complete window. In some very high resolution modes, it may not be possible to save the whole screen. The only way to avoid this problem is to ensure that your drawing window is not too large for the current graphics mode. If this situation occurs, **mallocerror()** is invoked. It is shown at the bottom of draw.c and does nothing more than abort the program. You might want to modify this error handler to make the program more user-friendly.

The next few statements set the drawing parameters and the drawing viewport coordinates. The code then proceeds through the outer **while** loop and the topmost **while** loop, which waits for the left mouse button to be pressed. As before, drawing does not begin until the left button is pressed and held down. In addition, the only way to exit the drawing routine is to click the mouse outside of the drawing window. Note that, on exit, the memory allocated for **covered1** and **covered2** is deallocated by calling the C function **free()**.

The next several lines initialize several important variables to the current coordinates of the mouse. We'll discuss these variables in a minute. Next, **getimage()** is called to save the screen located at the cursor. Although it is effectively saving only a point, this will begin our rubber-banding process.

Most of the complexity of the bottom **while** loop is due to the use of **getimage()** and **putimage()** to produce the rubber-banding effect. Keep in mind that these two functions do not clip their images relative to the current viewport. This means we must perform the clipping ourselves. The trick behind setting the size for a circle involves calculating the *absolute value* between the center point of the circle and the current mouse location. This value, which is saved in the variable **absradius**, is used by the clipping statements.

The first set of **if** statements in the **while** loop clips the current coordinates of the mouse to the drawing window. The process is illustrated in Figure 5.3. The clipped coordinates are saved in **cleft**, **cright**, **ctop**, and **cbottom**.

The next **if** statement tests whether the mouse has been moved from its previous position. If the mouse has been moved, the rubber-banding circle must be updated.

One other point to note about **drawcircle()** is that it does not draw the circle if the radius is zero. This is needed because the BGI function **circle()** will draw a circle of radius zero with a one-pixel radius. Since this is not what we want, we avoid drawing such circles.

Get Drawing

These interactive tools should provide everything you need to get started with your own drawing program. We've included a sample drawing program in Listing 5.5 to show you how the tools are accessed. If you feel adventurous, you might want to code up some additional tools to draw such figures as polygons and arcs.

CODE DESCRIPTION

Overview
The listings provided are used to create a set of interactive drawing tools for the BGI (Borland Graphics Interface).

Listings Available

Listing	*Description*	*Used with*
MOUSE.H	Header file that defines the structures used to control the mouse in graphics mode.	MOUSE.C DRAW.C. PAINT.C
DRAW.H	Header file that defines the function prototypes for the interactive drawing functions.	DRAW.C. PAINT.C
MOUSE.C	The library of functions for controlling the mouse.	------
DRAW.C	Main source file that defines the interactive drawing functions.	------
PAINT.C	Sample painting program that demonstrates how each of the drawing tools works.	------

How to Compile/Assemble

The C source files can be compiled with Borland C++ or Turbo C++. Make sure the header files DRAW.H and MOUSE.H can be located by the compiler.

Note: If you want to add additional drawing tools, you'll need to add functions to DRAW.C and you'll also need to update the header file DRAW.H.

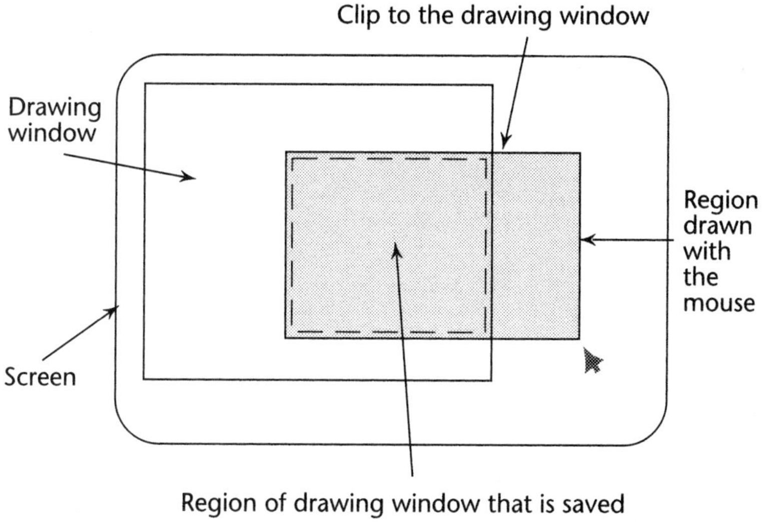

■ **FIGURE 5.3 Clipping the screen**

■ LISTING 5.1 MOUSE.H

```
#define RESET_MOUSE  0
#define SHOW_MOUSE  1
#define HIDE_MOUSE  2
#define GET_MOUSE_STATUS 3
#define PRESSED  5     /* Button presses */
#define RELEASED 6     /* Button releases */
#define LEFT_BUTTON  0    /* Use left button */

void mouse(int *m1, int *m2, int *m3, int *m4);
int  initmouse(void);
void getmousecoords(int *x, int *y);
void mousestatus(int stateofmouse);
int buttonstatus(int condition, int whichbutton);
```

■ LISTING 5.2 MOUSE.C

```
/* mouse.c - Routines to support a Microsoft compatible mouse.
   This package assumes that you are running in graphics mode. */
#include <dos.h>
#include <graphics.h>
#include <stdio.h>
#include "mouse.h"

/* Communicates with the mouse driver */
void mouse(int *m1, int *m2, int *m3, int *m4)
{
  union REGS inregs, outregs;
```

```
  inregs.x.ax = *m1;    inregs.x.bx = *m2;
  inregs.x.cx = *m3;    inregs.x.dx = *m4;
  int86(0x33,&inregs,&outregs);
  *m1 = outregs.x.ax;  *m2 = outregs.x.bx;
  *m3 = outregs.x.cx;  *m4 = outregs.x.dx;
}

/* Initialize the mouse */
int initmouse(void)
{
  int gmode, m1, m2, m3, m4;
  char far *memory = (char far *)0x004000049L;

  m1 = RESET_MOUSE;     mouse(&m1,&m2,&m3,&m4);
  if (m1) {
    /* Hercules card requires an extra step */
    gmode = getgraphmode();
    if (gmode == HERCMONOHI) {
      *memory = 0x06;
      m1 = RESET_MOUSE;  mouse(&m1,&m2,&m3,&m4);
    }
    mousestatus(SHOW_MOUSE);
    return(1);
  }
  else /* Mouse not found, return failure flag */
    return(0);
}

/* Hide or show the mouse */
void mousestatus(int stateofmouse)
{
  int m2, m3, m4;
  mouse(&stateofmouse,&m2,&m3,&m4);
}

/*  Get the current location of the mouse cursor */
void getmousecoords(int *x, int *y)
{
  int m1, m2;

  m1 = GET_MOUSE_STATUS;    mouse(&m1,&m2,x,y);
  /* Adjust for virtual coordinates of the mouse */
  if (getmaxx() == 319) (*x) /= 2;
}

/* Returns 1 if the mouse button condition specified occurred */
int buttonstatus(int condition, int whichbutton)
{
  int m3, m4;
  mouse(&condition,&whichbutton,&m3,&m4);
  if (whichbutton) return(1); else  return(0);
}
```

■ LISTING 5.3 DRAW.H

```
/*   draw.h  - Interactive drawing utilities */
void pencil(void);
void spraycan(void);
void drawlines(void);
void erase(void);
void drawcircle(void);
void mallocerror(void);
extern int globaldrawcolor;  /* Holds the drawing color to use */
extern int globallinestyle;  /* Holds the line style */
extern int wl, wt, wr, wb;
#define ERASERSIZE 3         /* Half the size of the eraser */
#define SPRAYSIZE 15         /* Size of spray can spray area */
```

■ LISTING 5.4 DRAW.C

```
/* draw.c - Interactive drawing tools used by the paint.c */
#include <stdio.h>
#include <graphics.h>
#include <alloc.h>
#include <stdlib.h>
#include <time.h>
#include "mouse.h"    /* Function prototypes for mouse */
#include "draw.h"     /* Function prototypes for draw.c */

int globaldrawcolor;  /* Holds active drawing color */
int globallinestyle;  /* Holds active line style */
int wl, wt, wr, wb;   /* Window bounds for drawing area */

/* This function emulates a pencil. While the left mouse button
   is pressed it draws a trail of connected lines. */
void pencil(void)
{
   int x, y, oldx, oldy;

   setviewport(wl,wt,wr,wb,1);  /* Define drawing viewport */
   setcolor(globaldrawcolor);   /* Set global drawing color */
   while (1) {
     while (!buttonstatus(PRESSED,LEFT_BUTTON)) ; /* Wait for */
     getmousecoords(&x,&y);  /* button press; get coordinates. */
     if (x < wl || x > wr || y < wt || y > wb) {
       setviewport(0,0,getmaxx(),getmaxy(),1);
       return;               /* Restore viewport to full screen */
     }                       /* and exit pencil routine */
     oldx = x;
     oldy = y;
     moveto(x-wl,y-wt);
     while (!buttonstatus(RELEASED,LEFT_BUTTON)) {
       getmousecoords(&x,&y);          /* If location has */
       if (x != oldx || y != oldy) {   /* changed, draw line */
           mousestatus(HIDE_MOUSE);      /* to it. Make sure to */
           lineto(x-wl,y-wt);            /* adjust mouse location */
```

```
            mousestatus(SHOW_MOUSE);      /* to current viewport. */
            oldx = x;  oldy = y;          /* Save mouse location */
        }
      }
    }
}

/*  This function resets a small screen area to the background
    color. Erasing is done by drawing a filled bar at the current
    mouse location. */
void erase(void)
{
   int x, y, oldx, oldy;

   setviewport(wl,wt,wr,wb,1);       /* Set drawing viewport */
   setcolor(getbkcolor());           /* Use background color */
   setfillstyle(SOLID_FILL,getbkcolor());  /* to erase screen */
   while (1) {
     while (!buttonstatus(PRESSED,LEFT_BUTTON));
     getmousecoords(&x,&y);          /* Get mouse location */
     if (x < wl || x > wr || y < wt || y > wb) {
       setviewport(0,0,getmaxx(),getmaxy(),1);
       return;                    /* Restore viewport and return */
     }
     oldx = x;
     oldy = y;
     mousestatus(HIDE_MOUSE);    /* Erase screen under mouse */
     bar(x-wl,y-wt,x-wl+ERASERSIZE,y-wt+ERASERSIZE);
     mousestatus(SHOW_MOUSE);
     while (!buttonstatus(RELEASED,LEFT_BUTTON)) { /* Continue */
       getmousecoords(&x,&y);           /* erasing as long */
       if (x != oldx || y != oldy) {    /* as the mouse is at */
            mousestatus(HIDE_MOUSE);       /* a new location and */
            bar(x-wl,y-wt,x-wl+ERASERSIZE,y-wt+ERASERSIZE);
            mousestatus(SHOW_MOUSE);       /* the left button is */
            oldx = x;   oldy = y;          /* pressed */
       }
     }
   }
}

/*  This function randomly paints pixels in a square region
    whenever the left mouse button is pressed */
void spraycan(void)
{
   int i, x, y;

   randomize();        /* Initialize random function */
   setviewport(wl,wt,wr,wb,1);   /* Set window to drawing window */
   while (1) {                     /* Wait until left button */
     while (!buttonstatus(PRESSED,LEFT_BUTTON)); /* is pressed */
     getmousecoords(&x,&y);
     if (x < wl || x > wr || y < wt || y > wb) {
       setviewport(0,0,getmaxx(),getmaxy(),1); /* Restore window */
```

```
      return;                              /* to full screen and */
    }                                      /* quit routine */
    while (!buttonstatus(RELEASED,LEFT_BUTTON)) {
      getmousecoords(&x, &y);         /* Continue spraying */
      mousestatus(HIDE_MOUSE);
      for (i=0; i<8; i++)
          putpixel(x-random(SPRAYSIZE)+5-wl,
            y-random(SPRAYSIZE)+5-wt, globaldrawcolor);
      for (i=0; i<8; i++)
          putpixel(x-random(SPRAYSIZE-2)+3-wl,
            y-random(SPRAYSIZE-2)+3-wt, globaldrawcolor);
      mousestatus(SHOW_MOUSE);
    }
  }
}

/* Draw a line while left mouse button is pressed. Use
   XOR_PUT to provide rubber-banding line feature.  */
void drawlines(void)
{
   int x1, y1, x2, y2, oldx2, oldy2;

   setviewport(wl,wt,wr,wb,1);     /* Use the drawing window */
   setlinestyle(globallinestyle,0,NORM_WIDTH);  /* and global */
   setcolor(globaldrawcolor);                   /* settings */
   while (1) {
     while (!buttonstatus(PRESSED,LEFT_BUTTON)) ;
     getmousecoords(&x1,&y1);
     if (x1 < wl || x1 > wr || y1 < wt || y1 > wb) {
       setviewport(0,0,getmaxx(),getmaxy(),1);
       setwritemode(COPY_PUT);
       return;
     }
     setwritemode(XOR_PUT); /* Use XOR_PUT to rubber-band lines */
     moveto(x1-wl,y1-wt);
     oldx2 = x1;   oldy2 = y1;
     while (!buttonstatus(RELEASED,LEFT_BUTTON)) {
       getmousecoords(&x2,&y2);
       if (x2 != oldx2 || y2 != oldy2) {
           mousestatus(HIDE_MOUSE);
           line(x1-wl,y1-wt,oldx2-wl,oldy2-wt);
           line(x1-wl,y1-wt,x2-wl,y2-wt);
           mousestatus(SHOW_MOUSE);
           oldx2 = x2;  oldy2 = y2;
       }
     }
     setwritemode(COPY_PUT);         /* Redraw line when set */
     mousestatus(HIDE_MOUSE);        /* so color will be */
     line(x1-wl,y1-wt,x2-wl,y2-wt); /* correct */
     mousestatus(SHOW_MOUSE);
   }
}

/*  Interactively draw a circle */
```

```
void drawcircle(void)
{
  int cleft, ctop, cright, cbottom, absradius;
  unsigned char far *covered1, *covered2;
  int centerx, centery, oldleft, oldtop;
  int halfx, newx, newy, oldx;

  halfx = (wr + wl) / 2;
  covered1 = malloc(imagesize(wl, wt, halfx, wb));
  covered2 = malloc(imagesize(halfx+1, wt, wr, wb));
  if (covered1 == NULL || covered2 == NULL) {
    mallocerror();
  }
  setcolor(globaldrawcolor);
  setviewport(wl, wt, wr, wb, 1);
  while (1) {
    while (!buttonstatus(PRESSED,LEFT_BUTTON)) ;
    getmousecoords(&centerx, &centery);
    if (centerx < wl || centerx > wr || centery < wt
                              || centery > wb) {
      setviewport(0, 0, getmaxx(), getmaxy(),1);
      free(covered2); free(covered1);
      return;
    }
    oldleft = centerx;  oldtop = centery;   oldx = centerx;
    mousestatus(HIDE_MOUSE);
    getimage(oldleft-wl,oldtop-wt,oldleft-wl,oldtop-wt,covered1);
    getimage(oldleft+1-wl, oldtop-wt, oldleft+1-wl,
                               oldtop-wt, covered2);
    mousestatus(SHOW_MOUSE);
    while (!buttonstatus(RELEASED,LEFT_BUTTON)) {
      getmousecoords(&newx, &newy);
      absradius = abs(centerx - newx);
      /* Clip the region that must be saved below the circle
       * to the boundaries of the drawing window */
      if (centerx-absradius < wl) cleft = wl;
        else cleft = centerx - absradius;
      if (centerx+absradius > wr) cright = wr;
        else cright = centerx + absradius;
      if (centery-absradius < wt) ctop = wt;
        else ctop = centery - absradius;
      if (centery+absradius > wb) cbottom = wb;
        else cbottom = centery + absradius;
      /* If the size of the circle has changed, redraw it */
      if (newx != oldx) {
         mousestatus(HIDE_MOUSE);
         putimage(oldleft-wl, oldtop-wt, covered1, COPY_PUT);
         putimage(centerx+1-wl, oldtop-wt, covered2, COPY_PUT);
         getimage(cleft-wl, ctop-wt, centerx-wl,
                  cbottom-wt, covered1);
         getimage(centerx+1-wl, ctop-wt, cright-wl,
                  cbottom-wt, covered2);
         if (absradius != 0)
           circle(centerx-wl, centery-wt, absradius);
```

```
            mousestatus(SHOW_MOUSE);
            oldleft = cleft;   oldtop = ctop;   oldx = newx;
          }
        }
      }
    }

    /* This function is called if a malloc() fails. Place your
       own error handler here. */
    void mallocerror(void)
    {
      closegraph();
      printf("Not enough memory");
      exit(1);
    }
```

■ LISTING 5.5 PAINT.C

```
/* paint.c - A simple paint program that demonstrates the
   interactive drawing tools in draw.c. Compile in the large model.
   Link with the BGI graphics library, mouse.c, and draw.c. */
#include <stdio.h>
#include <stdlib.h>
#include <graphics.h>
#include "draw.h"
#include "mouse.h"

void setupgraphics(void);
void drawscreen(void);
void paint(void);

int main(void) {
  setupgraphics();
  drawscreen();
  if (!initmouse()) {
    closegraph();
    printf("Mouse required.\n");
    exit(1);
  }
  paint();
  closegraph();
  return(0);
}

/* Sets the graphics mode, drawing parameters, and drawing
   window dimensions */
void setupgraphics(void)
{
  int gmode, gdriver=DETECT, errorcode;

  initgraph(&gdriver, &gmode, "\\tc\\bgi");
  if ((errorcode=graphresult()) != grOk) {
    printf("Graphics error: %s\n", grapherrormsg(errorcode));
    exit(1);
```

```
  }

  /* Set the coordinates of the drawing window */
  wt = 1;  wb = 400;
  if (wb > getmaxy()-1) wb = getmaxy() - 1;
  wl = textwidth("MenuWidth");
  wr = getmaxx() - 1;
  globaldrawcolor = WHITE;
  globallinestyle = SOLID_LINE;
}

/* Draws the paint program screen */
void drawscreen(void)
{
  setfillstyle(SOLID_FILL, EGA_BLUE);
  bar(0, 0, getmaxx(), getmaxy());
  setfillstyle(SOLID_FILL, EGA_BLACK);
  bar3d(wl-1, wt-1, wr+1, wb+1, 1, 0);

  /* Draw the screen border */
  rectangle(0, 0, wl-1, 120);
  outtextxy(4, 10, "Pencil");   line(0, 20, wl-1, 20);
  outtextxy(4, 30, "SprayCan"); line(0, 40, wl-1, 40);
  outtextxy(4, 50, "Erase");    line(0, 60, wl-1, 60);
  outtextxy(4, 70, "Lines");    line(0, 80, wl-1, 80);
  outtextxy(4, 90, "Circle");   line(0, 100, wl-1, 100);
  outtextxy(4, 110, "Quit");
}

/* The function used to select the paint routines */
void paint(void)
{
  int x, y;

  while (!buttonstatus(PRESSED,LEFT_BUTTON)) ;
  while (1) {
    while (!buttonstatus(RELEASED,LEFT_BUTTON)) ;
    getmousecoords(&x, &y);

    /* Is the mouse over a menu option? If so, execute
     * its corresponding drawing function. */
    if (x < wl && y < 120) {
      if (y < 20) pencil();
      else if (y < 40) spraycan();
      else if (y < 60) erase();
      else if (y < 80) drawlines();
      else if (y < 100) drawcircle();
      else return;  /* Quit option */
    }
    else  /* Flush the extra button press */
      while (!buttonstatus(PRESSED,LEFT_BUTTON)) ;
  }
}
```

Screen Typography

■ Marv Luse

Use the same graphics technology for screen displays as for laser printer output, with HP's Soft Font format.

User interface technology has matured dramatically in the past few years, especially on DOS systems. And nowhere is this more evident than in the gradual movement away from simple character-based presentation toward the use of graphics and typography to render the WYSIWYG display.

Nowadays, the DOS developer is finding it ever more necessary to understand typography. Where once it was sufficient to know how to poke a two-byte character/attribute pair into video memory, you must now be concerned with individual pixels and graphics modes, aspect ratios, quantities such as *leading* and *ascent*, and qualities such as *sans serif* or *black italic*.

But typography is still a bit of an arcane art to most developers. Here we'll look at the terminology and technology of typography and try to provide a solid introduction to this fascinating subject. Within this context, we'll also examine one font format in detail—the HP Soft Font. This is one of the more important formats, as it is both widely supported and widely available. We'll also look at a practical implementation of this format on-screen, using the Zortech C++ compiler and the Flash Graphics library provided with that compiler. This particular tool set provides all of the critical components required to implement high-speed bitmapped font support. But first, let's define some basic font terminology.

Typefaces, Typestyles, and Fonts

Nearly everyone uses the word "font" to refer to a particular typeface or typestyle. Strictly speaking, however, these terms have distinct meanings, and you should be aware of the distinctions among them.

Typeface refers to the particular style or look that is apparent in all of the individual characters comprising the typeface's symbol set. Almost everyone has heard of names such as Helvetica and Times Roman. These are typefaces, and they are easily recognized on the page by the unique look that they impart to text.

It is interesting to note that while a typeface pattern itself cannot be copyrighted, the *names* of typefaces may be trademarked, and those trademarks are heavily defended. Most of the standard typeface names are trademarks of a few of the larger typographic companies such as ITC and Linotype AG. For this reason, you cannot name a font of your own with a trademarked name without licensing the use of the name from its owner. This accounts for the large numbers of confusingly similar names for commercially available fonts—few companies actually elect to pay for the right to use a name. As an example, look-alikes for the Helvetica typeface are available under the names Helvette, Swiss, Geneva, and Aspen, to name just a few.

Typestyle refers to thematic variations on a given typeface. Bold, italic, and condensed are all examples of specific typestyles, and these are normally combined with a typeface name, as in Helvetica Bold. Curiously, there is no generally accepted term for indicating the plain, unadorned form of a typeface. Some commonly used adjectives are regular, roman, and book.

The term *font* is the most specific of the three: Strictly speaking, a font is a specific size of a specific typestyle of a specific typeface. Thus, 12-point Helvetica Bold is a font, while Helvetica by itself is more properly called a typeface. As I noted above, however, it is not uncommon to use the word font loosely in contexts to indicate any one of font, typestyle, or typeface.

Points, Pitch, and Leading

The typographer's customary unit of size is the *point*, and there are 72 points in an inch. When speaking of the size of a font, it is the font's character cell height that is being referenced. Note that characters are positioned with respect to a baseline that generally bisects the character cell in its lower half. The distance from the baseline to the top of the cell is referred to as the character's *ascent*, while the distance from the baseline to the bottom of the cell is the character's *descent*. Another important measurement is the height of a typical lower case letter, measured from the baseline. This distance is referred to as the font's *x-height*. These various metrics are illustrated in Figure 5.4.

Note that the vast majority of typefaces are designed to be rendered using *proportional spacing*, in which the widths of individual characters vary so as to occupy only as much horizontal space as necessary. This contrasts with the PC's typical ROM font, which is *monospaced,* meaning that all characters are the same width. With a monospaced font it makes sense to speak of the font's *pitch*, which is expressed as so many characters per inch (cpi). As an example, the default font of a typical dot matrix printer prints at a pitch of 10 cpi.

Returning to heights, note that lines of text are normally set with some whitespace between lines, so that the descender characters of one line do not touch the ascender characters of the line below. This whitespace is referred to as *leading* (rhymes with "bed-ding," not "feeding"). The term actually derives from the old practice of metal typesetting, where thin strips of lead were placed as spacers between lines of type.

When speaking of the height of a font, note that this measurement does not ordinarily include any leading. Thus, a 10-point font is typically set with a 2-point leading to yield an actual line height of 12 points. Recalling that there are 72 points in an inch, this example

■ **FIGURE 5.4 Font metrics**

would provide 72/12 = 6 lines of type per inch. These various measurements are illustrated in Figure 5.5.

The HP Soft Font Format

The HP Soft Font format is important because of its widespread use and availability. This makes it a logical choice for the developer who must provide font technology directly within an application. It's also an attractive choice for on-screen use when you consider that the same format can be used on most laser printers—so why use different formats for screen and hardcopy when one format will do?

What follows is a brief overview of the format. I've tried to avoid too much detail, preferring instead to concentrate on how to use the format.

An HP Soft Font file contains an ordered set of escape sequences, font and character descriptors, and character bitmaps. The escape sequences are used to identify what is to follow in the data stream and also to indicate, where appropriate, the number of bytes of data that follow.

Each font file contains a font descriptor, which is a data structure that provides information applicable to the font as a whole. Additionally, each character in the font contributes a character descriptor, which is a data structure providing metric information on a character. Finally, the character itself is represented by a character bitmap, which provides the actual image of the character.

Two aspects of the format are problematic. First, 16-bit or larger values are physically ordered MSB to LSB, which is backward relative to the byte ordering employed on Intel processors. As a result, having once read a descriptor into memory, you must first swap the bytes before using them.

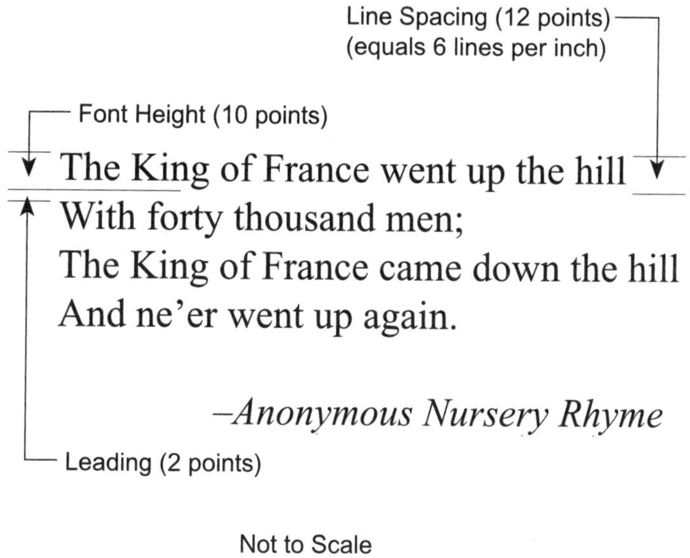

■ **FIGURE 5.5 Line height and spacing**

The second problem is that two sets of units are employed, dots and quarter-dots, and it can be confusing trying to keep these straight. Note that these are resolution-based units and are highly device-dependent: There are 300 dots per inch and 1200 quarter-dots per inch on the typical laser printer, and 82 dots per inch and 328 quarter-dots per inch on a 0.31mm-dot pitch monitor.

Font File Escape Sequences

Only three escape sequences are used in the typical HP font file. These are *define-font-descriptor, define-character-descriptor*, and *set-current-character-code.* The beginning of a sequence is indicated by the escape character, 1BH or 27 decimal, and the end of a sequence is signalled by the occurrence of a capital letter. Additional sequences are generally required to use the font on a printer, and these are provided by the application itself. These would include *specify-font-id* and *select-font.* The escape sequence syntax for the file-resident sequences is shown in Table 5.1.

Font File Data Structures

Two data structures are employed in an HP Soft Font file. One structure, the font descriptor, provides various qualitative and metric data that is applicable to the font as a whole. There will be a single instance of this structure, and it is the first element of the file (following its corresponding escape sequence). The other data structure is the character descriptor, and there will be one instance for each character in the font. A character's bitmap immediately follows its descriptor and can be thought of as being a part of the character descriptor. The escape sequence signalling the start of a character descriptor indicates the combined length of the descriptor and bitmap in bytes.

The data descriptors can be read or written using suitable C or C++ structure definitions. The HPFONT.HPP file illustrates the layout of the descriptors. Note that some fields and

■ TABLE 5.1 Font file escape sequences

Sequence	Example	Meaning
define-font-descriptor	Esc) s 2 4 8 W	Descriptor plus narrative data occupies the following 248 bytes.
set-current-char-code	Esc * c 6 5 E	Current character is ASCII 65 (a capital A).
define-char-descriptor	Esc (s 1 2 8 W	Descriptor plus character bitmap for current character occupies the next 128 bytes.

Note: Case of alphabetic characters in the sequences is significant in that an uppercase character indicates that the sequence is complete.

reserved areas may be dependent on PCL release level. The version given here is compatible with the LaserJet Series II firmware, and should work on any LaserJet. Also keep in mind the cautions regarding byte-ordering and measurement units noted earlier.

Many of the fields defined in the font and character descriptors are not actually needed to use the font. Indeed, HP printers themselves ignore the contents of a number of the fields. The simplest way of using a font in software would be reading in a descriptor as-is and simply ignoring unneeded fields. However, this would inflict a substantial memory penalty, so our approach here will be to define minimally functional structures that will be initialized from the font file's descriptors as they are read. This minimalist approach also serves to define a generic font type that is reasonably format-independent.

The Font Class Hierarchy

From a design standpoint, it is best to keep the structure and implementation details of fonts and characters as generic as possible. Although we are now dealing with the HP format on the backside and Zortech's Flash Graphics library at the front, we would like our design to be easily adaptable to other formats and display technologies. To this end, we define generic **Font** and **Character** classes.

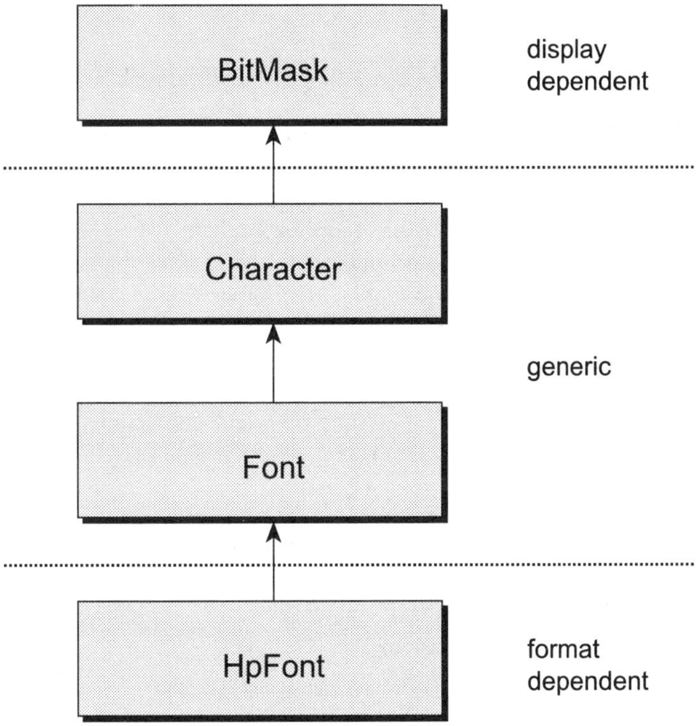

■ **FIGURE 5.6 Font class hierarchy**

The physical representation of a character and its library-specific methods are separated into a **BitMask** base class, from which the **Character** class is derived. The HP format-specific code is placed into a separate **HpFont** class, which is derived from class **Font**. Note that since **HpFont** inherits **Font**'s methods, **HpFont** only needs to provide suitable constructors to instantiate a **Font** from an HP font file. The hierarchy of these classes is shown in Figure 5.6.

The various classes are presented in separate source files as follows: BITMASK.HPP and BITMASK.CPP (Listings 5.6 and 5.7) contain the **BitMask** definition and the Flash Graphics-dependent code; CHARACTR.HPP and CHARACTR.CPP (Listings 5.8 and 5.9) contain the **Character** class definition; FONT.HPP and FONT.CPP (Listings 5.10 and 5.11) contain the generic **Font** class definition; and HPFONT.HPP and HPFONT.CPP (Listings 5.12 and 5.13) contain the code for the HP-specific derived class. FONTTEST.CPP (Listing 5.14) provides an example program to load a font and draw sample output to the screen. This program, as given, requires the Zortech C++ compiler for compilation.

Implementation Details

For the sake of illustration, character drawing capabilities have been kept to a minimum. It is only possible to specify where to draw a character or string and what color to use. The code could be modified to support additional features, such as justification, rotation, and additional pixel write modes.

The actual drawing is performed by the **fg_drawmatrix()** function from Zortech's Flash Graphics library. This function draws a *bitmask* rather than a *bitmap*; that is, only the foreground pixels of a monochrome image are drawn. This allows for a transparent background, on which characters appear as collections of lines and curves rather than as solid iconic images. Unfortunately, Borland's BGI library does not provide a corresponding function, so if you want to adapt this code for Borland's C++ you will have to either provide a **draw_mask()** function or adapt the code to use pixel or image drawing functions.

The sole purpose of the **HpFont** class is to instantiate an instance of class **Font**. Additional formats could be supported by deriving additional classes from **Font**, say for example a **GemFont** (for the GEM environment) or a **WinFont** class, for Windows. While you might think that **Font**'s methods should all be virtual, this is not necessary. Each supported format is translated into the single generic format represented by class **Font**, so there is no need to provide virtual function overrides in the derived classes.

Some Final Notes

The discussion of typography presented here provides a good background for the PC developer. It is certainly not exhaustive, however, and you might wish to pursue the topic further via one of the references listed.

The font technology implemented by the program listings is, of course, limited to bitmapped fonts. This is generally the preferable approach for on-screen use, since it is simpler to implement and provides the highest performance. The tradeoff is that each point size of each font requires a separate font file, which can lead to significant disk storage requirements if many sizes and typefaces are required.

Finally, don't forget that there is a plentiful supply of HP Soft Fonts from both commercial vendors and public domain sources. Also, many font generator software packages can be purchased. Two companies particularly worth mentioning that provide HP Soft Font generators are Bitstream, Inc., Cambridge, MA, and Digi-Fonts, Inc. of Golden, CO.

References

Binstock, Babcock, and Luse. *Programming the LaserJet in C.* Reading, Massachusetts: Addison-Wesley, 1991. Good general reference on the LaserJet and the HP Soft Font format.

Hewlett-Packard. *The LaserJet III Technical Reference Manual.* The definitive reference on the HP bitmapped Soft Font format.

Mendelson, Edward. "Fonts: The Elements of Type Style." *PC Magazine*, June 13, 1989: 206–292. Good coverage of font and font-related software sources.

Romano, Frank J. *The TypEncyclopedia.* New York: R.R. Bowker Company, 1984. A good basic reference on the subject of typography.

CODE DESCRIPTION

Overview

The listings provided are used to create a set of interactive drawing tools for the BGI (Borland Graphics Interface).

Listings Available

Listing	*Description*	*Used with*
BITMASK.HPP	Header file that defines the class used to represent a font bit mask.	BITMASK.CPP
CHARACTR.HPP	Header file that defines the class used to repesent characters.	CHARACTR.CPP
FONT.HPP	Header file that defines the class used to represent a font.	FONT.CPP
HPFONT.HPP	Header file that defines a class to represent HP Soft Fonts.	HPFONT.CPP
BITMASK.CPP	Source file that contains the methods for the bitmask class.	------
CHARACTR.CPP	Source file that contains methods for the Font and Character classes.	------
FONT.CPP	Source file that contains methods for the Font and Character classes.	------
HPFONT.CPP	Source file that contains the code to implement HP Soft fonts.	------
FONTEST.CPP	Font demonstration program.	------

How to Compile/Assemble

The C++ source files must be compiled with Zortech C++. Make sure the header files can be located by the compiler.

Note: The source files need to be compiled with Zortech C++ because the Flash Graphics are used. You can easily adapt the source files for another compiler, such as Borland C++, by removing the Flash Graphics calls and using the BGI.

■ LISTING 5.6 BITMASK.HPP

```
//    Definition of a Single-Plane Bitmap Class
#ifndef _BITMASK_HPP_
#define _BITMASK_HPP_

//........ BitMask Class
class BitMask
{
   protected:
      int   width;        // width in pixels
      int   height;       // height in pixels
      int   rowbytes;     // bytes per row
      char *mask;         // pointer to bitmask
   public:
      BitMask( );
      BitMask( int w, int h, char *m );
     ~BitMask( );
      virtual void draw( int x, int y, int clr );
};
#endif
```

■ LISTING 5.7 BITMASK.CPP

```
//   Methods for the BitMask Class
#include "fg.h"
#include "string.h"
#include "bitmask.hpp"

//........ default constructor
BitMask::BitMask( )
{
     width = height = rowbytes = 0;
     mask = 0;
}

//........ constructor using specified components
BitMask::BitMask( int w, int h, char *m )
{
     width    = w;
     height   = h;
     rowbytes = (w + 7) >> 3;
```

```
    if( (mask = new char[height*rowbytes]) != 0 )
       memcpy( mask, m, height*rowbytes );
}

//........ default destructor- needed to deallocate memory
BitMask::~BitMask( )
{
    if( mask ) delete mask;
}

//........ function to draw a bitmask using Zortech FG library
void BitMask::draw( int x, int y, int clr )
{
    fg_box_t  mask_area;

    mask_area[FG_X1] = mask_area[FG_Y1] = 0;
    mask_area[FG_X2] = width -1;
    mask_area[FG_Y2] = height -1;
    fg_drawmatrix( clr, FG_MODE_SET, -1, FG_ROTO,
                   x, y, mask, mask_area, fg.displaybox );
}
```

■ LISTING 5.8 CHARACTR.HPP

```
// Definition of a Character Class
#ifndef _CHARACTR_HPP_
#define _CHARACTR_HPP_
#include "BitMask.Hpp"

class Font;
class HpFont;

//........ Character Class
class Character : public BitMask
{
      friend class Font;
      friend class HpFont;
   protected:
      int   left_ofs;     // ref-pt to left edge dist
      int   top_ofs;      // ref-pt to top edge dist
      int   delta_x;      // ref-pt to next ref-pt dist
   public:
      Character( );
      Character( int w, int h, char *m );
     ~Character( );
      int  ch_delta( )  { return delta_x; }
      int  ch_width( )  { return width; }
      int  ch_height( ) { return height; }
      virtual void drawch( int x, int y, int clr );
};
#endif
```

■ LISTING 5.9 CHARACTR.CPP

```
//  Methods for Font and Character Classes
#include "string.h"
#include "charactr.hpp"

//........ default constructor
Character::Character( ) : BitMask( )
{
     left_ofs = 0;
     top_ofs  = 0;
     delta_x  = 0;
}

//........ constructor using specified components
Character::Character( int w, int h, char *m) : BitMask( w, h, m )
{
     left_ofs = 0;
     top_ofs  = h;
     delta_x  = w;
}

//........ default destructor (implied call to ~BitMask())
Character::~Character( )
{
}

//........ draw character
void Character::drawch( int x, int y, int clr )
{
     draw( x+left_ofs, y+top_ofs, clr );
}
```

■ LISTING 5.10 FONT.HPP

```
//  Definition for a generic Font Class
#ifndef _FONT_HPP_
#define _FONT_HPP_

#include "Charactr.Hpp"

//........ Font Class
class Font
{
   public:
      int        fstatus;    // font status flag
   protected:
      int        cell_w;     // cell width in pixels
      int        cell_h;     // cell height in pixels
      int        ascent;     // ascent dist in pixels
      int        descent;    // descent dist in pixels
      int        pitch;      // default pitch in pixels
      int        ch_cnt;     // allocated Character cnt
      int        min_ch;     // min ASCII char code
```

```
      int        max_ch;     // max ASCII char code
      Character *ch;         // allocated Character array
   public:
      Font( );
      Font( int bgn_ch, int end_ch );
     ~Font( );
      int chmin( void ) { return min_ch; }
      int chmax( void ) { return max_ch; }
      int chcnt( void ) { return ch_cnt; }
      int  strwidth( char *str );
      int  strheight( char *str );
      void drawstr( int x, int y, int clr, char *str );
};

// constants for Font.fstatus
const int fntNOINIT  =  0;   // font never initialized
const int fntOKAY    =  1;   // font successfully instantiated
const int fntFAILED  = -1;   // some kind of failure
#endif
```

■ LISTING 5.11 FONT.CPP

```
//  Methods for Font and Character Classes

#include "font.hpp"

//........ default constructor
Font::Font( )
{
     fstatus = fntNOINIT;
     cell_w = cell_h = 0;
     ascent = descent = 0;
     pitch = 0;
     ch_cnt = 0;
     min_ch = max_ch = 0;
     ch = 0;
}

//........ constructor that allocates char array
Font::Font( int bgn_ch, int end_ch )
{
     fstatus = fntNOINIT;
     cell_w = cell_h = 0;
     ascent = descent = 0;
     pitch = 0;
     ch_cnt = end_ch - bgn_ch + 1;
     min_ch = bgn_ch;
     max_ch = end_ch;
     ch = new Character[ch_cnt];
     if( ch == 0 )
        fstatus = fntFAILED;
}

//........ destructor
```

```
Font::~Font( )
{
     if( ch ) delete [ch_cnt] ch;
}

//........ compute string width
int Font::strwidth( char *str )
{
     int w = 0;
     while( *str )
     {
        if( (*str >= min_ch) && (*str <= max_ch) )
           w += ch[*str-min_ch].delta_x;
        str++;
     }
     return w;
}

//........ compute actual string height
int Font::strheight( char *str )
{
     int h = 0;
     while( *str )
     {
        if( (*str >= min_ch) && (*str <= max_ch) )
           if( ch[*str-min_ch].height > h )
              h = ch[*str-min_ch].height;
        str++;
     }
     return h;
}

//........ draw a string using Character.draw method
void Font::drawstr( int x, int y, int clr, char *str )
{
     while( *str )
     {
        if( (*str >= min_ch) && (*str <= max_ch) )
        {
           ch[*str-min_ch].drawch( x, y, clr );
           x += ch[*str-min_ch].delta_x;
        }
        str++;
     }
}
```

■ LISTING 5.12 HPFONT.HPP

```
// Definition for an HP Soft Font Class
#ifndef _HPFONT_HPP_
#define _HPFONT_HPP_
#include "Font.Hpp"

//........ macro to swap bytes in a 2-byte word
```

```
#define REV_WRD( w )  ( ((w>>8) & 0x00FF) | (w<<8) )
//........ constants for categorizing escape sequences
const int eFONTDESC = 1;        // define font descriptor
const int eCHARDESC = 2;        // define char descriptor
const int eCHARCODE = 3;        // specify current char code
const int eUNKNOWN  = 4;        // anything else
//........ constants indicating HP font status
const int hpNOINIT    = 0;      // uninitialized font
const int hpOKAY      = 1;      // all is well
const int hpNOTFOUND  = 101;    // disk file not found
const int hpIOERROR   = 102;    // io error, unexpected eof, etc.
const int hpBADFMT    = 103;    // format failure
const int hpOVRFLOW   = 104;    // internal buffer overflow
const int hpNOMEM     = 105;    // memory allocation failed

//........ font descriptor data structure
struct font_desc
{
    unsigned int   fd_size;        // font descriptor size
             char  resv_1;         // reserved
    unsigned char  font_type;      // font type
             int   resv_2;         // reserved
    unsigned int   bl_dist;        // baseline dist (D)
    unsigned int   cell_width;     // cell width (D)
    unsigned int   cell_height;    // cell height (D)
    unsigned char  orient;         // orientation
    unsigned char  proportional;   // 0=fixed, 1=proportional
    unsigned int   sym_set;        // symbol set
    unsigned int   pitch;          // pitch (QD)
    unsigned int   height;         // height (QD)
    unsigned int   xheight;        // x height (QD)
             char  wid_typ;        // width type
    unsigned char  style;          // style
             char  stroke_weight;  // stroke weight
    unsigned char  typeface;       // typeface
             char  resv_3;         // reserved
    unsigned char  serif_style;    // serif style
             int   resv_4;         // reserved
             char  ul_dist;        // underline dist (D)
    unsigned char  ul_height;      // underline height (D)
    unsigned int   txt_height;     // text height (QD)
    unsigned int   txt_width;      // text width  (QD)
             int   resv_5;         // reserved
             int   resv_6;         // reserved
    unsigned char  pitch_ext;      // pitch extended  (D/1024)
    unsigned char  height_ext;     // height extended (D/1024)
             int   resv_7;         // reserved
             int   resv_8;         // reserved
             int   resv_9;         // reserved
             char  font_name[16];  // font name
};

//........ character descriptor data structure
struct char_desc
```

```
{
    unsigned char  format;          // 4 for LaserJet family
             char  continue_flag;   // 0 normally
    unsigned char  desc_size;       // 14 for LaserJet family
    unsigned char  desc_class;      // 1=bitmap, 2=compressed
    unsigned char  orient;          // should match font_dec
             char  resv_1;          // reserved
             int   left_ofs;        // ref pt to bm left (D)
             int   top_ofs;         // ref pt to bm top  (D)
    unsigned int   char_width;      // bitmap width in pixels
    unsigned int   char_height;     // bitmap height in pixels
             int   delta_x;         // ref pt delta (QD)
    //............................... bitmap data follows here
};

//........ HP Soft Font Class
class HpFont : public Font
{
   public:
      int hpstatus;
      HpFont( );
      HpFont( char *path );
     ~HpFont( );
   private:
      void SetFontMetrics( font_desc& fd );
      void SetCharMetrics( Character&, char_desc& fc );
};
#endif
```

■ LISTING 5.13 HPFONT.CPP

```
//   Font implementation for HP Soft Font
#include "stdlib.h"
#include "stdio.h"
#include "ctype.h"
#include "HpFont.Hpp"

#define BUF_SIZ 128
static int cur_ch = 0;
static int hp_stat;

//............................. Skip next n bytes from a file
static int skip_inp( FILE *inp, int nbytes )
{
     int  n;
     char buf[BUF_SIZ];

     while( nbytes > 0 )
     {
        n = nbytes > BUF_SIZ ? BUF_SIZ : nbytes;
        if( fread(buf, n, 1, inp) != 1 )
           return 0;
        nbytes -= n;
     }
```

```
    return 1;
}

//........................ Determine char range from font type
static void char_range( int font_type, int& min_ch, int& max_ch )
{
    switch( font_type )
    {
        case 0 : // 7-bit, 32-127
                 min_ch = 32;
                 max_ch = 127;
                 break;
        case 1 : // 8-bit, 32-127 and 160-255
                 min_ch = 32;
                 max_ch = 255;
                 break;
        default: // 8-bit, everything
                 min_ch = 0;
                 max_ch = 255;
                 break;
    }
}

//................ Determine esq type and its numeric argument
static void get_esq_values( char esq_buf[], int& type, int& parm )
{
    int i;
    char  c1, c2, clast;

    /* extract group char and terminating char */
    c1 = esq_buf[1];
    c2 = esq_buf[2];
    i = 0;
    while( esq_buf[i] ) i++;
    clast = esq_buf[i-1];
    /* determine type */
    if( (c1==')') && (c2=='s') && (clast=='W') )
       type = eFONTDESC;
    else if( (c1=='(') && (c2=='s') && (clast=='W') )
       type = eCHARDESC;
    else if( (c1=='*') && (c2=='c') && (clast=='E') )
       type = eCHARCODE;
    else
       type = eUNKNOWN;
    /* get the sequence's value field */
    parm = 0;
    i    = 0;
    while( (esq_buf[i]) && (! isdigit(esq_buf[i])) ) i++;
    if( isdigit(esq_buf[i]) )
       parm = atoi( esq_buf+i );
}
//................... Read the next esc seq from the font file
static int get_esq( FILE *inp, char esq_buf[], int buf_len )
{
```

```
     int i, nbytes;

     nbytes = 0;
     while( (i=fgetc( inp )) != EOF )
     {
       if( nbytes == buf_len )
       {
          hp_stat = hpOVRFLOW;
          return 0;
       }
       esq_buf[nbytes++] = (char) i;
       // check for end of sequence
       if( isupper( i ) ) break;
     }
     // validity check - first char should be decimal 27
     if( (nbytes > 0) && (esq_buf[0] != 27) )
     {
        hp_stat = hpBADFMT;
        return 0;
     }
     // add a terminating null
     esq_buf[nbytes] = 0;

     return( nbytes );
}

//.................................... set font-related metrics
void HpFont::SetFontMetrics( font_desc& fd )
{
     cell_w  = REV_WRD( fd.cell_width );
     cell_h  = REV_WRD( fd.cell_height );
     ascent  = REV_WRD( fd.bl_dist );
     descent = cell_h - ascent;
     pitch   = REV_WRD( fd.pitch ) >> 2;
}

//.................................... set char-related metrics
void HpFont::SetCharMetrics( Character& c, char_desc& cd )
{
     c.left_ofs = REV_WRD( cd.left_ofs );
     c.top_ofs  = REV_WRD( cd.top_ofs );
     c.width    = REV_WRD( cd.char_width );
     c.height   = REV_WRD( cd.char_height );
     c.rowbytes = (c.width + 7) / 8;
     c.delta_x  = (REV_WRD( cd.delta_x ) + 3) >> 2;
}

//........................ default destructor
HpFont::~HpFont( )
{
}

//........................ instantiate a font from HP Soft Font
HpFont::HpFont( char *path ) : Font( )
```

```
{
     FILE       *inp;
     char        esq_buf[BUF_SIZ];
     font_desc  fd;
     char_desc  cd;
     int         n, esq_type, esq_parm;

     // open file
     if( (inp = fopen( path, "rb" )) == NULL )
     {
        hpstatus = hpNOTFOUND;
        fstatus  = fntFAILED;
        return;
     }
     cur_ch = 0;  // initialize static globals
     hp_stat = hpNOINIT;
     // scan the file and process
     while( (get_esq( inp, esq_buf, BUF_SIZ ) > 0) &&
            (hp_stat == hpNOINIT) )
     {
        // get escape sequence type and its numeric value field
        get_esq_values( esq_buf, esq_type, esq_parm );
        // process the sequence.....
        switch( esq_type )
        {
          case eFONTDESC:  //............... font descriptor
               // read the descriptor
               if( fread( &fd, sizeof(font_desc), 1, inp ) != 1 )
               {
                    hp_stat = hpIOERROR;
                    break;
               }
               // allocate the Character array, init font stuff
               char_range( (int) fd.font_type, min_ch, max_ch );
               ch_cnt = max_ch - min_ch + 1;
               ch = new Character[ch_cnt];
               if( ch == 0 )
               {
                    hp_stat = hpNOMEM;
                    break;
               }
               SetFontMetrics( fd );
               // skip any trailing info
               if( esq_parm > sizeof(font_desc) )
                    skip_inp( inp, esq_parm-sizeof(font_desc) );
               break;
          case eCHARDESC:  //............... char descriptor
               // read the descriptor
               if( fread( &cd, sizeof(char_desc), 1, inp ) != 1 )
               {
                    hp_stat = hpIOERROR;
                    break;
               }
               // is this a char we discard?
```

```
            if( (cur_ch < min_ch) || (cur_ch > max_ch) )
            {
                 skip_inp( inp, esq_parm-sizeof(char_desc) );
                 break;
            }
            // set char table entry
            Character *c = &ch[cur_ch-min_ch];
            SetCharMetrics( *c, cd );
            // allocate this char's bitmap
            int i = c->rowbytes * c->height;
            if( i )
            {
               c->mask = new char[i];
               if( c->mask == 0 )
               {
                  hp_stat = hpNOMEM;
                  break;
               }
            }
            else
               c->mask = 0;
            // get the bitmap which follows
            if( esq_parm > sizeof(char_desc) )
            {
               n = esq_parm - sizeof(char_desc);
               if( fread( c->mask, n, 1, inp ) != 1 )
               {
                  hp_stat = hpIOERROR;
                  break;
               }
            }
            break;
         case eCHARCODE:  //........ specify character code
            // save char code for later use
            cur_ch = esq_parm;
            break;
         case eUNKNOWN:  //........ unknown seq - ignore it
            break;
      }
   }
   fclose( inp );
   // update Font and HpFont status members
   if( hp_stat != hpNOINIT )
   {
      hpstatus = hp_stat;
      fstatus  = fntFAILED;
      return;
   }
   hpstatus = hpOKAY;
   fstatus  = fntOKAY;
   // set width of blank— may not have been a definition
   Character *b = &ch[32-min_ch];
   if( b->delta_x == 0 )
      b->delta_x = pitch;
}
```

■ LISTING 5.14 FONTEST.CPP

```
#include "Fg.H"
#include "HpFont.Hpp"
extern int cdecl getch( void );

int main( )
{
     fg_init();     // init for graphics
     // font_file is path to any valid HP Font File
     char *font_file = "AMER15.HP";
     HpFont hpF( font_file );  // instantiate an instance of HpFont
     char *greeting = "Hello, World"; // something to draw
     // draw it centered on the screen
     int x = ( fg.displaybox[FG_X1] + fg.displaybox[FG_X2]
               - hpF.strwidth( greeting ) ) / 2;
     int y = ( fg.displaybox[FG_Y1] + fg.displaybox[FG_Y2]
               - hpF.strheight( greeting ) ) / 2;
     int clr = fg.nsimulcolor - 1;  // use color white
     // and draw string greeting
     hpF.drawstr( x, y, clr, greeting );
     // wait for a keypress
     getch();
     // terminate graphics mode
     fg_term();
     return 0;
}
```

VGA Split-Screen Animation

■ Michael Abrash

Learn how to use some unique VGA tricks to master graphics animation.

Some folks ease into cold water slowly, one segment of one extremity at a time. Others grit their teeth and jump right in. If you're a novice with either the VGA or animation, this feature is the equivalent of tossing you into cold, deep water headfirst. There's a great deal to understand, and much of it will be skimmed over lightly, at best. However, this feature provides the most important ingredient for learning animation—a working example—and I've provided references at the end that should help you develop a better understanding of animation and the VGA. So grit your teeth and jump in; once you do come to comprehend everything covered here, you'll be well on your way to mastery of VGA animation.

The more experienced VGA programmers among you will have an easier time of it, but I'll warrant you'll find *something* unexpected in here. In particular, I'll discuss the little-appreciated use of the split screen to allow page flipping in high-resolution mode—the *only* way that's possible on a standard VGA.

Many people downgrade the PC as an animation platform. They're wrong; a VGA-equipped 286 or 386 is a good animation platform. Not everything one might wish, perhaps, but more than good enough for most purposes—if properly programmed. Now, programming the VGA well isn't trivial, but don't let anyone tell you it can't be done. It can—but there's only one way to learn how, and that's through experience.

A Brief Animation Primer

Computer animation consists of rapidly redrawing similar images at slightly differing locations, so that the eye interprets the successive images as a single object in motion over time. The fact that the world is an analog realm and the images displayed on a computer screen consist of discrete pixels updated at a maximum rate of about 70 Hz is irrelevant; your eye can interpret both real-world images and pixel patterns on the screen as objects in motion, and that's that.

One of the key problems of computer animation is that it takes time to redraw a screen, time during which the bitmap controlling the screen is in an intermediate state, with, quite possibly, many objects erased and others half-drawn. Even a briefly displayed partially updated screen can cause flicker at best, and can destroy the illusion of motion at worst.

Another problem of animation is that the screen must update often enough so that motion appears continuous. A moving object that moves just once every second, shifting by hundreds of pixels each time it does move, will appear to jump, not to move smoothly. Therefore, there are two overriding requirements for smooth animation: The bitmap must be updated quickly (once per frame—60 to 70 Hz—is ideal, although 30 Hz will do fine), and the process of redrawing the screen must be invisible to the user; only the end result should be seen. Both of these requirements are met by Listing 5.15 and ANIMATE2.ASM (see listings diskette).

A Sample Animation Program

Listings 5.15 and ANIMATE2.ASM together form a sample animation program, in which a single object bounces endlessly off other objects, with instructions and a count of bounces displayed at the bottom of the screen. These are too complex and involve too much VGA and animation knowledge for it to be possible for me to discuss the listings in exhaustive detail; instead, I'll cover the major elements in as much depth as possible, and leave it to you to explore the finer points—and, I hope, to experiment with and expand on the code.

Listing 5.15 is written in C. It could also have been written in assembly language, and would then have been somewhat faster. However, I wanted to make the point that assembly language, and, indeed, optimization in general, is needed only in the most critical portions of any program, and then only when the program would otherwise be too slow. Only in a highly performance-sensitive situation would the performance boost resulting from converting Listing 5.15 to assembly justify the time spent in coding and in fixing the bugs that would likely creep in. The sample program updates the screen at the maximum possible rate of once per frame even on an 8-MHz AT. In this case, faster performance would result only in a longer wait for the page to flip.

Write Mode 3

It's possible to update the bitmap very efficiently on the VGA, because the VGA can draw up to 8 pixels at once, and because the VGA provides a number of hardware features to speed up drawing. This feature makes considerable use of one particularly unusual hardware feature, write mode 3, which is like nothing you've ever seen.

Some background: In the VGA's high-resolution mode, mode 12H (640x480 with 16 colors, the mode in which the sample program runs), each byte of display memory controls eight adjacent pixels on the screen. (The color of each pixel is, in turn, controlled by four bits spread across four memory planes, but we need not concern ourselves with that here.) Now, there will often be times when we want to change some but not all of the pixels controlled by a particular byte of display memory. This is not easily done, for there is no way to write half a byte, or two bits, or such to memory; it's the whole byte or none of it at all.

You might think that using AND and OR to manipulate individual bits could solve the problem. Alas, not so. ANDing and ORing would work if the VGA had only one plane of memory, like a Hercules Graphics Adapter; but the VGA has four planes, and ANDing and ORing would work only if we selected and manipulated each plane separately, a process that would be hideously slow. No, with the VGA you must use the hardware assist features, or you might as well forget about real-time screen updates altogether. There is an amazing variety of ways to use the VGA's hardware, and I heartily recommend that you check out the references at the end of this article for a spectrum of VGA programming techniques; I can't discuss *everything* about the VGA in one feature, though, and write mode 3 will meet most of our needs.

Write mode 3 is useful when you want to set some but not all of the pixels in a single byte of display memory *to the same color*. That is, if you want to draw a number of pixels within a byte in a single color, write mode 3 is a good way to do it.

Write mode 3 works like this. First, set the Graphics Controller Mode register to write mode 3. (See ANIMATE2.ASM for code that does everything described here.) Next, set the Set/Reset register to the color with which you wish to draw, in the range 0–15. (It is not necessary to explicitly enable set/reset via the Enable Set/Reset register; write mode 3 does that automatically.) Then, to draw individual pixels within a single byte, simply read display memory (the data read doesn't matter; the read latches all four planes' data, a concept that I lack the space to explain here; see the references), and then write a byte to display memory with 1-bits where you want the color to be drawn and 0-bits where you want the current bitmap settings to be preserved. So, for example, if write mode 3 is enabled and the Set/Reset register is set to 1 (blue), then the following

```
mov dx,0a000h
mov es,dx
mov al,es:[0]
mov es:[0],0f0h
```

will change the first four pixels on the screen (the left nibble of the byte at offset 0 in display memory) to blue, and will leave the next four pixels (the right nibble of the byte at offset 0) unchanged.

Using one **MOV** to read from display memory and another to write to display memory is not particularly efficient. In Listing ANIMATE2.ASM (see listings diskette), I instead use **XCHG**, which reads and then writes a memory location in a single operation, as in

```
mov dx,0a000h
mov es,dx
mov al,0f0h
xchg   es:[0],al
```

Again, the actual value that's read is irrelevant. In general, the **XCHG** approach is faster and more compact than two **MOV**s.

If all pixels in a byte of display memory are to be drawn in a single color, it's not necessary to read before writing, because none of the information in display memory at that byte needs to be preserved; a simple write of 0FFH (to draw all bits) will set all eight pixels to the set/reset color:

```
mov dx,0a000h
mov es,dx
mov es:[di],0ffh
```

If you're familiar with VGA programming, you're no doubt aware that everything that can be done with write mode 3 can also be accomplished in write mode 0 or write mode 2 by using the Bit Mask register. However, setting the Bit Mask register requires at least one **OUT** per byte written, in addition to the read and write of display memory, and **OUT**s are often slower than display memory accesses, especially on 386s and 486s. One of the great virtues of write mode 3 is that it requires virtually no **OUT**s and is therefore substantially faster.

In short, write mode 3 is a good choice for single-color drawing that modifies individual pixels within display memory bytes. Not coincidentally, the sample application draws only single-color objects within the animation area; this allows write mode 3 to be used for all drawing, in keeping with our desire for speedy screen updates.

Drawing Text

We'll need text in the sample application; is that also a good use for write mode 3? Sometimes it is, but not in this case.

Each character in a font is represented by a pattern of bits, with 1-bits representing character pixels and 0-bits representing background pixels. Since we'll be using the 8x8 font stored in the BIOS ROM (a pointer to which can be obtained by calling a BIOS service, as illustrated by ANIMATE2.ASM), each character is exactly 8 bits, or 1 byte wide. We'll further insist that characters be placed on byte boundaries (that is, with their left edges only at pixels with X coordinates that are multiples of 8); this means that the character bytes in the font are automatically aligned with display memory, and no rotation or clipping of characters is needed. Finally, we'll draw all text in white.

Given the above assumptions, drawing text is easy; we simply copy each byte of each character to the appropriate location in display memory, and *voila*, we're done. Text copying is done in write mode 0, in which the byte written to display memory is copied to all four planes at once; hence, 1-bits turn into white (color value 0FH, with 1-bits in all four planes), and 0-bits turn into black (color value 0). This is faster than using write mode 3 because write mode 3 requires a read/write of display memory, while the write mode 0 approach requires only a write to display memory.

Is write mode 0 always the best way to do text? Not at all. The write mode 0 approach described above draws both foreground and background pixels within the character box, forcing the background pixels to black at the same time that it forces the foreground pixels to white. If you want to draw transparent text (that is, draw only the character pixels, not the surrounding background box), write mode 3 is ideal. Also, matters get far more complicated if characters that aren't eight pixels wide are drawn, or if characters are drawn starting at arbitrary pixel locations, without the multiple-of-8 column restriction, so that rotation and masking are required. Last, the Map Mask register can be used to draw text in colors other than white—but only if the background is black. Otherwise, the data remaining in the planes protected by the Map Mask will remain and can interfere with the colors of the text being drawn.

I'm not going to delve any deeper into the considerable issues of drawing VGA text; I just want to sensitize you to the existence of approaches other than the ones used in Listing 5.15. On the VGA, the rule is: If there's something you want to do, there probably are ten ways to do it, each with unique strengths and weaknesses. Your mission, should you decide to accept it, is to figure out which one is best for your particular use.

Page Flipping

Now that we're VGA experts and know how to update the screen reasonably quickly, it's time to get on to the fun stuff. Page flipping answers the second requirement for animation by keeping bitmap changes off the screen until they're complete. In other words, page flipping guarantees that partially updated bitmaps are never seen.

How is it possible to update a bitmap without seeing the changes as they're made? Easy—with page flipping, there are *two* bitmaps; the program shows you one bitmap while it updates the other. Conceptually, it's that simple. In practice, unfortunately, it's not so simple, because of the design of the VGA. To understand why that is, we must look at how the VGA turns bytes in display memory into pixels on the screen.

The VGA bitmap is a linear 64KB block of memory. Normally, the VGA picks up the first byte of memory (the byte at offset 0) and displays the corresponding eight pixels on the screen, then picks up the byte at offset 1 and displays the next eight pixels, and so on to the end of the screen. However, the offset of the first byte of display memory picked up during each frame is not fixed at 0. Rather, it is programmable by way of the Start Address High and Low registers, which together store the 16-bit offset in display memory where the bitmap to be displayed during the next frame starts. So, for example, in mode 10H (640x350, 16 colors), a large enough bitmap to store a complete screen of information can be stored at display memory offsets 0 through 27,999; and *another* full bitmap could be stored at offsets 28,000 through 55,999, as shown in Figure 5.7. (I'm discussing 640x350 mode for the moment for good reason; we'll get to 640x480 shortly.) When the Start Address registers are set to 0, the first bitmap (or page) is displayed; when they are set to 28,000, the

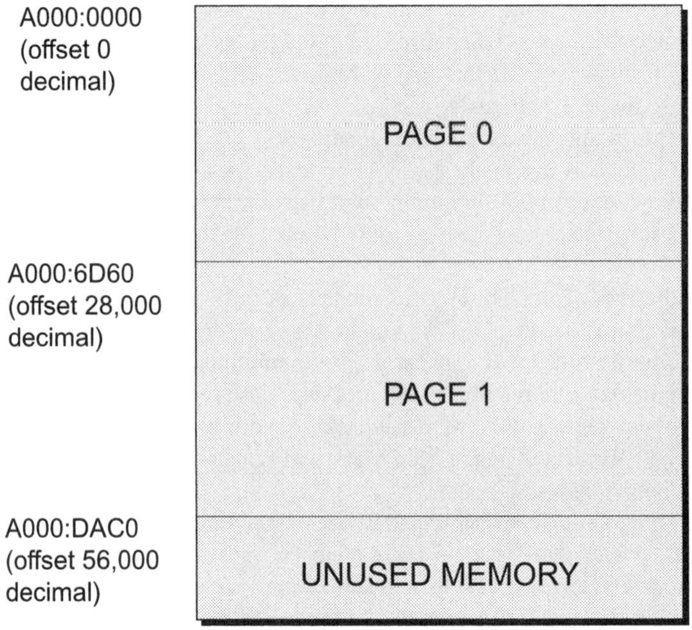

■ **FIGURE 5.7 Display memory for Mode 10H**

second bitmap is displayed. Page-flipped animation can be performed by displaying page 0 and drawing to page 1, then setting the start address to page 1 to display that page and drawing to page 0, and so on *ad infinitum.*

There's a hitch, though, and that hitch is knowing exactly when it is that the page has flipped. The page doesn't flip the instant that you set the Start Address registers. The VGA loads the starting offset from the Start Address registers once before starting each frame, then ignores those registers until the next frame comes around. This means that you can set the Start Address registers whenever you want—but the page actually being displayed doesn't change until after the VGA loads that new offset in preparation for the next frame.

The potential problem should be obvious. Suppose that page 1 is being displayed, and you're updating page 0. You finish drawing to page 0, set the Start Address registers to 0 to switch to displaying page 0, and start updating page 1, which is no longer displayed. Or is it? If the VGA was in the middle of the current frame, displaying page 1, when you set the Start Address registers, then page 1 is going to be displayed for the rest of the frame, no matter what you do with the Start Address registers. If you start updating page 1 right away, any changes you make may well show up on the screen, because page 0 hasn't yet flipped to being displayed in place of page 1—and that defeats the whole purpose of page flipping.

To avoid this problem, it is mandatory that you wait until you're sure the page has flipped. The Start Address registers are, according to my tests, loaded at the start of the Vertical Sync signal, and although that may not be the case with all clones, it is true of all the VGAs I've tested. The Vertical Sync status is provided as bit 3 of the Input Status 1 register, so it would seem that all you need to do to flip a page is set the new Start Address registers, wait for the start of the Vertical Sync pulse that indicates the page has flipped, and be on your merry way.

Almost—but not quite. (Do I hear teeth gnashing in the background?) The problem is this: Suppose that, by coincidence, you set one of the Start Address registers just before the start of Vertical Sync, and the other right after the start of Vertical Sync. Why, then, for one frame the Start Address High value for one page would be mixed with the Start Address Low value for the other page, and, depending on the start address values, the whole screen could appear to shift any number of pixels for a single, horrible frame. *This must never happen!* The solution is to set the Start Address registers when you're certain Vertical Sync is not about to start. The easiest way to know that is to check for the Display Enable status (bit 0 of the Input Status 1 register) being active; that means that bitmap-controlled pixels are being scanned onto the screen, and, since Vertical Sync happens in the middle of the vertical nondisplay portion of the frame, Vertical Sync can never be anywhere nearby if Display Enable is active.

So, to flip pages, you must complete all drawing to the nondisplayed page, wait for Display Enable to be active, set the new start address, and wait for Vertical Sync to be active. At that point, you can be fully confident that the page you just flipped off the screen is not displayed and can safely (invisibly) be updated. A side benefit of page flipping is that your program will automatically have a constant time base, with the rate at which new screens are drawn synchronized to the frame rate of the display (typically 60 or 70 Hz). However, complex updates may take more than one frame to complete, especially on slower processors; this can be compensated for by maintaining a count of new screens drawn and cross-referencing that to the BIOS timer count periodically, accelerating the overall pace of the animation (moving farther each time and the like) if updates are happening too slowly.

The Split Screen

So far, I've discussed page flipping in 640x350 mode. There's a reason for that; 640x350 is the highest-resolution standard mode in which there's enough display memory for two full pages on a standard VGA. It's possible to program the VGA to a nonstandard 640x400 mode and still have two full pages, but that's pretty much the limit. One 640x480 page takes 38,400 bytes of display memory, and clearly there isn't enough room in 64KB of display memory for two of *those* monster pages.

And yet, 640x480 is a wonderful mode in many ways. It offers a 1:1 aspect ratio (square pixels), and it provides by far the best resolution of any 16-color mode. Surely there's *some* way to bring the visual appeal of page flipping to this mode?

Sure there is—but it's an odd solution indeed. The VGA has a feature, known as the split screen, that allows you to force the offset from which the VGA fetches video data back to 0 after any desired scan line. For example, you can program the VGA to scan through display memory as usual until it finishes scan line number 338, and then get the first byte of information for scan line number 339 from offset 0 in display memory.

That, in turn, allows us to divvy up display memory into three areas, as shown in Figure 5.8. The area from 0 to 11,279 is reserved for the split screen, the area from 11,280 to 38,399 is used for page 0, and the area from 38,400 to 65,519 is used for page 1. This

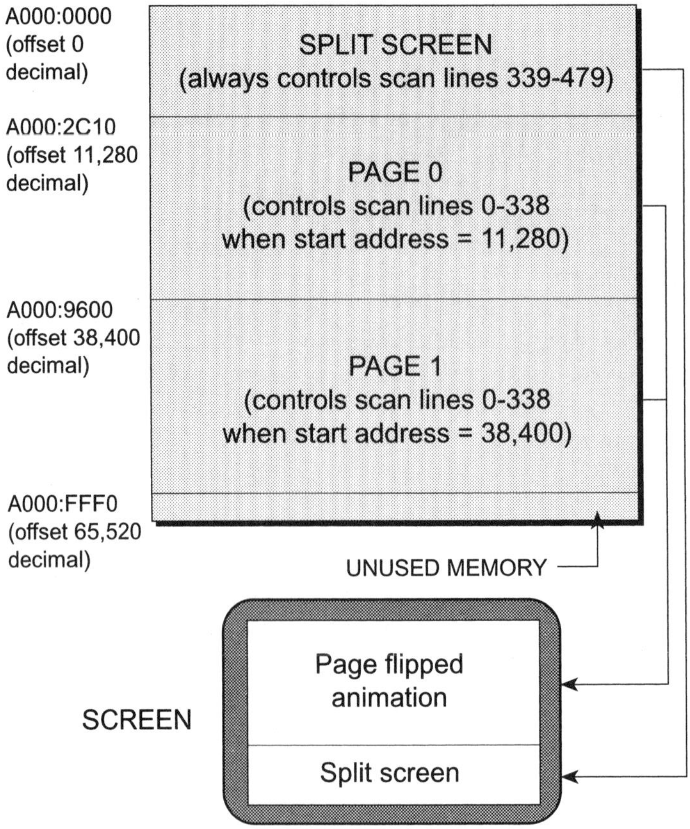

■ **FIGURE 5.8 Three areas of display memory**

allows page flipping to be performed in the top 339 scan lines (about 70%) of the screen, and leaves the bottom 141 scan lines free for nonanimation purposes, such as showing scores, instructions, statuses, and so on. (Note that the allocation of display memory and number of scan lines are dictated by the desire to have as many page-flipped scan lines as possible; you may, if you wish, have fewer page-flipped lines and reserve part of the bitmap for other uses, such as off-screen storage for images.)

The sample program uses the split screen and page flipping exactly as described above. The playfield through which the object bounces is the page-flipped portion of the screen, and the rectangle at the bottom containing the bounce count and the instructions is the split screen. Of course, to the user it all looks like one screen.

Very few animation applications use the entire screen for animation. If you can get by with 339 scan lines of animation, split-screen page flipping gives you the best combination of square pixels and high resolution possible on a standard VGA.

Taking the Jump

Is VGA animation worth all the fuss? *Mais oui*. Run the sample program; if you've never seen VGA animation before, you'll be amazed at how smooth it can be. Check out Listings 5.15 and ANIMATE2.ASM, read through the references, and write some code of your own. And, if you get frustrated, just run to the nearest cold lake or pool and jump right in. Like animation, it will feel great—once you get used to the water.

References

Abrash, Michael. *Power Graphics Programming*. Que, 1989.

Wilton, Richard. *Programmer's Guide to PC & PS/2 Video Systems*. Microsoft Press, 1987.

CODE DESCRIPTION

Overview

The listings provided are used to create fast PC graphics animation by using page-flipping techniques.

Listings Available

Listing	*Description*	*Used with*
ANIMATE1.C	C source file that demonstrates animation by using page-flipping in the top portion of the screen while displaying nonpage-flipped information in the split screen at the bottom of the screen.	------
ANIMATE2.ASM	ASM source file that contains the low-level animation routines (see listings diskette).	------

How to Compile/Assemble

Compile ANIMATE1.C with Borland C++ and assemble ANIMATE2.ASM with TASM.

■ LISTING 5.15 ANIMATE1.C

```
/* Split screen VGA animation program. Performs page flipping in the
top portion of the screen while displaying nonpage-flipped
information in the split screen at the bottom of the screen.
Compiled with Borland C++ in C compilation mode. */

#include <stdio.h>
#include <conio.h>
#include <dos.h>
#include <math.h>

#define SCREEN_SEG          0xA000
#define SCREEN_PIXWIDTH     640    /* in pixels */
#define SCREEN_WIDTH        80     /* in bytes */
```

```
#define SPLIT_START_LINE   339
#define SPLIT_LINES        141
#define NONSPLIT_LINES     339
#define SPLIT_START_OFFSET 0
#define PAGE0_START_OFFSET (SPLIT_LINES*SCREEN_WIDTH)
#define PAGE1_START_OFFSET ((SPLIT_LINES+NONSPLIT_LINES)*SCREEN_WIDTH)
#define CRTC_INDEX   0x3D4 /* CRT Controller Index register */
#define CRTC_DATA    0x3D5 /* CRT Controller Data register */
#define OVERFLOW     0x07  /* index of CRTC reg holding bit 8 of the
                              line the split screen starts after */
#define MAX_SCAN     0x09  /* index of CRTC reg holding bit 9 of the
                              line the split screen starts after */
#define LINE_COMPARE 0x18  /* index of CRTC reg holding lower 8 bits
                              of line split screen starts after */
#define NUM_BUMPERS  (sizeof(Bumpers)/sizeof(bumper))
#define BOUNCER_COLOR 15
#define BACK_COLOR   1     /* playfield background color */

typedef struct {  /* one solid bumper to be bounced off of */
   int LeftX,TopY,RightX,BottomY;
   int Color;
} bumper;

typedef struct {      /* one bit pattern to be used for drawing */
   int WidthInBytes;
   int Height;
   unsigned char *BitPattern;
} image;

typedef struct {  /* one bouncing object to move around the screen */
   int LeftX,TopY;         /* location */
   int Width,Height;       /* size in pixels */
   int DirX,DirY;          /* motion vectors */
   int CurrentX[2],CurrentY[2]; /* current location in each page */
   int Color;              /* color in which to be drawn */
   image *Rotation0;       /* rotations for handling the 8 possible */
   image *Rotation1;       /* intrabyte start address at which the */
   image *Rotation2;       /* left edge can be */
   image *Rotation3;
   image *Rotation4;
   image *Rotation5;
   image *Rotation6;
   image *Rotation7;
} bouncer;

void main(void);
void DrawBumperList(bumper *, int, unsigned int);
void DrawSplitScreen(void);
void EnableSplitScreen(void);
void MoveBouncer(bouncer *, bumper *, int);
extern void DrawRect(int,int,int,int,int,unsigned int,unsigned int);
extern void ShowPage(unsigned int);
extern void DrawImage(int,int,image **,int,unsigned int,
              unsigned int);
```

```
extern void ShowBounceCount(void);
extern void TextUp(char *,int,int,unsigned int,unsigned int);
extern void SetBIOS8x8Font(void);

bumper Bumpers[] = {/* All bumpers in the playfield */
   {0,0,19,339,2}, {0,0,639,19,2}, {620,0,639,339,2},
   {0,320,639,339,2}, {60,48,79,67,12}, {60,108,79,127,12},
   {60,168,79,187,12}, {60,228,79,247,12}, {120,68,131,131,13},
   {120,188,131,271,13}, {240,128,259,147,14}, {240,192,259,211,14},
   {208,160,227,179,14}, {272,160,291,179,14}, {228,272,231,319,11},
   {192,52,211,55,11}, {302,80,351,99,12}, {320,260,379,267,13},
   {380,120,387,267,13}, {420,60,579,63,11}, {428,110,571,113,11},
   {420,160,579,163,11}, {428,210,571,213,11}, {420,260,579,263,11} };

/* Image for bouncing object when left edge is aligned with bit 7 */
unsigned char _BouncerRotation0[] = {
   0xFF,0x0F,0xF0, 0xFE,0x07,0xF0, 0xFC,0x03,0xF0, 0xFC,0x03,0xF0,
   0xFE,0x07,0xF0, 0xFF,0xFF,0xF0, 0xCF,0xFF,0x30, 0x87,0xFE,0x10,
   0x07,0x0E,0x00, 0x07,0x0E,0x00, 0x07,0x0E,0x00, 0x07,0x0E,0x00,
   0x87,0xFE,0x10, 0xCF,0xFF,0x30, 0xFF,0xFF,0xF0, 0xFE,0x07,0xF0,
   0xFC,0x03,0xF0, 0xFC,0x03,0xF0, 0xFE,0x07,0xF0, 0xFF,0x0F,0xF0};
image BouncerRotation0 = {3, 20, _BouncerRotation0};

/* Image for bouncing object when left edge is aligned with bit 3 */
unsigned char _BouncerRotation4[] = {
   0x0F,0xF0,0xFF, 0x0F,0xE0,0x7F, 0x0F,0xC0,0x3F, 0x0F,0xC0,0x3F,
   0x0F,0xE0,0x7F, 0x0F,0xFF,0xFF, 0x0C,0xFF,0xF3, 0x08,0x7F,0xE1,
   0x00,0x70,0xE0, 0x00,0x70,0xE0, 0x00,0x70,0xE0, 0x00,0x70,0xE0,
   0x08,0x7F,0xE1, 0x0C,0xFF,0xF3, 0x0F,0xFF,0xFF, 0x0F,0xE0,0x7F,
   0x0F,0xC0,0x3F, 0x0F,0xC0,0x3F, 0x0F,0xE0,0x7F, 0x0F,0xF0,0xFF};
image BouncerRotation4 = {3, 20, _BouncerRotation4};

/* Initial settings for bouncing object. Only 2 rotations are needed
   because the object moves 4 pixels horizontally at a time */
bouncer Bouncer = {156,60,20,20,4,4,156,156,60,60,BOUNCER_COLOR,
   &BouncerRotation0,NULL,NULL,NULL,&BouncerRotation4,NULL,NULL,NULL};
unsigned int PageStartOffsets[2] =
   {PAGE0_START_OFFSET,PAGE1_START_OFFSET};
unsigned int BounceCount;

void main() {
   int DisplayedPage, NonDisplayedPage, Done, i;
   union REGS regset;

   regset.x.ax = 0x0012; /* set display to 640x480 16-color mode */
   int86(0x10, &regset, &regset);
   SetBIOS8x8Font();    /* set the pointer to the BIOS 8x8 font */
   EnableSplitScreen(); /* turn on the split screen */
   /* Display page 0 above the split screen */
   ShowPage(PageStartOffsets[DisplayedPage = 0]);
  /* Clear both pages to background and draw bumpers in each page */
   for (i=0; i<2; i++) {
      DrawRect(0,0,SCREEN_PIXWIDTH-1,NONSPLIT_LINES-1,BACK_COLOR,
            PageStartOffsets[i],SCREEN_SEG);
```

```
      DrawBumperList(Bumpers,NUM_BUMPERS,PageStartOffsets[i]);
   }
   DrawSplitScreen();   /* draw the static split screen info */
   BounceCount = 0;
   ShowBounceCount();   /* put up the initial zero count */
   /* Draw the bouncing object at its initial location */
   DrawImage(Bouncer.LeftX,Bouncer.TopY,&Bouncer.Rotation0,
         Bouncer.Color,PageStartOffsets[DisplayedPage],SCREEN_SEG);
   /* Move the object, draw it in the nondisplayed page, and flip the page until
Esc is pressed */
   Done = 0;
   do {
      NonDisplayedPage = DisplayedPage ^ 1;
      /* Erase at current location in the nondisplayed page */
      DrawRect(Bouncer.CurrentX[NonDisplayedPage],
            Bouncer.CurrentY[NonDisplayedPage],
            Bouncer.CurrentX[NonDisplayedPage]+Bouncer.Width-1,
            Bouncer.CurrentY[NonDisplayedPage]+Bouncer.Height-1,
               BACK_COLOR,PageStartOffsets[NonDisplayedPage],SCREEN_SEG);
      /* Move the bouncer */
      MoveBouncer(&Bouncer, Bumpers, NUM_BUMPERS);
      /* Draw at the new location in the nondisplayed page */
      DrawImage(Bouncer.LeftX,Bouncer.TopY,&Bouncer.Rotation0,
            Bouncer.Color,PageStartOffsets[NonDisplayedPage],
            SCREEN_SEG);
      /* Remember where the bouncer is in the nondisplayed page */
      Bouncer.CurrentX[NonDisplayedPage] = Bouncer.LeftX;
      Bouncer.CurrentY[NonDisplayedPage] = Bouncer.TopY;
      /* Flip to the page we just drew into */
      ShowPage(PageStartOffsets[DisplayedPage = NonDisplayedPage]);
      /* Respond to any keystroke */
      if (kbhit()) {
         switch (getch()) {
            case 0x1B:           /* Esc to end */
               Done = 1; break;
            case 0:              /* branch on the extended code */
               switch (getch()) {
                  case 0x48:  /* nudge up */
                     Bouncer.DirY = -abs(Bouncer.DirY); break;
                  case 0x4B:  /* nudge left */
                     Bouncer.DirX = -abs(Bouncer.DirX); break;
                  case 0x4D:  /* nudge right */
                     Bouncer.DirX = abs(Bouncer.DirX); break;
                  case 0x50:  /* nudge down */
                     Bouncer.DirY = abs(Bouncer.DirY); break;
               }
               break;
            default:
               break;
         }
      }
   } while (!Done);
   /* Restore text mode and done */
   regset.x.ax = 0x0003;
```

```
   int86(0x10, &regset, &regset);
}

/* Draws the specified list of bumpers into the specified page */
void DrawBumperList(bumper * Bumpers, int NumBumpers,
      unsigned int PageStartOffset)
{
   int i;

   for (i=0; i<NumBumpers; i++,Bumpers++) {
      DrawRect(Bumpers->LeftX,Bumpers->TopY,Bumpers->RightX,
      Bumpers->BottomY,Bumpers->Color,PageStartOffset,SCREEN_SEG);
   }
}

/* Displays the current bounce count */
void ShowBounceCount() {
   char CountASCII[7];

   itoa(BounceCount,CountASCII,10); /* convert the count to ASCII */
   TextUp(CountASCII,344,64,SPLIT_START_OFFSET,SCREEN_SEG);
}

/* Frames the split screen and fills it with various text */
void DrawSplitScreen() {
   DrawRect(0,0,SCREEN_PIXWIDTH-1,SPLIT_LINES-1,0,
         SPLIT_START_OFFSET,SCREEN_SEG);
   DrawRect(0,1,SCREEN_PIXWIDTH-1,4,15,SPLIT_START_OFFSET,
         SCREEN_SEG);
   DrawRect(0,SPLIT_LINES-4,SCREEN_PIXWIDTH-1,SPLIT_LINES-1,15,
         SPLIT_START_OFFSET,SCREEN_SEG);
   DrawRect(0,1,3,SPLIT_LINES-1,15,SPLIT_START_OFFSET,SCREEN_SEG);
   DrawRect(SCREEN_PIXWIDTH-4,1,SCREEN_PIXWIDTH-1,SPLIT_LINES-1,15,
         SPLIT_START_OFFSET,SCREEN_SEG);
   TextUp("This is the split screen area...",8,8,SPLIT_START_OFFSET,
         SCREEN_SEG);
   TextUp("Bounces: ",272,64,SPLIT_START_OFFSET,SCREEN_SEG);
   TextUp("\033: nudge left",520,78,SPLIT_START_OFFSET,SCREEN_SEG);
   TextUp("\032: nudge right",520,90,SPLIT_START_OFFSET,SCREEN_SEG);
   TextUp("\031: nudge down",520,102,SPLIT_START_OFFSET,SCREEN_SEG);
   TextUp("\030: nudge up",520,114,SPLIT_START_OFFSET,SCREEN_SEG);
   TextUp("Esc to end",520,126,SPLIT_START_OFFSET,SCREEN_SEG);
}

/* Turn on the split screen at the desired line (minus 1 because the
   split screen starts *after* the line specified by theLINE_
   COMPARE register) (bit 8 of the split screen start line is stored
   in the Overflow register, and bit 9 is in the Maximum Scan Line reg) */
   void EnableSplitScreen() {
   outp(CRTC_INDEX, LINE_COMPARE);
   outp(CRTC_DATA, (SPLIT_START_LINE - 1) & 0xFF);
   outp(CRTC_INDEX, OVERFLOW);
   outp(CRTC_DATA, (((((SPLIT_START_LINE - 1) & 0x100) >> 8) << 4) |
         (inp(CRTC_DATA) & ~0x10)));
```

```
   outp(CRTC_INDEX, MAX_SCAN);
   outp(CRTC_DATA, (((((SPLIT_START_LINE - 1) & 0x200) >> 9) << 6) |
         (inp(CRTC_DATA) & ~0x40)));
}

/* Moves the bouncer, bouncing if bumpers are hit */
void MoveBouncer(bouncer *Bouncer, bumper *BumperPtr, int NumBumpers) {
   int NewLeftX, NewTopY, NewRightX, NewBottomY, i;

   /* Move to new location, bouncing if necessary */
   NewLeftX = Bouncer->LeftX + Bouncer->DirX;   /* new coords */
   NewTopY = Bouncer->TopY + Bouncer->DirY;
   NewRightX = NewLeftX + Bouncer->Width - 1;
   NewBottomY = NewTopY + Bouncer->Height - 1;
   /* Compare new location to all bumpers, checking for bounce */
   for (i=0; i<NumBumpers; i++,BumperPtr++) {
      /* If moving puts the bouncer inside this bumper, bounce */
      if (  (NewLeftX <= BumperPtr->RightX) &&
            (NewRightX >= BumperPtr->LeftX) &&
            (NewTopY <= BumperPtr->BottomY) &&
            (NewBottomY >= BumperPtr->TopY) ) {
         /* The bouncer has tried to move into this bumper; figure
            out which edge(s) it crossed, and bounce accordingly */
         if (((Bouncer->LeftX > BumperPtr->RightX) &&
               (NewLeftX <= BumperPtr->RightX)) ||
               (((Bouncer->LeftX + Bouncer->Width - 1) <
               BumperPtr->LeftX) &&
               (NewRightX >= BumperPtr->LeftX))) {
          Bouncer->DirX = -Bouncer->DirX;  /* bounce horizontally */
          NewLeftX = Bouncer->LeftX + Bouncer->DirX;
         }
         if (((Bouncer->TopY > BumperPtr->BottomY) &&
               (NewTopY <= BumperPtr->BottomY)) ||
               (((Bouncer->TopY + Bouncer->Height - 1) <
               BumperPtr->TopY) &&
               (NewBottomY >= BumperPtr->TopY))) {
            Bouncer->DirY = -Bouncer->DirY; /* bounce vertically */
            NewTopY = Bouncer->TopY + Bouncer->DirY;
         }
         /* Update the bounce count display; turn over at 10000 */
         if (++BounceCount >= 10000) {
            TextUp("0    ",344,64,SPLIT_START_OFFSET,SCREEN_SEG);
            BounceCount = 0;
         } else {
            ShowBounceCount();
         }
      }
   }
   Bouncer->LeftX = NewLeftX; /* set the final new coordinates */
   Bouncer->TopY = NewTopY;
}
```

Hardcopy Dithering

■ Marv Luse

Learn how to use dithering techniques to simulate color effects on black and white printers.

Dithering is a graphics rendering technique that uses a matrix of printer dots or video pixels to represent a single image pixel. With dithering, an output device—the printer or video display—can simulate gray levels or colors that it cannot directly reproduce. Dithering is a classic example of "robbing Peter to pay Paul." That is, it "robs" image space to "pay" intensity or color in the reproduction.

Graphics programs like Windows Paintbrush use dithering to render multicolor or gray scale images on standard "bi-level" devices such as dot matrix and laser printers. While the printers themselves can only produce black dots on white paper, a dithered graphics image will appear to have different shades of gray, with each gray level corresponding to a color or gray level in the original image. Since dithering is a general technique, it is equally suited to rendering 256-color images on an eight-color printer, or displaying exotic colors on a video monitor with a limited color palette.

Besides being useful, dithering is an interesting subject. Many of its principles derive from fields far removed from computer programming: the science of light, the physiological characteristics of the human eye, and the brain's response to visual input. The programming of effective dithering techniques requires an appreciation for these factors.

Black on Black

The typical PC configuration with a color monitor and dot matrix (or laser) printer is the classic setting for dithering. The monitor can display many color and intensity combinations, typically 16 or 256. The lowly printer can display just two: a black dot or nothing (a "white" dot). If you attempt to copy the monitor's screen image to the printer, a pixel-for-pixel rendering of yellow text on a blue background will give you black text on a black background; not a particularly useful result. Dithering the same image would produce light gray text on a dark gray background, and while not in living color, it would at least be readable.

In the simplest dithering implementation, we replace each pixel in the color image by a square *cell* of dots in the printed image. We can use cells having four or 16 dots by selecting square cells with two or four dots per side. By controlling how many dots in a cell actually print, we create the illusion of large pixels of varying intensity. (While it might appear that the printed image must then be four or 16 times the size of the source image, this is not actually the case, as we shall see.)

The Eye of the Beholder

The human eye is an optical sensor and has a known set of response characteristics. For instance, the eye cannot generally perceive objects to a resolution below about 1 minute of arc. At a distance of 10 inches, a typical viewing distance, this corresponds to an object of about 0.003 inches in width—about the size of the dots printed by a 300 dpi laser printer.

But, even before this resolution limit is reached, the human brain performs spatial integration on complex imagery. The brain averages the intensity values in small areas to reduce an image's complexity and resolution. It is this mechanism that allows dithering to work. Thus, the five dithering cells illustrated in Figure 5.9, when reproduced at a sufficiently small scale, would be perceived as dots of differing intensity.

The eye's response to intensities is logarithmic, not linear. Pairs of light sources will appear to differ by the same intensity as long as their intensity *ratios* are the same. For example, in the typical three-way light bulb, with ratings of 50, 100, and 150 watts, the 150-watt setting may not appear to be much of an improvement over the 100-watt setting. To create uniform intensity steps between settings, the bulb would need ratings of 50, 100, and 200 watts. These ratings give the same intensity ratio of 2 (100/50 and 200/100) between settings.

Another important characteristic of the eye is its sensitivity to intensity changes; that is, the smallest intensity change that it can detect. This is an important consideration in producing what is known as a continuous-tone image, such as that found in the typical photograph. In such an image, discrete intensity changes are below the level detectable by the human eye, and the image appears to contain a continuous intensity spectrum.

The smallest detectable intensity ratio to the human eye is about 1.01. Using logarithms based on this number, the image's intensity range determines how many gray levels are required to produce an optimum rendition of the image. Thus, if we are dealing with an intensity range of I0 to I1 then the required number of levels would be

$$n = \log_{1.01} (I1/I0).$$

The ratio I1/I0 is the image's *dynamic range*. Typical values for printed materials are in the range 10–100, giving values for *n* of roughly 250–450. Note that this indicates that a 256-level image can be printed with good results on some media, but not so well on others. A representative example of low dynamic range media is a black and white newspaper photograph.

Halftone Approximation

In the case of achromatic, or gray-scale images, *intensity* is the only property we need to consider with respect to its rendition. The dithering of such images is referred to as *halftoning*. (Note that a color image has other properties associated with it, such as the hue and saturation values of its colors. These properties require consideration of the eye's response to light wavelength, among other factors.)

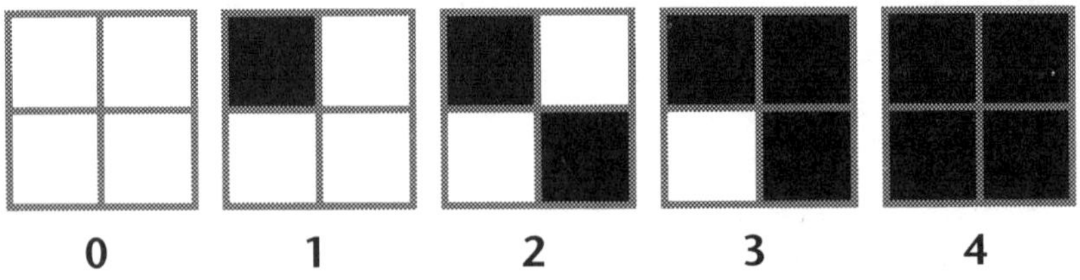

■ **FIGURE 5.9 Example of a five-level 2x2 dither set**

We now turn to the actual construction of halftone patterns, or dither cells. When doing so, we need to keep a number of basic principles in mind. First, photographic reproduction is generally best if cells approximate solid dots of varying radii. This technique is referred to as a *clustered-dot order* dither.

Second, it is best if the progression from one cell to the next is additive in nature. This means that if cell **N** has more dots than cell **M**, then cell **N** should contain all the dots in cell **M**. To put it another way, if a given dot is set in cell **M**, then all cells occurring *after* **M** will have that dot set too.

A third consideration is that dither patterns should be constructed so that they do not introduce visual artifacts into an image. For instance, a square dither cell with all dots on a diagonal set would, when replicated in adjacent positions, create a hatching pattern in a dithered image. These various considerations are illustrated graphically in Figure 5.10.

Dither Matrices

The easiest way to represent a dither progression is with a dither matrix. This is an *NxM* matrix, corresponding to an *NxM* cell size, in which the matrix entries define the order in which dots are turned on within the cells. For example, we can uniquely define the simple dither patterns of Figure 5.9 by the following matrix:

```
|  9  5 16 12 |
| 13  1  4  8 |
|  6  2  3 15 |
| 10 14  7 11 |
```

You can conveniently program dithers of 8x8 and smaller as two-dimensional arrays of unsigned chars. Each array byte corresponds to one row of a cell, and the second index of the array accesses a given row within a cell. A dot is printed for each 1-bit within a cell. For instance, the 4x4 dither matrix above yields the following array:

```
unsigned char lin_4x4[16][4] =
{                           /* bits on: */
 { 0x00, 0x00, 0x00, 0x00, }, /* 00 */
 { 0x00, 0x04, 0x00, 0x00, }, /* 01 */
 { 0x00, 0x04, 0x04, 0x00, }, /* 02 */
 { 0x00, 0x04, 0x06, 0x00, }, /* 03 */
 { 0x00, 0x06, 0x06, 0x00, }, /* 04 */
 { 0x04, 0x06, 0x06, 0x00, }, /* 05 */
 { 0x04, 0x06, 0x0E, 0x00, }, /* 06 */
 { 0x04, 0x06, 0x0E, 0x02, }, /* 07 */
 { 0x04, 0x07, 0x0E, 0x02, }, /* 08 */
 { 0x0C, 0x07, 0x0E, 0x02, }, /* 09 */
 { 0x0C, 0x07, 0x0E, 0x0A, }, /* 10 */
 { 0x0D, 0x07, 0x0E, 0x0B, }, /* 11 */
 { 0x0D, 0x07, 0x0E, 0x0B, }, /* 12 */
 { 0x0D, 0x07, 0x0E, 0x0F, }, /* 13 */
 { 0x0D, 0x0F, 0x0E, 0x0F, }, /* 14 */
 { 0x0F, 0x0F, 0x0F, 0x0F, }  /* 16 */
};
```

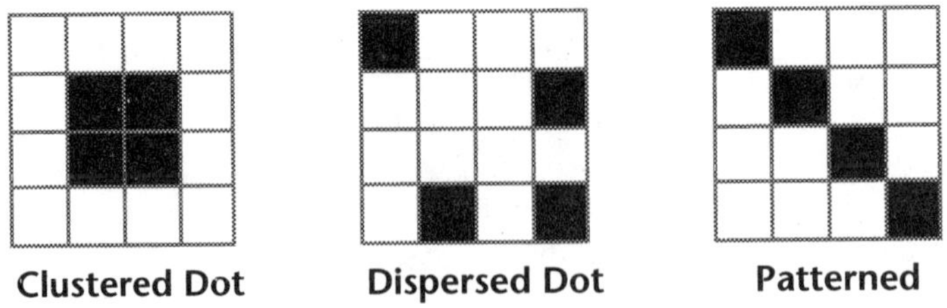

■ **FIGURE 5.10 Examples of dithering types**

The array's first index selects the dither cell for a given pixel attribute value (i.e., gray level or color). Note that a 4x4 dither generates 17 possible cells, with 0 to 16 bits set on within a cell. In actual practice only 16 are used. The best candidate for omission is the next to last cell arrangement, with 15 bits on. This has the least impact on perceived intensity ratios while still providing a 16-level set from solid white (all bits off) to solid black (all bits on).

The easy way to generate the byte values for a dither array is to write a small program to output the values given in the dither matrix. (This beats marking up a whole pad of graph paper with checkerboard patterns and hex digits!) Listing 5.16 provides the C source code for this operation. This code will output either a linear dither or a logarithmic dither. With only 16 bits to work with in a 4x4 cell, the logarithmic progression is roughly approximated using an eight-step scale.

Note that while the logarithmic dither more closely matches the logarithmic intensity response of the human eye, it may not be the best choice in some circumstances. Given the dynamic ranges of printed media, the fewer levels of the logarithmic scheme may produce a coarser looking image.

Also note that, while a large number of levels is desirable, the larger spatial sizes of the resulting dither cells can degrade image resolution.

Many developers are surprised to learn that a 300-dpi laser printer cannot, in most cases, produce a useful 256-level dither. A 256-level dither requires at least a 16x16 cell size, which is far too big for a 300-dpi device. In most cases, even an 8x8 cell is too big. Keep in mind that, while the typical VGA monitor has perhaps only one-fourth of the laser printer's spatial resolution, it possesses 32 times as much intensity resolution—6 bits of primary intensity versus 1 bit for the printer.

Printed images with 256-level dithering are realistically attainable only on a linotronic or similar printing device. These have 2400-dpi capability—eight times better than the laser printer. That translates into 64 times the number of useful halftone values.

Fade to Gray

At this point you're probably wondering how halftoning is actually performed in practice. We're getting there, but we must first consider how to convert a color image into gray levels for rendering on a gray-level device. This is a necessary accommodation to the real world, as the most common dithering situation is rendering a 16-color screen image on a black and white printer.

Recall that the video driver uses pixel attribute values from the graphics display to perform a table lookup. The pixel value selects a palette entry, which consists of an "RGB" (Red-Green-Blue) triplet that defines the relative primary color intensities for that pixel value.

If we treat each RGB triplet as a point in a three-dimensional space, then each color's relative intensity is proportional to the distance from the origin (0,0,0) to the point (r,g,b). These distance values must of course be normalized before they can be used.

A VGA-compatible display uses a 6-bit quantity for each primary intensity, yielding values in the range 0–63. The point (0,0,0) represents black and (63,63,63) represents white. The "distance" between these two points is the square root of 3 times 63, roughly 109. This leads to the following relation for defining the relative intensity of a VGA color on a scale of 0 to 1:

```
      Sqrt(r^2+g^2+b^2)
I  = ------------------
             109
```

The resulting value of **I**, between 0 and 1, is multiplied by the number of cells in our dithering set to yield an index for selecting the appropriate dither cell. This is best done beforehand, and when actually processing the image each pixel value is used to look up a corresponding dithering index, which then selects the appropriate dither cell. Note that **I** increases toward white with an RGB monitor, while dither cell indexes increase toward black (assuming that the number of 1-bits per cell increases with index). This requires in practice that either the order of dither cells be reversed in the dither array or the complement of **I (1.0 – I)** be used to compute dither indexes.

From Theory to Practice

For this discussion we'll assume that we are printing a VGA mode 12H image, 640x480 pixels and 16 colors, on a black-and-white printer. Further, we will use the 4x4 16-level dithering set described previously. Note that the number of colors and number of dither cells are not related, and are only coincidentally equal here.

The default mode 12H VGA palette is usually something like that shown in Table 5.2. Our "palette," which originally contained RGB intensities, now consists of dither cell indexes computed as **(1.0 – I)*16**; that is,

```
int dither_pal[16] =
{
  16, 9, 9, 7, 9, 7, 9, 5,
  10, 5, 5, 2, 5, 2, 2, 0
};
```

By design, this set of indices should accurately reproduce the relative light intensities from the original image. As a rule, this approach gives the best results.

Note, however, that you can manipulate the dither palette for alternative approaches. Suppose you wish to be able to distinguish *each* of the original 16 colors. In that case, each

■ TABLE 5.2 Relative intensities for VGA Mode 12H

Index	Red	Grn	Blu	Color	1.0 – I
0	0	0	0	Black	1.000
1	0	0	42	Blue	0.615
2	0	42	0	Green	0.615
3	0	42	42	Cyan	0.456
4	2	0	0	Red	0.615
5	2	0	42	Magenta	0.456
6	2	21	0	Brown	0.570
7	42	42	42	Light Gray	0.333
8	21	21	21	Dark Gray	0.667
9	21	21	63	Light Blue	0.362
10	21	63	21	Light Green	0.362
11	21	63	63	Light Cyan	0.161
12	63	21	21	Light Red	0.362
13	63	1	63	Light Magenta	0.161
14	63	63	21	Yellow	0.161
15	63	63	63	White	0.000

color could be assigned its own dither index, and all 16 dither cells would be used. If so, you would need to force-rank the pixel index values that share common (1.0 – I) values, based on perceived relative intensity. (For example, you might decide that blue is darker than red, and red is darker than green.)

The 1-to-1 Solution

Earlier, I mentioned that using an *N*x*N* dot matrix for dithering does not necessarily force the rendered image to be *N*-squared times larger than the original image. You can produce a dithered image that is *exactly the same size* as the original image. The trick is as follows:

Let's suppose we wish to render the image 1-to-1, with a dot on the page for each pixel on the screen. We need to determine three quantities in order to render the dot corresponding to the pixel located at (x,y):

1. Which dither palette cell corresponds to the pixel's attribute value:

```
cell = dither_pal[ pixel(x,y) ];
```

2. Which row of the dither cell corresponds to the image's "y":

```
row = y % cell_hgt;
```

3. Which bit in the cell row corresponds to the image's "x":

```
bit = 1 << cell_wid - ((x%cell_wid) + 1);
```

Having determined these values, we can isolate the one bit in the dither cell that will represent the image pixel:

```
lin_4x4[cell][row] & bit
```

The corresponding bit in the printed image takes this value. To see the computations in context refer to Listing 5.18, which shows a typical implementation.

In the case of 1-to-1 scaling each source pixel is represented by only *one* dot from the dither cell, and it would seem that the dithered image would be missing a lot of detail. Note, however, that the dither cell dot selected for each pixel is related to the pixel's location. You should be able to prove to yourself that a *block* of image pixels having the same dimension as the dither cell will produce one complete dither cell in the rendered image.

Most image features tend to be large relative to a single dithering cell, and even where they are not, adjacent features often have closely related colors or gray levels. This tends to produce lower spatial frequencies in the dithered image. That is, most real-world imagery possesses *spatial coherence.*

Dithering does, however, reduce spatial resolution overall. In this sense it is equivalent to filtering an image's spatial features with a low-pass frequency filter.

Screen Angles

There remains one important concept that we have yet to touch on, and that is screen angle. You've probably at least heard the term if you've ever had anything to do with the printing business.

In the traditional phototypesetting process, a continuous-tone image, such as a photograph or other "live" artwork, is printed by first taking a photograph of it through a fine wire screen. The screened photographic negative is then used in the construction of a copper plate that carries an etching of the negative. It is this copper plate, a component of the printing press, that actually places ink on the paper being printed.

The screen used in phototypesetting can be positioned at various angles of rotation about the axis represented by the direction of the camera's view. This angle is known as the screen angle, and it can affect the perceived fidelity of the printed image. Most black-and-white newspaper photographs, for instance, are reproduced using a 45-degree screen angle, which is visually less rigid than the "squarish" effect of a 0-degree screen.

A screen angle can be incorporated into a dithering algorithm by varying the spacing and orientation of the sampling of the source image. Note that the examples presented are hard-wired in this respect and produce a 0-degree screen angle.

Fade to Black

The program presented in Listing 5.17 is designed to provide a side-by-side comparison of an eight-level gray-scale image with its bi-level dithered counterpart. For ease of implementation the program generates output on a VGA display. Note, however, that a typical video display has both lower resolution and a very much higher dynamic range than a typical printed page. Both of these factors work against the effectiveness of a dithered representation, so the results shown on-screen are not as good as the result obtained on an average laser printer.

For the reader interested in additional information on dithering, get a copy of Foley *et al. Computer Graphics Principles and Practice,* 2nd edition. (Addison-Wesley, 1990; ISBN 0-201-12110-7.) This is easily the single best book on computer graphics ever printed, and belongs in the library of every developer.

CODE DESCRIPTION

Overview

The listings provided are used to demonstrate how different dithering techniques are used to display color images in black and white.

Listings Available

Listing	*Description*	*Used with*
DITHER1.C	C source file that contains a set of functions for dithering images using a 4x4 cell.	------
DITHER2.C	C source file that contains a set of functions for dithering images using a 8x8 cell.	------

How to Compile/Assemble

The C source files can be compiled with Borland C++ or Turbo C++.

■ LISTING 5.16 DITHER1.C

```
/* File: DITHER1.C   By: Marv Luse, Autumn Hill Software */
/*                                                        */
/* Desc: Code for computing 4x4 dither cells with either  */
/*       16 linear steps or 8 logs steps, given a 4x4     */
/*       dither matrix as input.                          */
#include "stdlib.h"
#include "stdio.h"
#include "math.h"

/* types applicable to 4x4 dithering */
typedef int DITHER_MATRIX[4][4];
typedef unsigned char DITHER_CELL[4];

/* dit_mat determines dot-order within cell */
DITHER_MATRIX dit_mat = {
   {  9,  5, 16, 12 }, { 13,  1,  4,  8 },
   {  6,  2,  3, 15 }, { 10, 14,  7, 11 },};

/* dit_cells contains 4x4 dither patterns */
DITHER_CELL dit_cells[16] = {
  { 0x00, 0x00, 0x00, 0x00 },{ 0x00, 0x00, 0x00, 0x00 }, /*  0,1  */
  { 0x00, 0x00, 0x00, 0x00 },{ 0x00, 0x00, 0x00, 0x00 }, /*  2,3  */
  { 0x00, 0x00, 0x00, 0x00 },{ 0x00, 0x00, 0x00, 0x00 }, /*  4,5  */
  { 0x00, 0x00, 0x00, 0x00 },{ 0x00, 0x00, 0x00, 0x00 }, /*  6,7  */
  { 0x00, 0x00, 0x00, 0x00 },{ 0x00, 0x00, 0x00, 0x00 }, /*  8,9  */
  { 0x00, 0x00, 0x00, 0x00 },{ 0x00, 0x00, 0x00, 0x00 }, /* 10,11 */
```

```
  { 0x00, 0x00, 0x00, 0x00 },{ 0x00, 0x00, 0x00, 0x00 }, /* 12,13 */
  { 0x00, 0x00, 0x00, 0x00 },{ 0x00, 0x00, 0x00, 0x00 }, /* 14,15 */
};
/*---------------------------------*/
/* determine dot count at each step of log intensity scl  */
/*---------------------------------*/
void compute_log_steps( int dot_cnt[], int nlvls, int ndots ) {
    int    i;
    double r, ri;

/* compute step intensity ratio */
    r = pow( ndots, 1.0/(nlvls-1.0) );
/* index 0 always has 0 dots on */
    dot_cnt[0] = 0;
/* compute number of dots in remaining levels */
    for( i=1, ri=r;  i<nlvls;  i++, ri*=r )
       dot_cnt[i] = (int) (ri + 0.5);
}
/*---------------------------------*/
/* create an 8-level 4x4 logarithmic intensity dither      */
/*---------------------------------*/
void log_4x4_dither(  DITHER_MATRIX dm, DITHER_CELL dc[] ) {
    int i, j, n, cnt[8];
    unsigned char mask;

/* determine dots/cell for each level */
    compute_log_steps( cnt, 8, 16 );
/* determine dither cells */
    for( n=0; n<8; n++ ) {              /* cell n          */
       for( i=0; i<4; i++ ) {           /* byte i of cell n */
          dc[n][i] = 0;
          for( j=0; j<4; j++ ) {        /* bit j of byte i  */
             mask = 0x08 >> j;
             if( dm[i][j] <= cnt[n] ) dc[n][i] |= mask;
          }
       }
    }
}
/*---------------------------------*/
/* create a 16-level 4x4 linear intensity dither          */
/*---------------------------------*/
void lin_4x4_dither(  DITHER_MATRIX dm, DITHER_CELL dc[] ) {
    int i, j, n;
    unsigned char mask;

/* determine dither cells */
    for( n=0; n<16; n++ ) {             /* cell n          */
       for( i=0; i<4; i++ ) {           /* byte i of cell n */
          dc[n][i] = 0;
          for( j=0; j<4; j++ ) {        /* bit j of byte i  */
             mask = 0x08 >> j;
             if( dm[i][j] <= n ) dc[n][i] |= mask;
          }
       }
```

```
    }
}
/*-------------------------------------------------*/
/* print the data-initialization of a 4x4 dither set      */
/*-------------------------------------------------*/
void print_dither(  char *name, DITHER_CELL dc[], int ncells ) {
    int i, j;

    printf( "DITHER_CELL %s[] =\n", name );
    printf( "{\n" );
    for( i=0; i<ncells; i++ ) {
       printf( "    {" );
       for( j=0; j<4; j++ ) printf( " 0x%02X,", dc[i][j] );
       printf( " },\n" );
    }
    printf( "};\n" );
}
/*-------------------------------------------------*/
/* main to exercise the code...                            */
/*-------------------------------------------------*/
void main( void ) {
     int i, j;

     printf( "4x4 Dither Matrix...\n" );
     printf( "\n" );
     for( i=0; i<4; i++ ) {
        printf( "  %c", 179 );
        for( j=0; j<4; j++ ) printf( " %2d", dit_mat[i][j] );
        printf( " %c\n", 179 );
     }
     printf( "\n" );
     printf( "4x4 16-level Linear Dither...\n" ); printf( "\n" );
     lin_4x4_dither( dit_mat, dit_cells );
     print_dither( "lin_4x4", dit_cells, 16 ); printf( "\n" );
     printf( "4x4 8-level Logarithmic Dither...\n" );
     printf( "\n" );
     log_4x4_dither( dit_mat, dit_cells );
     print_dither( "log_4x4", dit_cells, 8 ); printf( "\n" );
}
```

■ LISTING 5.17 DITHER2.C

```
/* File: DITHER2.C   By: Marv Luse, Autumn Hill Software */
/*                                                        */
/* Desc: Program to illustrate the results of dithering.  */
/*       An 8-level filled circular region is dithered    */
/*       and rendered as a bi-level image.  Result is     */
/*       shown on-screen using Borland C++ and BGI.       */
/*       (Use Options-Compiler-Source = "Borland C++")    */
#include "stdlib.h"
#include "stdio.h"
#include "conio.h"
#include "dos.h"
#include "graphics.h"
```

```
/*--------------------------------*/
/* Dithering types and data                              */
/*--------------------------------*/
typedef unsigned char DITHER_CELL[4];
DITHER_CELL log_4x4[] = {
  { 0x00, 0x00, 0x00, 0x00, }, { 0x00, 0x04, 0x00, 0x00, },
  { 0x00, 0x04, 0x04, 0x00, }, { 0x00, 0x04, 0x06, 0x00, },
  { 0x04, 0x06, 0x06, 0x00, }, { 0x04, 0x06, 0x0E, 0x02, },
  { 0x0C, 0x07, 0x0E, 0x0B, }, { 0x0F, 0x0F, 0x0F, 0x0F, },};
/*--------------------------------*/
/* Variables to create 8-level pixel array               */
/*--------------------------------*/
#define pxWIDTH     175
#define pxHEIGHT    175
#define pxRADIUS     80
char pxl_array[pxHEIGHT][pxWIDTH];
/*--------------------------------*/
/*  compute integer square root                          */
/*--------------------------------*/
int isqrt( int n ) {
    long xnew, xold, y, d;
    y    = n; /* initialize */
    xnew = y;
    xold = y / 2;
    d    = xold;
/* compute integer part of square root */
    while( (d > 1) && (xold > 0) ) {
         xnew = xold;  xnew += y/xold;  xnew /= 2;
         d = xold - xnew;
         xold = xnew;
    }
/* if desired, round to nearest integer */
    xold = xnew + 1;
    if( (n - xnew*xnew) > (xold*xold - n) )
        xnew++;
    return( (int) xnew );
}
/*--------------------------------*/
/* Build filled circular image                           */
/*--------------------------------*/
void create_image( void ) {
    int   i, j, xo, yo;
    int   d, dx, dy, dxy;

    xo = pxWIDTH / 2;     /* center of circle */
    yo = pxHEIGHT / 2;
/* compute pixel values for filled circle */
    for( i=0; i<pxHEIGHT; i++ ) {
       dy = i - yo;
       for( j=0; j<pxWIDTH; j++ ) {
          dx = j - xo;
          dxy = dx*dx + dy*dy;
          d  = isqrt( dxy );
          if( d <= pxRADIUS ) {
```

```
            d *= 7;
            d /= pxRADIUS;
            pxl_array[i][j] = d;
         }
         else
            pxl_array[i][j] = 0;
      }
   }
}
/*-------------------------------*/
/* Draw 8-level version of circle                         */
/*-------------------------------*/
void draw_color_image( void ) {
   int i, j;

    for( i=0; i<pxHEIGHT; i++ ) {
       for( j=0; j<pxWIDTH; j++ ) {
          putpixel( j, i, pxl_array[i][j] );
       }
    }
}
/*-------------------------------*/
/* Draw dithered version of circle                        */
/*-------------------------------*/
void draw_dithered_image( void ) {
    int           i, j, r, p;
    unsigned char mask;

    for( i=0; i<pxHEIGHT; i++ ) {
       r  = i % 4;
       mask = 0x08;
       for( j=0; j<pxWIDTH; j++ ) {
          p  = pxl_array[i][j];
          if( log_4x4[p][r] & mask )
              putpixel( pxWIDTH+j+5, i, 7 );
          if( (mask>>=1) == 0 ) mask = 0x08;
       }
    }
}
/* Get contents of specified VGA palette register...                    */
int get_vga_pal_register( int reg_no ) {
     union REGS r;

     r.h.ah = 0x10;                  /* function 10h */
     r.h.al = 0x07;                  /* subfunction 07h */
     r.h.bl = (unsigned char) reg_no; /* register number */
     int86( 0x10, &r, &r );
     return( (int) r.h.bh );
}

/* Set contents of specified VGA DAC register...                        */

void set_vga_dac_register( int reg_no, unsigned char rgb[] ) {
     union REGS r;
```

```
        r.h.ah = 0x10;        /* function 10h */
        r.h.al = 0x10;        /* subfunction 10h */
        r.x.bx = reg_no;      /* register number */
        r.h.dh = rgb[0];      /* 6-bit red component */
        r.h.ch = rgb[1];      /* 6-bit grn component */
        r.h.cl = rgb[2];      /* 6-bit blu component */
        int86( 0x10, &r, &r );
}
/*--------------------------------*/
/* Main to illustrate dithering visually                    */
/*--------------------------------*/
void main( void ) {
        int  i, dac, gDrvr=0, gMode;
        unsigned char rgb[3];

        printf( "building image, please wait..." );
        create_image();
        printf( "done\n" );
        initgraph( &gDrvr, &gMode, "" );
        /* modify VGA palette to show 8 gray scales */
        for( i=0; i<8; i++ ) {
           dac = get_vga_pal_register( i );
           rgb[0] = rgb[1] = rgb[2] = i << 3;
           set_vga_dac_register( dac, rgb );
        }
        draw_color_image();
        draw_dithered_image();
        getch();
        closegraph();
}
```

Fast Bezier Curves in Windows

■ Michael Bertrand

Here's how to draw Bezier curves quickly enough to rubber-band them on-screen.

Bezier curves are widely used in computer graphics. PostScript uses these curves as building blocks, for example; defining even circles in terms of Beziers. Many modern illustration programs for the PC and the Apple Macintosh implement Bezier curves in a direct way, allowing users to create and interactively edit the curves to create complex images.

These curves possess several properties that have led to their widespread adoption in computer graphics applications:

- Because they are defined in terms of a few points, Bezier curves can be identified with these points in the graphics database.
- Efficient algorithms generate the entire curve from the defining points.
- The defining points intuitively describe the curve.

Four Defining Points

A Bezier curve is defined by four points called control1, handle1, handle2, and control2 (abbreviated here as ctrl1, hand1, hand2, and ctrl2). The curve begins at ctrl1 and proceeds toward hand1; at the other end, we can think of it as starting from ctrl2 and proceeding toward hand2. In each case, the curve gradually pulls away from the associated handle in its movement toward the other handle/control. The handles are points of attraction for the curve; the curve starts from ctrl1 toward hand1, but gradually pulls toward hand2 as the attractive force of hand1 diminishes and the attractive force of hand2 increases. The further away hand1 is from ctrl1, the longer the curve will be pulled toward ctrl1 before breaking toward hand2.

Bezier curves take several forms, as shown in the screen shot given in Figure 5.11. Vectors connecting each control point to its handle are shown as well as the Bezier curve they define. This example is about as complex as four-point Beziers get; more complex Bezier curves require a series of Beziers joined together in a continuous path.

de Casteljau Construction

Beziers must be drawn quickly to be dragged, or rubber-banded, on the screen, since the curves are being drawn and erased constantly with each mouse movement. We also need fast Bezier-drawing routines to render a complex image comprising perhaps hundreds of individual Beziers in a reasonable time.

The de Casteljau algorithm is a fast integer-based method for calculating points along a Bezier curve, given the four original defining points. The calculated points can then be connected by line segments to give the impression of a smooth curve. The de Casteljau

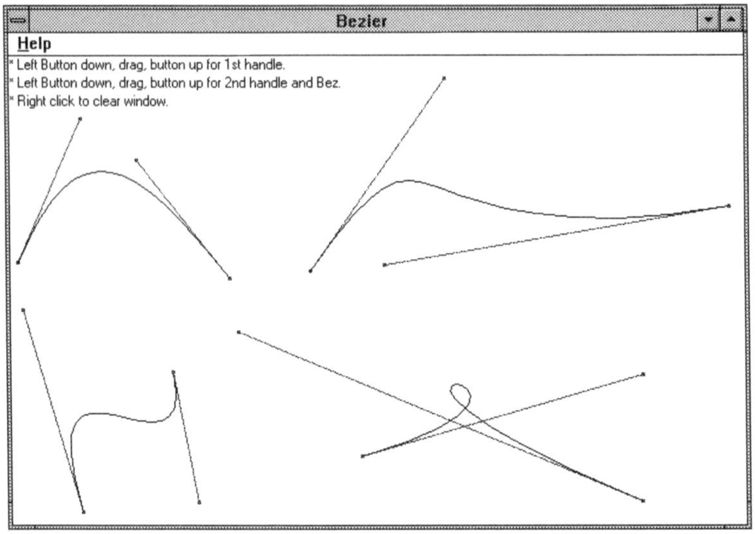

■ **FIGURE 5.11 Sample Bezier curves**

algorithm breaks a Bezier curve into two separate pieces, left and right, each of which is itself a Bezier curve.

The key to the efficiency of this algorithm is the astounding simplicity of the math, which involves taking simple averages to calculate de Casteljau construction points: First average the original defining points (the q's shown below are the averages), then average the averages (r's), then take a final average (s0):

```
ctrl1  = p0
     q0
hand1  = p1        r0
           q1          s0
hand2  = p2        r1
           q2
ctrl2  = p3
```

That is: q0 = (p0 + p1)/2, r0 = (q0 + q1)/2, and so on. The actual calculations will be with coordinates, not points, but it helps to think in terms of points, keeping in mind that the "average" of two points is the point midway between the two. It turns out that s0 is the midpoint of the Bezier curve. What's more, (p0, q0, r0, s0) are (ctrl, hand, hand, ctrl) for a Bezier coinciding with the left half of the original Bezier; and (p3, q2, r1, s0) are (ctrl, hand, hand, ctrl) for another Bezier coinciding with the right half of the original Bezier.

The procedure can be repeated: The midpoint of the left sub-Bezier is one-fourth of the way along the original curve; and the midpoint of the right sub-Bezier is three-fourths of the way along the original curve. The subdivision process can be repeated indefinitely to generate 2, 4, 8, 16, . . . , 2^n sub-Beziers and 3, 5, 9, 17, . . , 2^{n+1} points along the original curve. Like other subdivision processes, the de Casteljau algorithm lends itself to recursive implementation. Averaging entails dividing by 2, which can be done quickly as a shift-right operation because we are dealing with integers.

The de Casteljau construction is illustrated in Figure 5.12, where the p's are the controls and handles of the original Bezier curve. q0 is midway between p0 and p1, r0 is midway between q0 and q1, and so on. Observe that

1. s0 is the midpoint of the original Bezier curve.
2. (p0, q0, r0, s0) are (ctrl1, hand1,hand2, ctrl2) of a sub-Bezier coinciding with the left half of the original Bezier curve.
3. (p3, q2, r1, s0) are (ctrl1, hand1, hand2, ctrl2) of a sub-Bezier coinciding with the right half of the original Bezier curve.

After the first step illustrated here, we have three points on the curve:

- The original control point, p0
- The midpoint of the original Bezier curve
- The original control point, p3

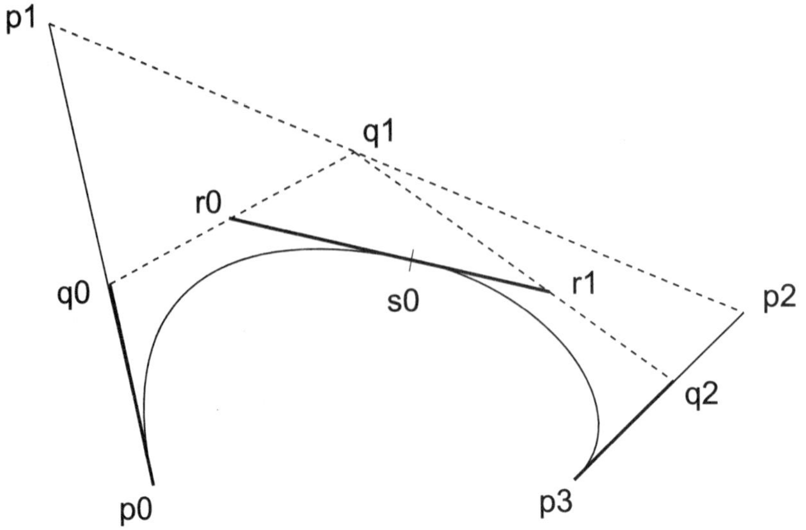

■ **FIGURE 5.12 The de Casteljau construction screen image**

Applying the procedure again to the left and right sub-Beziers generates their midpoints, giving five points on the original Bezier. Subdividing these four sub-Beziers then gives us nine points on the original curve, and so on. Stopping at four subdivision levels and 17 points produces smooth curves at VGA resolution. The number of subdivisions, or recursive depth, is **BEZ_DEPTH** in the program. **NUM_BEZPTS** is the number of points generated along the Bezier curve, and is used to allocate an array to hold the Bezier points. Therefore, make sure that

```
NUM_BEZPTS >= 2^BEZ_DEPTH + 1
```

Increasing **BEZ_DEPTH** results in more line segments in the Bezier curve, hence a smoother curve—at least up to a point. We reach diminishing returns in increasing **BEZ_-DEPTH** too much, since the accumulated error of repeated averaging eventually throws the calculations off by one or more pixels. Remember that **BEZ_DEPTH** is an exponent, so increasing **BEZ_DEPTH** by 1 doubles the number of segments.

Since the recursion proceeds to the maximum depth down the far left branch, the first curve point actually generated is the point immediately following p0 = ctrl1 along the Bezier. The remaining points are also generated in order (from p0 = ctrl1 to p3 = ctrl2), a nice side effect of the recursive implementation. Another point is collected into an array every time the recursion reaches its finest subdivision level, and the points are in order!

Writing Tools in Windows

We want to show off our fast Bezier-drawing through an interactive Bezier tool. If the curve rubber-bands well on the screen, then we can claim to have a good algorithm.

Interactive tools in Windows are constructed with the concept of "system state." The **Window** procedure passes mouse messages to **BezTool()**, which maintains a key static variable, **iState**, which takes four values summarized in Table 5.3.

BezTool()'s action depends on **iState**, which in turn depends on the sequence of mouse messages that have recently streamed into the tool. Until the first **WM_LBUTTONDOWN** message is received, **iState** remains **NOT_STARTED** because nothing has been done. The first **WM_LBUTTONDOWN** triggers a state transition to **DRAG_HAND1**. In this state, the tool responds to **WM_MOUSEMOVE**s by rubber-banding the first handle in XOR mode. **WM_LBUTTONUP** then causes a state transition to **WAIT_FOR_CTRL2**. Nothing happens until another **WM_LBUTTONDOWN** is received, which changes **iState** to **DRAG_HAND2**; in this state, **WM_MOUSEMOVE** messages cause rubber-banding of both the second handle and the Bezier curve as a whole. **WM_LBUTTONUP** now causes a final state transition back to **NOT_STARTED**. The final handle and Bezier are frozen, and the tool is again ready to start another Bezier.

BezTool() calls **DrawHandle()** and **DrawBez()** to draw the figures (which in turn call Windows' GDI calls **MoveTo()**, **LineTo()**, and **Polyline()**). Each mouse move causes two calls to these routines. The first call draws over the figure exactly where it had been drawn the first time. Since we are in XOR drawing mode, drawing over the original figure erases it. The second call then draws at the new location. Static variables must be used if the user points are to be remembered for the next pass through the tool so previous figures can be erased.

Windows and Graphics Programming

Windows is a natural medium for this kind of programming (See Listing 5.19.) Mouse events are sent to our window procedure automatically, enabling us to build interactive mouse-driven tools. The GDI system provides line drawing, including the **R2_NOTXORPEN** ROP code that allows us to draw in XOR mode.

Windows has a built-in coordinate system and mapping modes so we can change our working range of numbers. The Beziers would not display nearly as nicely were we restricted to screen coordinates of about 500x500 pixels. By setting the **MM_ISOTROPIC** mapping mode and adjusting the Window Extent and Viewport Extent in **BezTool()**, we can expand the range to [–15,000, +15,000] which minimizes the negative side effects of calculations with small integers.

■ TABLE 5.3 IState's four possible values

Value	Description
NOT_STARTED	tool has not been started
DRAG_HAND1	dragging handle1
WAIT_FOR_CTRL2	waiting for control2 to be entered
DRAG_HAND2	dragging handle2 and Bezier

TIP: To create BEZ.EXE, you'll need several files in addition to BEZ.C, including some with no ASCII representation. These files are present in a file called BEZ.ZIP, contained within the listings disk.

References

Foley, James D., Andries van Dam, Steven K. Feiner, and John F. Hughes, *Computer Graphics:Principles and Practice*, Addison-Wesley (2nd ed., 1990), pp 507ff.

CODE DESCRIPTION

Overview

The listings provided are used to draw fast Bezier curves in Windows.

Listings Available

Listing	*Description*	*Used with*
BEZ.C	C source file that draws Bezier curves in Windows.	------

How to Compile/Assemble

Apart from the BEZ.C source file listed here, you will also need the following files, which can be found on the source code diskette: BEZ.H, BEZ.RC, BEZ.DEF, BEZ.ICO, BEZ.RES, and BEZ. BEZ contains a makefile for compiling and linking the application.

■ LISTING 5.18 BEZ.C

```
/* BEZ.C : Program to draw Bezier curves and their handles
   interactively. User draws first handle by dragging, then second
   handle; the Bezier curve rubber-bands together with the second
   handle. Demonstrates the de Casteljau algorithm for fast
   calculation of Bezier points.
   Copyright (c) 1991, Michael A. Bertrand.   */

#include <windows.h>
#include "bez.h"

HPEN   hRedPen;             /* red pen for handles. */
int    LogPerDevice;        /* #logical units per device unit
                               (both axes). */
WORD   cxClient;            /* size of client area (x). */
WORD   cyClient;            /* size of client area (y). */
HANDLE hInst;               /* current instance */
POINT  BezPts[NUM_BEZPTS]; /* array of pts along Bezier curve */
POINT  *PtrBezPts;          /* pointer into BezPts[] array */

char Instr1[] =
  "* Left Button down, drag, button up for 1st handle.";
char Instr2[] =
```

```
  "* Left Button down, drag, button up for 2nd handle and Bez.";
char Instr3[] = "* Right click to clear window.";

int PASCAL WinMain(HANDLE hInstance, HANDLE hPrevInstance,
           LPSTR lpszCmdLine, int nCmdShow)
/*
  USE:  Register window and set dispach message loop.
  IN:   hInstance,hPrevInstance,lpszCmdLine,nCmdShow : standard
        WinMain parms
*/
{
  static char szAppName [] = "Bezier";
  static char szIconName[] = "BezIcon";
  static char szMenuName[] = "BezMenu";

  HWND     hWnd;    /* handle to WinMain's window */
  MSG      msg;     /* message dispached to window */
  WNDCLASS wc;      /* for registering window */

  /* Save instance handle in global var
     so can use for "About" dialog box. */
  hInst = hInstance;

  /* Register application window class. */
  if (!hPrevInstance)
    {
    wc.style         = CS_HREDRAW | CS_VREDRAW;
    wc.lpfnWndProc   = WndProc;  /* fn to get window's messages */
    wc.cbClsExtra    = 0;
    wc.cbWndExtra    = 0;
    wc.hInstance     = hInstance;
    wc.hIcon         = LoadIcon(hInstance, szIconName);
    wc.hCursor       = LoadCursor(NULL, IDC_ARROW);
    wc.hbrBackground = GetStockObject(WHITE_BRUSH);
    wc.lpszMenuName  = szMenuName;  /* menu resource in RC file */
    wc.lpszClassName = szAppName;   /* name used in call to
             CreateWindow() */

    if (!RegisterClass(&wc))
      return(FALSE);
    }

    /* Initialize specific instance. */
    hWnd = CreateWindow(szAppName, szAppName, WS_OVERLAPPEDWINDOW,
                        CW_USEDEFAULT, CW_USEDEFAULT, CW_USEDEFAULT,
                        CW_USEDEFAULT, NULL, NULL, hInstance, NULL);

  ShowWindow(hWnd, nCmdShow); /* display the window */
  UpdateWindow(hWnd);        /* update client area; send WM_PAINT */

  /* Read msgs from app que and dispatch them to appropriate win
     function. Continues until GetMessage() returns NULL when it
     receives WM_QUIT. */
  while (GetMessage(&msg, NULL, NULL, NULL))
```

```
    {
    TranslateMessage(&msg);  /* process char input from keyboard */
    DispatchMessage(&msg);   /* pass message to window function */
    }
  return(msg.wParam);
}

long FAR PASCAL WndProc(HWND hWnd, unsigned iMessage,
                        WORD wParam, LONG lParam)
/*
  USE: Application's window procedure : all app's messages come here.
  IN:  hWnd,iMessage,wParam,lParam : standard Windows proc parameters
*/
{
  HDC         hDC;  /* must generate our own handle to DC to draw */
  PAINTSTRUCT ps;         /* needed when receive WM_PAINT message */
  FARPROC     lpProcAbout;      /* pointer to "AboutBez" function */

  switch(iMessage)
    {
    case WM_CREATE:
      /* Create hRedPen once and store as global. */
      hRedPen = CreatePen(PS_SOLID, 1, RGB(255, 0, 0));
      break;  /* WM_CREATE */

    case WM_SIZE:
      /* Get client area size into globals when window resized. */
      cxClient = LOWORD(lParam);
      cyClient = HIWORD(lParam);
      break;  /* WM_SIZE */

    case WM_COMMAND:
      if (wParam == IDM_ABOUT)
        {
        /* "About" menu item chosen by user :
            call "AboutBez" function. */
        lpProcAbout = MakeProcInstance(AboutBez, hInst);
        DialogBox (hInst, "AboutBez", hWnd, lpProcAbout);
        FreeProcInstance(lpProcAbout);
        }
      break;  /* WM_COMMAND */

    case WM_PAINT:
      /* Repaint instructions at upper left of window. */
      hDC = BeginPaint(hWnd, &ps);
      SelectObject(hDC, GetStockObject(ANSI_VAR_FONT));
      TextOut(hDC, 0,  0, Instr1, lstrlen(Instr1));
      TextOut(hDC, 0, 15, Instr2, lstrlen(Instr2));
      TextOut(hDC, 0, 30, Instr3, lstrlen(Instr3));
      EndPaint(hWnd, &ps);
      break;  /* WM_PAINT */

    case WM_LBUTTONDOWN:
    case WM_RBUTTONDOWN:
    case WM_MOUSEMOVE:
```

```
    case WM_LBUTTONUP:
      /* Mouse events passed on to BezTool() for processing. */
      BezTool(hWnd, iMessage, lParam);
      break;  /* WM_LBUTTONDOWN... */

    case WM_DESTROY:
      /* Destroy window & delete pen when application terminated. */
      DeleteObject(hRedPen);
      PostQuitMessage(0);
      break;  /* WM_DESTROY */
    default:
      return(DefWindowProc(hWnd, iMessage, wParam, lParam));
    }  /* switch(iMessage) */
  return(0L);
}

void NEAR PASCAL BezTool(HWND hWnd, unsigned iMessage, LONG lParam)
/*
USE:  Process mouse event to draw handles and Bezier curve.
IN:   hWnd      : handle to window
      iMessage : mouse event (WM_LBUTTONDOWN, etc.)
      lParam    : mouse coords (x == loword, y == hiword)
NOTE: This is the interactive Bezier drawing tool which processes
WM_RBUTTONDOWN, WM_LBUTTONDOWN, WM_MOUSEMOVE, and WM_LBUTTONUP
messages. BezTool() is called repeatedly as the user draws. The
current state of the tool is maintained in the key static variable
iState. iState's value, as set last time thru the tool, determines
the tool's action this time thru. Bezier control and handle points,
as input by the user, are also maintained as statics so BezTool()
remembers them the next time thru.
*/
{
  HDC    hDC;        /* must generate our own handle to DC to draw */
  WORD   maxClient; /* larger of (cxClient, cyClient) */
  POINT  inPt;       /* incoming point */
  POINT  pts[2]; /* to get LogPerDevice, #logical units/dev. unit */
  /* user-entered Bez control & handle (1st): */
  static POINT ctrl1, hand1;
  /* user-entered Bez control & handle (2nd): */
  static POINT ctrl2, hand2;
  static int iState;  /* BezTool()'s state : DRAG_HAND1, etc. */

  hDC = GetDC(hWnd);

  /* Set extents and origin so will be working
     in range [-15000, +15000]. */
  SetMapMode(hDC, MM_ISOTROPIC);
  SetWindowExt(hDC, 30000, 30000);
  maxClient = (cxClient > cyClient) ? cxClient : cyClient;
  SetViewportExt(hDC, maxClient, -maxClient);
  SetViewportOrg(hDC, cxClient >> 1, cyClient >> 1);

  /* Calculate #logical units per device unit -
     will need later when draw little 3x3 boxes in DrawHandle(). */
```

```
pts[0].x = pts[0].y = 0;
pts[1].x = pts[1].y = 1;
DPtoLP(hDC, pts, 2);
LogPerDevice = (pts[1].x > pts[0].x) ? (pts[1].x - pts[0].x) :
                                      (pts[0].x - pts[1].x);

/* Incoming point in device coordinates. */
inPt.x = LOWORD(lParam);
inPt.y = HIWORD(lParam);
/* Convert to logical coordinates. */
DPtoLP(hDC, &inPt, 1);

switch(iMessage)
  {
  case WM_RBUTTONDOWN:
    /* Erase client area if not in middle of Bez. */
    if (iState == NOT_STARTED)
      InvalidateRect(hWnd, NULL, TRUE);
    break;  /* WM_RBUTTONDOWN */

  case WM_LBUTTONDOWN:
    switch(iState)
      {
      case NOT_STARTED:
        iState = DRAG_HAND1;          /* starting drag */
        hand1.x = ctrl1.x = inPt.x;  /* store user point
        hand1.y = ctrl1.y = inPt.y;     in statics */
        break;  /* NOT_STARTED */
      case WAIT_FOR_CTRL2:
        iState = DRAG_HAND2;          /* starting drag */
        hand2.x = ctrl2.x = inPt.x;  /* store user point
        hand2.y = ctrl2.y = inPt.y;     in statics */
        SetROP2(hDC, R2_NOTXORPEN);  /* draw in XOR */
        DrawBez(hDC, ctrl1, hand1, hand2, ctrl2);
        break;  /* NOT_STARTED */
      }  /* switch(iState) */
    break;  /* WM_LBUTTONDOWN */

  case WM_MOUSEMOVE:
    switch(iState)
      {
      case DRAG_HAND1:
        SetROP2(hDC, R2_NOTXORPEN);      /* draw in XOR */
        DrawHandle(hDC, ctrl1, hand1);  /* erase old */
        hand1.x = inPt.x;                /* get new handle */
        hand1.y = inPt.y;
        DrawHandle(hDC, ctrl1, hand1);  /* draw new */
        break;  /* DRAG_HAND1 */
      case DRAG_HAND2:
        SetROP2(hDC, R2_NOTXORPEN);      /* draw in XOR */
        DrawHandle(hDC, ctrl2, hand2);  /* erase old */
        DrawBez(hDC, ctrl1, hand1, hand2, ctrl2);
        hand2.x = inPt.x;                /* get new handle */
        hand2.y = inPt.y;
```

```
          DrawHandle(hDC, ctrl2, hand2);  /* draw new */
          DrawBez(hDC, ctrl1, hand1, hand2, ctrl2);
          break;  /* DRAG_HAND1 */
        }  /* switch(iState) */
      break;  /* WM_MOUSEMOVE */

    case WM_LBUTTONUP:
      switch(iState)
        {
        case DRAG_HAND1:
          iState = WAIT_FOR_CTRL2;
          SetROP2(hDC, R2_COPYPEN); /* COPY pen for final handle */
          DrawHandle(hDC, ctrl1, hand1);    /* draw in COPY mode */
          break;  /* DRAG_HAND1 */
        case DRAG_HAND2:
          iState = NOT_STARTED;
          SetROP2(hDC, R2_COPYPEN); /* COPY pen for final handle */
          DrawHandle(hDC, ctrl2, hand2);    /* draw in COPY mode */
          DrawBez(hDC, ctrl1, hand1, hand2, ctrl2);
          break;  /* DRAG_HAND2 */
        }  /* switch(iState) */
      break;  /* WM_LBUTTONUP */
    }  /* switch(iMessage) */

  ReleaseDC(hWnd, hDC);
}

BOOL FAR PASCAL AboutBez(HWND hDlg, unsigned iMessage,
                         WORD wParam, LONG lParam)
/*
USE:  Application's "About" dialog box function.
IN:   hDlg     : handle to dialog box
      iMessage : message type
      wParam   : auxiliary message info (act on IDOK, IDCANCEL)
      lParam   : unused
RET:  Return TRUE if processed appropriate message, FALSE otherwise.
NOTE: Closes "About" box only when user clicks OK button
      or system close. */
{
  switch (iMessage)
    {
    case WM_INITDIALOG:        /* initialize dialog box */
      return (TRUE);
    case WM_COMMAND:           /* received a command */
/* IDOK if OK box selected; IDCANCEL if system menu close command */
      if (wParam == IDOK || wParam == IDCANCEL)
        {
        EndDialog(hDlg, TRUE);  /* exit dialog box */
        return(TRUE);           /* did proccess message */
        }
      break;  /* WM_COMMAND */
    }  /* switch (iMessage) */
  return (FALSE);               /* did not process message */
}
```

```
void NEAR PASCAL DrawBez(HDC hDC, POINT ctrl1, POINT hand1,
                         POINT hand2, POINT ctrl2)
/*
USE:  Draw Bezier curve given control and handle points.
IN:   ctrl1,hand1,hand2,ctrl2 : control and handle points for Bezier
NOTE: Set up, then call SubDivideBez(), the recursive de Casteljau
routine, generate points along the Bez. Windows' Polyline() displays
the Bez as a polygon. BEZ_DEPTH = recursive depth of de Casteljau.
Initial POINT ctrl1 loaded here, then recursive routine calculates
and loads the remaining 2^BEZ_DEPTH = (NUM_BEZPTS - 1) de Casteljau
pts. */
{
  PtrBezPts = BezPts;         /* init ptr to start of array */
  *PtrBezPts++ = ctrl1;       /* first control point special case */
  /* calc pts */
  SubDivideBez(ctrl1, hand1, hand2, ctrl2, BEZ_DEPTH);
  Polyline(hDC, BezPts, NUM_BEZPTS);  /* call Windows to draw */
}

void NEAR PASCAL SubDivideBez(POINT p0, POINT p1,
                              POINT p2, POINT p3, int depth)
/*
  USE:  Calculate de Casteljau construction points and break Bez
        in two.
  IN:   p0,p1,p2,p3 : control/handle/handle/control for Bez to
        subdivide depth: current recursive depth of algorithm.
  NOTE: Calculates the de Casteljau construction points so the
  Bezier can be subdivided into 2 parts (left, then right) by
  recursive calls to this routine. Recursion is broken off when
  depth, decremented once for each recursion level, becomes 0.
  This is the finest level of subdivision; the right-most point on
  the small subdivided Bezier is also a point on the original
  Bezier, so we load it into global array BezPts[] (thru PtrBezPts
  which points into the array). */
{
  /* de Casteljau construction points: */
  POINT q0, q1, q2, r0, r1, s0;

  /* depth == 0 means we are at the finest subdivision level:
  grab point into global array and return, breaking off recursion.
  */
  if (!depth)
    {
    *PtrBezPts++ = p3;
    return;
    }

  /* Calculate de Casteljau construction points as averages of
     previous points (ie, midway points); note shift right is
     fast division by 2. */
  /* q's are midway between 4 incoming control and handle points. */
  q0.x = (p0.x + p1.x) >> 1;  q0.y = (p0.y + p1.y) >> 1;
  q1.x = (p1.x + p2.x) >> 1;  q1.y = (p1.y + p2.y) >> 1;
  q2.x = (p2.x + p3.x) >> 1;  q2.y = (p2.y + p3.y) >> 1;
```

```
    /* r's are midway between 3 q's. */
    r0.x = (q0.x + q1.x) >> 1;  r0.y = (q0.y + q1.y) >> 1;
    r1.x = (q1.x + q2.x) >> 1;  r1.y = (q1.y + q2.y) >> 1;

    /* s0 is midway between 2 r's and is in middle of original Bez. */
    s0.x = (r0.x + r1.x) >> 1;  s0.y = (r0.y + r1.y) >> 1;

    /* Decrement depth; subdivide incoming Bez into 2 parts:
       left, then right.*/
    SubDivideBez(p0, q0, r0, s0, --depth);
    SubDivideBez(s0, r1, q2, p3,   depth);
  }

void NEAR PASCAL DrawHandle(HDC hDC, POINT p, POINT q)
/*
  USE:  Draws handle on screen from p to q with hRedPen.
  IN:   hDC : handle to display context
        p,q : handle start and end points
  NOTE: Don't CreatePen or delete—these are done globally once
        only.
  Handles are drawn with little 3x3 pixel boxes at each end.
  Each pixel is LogPerDevice logical units; logical units must be
  used for the boxes since we are in MM_ISOTROPIC mapping mode.
*/
{
  HPEN origPen;     /* DC's original pen */
  int  xLeft;       /* left coord of little box at end of handle */
  int  xRight;      /* right coord of little box */
  int  y;           /* y coord of little box */

  /* Save original pen, select red pen. */
  origPen = SelectObject(hDC, hRedPen);

  /* Draw handle. */
  MoveTo(hDC, p.x, p.y);  LineTo(hDC, q.x, q.y);

  /* Set left and right coords around q.x (3 pixels). Remember
     Windows lines do not draw last pixel. */
  xLeft  = q.x - LogPerDevice;
  xRight = q.x + (LogPerDevice << 1);

  /* Init y coord 1 pixel below q.y. */
  y = q.y - LogPerDevice;

  /* Draw little box : 3x3 pixels. */
  MoveTo(hDC, xLeft, y); LineTo(hDC, xRight, y);  y += LogPerDevice;
  MoveTo(hDC, xLeft, y); LineTo(hDC, xRight, y);  y += LogPerDevice;
  MoveTo(hDC, xLeft, y); LineTo(hDC, xRight, y);  y += LogPerDevice;

  /* Re-select original pen. */
  SelectObject(hDC, origPen);
}
```

POSTNET Barcodes in C

■ Brian Cheetham

Here's a useful technique for printing ZIP+4 bar codes.

If you're not in the mailing business, you may be unaware of the strides that the U.S. Postal Service has made toward automation in recent years. Yep, those dependable guys and gals who deliver your mail through sleet and snow and freezing rain are also interested in doing it better, faster, and cheaper.

Central to this effort is the USPS POSTNET bar code. If you've noticed funny looking lines at the bottom of some of your mail, you've seen POSTNET in action. POSTNET is a fairly simple bar code specification that defines bar codes for the digits 0–9. Each digit is composed of a unique combination of two long bars and three short bars. A full POSTNET bar code sequence consists of a starting long bar, five bars for each of the nine digits in the ZIP+4 code, five bars for a checksum digit, and an ending long bar, for a total of 52 bars. (In the near future, the USPS will be adding delivery *point* to the specification. Delivery point simply adds the last two digits of the street address to the ZIP+4 code, for a total of 62 bars.) The encoding of the bars for each digit is shown in the comments in Listing 5.19, beside the definition for the code array.

Listing 5.19 is a short program that implements POSTNET bar coding (as currently defined by the USPS) on LaserJet printers. Note: While Listing 5.19 prints the bar code along the bottom edge of the envelope, recent changes by the USPS allow you to print the bar code within the "address block" of the envelope as well. This is particularly useful when printing mailing labels. Business mailers may qualify for certain discounts by using bar codes. Additionally, individuals may soon be eligible for discounts for using bar codes, subject to USPS approval. Contact the Postal Service for current information.

CODE DESCRIPTION

Overview

The listings provided can be used to draw bar codes on LaserJet printers.

Listings Available

Listing	*Description*	*Used with*
POSTNET.C	The source file for the barcode program.	------

How to Compile/Assemble

The C source file can be compiled with any C/C++ compiler.

■ **LISTING 5.19 POSTNET.C**

```
#include <ctype.h>
#include <stdio.h>
#include <stdlib.h>
```

```
#include <string.h>

#define LONGBAR  33
#define SHORTBAR 32

void  postnet(char *),
      printbar(int);

void main(int argc, char *argv[]) {
/*--------------------------------*/
/*  main function - syntax: Postnet zip_code LETTER|BUSINESS   */
/*--------------------------------*/

if (argc < 3) {
  printf("Usage:  Envelope zip_code LETTER|BUSINESS\n");
  exit(1);
}

if (stricmp(argv[2], "LETTER") == 0)    // size of envelope parm
  fprintf(stdprn, "\033*p1640x1200Y"); // initialize print posn
else
  if (stricmp(argv[2], "BUSINESS") == 0)
    fprintf(stdprn, "\033*p1715x1200Y");
  else {
    printf("Usage:  Envelope zip_code LETTER|BUSINESS\n");
    exit(1);
    }

postnet(argv[1]);           // print the US PostNet barcode
fprintf(stdprn, "\033E");  // reset & form feed
}

void postnet(char *zip_code) {
/*  postnet - print US Postal Service PostNet barcode.  */
int checksum = 0,
    code[10] = {       // |-len-|-data-|
                184,  //  1 0 1 1 1 0 0 0\
                163,  //  1 0 1 0 0 0 1 1 \       len:
                165,  //  1 0 1 0 0 1 0 1  \      # of bars
                166,  //  1 0 1 0 0 1 1 0   \     in code
                169,  //  1 0 1 0 1 0 0 1    \
                170,  //  1 0 1 0 1 0 1 0    /
                172,  //  1 0 1 0 1 1 0 0   /    data bits:
                177,  //  1 0 1 1 0 0 0 1  /     0 = short bar
                178,  //  1 0 1 1 0 0 1 0 /      1 = long bar
                180}, //  1 0 1 1 0 1 0 0/
    i,
    len;

len = strlen(zip_code);
printbar(LONGBAR);              // start with LONGBAR
for (i = 0; i < len; i++)       // print each digit
  if (isdigit(zip_code[i])) {
    printbar(code[zip_code[i] - '0']);
```

```
    checksum = checksum + (zip_code[i] - '0');
  }

checksum %= 10;                      // get remainder
printbar(code[10 - checksum]);       // print checksum
printbar(LONGBAR);                   // end with LONGBAR

}

void printbar(int code) {
/*  printbar() - print the bar(s) for a single code. */
int     i,
    len;

len = (code >> 5) & 0x07;
for (i = len - 1; i >= 0; i—)
  if ((code & (1 << i)) != 0) {     // if bit == 1, long bar
    fprintf(stdprn, "\033*c38a4b0P"); // draw rectangle 38x4 dots
    fprintf(stdprn, "\033*p-14Y");  // move 14 dots (Y) for next
    } else {                        // else, short bar
    fprintf(stdprn, "\033*p+21X");    // move 21 dots (X)
    fprintf(stdprn, "\033*c17a4b0P"); // draw rectangle 17x4 dots
    fprintf(stdprn, "\033*p-21x-14Y");// move back 21 dots (X) &
    }                                   // 14 dots (Y) for next bar
}
```

6

User Interface Programming

No one could accuse our industry of ignoring the user interface issue. UIs have become a bit of an obsession these days, with a lot of predictable griping. Seventy percent of an application is UI! How appalling!

Well, maybe not.

You have to look at it this way: A program exists to get some work done, and the user interface is the part of a program that organizes the process of doing the work. How well or how poorly the work process is organized can make an enormous difference in how much work gets done per unit time.

Most intelligent developers are beginning to recognize this—which doesn't mean that we've arrived at a consensus of what a good UI is, let alone how to implement one. The issue of expert user access versus beginning user access is still unresolved. A program that forces both beginners and experts down all the same paths is wasting the time of the experts.

I guess this means that we're still living in interesting times, in the sense of the old Chinese curse.

What we can do, regardless of unresolved issues, is know how the basic components of user interfaces work, so that we can continue the evolution of UI concepts. That's what we're up to in this chapter. Bryan Flamig's piece on 3-D graphics windows will appeal to those who persist in rolling their own GUI—for which there may still be good reason. (The industry's best-kept secret seems to be the simple truth that you can't always use Microsoft Windows!)

Borland gave the text-mode UI new life when it released Turbo Vision, an ambitious application interface for TurboPascal and Borland C++. Kevin Dean tells us how to "fake" multitasking in Turbo Vision by using the **idle()** function, as well as how to make Turbo Vision jive with the notion of C++ streams.

Three-Dimensional Graphics Windows

■ Bryan Flamig

Here's a useful trick for creating simple 3-D graphics windows.

Many of the contemporary graphical interfaces have been going to a 3-D look lately. It's easy to be impressed by such interfaces, thinking that the programmers who designed them must be really hot.

It turns out that getting this look is not very difficult, as **BOX3D_EX.C** (Listing 6.1) shows. Listing 6.1 works best in one of the color EGA or VGA modes. The program contains the function **Box3d()**, which, when given the location, size, border width, color, and style, draws a box either convex (appearing to stick out of the screen), or concave (appearing to be sunken in).

The secret lies in setting up two colors—the sun color and the shadow color—that are used on the border of the box (see Figure 6.1). Imagine a light shining on the box from one side. The portion of the border where the light hits is given the sun color, and the portion where the light doesn't hit is given the shadow color. By swapping these two colors, you can make your box appear concave or convex. The **Box3d()** function interprets the colors as though the light comes from the "northwest" corner of the screen.

The heart of the function is the **for** loop that draws the border. Each time through the loop, it draws four line segments, making one circuit around the border. It starts at the outer edge of the box and works inward until the border is **Bw** pixels wide. Then, the interior is filled to the interior color **FillC**.

The example draws a cyan-colored concave box inside a convex box. If you try experimenting with different color sets, you'll find that few sets work very well. The cyan color set is probably the best one, unless you modify the standard color palette.

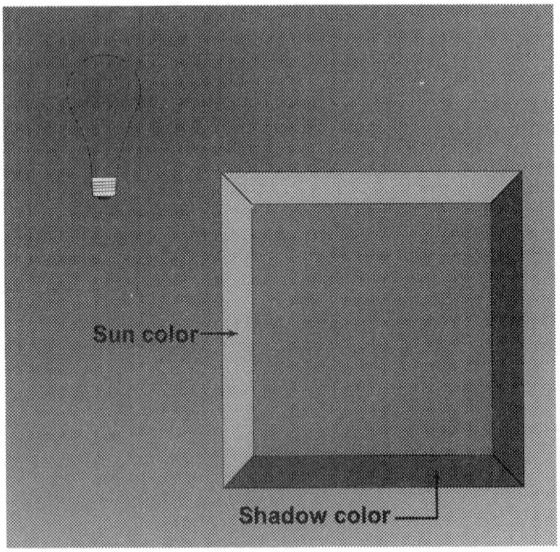

■ **FIGURE 6.1 Sun color and the shadow color**

CODE DESCRIPTION

Overview

This is a short procedure written in C that will display a three-dimensional box on the screen.

Listings Available

Listing	*Description*	*Used With*
BOX3D_EX.C	Draws a 3D box on the screen	------

How to Compile/Assemble

Can be compiled and linked with any C/C++ compiler.
Changing **SunC** and **ShadowC** and **Style3d** in the call to **Box3d()**, will result in different effects.

■ LISTING 6.1 BOX3D_EX.C

```
/*  Draws a 3D box with top-left corner (Xul, Yul) and bottom-right corner (Xlr,
Ylr). A border width of Bw and a border style of Bs (either Concave or Convex)
is used. The sun color is SunC, the shadow color is ShadowC, and the interior
fill color is FillC. */

#include <graphics.h>
#include <stdlib.h>
#include <stdio.h>
#include <conio.h>

typedef enum _Style3d {Concave, Convex} Style3d;

void Box3d(int Xul,int Yul,int Xlr,int Ylr,
           int Bw, int SunC, int ShadowC, int FillC,
           Style3d Bs)
{
int I,T;

  if (Bs == Concave)
  { /* Swap sun and shadow colors */
    T = ShadowC;
    ShadowC = SunC;
    SunC = T;
  }
  /* For each circuit around the border: */
  for (I = 0; I < Bw; I++)
  {
    setcolor(SunC);
    moveto(Xul+I, Ylr-I);      /* Draw top/left sides */
    lineto(Xul+I, Yul+I);
    lineto(Xlr-I, Yul+I);
    setcolor(ShadowC);
    moveto(Xlr-I, Yul+I+1);    /* Draw bottom/right sides */
    lineto(Xlr-I, Ylr-I);
    lineto(Xul+I+1, Ylr-I);
```

```
    };
    /* Fill the interior */
    setfillstyle(SOLID_FILL,FillC);
    bar(Xul+Bw, Yul+Bw, Xlr-Bw, Ylr-Bw);
};

void main(void)
{
int Gdriver = DETECT, Gmode, errCode;

    getch();
    initgraph(&Gdriver,&Gmode,"");
    //set this string to the place where your graphics drivers can be found
    errCode = graphresult();
    if (errCode != grOk)
    {
     fprintf(stderr, "Graphics error:  %s\n",grapherrormsg(errCode));
      exit(1);
    };
    Box3d(5, 5, 100, 100, 3, LIGHTCYAN, DARKGRAY, CYAN, Convex);
    Box3d(42, 42, 62, 62, 3, LIGHTCYAN, DARKGRAY, CYAN, Concave);
    getch();
    closegraph();
}
```

Determining When Windows Overlap

■ Bryan Flamig

Learn how to develop a useful algorithm to check for overlapping windows.

One of the problems you'll encounter when writing a robust overlapping-windows package is how to tell when one window overlaps another, so that you can update the window images efficiently. It turns out that a very simple yet elegant algorithm can be used to determine when windows overlap.

One problem-solving method that often works well is to do a case analysis of the problem at hand. In the window overlap problem, windows can be treated as rectangular regions, and then we can list all possible ways that two rectangles can intersect each other. There are eight cases in all, as shown in Figure 6.2. Note that, in these cases, we're not concerned about which rectangle is on top, or which is to the left or right, but only whether the two rectangles intersect.

By studying the eight cases, we can develop the following simple rule: The rectangles can intersect only if their horizontal extents intersect *and* if their vertical extents intersect. OVERLAP.C (Listing 6.2) shows a C function that tests for rectangle intersection by checking the horizontal and vertical extents. It takes only four compares to do this checking.

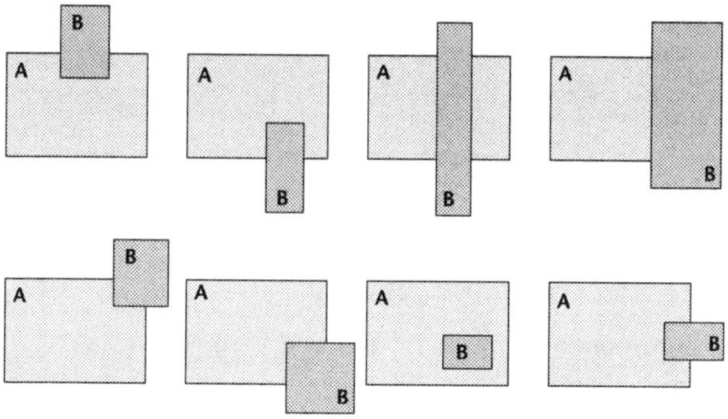

■ **FIGURE 6.2 The eight cases for overlapping rectangles**

Only "proper" intersections are considered here. That is, a rectangle isn't considered to intersect with itself. We check for this case by comparing rectangle pointers.

CODE DESCRIPTION

Overview

This is a short procedure written in C which will determine whether the coordinates of two windows overlap.

Listings Available

Listing	*Description*	*Used with*
OVERLAP.C	Contains the function Overlap().	------

How to Compile/Assemble

Can be compiled and linked with any C/C++ compiler.

■ LISTING 6.2 OVERLAP.C

```
typedef struct _Rect {
        int Xul, Yul;  //Upper left-hand corner
        int Xlr, Ylr;  //Lower right-hand corner
        } Rect;

char Overlap(Rect *A, Rect *B)
{
    if (A == B)
       return 0;    //Not allowed to intersect with itself

    return !((A->Xul > B->Xlr) ||  (A->Xlr < B->Xul) ||
        (A->Yul > B->Ylr) || (A->Ylr < B->Yul));
}
```

Turbo Vision's Idle Moments

■ Kevin Dean

Put the dead time between user keystrokes to good use by studying the lore of the ***idle()*** *function.*

Most programs spend most of their time waiting for keyboard input. Even if you graduated with first-class honors from the Wonder Wizard Typing School, you'll never keep up with even the simplest program's demands on the keyboard. What happens to all that wasted CPU time?

The answer to that depends more on the operating system than anything else. Most operating systems, even early versions of DOS, have some way of telling when a program is idling. In DOS, if a program is blocked waiting for data from the keyboard, the "DOS OK" INT 28H is generated in a loop that looks something like this:

```
while not key pressed:
  generate idle INT 28H;
end while
return pressed key.
```

Many TSRs use this interrupt to do background processing. For example, the DOS PRINT program hooks into the DOS OK interrupt and prints files when the computer is not otherwise engaged. Multitasking environments like Windows and DESQview also watch for idle time and switch to another program when they detect it.

Idling with Turbo Vision

Turbo Vision has its own idling routine. You may have seen casual references to it, but not much more than statements that the **idle()** member function of **TApplication** is called when no event is ready. There are no rules about when we can use it and only one rule about how: We must call the **idle()** routine of the base application class to make sure that all other idle tasks are handled properly.

Because the **idle()** function is called only when no events are pending, we know two things for certain: Nothing else is happening, and that our program is the active one. This is obvious and not very profound, I know; but the biggest problems that TSRs and multitaskers face are those of DOS reëntrancy and context switching. If our program is doing anything at all in DOS, it takes some doing to find out what and whether or not it can be interrupted. A TSR or multitasker also has to change the context to fool DOS into believing that the TSR or new program is the currently active program.

Turbo Vision's **idle()** function is a gift by comparison. For **idle()** to be called, **getEvent()** must have no events pending; and for **getEvent()** to be called, the program must be blocked waiting for input. We're not in DOS and the context is already that of our own program. We have free rein, almost.

I say "almost" because, although we can always use the idle time, there are times when we *shouldn't*. The rules depend on the application, and the ones I have created are only guidelines. If, for example, you have BGI graphics on the screen, the last thing you want your idle routines doing is popping up dialog boxes!

Turbo Vision's **idle()** function has a number of advantages, including

- Access to all Turbo Vision resources
- Access to all DOS functions
- The ability to send messages or create events that will be responded to by other parts of the program

The sample program presented here is based on Borland's FILEVIEW, which is included with Turbo Vision for C++. FILEVIEW.HHG (LISTING 6.3), lists the changes to the original FILEVIEW.H. (The complete source for the program is available on the listings diskette included with this book.) Similar files are in FILEVIEW.CHG (Listing 6.4) and FVIEWER.CPP (Listing 6.5).

TIP: The ellipses (. . .) in all three listings files represent parts of the file that were not printed in this book.

Two new files, PRFILE.H and PRFILE.CPP, are given in Listings 6.6 and 6.7. Wherever possible, I have put the new code in PRFILE.H and PRFILE.CPP.

Changes to Borland's Code

The **cmPrintFile** command has been added to the application in PRFILE.H. Because this command is not one of TV's default commands, we have to add an event handler for it. A **TFileViewer** is the only view that can reasonably handle this event, so two new member functions, **handleEvent()** and **printFile()**, have been added to its class definition in FILEVIEW.H. We should also disable the **cmPrintFile** command if no files are open, so a new static member, **filesOpen**, has been added to **TFileViewer** to keep track of the number of open files.

In FILEVIEW.CPP, TVCMDS.H has been removed from the include file list (it wasn't being used anyway) and PRFILE.H has been added. The **TFileViewer** constructor enables the **cmPrintFile** command if this is the first file opened, and the destructor disables the command if this is the last file closed. Finally, there is a bug in the **TFileWindow** constructor: the first file opened should be assigned a window number of 1 but is instead assigned a window number of 0 because of the placement of the increment operator.

Most of the changes to FVIEWER.CPP define the interface to the background printer: disabling the **cmPrintFile** command in the application constructor, adding the Print option to the menu, adding the **idle()** function to the application, and handling the **cmQuit** command in the **handleEvent()** member. If the **cmQuit** makes it to **TProgram::handleEvent()**, the application is closed. By checking for **cmQuit** first, we can do any shutdown procedures and, if any of the procedures fail, clear the event. In this case, we attempt to cancel the print queue. If the queue isn't canceled, the **cmQuit** event is cleared before it can be passed any farther down the line.

The **TFileViewerApp::idle()** function calls the base class **idle()** function and prints from the default queue.

The Print Queue

PRFILE.H defines two classes, **TPrintFile** and **TPrintQueue**, that work together to implement print queues. **TPrintFile**, derived from **TObject**, holds a copy of the filename to be printed. **TPrintQueue** is a **TNSCollection** of **TPrintFile** pointers with additional members to define the printer port, current file, file buffer, and whether or not the printer error dialog box is open. The **printQueue** static member is the default queue used throughout the program.

One failing of the TV collection classes is that they collect **void*** pointers, not **TObject*** pointers. When any of the **free()** member functions of the collection classes are called, they remove a **void*** pointer and delete it. As a result, the destructor for the **TPrintFile** object (or anything else derived from **TObject**) is not called. The **TPrintQueue** functions **removeFile()** and **removeAll()** properly delete **TPrintFile** objects and remove them from the collection.

The **cancel()** member of **TPrintQueue** is called when **cmQuit** is received by the application. If any files are still in the queue when this function is called, a dialog box pops up asking the user to confirm the command. If the user confirms the exit, the print queue is purged. If not, the event is cleared by **TFileViewerApp::handleEvent()** and the program resumes.

The print() Function

Finally, there is the **print()** function itself. This is the function called while the program is idling, so it merits special study.

The most important rule for an idle function is that it must not take so much time that we affect user response time. If the user presses F3 to open the file dialog box, the dialog box should come up instantly, not five seconds later. If the idle function has several things to do, only one thing should be done each time the function is called. The idle function is called several times a second, so we lose nothing by breaking our task down into smaller pieces.

The best way to design an idle function is to design it as though it were a regular function and then break it down into its components. The **print()** function, if it were not an idle function, would look like this:

```
for each file in the queue
  open the file;
  while not end of file
    read data into buffer;
    for each character in the buffer
      print the character;
      if error while printing
        ask the user to fix the problem;
  print a formfeed;
  close the file;
  remove the file from the queue.
```

There are three time-consuming tasks here: opening a file, reading data into the buffer, and printing the data. The other tasks, closing the file and removing it from the queue, have negligible overhead. The **print()** function can be rewritten as follows:

```
if data in buffer
  for some small length of time
    check the printer status;
    if printer error
      ask the user to fix the problem;
    else if printer available
      print the next character in the buffer;
else if file is open
  read data into buffer;
  if end of file
    add formfeed to buffer;
    close file;
else if file is waiting in print queue
  open the next file;
  remove file from queue.
```

What we have done is turn the original loop inside out.

If an error occurs, such as the printer running out of paper, we need to alert the user. A simple dialog box pops up with an error message asking the user to retry the operation, cancel the file, or purge the entire queue. This is the only part of the idle function that interacts with Turbo Vision itself, so it is here that we need to be sure that it is safe to pop up. To be sure that we may interrupt the user, we check the top view. If the application isn't the top view (e.g., if the user has another dialog box open or a menu pulled down), we skip the error message and exit the **print()** function immediately.

We deal with errors only when the application is the top view. This is not a restriction placed by Turbo Vision, but rather by good interface design: Don't confuse the user with things like multiple dialog boxes. The full range of checks depends on the application.

Now it gets interesting: If we open a dialog box in the idle function, it's going to have to get input from the user and so it's going to spend a certain amount of time idling. While the application is idling, the **print()** function continues to check the status of the printer. If the printer becomes available while the dialog box is open (i.e., when **dialogOpen** is True), we can signal the fact by putting a **cmCancel** command into the event queue with **putEvent()** (as I have done here) or by sending the command through the **message()** function (also shown, but not used). Either of these will close the error dialog box and return control to the application and the background printer.

Busy Being idle()

With Turbo Vision's **idle()** function and a little planning, we can make good use of spare CPU time. We have access to all Turbo Vision resources and can do anything we please as long as we don't slow down response time or confuse the user. We can even send events or messages to any view in Turbo Vision, including views in other levels of the **idle()** function.

CODE DESCRIPTION

Overview

Listing	*Description*	*Used With*
FILEVIEW.HHG	Changes to FileView.HPP	------
FILEVIEW.CHG	Changes to FileView.CPP	------
FVIEWER.CHG	Changes to FViewer.CPP	------
PRFILE.H		------
PRFILE.CPP		------

How to Compile/Assemble

Must be compiled with Turbo Vision and C++ compiler

■ LISTING 6.3 FILEVIEW.HHG

```
. . .
#if !defined( __FILEVIEW_H )
#define __FILEVIEW_H

class TFileViewer : public TScroller
{
public:
...
    // PRFILE CHANGE: added handleEvent(TEvent&) and printFile()
    // functions.
    void handleEvent(TEvent& event);
    void printFile();

    // PRFILE CHANGE: added filesOpen member.
    static int filesOpen;
...
};
...
#endif
```

■ LISTING 6.4 FILEVIEW.CHG

```
. . .
// PRFILE CHANGE: removed #include "tvcmds.h".
#include "fileview.h"

// PRFILE CHANGE: added #include "prfile.h".
#include "prfile.h"

const char * const TFileViewer::name = "TFileViewer";

TFileViewer::TFileViewer( const TRect& bounds,
            TScrollBar *aHScrollBar,
            TScrollBar *aVScrollBar,
            const char *aFileName) :
    TScroller( bounds, aHScrollBar, aVScrollBar )
```

```
{
...
    // PRFILE CHANGE: added enable of cmPrintFile.
    if (!filesOpen++)
      enableCommand(cmPrintFile);
}

TFileViewer::~TFileViewer()
{
    // PRFILE CHANGE: added disable of cmPrintFile.
    if (!—filesOpen)
      disableCommand(cmPrintFile);
...
}
...
TFileWindow::TFileWindow( const char *fileName ) :
    // PRFILE CHANGE: changed winNumber++ to ++winNumber (bug).
    TWindow( TProgram::deskTop->getExtent(), fileName, ++winNumber),
    TWindowInit( &TFileWindow::initFrame )
{
...
}
```

■ LISTING 6.5 FVIEWER.CHG

```
. . .
#if !defined( __FILEVIEW_H )
#include "FileView.h"
#endif  // __FILEVIEW_H
// PRFILE CHANGE: added #include "prfile.h".
#include "prfile.h"

class TFileViewerApp : public TApplication
{
public:
...
    // PRFILE CHANGE: added idle() function.
    virtual void idle();
...
};

TFileViewerApp::TFileViewerApp() :
    TProgInit( &TFileViewerApp::initStatusLine,
           &TFileViewerApp::initMenuBar,
           &TFileViewerApp::initDeskTop
         )
{
    // PRFILE CHANGE: added disable of cmPrintFile.
    // No files open; none can be printed.
    disableCommand(cmPrintFile);
}
...
void TFileViewerApp::handleEvent( TEvent& event )
{
    // PRFILE CHANGE: added handler for cmQuit.
```

```
    // Attempt to cancel print queue; clear quit event if failed.
    if (event.what == evCommand && event.message.command == cmQuit
    && !TPrintQueue::printQueue.cancel())
    clearEvent( event );

    TApplication::handleEvent( event );
...
}

TMenuBar *TFileViewerApp::initMenuBar( TRect r )
{
    r.b.y = r.a.y+1;

    return new TMenuBar( r,
      *new TSubMenu( "~F~ile", kbAltF ) +
    *new TMenuItem( "~O~pen...", cmFileOpen, kbF3,
    hcNoContext, "F3" ) +
    *new TMenuItem( "~C~hange dir...", cmChangeDir,
    kbNoKey ) +
    // PRFILE CHANGE: added ~P~rint menu item.
    *new TMenuItem( "~P~rint", cmPrintFile, kbNoKey ) +
    *new TMenuItem( "E~x~it", cmQuit, kbAltX,
    hcNoContext, "Alt-X" ) +
...
}
...
// PRFILE CHANGE: defined TFileViewerApp::idle() function.
void TFileViewerApp::idle()
{
TApplication::idle();
TPrintQueue::printQueue.print();
}
```

■ LISTING 6.6 PRFILE.H

```
#include <fstream.h>

#define Uses_TNSCollection
#define Uses_TObject
#include <tv.h>

class TPrintFile : public TObject
  {
  const char *_name;

  public:

  TPrintFile(const char *name);

  virtual ~TPrintFile();

  const char *name()
  {
  return (_name);
  }
```

```
  };

class TPrintQueue : public TNSCollection
  {
  enum
    {
    timeOut     = 0x01,
    ioError     = 0x08,
    selected    = 0x10,
    outOfPaper  = 0x20,
    acknowledge = 0x40,
    notBusy     = 0x80
    };

  enum
    {
    printChar, initPrinter, readStatus
    };

  int _port;      // Printer port number.
  ifstream f;     // Printer input file.
  char buffer[1024];  // Printer buffer.
  char *bufend;     // End of buffer.
  const char *bufptr;  // Current index into buffer.
  Boolean dialogOpen;  // True if error dialog box is open.

  public:

  static TPrintQueue printQueue;

  // Should be private.
  TPrintQueue(int port);

  void removeFile();

  void removeAll();

  Boolean cancel();

  void print();
  };

const int cmPrintFile    = 100;
```

■ LISTING 6.7 PRFILE.CPP

```
#include <bios.h>
#include <dos.h>
#include <string.h>

#define Uses_TApplication
#define Uses_TButton
#define Uses_TDeskTop
#define Uses_TDialog
#define Uses_TEvent
```

```
#define Uses_TLabel
#define Uses_TProgram
#define Uses_TRadioButtons
#define Uses_TSItem
#define Uses_TView
#include <tv.h>

#include "fileview.h"
#include "prfile.h"

int TFileViewer::filesOpen = 0;

void TFileViewer::handleEvent(TEvent& event)
{
TScroller::handleEvent(event);
if (event.what == evCommand)
  switch (event.message.command)
    {
    case cmPrintFile:
      printFile();
      clearEvent( event );
      break;
    }
}

TPrintFile::TPrintFile(const char *name) : TObject(),
_name(newStr(name))
{
}

TPrintFile::~TPrintFile()
{
delete _name;
}

TPrintQueue::TPrintQueue(int port) : TNSCollection(10, 5),
_port(port - 1), bufend(buffer), bufptr(buffer), dialogOpen(False)
{
}

void TPrintQueue::removeFile()
{
delete (TPrintFile*)at(0);
atRemove(0);
}

void TPrintQueue::removeAll()
{
while (count)
  removeFile();
}

Boolean TPrintQueue::cancel()
{
Boolean cancelled;
```

```
  // Queue active if files remaining or buffer not empty.
  if (count || bufptr != bufend)
    {
    TDialog *errdlg = new TDialog(TRect(0, 0, 29, 8),
              "Printer Warning");
    errdlg->options |= ofCentered;
    if (errdlg)
      {
      errdlg->insert(new TLabel(TRect(1, 1, 27, 2),
                  "Print queue is not empty.", 0));
      errdlg->insert(new TLabel(TRect(1, 2, 24, 3),
                  "Exiting will purge all", 0));
      errdlg->insert(new TLabel(TRect(1, 3, 13, 4),
                  "print jobs.", 0));

      errdlg->insert(new TButton(TRect(1, 5, 13, 7), "E~x~it",
                  cmOK, bfNormal));
      errdlg->insert(new TButton(TRect(15, 5, 27, 7), "Cancel",
                  cmCancel, bfDefault));
      if (lowMemory())
        {
        destroy(errdlg);
        cancelled = True;
        }
      else
        {
        // Alert user with error tone.
        sound(880);
        delay(100);
        sound(554);
        delay(100);
        nosound();

        switch (TProgram::deskTop->execView(errdlg))
      {
      case cmCancel:
        cancelled = False;
        break;

      case cmOK:
        cancelled = True;
        break;
      }

        destroy(errdlg);
        }
      }

    if (cancelled)
      removeAll();
    }
  else
    cancelled = True;

  return (cancelled);
```

```
}

void TPrintQueue::print()
{
if (bufptr != bufend)
  for (int i = 0, printOk = True; i < 100 && bufptr != bufend &&
       printOk; i++)
    {
    char *errmessage = 0;
    int printStat = biosprint(readStatus, 0, _port);

    if (printStat & outOfPaper)
      errmessage = "Out of paper.";
    else if (!(printStat & selected))
      errmessage = "Offline.";
    else if (printStat & (timeOut | ioError))
      errmessage = "I/O error.";
    else if (printStat & notBusy)
      // If the dialog box is open (user is being asked to reply to
      // an error), error has been cleared so clear dialog box.
      if (dialogOpen)
      {
       TEvent cancelEvent;

       cancelEvent.what = evCommand;
       cancelEvent.message.command = cmCancel;
       cancelEvent.message.infoPtr = 0;
       TProgram::application->putEvent(cancelEvent);

       // Instead of putEvent(), could also use:
       // message(TProgram::application, evCommand, cmCancel, 0);

       // Abort this invocation of the idle() routine.
       printOk = False;
      }
      else
       biosprint(printChar, *bufptr++, _port);
       if (errmessage)
       // If dialogOpen is True, this test will fail anyway.
       if (TProgram::application->TopView() == TProgram::application)
       {
        TDialog *errdlg = new TDialog(TRect(0, 0, 35, 5),
                        "Printer Error");
        errdlg->options |= ofCentered;
        if (errdlg)
         {
          errdlg->insert(new TLabel(TRect(1, 1, strlen(errmessage) +
                      2, 2), errmessage, 0));

          errdlg->insert(new TRadioButtons(TRect(16, 1, 33, 4),
                    new TSItem("~R~etry",
                    new TSItem("~C~ancel file",
                    new TSItem("~P~urge queue", 0)))));

          errdlg->insert(new TButton(TRect(1, 2, 15, 4), "O~K~",
```

```
                    cmOK, bfDefault));

          if (lowMemory())
            {
            destroy(errdlg);
            printOk = False;
            }
          else
            {
            ushort response = 0;
            errdlg->setData(&response);

            // Alert user with error tone.
            sound(880);
            delay(100);
            sound(554);
            delay(100);
            nosound();

            dialogOpen = True;
            switch (TProgram::deskTop->execView(errdlg))
            {
              case cmCancel:
                break;

              case cmOK:
                errdlg->getData(&response);
              switch (response)
               {
                  case 0:
                    break;

                  case 2:
                    removeAll();

                  case 1:
                    f.close();
                    bufptr = bufend;
                    break;
              }
              break;
            }

        destroy(errdlg);
        dialogOpen = False;
          }
        }
      }
       else
     // Application is not modal view; wait until it is.
    printOk = False;
     }
else if (f.rdbuf()->is_open())
  {
  f.read(buffer, sizeof(buffer));
```

```
    bufend = buffer + f.gcount();
    bufptr = buffer;

    // If end of file, close file and add formfeed.
    if (bufend != buffer + sizeof(buffer))
      {
      f.close();
      *bufend++ = '\f';
      }
    }
  else if (count)
    {
    f.open(((TPrintFile*)at(0))->name(), ios::in | ios::binary);
    removeFile();
    }
  }
// Create print queue on port LPT1.
TPrintQueue TPrintQueue::printQueue(1);

void TFileViewer::printFile()
{
TPrintQueue::printQueue.insert(new TPrintFile(fileName));
}
```

TV I/O with C++ Streams

■ Kevin Dean

Learn how to use C++ streams in Turbo Vision to control formatted I/O.

One of the first things Borland warns against when Turbo Vision is used for C++ is the use of **printf()**, **puts()**, and the standard C++ stream I/O to write to the screen. Because they're not part of TV, there is nothing to prevent these functions from obliterating or being obliterated by a TV window. Very often, however, we need to display formatted I/O and we would either have to write our own output formatters or write the output to a string (via **sprintf()** or the **strstream** classes) and then to the screen.

Fortunately, Borland has extended C++ streams to include Turbo Vision windows. The classes they have defined in TEXTVIEW.H are **TTextDevice** (derived from **TScroller** and **streambuf**), **TTerminal** (a buffered **TTextDevice**), and **otstream** (derived from **ostream**). By creating a **TTerminal** view in a window and passing it to the constructor of **otstream**, we have a C++ stream that can be used as follows:

```
ot << "Value of 'X' is " << setw(4) << X << endl;
```

No Extra Coding Required

Some time ago, I wrote a communications package that monitored several devices and displayed status and error messages through **cout** and **cerr**, respectively. It wasn't the prettiest interface, and the only real problem was reviewing the messages if several of them came in while the system was unattended—the old messages had scrolled off the screen. With Turbo Vision, I was able to clean up the interface and review messages, again thanks to the TV extensions to C++ streams, without having to change much code.

A little-known property of the standard stream objects **cin**, **cout**, **cerr**, and **clog** (a buffered version of **cerr**) is that they can be redirected by assigning stream buffers or other streams to them. By assigning **TTerminal** views to them (**TTerminal** being derived from **streambuf**), I got the message-review capability that was needed as well as the cleaner TV interface I wanted. None of my code that used **cout** or **cerr** had to be changed.

The **TOutputWindow** constructor in TVOUTERR.CPP creates a **TTerminal** view, assigns it to a stream, writes to that stream, and then copies that stream to **cout** or **cerr**, whichever has been passed to the constructor (see Listing 6.8). The member function **TOutputWindow::attach()** attaches the **TTerminal** view to a formatted output stream.

■ LISTING 6.8 TVOUTERR.CPP

```
#include <iostream.h>

#define Uses_otstream
#define Uses_TApplication
#define Uses_TDeskTop
#define Uses_TRect
#define Uses_TTerminal
#define Uses_TWindow
#include <tv.h>

class TOutputWindow : public TWindow
  {
  TTerminal *_term;

  public:

  TOutputWindow(TRect bounds, const char *title,
  ostream_withassign& ostr, ushort bufsize);

  void attach(ostream_withassign& ostr)
  {
  // Attach TTerminal stream buffer to I/O stream.
  ostr = _term;
  }
  };

class TOutErr : public TApplication
  {
  ostream_withassign _old_cout;
  ostream_withassign _old_cerr;
  ostream_withassign _old_clog;

  public:

  TOutErr(TRect& outbounds, ushort outbufsize, TRect& errbounds,
  ushort errbufsize);
```

```
  ~TOutErr();

  virtual void run();
  };

TOutputWindow::TOutputWindow(TRect bounds, const char *title,
ostream_withassign& ostr, ushort bufsize) :
TWindowInit(&TOutputWindow::initFrame),
TWindow(bounds, title, wnNoNumber)
{

// Terminal view should cover entire window.
bounds = getExtent();
bounds.grow(-1, -1);

// Create terminal view and add to window.
_term = new TTerminal(bounds,
standardScrollBar(sbHorizontal | sbHandleKeyboard),
standardScrollBar(sbVertical | sbHandleKeyboard), bufsize);
insert(_term);

// Create TV output stream.
otstream ot(_term);

ot << "Terminal window \"" << title << "\" created." << endl;

// Copy output stream; normally attach(ostr) would be sufficient.
ostr = ot;
}

TOutErr::TOutErr(TRect& outbounds, ushort outbufsize,
TRect& errbounds, ushort errbufsize) :
TProgInit(&TOutErr::initStatusLine, &TOutErr::initMenuBar,
&TOutErr::initDeskTop)
{
// Save current I/O assignments.
_old_cout = cout;
_old_cerr = cerr;
_old_clog = clog;

TOutputWindow *tow;

// Create standard output window.
tow = new TOutputWindow(outbounds, "Standard Output", cout,
outbufsize);
deskTop->insert(tow);

// Create standard error window and attach to log stream.
tow = new TOutputWindow(errbounds, "Standard Error", cerr,
errbufsize);
tow->attach(clog);
deskTop->insert(tow);
}

TOutErr::~TOutErr()
```

```
{
// Restore old I/O assignments.
cout = _old_cout;
cerr = _old_cerr;
clog = _old_clog;
}

void TOutErr::run()
{
cout << "Testing standard output:";
for (int i = 0; i < 10; i++)
  cout << ' ' << i;
cout << endl;

cerr << "Testing standard error:";
for (; i < 20; i++)
  cerr << ' ' << i;
cerr << endl;

clog << "Testing log:";
for (; i < 30; i++)
  clog << ' ' << i;
clog << endl;

TApplication::run();
}

int main()
{
TOutErr outerr(TRect(0, 0, 80, 15), 8192, TRect(0, 15, 80, 23),
2048);
outerr.run();
return (0);
}
```

Accepting Default Numbers in C

■ William G. Nettles

*Here's a clever technique for enhancing the **gets()** function.*

User friendly input should allow for simply pressing the **Enter** key to accept a default value. In C, entry of numerical data is usually handled with the **scanf()** family of functions, which will *not* accept an empty entry. However, the **gets()** function *will* accept an empty string as input.

Using **gets()** as a starting point, you can write a "get" function for numerical data that will accept default values. See DEFAULT.C (Listing 6.9). If the string entered is **NULL**, the default value (passed as an argument to the function) is returned; otherwise, the string is converted to the appropriate type using the **atoi()** family of functions.

The functions **getint()** and **getdouble()** will accept either a constant or a variable and return a value of the proper type.

CODE DESCRIPTION

Overview

A short program that demonstrates the use of two I/O functions which accept default values.

Listings Available

Listing	*Description*	*Used With*
DEFAULT.C	Demo program which uses **getint()** and **getdouble().**	------

How to Compile/Assemble

Can be compiled and linked with any C/C++ compiler.

■ LISTING 6.9 DEFAULT.C

```
#include <stdio.h>
#include <stdlib.h>

int getint(int deflt)
{
char buf[32];

   gets(buf);
   if (!buf[0])
      return(deflt);
   else
    return(atoi(buf));
}

double getdouble(double deflt)
{
char buf[32];

   gets(buf);
   if (!buf[0])
      return(deflt);
   else
    return(atof(buf));
}

void main(void)
{
int i = 12;
double a = 15.7;

   printf("Enter a new value for i (default %d):", i);
   i = getint(12);
  printf("The value of i is now %d \n",i);

   printf("Enter a new value for a (default %e):", a);
   a = getdouble(a);
   printf("The value of a is %e \n", a);
}
```

7

Printers and Printers Programming

There's been talk about the "paperless office" since before there were PCs—I remember that schtick being old when I was working at Xerox in the late 1970s and early 1980s. Perhaps that was just poor Xerox feeling guilty for inventing the photocopier. The cheaper and better our printers get, the more we use them. Just look at your company waste paper bin sometimes. Sheesh.

There just must be something about paper, I guess.

I have a theory on that. Our eyes evolved looking at reflected rather than generated light. What this means is still a little unclear, but there must be something to it, because my eyes tire more quickly staring at a screen than reading paper.

And paper, of course, has an edge-to-edge resolution of 2000 dpi or more. Our screens have a way to go yet.

So let's not be so quick to condemn a medium that's been with us for 3000 years. Our printers have never been better, or cheaper, and there's plenty to be done to make them operate at peak efficiency. DOS, for example, contains all the hooks for print spooling, as Nicholas Temple points out. Chuck Somerville has a solid fix for a problem that bedevils everyone sooner or later—directing output to the printer when the printer is powered-down or off-line.

Admit it: Paper's cool. If that's settled, let's make the most of it.

Direct Printer Output

■ Allen L. Wyatt

Here's an easy way to send important data to your printer.

Do you have to start up your word processor just to send a few bytes to the printer? Even sending an initialization string this way can be a real hassle, so I developed a short utility that sends its parameters directly to the printer. Anything enclosed in single quotes is sent as literal; any other values are considered to be decimal ASCII values. For example, the following is a representation of how PRNT.COM handles parameters:

```
PRNT 15  Sends a byte value of 0x15 to the printer
PRNT 27 71  Turns on Bold Face for an Epson
PRNT 27 'E'  Sends ESC-E sequence to printer (reset LaserJet)
PRNT 13 10 12  Sends CR/LF and FormFeed
```

You can even get fancy with your lines, as in the following, which does a CR/LF, prints a string, tabs twice, amd prints another string.

```
PRNT 13 10 'This is a test' 9 9 'Another test'
```

The Program

The attached file is PRNT.ASM (Listing 7.1), which must be assembled, linked, and converted to a COM file using EXE2BIN. Using TLINK's /t option will also work. If you use the program without parameters, a help message is displayed.

An interesting thing to note about PRNT.ASM is the first line of the data area:

```
DB 8,8,8,32,32,32
```

These six bytes are used in conjunction with the three bytes (8, 32, 26) at the end of the help notice. These nine extra bytes are included in case a user tries to type the COM file. In this case, what the user will see is the help screen.

The first three bytes of the PRNT.COM are the jump to the beginning of the code (**JMP PBEGIN**). The 8,8,8 will backspace over the characters displayed and the 32,32,32 blanks them out. Likewise, the trailing 8 and 32 are used to wipe out the '$' character at the end of the help message. The 26 provides a CTRL-Z to fool the TYPE command into thinking that the end of the file has been reached. Because of this trick, there is no difference on the display between PRNT and TYPE PRNT.COM. Try it and see.

Error Messages

If the user types in a number that is too large, as in PRNT 2345, a message is displayed to indicate a parameter error has occurred. Additionally, if part of a line was already sent to the printer when the error was detected, the user is informed of this.

This is a great multipurpose utility that can be used in batch files. For example, the following is a batch file I use to configure my HP LaserJet printer:

```
prnt 27 '(8U' 27 '&l1O'
prnt 27 '(s0p16.66h8.5v0s-1b0T'
prnt 27 '&l5.4545c66F'
pent 27 '&a2L'
```

The following is one I use to set the number of copies the LaserJet will print. I provide the quantity as a parameter to the batch file:

```
prnt 27 '&l%1X'
```

Well, you get the idea.

CODE DESCRIPTION

Overview

Complete assembly language program to output its command directly to LPT1:

Listings Available

Listing	*Description*	*Used with*
PRNT.ASM	Assembly language .COM program to output its command line directly to LPT1.	------

How to Compile/Assemble

Can be assembled with MASM or TASM. Use /t option with TLINK or EXE2BIN to produce .COM program

---

TIP: To change the printer being output to, change the value placed in DX in the function **PRINT** before the call to INT17H (0 = LPT1:, 1 = LPT2:, 2 = LPT3:)

■ LISTING 7.1 PRNT.ASM

```
page 60, 132
;
;Author: Allen L. Wyatt
;Program: Prnt.COM
;
;
PUBLIC PRNT

CODE SEGMENT PARA PUBLIC 'CODE'
     ASSUME CS:CODE

     ORG 100H
```

```
PRNT PROC FAR
     JMP PBEGIN

;------------
;DATA AREA
;------------
       DB 8,8,8,32,32,32
COPYR  DB 13,10
       DB 'PRNT.COM - ', 13,10,13,10
       DB 'To use, enter PRNT followed by the ASCII decimal',13,10
       DB 'values of the characters to be sent to the printer',13,10
       DB '(LPT1:).  Anything without single quotes (',39,') is',13,10
       DB 'considered literal text and sent as is.',13,10
       DB 'Examples: ',13,10
       DB '   PRNT 12       causes a form feed character to be sent',13,10
       DB '   PRNT 27 ',39,'E',39,'   causes ESC-E to be sent',13,10
          DB '     PRNT ', 39, 'Howdy!',39,' sends the text string to the
printer',13,10
       DB 13,10,13,10,'$'
       DB 8,32,26

TRUE EQU -1
FALSE EQU 0

LITERAL DB 0
PARTIAL_FLAG DB 0

ERR_MSG DB   'Parameter error',13,10,'$'
ERR_MSG2 DB  'Partial Line Sent',13,10,'$'

;-----------------
;START OF PROGRAM
;-----------------

PBEGIN:         CMP   BYTE PTR CS:80h,2 ; Check length of parameters
                JA    PB1               ; Jump if > 2
                MOV   DX, OFFSET COPYR  ; Point to the Help Screen
                MOV   AH, 9             ; Use DOS to Output
                INT   21h               ;
                JMP   DONE              ; Exit Early

PB1:            MOV   SI, 82h            ; Point to first parameter
                MOV   LITERAL, FALSE    ; Reset Literal and Partial
                MOV   PARTIAL_FLAG, FALSE

PB2:            MOV   BX, 0
                MOV   AX, 0
                MOV   DX, 0

NEXT_CHAR:      MOV   BL,[SI]           ; Get Character
                INC   SI                ; Point to Next One
                CMP   BL, 39            ; Apostrophe
                JNE   NC1
                XOR   LITERAL, TRUE     ; Toggle Status
                CMP   LITERAL, TRUE     ; Are we in a literal?
```

```
                JNE   PB2                  ; No, so start fresh
                JE    PRINT                ; Yes, so try to print

NC1:            CMP   LITERAL, TRUE        ; Inside a literal?
                JNE   NC2                  ; No, continue
                CMP   BL, 0Dh              ; Was it a carriage return?
                JE    DONE                 ; If yes, go to finish
                MOV   AX, BX
                JMP   PRINT                ; Else print it

NC2:            CMP   BL, 0Dh              ; Was it a carriage return?
                JE    PRINT                ; If Yes, go print
                CMP   BL, ' '              ; Was it a space?
                JE    PRINT                ; If Yes, print what we have
                CMP   BL, '0'              ; < 0?
                JL    ERR
                CMP   BL, '9'              ; > 9?
                JG    ERR
                AND   BL, 0Fh              ; Make number
                MOV   CX, 10
                MUL   CX
                ADD   AX, BX               ; Add current character
                JMP   NEXT_CHAR

;****Try to print what is in DX:AX
PRINT:          CMP   DX, 0                ; Number is out of range
                JNE   ERR
                CMP   AX, 255              ; Also out of range
                JA    ERR
                CMP   AX,0                 ; Any number there?
                JE    PR_EXIT              ; If no, exit printing
                MOV   DX, 0                ; Printer (0=LPT1:)
                MOV   AH, 0                ; Service 0
                INT   17h                  ; BIOS Call to print AL
                                           ; We've sent something
                MOV   PARTIAL_FLAG, TRUE

PR_EXIT:        CMP   BL, 0Dh              ; Was the character a CR?
                JNE   PB2                  ; If not, continue
                JE    DONE                 ; If yes, then exit

;****Error Message
ERR:            MOV   DX, OFFSET ERR_MSG
                MOV   AH, 9
                INT   21h
                CMP   PARTIAL_FLAG, TRUE
                JNE   DONE
                MOV   DX, OFFSET ERR_MSG2
                MOV   AH, 9
                INT   21h

DONE:           INT   20h
PRNT            ENDP
;----------------
CODE ENDS
     END    PRNT
```

Enabling and Disabling the PrtScr Key

■ Mike Bernard

A clever trick for controlling the PrtScr key.

It can be useful to disable the print-screen capabilities of a PC, especially when running on a laptop. Listing 7.2 presents a short function to do this.

First, some background. The ROM BIOS stores the status of print-screen operations at address 0050:0000h. This location contains one of three possible values:

```
00H    Ready for screen print
01H    Screen print is in progress
FFH    Error occurred in last screen print
```

If a screen print is in progress, BIOS will not allow another one to be initiated. This means that if a 1 value is written to this address, the print screen capability will be disabled. The PrtScr key can be reenabled by writing a 0 value to 0050:0000h.

CODE DESCRIPTION

Overview

Function call which will turn the PrtScr key off and on. Uses Borland C++'s **pokeb** macro defined in the DOS.H file to access 0050:0000h.

Listings Available

Listing	*Description*	*Used with*
PRINTSCR.C	C source file that defines the **print_screen()** function.	------

How to Compile/Assemble

Can be compiled and linked with any C/C++ compiler.

■ LISTING 7.2 PRINTSCR.C

```
#include <dos.h>
void print_screen(int turn_on)
{
   if (turn_on)
     pokeb(0x0050, 0x0000, 0);
   else
     pokeb(0x0050, 0x0000, 1);
}
```

Breaking Out of the Hung Printer Trap

■ Chuck Somerville

Here's a useful TSR to check the status of the printer.

If you've ever mistakenly directed an application program to print something, or inadvertently pressed Shift-PrtScr when your parallel printer was unavailable, then you've probably observed that when the ROM BIOS parallel printer service routine is busy checking and rechecking to see if the printer's ready, nothing short of Alt-Ctrl-Del or the Big Red Switch will get its attention.

Listing 7.3 shows a short TSR that provides a front end to the BIOS parallel printer service (INT 17H). This front end checks the printer status to see if it's busy, and then checks the keyboard to see if the escape key (ESC) has been pressed. If ESC was pressed, then the routine just performs an **IRET** to the caller as if the character had been printed.

TIP: An interesting feature in this program is the need to save the old address of the INT 17H vector for use by the TSR itself. Subfunction 02H of this interrupt is used to query the printer status. This is accomplished by pushing the flags with **PUSHF** and making a far call to the saved address to simulate an interrupt.

Since the routine does not consume the ESC character from the type ahead buffer, all subsequent characters sent to the printer are dropped until the application collects the ESC from the keyboard buffer. This lets you kill a lengthy print command with one keypress. A mistakenly entered COPY XXX LPT1: will run to completion without printing.

To take advantage of this TSR inside a C program, the test for ESC might be coded like this:

```
if(kbhit()) if(0x1B == getch()) exit(8);
```

The TSR in Listing 7.3 is the bare minimum to get the job done. You could add code to recognize a hot key or an escape sequence in the print data stream to enable/disable the keyboard checking. Code could also be added to check for prior installation of the TSR (to prevent loading it twice) or perhaps to unload it.

CODE DESCRIPTION

Overview

Assembly language TSR which monitors INT17H to see if the printer is hung. Allows the user to press ESC to get control back to the application.

Listings Available

Listing	*Description*	*Used with*
LPTESC.ASM	TSR program to hook Int 17H to check for hung printer status.	------

How to Compile/Assemble

MASM or TASM. Use TLINK's /t option or EXE2BIN to create a .COM program.

■ LISTING 7.3 LPTESC.ASM

```
;  LPTESC.COM  -  INT 17H front end: allow ESC key to break
;          out of hung parallel printer I/O attempts.
;          Chuck Somerville - Dayton, OH

     .MODEL  TINY           ; Be a .COM program.
     .CODE                  ; Shorthand...
     ORG     0100H          ;  our segment name will be _TEXT
START:
     JMP     SHORT INSTALL
     ASSUME  CS:_TEXT,DS:NOTHING,ES:NOTHING,SS:NOTHING ; ISR environment
OLD_IO  DD      ?              ; Old INT 17H address
OLDDX   DW      ?              ; Printer unit: 0 = LPT1:, 1 = LPT2:, etc.
OLDAX   DW      ?              ; Character to print
NEW_IO:                        ; TSR entry point
     PUSHF                  ; save flags
     CMP     AH,0           ; Request = 00H (print character)?
     JNE     GO_BIOS2       ; ..no,  then just go to the BIOS code
     STI                    ; ..yes, re-enable interrupts
     MOV     CS:OLDDX,DX    ;  save printer unit
     MOV     CS:OLDAX,AX    ;  save function and char to print
LPT_WAIT:
     MOV     AH,2           ;  set up GET STATUS request
     PUSHF                  ;  simulate INT with PUSHF
     CALL    CS:OLD_IO      ;  and a far call
     AND     AH,10111001B   ;  mask off unwanted bits
     CMP     AH,10010000B   ;  printer selected and ready?
     JE      GO_BIOS1       ;  ..yes, go print
     MOV     AH,1           ;  ..no,  set up for keyboard check
     INT     16H            ;      BIOS keyboard service
     JZ      LPT_WAIT       ;      no character: loop some more
     CMP     AL,1BH         ;      character: is it ESC?
     JNE     LPT_WAIT       ;      ..no,  loop some more
     MOV     AX,CS:OLDAX    ;      ..yes, restore func and char
     POPF                   ;             restore flags
     IRET                   ;             and return w/o print
GO_BIOS1:
     MOV     AX,CS:OLDAX    ; restore original function and character
GO_BIOS2:
     POPF                   ; restore flags
```

```
    JMP     CS:OLD_IO       ; JMP to BIOS (it'll IRET)

    ASSUME  DS:_TEXT,ES:_TEXT,SS:_TEXT ; Normal .COM environment
INSTALL:
    MOV     AX,3517H        ; Get current BIOS INT 17H vector
    INT     21H
    MOV     WORD PTR OLD_IO,BX ; Save current INT 17H vector
    MOV     WORD PTR OLD_IO[2],ES
    MOV     DX,OFFSET NEW_IO
    MOV     AX,2517H        ; Make INT 17H come to us
    INT     21H
    CALL    @@              ; Push message's offset on stack
    DB      13,10
    DB      "Interrupt handler installed.  ESCape key interrupts",13,10
    DB      "busy or offline parallel printer waits.",10,"$"
@@:     POP     DX          ; Pop offset into DX (old CP/M trick)
    MOV     AH,9            ; Tell 'em we're installed.
    INT     21H
    MOV     AX,3100H        ; T. & S. R., DOS ERRORLEVEL = 0
    MOV     DX,(INSTALL - START + 256 + 15) SHR 4 ; DX = Size
    INT     21H             ;  in paragraphs of block to keep
    END     START
```

Printer/Aux Device Access with C++ Streams

■ Kevin Dean

Learn how to use C++ streams to access the printer and auxiliary devices.

One thing missing from the Turbo C++ streams implementation is access to the printer and auxiliary devices, referred to as **stdprn** and **stdaux** in the traditional C header file STDIO.H. To access them, use the **fstream** (file stream) class to attach the names **cprn** and **caux** to their respective DOS file handles. Listing 7.4 is the source file PRNAUX.CPP that defines the streams; PRNAUX.HPP (Listing 7.5) is the header file to include with each module that uses either stream.

There is one restriction: Assignment of any stream to either **cprn** or **caux** is not allowed because the assignment operator has not been defined for the **fstream** class. For example, the following two assignments are legal:

```
cerr = cout;  // Redirect error to standard output
cerr = cprn;  // Redirect error to printer
```

However, these two are not:

```
cprn = cout;  // Redirect printer to standard output
cprn = caux;  // Redirect printer to auxiliary output
```

CODE DESCRIPTION

Overview

A C++ source and header file that allow you to access **stdprn** and **stdaux** using stream I/O.

Listings Available

Listing	*Description*	*Used with*
PRNAUX.HPP	C++ header file that defines the names cprn and caux.	PRNAUX.CPP
PRNAUX.CPP	C++ source file that initializes cprn and caux as file handles.	------

How to Compile/Assemble

Can be compiled and linked with the Borland C++ compiler.

■ LISTING 7.4 PRNAUX.CPP

```
#include <prnaux.hpp>    // prnaux.hpp #includes fstream.h

// DOS opens both files for read and write.
fstream cprn(4);        // DOS file handle 4 is stdprn
fstream caux(3);        // DOS file handle 3 is stdaux
```

■ LISTING 7.5 PRNAUX.HPP

```
include <fstream.h>

extern fstream cprn;
extern fstream caux;
```

Background Printing In Turbo C

■ Nicholas L. Temple III

A useful utility for setting up and controlling your background printing.

Many times in a program, it would be nice to print a file while doing something else. Here is a simple spooling program that replaces C's **getch()** function with one that supports background printing while waiting for a keystroke (Listing 7.6).

In this example, the new function is called **v_getch()**. Whenever **v_getch()** finds a keystroke waiting, it returns the character to the calling program, or else it continuously calls **spool()** to process any printing that needs to be serviced.

When **spool()** is called, it checks the status of **sp_print** to see if it has a file it should be printing. If this is TRUE, it reads a line from the file and prints it. Otherwise it returns. If the file is done, or a printer error occurs, the function closes the file and updates **sp_print** to stop printing.

To initiate the printing of a file, **print()** is called with the pathname of the file to be printed. If the spooler is already busy, or if the filename is invalid, the function returns TRUE, and nothing is done. Otherwise, print will open the file and set a global variable to the designated file. The variable **sp_print** is set to TRUE, informing the spooler that it has a file to print. This variable is a global flag value which is set to TRUE whenever a file is in the process of being printed.

Because only one file should be printed at any one time, programs wishing to use **print()** can query whether the spooler is busy by calling **is_printing()**, which returns the status of **sp_print**.

A few cautions. If a line overruns the buffer, it can destroy other data, potentially crashing the program. In this example, the length of the buffer is set to 200 bytes, which should be ample, but it is something to bear in mind when adding this code to your programs. Also notice that no error messages are reported; you may want your host program to check the printer status and relay information to the user. To ensure an orderly shutdown and that the entire file has been printed, call **spool()** until **is_printing()** returns FALSE.

TIP: If your program doesn't need keyboard input or isn't going to be calling **v_getch()** for a while, **spool()** can still be called directly (during a sort, for instance) so background printing can continue.

CODE DESCRIPTION

Overview

Two modules which demonstrate a simple print spooling program. The example program makes use of time normally spent waiting for keyboard input to spool printing.

Listings Available

Listing	*Description*	*Used with*
XPRINT.ASM	Handles the printing of characters.	SPOOL.C
SPOOLER.C	Example of using XPRINT.ASM as a spooler.	------

How to Compile/Assemble

Can be compiled and linked with any C/C++ compiler and assembler.

■ LISTING 7.6 SPOOLER.C

```
/* spooler.c */

#include <stdio.h>
#include <string.h>
#include <conio.h>
```

```
/* Prototype */
int  xprint(char t);             /* Defined in ASM file        */

#define TRUE  1
#define FALSE 0
#define MAX_BUFF 200            /* Buffer Size         */

int sp_print     = FALSE;       /* spooler active?     */
FILE * printfile = NULL;        /* current file        */


int is_printing(void)
{                               /* Status function     */
  return(sp_print);
}

int print (char * path)
{
  if (sp_print) return (TRUE);   /* If printing, abort   */
  printfile = fopen(path, "r");  /* Open the file        */
  if (!printfile) return(TRUE);  /* No file, abort       */
  sp_print = TRUE;               /* Tell system busy     */
  return(FALSE);                 /* O.K.                 */
}

void sp_abort(void)              /* Printer error - abort */
{
  fclose(printfile);             /* Close the file        */
  xprint(0x0d);                  /* CR                    */
  xprint(0x0c);                  /* FF                    */
  printfile = NULL;              /* Tell system not printing */
  sp_print = FALSE;
}

void spool(void)
{
  static char printbuff[MAX_BUFF];      /* Local buffer     */
  register int len;                     /* Length of buffer */
  register int pntr;                    /* Pointer          */

  if (!sp_print) return;                /* Not active, quit */
  if(!feof(printfile))
  {
    fgets(printbuff, MAX_BUFF, printfile);
    len = strlen(printbuff);            /* Get next line    */
    for(pntr = 0; pntr < len; pntr++)   /* Print it         */
      if(xprint(printbuff[pntr]))
        sp_abort();                     /* Error? quit      */
  }
  else
    sp_abort();                         /* quit             */
}

int v_getch(void)
```

```
{
    while (!kbhit())                    /* If no key        */
      spool();                          /* Print a line     */
    return(getch());                    /* Else return key  */
}
```

■ LISTING 7.7 XPRINT.ASM

```
; XPRINT.ASM
; Extended Keyboard Driver
; (C)1992 Nick Temple, Tek Industries.  All Rights Reserved.

.MODEL small
PUBLIC _xprint

.CODE

; int xprint(char t);
; Short C procedure to print a single character to printer #0
;
; RETURNS:
;
;   FALSE (0)  if character printed
;       TRUE  (!0)  if there was an error

ARG1      equ  word ptr [bp+4] ; small model stack

_xprint  PROC
       push bp               ; make stack frame
       mov  bp, sp
       mov  ah, 02h          ; get printer status
       xor  dx, dx           ; for printer #0
       int  17h              ; call BIOS
       and  ah, 29h          ; mask bits
       jnz    xp_exit          ; if(ah) return(TRUE)

       mov  ax, ARG1   ; get character from stack
       xor  ah, ah  ; function 0 (print char)
       int  17h              ; call BIOS
       xor  ax, ax           ; clear ax (FALSE)
xp_exit: pop  bp               ; restore caller's stack
       ret                     ; return!
_xprint     ENDP
       END
```

8

Programming the Serial Port

I've always been fascinated by serial port programming. It was one of those things I did back at Xerox, when I was not marking time fighting with COBOL and other mainframe stuff. Most of what I did, granted, was on the Z80, but the fundamental principles are the same.

The serial port is the most malleable door between the PC software and the hardware. If you understand it thoroughly, you can connect your PC to virtually anything. This, I think, is one of its attractions to old-school people (like me) who came to computers from discrete digital logic. (That is, we did things by strapping 7400s together and watching waveforms on triggered-sweep scopes.) To hardware people, serial port programming smells distinctly like home.

There's a lot of information in this chapter, and it operates on a number of levels. First of all, Brett Glass presents one of the best introductions to serial port programming ever published. If, having read Brett's piece, the lights don't come on, you need to change a few bulbs.

At the other end of the scale, Kevin Weeks constructs an elegant object-oriented C++ shell around the serial port to shield the programmer from the gritty details of having to futz individual registers. Kevin's code is wonderful. Read it closely. It's one of the best arguments for object-oriented design that I've ever seen.

Poking Your Way to COM3 and COM4

■ Jack Mefford

Here's a useful technique for accessing the ports COM3 and COM4.

It's not uncommon to find yourself wishing for more than the two serial ports COM1 and COM2. Perhaps you have a modem, a serial mouse, and an optical scanner and are tired of having to swap cables every time you change applications. Actually, the BIOS does allow you to specify two more COM ports. You just have to tell the BIOS where to find them in the I/O address space.

The BIOS reserves a word-entry table starting at 0040:0000h that contains the I/O base address for each COM port. The first two entries are initialized during the boot process to 03F8H and 02F8H for COM1 and COM2, respectively (see Figure 8.1). The next two words are reserved for COM3 and COM4 and are initially zeros. Just poke the port addresses for the serial cards you wish to add. For example, in Turbo C it could be done this way:

```
poke(0x0040,0x0004,0x03E8);   /*Put COM3 at 03E8H*/
poke(0x0040,0x0006,0x02E8);   /*Put COM4 at 02E8H*/
```

After executing these lines, if you are writing your own application program, you can then use all the normal INT 14 functions to access the new COM ports. If you are running a commercial application, you must configure it to use COM3 or COM4. Unfortunately, not all applications allow this.

TIP: To use the **poke()** function make sure you include the DOS.H header file in your program.

Some warnings are in order. First, you must choose I/O addresses that are not already used by the system or other cards. Normally, you would use 03E8H for COM3 and 02E8H for COM4, as shown in our example. Other possibilities are 02E0H, 02F0H, and 03E0H.

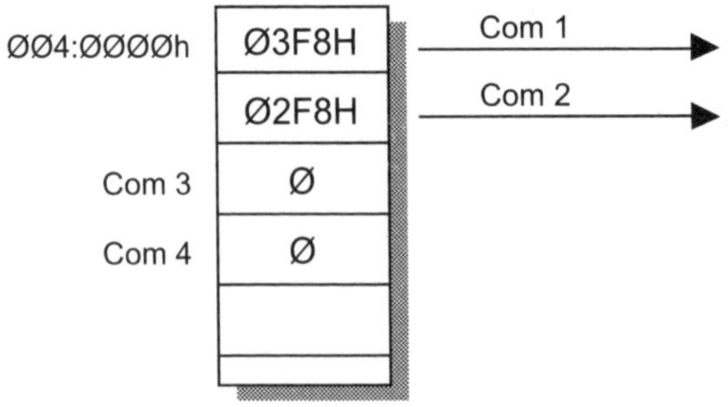

■ **FIGURE 8.1 Accessing COM ports**

Second, if you change COM ports, you must have serial cards with jumpers or switches that allow you to select addresses other than the standard 03F8H and 02F8H used by COM1 and COM2. Check the serial card's manual before you buy. Finally, IRQ3 is shared by COM ports 2 and up. This means that interrupt-driven serial port applications must be well-behaved and pass on the hook to the interrupt handler. Otherwise, only one of the applications will be able to run.

Inside the Serial Hardware

■ Brett Glass

The UART is the shop foreman of the PC's serial adapter. Here's how to put it to work.

Interested in writing a blockbuster communications program for the IBM PC and kin? If so, be prepared to do a little hacking. The IBM PC's system software—the BIOS and DOS—provide woefully inadequate support for asynchronous serial communications, leaving serious software developers no choice but to go directly to the hardware to make things work right. Here are some hardware-oriented details of the techniques you'll need in order to use the IBM PC's serial ports.

What IBM and Microsoft Left Out

When IBM released the IBM PC in 1981, it provided simple ways to access nearly every component of the computer—including the screen, the disk drives, and the parallel port—via BIOS and DOS. While the system software wasn't necessarily the fastest way to do things (BIOS screen writes, for example, were relatively slow), these low-level tools were at least adequate for simple applications.

Alas, this was not true of the serial port services. The IBM PC BIOS calls that control the serial port insisted on using a peculiar RTS/DTR (request to send/data terminal ready) handshake sequence that causes many modems to hang up. What's more, they also used polled rather than interrupt-driven I/O. This means the machine could drop characters during a disk access, a screen update, or any other operation that prevented an application program from polling the port for two character times (only two milliseconds at 9600 baud). The DOS serial port functions were even worse. DOS did include a device, AUX:, that in theory mapped to the serial port. In practice, however, this device was quirky and virtually useless. It not only suffered from the character-dropping problems of the BIOS when receiving characters, but hoarded outgoing characters and spit them out in bursts—that is, when they emerged at all.

It would have been nice if, in the early days of the PC, a third party had been able to set a standard for an add-on serial port driver. (The FOSIL driver, created for the FIDO BBS program, did this but, alas, never managed to gain widespread acceptance.) Thus, to do serious serial communications, you must bypass both the BIOS and DOS and program down to the bare metal. If this sounds intimidating, don't worry, it really isn't as hard as it seems at first glance.

What You Need to Know

To write an interrupt-driven serial communications program for the PC, you'll need to understand:

- How to control the Asynchronous Communications Adapter
- How to write an interrupt service routine for the 8086
- How to manage the PC's Intel 8259 interrupt controller
- A bit about data structures and buffering

The IBM Asynchronous Communications Adapter

The first (and most important) component you'll need to understand is the Asynchronous Communications Adapter—your PC's serial card. It is instructive to note that the architecture of this card, and the hardware and software that support it, reveal the worst kludges in the design of the original IBM PC.

Had they had more foresight, IBM's designers might have found a way to allow for many serial ports on any PC. Unfortunately, they designed the PC's bus so that the 8088's eight nonmaskable interrupts—five of which appeared on the bus—could not be used by more than one peripheral each. By the time all the other peripherals had been assigned interrupts, there were only two interrupts left: IRQ4 and IRQ3. These became the interrupts for COM1: and COM2: respectively (see Table 8.1).

A peek inside the BIOS, however, shows that IBM may originally have intended to offer more serial ports. At boot time, the IBM PC BIOS creates a list of the available serial ports in low RAM. The table entries in the list and their addresses are shown in Table 8.2.

Any unused table entries are set to 0. This makes the BIOS table useful if you want to make sure a serial port is available for use. Many system programs—such as mouse drivers—zero out the entry for a port they're using. This is a signal that other software should not try to access that port.

The four entries in Table 8.2 suggest that one of the designers thought the PC would contain as many as four serial ports. The format of this table also bears a telltale sign of a serious lack of foresight: It doesn't have entries for the interrupt numbers of the ports. This means that one could not make a serial adapter that used some other interrupt (say, one of the eight additional interrupts on the AT) and set the table to convey the number of that interrupt to the software.

The inconsistencies don't end here. The specification for the BIOS service called "Equipment Determination"—invoked by INT 11—suggests yet another maximum number of serial ports. This function returns a 16-bit word in which *three* bits are reserved for the number of ports, suggesting that yet another designer planned for as many as seven ports.

■ TABLE 8.1 Serial ports

Port	Interrupt	I/O Addresses
COM1:	IRQ 4	3F8h-3FFh
COM2:	IRQ 3	2F8h-2FFh

■ **TABLE 8.2 Serial port list**

Low RAM Location	I/O Address of
0040:0000h	COM1:
0040:0002h	COM2:
0040:0004h	COM3:
0040:0006h	COM4:

A Poor de facto Standard

While few PC users needed seven serial ports, many needed more than two. Responding to this need, Quadram, AST, and other PC board makers created de facto standards for two more serial ports: COM3: and COM4:. Table 8.3 shows the interrupts and addresses for these additional ports. (Many clone BIOSes search for these ports and insert their I/O addresses in the BIOS list shown in Table 8.2.)

It doesn't take much scrutiny to see a potential pitfall in these definitions, however: They use the same interrupts as COM1: and COM2:. This is a serious problem because, as mentioned earlier, interrupts on the IBM PC bus were not meant to be shared. The IBM serial card—and all true compatibles—drive the interrupt lines with tri-state drivers, rather than open-collector drivers. If two cards attempt to share an interrupt line, it's possible to miss interrupts or even ruin chips on the cards.

Because many IBM-compatible computers have three or four serial ports, this problem has the potential to crop up on many users' machines. Yet it doesn't in many cases. Why not? Because serial communications that go through DOS or the BIOS do not use interrupts. If printer output were redirected to COM1: (via the DOS MODE command), and COM3: were being used by a terminal program that did interrupt-driven I/O, there would be no conflict because COM1: would not try to control the interrupt line. However, if COM1: were being used by a mouse driver (which is also interrupt-driven), the terminal emulator might hang when the mouse was moved. For this reason, it's prudent to avoid the use of COM3: or COM4:, although you may have to support them in a terminal program.

The 8250 UART Family

Inside the Asynchronous Communications Adapter is a chip called the UART (Universal Asynchronous Receiver and Transmitter). The chip used in the original IBM PC, called the 8250B, was introduced by National Semiconductor around 1980. It contained a single serial port and a baud rate generator.

Later generations of the chip fixed bugs, added more features, and allowed the UART to work with faster CPUs. The IBM PC AT, for instance, used a UART called the 16450 (note

TABLE 8.3 Other serial ports

Port	Interrupt	I/O Addresses
COM3:	IRQ 4	3E8h-3EFh
COM4:	IRQ 3	2E8h-2EFh

the doubling of the first two digits), and the PS/2 line uses the 16550. This last chip, while downward-compatible with others, adds 16-character FIFO buffers on both the transmitter and receiver. This extra hardware helps solve problems with dropped characters—especially under operating systems OS/2, which take a long time to service interrupts.

The eight I/O ports reserved for each serial port are mapped to the UART's registers (shown in Figure 8.2). A solid understanding of these registers is key to writing a good serial communications package.

Setting Up the UART

We'll begin our tour of the UART in the middle of the register set, with the Line Control Register (LCR). This is likely to be the first register your program touches when it configures the UART, because it contains the bits that set the character size, parity, and number of stop bits. To set the character size, you set the Word Length Select Bits as shown in Table 8.4.

Three bits in this register can tell the UART to send and check a parity bit on each character. Table 8.5 shows how to set these bits for different kinds of parity.

The LCR also contains a "Send Break" bit, which sends a "break" signal when set. It also contains another important bit: the Divisor Latch Access Bit (DLAB). When DLAB is set to 1, the Divisor Latches (DLL and DLM, shown at the bottom of Figure 8.2) take over the addresses of the RBR and THR. These latches contain a 16-bit number that controls the baud rate. The values you'll need to produce some common baud rates are shown in Table 8.6. Once you've set the baud rate, remember to clear DLAB before attempting to use the UART! Also, don't rely on registers other than DLM, DLL, and LCR being available while DLAB is set; I've discovered the hard way that different manufacturers handle this situation differently.

■ **TABLE 8.4 Character size**

Bits/Char	WLS1	WLS0
5	0	0
6	0	1
7	1	0
8	1	1

■ **TABLE 8.5 Setting parity**

Parity	PEN	EPS	Stick	Parity
None	0	X	X	
Odd	1	0	0	
Even	1	1	0	
Always	0	1	0	1
Always	1	1	1	1

Register Name	Address/Access Restrictions	Bit 7	Bit 6	Bit 5	Bit 4	Bit 3	Bit 2	Bit 1	Bit 0
Receiver Buffer Register (RBR)	Base+0 Read-Only When DLAB=0	← Incoming Data →							
Transmitter Holding Register (THR)	Base+0 Write-Only When DLAB=0	← Outgoing Data →							
Interrupt Enable Register (IER)	Base+1 Read/Write When DLAB=0					Enable Data Set Status Interrupt (EDSSI)	Enable Line Status Interrupt (ELSI)	Enable Transmit Buffer Empty Interrupt (ETBEI)	Enable Receive Buffer Full Interrupt (ERBFI)
Interrupt Identification Register (IIR)	Base+2 Read-Only	FIFOs Enabled (16550 Only)	FIFOs Enabled (16550 Only)				Interrupt ID Bit 1	Interrupt ID Bit 0	0=Interrupt Pending
FIFO Control Register (FCR)	Base+2 Write-Only (16550 Only)	Receiver Trigger (MSB)	Receiver Trigger (LSB)			DMA Mode Select	Transmit FIFO Reset	Receive FIFO Reset	FIFO Enable
Line Control Register (LCR)	Base+3 Read/Write	Devisor Latch Access Bit (DLAB)	Send Break	Stick Parity	Even Parity Select (EPS)	Parity Enable (PEN)	Stop Bits (STB)	Word Length Select Bit 1 (WLS1)	Word Length Select Bit 0 (WLS0)
Modem Control Register (MCR)	Base+4 Read/Write				Loop	Out 2 (Enables Interrupts on PC)	Out 1 (Resets some internal Modems)	Request to Send (RTS)	Data Terminal Ready (DTR)
Line Status Register (LSR)	Base+5 Read/Write		Transmit Shift Register Empty (TSRE)	Transmit Hold Register Empty (THRE)	Break Interrupt (BI)	Framing Error (FE)	Parity Error (PE)	Overrun Error (OR)	Data Ready (DR)
Modem Status Register (MSR)	Base+6 Read/Write	Receiver Line Signal Detect (RLSD)	Ring Indicator (RI)	Data Set Ready (DSR)	Clear to Send (CTS)	Delta RLSD (DRLSD)	Trailing Edge Ring Indicator (TERI)	Delta DSR (DDSR)	Delta CTS (DCTS)
Scratch Register (SCR)	Base+7 Read/Write (16450/550 Only)	← Arbitrary Data →							
Device Latch LS Byte (DLL)	Base+0 Read/Write when DLAB=1	← LSB of Divisor →							
Device Latch MS Byte (DLM)	Base+1 Read/Write when DLAB=1	← MSB of Divisor →							

■ **FIGURE 8.2 The IBM PC UART registers**

■ **TABLE 8.6 Baud rate factors**

Baud Rate	Divisor
110	1047
300	384
1200	96
2400	48
4800	24
9600	12

Handling the Modem

Next, take a look at Figure 8.2 for the Modem Control Register (MCR). The MCR contains several very important bits. Data Terminal Ready (DTR) must be turned on before many modems will acknowledge characters from a serial port; in fact, many modems hang up when DTR is turned off. Therefore, your program should set DTR whenever it wants to talk to a modem. Request to Send (RTS) may also need to be set before you can transmit.

Two other bits in this register, Out 1 and Out 2, go to general-purpose output pins on the UART. When IBM designed the Asynchronous Communications Adapter, it didn't use Out 1, but made Out 2 the signal that turned on the card's interrupt driver. (This was documented only in the schematic, so many programmers had a difficult time figuring out why interrupts did not work.) If you are using interrupts, you must turn on Out 2!

Out 1, originally unused by IBM, is used in different ways by other vendors. For example, it's the reset signal for the onboard microprocessor of many "smart" modems, including many of Hayes' internal models. To avoid compatibility problems, it's best to leave this bit alone.

Transmitting and Receiving Data

To receive and transmit characters, your program reads and writes two registers: the Receive Buffer Register (RBR) for incoming characters, and the Transmit Holding Register (THR) for outgoing characters. These registers share the same I/O address; one is read-only, the other write-only.

Your program should not access these registers indiscriminately, however. If the CPU attempts to read an incoming character from the RBR, but none has come in, you will get another copy of the character most recently received. The situation is similar with the THR. If the UART hasn't yet been able to transmit a character written to the THR and the CPU writes another character to this register, the first character will be overwritten and lost.

These problems can be avoided in one of two ways: The CPU can check a bit in one of the UART's status registers to make sure the RBR or THR is ready to be accessed, or it can wait for the UART to generate an interrupt that signals one of these two conditions. Since a received character must be removed from the RBR immediately to make room for the next, nearly all professional communications programs use interrupts to signal incoming data–that is, an "interrupt-driven" receive. However, since no data will be lost if a program waits a little longer to *send* characters, it's fine in most cases to poll a status bit during transmission to see if the previous character has left the UART. This scheme—"interrupt-driven receive and polled transmit"—is popular because it keeps the interrupt service routine short and simple.

Enabling and Identifying Interrupts

To configure the UART to generate interrupts, your software must set one or more bits in the Interrupt Enable Register (IER). Each of the four defined bits in this register turns on a different kind of interrupt: Receive Buffer Full, Transmit Buffer Empty, Line Status, or Data Set Status. The Receive Buffer Full interrupt—the only one needed for interrupt-driven receive—will occur when a character is ready to be read from the RBR.

The Transmit Buffer Empty interrupt occurs when the UART is ready to take a new character into the THR. The Line Status interrupt indicates that the UART has encountered a "break" signal, a framing error, a parity error, or an overrun error; finally, the Status Interrupt indicates that Clear to Send (CTS), Carrier Detect (also called Receive Line Signal Detect), or Data Set Ready (DSR) has changed, or RI (Ring Indicator) has been de-asserted.

When an interrupt comes in, the interrupt service routine (ISR) must be prepared to handle any condition for which an interrupt is enabled. To do this, it first reads the Interrupt Identification Register (IIR). The three least significant bits of this register contain a code that says whether there's really an interrupt condition (to eliminate false alarms) and, if there is an interrupt, which of the four kinds of interrupts it is. Of course, the ISR can skip this step if only one kind of interrupt is enabled.

Status Registers

The Line Status Register (LSR) contains information on the internal state of the UART. The Data Ready (DR) bit is set when data is available in the RBR; this is the bit to test when doing polled receive. The Overrun Error (OR), Parity Error (PE), and Framing Error (FE) bits indicate errors encountered as characters are received, while the Break Interrupt (BI) bit indicates that a "break" signal—literally, a signal that looks like the wire was temporarily broken—has been received.

The Transmit Hold Register Empty (THRE) bit, when set, indicates that it's OK to write to the THR; this is the bit to test when doing polled transmit. Finally, the Transmit Shift Register Empty (TSRE) bit indicates that the UART has finished transmitting all the characters it's been asked to send. (The THR, which holds a character on its way to the UART's shift register, becomes empty before the shift register does.) Each of these bits can trigger an interrupt if IER is set to allow it.

The Modem Status Register (MSR) reflects the status of the RS-232 signal lines. Clear to Send (CTS) is a hardware handshake signal that tells your PC that it's OK to send characters on the serial line. Data Set Ready (DSR) indicates that the modem is ready to accept characters. Received Line Signal Detect (RLSD) indicates that a carrier is present, and RI (Ring Indicator) indicates the phone line is ringing.

The Delta CTS (DCTS), Delta DSR (DDSR), Trailing Edge Ring Indicator (TERI), and Delta RLSD (DRLSD) bits signal significant changes in the other bits, and trigger a Modem Status interrupt if IER is set to allow it. (Note that detecting the trailing edge of Ring Indicator is important because it lets the computer pick up between rings instead of during them—avoiding the high-voltage signal that rings the bells on most phones.)

Special UART Registers and Bits

The Scratch Register (SCR) is exactly that: an eight-bit register that can be written and read back. Most of the time, this register is used only for testing, but a few programs use it for other things. For instance, some OS/2 serial drivers use this register to hold a received character during a transition between Real and Protected Modes.

Finally, the top-of-the-line 16550 has a special write-only register to control the FIFOs: the FIFO Control Register (FCR). Because this register is write-only, the UART confirms that it's using the FIFOs by setting the top two bits of the IIR—the ones marked "FIFOs Enabled." After enabling the FIFOs, the software can ask to be notified of incoming characters only when there's a certain number of them already in the FIFO, reducing the number of interrupts required to collect them.

Unimplemented UART Bits

The bits that haven't been marked with any function in Figure 8.2 (such as IER bits 4–7) are not currently implemented, but that doesn't mean they will remain so in the future. The safest course is to avoid altering them to prevent incompatibility with later versions of the UART.

Interrupts on the IBM PC

The IBM PC handles interrupts using the facilities of the Intel 8259 interrupt controller—which works in concert with the 808X series of microprocessors. The 8259 prioritizes and filters interrupts, making sure that only legitimate requests are handled, and that those are handled in the right order.

To use interrupt-driven communications, your program must tell the 8259 to respond to interrupt requests from the serial port. Then, after each interrupt has been serviced, the interrupt service routine must send an End of Interrupt (EOI) command to the 8259 before more serial interrupts will arrive.

Here's how to tell the 8259 to handle serial port interrupts. One of the registers in the 8259, Operation Control Word 1 (OCW1), is addressed at Port 21H and contains an eight-bit interrupt mask. To enable a hardware interrupt, you must clear the corresponding bit—Bit 3 for IRQ 3, and Bit 4 for IRQ 4. You need do this only once when you start interrupt-driven communications, but remember to set the mask bit again before the program terminates.

■ TABLE 8.7 8259 registers and commands

Action	Procedure
Enable IRQ 4	OCW1 = OCW1 & 0x0EF
Disable IRQ 4	OCW1 = OCW1 | 0x010
Enable IRQ 3	OCW1 = OCW1 & 0x0F7
Disable IRQ3	OCW1 = OCW1 | 0x008
EOI Command	OCW2 = 0x020

(OCW1 = Port 20h, OCW2 = Port 21h)

Issue the EOI command by writing the value 20H to Operation Control Word 1 (OCW1), which is addressed at Port 20H. Don't forget to issue the EOI command before the end of your interrupt service routine.

The 8259-specific operations you'll need to perform are summarized in Table 8.7.

Writing Your Interrupt Service Routine

Finally, you'll need to write an interrupt service routine to handle received characters. The exact way you implement your ISR depends on your choice of language (C, C++, Pascal, and so on); many popular compilers, such as Borland C++, let you service interrupts without dropping down to assembly language. Whatever language you use, your ISR should be able to add characters to a circular buffer, which the communications program can then empty. Remember to restore all registers and send an EOI before the end of the routine. Also make sure there is no inconsistency problem if an interrupt occurs just as the main program is removing a character from the buffer.

Use DOS calls, not direct memory writes, to set the interrupt vector to your ISR. Remember that the vector number you'll give to DOS will be the IRQ number plus 8; that is, for IRQ 4 you'd specify 12 (decimal).

Putting It All Together

Figure 8.3 shows pseudocode for a simple communications program. This program takes all the necessary steps to set up the UART, install an interrupt service routine, handle user keystrokes, and exit on command. You should be able to use this example as the basis for implementing your own program.

■ FIGURE 8.3 Pseudocode for a communications program

```
Is the UART in the BIOS list?
  If not, exit to DOS
Set up the hardware:
  Initialize circular buffer
  IER := 0; (Disable UART interrupts)
  Point interrupt vector at ISR
  DLAB := 1
  Set baud rate
  DLAB := 0
  Set data bits, parity in LCR
  Set DTR, RTS, OUT2 in MCR
  Enable IRQ in OCW1
  IER := 1 (Enable receive interrupts)

Main Loop:
  Characters available in circular buffer?
    If so, fetch and display them,
      and update the buffer pointers.
  Is keystroke pending in keyboard buffer?
    If not, begin Main Loop again...
    If so, fetch the keystroke.
  Test the keystroke fetched
```

```
        Is it the exit key?
          If so, go to Exit Tasks...
        (Put other keystroke tests here)
      Test for Ready to Transmit:
        Is Transmit Holding Register empty?
        If not, go back to Test for Ready...
        If so, Load keystroke into THR
      Go to Main Loop...

    Exit Tasks:
      IER := 0 (Disable UART interrupts)
      Disable IRQ in OCW1
      DSR, RTS, OUT2 off in MCR
      Restore interrupt vector
      Exit to DOS
```

References

Data Communications/LAN/UARTS Handbook. National Semiconductor, PO Box 58090, Santa Clara, CA 95052 (408)721-5000

Eggebrecht, Lewis C. *Interfacing to the IBM Personal Computer.* Indianapolis: Howard W. Sams & Co. 1983. ISBN: 0-672-22027-X.

Technical Reference, Personal Computer AT. Part #1502243 IBM Corporation, Armonk, NY.

Foster, John and John Choisser. *The XT-AT Handbook*, Second Edition. San Diego: Annabooks 1989. ISBN: 0-929392-00-0

Extendible Serial Port Objects

■ Kevin Weeks

The way to add extendibility to an assembly language core is to build a C++ wrapper around it.

Working with RS-232 ports in the real world is a lot like rebuilding, modifying, and updating vintage homes. For instance, recently I wrote a device driver and support programs that enable one computer to transparently (through a DOS block device driver) access another computer's hard disk via an RS-232 connection. Last year I had to communicate with an embedded controller via a serial link and I also wrote an HP plotter driver. The year before that it was remote, radio-linked ASCII terminals.

Along the way, I've developed a fairly standard collection of communication routines written in assembly language. Unfortunately, these routines have to be modified for almost every application. What I really need is a way to extend the existing assembly language routines without having to modify them. What is needed is an extendible communications object.

The View from a Height

What nearly all serial communications applications have in common is a need to move data from one point to another over a serial link. This is where most of the action is, and I felt that this is where my assembly language primitives would be most useful.

What differs from application to application are things like hardware handshaking, flow control, and block transfer protocols. These are things that can be added to the assembly language core by extension, in a layered fashion, using C++ object-oriented features. The basic C++ class **Serial_Comm** is simply a software gadget for moving bytes of data from one point to another through a serial link. It's interrupt driven on both input and output; it was designed to be extended, and to make that extension as easy as possible. This base class is little more than a thin C++ wrapper around the assembly language primitives.

Other features can be added by extending the base class. Later on, I'll use the XON/XOFF flow control feature as an example of how this is done. With XON/XOFF in place, the extended class could then communicate reliably with an HP plotter. Other extensions (like the XMODEM file transfer protocol) could be done the same way with little additional effort.

The C++ Shell

The first step in moving to OOP is to produce a "simple and affordable" C++ structure. Class **Serial_Comm** is this structure. SERIAL.HPP (Listing 8.1) begins with a series of enumeration types; **Bool**, **Baud_Rate**, **Parity**, and so on.

TIP: This is a good example of how C++'s type checking can help the programmer. In Standard C the **enum** type doesn't really constitute the creation of a new type, since no type checking is provided. For instance, we can declare the following in C:

```
enum Bool {FALSE,TRUE = -1};
```

There is nothing in C, however, to prevent this:

```
Bool return_value;
return_value = 4;
```

In C++, on the other hand, the above assignment causes the compiler to generate a warning message. This type checking can eliminate a lot of errors.

TIP: One caveat when using Borland's C++ compiler: Be sure to specify that enums be treated as integers (this is controlled by a compiler switch). There is a bug in the compiler that can cause misalignment and consequent misassignment of values if the compiler is allowed to default to using byte-size enums.

Serial_Comm, in general, passes all messages (function calls) straight through to the appropriate assembler routine. If you'll examine Listing 8.1 you'll see that a number of the method declarations, (**get_baud_ rate()** and **get_port()**, for instance) are followed immediately by the name of the assembly code that implements them. This looks like a double call, first to the C++ method and then to the assembly language function, but it's not. These methods are intrinsically inline. The C++ call disappears and only the assembly call remains in your .EXE file. This is as close to a free lunch as you can get (See Listing 8.2). You receive the benefits of encapsulation and abstraction (your program doesn't have to know that the low-level routines exist or how they're implemented), and the call to the assembly functions is direct and, consequently, as efficient as you can get.

In addition to providing access to the lower-level assembly language functions, **Serial_Comm** adds methods for getting and setting the communication parameters. The class data members should be self-evident with the exception of **open_flag**. Since there's not a way to simultaneously handle two comm ports at once, it is necessary to prohibit this possibility. This prohibition is accomplished by declaring **open_flag** as a static data member (attribute). Static attributes are created once and are shared by all instances of the class. Since this is the case, we can create as many instances of **Serial_Comm** as we want but they share the same **open_flag**. **open_flag** is defined as a pointer to **Serial_Comm**.

This definition allows us to kill two birds with one stone: If **open_ flag** equals **NULL** then the port is available; if **open_flag** is not equal to **NULL** then the address stored in it indicates which instance currently owns the hardware port. Any attempt to open a class instance when **open_flag** already contains a legal instance address will result in an error. All methods that actually access the low-level assembly routines check to make sure that **open_flag** is either **NULL** or belongs to the instance in question.

Assembler Foundations

The original assembly routines were written a while ago and (to object-oriented eyes) are downright incestuous. By this I mean that the various routines, **open()**, **close()**, **read()**, **write()**, and so on, were too heavily coupled and the interrelationships were rather haphazard. In addition, the basic routines didn't provide any handshaking. This was the primary reason these routines have had to be modified for specific applications. A further complication is that one protocol may need to be implemented at the assembly level (XON/XOFF comes up) while another protocol, transfer packet for instance, should be implemented by the high level language.

I did give some thought to reimplementing the actual bottom-level communications routines in C++, but concerns about efficiency in an interrupt service routine persuaded me otherwise. To make best use of the assembly language routines inside an extendable C++ shell, I had to determine what sort of changes should be made to the existing routines.

As mentioned earlier, I began the project by designing a standard C++ class to describe what the assembly routines had to do. The actual code is not implemented as some sort of assembly-level OOP hybrid. However, I've found that describing an assembly language problem in a higher level language is an outstanding design aid. At any rate, I needed to find a way to modify the assembly stuff so that

1. The routines can be extended painlessly.
2. They are orthogonal (no duplication of function)
3. They provide a complete set of basic capabilities.

The following code shows the class version of the assembly language object:

```
class RS_232_asm
{
   public:
     int      open(int port, unsigned int params);
     void     close(void);
     int      read(void *buffer);
     int      write(void *buffer, int length);
     int      read_char(void);
     int      write_char(unsigned char chr);
     unsigned int      get_status(void);
     int      get_chars_recvd(void);
     int      get_chars_sent(void);
     void     clr_read_buffer(void);
     void     clr_write_buffer(void);
     void     stop_sending(unsigned char *control_str);
     void     start_sending(unsigned char *control_str);
   private:
     void              *receive_buffer;
     int               recv_buf_tail;
     void              *write_buffer;
     int               write_buf_tail;
     int               write_msg_length;
     unsigned int      com_status;
     unsigned int      flags;
     unsigned char     interrupt_num;
     unsigned char     interrupt_mask;
     unsigned char     interrupt_enable;
     unsigned int      old_interrupt_offset;
     unsigned int      old_interrupt_segment;
};
```

The obvious functions are opening and closing the port, reading and writing both individual characters and blocks of characters, and starting over when necessary (**clr_recv_buffer** and **clr_write_buffer**). Since low-level handshaking consists of start and stop commands, generic **stop_sending** and **start_sending** methods provide support for handshaking.

The problem of extendibility is solved by providing for an optional, external function that can be tested for and called when handshaking is enabled. The code listed next shows an assembly language code excerpt demonstrating this. The key is that the call to the handshaking routine is not directly to an assembly language label, but to an address stored at the location **hand_shake**, the contents of which may be changed at any time.

```
recv_char proc near
   mov     dx,com_port            ; get com port address
```

```
        in      al,dx               ; & read character

        test    com_status,HAND_SHAKING ; check for hand-shaking
        jz      rc_save             ; no hand-shaking so save
                                    ; else
        mov     ah,RECV_TEST        ; set ah to function code
        push    ax                  ; (al = character)
        call    [hand_shake]
        add     sp,2                ; adjust stack
        test    ah,0ffh             ; see if ah is zero
        jz      rc_save             ; if it is, save the byte
                                    ; else
        jmp     rc_out              ; exit
    rc_save:
...
```

There are four parts to a handshaking process: stop sending when requested by the other machine, restart sending when requested, and the reverse: request the other machine to stop sending, and request the other machine to restart sending. This may seem obvious, but it's essential to clarify what's important. Thus, we can establish the methods needed and also design a suitably flexible means of performing these actions.

XON/OFF

I'll demonstrate the process using XON/XOFF flow control as an example. Whenever a character is received and handshaking is enabled, the external module (**hand_shake**) is called and passed a function code—**CHAR_RECVD**—and the character received. This function code instructs **hand_shake** to examine the character sent. When a Control-S (XOFF) is detected, the base module's **stop_sending** function is called by **hand_shake**. The **stop_sending** function turns off the **TRANSMIT** interrupt.

If **hand_shake** is passed a Control-Q (XON) then **start_sending** is called, which reverses the previous operation. Then, **hand_shake** returns an integer to its caller. If the high byte of the integer is 0 then the value in the low byte is saved. Otherwise, **recv_char** exits immediately. The original **recv_char** routine remains ignorant of any details. We've now dealt with the other machine telling us when to stop or start, but how do we tell it to do the same?

Controlling the other machine is accomplished in the same external module. When called by **recv_ char, hand_shake** issues a call to **com_chars_recvd**, which returns the number of bytes in the receive buffer, and to **com_get_status**. If the number of bytes received is above an arbitrary threshold, **hand_shake** does one of two things. In the first case, if the main module is already sending (as determined by the call to **com_ get_status**) an internal flag is set. The next time **send_char** issues its call to **hand_shake, hand_shake** replaces the character sent to it with an XOFF for **send_char** to send. If the main module isn't currently sending, a call to **com_write** is made. The **send_ char** routine checks to see if the high byte of the return value is 0, and if so, **send_char** increments write buffer's tail. We've now accomplished:

1. The lowest level methods are in assembly language, which provides speed and efficiency. (The C++ methods provide platform independence.)

2. The routines are orthogonal and have low cohesion. This means that no single routine duplicates any other routine's function, and no routine knows any more than it absolutely has to about any other routine. The benefit is that side-effects resulting from a change to some particular routine are minimized.
3. The base assembler object is extendable through the provision of an external handshaking function. The fact that this function is external should also reduce or eliminate side-effects from changing the particular handshaking procedure used. Additionally, the external routine can be used for other purposes.
4. Finally, because the handshaking routine is external and isn't linked until runtime, it is possible to support multiple types of handshaking (or none at all) in a single program without adding significant complexity.

A Room on the Side

In **Serial_Comm** we have a nice little "two-room" base class. Let's extend it. The first extension is an **Xon_Xoff** class. This addition produces an object suitable for ASCII text transfers; driving a plotter, for instance. XON_XOFF.HPP and XON_XOFF.CPP (Listings 8.3 and 8.4) provide this capability. As you can see from the listings, the **Xon_Xoff** class itself has almost nothing in it. The constructor and destructor simply provide a path to the **Serial_Comm** constructor and destructor.

The **open()** and **close()** methods are redefined so that the handshaking function can be passed to the assembly language module, and that's it! All other methods are supplied by the base class. The actual handshaking routine, **xon_xoff_handler()**, is written in C. This was done to provide a clear example of how a handshaking routine should be coded. As a rule, however, I recommend writing any actual handshaking routines in assembler for maximum code performance. Since all lower priority interrupts are disabled until the communications interrupt ends, one should get in and get out as quickly as possible.

The next class on the list (**Msg_Packet**, Listings 8.5 and 8.6) implements a message packet protocol. The implementation is similar to one we use at my office for communicating with the spectrum analyzers we produce. A packet consists of a message-type code, a binary value specifying the message length in bytes, the message packet itself, and a terminating CRC value. The structure of a packet is shown in Table 8.8.

The CRC is checked when the **read()** method is called. If the packet is OK an ACK is returned; otherwise a NAK is returned and **read()** waits for the packet to be retransmitted. Two new data attributes and methods were added to support this. **re_trys** is the number of times to attempt a transmission or receipt before giving up and **timeout** is the time to wait between bytes received.

New versions of **read()** and **write()** are also implemented. These versions provide for passing and returning the message type and length. The **clr_xxxx_buffer()** methods are completely overridden because **Msg_Packet** maintains its own local buffers in addition to

■ **TABLE 8.8 Message packet structure**

Field:	**Type**	**Length**	**Message Packet**	**CRC**
# of bytes:	2	2	0 - 1024	2

the low-level buffers used by the assembly module. The higher level buffers enable client programs to peek at what has been received (using the new **get_xxxx()** methods) without emptying the buffer and to preset an outgoing packet (with the new **set_xxx()** methods) without sending.

There is a weakness in the **Msg_Packet** class. The fact that the CRC isn't checked until either **read()** or **get_recv_message()** is called means that a program using this class must check for packets on a frequent basis to ensure the other machine doesn't time out waiting for an ACK.

In Closing. . .

Object-oriented programming (OOP) is more a matter of the way you think about programs ("active data" as Jeff Duntemann says) than any particular syntax. As is demonstrated here, that way of thinking can be applied to assembly language, or even FORTRAN. Then why use an OOP language? In many ways, object-oriented programming using an object-oriented language allows the programmer to design his or her own special purpose language for a particular problem. An added benefit is that if you do a good job of defining the objects used, then these components can be reused in solving other problems. OOP brings us one step closer to component-level software design.

CODE DESCRIPTION

Overview

The code provided includes a complete set of serial communications functions in C++. The functions serve as high-level wrappers around low-level assembly code.

Listings Available

Listing	*Description*	*Used with*
SERIAL.HPP	Defines data types and **Serial_Comm** class.	------
SERIAL.CPP	Implements methods for **Serial_Comm**.	------
XON_XOFF.HPP	Extends **Serial_Comm** to include XON/OFF.	------
XON_XOFF.CPP	Implements **Xon_Xoff** Class.	------
MSG_PCKT.HPP	Defines **Msg_Packet** Class.	------
MSG_PCKT.CPP	Implements **Msg_Packet** methods and **timer()** function.	------

How to Compile/Assemble

Can be compiled and linked with Turbo, Borland, Zortech C++ compiler.

Note: The assembly language module is not included in the printed listings, but is present on the listings diskette included with the book.

■ LISTING 8.1 SERIAL.HPP

```
/*   Written by Kevin D. Weeks
 *   Compiles and runs under Turbo C++ and Zortech C++. */
```

```
#if !defined(COMM_HPP)
#define COMM_HPP
// These enum types perform two functions: They are checked
// for type by the compiler to prevent an invalid parameter from
// being passed, and they function as indices into the tables
// defined at the end of the class definition
enum Com_Port { Com_1, Com_2 };
enum Baud_Rate
    {   Baud_110, Baud_150, Baud_300, Baud_600, Baud_1200,
        Baud_2400, Baud_4800, Baud_9600 };
enum Parity { Odd_Parity, Even_Parity, No_Parity };
enum Stop_Bits {   Stop_Bits_1, Stop_Bits_2 };
enum Data_Bits {   Data_Bits_7, Data_Bits_8 };
enum Bool {   FALSE, TRUE };
enum Result {   OK, ERROR = -1 };
// define a handshaking function type
typedef   int(*HAND_SHAKE)(int);
// assembly function prototypes
extern "C"
{
    Result  com_open(int port, unsigned int parameters);
    void    com_close(void);
    int     com_read(void *buffer);
    Result  com_write(int num_bytes, void *buffer);
    int     com_read_char(void);
    Result  com_write_char(unsigned char chr);
    void    com_start_sending(void);
    void    com_stop_sending(void);
    unsigned int    com_get_status(void);
    int     com_chars_recvd(void);
    int     com_chars_sent(void);
    void    com_set_buffers(unsigned char *recv_buffer,
                        unsigned char *send_buffer, int length);
    void    com_set_handshake(HAND_SHAKE);
    void    com_clr_recv_buf(void);
    void    com_clr_send_buf(void);
};
// Define bit flags returned by com_get_status(). Note that bits
// 0 - 3 indicate current status, 4 - 7 indicate line errors,
// and 8 - 10 indicate execution errors
typedef union
{
    unsigned int    value;
    struct {
        unsigned    port_open : 1;
        unsigned    char_received : 1;
        unsigned    sending_message : 1;
        unsigned    hand_shaking : 1;
        unsigned    overrun_err : 1;
        unsigned    parity_err : 1;
        unsigned    framing_err : 1;
        unsigned    break_received : 1;
        unsigned    buffer_overflow : 1;
        unsigned    invalid_port : 1;
        unsigned    port_not_found : 1;
```

```
    } flag;
} Comm_Status;

#define DEFAULT_BUF_SIZE    1024
/* Methods marked with a "// *" will return an error unless
*  the port is owned by current instance of the class. */
class Serial_Comm
{
  public:
    // constructors
        Serial_Comm(void);
        Serial_Comm(Com_Port port, Baud_Rate baud, Parity par,
                    Stop_Bits stop, Data_Bits data);
    // destructor
        ~Serial_Comm(void);
    // first group of methods provide for actually accessing data
    // they return an ERROR or -1 if the port is unowned or is
    // owned by another instance of the class
    Result          open(void);
    void            close(void);
    int             read(void *client_buffer);
    Result          write(void *client_buffer, int length);
    int             read_char(void);
    Result          write_char(unsigned char);
    // Next two methods allow starting over. Note that clr_send_
    // buffer disables sending if sending is enabled. They
    // return an ERROR if another instance owns the port.
    Result          clr_recv_buffer(void);
    Result          clr_send_buffer(void);
    // get_status() returns a 0 if the port is owned by another.
    Comm_Status     get_status(void);
    // Next two methods return an ERROR if the port is owned
    // by another instance. In both caes 0 is a valid return value.
    int             get_bytes_recvd(void);
    int             get_bytes_sent(void);
    // The remaining methods will function whether the instance
    // in question owns the port or not.
    Com_Port        get_port(void) { return com_port; };
    Baud_Rate       get_baud_rate(void) { return baud_rate; };
    Parity          get_parity(void) { return parity; };
    Stop_Bits       get_stop_bits(void) { return stop_bits; };
    Data_Bits       get_data_bits(void) { return data_bits; };
    int             get_buffer_size(void) { return buffer_size; };
    // If port is open AND owned by the instance called,
    // then it will be closed before parameters are changed and
    // then re-opened. Since closing the port causes data in
    // the send or receive buffers to be discarded, these
    // methods should be used carefully.
    void            set_port(Com_Port port);
    void            set_baud_rate(Baud_Rate baud);
    void            set_parity(Parity par);
    void            set_stop_bits(Stop_Bits stop);
    void            set_data_bits(Data_Bits data);
    Result          set_buffer_size(int size);
```

```
protected:
// the following attributes are shared by all instances of
// the class and descendants
  static Serial_Comm      *open_flag;
  static unsigned int     baud_table[8];
  static unsigned int     parity_table[3];
  static unsigned int     stop_table[2];
  static unsigned int     data_table[2];
private:
// These attributes are accessible through methods so keep
// them private
  int             buffer_size;
  unsigned char   *recv_buffer;
  unsigned char   *send_buffer;
  Com_Port        com_port;
  Baud_Rate       baud_rate;
  Parity          parity;
  Stop_Bits       stop_bits;
  Data_Bits       data_bits;
};
#endif
```

■ LISTING 8.2 SERIAL.CPP

```
#include <stdio.h>
#include "serial.hpp"
// Initialize tables for use by Int 14h. Enum's defined in
// SERIAL.HPP (Buad_Rate, Parity) index into these tables
unsigned int Serial_Comm::baud_table[8] = {0,0x20,0x40,0x60,
                                        0x80,0xa0,0xc0,0xe0};
unsigned int Serial_Comm::parity_table[3] = {8,0x18,0};
unsigned int Serial_Comm::stop_table[2] = {0,4};
unsigned int Serial_Comm::data_table[2] = {2,3};
Serial_Comm  *Serial_Comm::open_flag = NULL;
/* Null constructor-sets the data attributes to arbitrary
*  defaults. If some other values seem better, use them.  */
Serial_Comm::Serial_Comm(void)
{
    com_port = Com_1;
    baud_rate = Baud_1200;
    parity = No_Parity;
    stop_bits = Stop_Bits_1;
    data_bits = Data_Bits_8;
    buffer_size = DEFAULT_BUF_SIZE;
    recv_buffer = new unsigned char[buffer_size];
    send_buffer = new unsigned char[buffer_size];
}

/* Constructor-allows the user to specify start-up parameters. */
Serial_Comm::Serial_Comm(Com_Port port, Baud_Rate baud, Parity par,
                         Stop_Bits stop, Data_Bits data)
{
    unsigned int    parameters;
    com_port = port;
```

```
    baud_rate = baud;
    parity = par;
    stop_bits = stop;
    data_bits = data;
    buffer_size = DEFAULT_BUF_SIZE;
    recv_buffer = new unsigned char[buffer_size];
    send_buffer = new unsigned char[buffer_size];
}

/* Destructor-closes the port if open and owned by this
*  instance and frees the buffers. */
Serial_Comm::~Serial_Comm(void)
{
    close();
    delete [buffer_size] recv_buffer;
    delete [buffer_size] send_buffer;
    recv_buffer = send_buffer = NULL;
}

/* First, set local buffers for the assembly module. Then open
*  port and claim it. Fails if someone else owns the port. */
Result  Serial_Comm::open(void)
{
    unsigned int    parameters;
    if (open_flag) return ERROR;
    com_set_buffers(recv_buffer,send_buffer,buffer_size);
    parameters = baud_table[baud_rate] | parity_table[parity] |
                 stop_table[stop_bits] | data_table[data_bits];
    if (com_open(com_port,parameters) != ERROR) {
        open_flag = this;                   // claim the port
        return OK;
    }
    return ERROR;
}

/* If port is open and belongs to this instance, close it. */
void    Serial_Comm::close(void)
{
    if (open_flag == this) {
        com_close();
        open_flag = NULL;
    }
}

/* Read whatever's in the local buffer into client's buffer.
*  Fail if someone else owns the port. */
int  Serial_Comm::read(void *client_buffer)
{
    if (open_flag == this) return com_read(client_buffer);
    else return -1;
}

/* Write the client's buffer. Fails if already sending or if
*  someone else owns the port. */
```

```
Result   Serial_Comm::write(void *buffer, int num_bytes)
{
    if (open_flag == this)
      return (Result)com_write(num_bytes,buffer);
    else return ERROR;
}

/*  Read a single character from the receive buffer. */
int     Serial_Comm::read_char(void)
{
    if (open_flag == this) return com_read_char();
    else return -1;
}

/* Write a character out the port. Note: this method will
*  fail if a message is currently being sent. */
Result   Serial_Comm::write_char(unsigned char chr)
{
    if (open_flag == this) return com_write_char(chr);
    else return ERROR;
}

/*  Clear and reinitialize the receive buffer. */
Result  Serial_Comm::clr_recv_buffer(void)
{
    if (open_flag == this || open_flag == NULL) {
        com_clr_recv_buf();
        return OK;
    }
    return ERROR;
}

/* Clear and reinitialize send buffer. If currently sending
*  the remainder of the message will be discarded and the
*  transmit interrupt disabled. */
Result  Serial_Comm::clr_send_buffer(void)
{
    if (open_flag == this || open_flag == NULL) {
        com_clr_send_buf();
        return OK;
    }
    return ERROR;
}

/* Get the current port status. */
Comm_Status  Serial_Comm::get_status(void)
{
    Comm_Status stat;
    if (open_flag == this || open_flag == NULL)
        stat.value = com_get_status();
    else stat.value = 0;
    return stat;
}
```

```
/*  Returns the number of bytes in the receive buffer. */
int  Serial_Comm::get_bytes_recvd(void)
{
    if (open_flag == this) return com_chars_recvd();
    else return -1;
}

/* Returns number of bytes sent from the current message. */
int  Serial_Comm::get_bytes_sent(void)
{
    if (open_flag == this) return com_chars_sent();
    else return -1;
}

/* Specifies the com port to use. */
void    Serial_Comm::set_port(Com_Port port)
{
    com_port = port;
    if (open_flag == this) {
        close();
        open();
    }
}

/* Specifies the baud rate. */
void    Serial_Comm::set_baud_rate(Baud_Rate baud)
{
    baud_rate = baud;
    if (open_flag == this) {
        close();
        open();
    }
}

/* Specifies the parity. */
void    Serial_Comm::set_parity(Parity par)
{
    parity = par;
    if (open_flag == this) {
        close();
        open();
    }
}

/* Specifies the number of stop bits. */
void    Serial_Comm::set_stop_bits(Stop_Bits stop)
{
    stop_bits = stop;
    if (open_flag == this) {
        close();
        open();
    }
}
```

```
/* Specifies the number of data bits. */
void    Serial_Comm::set_data_bits(Data_Bits data)
{
    data_bits = data;
    if (open_flag == this) {
        close();
        open();
    }
}

/*  Specifies the size of low-level buffers. */
Result      Serial_Comm::set_buffer_size(int size)
{
    Bool    port_open = FALSE;
    // close the port if it's open and owned by this instance
    if (open_flag == this) {
        port_open = TRUE;
        close();
    }
    // free the original buffers, then change the buffer size
    // and re-allocate the buffers
    delete [buffer_size] recv_buffer;
    delete [buffer_size] send_buffer;
    buffer_size = size;
    recv_buffer = new unsigned char[buffer_size];
    send_buffer = new unsigned char[buffer_size];
    // if the port was open re-open it and re-set the buffers
    if (port_open == TRUE) {
        com_set_buffers(recv_buffer,send_buffer,buffer_size);
        return open();
    }
    return OK;
}

unsigned int clock_ticks(int start)
{
    static long     reference;
    static long far *bios_clock = (long far *)0x0040006c;

    if (start)
        reference = *bios_clock;
    return (unsigned int)((*bios_clock - reference) / 2);
}
```

■ LISTING 8.3 XON_XOFF.HPP

```
#if !defined(XON_XOFF_HPP)
#define XON_XOFF_HPP
#include "serial.hpp"
class Xon_Xoff : public Serial_Comm
{
  public:
  // constructor—provides a path to Serial_Comm constructor
```

```
          Xon_Xoff(Com_Port port, Baud_Rate baud, Parity par,
                   Stop_Bits stop, Data_Bits data) :
                   Serial_Comm(port, baud, par, stop, data) {};
   // destructor - also empty
             ~Xon_Xoff(void) {};
   // replace Serial_Comm's open and close methods
     Result  open(void);
     void    close(void);
};
#endif
```

■ LISTING 8.4 XON_XOFF.CPP

```
#include <stdio.h>
#include "xon_xoff.hpp"
// handshake function codes
#define RECV_TEST   1
#define SEND_TEST   2
#define BUF_EMPTY   3
#define XON         17
#define XOFF        19
int     xon_xoff_handler(int function_code);

/* Method replaces Serial_Comm's open to allow for setting the
*  hand-shaking function. */
Result  Xon_Xoff::open(void)
{
    // make sure no one has the com port, then set hand-
    // shaking and call Serial_Comm to open the port
    if (open_flag == NULL) {
        com_set_handshake(xon_xoff_handler);
        return Serial_Comm::open();
    }
    return ERROR;
}

/* Method replaces Serial_Comm's close to allow for re-setting
*   the hand-shaking function. */
void    Xon_Xoff::close(void)
{
    if (open_flag == this || open_flag == NULL) {
        com_set_handshake(NULL);
        Serial_Comm::close();
    }
}

/* This function actually performs hand-shaking. Although the
*  assembly routines are coded to support calls to C functions,
*  it is better practice to code this function in assembler
*  so that it operates as fast as possible.
*  The high byte of function_code contains the function code
*  from the assembly routine.The low byte of the function code
*  contains either the byte received or the byte to be sent. */
#pragma option -N-              // turn off stack checking
```

```
int     xon_xoff_handler(int function_code)
{
    // state flags
    static Bool send_xoff = FALSE;
    static Bool send_xon = FALSE;
    static Bool sending_halted = FALSE;
    static Bool xoff_sent = FALSE;
    Comm_Status stat;
    switch (function_code >> 8) {  // determine function code
        case RECV_TEST:
            stat.value = com_get_status();
           // turn off receiving if there are < 64 bytes
           // free in the receive buffer
            if (com_chars_recvd() > 960)
                if (stat.flag.sending_message)
                    send_xoff = TRUE;
                else {
                    xoff_sent = TRUE;
                    com_write_char(XOFF);
                }
            if ((function_code & 0x00ff) == XOFF)
                // if XOFF received then stop sending
                if (stat.flag.sending_message) {
                    com_stop_sending();
                    sending_halted = TRUE;
                    return 0xff00;
                }
            if ((function_code & 0x00ff) == XON)
                // if XON received then start sending
                if (sending_halted) {
                    com_start_sending();
                    sending_halted = FALSE;
                    return 0xff00;
                }
            // clear high byte so the character will be saved
            return (function_code & 0x00ff);
        case SEND_TEST:
            if (send_xon) {
                send_xon = FALSE;
                xoff_sent = FALSE;
                return (0xff00 | XON);
            }
            if (send_xoff) {
                send_xoff = FALSE;
                xoff_sent = TRUE;
                return (0xff00 | XOFF);
            }
            // clear high byte so send_tail will be incremented
            return (function_code & 0x00ff);
        case BUF_EMPTY:
            stat.value = com_get_status();
            if (xoff_sent)
                // if sending was stopped then restart it
                if (stat.flag.sending_message)
```

```
                    send_xon = TRUE;
                else {
                    com_write_char(XON);
                    xoff_sent = FALSE;
                }
            return 0;
    };
}
#pragma option -N+    // turn stack checking back on
```

■ LISTING 8.5 MSG_PCKT.HPP

```
#if !defined(MSG_PCKT_HPP)
#define MSG_PCKT_HPP
#include "serial.hpp"
// these types are used to control file transfer between two
// devices.
enum Msg_Type
{
    NO_MESSAGE,       // used as a response to get_msg_type()
    END_OF_PROCESS,   // designates end of load data or file
    PROGRAM_INQUIRE,  // requests list of programs for upload
    LOAD_PROGRAM,     // requests that a program be uploaded
    DATA_INQUIRE,     // requests list of data files
    DATA_UPLOAD,      // requests that a data file be uploaded
    DATA_DOWNLOAD,    // requests that a data file be downloaded
    MSG_ERROR         // general error
};
// this structure is used to monitor internal object status
struct Msg_Status
{
    unsigned int    type_read : 1;
    unsigned int    size_read : 1;
    unsigned int    msg_read : 1;
};
struct Msg_Buffer
{
    Msg_Type        type;
    int             length;
    unsigned char   msg[1026];
};

class Msg_Packet : public Serial_Comm
{
  public:
    // constructors and destructor
       Msg_Packet(void);
       Msg_Packet(Com_Port port, Baud_Rate baud, Parity par,
                  Stop_Bits stop, Data_Bits data);
       ~Msg_Packet(void) {};
    // methods provide support for packet parameters. Note
    // that the read() and write() methods in Serial_Comm
    // are still accessable
    Result  read(Msg_Type *type, int *msg_size, void *buffer);
```

```
    Result  write(Msg_Type type, int msg_size, void *buffer);
    // methods replace their originals in Serial_Comm
    void    clr_recv_buffer(void);
    void    clr_send_buffer(void);
    // methods are non-destructive (unlike the read() method)
    // they allow the user to peek at what's in the buffer
    // without committing
    Msg_Type get_recv_msg_type(void);
    int      get_recv_msg_size(void);
    Result   get_recv_message(void *buffer);
    // these three methods are also non-committal. nothing is
    // actually sent until send_message() is called
    void     set_send_msg_type(Msg_Type type)
             { send_msg_buffer.type = type; };
    Result   set_send_msg_size(int size);
    void     set_send_message(void *buffer)
          {memcpy(send_msg_buffer.msg,buffer,get_buffer_size());};
    Result   send_message(void);
    int      get_timeout(void) { return timeout; };
    int      get_retrys(void) { return re_trys; };
    void     set_timeout(int tenths) { timeout = tenths; };
    void     set_retrys(int num_trys) { re_trys = num_trys; };
    // these methods disable the base class' methods.
    // buffer_size is hard coded and input and output MUST take
    // place through the read() and write() methods above
    Result   set_buffer_size(void) { return ERROR; };
    int      read_char(void) { return ERROR; };
    Result   write_char(void) { return ERROR; };
  private:
    Msg_Status      status;
    int             timeout;
    int             re_trys;
    Msg_Buffer      recv_msg_buffer;
    Msg_Buffer      send_msg_buffer;
};
#endif
```

■ LISTING 8.6 MSG_PCKT.CPP

```
#if defined(__TURCOC__)
    #include <mem.h>         // memset() prototype in Turbo
#else
    #include <string.h>      // memset() prototype in Zortech
#endif
#include "msg_pckt.hpp"
// timer function codes
#define MARK    1
#define ELAPSED 2
// protocol codes
#define ACK     6
#define NAK     21
// these two functions are not part of the class but are
// included here for convenience.
unsigned int  timer(int function);
```

```
unsigned int  calc_crc(void *buffer, int length);
/* Null constructor-difference between this constructor and
*  next one is the use of Serial_Comm's default parameters. */
Msg_Packet::Msg_Packet(void) : Serial_Comm()
{
    timeout = 50;
    re_trys = 3;
    memset(&recv_msg_buffer,'\0',sizeof(recv_msg_buffer));
    memset(&send_msg_buffer,'\0',sizeof(send_msg_buffer));
    // initialize buffer size to the default plus the other
    // packet members
    Serial_Comm::set_buffer_size(DEFAULT_BUF_SIZE +
                sizeof(Msg_Type)+sizeof(char *)+sizeof(int));
    status.type_read = status.size_read=status.msg_read=FALSE;
}

/* Constructor-communication parameters are specified. */
Msg_Packet::Msg_Packet(Com_Port port, Baud_Rate baud, Parity par,
                       Stop_Bits stop, Data_Bits data) :
                       Serial_Comm(port,baud,par,stop,data)
{
    timeout = 50; re_trys = 3;
    memset(&recv_msg_buffer,'\0',sizeof(recv_msg_buffer));
    memset(&send_msg_buffer,'\0',sizeof(send_msg_buffer));
    // initialize the buffer size to the default plus the other
    // packet members
    Serial_Comm::set_buffer_size(DEFAULT_BUF_SIZE+sizeof(Msg_Type)
                  + sizeof(char *) + sizeof(int));
    status.type_read = status.size_read = status.msg_read=FALSE;
}

/* Supports message type and size. Will not return until either
*  a message is received, or the timeout or retry values have
*  been exceeded. */
Result  Msg_Packet::read(Msg_Type *type, int *msg_size, void *buffer)
{
    int     bytes_read;
    *type = get_recv_msg_type();
    if ((*type == MSG_ERROR) || (*type == NO_MESSAGE))
        return ERROR;
    *msg_size = get_recv_msg_size();
    get_recv_message(buffer);
    status.type_read = status.size_read = status.msg_read = FALSE;
    recv_msg_buffer.type = NO_MESSAGE;
    recv_msg_buffer.length = 0;
    return OK;
}

/* Supports message type and size. Will not return until
*  message is ACKnowledged or the retry and timeout values have
*  been exceeded. */
Result  Msg_Packet::write(Msg_Type type, int msg_size, void *buffer)
{
    set_send_msg_type(type);
```

```
    if (set_send_msg_size(msg_size) == ERROR)
        return ERROR;
    set_send_message(buffer);
    return send_message();
}

/* Returns message type. If the type has already been read it is
*  returned immediately, otherwise this method waits for up to
*  timeout tenths of a second for a message to be received. */
Msg_Type    Msg_Packet::get_recv_msg_type(void)
{
    Msg_Type    ret_value;
    if (open_flag != this) return NO_MESSAGE;
    if (status.type_read == TRUE)   // type acquired-return it
        return recv_msg_buffer.type;
    timer(MARK);                        // start the timer
    do {            // loop until type is received or timeout
        if (com_chars_recvd() >= 2) {   // check word size type
            // first read the message type low byte
            if ((recv_msg_buffer.type =
                    (Msg_Type)com_read_char()) == ERROR)
                break;
            com_read_char();     // throw away high byte
            status.type_read = TRUE;
            return recv_msg_buffer.type;
        }
    } while (timer(ELAPSED) < timeout);
    recv_msg_buffer.type = NO_MESSAGE;
    return MSG_ERROR;
}

/* Returns message size. If size has already been read it is
*  returned immediately, otherwise this method waits for up to
*  timeout tenths of a second for a message to be received. */
int     Msg_Packet::get_recv_msg_size(void)
{
    int     ret_value;
    if (open_flag != this) return (int)ERROR;
    // if the type hasn't been read yet, read it
    if (get_recv_msg_type() == MSG_ERROR) return (int)ERROR;
    // if the size has already been read return it
    if (status.size_read == TRUE)
        return (recv_msg_buffer.length);
    timer(MARK);                        // start the timer
    do {            // loop until size is received or timeout
        if (com_chars_recvd() >= 2) {   // size is two bytes long
          if ((recv_msg_buffer.length = com_read_char()) == ERROR)
              break;
          if ((ret_value = com_read_char()) == ERROR) break;
          recv_msg_buffer.length &= ret_value << 8;
          status.size_read = TRUE;
          return recv_msg_buffer.length;
        }
    } while (timer(ELAPSED) < timeout);
```

```
    recv_msg_buffer.type = MSG_ERROR;
    return (int)ERROR;
}

/* Return message received. This method will try up to re_trys
*  times to read a message. Once successfully read, the message
*  is returned but not destroyed. */
Result  Msg_Packet::get_recv_message(void *buffer)
{
    int               retry_counter = 0;
    int               ret_value;
    int               bytes_read;
    unsigned int      crc;
    if (open_flag != this) return ERROR;
    // if the message has already been read then just return it
    if (status.msg_read) {
      memcpy(buffer,recv_msg_buffer.msg,recv_msg_buffer.length);
      return OK;
    }
            // loop until either a complete message has
    do {    //  been read or until re_trys is exceeded.
        // get the message type
        if (get_recv_msg_type() != MSG_ERROR)
          if (get_recv_msg_size() != -1){ // get message size
            timer(MARK);                  // start timer
              bytes_read = 0;
              do {
                 if ((ret_value = com_read
                 (&recv_msg_buffer.msg[bytes_read])) == ERROR)
                    break;
                 else {
                    bytes_read += ret_value;
                    if (bytes_read >= recv_msg_buffer.length) {
                        // add 4 to allow for type & size
                        crc = calc_crc(&recv_msg_buffer,
                            recv_msg_buffer.length + 4);
                        if (crc == (unsigned int) recv_msg_buffer
                                  .msg[recv_msg_buffer.length]) {
                              com_write_char(ACK);
                              status.msg_read = TRUE;
                              memcpy(buffer,recv_msg_buffer.msg,
                                  recv_msg_buffer.length);
                              return OK;
                         } else {
                              com_write_char(NAK);
                              status.type_read = FALSE;
                              status.size_read = FALSE;
                         }
                    }
                 }
              } while (timer(ELAPSED) < timeout);
          }
    } while (++retry_counter < re_trys);
    status.type_read = status.size_read = status.msg_read = FALSE;
```

```
    return ERROR;
}

/* Sets the size of the message to be sent. */
Result  Msg_Packet::set_send_msg_size(int size)
{
    if (size <= get_buffer_size()) {
        send_msg_buffer.length = size;
        return OK;
    }
    return ERROR;
}

Result  Msg_Packet::send_message(void)
{
    int             response;
    int             retry_counter;
    unsigned int    t;
    if (send_msg_buffer.type == NO_MESSAGE) return ERROR;
    // calculate the crc
    send_msg_buffer.msg[send_msg_buffer.length] =
            calc_crc(&send_msg_buffer,send_msg_buffer.length+4);
    // if currently sending wait until current message is out
    timer(MARK);
    while (get_status().flag.sending_message)
        if (timer(ELAPSED) > timeout) return ERROR;
    // loop until message has been sent or re_trys exceeded
    do {
        if ((Result)com_write(send_msg_buffer.length + 6,
                              &send_msg_buffer) != ERROR) {
            // wait until the message is gone
            timer(MARK);
            while (get_status().flag.sending_message)
                if (timer(ELAPSED) > timeout) return ERROR;
            // now wait until the ACK or NAK is received
            timer(MARK);
            while (!get_status().flag.char_received)
                if (timer(ELAPSED) > timeout) break;
            if (get_status().flag.char_received) {
                response = com_read_char();
                if (response == ACK) return OK;
            }
        }
    } while (++retry_counter < re_trys);
    return ERROR;
}

/* This function is not a member of Msg_Packet. The clock starts
*  when it is passed the MARK code. Thereafter it returns
* (approximately) the number of tenths of a second that have passed
* since MARK */
unsigned int timer(int function)
{
    static long     reference;
```

```
    static long far *bios_clock = (long far *)0x0040006c;
    if (function == MARK) reference = *bios_clock;
    return (unsigned int)((*bios_clock - reference) / 2);
}

/* This function is also not a member of Msg_Packet. It calculates a
*  CRC value which is then used to detect message corruption. */
unsigned int    calc_crc(unsigned char *buffer, int length)
{
    unsigned int    cur_crc;
    int             i, j;
    for (i = 0; i < length; i++) {
        // xor current byte with crc hi-byte
        cur_crc ^= (unsigned int)*buffer << 8;
        // shift crc left 8 times checking to see if MSB is on
        for (j = 0; j < 8; j++)
            if (cur_crc & 0x8000)           // if MSB on
                // shift left and xor with prime
                cur_crc = (cur_crc << 1) ^ 0x1021;
            else
                cur_crc <<= 1;              // just shift left
        ++buffer;
    }
    return cur_crc;
}
```

9

Managing Memory

In the best of worlds, "managing memory" would be as serious a problem as "walking"—but we work in a world where IBM put the BIOS, video buffers, and other system machinery at the top of memory rather than at the bottom, creating a barrier at 640K that we have spent years and years transcending. Furthermore, Intel hasn't helped by forcing us to carry around the baggage of the antediluvian 8080 CPU in the form of 64K segments and all the complexities they imply.

It's not for nothing that "memory" and "mess" both begin with "m."

Industry analyst Brett Glass takes the opposite view and holds that our segmented, divided memory system is an opportunity in disguise, since it is enormously flexible, and the newer Intel processors provide a multitude of ways to protect against wayward memory accesses, all of them based in some ways on segmented memory. So perhaps it's not as bad as it looks. Perhaps we just haven't grokked our own memory architecture in its fullness.

Maybe all we need is a few more years.

In the meantime, this chapter provides some ammunition in your war on muddled memory management. For starters, Daev Rohr can give you your bearings in the area of DOS extenders, where a clever system routine intermediates between real-mode DOS and a program running in protected mode. Terrence Vaughn explains the difference between far pointers and huge pointers, and David Stafford explains how to minimize overhead in dynamically-allocated records. Finally, Richard Sadowsky and Michael Abrash each provide their own carefully considered advice on how to use memory effectively and quickly.

In memory management, as almost anywhere, the more you know, the better off you are—and in the memory game, the payoff is higher than most.

Guaranteeing Word-Sized Block Moves

■ Cye Waldman

Here's a useful trick for quickly moving an arbitrary number of bytes.

Routines to move blocks of bytes from one location in memory to another are common. These routines can be made more efficient when even numbers of bytes are to be moved because they can be moved two bytes (one word) at a time. Unfortunately, life doesn't always hand us bytes in even-sized blocks. So, in a truly general-purpose routine we are limited to moving a single byte at a time, right? Not so. The following code fragment shows how to deal with arbitrary numbers of bytes most efficiently. Instead of using this for a **Moveleft** routine:

```
cld                        ; Auto increment si & di
rep     movsb          ; Move while cx <> 0
```

try this:

```
cld             ; Auto increment si & di
shr    cx,1     ; cx <- cx DIV 2
jae    @@10     ; Jump if cx=0
                    ; (i.e., an even number of bytes)
movsb           ; ... Else move just the first byte
@@10:
rep    movsw    ; Move all, or the remaining bytes
```

Here we are testing whether there's an even number of bytes in the block. If the number is odd, you move the first byte by itself (making the remainder of the block an even number of bytes), then fall into the true word-sized block move. This effectively doubles the speed of the **MoveLeft** routine for large numbers of bytes.

Normalizing Huge Pointers

■ Terrence Vaughn

Save some time by treating a huge pointer as a far one.

A huge pointer (like a far pointer) is a 32-bit pointer containing a segment and an offset. Unlike the far pointer, however, arithmetic on huge pointers operates on *both* the offset and segment. A huge pointer can't "wrap around" in the normal DOS address space and allows the pointer to point to objects (such as dynamic arrays) that are larger than 64K. The more complicated arithmetic, which makes huge pointers work, unfortunately also makes them slower to manipulate. However, if you're going to access less than 64K of memory *and* if the pointer is *normalized*, it is possible to assign a huge pointer's value to a far pointer for greater speed.

In the Intel scheme of things the segment is the paragraph number and the offset is the byte count offset from the start of the segment. Because a paragraph is 16 bytes, no location in memory is farther than 16 bytes from a paragraph boundary. The segment portion of a normalized pointer specifies the closest paragraph boundary less than the address in question. This being the case, a normalized offset can never exceed 0x0F (see Figure 9.1). For example, 0010:0009h is normalized; 0000:0109h is not. Using huge pointers that aren't normalized can result in errors during comparisons and other operations.

Because they don't wrap around when the offset reaches 0xFFFF, huge pointers are a necessity when you are using large data on the far heap. Unfortunately, huge pointers aren't part of the ANSI standard. Rather, they're specific to the Intel 80x86 architecture—so what you get when you use them depends on your compiler. With Turbo C (and Borland C++), a simple nudge like adding zero will normalize a huge pointer. (Keep in mind that optimizing compilers typically ignore additions of 0). QuickC requires a hammer like the **normalize()** function shown in Listing 9.1. Although QuickC performs accurate math on huge pointers, it *doesn't* normalize pointers before comparisons involving them. Microsoft C/C++ allegedly will always normalize pointers.

Listing 9.1 simply shows what your compiler thinks about huge pointers. The **normalize()** function will work with any 32-bit pointer. Since only the lowest four bits of the offset contain the byte count from the closest paragraph boundary, shifting the other 12 bits over and adding them to the segment gives you a normalized pointer. If your compiled program reports unequal pointers or incorrect subtraction, you'll need to force normalization on your huge pointers.

CODE DESCRIPTION

Overview

The program provided shows how huge pointers are normalized.

Listings Available

Listing	*Description*	*Used with*
TESTHP.C	Test program for checking whether huge pointers are normalized.	------

How to Compile/Assemble

The listing can be compiled and linked with any C/C++ compiler.

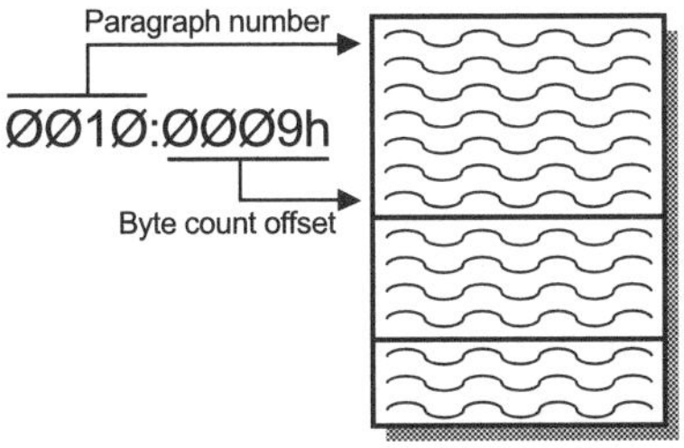

■ **FIGURE 9.1 Accessing memory with normalized pointers**

■ LISTING 9.1 TESTHP.C

```
#include <stdio.h>
void huge *normalize(void huge *);

main() {

 char far *cp;
 char huge *hp, huge *hp1;
 long l;

 cp = (char far *)0x2FFF00F2L; /* An easily visible address */
 hp = (char huge *)cp;         /* Normalized * = 300E:0002   */
 /* Did the cast have any effect? */
 printf("far * =  %Fp\n",cp);
 printf("huge * = %Fp\n",hp);
 hp1 = hp;
 hp1+=0;                      /* This works with TurboC */
 printf("huge * +0 = %Fp\n",hp1);
 hp1 = normalize(hp);         /* Force normalization  */
 printf("Normalized * = %Fp\n",hp1);
 if(hp == hp1) printf("Pointers equal.\n");
 else printf("Pointers not equal.\n");
 l = (long)(hp1 - hp);        /* Test pointer subtraction */
 printf("%s subtraction= %li\n\n", (l) ? "Incorrect":"Correct", l);
}

void huge *normalize(void huge *hp) {

 unsigned long base, para;

 base = (unsigned long) hp&0xFFFF000FL;
 para = (unsigned long) hp&0x0000FFF0L;
 para <<= 12;
 return(void huge *)(base + para);
}
```

Spotting a Wandering Pointer in C++

■ Kevin Dean

Overload the new and delete operators to check for incorrect memory deletions.

C++ has added memory management operators **new()** and **delete()** to the language, analogous to Pascal's **New** and **Dispose**. They are implemented as library functions and it's perfectly permissible (and sometimes encouraged) to override the default library functions with your own. The usual, but by no means standard, implementation is simply to pass the request on to the runtime library routines **malloc()** and **free()** to get and release the required memory. As long as the call to **new()** returns a pointer to an otherwise unused piece of memory, the call is valid.

Recently, one of my C++ programs that relied extensively on dynamic memory allocation went wandering into the sunset every time it ran. Some careful debugging revealed that the program was trashing the memory allocation tables. But I still couldn't find the bug.

I suspected the program was deleting memory it hadn't allocated and, with the help of the code in Listing 9.2, I created my own version of **delete()** to find out where and why. By setting a breakpoint at the indicated spot, it was possible to single-step back to the calling function, find the offending line, and find the reason the program was trying to deallocate memory it didn't own.

TIP: Borland C++ users may also wish to check out the **heap. . . ()** functions. If properly embedded in the **new()** and **delete()** functions, they can add an extra layer of debugging during software development.

CODE DESCRIPTION

Overview

The listing provided shows how the C++ new and delete operators can be overloaded for greater flexibility.

Listings Available

Listing	*Description*	*Used with*
NEWDEL.CPP	Example of overloading new and delete operators to check for incorrect deletions.	------

How to Compile/Assemble

This listing an be compiled and linked with any C/C++ compiler.

■ LISTING 9.2 NEWDEL.CPP

```
#include <alloc.h>
#include <iostream.h>

#define TABLE_SIZE  100
static void *validaddr[TABLE_SIZE];

// Call C malloc() function and save pointer in internal table.
void *operator new(size_t s)
{
void *p = malloc(s);

// Search for free space in table.
for (int i = 0; i < TABLE_SIZE && validaddr[i] != 0; i++);

// Insert pointer into table if space found.
if (i != TABLE_SIZE)
  validaddr[i] = p;
```

```
return (p);
}

///
// Test pointer for validity before deleting it.
void operator delete(void *p)
{
if (p)
  {
  for (int i = 0; i < TABLE_SIZE && p != validaddr[i]; i++);
  if (i != TABLE_SIZE)
    {
    validaddr[i] = 0;
    free(p);
    }
  else
    // *** SET BREAKPOINT HERE ***
    cerr << "MEM MGR ERROR: delete called with invalid pointer "
    << p << '.' << endl;
  }
}
```

Minimizing Overhead in Dynamic Records

■ David Stafford

Streamline the storage requirements for your dynamic records with these useful techniques.

Managing dynamic records may seem like old hat, but there are some nonobvious tricks to reduce their memory overhead. Consider the **EMPLOYEE** structure definition shown below. It is designed as a record in a doubly linked list, with fields for name, phone number, social security number, and salary:

```
struct EMPLOYEE
  {
  struct EMPLOYEE *Prev, *Next;
  char Name[40];
  char PhoneNum[10];
  long SocSecNum, Salary;
  };
```

As simple as it seems, there is a great deal of room for improvement. Look at the size of that structure. Assuming near (two-byte) pointers, it totals 62 bytes. If we have 30K of near heap available, that would limit us to a maximum of about 400 records. If the average employee name comes to only 20 characters, much of the space within the record is going to be wasted. How can we fix this?

Beginning programmers might try to avoid using a fixed array and instead change the **Name** declaration to a pointer and dynamically allocate memory for the name field on the heap. They will be surprised to find that it does not save any space, and in fact may use *more* space than if they stayed with the fixed array. This is because there is a fixed amount of overhead involved in maintaining each memory block in the heap. The smaller each allocation is (and hence the more needed) the greater the overhead. The experienced programmer always avoids allocating small blocks like this when possible.

Does this mean we have to stick with the fixed array and its waste of space? Not at all. Do this: Move the **Name** field to the end of the structure and change its length to 1:

```
struct EMPLOYEE
  {
  struct EMPLOYEE *Prev, *Next;
  char PhoneNum[10];
  long SocSecNum, Salary;
  char Name[1];
  };
```

Now, when you need to create a new record on the heap, do this:

```
malloc(sizeof(struct EMPLOYEE) + strlen(name));
```

This allocates the *exact* space required for *each* individual record with *no* waste. The average record size drops from 62 to 42 bytes and we can store close to 600 records instead of only 400.

The idea is to put the variable-length field at the end of the record and stretch the record to accommodate the field's exact length. Now, what if you have more than one variable-length field within a record? There are two possibilities. The simplest is to put the one that would save the most space at the end of the record and leave the other one a fixed-length array. The more complex but more efficient approach is to merge the two fields and use a delimiter to separate them or keep pointers for each field. Here is an example of a single large field with separate pointers for the two strings stored in the field:

```
struct BOOK
  {
  struct BOOK *Prev, *Next;
  char *Title, *Author;
  char Strings[1];
  };
```

And here's a code fragment to show how it would be used:

```
nubook = malloc(sizeof(struct BOOK) +
         strlen(title) +
         strlen(author) + 1);

nubook->Title  = nubook->Strings;
nubook->Author = nubook->Strings +
                 strlen(title) + 1;
strcpy(nubook->Title,  title);
strcpy(nubook->Author, author);
```

Although I put it in the example for clarity, we do not need the **Title** pointer, because it always points to **nubook->Strings**. If we are very short on space and don't mind a small performance penalty, we could also eliminate the **Author** pointer and just search past the first NULL (ASCIIZ) string terminator for the author string whenever we need it.

The only caution is that if the size of the variable-length field within an already-allocated record must grow, you will then have to release and reallocate the entire record.

Word-Sized *Backwards* Block Moves

■ Michael Abrash

Here's a useful technique for quickly copying blocks of memory backwards.

In "Guaranteeing Word-Sized Block Moves" earlier in Chapter 9, Cye Waldman presented the following code to perform what he referred to as **MoveLeft**. Here's a corresponding **MoveRight** function. You might think that to copy in the opposite direction, you would simply need to **std** instead of **cld**. Not so. By "**MoveRight**," we mean first copying from the highest address in the source block to the highest address in the destination block, then copying between progressively lower addresses; that is, copying backwards from the normal direction, as is sometimes necessary in order to copy correctly when the source and destination blocks overlap. Copying backwards with **movs** is indeed effected by **std**. However, when **std** is in effect, the proper address at which to start **rep movsb** to copy a block and the proper address at which to start **rep movsw** to copy the same block are not identical, owing to the way the 80x86 stores words in memory, as shown by the code fragment below. (The addresses are, however, the same when **cld** is in effect.)

```
;Copies a block of memory backwards, starting at the
; high end and progressing toward the low end
;DS:SI = highest address in the source block
;ES:DI = highest address in the destination block
;CX = # of bytes to copy

    std         ;cause MOVS to decrement SI & DI
    shr   cx,1      ;count of words to copy
    jnc   NoOddByte ;no odd byte to copy
    movsb       ;copy the odd byte
NoOddByte:
    dec   si    ;point to the start of the next
    dec   di    ; source and dest words to copy
    rep   movsw ;copy the rest of the block a
                ; word at a time
    inc   si    ;point to the byte before the
    inc   di    ; start of each block
    cld         ;cause string instructions to
                ; increment pointers
```

Let's assume that on entry, DS:SI points to the last byte (the highest address) of the source block, and ES:DI points to the last byte of the destination block. Those pointers are correct for **movsb**. However, they are *not* correct for **movsw**; after the odd byte, if there is one, is copied, both SI and DI must be decremented by one to point to the next word to copy. Otherwise, **movsw** will work with blocks that are positioned 1 byte too high in memory. The code shown on page 306 properly copies blocks of memory backward.

TIP: The two final **inc** instructions convert SI and DI back from word-copy to byte-copy mode. That's not necessary, but it's handy because it leaves SI and DI properly positioned to be used for another copy later. Likewise, the final **cld** isn't necessary, but leaving the Direction Flag cleared by default avoids a whole class of subtle bugs.

The DOS Extender Solution

■ Daev Roehr

Master the art of DOS extenders to squeeze more memory out of your system.

You can always use more money—or more memory. As programmers attempt to shoehorn the latest fad GUI, mouse support, macro recorder, and online help (not to mention the actual program!) into low DOS memory, the 640K barrier starts looking pretty formidable.

One solution to the memory crisis is the *DOS extender.* DOS extenders have been around for some years, and are in use by many of the leading software product vendors: Lotus, Autodesk, Ashton-Tate, Borland, and even Microsoft, which provides an extender for use with Windows.

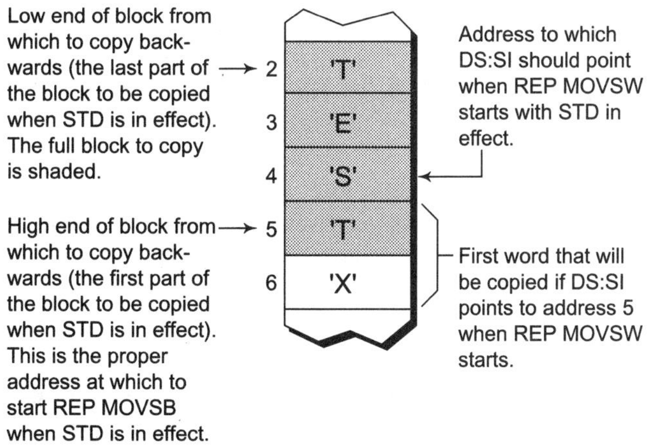

■ **FIGURE 9.2 Starting addresses for moves**

This article introduces DOS extenders, discusses why or why not to use them, and provides some sample code demonstrating DOS extenders in action. I will not discuss the numerous subtleties of 86-family protected mode, such as ring and I/O protection, protected mode interrupt service routines, real/protected mode switching mechanics, or similar arcana. These subjects are usually irrelevant to application implementation (as opposed to operating system design) and confuse the real issue of "How tough are these things to use?" with the lesser issue, "How complicated can I make my life?"

Why Use a DOS Extender?

In a word, *memory*! Unlike that great hack job we call EMS, accessing additional memory through a DOS extender doesn't require massive program reorganization. With DOS extender support, your application can effortlessly access more memory for both code and data. The DOS extender vendor provides function libraries containing replacement **malloc()**, **free()**, **int86()**, and other functions that work transparently with the DOS extender code itself.

Another reason to use an extender is that your program will be more robust, and easier to debug. For example, NULL or invalid pointers, incorrect array indexing, and trashed stacks are all illegal in protected mode (the necessary magic for all DOS extenders) and are caught by the CPU hardware. Instead of crashing your system, a DOS extender will politely show you the offending code! How's that for friendly?

Modes for the Code

Intel processors, starting with the 80286, support several different *modes* for CPU operation. One of these modes, referred to as *protected mode,* among numerous other things, changes the addressing scheme used by the CPU. When the CPU is operating in protected mode, it can directly access more memory, from 16 megabytes on a 286 to 4 gigabytes on a 386. "Aha," you say, "this sounds like OS/2. No thanks!" Not true. OS/2's biggest problem was that it forced a massive software change; that is, a new operating system, new APIs, new programming techniques, and so on. Unlike OS/2, DOS extenders require minimal recoding of your product, which will run like any other DOS program. Better still, you can use most of your standard DOS development tools.

The Catch

Nothing is a total solution in the computer racket, and power does not come without cost. DOS extenders are no exception. Consider:

1. Older 8088-based PCs can't use DOS extenders, because of the need for at least an 80286 processor.
2. You will need "extended memory" to use a DOS extender. Extended memory is that memory located above the first megabyte of the PC's address space, and the more you have the better.
3. You need to make sure that your compiler, linker, DOS extender, and any involved third-party libraries are all compatible and in sync, version-wise. Get the specific

version numbers that were tested together, and only upgrade when everything is verified—unless you *like* massive frustration!

4. System calls to BIOS or DOS will not be as fast as in real mode. BIOS and DOS are real-mode programs. The DOS extender intercepts calls to DOS and BIOS. When a DOS or BIOS call is made, it switches back to real mode, executes the DOS or BIOS code, and then returns to protected mode. This whole process is fairly involved from a machine-cycles perspective, and a program that makes lots of DOS or BIOS calls will show some speed degradation.
5. You will have some source code changes to make if you have written interrupt service routines, if you directly reference absolute memory addresses, or if you monkey around with interrupt vectors.
6. There are a few programming tricks that are not allowed in protected mode, such as using segment registers to hold scratch values in assembly language work. Segment registers have new jobs and new responsibilities, and cannot be considered "general-purpose" registers anymore.

With regard to item 5 above, many programs do a certain number of absolute reads of or writes to memory, mostly in connection with video display output and DOS/BIOS data areas. Most DOS extenders take this into account, and allow such absolute writes or reads with the addition of necessary but small code changes.

Brothers but Not Twins

There are two kinds of DOS extenders: 16-bit and 32-bit, sometimes referred to as 286 and 386 extenders, respectively. The names refer to the minimum required processor; that is, a 286 extender will run on a 386 CPU, but not vice versa. Why, then, limit your market by using a 32-bit extender? Well, there are a few reasons:

- A segment load in protected mode is *very* bad for performance, taking at least 19 clocks. Since the 386 general registers are all 32 bits (and 32 bits can express address values up to 4 gigabytes), a 386 extender can address that full 4 gigabytes of memory *without* segment loads. The 286, with only 16-bit registers, cannot avoid segment loads.
- With a 286 extender, a single object cannot exceed the size of a 286 segment, 64K. If you work with large objects, a 386 extender is much faster (no segment loads, remember?) and eliminates a lot of frustration.
- A 16-bit DOS extender has a maximum address space of "only" 16 megabytes. This sounds like more than enough, but if you have a *really* big program (or use a great deal of data), you could still run out of memory.

A Code Example

There are several companies currently producing DOS extenders. Phar Lap is a major vendor selling both a 16-bit and a 32-bit extender, so I'll use them to illustrate how easy it is to incorporate a DOS extender into your application.

First, let's build a DOS real-mode program that walks the heap. This is a good sample illustrating transparent portability, as it is hooked into the memory system at a fairly low level. I compiled Listing 9.3, LIST.C, with Microsoft C version 6.0A. Listings 9.4, 9.5, and 9.6 are supporting files necessary to create the executable from Listing 9.3. Read LIST.C carefully, paying attention to the C functions that allocate, free, and reference memory. Here's the program output:

```
512 nodes: 0 seconds
769 nodes: 0 seconds
Allocated 393K
far heap used=404310
free=392
blks=1548
status=ok
```

As you can see, under ordinary (nonextended) DOS, I had a whopping 393K of heap available on my 3-megabyte 386 machine. Obviously, there's nothing new here since the 8088 days. Now, let's build a 286 protected-mode program. The Phar Lap 286 extender is a little like a runtime version of OS/2 (but just a little!) and uses the OS/2 versions of the Microsoft C 6.0A compiler, linker, librarian, and debugger. (I consider that a pretty clever trick.)

So where's the new program listing? There isn't one. *No* changes to Listing 9.3 were required to compile and run it in protected mode. I merely had to recompile and relink LIST.C with the OS/2 utilities and libraries as mentioned above, and run the resulting LIST.EXE executable file by way of the 286 extender run utility. At the command line, you execute RUN286.EXE, and pass the name of the application as a command line parameter:

```
C:\>run286 list
```

The displayed output is considerably different this time:

```
512 nodes: 1 seconds
1024 nodes: 1 seconds
1536 nodes: 1 seconds
2048 nodes: 2 seconds
2560 nodes: 2 seconds
3072 nodes: 3 seconds
3584 nodes: 4 seconds
4096 nodes: 5 seconds
4348 nodes: 7 seconds
Allocated 2224K
far heap used=2279724
free=1090
blks=8724
status=ok
```

Obviously, we're not in 8088-land anymore. Please keep in mind that there were *no* source code changes, and that this sample did some interesting and complicated things with the heap.

From 16 to 32 Bits

Now let's see what a 386 extender can do. The 386 version of LIST.C required some minor source code changes, but only because I had to switch C compilers. Had Microsoft C 6.0A the ability to generate 32-bit code, I wouldn't have had to make any changes at all. When I do 32-bit work I use the Watcom 8.0 C compiler, and I used it here. After a few minor changes for the differences in heap management syntax between compilers, I recompiled and relinked for 32-bit mode. Running the application is done the same way, through a protected-mode run utility called RUN386.EXE. LIST.EXE's output follows:

```
512 nodes: 0 seconds
1024 nodes: 0 seconds
1536 nodes: 0 seconds
2048 nodes: 0 seconds
2560 nodes: 0 seconds
3072 nodes: 0 seconds
3584 nodes: 0 seconds
4096 nodes: 0 seconds
4434 nodes: 0 seconds
Allocated 2268K
far heap used=2359964
free=268
blks=8873
status=ok
```

Apart from the tremendous increase in execution speed, these results may be a little difficult to interpret. The memory size values are not identical to those of the 286, but they don't differ much. I suspect that the differing memory sizes probably have more to do with the change in compilers, and not the change to the 386 DOS extender.

As you can see, the **malloc()** process was considerably faster here than with the 286 extender. It appears that Watcom's heap system is more efficient than Microsoft's, but that alone couldn't account for all of the difference. As I explained before, a 32-bit extender is more efficient when dealing with 32-bit pointers, and this test case seems to bear that out.

Virtual Memory

The 386 CPU has memory management hardware on the chip. This hardware support allows a virtual memory system to be created. Virtual memory will let you run programs larger than will fit in your RAM system. This is done by using part of your hard disk as a dynamic extension of system memory, bringing code or data from disk into system memory as needed. This technique is used by other operating platforms like UNIX, Windows 3.0, and OS/2.

Phar Lap has implemented a virtual memory system as part of their 386 development kit. In working with their product, I limited virtual memory to 16 megabytes, since 4 gigabytes is (somewhat!) larger than my available disk space. Let's fire up LIST.C with the virtual memory manager and see what happens. Again, LIST.EXE is run from the command line by way of the RUN386.EXE utility, with the following command line:

```
C:\>run386 -maxp 1000000h -vm vmmdrv list
```

The additional command-line parameters instruct RUN386 to set up a 16MB virtual memory system. The output follows:

```
512 nodes: 0 seconds
1024 nodes: 0 seconds
1536 nodes: 0 seconds
2048 nodes: 0 seconds
2560 nodes: 0 seconds
3072 nodes: 0 seconds
3584 nodes: 0 seconds
4096 nodes: 0 seconds
4608 nodes: 1 seconds
5120 nodes: 3 seconds
```

. . .

The output has been trimmed considerably. . . .)

. . .

```
30720 nodes: 245 seconds
31232 nodes: 253 seconds
31473 nodes: 257 seconds
Allocated 16105K
far heap used=16745100
free=236
blks=62951
status=ok
```

Once again, no special coding is required once the compiler's syntactic requirements are met. Using the standard C **malloc()** function the program effortlessly allocated a 16-megabyte heap on my 3-megabyte 386 system. Life should be so simple all the time. . . .

Notice the time jump between nodes 4096 and 4608. At this point, my system ran out of physical memory. Rather than bottoming out with an out-of-memory error, the virtual memory system started allocating from virtual memory located on the hard disk. This allowed the use of a ridiculous amount of memory, without any messy EMS calls.

So What Are You Waiting For?

Even without the intimate details of how they work, you now have a feeling for how simple they are to use. DOS extenders can solve PC memory problems, and do it easily. As an example, Metagraphics' MetaWINDOW C headers and sample C code worked across the entire spectrum of DOS, 286, and 386 DOS extenders, with only minor, compiler-related changes. Moving to a DOS extender is more a tools issue (editors, compilers, third-party libraries, and so on) than an underlying technology issue.

There is some downside—DOS extenders will not run on older 8086/8088 systems, are closely tied to individual (mostly C) language compilers, and do impose a performance overhead for some system services. As I would put it, "You can have your cake and eat it, too—but you gotta find a good baker."

CODE DESCRIPTION

Overview

Example program which uses the Phar Lap DOS Extender to demonstrate the use of extended memory under DOS. The 286 version uses Microsoft C, the 386 version uses Watcom C.

Listings Available

Listing	*Description*	*Used with*
LIST.C	Example program which uses function calls in HEAPSTAT.C to allocate memory.	------
HEAPSTAT.C	Heap Status routines for use with Phar Lap DOS Extender.	------
HEAPSTAT.H	Header files for use with HEAPSTAT.C.	------
SMAKE.BAT	Batch file to control creation of the example program.	------

How to Compile/Assemble

Use SMAKE /86 for Real Mode; SMAKE /286 for 16-bit Protected Mode; SMAKE / 386 for 32-bit Protected Mode.

This program should be easy to modify for use with any C/C++ compiler that produces protected-mode code. Consult your DOS Extender documentation for further information.

■ LISTING 9.3 LIST.C

```
/* usage: list [nodesize]
Allocates and frees a lot of memory; uses linked list.
You can specify node size, default is 512 bytes.
This is based on a sample routine distributed by Phar Lap as part
of their DOS extender product.  Modified to work with the Watcom
heap system to illustrate 386 DOS extenders.  Used by permission.
    Compile with the batch file SMAKE.BAT * /

#include <stdlib.h>
#include <stdio.h>
#include <malloc.h>
#include <time.h>
#include "heapstat.h"

typedef struct node {
    unsigned long num;
    void *data;
    struct node *next;
    } NODE;

main(int argc, char *argv[])
{
```

```
    HEAP_STATS h;
    NODE *p, *q;
    time_t t1, t2;
    unsigned long nodes = 0;
    unsigned nodesize = (argc > 1) ? atoi(argv[1]) : 512;

    time(&t1);
    for (q=NULL; ; q->next = p)
    {
        p = q;
        if ((q = malloc(sizeof(NODE))) == NULL)
            break;
        if ((q->data = malloc(nodesize)) == NULL)
        {
            free(q);
            break;
        }
        q->num = nodes++;
        if ((nodes % 512) == 0)
            printf("%lu nodes: %lu seconds\n",
                nodes, time(&t2) - t1);
    }
    printf("%lu nodes: %lu seconds\n",
        nodes, time(&t2) - t1);
    printf("Allocated %uK\n",
        (nodes * (sizeof(NODE)+nodesize)) >> 10);
    heap_stats(FARHEAP, &h);
    print_heap_stats(&h);
    for ( ; p != NULL; p = q)
    {
        q = p->next;
        if (p->num != --nodes)
            printf("list corrupt: nodes=%lu num=%lu\n",
                nodes, p->num);
        free(p->data);
        free(p);
    }
    puts(nodes? "fail" : "ok");
    return nodes;
}
```

■ LISTING 9.4 HEAPSTAT.C

```
/* Heap status routines for Microsoft C */
#include <stdlib.h>
#include <malloc.h>
#include "heapstat.h"
#ifdef __WATCOMC__
                /* there isn't a far version in 386 mode */
#define _fheapwalk _heapwalk
#define _fheapchk  _heapchk
                /* also typedef difference in malloc.h */
int (*walkf[2])(struct _heapinfo *phi) = { _nheapwalk, _fheapwalk };
/* Watcom uses different return values for heap management */
```

```
static char *heap_status[] = { "ok", "empty", "bad-begin",
    "bad-node", "end", "bad-ptr" };
#else /* Microsoft C heap stuff */
int (*walkf[2])(_HEAPINFO *phi) =   { _nheapwalk, _fheapwalk };
static char *heap_status[] = { "?free?", "empty", "ok", "bad-begin",
    "bad-node", "end", "bad-ptr" };
#endif

int (*statf[2])(void) = { _nheapchk, _fheapchk } ;

void heap_stats(HEAP h, HEAP_STATS *hs)
{
    struct _heapinfo hi;

    hs->heap = h;
    hs->used = hs->free = hs->blks = 0;
    hi._pentry = 0;
    /* walk the heap, calling walk function for each block */
    while ((*walkf[h])(&hi) == _HEAPOK)
    {
        switch (hi._useflag)
        {
            case _USEDENTRY: hs->used += hi._size; break;
            case _FREEENTRY: hs->free += hi._size; break;
        }
        hs->blks++;
    }
    hs->status = (*statf[h])();

#ifdef __WATCOMC__    /* Watcom uses positive numbers */
  hs->status_str = heap_status[ hs->status];
#else
  hs->status_str = heap_status[- hs->status];
#endif
}

void print_heap_stats(HEAP_STATS *hs)
{
  printf("%s heap used=%lu free=%lu blks=%lu status=%s\n",
        (hs->heap == NEARHEAP) ? "near" : "far",
        hs->used, hs->free,
        hs->blks, hs->status_str);
}
```

■ LISTING 9.5 HEAPSTAT.H

```
/* Heap status routines for Microsoft C */
#ifndef HEAPSTAT_H
#define HEAPSTAT_H
typedef enum { NEARHEAP, FARHEAP } HEAP;

typedef struct {
    HEAP heap;
    unsigned long free;
```

```
    unsigned long used;
    unsigned long blks;
    char *status_str;
    int status;
    } HEAP_STATS;

void heap_stats(HEAP h, HEAP_STATS *hs);
void print_heap_stats(HEAP_STATS *hs);
#endif
```

■ LISTING 9.6 SMAKE.BAT

```
ECHO OFF
echo Build Procedure for sample program LIST.C
echo =============================================
if .%1 == ./h goto help
if .%1 == .   goto help
if .%1 == ./86 goto realmode
if .%1 == ./286 goto pm286
if .%1 == ./386 goto pm386
goto badopt
:realmode:
echo Making real mode version of LIST.C
echo =============================================
cl -AL list.c heapstat.c
if errorlevel 1 goto err
goto end

:pm286
echo Making Phar Lap 286-DOS version of LIST.C
echo =============================================
run286 cl -AL -Lp list.c heapstat.c
if errorlevel 1 goto err
goto end

:pm386
echo Making Phar Lap 386-DOS version of LIST.C
echo =============================================
wcl386  list.c heapstat.c  /d2  /k20000
if errorlevel 1 goto err
goto end

:err
ECHO An error occurred during build
goto end

:badopt
ECHO Error, "%1" is not a valid argument
:help
ECHO .
ECHO HELP
ECHO  Valid options are
ECHO .
ECHO  /86    standard DOS real mode, using Microsoft C 6.0A
```

```
ECHO  /286   286 DOS protected mode, using Microsoft C 6.0A
ECHO  /386   386 DOS protected mode, using Watcom C 8.0
:end
```

Determining True Extended Memory Size

■ Richard Sadowsky

Use the DOS List of Lists to detect the actual amount of extended memory available.

When an XMS driver is installed, you cannot easily determine the actual amount of extended memory installed in a machine. One technique is to peek at CMOS RAM. An easier and faster if less obvious technique is to get the value from the DOS List of Lists. The List of Lists is a large internal data structure that DOS uses to hold a variety of useful information. For DOS 4.x and later, this list includes the amount of extended memory above the base conventional memory. The program in Listing 9.7 shows how to access this information. The DOS MEM.EXE program uses the DOS List of Lists to obtain the amount of free extended memory.

Note that the amount of extended memory physically *installed* may be much different from the amount of extended memory currently available. To find how much extended memory is available (rather than installed), use XMS function 8. This assumes, of course, that an XMS driver such as HIMEM, QEMM386, or 386MAX is present in the system.

CODE DESCRIPTION

Overview

Example program which calculates the actual amount of extended memory installed in a PC.

Listings Available

Listing	*Description*	*Used with*
EXTMEM.C	Example program that uses the DOS List of Lists to determine the amount of extended memory installed.	------

How to Compile/Assemble

The listing can be compiled and linked with any C/C++ compiler. This program may be compiled using the Large memory model to work properly.

■ LISTING 9.7 EXTMEM.C

```
/*extmem.c*/

#include <dos.h>
#include <stdio.h>
```

```
void * GetListOfLists(void)
{
struct REGPACK regs;

      regs.r_ax = 0x52 << 8;
      intr(0x21,&regs);
      return MK_FP(regs.r_es,regs.r_bx);
}

int ExtMemInK(void)
{
char *p;
     p = GetListOfLists();
     p += 0x45;               /*extended mem in K at offset 0x45*/

     return *(int*)p;         /*convert to int before returning */
}

void main(void)
{
  if (_osmajor < 4)
    printf("Requires DOS 4 or greater\n");
  else
    printf("%dK in extended memory\n",ExtMemInK());
}
```

TIP: The way this program makes use of pointer arithmetic illustrates a special problem with odd offsets into data structures. In C, when a value is added to a pointer, the size of what the pointer points to is taken into account when the result is calculated. The value we want in the DOS List of Lists is at 0x45, but it is an integer. Attempting to add 0x45 to an **int *** will cause 0x8A to be added instead, so we use a **char *** and then cast the pointer when the result is returned to make sure **ExtMemInK** returns an **int**.

10

Sorting and Searching Methods

"Information," the old sage said, "is nothing more than data you can lay hands on when you need it."

True, true. So the difference between raw data and useful information is often nothing more than some sort of predictable order, allowing a quick search to the desired point.

Sorting and searching go together; without sorting, all searches are sequential and totally unpredictable. You're sure to find what you're looking for between the beginning and the end of your file—unless what you want wasn't there at all.

You can do better than that. We can help. In this chapter, Kevin Weeks presents a clever way to sort on more than one field at a time—while performing the sort only once. And Larry Weibel shows how to squeeze a little extra performance out of your comfortable old binary search.

Seek, and—with a reasonable algorithm—ye shall find.

Multifield Sorting

■ Kevin Weeks

Develop a useful function for performing a multifield sort operation.

Suppose you want to sort a file composed of, say, a DOS disk directory. Suppose further that you want to sort by file extension, name, date, and time—in that order. If you're using a compiler that provides a sort procedure, the hard part is taken care of. For example, **qsort()**, an implementation of the quicksort algorithm, is provided with all standard C compilers. However, you still have to come up with the logic for handling the hierarchy of multiple sort fields, and that's where this technique could prove useful.

As one of its parameters, **qsort()** is passed the name of a function that actually performs the comparison of two items during the sort process:

```
qsort(list,num_elements,element_width,compare_function);
```

The compare function (named **compare_function** here) is then called by **qsort()** and passed two elements from the list being sorted. The compare function's job is to compare the two elements and return one of three results based on the comparison. If the first element is greater than the second element, positive one (1) is returned. If the first element is less than the second, negative one (–1) is returned. Finally, should the two elements be equal, zero (0) is returned to **qsort()**.

The brute-force solution to the multifield sort problem is to first call **qsort()** with a compare function for the file extension. Next, break up the main list into smaller lists based on file extension and call **qsort()** again but this time specifying a compare function that sorts by filename. This process is repeated for each additional field on which information is to be sorted. After all sorts have been completed, the lists must be recombined. This brute-force approach requires a fair bit of code even if the smaller lists are just pointers to subsections of the main list. There's an easier way.

A single compare function can be written to test *all* of the fields in order of precedence. If you'll look at the code in Listing 10.1 you'll see that the function **dir_compare()** first performs a test on the extension using **strcmp()**. If the extensions are nonequal the result is returned to **qsort()** which then orders the two elements. However, if the extensions are equal then **dir_compare()** moves on to compare the names. If both the names and the extensions are equal then the dates and finally the times are compared. All necessary comparisons are made, even though only a single compare function is called.

Although I'm sure this algorithm is in the literature somewhere, I've never run across it. Is it quicker than the brute-force approach? Probably not, but I've never bothered to find out because it is definitely easier to code.

CODE DESCRIPTION

Overview

A short example piece of code which demonstrates performing multiple field comparisons in a single function to be supplied to a routine like **qsort()**.

Listings Available

Listing	*Description*	*Used with*
DIRCOMP.C	Program that performs multifield sorting.	------

How to Compile/Assemble

Can be compiled and linked with any C/C++ compiler.

■ LISTING 10.1 DIRCOMP.C

```
int dir_compare(char file_1[], char file_2[])
{
    int     result;

    // compare extensions
    result = strncmp(&file1[9],&file2[9],3);
    // if they aren't equal return the result
    if (result != 0)
        return(result);

    // extensions were equal so compare names
    result = strncmp(&file1[0],&file2[0],8);
    if (result != 0)
        return(result);
    // datecmp() is assumed to compare directory style dates
    result = datecmp(&file1[23],&file2[23]);
    if (result != 0)
        return(result);
    // timecmp() is assumed to compare directory style times
    result = timecmp(&file1[33],&file2[33]);
    // return whatever the result of timecmp() was
    return(result);
}
```

Speeding Up Binary Searches

■ Larry Weibel

Speed up your binary searches by using a special "presearching" trick.

Most C compilers today include a **bsearch** function in their runtime library. The **bsearch** function is used to perform a binary search on sorted arrays of records. **bsearch** takes several parameters including the key to search for, the address of the start of the sorted array, the size of an array entry, and the address of a user-supplied function that compares two values from the array.

When your program calls **bsearch**, it will then call the user-provided function every time it needs to evaluate values from the array. This is all fairly straightforward, but sometimes your program can't afford the (sometimes considerable) overhead of all those function calls. Here's a technique that can be used for really speeding up binary searches by "presearching" the array.

Begin by setting up a structure to contain the entries to be searched. This structure should contain the "key" to be looked for as well as two pointers. One pointer will be used to point toward entries with lower values; the other will point toward the higher values.

```
#define BSRCHTBLMAX 1000
unsigned long numrecs;

struct BSRCHTBL
{
long keyvalue;
/*any other pertinent data would go here */
struct BSRCHTBL *lower;
struct BSRCHTBL *higher;
} bsrchtbl[BSRCHTBLMAX];
```

Once this table has been filled with **numrec** worth of **keyvalue**s and sorted, the pointers need to be initialized. During the first loop, all pointers are initialized to **NULL**. The outer loops move through the array first by every second entry, then by every fourth, then by every eighth, and so on. The inner loop uses half the value of the outer step to adjust the upper and lower pointers.

```
int mid, x, y, z;
struct BSRCHTBL;

for (x = 0; x < numrecs; x++)
    bsrchtbl[x].lower = bsrchtbl[x].higher = NULL;

for (x = 1; x < numrecs; x <<=1)
    for (y = (x << 1) - 1; y < numrecs; y += (x << 1))
    {
      mid = y;
      bsrchtbl[y].lower = bsrchtbl + y - x;
      z = x;
      while ((y + z) >= numrecs)
        z >>=1;
      if (z)
        bsrchtbl[y].higher = bsrchtbl + y + z;
    }
midptr = bsrchtbl + mid;
```

The check of **z** prevents the higher pointer from ever being beyond the end of the number of records actually in the table. This results in a binary search routine that requires no subscript computations and no limit checking.

midptr is initialized to what would be the exact center of the array if the number of elements in the array were rounded up to the nearest power of two. This is the proper starting location for examining a "presearched" array.

At this point, the search table is filled and can be searched as follows:

```
register struct BSRCHTBL *srchptr;
long key_to_find;

srchptr = midptr;
key_to_find = (value to search for);
while (srchptr != NULL)
{
    if (srchptr->keyvalue == key_to_find)
       break;
    if (srchptr->keyvalue > key_to_find)
       srchptr = srchptr->lower;
    else
       srchptr = srchptr->higher;
}
if (srchptr != NULL)
    /*key_to_find was found */
else
    /*key_to_find was not found*/
```

The search proceeds by following the pointers through the even elements. All of the odd numbered entries' pointers contain **NULL** because they represent the last nodes to be checked in the binary search. An odd location is checked only if the even elements on either side have already been checked, and by then either it is the one being searched for or the search key is not found.

And that's all there is to it. At first it does seem complicated, but by setting up the pointers ahead of time, you can avoid the overhead of numerous calls to a user-supplied function that normal system-supplied **bsearch** routines require. This will result in considerable performance improvement.

11

Manipulating String Data

I remember when the mark of a good BASIC interpreter was whether it could handle strings. That strings could be considered a dazzling sales gimmick rather than a core product feature gives you some idea of how far we've come.

Much of the information we process, store, and retrieve is ordinary text, and without string variables to hold it, we'd be doing backflips just trying to get the screen to say "Hi!" Modern languages tend to have do-everything string libraries, and getting good at string handling is one of those skills you either develop or go back to selling shower curtains.

In this chapter we're taking string handling a little beyond what comes in the box with your C++ compiler. Scott Bussinger shows how to compress strings and save a little space—which may become essential when your help file starts pushing 200K and shows no sign of leveling off. David Clark takes up the question of defining a standard format for proper names, and how to convert to such a format so that spotting duplicate names is easier. Other short tips by Brian Cheetham, Kas Thomas, and Leland Van Allen build on the fundamental string-handling skillset to do things with strings that they don't always teach you in school.

A Simple String Compression Algorithm

■ Scott Bussinger

Here are two useful encryption and decryption functions to help you compress string data.

Often the keys used in database application index files are quite long and are derived from data like proper names, which contain a very limited subset of the ASCII character set. By performing a little data compression on these keys before adding them to an index file, you can both save a substantial amount of disk space and improve the access speed.

Although there are lots of sophisticated data compression schemes, here's a simple algorithm that has a couple of very handy features: Simply map each eight-bit character into five or six bits and pack these shorter bit sequences end-to-end into consecutive eight-bit bytes. In the case of names, digits and punctuation are treated as blanks and lowercase letters can be treated as uppercase letters. This allows you to pack each character into five bits. The algorithm is simple and fast, and in addition to achieving almost 40% compression, the resulting string is a constant length and is still kept in sortable order. Furthermore, the algorithm automatically eliminates differences in duplicate names that result only from variations in capitalization. This feature turns aside the need to force names to uppercase before trying to add their derived keys to the index file.

Listing 11.1 (PACKUP.C) shows two functions, one to encrypt and the other to decrypt eight-bit values to five-bit values. To make these routines as useful as possible, I've hard-coded some special cases into the algorithm. For example, the packing function **Pack** specifically checks a character to see if it is a space character (20h) or a numeric character "1" through "9." These two cases are assigned special values so they can be decoded later. Unfortunately, five bits is not enough to hold 26 characters *and* ten digits. This method simply encodes all digit values as a special character, which the decode routine extracts as "#." Similarly, all other characters outside of "a"–"z" (and "A"–"Z") are decoded as "@". If these characters are significant, you'll want to change to a six-bit compression scheme. That algorithm would essentially be the same as the five-bit one.

The major hurdle in converting from an eight-bit to a five-bit representation of information, apart from loss of data, is the fact that most machines are byte-addressable. This means that not only must they read and write eight (or 16 or 32) bits at a time, these reads and writes *must* occur on an eight-bit boundary. The key to surmounting this hurdle lies in using nondestructive ANDs and ORs in conjunction with bitmap masks.

In **Pack**, capturing five bits from eight is accomplished by means of a bitmask (0x1f) that is ANDed with the byte in question. This part is fairly straightforward since the values being read are always eight bits and always reside on eight-bit boundaries. The five-bit value must then be shifted left to match the current *bit* position in the target array (**ShiftFactor**) and an index is maintained to point to the correct *byte* position in the packed string (**j**). Two writes to the packed string are necessary (one to **ResultStr[j]** and one to **ResultStr[j+1]**), since occasionally one of the five-bit values will overlap into the next byte. Remember, in this scheme, both "a" and "A" are encoded as 01h, "b" and "B" are encoded as 02h, and so on. Space characters and digits are treated as special cases, as mentioned above. All other characters are encoded as 00h.

In **Unpack**, the reverse takes place. An index into the correct starting byte of the packed array (**byte_index**) is maintained as well as the current bit-shift factor (**shift**). In this case, it is necessary to *read* two bytes since more often than not, a five-bit value will start in one byte and end in another. Getting two bytes is accomplished by typecasting the pointer **int_ptr**. Once the five bits have been extracted from the array, their proper (capitalized) values are converted to eight bits and assigned to the return array. **Unpack** needs an extra parameter to specify how many characters to extract from the packed array; this is necessary because using this algorithm, the normal **NULL** terminator can easily turn up unexpectedly in a compressed string.

TIP: When passing the second array to **Pack** (parameter **ResultStr**), make sure it contains all zeroes, since the routine simply ANDs values to place them into the array.

CODE DESCRIPTION

Overview

Two functions which demonstrate a simple 8:5 text compression scheme. One function, **Pack**, compresses strings, the other **Unpack** expands them.

Listings Available

Listing	*Description*	*Used with*
PACKUP.C	Contains the two functions **Pack()** and **Unpack()** for use with other programs.	------

How to Compile/Assemble

Can be compiled and linked with any C/C++ compiler.

■ LISTING 11.1 PACKUP.C

```
#define SPACE 0x20
#define NUMBER 0x23
#define PACKED_SPACE 27
#define PACKED_NUMBER 28

#include <string.h>
#include <stdio.h>
#define LOBYTE(a) (char)(a & 0x00FF)
#define HIBYTE(a) (char)((a & 0xFF00) >> 8)

void Pack(char *Original, char *ResultStr)
{
  /* Take a string of characters and compress it down at a ratio
    of 5:8 by converting all characters into a 5 bit code. Only
    letters are unique, numbers are bunched together as are
    punctuation marks. */
int i, j;
```

```
int BitMask;
int ShiftFactor;
int Limit;

  j = 0;  /*index into compressed string */
  ShiftFactor = 0;
  Limit = strlen(Original);
  for (i = 0; i < Limit; i++)
     /* Pack each character */
  {
    BitMask = 0x0;  /*default value*/

    /*check for special cases*/
    if (Original[i] == SPACE)
       BitMask = PACKED_SPACE;
    else
       if (Original[i] >= '0' && Original[i] <= '9')
          BitMask = PACKED_NUMBER;
       else
    /*check for alpha character*/
          if ((Original[i] >= 'a' && Original[i] <= 'z') ||
              (Original[i] >= 'A' && Original[i] <= 'Z'))
            BitMask = Original[i] & 0x1F; /*take only the low five bits */
    BitMask = BitMask << ShiftFactor;  /*BitMask may exceed 255 after shift*/
    ResultStr[j] = ResultStr[j] | LOBYTE(BitMask);
    ResultStr[j+1] = ResultStr[j+1] |  HIBYTE(BitMask);
    ShiftFactor = (ShiftFactor+5)%8;   /*get next five bits*/
    if (ShiftFactor < 5)
      j++;          /*move to next byte if the shift factor has wrapped*/
   };
};

void Unpack(char *packed, char *unpacked, int size)
{
int shift = 0;
int byte_index = 0;
int new_index = 0;
int *int_ptr;
char new_char;

     while (new_index < size)
     {
        /*get two bytes in case new character straddles boundary*/
        int_ptr = (int *)&packed[byte_index];
        /*extract the correct five bits*/
        new_char = ((0x1f << shift) & *int_ptr) >> shift;
        /*if shift value will wrap, go to next byte in packed string*/
        if (shift > 2)
           byte_index++;
        shift = (shift+5)%8;
        /*translate the character, as needed*/
        if (new_char == PACKED_SPACE)
           unpacked[new_index] = SPACE;
        else
        if (new_char == PACKED_NUMBER)
```

```
            unpacked[new_index] = NUMBER;
        else
            unpacked[new_index] = (char)(new_char + 'A'-1);
        new_index++;
    }
    unpacked[new_index] = 0x0;  /*terminate the string */
}
```

Quick Parsing of Command-Line Switches

■ Kas Thomas

Use a type-casting trick to efficiently parse command line switches.

Here's a useful way of parsing the command line in C. When searching for switches (options) in the command line tail, try type-casting the string pointers to pointers-to-int, and refer to the switches by their literal values. Thus, in C:

```
while(argc— && **argv++)      /* while there are aguments */
  switch (*( (int *) *argv))
    {
      case '-A':    /* Fall through */
      case '/a':
      case '-a': break /* code goes here */

      case '-B':    /* Fall through */
      case '/b':
      case '-b': break /* code goes here */
      default :
    }
```

Values like "-a" and "-b" are seen by the compiler as their literal word values (in this case 0x612D and 0x622D, respectively). By casting ***argv** to a pointer-to-int and performing indirection on it, you are obtaining a word value that can be compared directly against the literal value in the **switch** statement. The result is fewer lines of code, code that's easy to read, and quick execution at runtime. What more could you want?

Normalizing Proper Names

■ David D. Clark

Get your strings in order using this flexible normalizing program.

The proper handling of proper names in a database presents some unique programming challenges, especially when a full name resides in a single string. Since surnames are more diverse than given names, sorting and searching for proper names has traditionally meant that the name strings be "normalized" to the "last name first" format, as in "Clark, David D."

While the normalized format facilitates database sorting and searching, it complicates *data entry*. The "raw data" for the names is usually *not* normalized, appearing as "David D. Clark." The person entering the data has to rearrange the name, which presents the first opportunity for database errors. Compounding the problem are the various capitalizations, hyphenations, and affectations that are unique to proper names.

Clearly, data entry would be quicker and easier if proper names could be entered in "raw" (unnormalized) form. Ignoring capitalization during data entry would also save time, since the typist doesn't have to fiddle with the shift key. All we need then is a function to normalize the raw input string; that is, to rearrange the name to "last name first" order, and to restore the capitalization according to some general rules. My **NormalizeName()** routine is just such a function.

About NormalizeName()

Listing 11.2 (NORMNAME.C) contains the **NormalizeName()** function, along with its various helper functions. **NormalizeName()** expects a single string argument (the unnormalized proper name) and returns a pointer to the normalized copy of the string. Ideally, the input string should be in lowercase, with no leading, trailing, or redundant interior white space. If you uncomment the **#define NEEDCLEANING** line in the listing, the local **CleanString()** function will "pretreat" the input string by removing redundant spaces, control characters, and so on.

(While **CleanString()** does the job, you may be able to find a more efficient string clean-up routine in a function library. If so, you can use it in place of **CleanString()**.)

As alluded to above, normalizing a proper name involves two basic tasks: capitalization and rearrangement. Let's look at these two tasks individually.

Capitalization

The **NormalizeName()** function does its capitalization based on five rules that I derived from reviewing the phone book (a large cast of characters, but very little plot!). These begin with the obvious general rule, Rule 1: The first character in every name should be capitalized. Rule 2 requires that every character following a space in a proper name be capitalized. These two rules take care of about 80% of the capitalization required.

Hyphenated names ("Jane Q. Smith-Jones") lead to Rule 3: Capitalize any character that appears after a hyphen. Another common situation involves names derived from Irish, French, or Italian, such as O'Malley, D'Arcy, or D'Antini. For these, we use Rule 4: Capitalize every character after an apostrophe. (This may not always apply with some Italian or French surnames.)

Rules 2 through 4 dictate a common general operation: Capitalize any character that appears after a "special" character, space, hyphen, or apostrophe. This suggests that a single code function could scan a string, searching for the special characters that trigger subsequent capitalization. This is exactly how the helper function, **DoCapAfterChar()** works.

The function **DoCapAfterChar()** accepts as its argument a pointer to the string to be operated on. After checking that the string pointer argument is not **NULL** and that the string is not empty, the function moves through the string, one character at a time, looking for a match with any of the special characters defined by the global variable **CapAfterCharList**. If a match is found, the character after the match is converted to upper case with a call to the library function **toupper()**.

The **CapAfterCharList** array of characters contains the characters discussed above, the space, apostrophe, and hyphen, as well as a "nonbreaking" or "hard" space character denoted by "\xff." On the IBM PC and its look-alikes, this character looks just like a space when displayed on the screen. The user can enter such a character from the keyboard by holding down the Alt key, typing "2," "5," and "5" on the numeric keypad, and then releasing the Alt key.

When entering a name, the user can use the nonbreaking space character to prevent the two adjacent parts of the name from being separated during the rearrangement phase. This might be necessary for doubled (but not hyphenated) surnames, such as "Billy Big Mountain."(As you'll see below, the **DoNonBreakingPrefixes()** helper function can pick up many common occurrences of this type *without* the need for the user-entered nonbreaking space.)

The **while** loop control statement in the **DoCapAfterChar()** function may look a little odd, since it tests the character *after* the one pointed to by **t**. Since we are interested in capitalizing that next character, however, it is only natural to check that there is something to capitalize. Also, the repeated use of the expression ***(t + 1)** may look inefficient, but most C/C++ compilers will generate good code for it, with no redundant loads or adds.

McRule No. 5

Another rule can be derived for certain Scottish surnames such as "McAllister" or "MacAllister." It is easy to check for "Mc," which leads to Rule 5: Capitalize the character that follows "Mc." So far, I have found no exceptions to this rule.

The **CapAfterStr()** helper function easily handles the "Mc" cases. Note that the search for "Mc" comes after all other capitalizations. If "mc" occurs at the beginning of a name, it will be capitalized by Rule 1 or Rule 2 above. Since the search is case specific, only the "Mc" at the beginning of a name will be capitalized while any "mc" embedded in the middle of a string will not be converted.

CapAfterStr() is somewhat analogous to the **DoCapAfterChar()** function described above; **CapAfterStr()** searches one string (**s**) for occurrences of a second *substring* of length **patlen**. If it finds a match, it capitalizes the first character after the match. If the end of the input string has not yet been reached, the search continues.

MacProblems

We are still left with the case for "Mac" names. "Mac" can appear at the beginning of many names that do not need additional capitalization: Macchio, Mace, Macy, Mack, and so on. Similar situations exist with names preceded by "De" or "Del" such as "DeLong" or "DelVecchio." In some variations of the spellings, the "De" or "Del" are separated from the remainder of the name by a space producing the correct capitalization by Rule 2.

These special cases are beyond the capacity of **NormalizeName()**, and must be left to the tender mercies of the user who may enter the correct capital directly. One possible solution is to build a list of Scottish, Italian, and Spanish surnames into the program. Then, when one of the special cases in a name is encountered, the list could be searched for a match.

Rearrangement

Compared to capitalization, normalizing the arrangement of a proper name would be a piece of cake, were it not for one or two exceptions. (We'll get to these in a moment.)

It is possible that the user may enter the name in last name first format to begin with. To check this, the function simply looks for the presence of a comma. If one is found, the function assumes that the last name is already first in the string and processing stops.

If the string does not contain a comma, the function assumes that the last name is indeed last in the string and must be rearranged. The strategy used by **NormalizeName()** to rearrange the name is simple:

1. Create a temporary string variable, three bytes larger than the length of the original. (One byte is for a comma character after the last name during rearrangement. The second byte allows for adding a period, if needed, to a "Jr" or "Sr" suffix. The third byte just makes me feel better.)
2. Check for nonbreaking prefixes (described below) and connect them with nonbreaking space characters. For example, "Susan St. James" should be rearranged to "St. James, Susan," not "James, Susan St." The variable **NonBreakingPrefixList** is an easily extensible list of nonbreaking prefixes, like "St." or "Del." The **DoNonBreakingPrefixes()** does the search for the nonbreaking prefixes.
3. Check for common suffixes, such as "Jr," "Sr," and "III," using the **LookForSuffixes()** function. If one is found, disconnect it from the name by placing a "\0" in front of it and return its position; otherwise, return NULL. The result of the suffix search is stored in the local variable **Suffix**.
4. If a surname is present, copy it to the beginning of the temporary variable and append a comma. Then copy the rest of the name to the temporary variable.
5. If a suffix was detected, append a space to the temporary variable and append the **Suffix** variable contents.
6. Remove any nonbreaking spaces from the temporary variable, using a call to **RemoveHardSpaces()**. (Although the nonbreaking space character looks like a normal space on the display screen, it has a different character code and will not sort the same. Since names are often sorted, we replace the nonbreaking spaces with real space characters.)
7. Copy the temporary string back into the original string.
8. Release the space occupied by the temporary string.

Test Program

NORMNAME.C includes a simple test program that will be compiled if you uncomment the **#define GENTESTPROGRAM** line. The program simply accepts names from the standard input and writes their normalized representation to the standard output. The program will continue to accept and normalize names until an End-Of-File character (Ctrl-Z on MS-DOS computers) is encountered. Using the program is an easy way to observe the results of normalizing names. Table 11.1 (Examples of Normalization) contains several examples of sample input and the normalized form produced by **NormalizeName()**.

Limits and Opportunities

There are still a few things that the current version of **NormalizeName()** won't do. In addition to the "Mac" prefix problem, the function does not handle honorifics and titles such as "Mr.," "Ms.," "Dr.," "Baron," "Her Majesty," "King," and so on. I do not believe such a capability would be useful in most applications, particularly if the normalized names were to be sorted. An alternative might be to write another function that parses its input into two strings: a title and a normalized name.

Obviously, the function does not know everything about every type of name from every ethnic background. There are undoubtedly additional capitalization and rearrangement rules. For example, it should be easy to handle Native American surnames consisting of an adjective and a noun, like "John Running Bear" or "Bob Screaming Owl." But the general rules won't apply to "James Rain in the Face."

One feature that should be easy to add is the automatic addition of periods to initials. If the user types "j q smith," it should be simple to return "Smith, J. Q."

One way to make the function a little more efficient is to perform all the capitalizations in a single pass through the string instead of several successive passes. As far as the user is concerned, however, the function is instantaneous; there is no noticeable delay between entering a name and the appearance of the normalized output in the test program, even on a 4.77-MHz 8088 machine.

■ TABLE 11.1 Examples of Normalization

Original	Normalized
smith	Smith
j. smith	Smith, J.
john smith	Smith, John
j. q. smith	Smith, J. Q.
j. quincy smith	Smith, J. Quincy
john q. smith	Smith, John Q.
jane q. smith-jones	Smith-Jones, Jane Q.
john q. smythe-jones iii	Smythe-Jones, John Q. III
susan st. james	St. James, Susan
martin luther king jr	King, Martin Luther Jr.
peter o'toole	O'Toole, Peter
john mcallister	McAllister, John
clark, david d	Clark, David D.
Clark, David D.	Clark, David D.

Names, Right-Side-Out

Many of the database applications we write require the repetitive input of proper names. The **NormalizeName()** function can make those applications a little more bulletproof and much easier to use. The function's design improves the more I use it because I am exposed to more and more names.

CODE DESCRIPTION

Overview

Program that demonstrates a method of normalizing (last name first, first name last) many common names.

Listings Available

Listing	*Description*	*Used with*
NORMNAME.C	Example program that demonstrates how to normalize data.	------

How to Compile/Assemble

Can be compiled and linked with any C/C++ compiler. Uncomment the definition of **GENTESTPROGRAM** to use the example program. **NEEDCLEANING** macro controls whether function **CleanString** is included in the program.

■ LISTING 11.2 NORMNAME.C

```
/* NormalizeName() and helper functions. */
#include <stdio.h>
#include <stdlib.h>
#include <ctype.h>
#include <string.h>

/*#define NEEDCLEANING*/   /* uncomment to compile CleanString */
/*#define GENTESTPROGRAM*/ /* uncomment to compile main */
#define HARDSPACE '\xff' /* a 'hard', i.e. nonbreaking, space */

extern char *strupr(char *s); /* not prototyped in ANSI string.h */

/* Special characters to capitalize after: space,
   apostrophe, hyphen, and HARDSPACE. */
static char CapAfterCharList[] = " '-\xff";

/*  The list of nonbreaking prefixes. */
static char *NonBreakingPrefixList[] = {
      "St.","De","Del","Della","Di","De La",
      "Running",
      0
      };

#if defined(NEEDCLEANING)
```

```
/* ---------- CleanString ---------- */
static void CleanString(register char *s) {
  register char *t;
  for (t = s; *t; t++) /* convert control chars to spaces */
  if (iscntrl(*t)) *t = ' ';
  for (t = s; isspace(*t); t++); /* remove leading spaces */
  if (t != s) strcpy(s, t);
  /* remove trailing spaces */
  for (t = s + strlen(s) - 1; isspace(*t); t—);
  *(t + 1) = '\0';
  /* remove redundant internal spaces */
  if (*s) {  /* check that there's still something there */
    for (t = s; *t;) {
      while (*t && *t != ' ') {    /* find a blank */
        *s = *t;
        s++;
        t++;
      }
      *s = *t;              /* copy one blank */
      if (*t) {
        s++;
        t++;
        while (*t && *t == ' ') t++;
      } /* find next nonblank */
    }
  }
  return;
}
#endif

/* ---------- DoCapAfterChar ---------- */
static void DoCapAfterChar(char *s){
  register char *p, *t;
  /* check for NULL pointer or zero length string */
  if ((s == (char *) NULL) || !(*s)) return;
  for (p = CapAfterCharList; *p; p++) {
  /* move through the string, one char at a time */
    t = s;
    while (*(t + 1) != '\0') { /* terminate if '\0' */
      if (*t == *p)
        *(t + 1) = toupper(*(t + 1));
        t++;
    }
  }
  return;
}

/* ---------- CapAfterStr ---------- */
static void CapAfterStr(register char *s, char const * const pat) {
  int patlen;
  char *stop;

  /* check for NULL pointers and zero length strings */
  if ((s == (char *) NULL) || !(*s) || (pat == (char *) NULL) ||
  !(*pat))
```

```
      return;

    patlen = strlen(pat);      /* length of pattern */
    stop = s + strlen(s);     /* stop points to end of string ('\0') */
    while (1) {
     if ((s = strstr(s, pat)) == (char *) NULL)   /* look for match */
        return;          /* no more matches, so return */
    /* point to char after pattern and check for end of string */
      if ((s += patlen) >= stop)
        return;          /* don't cap past the end of the string */
      *s = toupper(*s);    /* capitalize char after matched pattern */
    }
  }

/* ---------- DoNonBreakingPrefixes ---------- */
static void DoNonBreakingPrefixes(char *s) {
  int patlen;
  char *t, **listp;
  for (listp = NonBreakingPrefixList; *listp; listp++) {
    patlen = strlen(*listp);
    t = s;
    while (1) {
      if ((t = strstr(t, *listp)) == (char *) NULL)
        break;                /* no more matches */
      if (*(t + patlen) != ' ')
        break;                /* past end of string? */
      (*(t + patlen) = HARDSPACE);
      t += patlen;             /* move past match */
    }
  }
}

/* ---------- RemoveHardSpaces ----------- */
static void RemoveHardSpaces(register char *s) {
  while (s != (char *) NULL)
    if ((s = strchr(s, HARDSPACE)) != (char *) NULL)
      *s = ' ';
}

/* --------- LookForSuffixes ----------- */
static char *LookForSuffixes(char *s) {
  char *sptr;
  if ((sptr = strstr(s, " Jr")) != (char *) NULL) {
    if (*(sptr + 3) == '\0') /* needs a period */
      strcat(sptr, ".");
  }
  else if ((sptr = strstr(s, " Sr")) != (char *) NULL) {
    if (*(sptr + 3) == '\0') /* needs a period */
      strcat(sptr, ".");
  }
  else if ((sptr = strstr(s, " Iii")) != (char *) NULL)
    strupr(sptr);
  else if ((sptr = strstr(s, " Iv")) != (char *) NULL)
    strupr(sptr);
```

```
  else if ((sptr = strstr(s, " III")) != (char *) NULL)
  /* don't need to do anything */;
  else if ((sptr = strstr(s, " IV")) != (char *) NULL)
  /* don't need to do anything */;
  if (sptr != (char *) NULL)
    *sptr++ = '\0';     /* disconnect and point to suffix */
  return (sptr);
}

/* ---------- NormalizeName ---------- */
char *NormalizeName(char *s) {
  char *LastName, *Suffix, *TempString;
#if defined(NEEDCLEANING)
  CleanString(s);      /* clean up the string */
#endif

/* capitalization section */
  *s = toupper(*s);          /* always capitalize first char */
  DoCapAfterChar(s);
  CapAfterStr(s, "Mc");      /* always capitalize after Mc */
/* name rearrangement section */
  if (strchr(s, ',') == (char *) NULL) { /* put first name last */
/* allocate a temporary buffer to build new copy of string */
    if ((TempString = (char *) malloc(strlen(s) + 3)) !=
    (char *) NULL) {    /* connect any nonbreaking prefixes */
      DoNonBreakingPrefixes(s);
      Suffix = LookForSuffixes(s);   /* disconnect suffixes */
      if ((LastName = strrchr(s, ' ')) != (char *) NULL) {
        strcpy(TempString, LastName + 1);  /* copy last name */
        strcat(TempString, ", ");          /* append comma */
        strncat(TempString, s, (LastName - s)); /* append rest */
        if (Suffix != (char *) NULL) {     /* reconnect suffixes */
          strcat(TempString, " ");
          strcat(TempString, Suffix);
        }
        RemoveHardSpaces(TempString);
        strcpy(s, TempString); /* copy back to original string */
      }
      free(TempString);         /* release temporary buffer */
    }
  }
  return (s);    /* return pointer to normalized string */
}

/* ---------- Test Program ---------- */
#if defined(GENTESTPROGRAM)
#define   NAMESIZE  80
void main(void) {
  char buf[NAMESIZE];
  fputs("Testing\n", stdout);
  while (fgets(buf, (NAMESIZE - 2), stdin) != NULL) {
    if (strchr(buf, '\n') != NULL)      /* remove newline */
      *(strchr(buf, '\n')) = '\0';
    fputs("->", stdout);
```

```
      fputs(NormalizeName(buf), stdout);
      fputs("<-\n", stdout);
    }
    exit(0);
  }
#endif
```

Smart Numerical Storage

■ Brian Cheetham

Develop a set of macros to quickly store numeric data.

Most programmers at one time or another will have the need to store a number—such as the number of records in a data file—to disk. Although you can do this by making a call to **fprintf()**, there is a better way.

The Intel family of microprocessors stores values with the least significant byte first. This means that the number 0x0100, for example, is stored in memory with two (hex) bytes as follows: 00 01. Why is this important?

Simple. With **fprintf()** we store the number 256 as the string "256." First of all, the string takes up unnecessary space in our data file. While the example of 256 only wastes one byte, it's easy to see that the larger the number, the more the space that's wasted. In addition, calling **fprintf()** can waste something else—time.

If we store the hex values instead of the string representation of the values, we can save both space and time. The macros shown in Listing 11.3 (NUMERIC.C) demonstrate compact functions to convert both **int**s and **long**s to and from their internal representations.

When would you want to take advantage of this technique? Consider a typical B-Tree algorithm that needs to store record pointers for each node in the tree. In such an algorithm, both space and time are at a premium.

CODE DESCRIPTION

Overview

Sample program which demonstrates the use of **itols**, **ltols**, **lstoi**, and **lstol** macros that store data in the native Intel format.

Listings Available

Listing	*Description*	*Used with*
NUMERIC.C	Self contained example program.	------

How to Compile/Assemble

Can be compiled and linked with any C/C++ compiler.

■ **LISTING 11.3 NUMERIC.C**

```
#include <stdio.h>

/* Least Significant format to int */
#define lstoi(a) (* (int *) (a))

/* int to Least Significant format */
#define itols(a, b) (a = (unsigned char *) &b)

/* Least Significant format to long */
#define lstol(a) (* (long *) (a))

/* long to Least Significant format - same as itols() */
#define ltols(a, b) (a = (unsigned char *) &b)

void main(void)
{
unsigned  char  *i_str,  *l_str;
int    i, j;
long   l, m;

    i = 256;
    l = 100000L;

    /*-
     *- note that since ?_str becomes a pointer to
     *- the value, no initialization or storage
     *- space is needed
    -*/

    itols(i_str, i);
    ltols(l_str, l);
    /*- now you could use write() to write to disk */

    j = lstoi(i_str);
    m = lstol(l_str);

    printf("i=%d == j=%d, l=%ld == m=%ld\n", i, j, l, m);

}
```

Generating Ordinal Suffixes in C

■ Leland Van Allen

Here's a handy macro that returns the ordinal suffix for a specified number.

It's often useful to be able to generate the ordinal equivalent of cardinal values in string form for display or printing of numeric adjectives. That is, words like 3rd, 40th, 72nd, or

91st. The C macro in Listing 11.4 (ORDSFX.C) returns the correct ordinal suffix for the integer argument **x**. An example call follows:

```
if (csfail)
{
  printf( "Line check-sum failure-"
          "- %d%s line!  Aborting!",linnum,ordsfx(linnum));
  exit(1);
}
```

I would like to thank James Scandale for correcting a mistake in my original code.

TIP: At first look, the macro construction seems more complicated than necessary. The reason for this is the fact that some ordinal numbers, specifically those ending in 11, 12, and 13, actually use the "-th" suffix and not the "-st," "-nd," or "rd" you might expect. This is true no matter how large the number is (e.g. 212th, 4311th, 333313th, and so on). To be accurate, the macro must first test to see if the value lies in the "teens." If it does, the correct suffix will always be "-th." Otherwise, the macro will return a value based on the final digit of the value given.

CODE DESCRIPTION

Overview

A simple macro to be included with a program, either in the main function or in a header file.

Listings Available

Listing	*Description*	*Used with*
ORDSFX.C	Short macro which returns a two-character string that represents the ordinal suffix for the specified number.	------

How to Compile/Assemble

Can be compiled and linked with any C/C++ compiler.

■ LISTING 11.4 ORDSFX.C

```
#define ordsfx(x)  (((x)%100)>10 && ((x)%100)<14 ? "th" :\
                                  (x)%10 == 1 ? "st" :\
                                  (x)%10 == 2 ? "nd" :\
                                  (x)%10 == 3 ? "rd" :\
                                               "th")
```

12

Data Structures

Anyone who's ever moved knows that books on a shelf are a lot easier to locate and use than books tossed into a big box and shoved into a corner of the garage. That's the essence of structuring data: Put it somewhere close by in a convenient arrangement in some predictable order.

The arrangement and the order can be whatever serves the needs of the application. Arrays are fast but inflexible, whereas linked lists are infinitely mutable but significantly slower and trickier to manage. A great many PhDs have been earned studying the subtleties of arranging data in memory. I suspect a few more will be earned over time as well. The last chapter on data structures has definitely *not* been written.

I thought I had seen most of it on my cruise through Knuth, but Bruce Schneier definitely tossed me a new one with his article on splay trees, which are binary trees that adjust themselves after each access to gradually and automatically bring the most frequently sought nodes closer to the root. Amazing notion!

Nicholas Wilt's piece on binary heaps, while less surprising, is a more generally useful technique that everyone should have in his or her arsenal. The same author also presents bit vectors, which have long been part of the definition of Pascal as sets, but which need to be synthesized for use in the C/C++ world.

Structuring data is one of the few areas of programming that remain more or less unfettered by the gradual encroachment of the platform. Microsoft Windows demands that program structure conform to its own needs, but data—well, data can be what it needs to be, and right-brain brilliance can still make a difference.

The Binary Heap

■ Nicholas Wilt

Use a general purpose binary heap class as a resource for sorting or prioritizing data in C++ objects.

We generally think of the heap in conventional, non-OOP, terms: It's a data resource that we manage through library functions, like **malloc()** and **free()**. This is hardly an example of the data-*cum*-code encapsulation that we enjoy with object-oriented programming. But, it *could* be.

It's easy to conceive of the heap in terms of a C++ class, with the data (the heap space) and the management functions welded together in one object. We do *not* propose taking on *universal* heap management; however, we can stake out a small corner of the heap universe and create a heap class that serves one very useful function: sorting or prioritizing data. For this application, we need a heap object that gives us "binary tree" capabilities—a *binary heap.*

So, What Is It?

The binary heap is a C++ object class that combines a heap data structure with two user functions. **Insert()** inserts an object (or stand-alone data element) into the heap space, while **Extract()** extracts the current "ranking" object (or data element) from the managed heap space.

In this context, *"ranking"* refers to the element ("node") in the heap that has the minimum or maximum value of some data item. This could be the highest or lowest numeric value, or an ASCII character's alphabetic ranking. As we will see, the user determines the criteria for testing the relative ranking of any two nodes in the heap. The binary heap acts on the test result and doesn't even concern itself with the *type* of data. Its member functions are entirely general purpose.

A binary heap has many uses, the most obvious being for sorting. As our example program demonstrates, you **Insert()** *N* elements, then do *N* **Extract()** calls. You can also alternate the individual **Insert()** and **Extract()** function calls. The priority queues in operating systems use this technique.

Why Not Linked Lists?

Looking at the user functions, you might conclude that implementing them would be simple: Just maintain a linked list. For the **Insert()** function, insert the object in the order of its ranking. When performing the **Extract()**, just remove the head of the linked list.

Alternatively, you could maintain an unordered list. Then, inserting an element is fast (just add to the head of the list); however, you have to traverse the entire list to find the ranking element and extract it.

Binary heaps let you implement the **Insert()** and **Extract()** operations more efficiently than either of the linked-list approaches. For a binary heap with *N* elements, it takes time proportional to log*N* (the logarithm of *N*) to insert or extract an element. A sequence of *N*

Insert() and **Extract()** calls requires time on the order of $N \log N$. By contrast, a sequence of N **Insert()** and **Extract()** operations on either of the above linked-list data structures would require time on the order of N^2.

Replacing "N-squared" type algorithms with "$N\log N$" algorithms is a routine practice in programming sorting applications. Quicksort offers an "$N\log N$" sorting algorithm to replace the many "N-squared" algorithms, such as Insertion Sort. The speed-up is impressive: for $N = 1000$, $N\log N$ is 6,907, while N^2 is 1,000,000. The disparity increases as N gets larger.

How Does It Work?

A binary heap can be thought of as a cross between an array and a binary tree. Figure 12.1 illustrates the shape of a binary heap; it is a binary tree, balanced except for the lower right-hand corner. Such a tree can be embodied in a simple array. If we start numbering from 0, the indices for the *children* of any node "I" are

```
Left Child = 2*I+1
Right Child = 2*I+2
```

The index for the parent of node "J" is

```
Parent = (J-1)/2
```

With the background established, we can define the heap property, which must always be true for the binary heap: *The parent of a node always outranks the node itself.* The notion of "rank" can be anything, as long as the elements can be compared. Figure 12.1 demonstrates the heap property when the elements in the heap are integers and ranking involves ascending numeric value.

Insert() places the node being added *at the end* of the heap. If the new node outranks its parent, the heap property is violated; therefore, the new node must swap places with its parent. If, after this first swap, the new node still outranks its new parent, another swap is required. The new node percolates up the heap, swapping positions with its parent until the heap property is restored.

Figure 12.2 illustrates the insert/sift process. Note that a binary heap with "n" levels can hold "*Nmax*" elements, where *Nmax* equals 2^{n-1}. The *maximum* number of swaps required after an **Insert()** would be n–1.

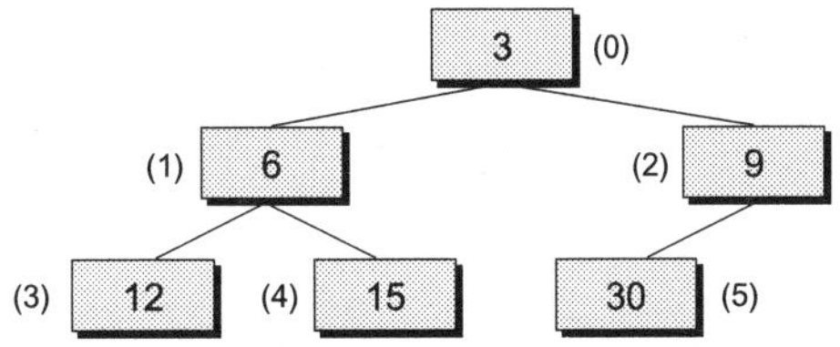

The numbers in parentheses are the array subscripts of the heap elements (numbering from 0).

■ **FIGURE 12.1 A simple binary heap**

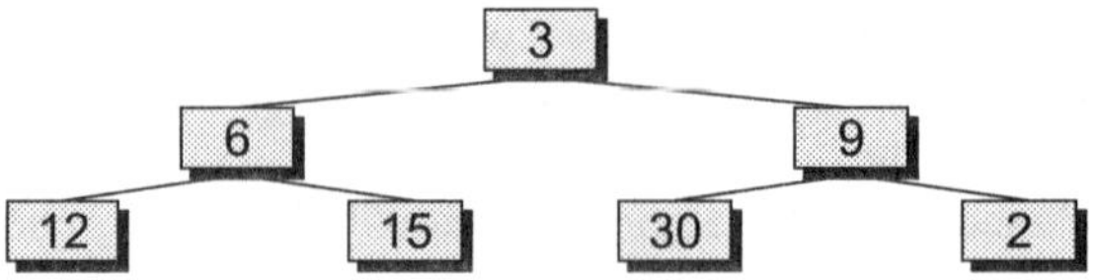

Step 1.
Put 2 at the end of the heap array: 2 < 9, so we have to shift it up.

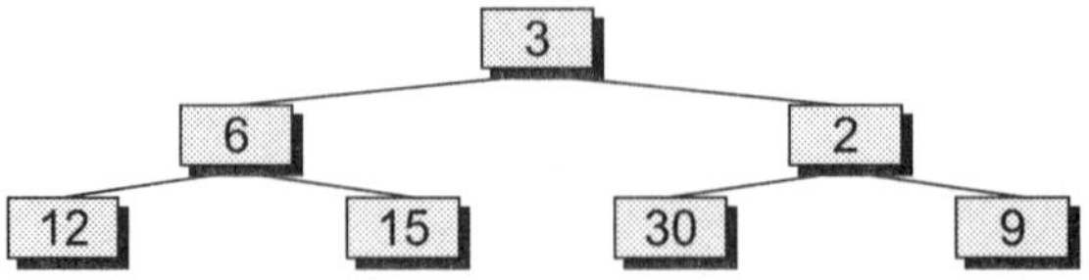

Step 2.
2 has been swapped with 9, but 2 < 3, so we must continue.

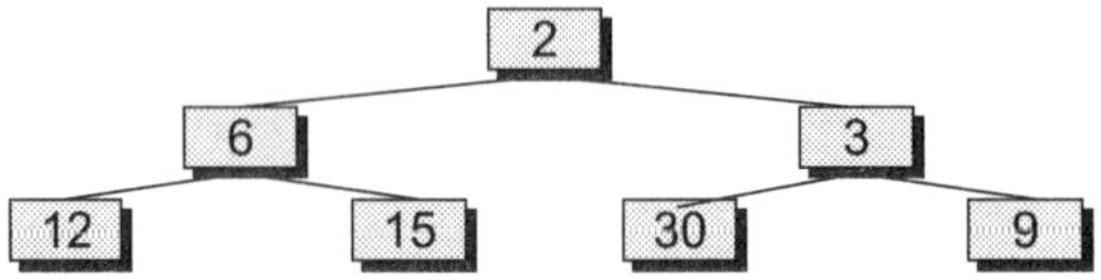

Step 3.
2 has been swapped with 3: it is the new minimum value in the heap, and has been sifted to the top. Note that the heap property now holds throughout the heap.

■ **FIGURE 12.2 Inserting a number**

By maintaining the heap property, it is simple for **Extract()** to find the "ranking node" from the heap; the *first* node (the root of the tree) is always the ranking element. When **Extract()** removes the first element, it creates a hole at the top of the heap. We then move the *last* element in the heap into the hole, choosing it because its movement does not disturb the rest of the ranking structure. Nevertheless, promoting the last element violates the heap property. The new first element must "sift down" into the heap; that is, swap places with the lower ranking of its children until the heap property is restored.

Figure 12.3 illustrates this process. As with **Insert()**, an **Extract()** from a binary heap of "*n*" levels would require up to *n*–1 swaps.

The Heap Class

The code in Listings 12.1 (HEAP.HPP) and 12.2 (HEAP.CPP) create a C++ class, **Heap()**, that implements the binary heap. The constructor, **Heap::Heap()**, takes one parameter: a pointer to the user-defined comparison function (**ComparisonFunction**).

The comparison function takes two pointers to objects in the heap (designated by **a** and **b**) and returns an integer based on the comparison. Whenever the **Heap** class has to decide whether to swap two elements, it calls the comparison function. The return value reflects the relative ranking of the items. For example,

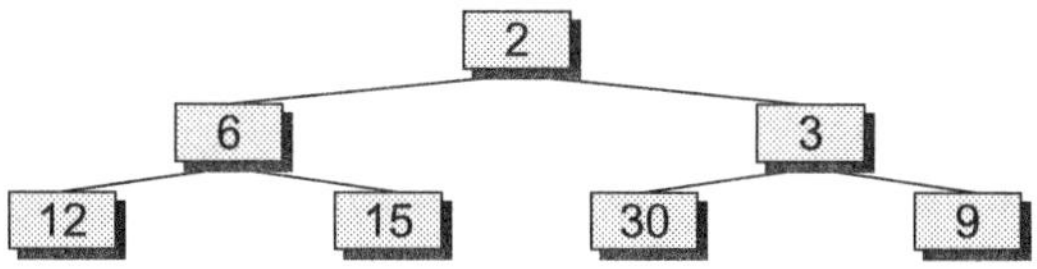

Step 1.
Remove the 2, move the 9 into its place, and delete the last entry in the heap.

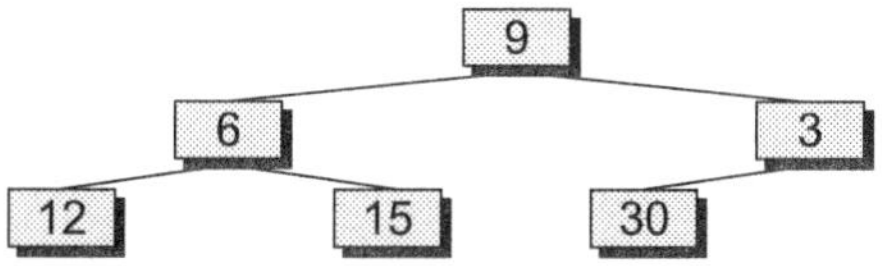

Step 2.
Fix up the heap property by swapping 9 with the smaller of its children.

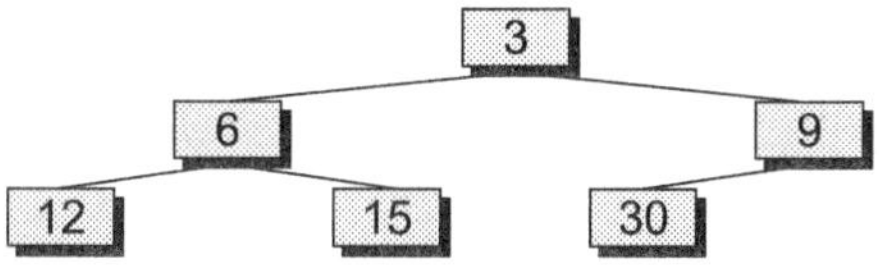

Step 3.
After swapping 9 with 3, the heap property holds throughout the heap.

■ **FIGURE 12.3 Extracting the minimum**

Condition	**Return Value**
a < b	Negative (**b** outranks **a**)
a == b	0 (**a** and **b** have same rank)
a > b	Positive (**a** outranks **b**)

By using only the pointer to the comparison function, we make the **Heap** class truly versatile. Besides letting the **Heap** class deal with all possible data types, we need only switch the sense of the comparison to extract a "maximum" instead of a "minimum." (The demonstration program, DEMO.CPP, uses both ordering techniques.)

Note also that the **Heap** class does not directly keep track of the objects contained in the heap. Rather, it stores pointers to the objects. (Therefore, you must never free objects stored in the heap *before* removing them from the binary heap. If you allocate memory, insert a pointer to it into the binary heap, and then free the object's memory, the binary heap contains a pointer to freed memory—producing the *old* definition for OOPS!)

You call **Heap::Insert** with a pointer to the object to insert into the heap. This pointer must be cast to **void** *. **Heap::Extract** returns a pointer (**void** *) to the ranking element. This second pointer must be cast to the correct data type, or to 0 (the null pointer) if there are no elements in the heap.

The private **SiftUp()** and **SiftDown()** functions handle the respective upward and downward adjustments following **Insert()** and **Extract()** operations. These functions make the calls to the user's comparison function.

The Demo Program

Listing 12.3 (HEAPDEMO.CPP) is a small program that demonstrates the use of **Heap** class objects. It sorts integers in ascending order, and characters in descending order. You can compile the demo with the Turbo C++ command line compiler, using the Make file included on disk. You can also use the Turbo C++ IDE; just create a project file that includes both HEAP.CPP and DEMO.CPP.

The program illustrates the typecasting requirements and parameter formats for the user functions. It also shows the general form of comparison functions. Since our demo deals only with local integer and character data, you might consider expanding it to use data in some simple C++ objects. The general utility of the **Heap** class for sorting objects should then be even more apparent.

CODE DESCRIPTION

Overview

Example program that demonstrates the use of a general purpose binary heap.

Listings Available

Listing	*Description*	*Used with*
HEAP.HPP	Contains the definition of class **Heap**.	------
HEAP.CPP	Contains the implementation of HEAP.HPP.	------
HEAPDEMO.CPP	Uses the code and definitions in HEAP.HPP and HEAP.CPP to demonstrate the use of a binary heap to sort and store values.	------

How to Compile/Assemble

Can be compiled and linked with any C++ compiler using Large Memory Model. HEAPDEMO depends on HEAP.CPP.

■ LISTING 12.1 HEAP.HPP

```
// Header file for Heap class.
#define DEFSIZE 10  // Default heap size

class Heap {
private:
  void **elms;
  int n;
  int maxsize;
  int (*comp)(void *, void *);
  void SiftUp();
  void SiftDown();
public:
  Heap(int (*ComparisonFunction)(void *, void *));
  ~Heap();
  void Insert(void *);
  void *Extract();
};
```

■ LISTING 12.2 HEAP.CPP

```
// C++ code implementing binary heaps.
#include <alloc.h>
#include "heap.hpp"

// ---------------------------------
// Constructor:  Takes a pointer to a comparison function akin to
//               those used by bsearch() and qsort().
// ---------------------------------
Heap::Heap(int (*ComparisonFunction)(void *, void *))
{
  elms = (void **) malloc(DEFSIZE * sizeof(void *));
  n = 0;
  maxsize = DEFSIZE;
  comp = ComparisonFunction;
}

// ---------------------------------
// Destructor: Free the allocated memory.
// ---------------------------------
Heap::~Heap()
{
  free(elms);
}

// ---------------------------------
// SiftUp(): Restores the heap property if broken at the bottom.
// ---------------------------------
void Heap::SiftUp()
{
  int i = n - 1;

  while (i) {
    int p = (i-1) >> 1;
    void *temp;
    if ((*comp)(elms[p], elms[i]) <= 0)
      break;
    temp = elms[i];
    elms[i] = elms[p];
    elms[p] = temp;
    i = p;
  }
}

// ---------------------------------
// SiftDown(): Restores the heap property if broken at the top.
// ---------------------------------
void Heap::SiftDown()
{
  int i = 0;
  int c;

  while ( (c = i+i+1) < n) {
    void *temp;
```

```
      if (c+1 < n)
        c += ((*comp)(elms[c+1], elms[c]) < 0);
        if ((*comp)(elms[i], elms[c]) <= 0)
      break;
        temp = elms[i];
        elms[i] = elms[c];
        elms[c] = temp;
        i = c;
    }
}

// ----------------------------------
// Insert(): Insert an element into the heap and restore the heap
//           property.
// ----------------------------------
void Heap::Insert(void *ptr)
{
  if (++n >= maxsize) {
    maxsize <<= 1;
    elms = (void **) realloc(elms, maxsize * sizeof(void *));
  }
  elms[n-1] = ptr;
  SiftUp();
}

// ----------------------------------
// Extract(): Extract the ranking element from the heap and
//            restore the heap property.
// ----------------------------------
void *Heap::Extract()
{
  void *ret;

  if (! n)
    return 0;
  ret = elms[0];
  elms[0] = elms[--n];
  SiftDown();
  return ret;
}
```

■ LISTING 12.3 HEAPDEMO.CPP

```
// C++ code for demonstration of Heap class.
// Depends on HEAP.CPP

#include <iostream.h>
#include "heap.hpp"

// ------------------------------
// This is the comparison function for ASCENDING integers
// ------------------------------
int comp_ints(void *a, void *b)
{
  return( *((int *) a) - *((int *) b));
```

```
}

// --------------------------------
// This is the comparison function for DESCENDING characters
// --------------------------------
int comp_char(void *a, void *b)
{
  return( *((char *) b) - *((char *) a));
}

main()
{
  // An unordered set of integers
  int numbers[20] = {1, 2, 4, 5, 3,
         19, 15, 18, 0, 13,
         11, 14, 12, 16, 17,
         6, 9, 8, 7, 10};

  // An unordered set of characters
  char letters[34] = {"THEQUICKBROWNFOXJUMPSOVERLAZYDOGS"};
                   // 123456789012345678901234567890123

  Heap h(comp_ints);  // A heap instance for the integers
  Heap ch(comp_char); // A heap instance for the characters

  int i;

// --------------------------------
// Start with the integer data...
// --------------------------------
  // Print out numbers before sorting
  for (i = 0; i < 20; i++)
    cout << numbers[i] << ' ';
  cout << '\n';

  // Insert numbers into heap
  for (i = 0; i < 20; i++)
    h.Insert(numbers+i);

  // Print out numbers in order extracted from heap
  // (In this case, in ASCENDING order.)
  for (i = 0; i < 20; i++)
    cout << *((int *) h.Extract()) << ' ';
  cout << '\n';

// Now, try the character data...
  // Print out letters before sorting
  for (i = 0; i < 33; i++)
    cout << letters[i] << ' ';
  cout << '\n';
  // Insert letters into heap
  for (i = 0; i < 33; i++)
    ch.Insert(letters+i);
  // Print out letters in order extracted from heap
  // (In this case, in DESCENDING order.)
```

```
    for (i = 0; i < 33; i++)
      cout << *((char *) ch.Extract()) << ' ';
    cout << '\n';
}
```

A Bit Vector Class in C++

■ Nicholas Wilt

Packed arrays of Boolean flags (bit vectors) can be mighty handy, and are very compact for what they do.

A bit vector is an array of individually addressable bits. It is used to efficiently store arrays of Boolean values, such that a single bit is all that is required to store a truth value. By packing the bits efficiently, bit vectors allow programmers to store arrays of related Boolean values in as small a space as can be done. Pascal sets express the bit vector idea in a limited way for the Pascal language, in that up to 256 Boolean elements may be stored in only 32 bytes.

Bit vectors have a variety of uses. An *N*-element bit vector can be used to guarantee that a sequence of random numbers in the range [0..*N*-1] will not contain duplicates. The method works like this: First allocate an *N*-element bit vector and initialize all the elements to 0. For each random number generated, set the corresponding element in the bit vector to 1. Then, after generating each new random number, check the bit vector to see whether that number has already been generated. Keep "pulling" random numbers until one is found whose element in the bit vector is not set to 1, and then repeat the process for each unique random number desired.

Another interesting application for bit vectors is in the UNIX utility "spell." Spell is a rudimentary spell-checker that prints out each word in its input that is not in its dictionary. The "dictionary" is not a list of words, but a bit vector with 2^{27} elements. A hash function transforms a word into a 27-bit index in the hash table; the bits corresponding to valid English words contain 1's, while all other bits in the bit vector contain 0's. To check whether a word is valid, the program hashes the word to a 27-bit value and checks whether the corresponding bit in the bit vector is 1. The chance of error is small, since the bit vector is sparse. (2^{27} is much larger than the number of words in the English language.)

As mentioned, bit vectors can be used to implement sets. Each element in the vector tells whether the corresponding element is in the set or not. The bit vectors presented (Listings 12.4 and 12.5) are both more and less powerful than the sets available in Pascal; C++ lacks built-in language support for set operations, but the **BitVect** class can manipulate far larger sets.

Bit Vector Operations

If you number the set elements from 0 to *N*-1, an *N*-element bit vector is the same as an *N*-element set. To take the intersection of two sets, AND the bit vectors together. To take the union, OR them. To take the complement, NOT them. To compute the set difference X – Y, clear all the bits in X corresponding to 1-bits in Y.

Figure 12.4 depicts some of these operations on ten-element bit vectors. After constructing two bit vectors, the results of Boolean operations on the bit vectors are shown. They should look familiar; with the exception of set difference, operations on bit vectors are exactly like Boolean operations on integers.

Enter BitVect

BitVect is a C++ class that encapsulates the idea of a bit vector. The constructors allow you to specify a number **N** of bits in the vector. Then member functions define the operations you can perform on bit vectors:

- The constructor can initialize all bits to 0 or 1.
- **SetBit()** sets a given bit to 0 or 1.
- **GetBit()** retrieves the value of a given bit.
- The [] operator has been overloaded for the **GetBit** operation as well, so the bit vector can be treated more literally as an array.
- The Boolean operators have been overloaded so that all the bits in the vector can be manipulated at once.

The bit vectors are implemented as an array of bytes, or "unsigned chars" in C parlance. Since the bits are packed, we only need about *N*/8 bytes of storage for *N* bits. Of course, we have to round *N*/8 up (e.g., a 9-bit vector requires 2 bytes).

All example bit vectors in this figure are ten elements long.
Note the starting values for A and B.

```
C = A | B       0111010000  (A)
             OR 0000000001  (B)
              = 0111010001  (C)

    C & A       0111010001  (C)
            AND 0111010000  (A)
              = 0111010000

       ~A   NOT 0111010000  (A)
              = 1000101111

    C - A       0111010001  (C)
              - 0111010000  (A)
              = 0000000001
```

The operator symbols demonstrated above are overloaded for bit vectors in BITVECT.CPP (Listing 12.5).

■ **FIGURE 12.4 Bit vector operations**

This bit-packing means we can manipulate fairly large arrays of bits. A bit vector with 2^{18} (262,144) elements requires only 32K to store. This is why the indices into the bit vectors are declared **long**: Even if we limit the bit vector's size to 64K, it can contain a greater number of bits than a 16-bit integer can express.

The **BitVect** class could be improved. Some of the functions might be better placed inline for efficiency. The **vect** member could be redeclared as **huge**, allowing larger bit vectors to be manipulated by the class at some cost in performance. **BitVect::SetRange** could be made more efficient, and several of the functions should range-check their arguments. The overloaded operator functions should make sure to operate only on bit vectors of the same size.

Listing 12.6, SETS.CPP, uses bit vectors as sets of characters. It generates bit vectors corresponding to the sets of capital and lowercase letters, and the set {A, E, I, O, U, a, e, i, o, u} of vowels. Then it uses various set operations (OR for union, AND for intersection, and so on) to generate other sets of characters. The set of consonants, for example, is the set of upper and lowercase letters minus the set of vowels. After computing the sets, SETS.CPP uses them to look at a test string and print out only those characters that are in the set. Thus, "([StringToLookAt])," the test string in SETS.CPP, becomes "StrngTLkT" when only the consonants are printed.

Only a few of the possible applications for bit vectors have been covered here, but I hope you now have enough ammunition to pursue them on your own.

CODE DESCRIPTION

Overview

Example program on using bitvector classes. The program performs a series of bit operations on the string "([StringToLookAt])".

Listings Available

Listing	*Description*	*Used with*
BITVECT.HPP	Describes the **BitVector** class.	------
BITVECT.CPP	Implements the **BitVector** class described in BITVECT.CPP.	------
SETS.CPP	Example program which exercises methods and data in BITVECT.CPP.	------

How to Compile/Assemble

Can be compiled and linked with any C++ compiler.

■ LISTING 12.4 BITVECT.HPP

```
// Header file for the bit vector class.

class BitVect {
  unsigned char *vect; // Vector that contains the bits
  int numbytes;      // Number of bytes in vect
  long numbits;      // Number of bits in vector
```

```
public:
  // Copy constructor.
  BitVect(const BitVect&);
  // Constructor takes the number of elements in the bit vector.
  BitVect(long n);
  // Constructor takes the number of elements in the bit vector
  // and the initial value to give all the bits.
  BitVect(long n, int val);
  ~BitVect();
  // Functions to extract bits out of the vector.
  int operator[] (long); // Subscripts into the bit vector
  int GetBit(long);    // Same as overloaded [].

  // Sets bit to 1 or 0 (1 if val is nonzero, 0 otherwise).
  void SetBit(long inx, int val);
  void SetRange(long min, long max, int val);

  // Boolean operations on bit vectors using overloaded operators.
  BitVect operator~ ();
  BitVect& operator|= (BitVect& x);
  BitVect& operator&= (BitVect& x);
  BitVect& operator-= (BitVect& x);
  friend BitVect operator| (BitVect& x, BitVect& y);
  friend BitVect operator& (BitVect& x, BitVect& y);
  friend BitVect operator- (BitVect& x, BitVect& y);
};
```

■ LISTING 12.5 BITVECT.CPP

```
// Implementation of BitVect (bit vector) class.


#include <mem.h>
#include "bitvect.hpp"

BitVect::BitVect(const BitVect& x)
{
  numbytes = x.numbytes;
  numbits = x.numbits;
  vect = new unsigned char[numbytes];
  memcpy(vect, x.vect, numbytes);
}

BitVect::BitVect(long NumElms): numbits(NumElms)
{
  numbytes = (numbits+7) >> 3;
  vect = new unsigned char[numbytes];
}

BitVect::BitVect(long NumElms, int val): numbits(NumElms)
{
  numbytes = (numbits+7) >> 3;
  vect = new unsigned char[numbytes];
  memset(vect, (val) ? 0xff : 0, numbytes);
}
```

```
BitVect::~BitVect()
{
  delete vect;
}

// BitVect x[inx] returns the inx'th element of x (a 0 or 1).
// No range checking is performed.
int BitVect::operator[] (long inx)
{
  return (vect[inx>>3] & (1 << (inx & 7))) != 0;
}

// Same as operator[]. May be more intuitive at times.
int BitVect::GetBit(long inx)
{
  return (*this)[inx];
}

// Sets the inx'th bit in the vector to 1 or 0.
void BitVect::SetBit(long inx, int on)
{
  if (on)
    vect[inx>>3] |= (1 << (inx & 7));
  else
    vect[inx>>3] &= ~(1 << (inx & 7));
}

// Sets the given range of bits to the given value.
void BitVect::SetRange(long min, long max, int on)
{
  long truemin, truemax;

  truemin = (min < max) ? min : max;
  truemax = (max > min) ? max : min;
  for (long i = truemin; i <= truemax; i++)
    SetBit(i, on);
}

// NOT's the bit vector—all the 0's become 1's and vice versa.
BitVect BitVect::operator~()
{
  BitVect ret(numbits);
  unsigned char *src = vect;
  unsigned char *dst = ret.vect;
  for (int cnt = numbytes; cnt—; src++, dst++)
    *dst = ~*src;
  return ret;
}

// OR's the bit vector with another.  They should be the same size,
// but this is not checked for.
BitVect& BitVect::operator|= (BitVect& x)
{
  unsigned char *src = x.vect;
  unsigned char *dst = vect;
```

```
  for (int cnt = numbytes; cnt--; src++, dst++)
    *dst |= *src;
  return *this;
}

// AND's the bit vector with another.  They should be the same
// size, but this is not checked for.
BitVect& BitVect::operator&= (BitVect& x)
{
  unsigned char *src = x.vect;
  unsigned char *dst = vect;
  for (int cnt = numbytes; cnt--; src++, dst++)
    *dst &= *src;
  return *this;
}

// Set difference: if the ith element is in *this, and it's
// also in x, remove it from *this.
BitVect& BitVect::operator-= (BitVect& x)
{
  for (long i = 0; i < numbits; i++)
    if (x[i])
      SetBit(i, 0);
  return *this;
}

// OR's two bit vectors together, generating a third.
BitVect operator| (BitVect& x, BitVect& y)
{
  BitVect ret(x);
  ret |= y;
  return ret;
}

// AND's two bit vectors another, generating a third.
BitVect operator& (BitVect& x, BitVect& y)
{
  BitVect ret(x);
  ret &= y;
  return ret;
}

// Returns set difference x - y.
BitVect operator- (BitVect& x, BitVect& y)
{
  BitVect ret(x);
  ret -= y;
  return ret;
}
```

■ LISTING 12.6 SETS.CPP

```
// Test program for BitVect (bit vector) class.

#include <iostream.h>
```

```
#include <stdlib.h>
#include <alloc.h>

#include "bitvect.hpp"

// This program uses bit vectors to implement sets of characters.
// The CapitalLetters function returns a 256-element bit vector
// with the bits corresponding to capital letters set.
// LowercaseLetters returns a 256-element bit vector with the bits
// corresponding to lowercase letters set.

BitVect CapitalLetters()
{
  BitVect ret(256, 0);
  ret.SetRange((long) 'A', (long) 'Z', 1);
  return ret;
}

BitVect LowercaseLetters()
{
  BitVect ret(256, 0);
  ret.SetRange((long) 'a', (long) 'z', 1);
  return ret;
}

BitVect Vowels()
{
  BitVect ret(256, 0);
  ret.SetBit((long) 'a', 1);    ret.SetBit((long) 'A', 1);
  ret.SetBit((long) 'e', 1);    ret.SetBit((long) 'E', 1);
  ret.SetBit((long) 'i', 1);    ret.SetBit((long) 'I', 1);
  ret.SetBit((long) 'o', 1);    ret.SetBit((long) 'O', 1);
  ret.SetBit((long) 'u', 1);    ret.SetBit((long) 'U', 1);
  return ret;
}

// Given a string and a bit vector, prints out only
// the characters in the string that are members
// of the set described by the bit vector.
void
PrintString(unsigned char *s, BitVect& x)
{
  while (*s) {
    if (x[*s])
      cout << *s;
    s++;
  }
  cout << '\n';
}

int main()
{
  char *StringToLookAt = "([StringToLookAt])";

  BitVect iscapital = CapitalLetters();
```

```
    BitVect islowercase = LowercaseLetters();
    BitVect iseither = iscapital | islowercase;
    BitVect isneither = ~iseither;
    BitVect isvowel = Vowels();
    BitVect isconsonant = iseither - isvowel;

    cout << "String to look at: " << StringToLookAt << '\n';

    cout << "Capitals only: ";
    PrintString((unsigned char *) StringToLookAt, iscapital);

    cout << "Lowercase only: ";
    PrintString((unsigned char *) StringToLookAt, islowercase);

    cout << "Capitals or lowercase: ";
    PrintString((unsigned char *) StringToLookAt, iseither);

    cout << "Neither capitals nor lowercase: ";
    PrintString((unsigned char *) StringToLookAt, isneither);

    cout << "Vowels only: ";
    PrintString((unsigned char *) StringToLookAt, isvowel);

    cout << "Consonants only: ";
    PrintString((unsigned char *) StringToLookAt, isconsonant);

    return 0;
}
```

Splay Trees

■ Bruce Schneier

Use these splaying algorithms to implement binary trees that adjust themselves toward the fastest access time.

Binary trees are much more efficient data structures than linked lists, because the tree's branched structure shortens the search path for any given piece of data. Still, if the tree is poorly balanced or if the particular piece of data you always want is way out on a leaf somewhere, the performance benefit might not be worth the cost of all those tree operations.

Tree-balancing algorithms are described in almost every data structures book (read Knuth's *The Art of Computer Programming Volume 3: Searching and Sorting;* Sedgewick's *Algorithms;* or Cormen, Leiserson, and Rivest's *Introduction to Algorithms*), but they are mostly concerned with simple balancing operations that don't take into account how the tree is used.

Various self-adjusting techniques have been invented in an effort to improve the performance of binary trees. These techniques are designed to make tree operations more efficient, depending on how frequently each piece of data is actually accessed. For example, if 80% of data access operations retrieves only 20% of the data, the accesses would be far more efficient if that 20% of the data were close to the root of the tree. The rest of the data, which is only accessed 20% of the time, could be down toward the leaves with little loss of performance. If you know those percentages when you build the tree, you could carefully position each piece of data based on its frequency of access. In the far more likely case that you don't know the frequencies, you have to continuously modify the tree pointers as nodes are inserted, deleted, and searched.

Rotating Trees

Binary trees are most easily modified through *rotation*. Rotation algorithms are well defined and can be found in any of the references listed above. Examples of left and right rotation are shown in Figure 12.5.

A simple self-adjusting technique would be to rotate a node every time it is accessed. This would move the accessed node one notch up the tree. Nodes that are frequently accessed would slowly bubble up to the top of the tree, while nodes that are infrequently accessed would be pushed farther down toward the leaves. Another, more dramatic self-adjusting technique would be to keep rotating an accessed node until it actually becomes the root.

Splaying Trees

Although both of these techniques work in theory, neither is terribly efficient in practice. Since all the rotations take a certain amount of time, overall access times can be long. In an effort to improve performance, Daniel Sleator and Robert Tarjan have developed a technique called *splaying*. Splaying accomplishes the same thing as the "move to the root" rotation technique, but it does so far more efficiently.

The splaying algorithm is straightforward. To splay a tree at node x, do the following until x becomes the root of the tree:

Case 1 (zig) If the parent of x is the root, rotate x with its parent, so that x becomes the root of the tree. (If x is a left child, then rotate right at x; if x is a right child, then rotate left at x.)

Case 2 (zig-zig) If the parent of x is not the root, and if x and the parent of x are both left children or both right children, then first rotate the parent of x with the grandparent of x, and then rotate x with the parent of x.

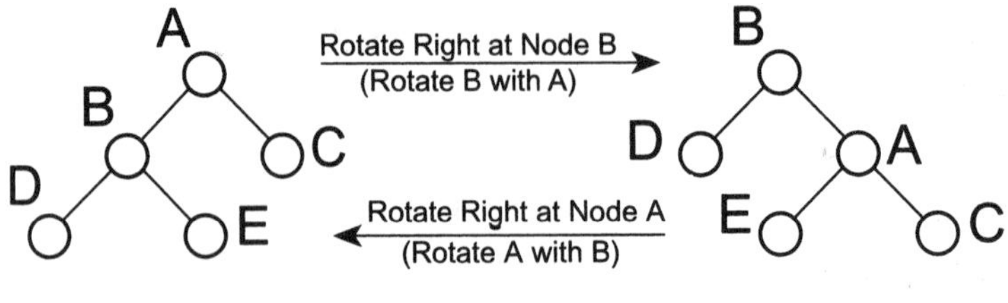

■ **FIGURE 12.5 Left and right rotations**

Case 3 (zig-zag) If the parent of x is not the root, and if x is a left child and the parent of x is a right child (or vice versa), first rotate x with the parent of x and then rotate x with the new parent of x.

Figure 12.6 shows an example of splaying. Notice that the difference in the longest and shortest path length of the resultant tree is smaller: i.e., the tree ends up more balanced after splaying. This is a nice side effect.

Using and Maintaining Your Trees

The code listings implement splay trees in C. Listing 12.7 (SPLAY.H) is a header file defining functions that implement the three basic operations (access, insert, and delete) commonly performed on binary trees. (Note in perusing the code that the names of the operations are not the same as the names of the functions that implement them!) The operations are implemented to incorporate the splaying algorithm, and are carried out as follows:

access(x,t) To access node x in a binary tree t, search t looking for x. If x is found in t, splay t at x. If x is not found in t, splay t at the last non-null reached during the search. This operation is implemented in Listing 12.8 as **splay()**.

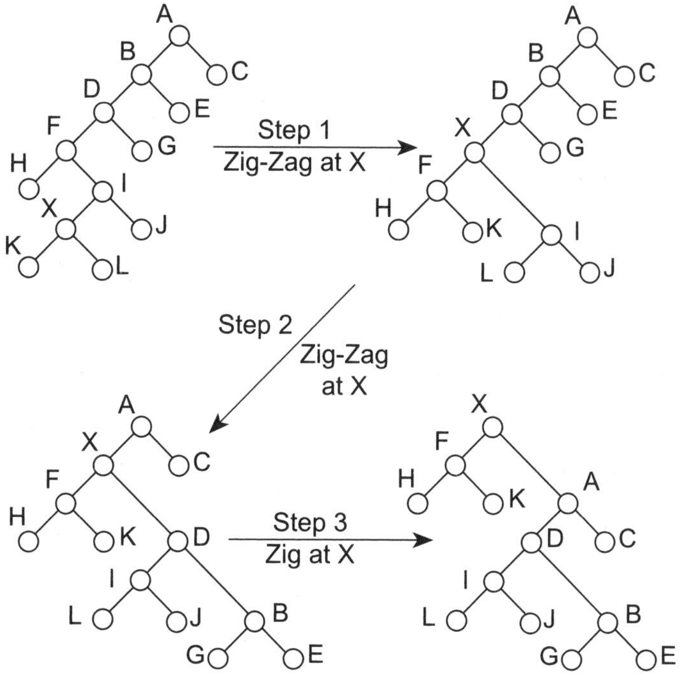

■ **FIGURE 12.6 Splaying at X**

join(t1,t2) To join two binary search trees (this function returns a single binary search tree that contains all the nodes of t1 and t2—the root of t1 is assumed to be less than the root of t2), first access the largest item in t1. After the access, the splaying operation makes the largest item the root of t1. Since t1 now has no right child, simply make t2 the right child of t1's root.

split(x,t) To split t at x (this function returns two binary trees, t1 and t2—one with all the items in the original less than or equal to the value of x and the other with all the items in the original tree greater than the value of x), first access node x in t. Break the right link of the root: t1 is the original tree without the right link, and t2 is the right link.

Split and join are not very common binary tree operations, but it is useful to define the insert and delete operations in these terms:

insert (x,t) To insert x into t, first split t at x. Then reform t with new node x as the root, t1 as the left subtree, and t2 as the right subtree. This operation is implemented in Listing 12.8 as **splayinsert()**.

delete (x,t) To delete x from t, first access x in t. Then replace t with a join of the root's left and right subtrees. The old root, x, is deleted. This operation is implemented in Listing 12.8 as **splaydelete()**.

The point of this whole discussion is to provide an efficient alternative to standard tree-balancing operations. The algorithms are simple to implement, and the speed-up can be impressive. They are ideally suited for priority queues, because operations that delete the minimum-valued node tend to unbalance the tree in such a way as to bring the lower-valued nodes nearer the root.

Adaptable Algorithms

One neat thing about splay trees is that they start to resemble the ways in which you use them. If nodes tend to be inserted and deleted in a last-in first-out manner, like a stack, then eventually the tree starts to resemble a stack: Recently inserted nodes generally hang out around the root of the tree. If nodes tend to be inserted and deleted in a first-in first-out manner, like a queue, then the tree starts to resemble a queue with the oldest nodes near the root of the tree. And if the usage changes from stack-like to queue-like, then the tree changes likewise in response.

Splay trees are not suitable for all applications. If you're accessing nodes more or less randomly, the self-adjusting properties won't speed things up much. Also, splay tree algorithms do many more node comparisons than simple tree algorithms; so if your comparison algorithm is very slow, then splay trees might actually be slower than simple binary trees. The applications where splay trees really shine are those where nodes are *not* accessed randomly. For example (as mentioned earlier), priority queues can be efficiently implemented as splay trees.

As a general rule, if the splay tree can modify itself to take advantage of the way nodes are inserted, deleted, and accessed, then implementing it will significantly improve performance over that of a "fixed-shape" binary tree.

References

Sleator, D.D., and Tarjan, R.E. "Self-Adjusting Binary Search Trees." *Journal of the ACM, 32* (July 1985), 652–686.

Tarjan, R.E. *Data Structures and Network Algorithms,* Society for Industrial and Applied Mathematics, 1983.

CODE DESCRIPTION

Overview

Demonstrates algorithm for splaying binary trees. Ten integers are inserted into the tree and then random values are searched for.

Listings Available

Listing	*Description*	*Used with*
SPLAY.H	Contains the basic Node definition and prototypes for the basic functions.	------
SPLAY.C	Implements the splaying algorithm and contains a short example program to use it.	------

How to Compile/Assemble

Can be compiled and linked with any C/C++ compiler. Macro **TESTING** is used to control whether example program is created.

■ LISTING 12.7 SPLAY.H

```
/*
 * SPLAY.H - function prototypes for splay tree access
 */
typedef struct _node {
long data;
struct _node *left,*right;
} node;

// typdef node struct _node;

node *splay (long x,  node *root);
node *splayinsert (long x,  node *root);
node *splaydelete (long x,  node *root);
```

■ LISTING 12.8 SPLAY.C

```
/* Splay tree implementation

The splay routines are called in the following manner:

    root=splay(arg,root);            Search
    root=splayinsert(arg,root);      Insert
    root=splaydelete(arg,root);      Delete
*/

#define TESTING      /* comment if not testing */
#include <stdlib.h>
#include <stdio.h>
#include <conio.h>

#include "splay.h"
#define key long

// struct node { long data; struct node *left,*right; };
typedef struct nrec_ {  node *left,*right; }nrec ;

#define false 0
#define true 1

 node *rrot(node *root)
{  node *temp,*templ,*p;
  p=root;
  if (p!=NULL)
    { if (p->left!=NULL)
    { temp=p; templ=p->left->right;
      p=temp->left; p->right=temp; temp->left=templ;
    }
    }
  return(p);
}

 node *lrot(node *root)
{  node *temp,*templ,*p;
  p=root;
  if (p!=NULL)
    { if (p->right!=NULL)
    { temp=p; templ=p->right->left;
      p=temp->right; p->left=temp; temp->right=templ;
    }
    }
  return(p);
}

 node *lnkright(node *root,nrec *r)
{  node *temp,*p;
  p=root;
  if (p->left!=NULL)
    { temp=p->left; p->left=NULL;
      if (r->left==NULL)
```

```
        { r->left=p; r->right=p; }
      else
        { r->right->left=p; r->right=r->right->left; }
      p=temp;
    }
   return(p);
}

 node *lnkleft(node *root,nrec *l)
{  node *temp,*p;
  p=root;
  if (p->right!=NULL)
    { temp=p->right; p->right=NULL;
      if (l->left==NULL)
        { l->left=p; l->right=p; }
      else
        { l->right->right=p; l->right=l->right->right; }
      p=temp;
    }
   return(p);
}

 void assemble(node *p,nrec *l,nrec *r)
{  node *temp,*temp1;
  temp=p->left; temp1=p->right;
  if (l->left!=NULL)
    { p->left=l->left; l->right->right=temp; }
  if (r->left!=NULL)
    {  p->right=r->left; r->right->left=temp1;}
}

 node *splay(key x,node *root)
{   nrec l,r;                /* Temp subtrees */
   node *p;
  int done;                        /* Process boolean */
  p=root;
  l.left=l.right=r.left=r.right=NULL;
  done=false;
  if (p!=NULL)
    { do
       {if (x<p->data)
      { if (p->left!=NULL)
          { if (x==p->left->data) p=lnkright(p,&r);
       else
       if (x<p->left->data)
         { p=rrot(p); p=lnkright(p,&r); }
       else
       if (x>p->left->data)
         { p=lnkright(p,&r); p=lnkleft(p,&l); }
          } else done=true;
      }
    else
    if (x>p->data)
      { if (p->right!=NULL)
          { if (x==p->right->data) p=lnkleft(p,&l);
```

```
        else
        if (x>p->right->data)
          { p=lrot(p); p=lnkleft(p,&l); }
        else
        if (x<p->right->data)
          { p=lnkleft(p,&l); p=lnkright(p,&r); }
            } else done=true;
        }
    }
       while ((p->data!=x) && !done);
       assemble(p,&l,&r);
    }
   return(p);
}

 node *splayinsert(key x,node *root)
{  node *p;

  root=splay(x,root);
  if ((root==NULL) || (root->data!=x))
    { p=( node *) malloc(sizeof(node));
      p->data=x; p->left=p->right=NULL;
      if ((root!=NULL) && (x<root->data))
        { p->right=root; p->left=root->left;
          root->left=NULL;
        }
      else
      if ((root!=NULL) && (x>root->data))
        { p->left=root; p->right=root->right;
      root->right=NULL;
    }
      root=p;
     }
  return(root);
}

/* NOTE: SPLAYDELETE is currently set up to deal with integer keys.
   If you want to deal with strings, you will have to build an
   appropriate character array all of whose bytes have the maximum
   ASCII value on your machine.   */
 node *splaydelete(x,root)
key x;
 node *root;
{  node *temp1,*temp2;
  key max=2147483647L;

  root=splay(x,root);
  if ((root!=NULL) && (root->data==x))
    { temp1=root->left; temp2=root->right;
      if (temp1!=NULL)
    { temp1=splay(max,temp1);
      temp1->right=temp2;
    } else temp1=temp2;
      free((char *) root);
      root=temp1;
    }
```

```
  return(root);
}

#ifdef TESTING
void main (void) {
  int x;
  key z;
   node *root = NULL;

  puts ("fill tree");
  root = splayinsert (-1L, root);
  for (x=0; x<10; x++) {
    z = random (10);
    root = splayinsert (z, root);
    printf ("%02ld  ", root->data);
  }
  puts ("\nsearch tree");

  for (x=0; x<100; x++) {
    z = random (10);
    root = splay (z, root);
    printf ("Search for %02ld. %sfound.  Root = %02ld\n", z,
       (root->data == z) ? "    " : "Not ", root->data);
  }
  puts ("\ndone");
}
#endif
```

Inheriting Data Structures in C

■ Tom DePew

Here's a useful trick you can use to implement inheritance with C programs.

Object-oriented techniques can be applied in standard C to reuse functions and data structures. Often, you can define a base data structure and create functions that operate on the structure. Later, you can add more functions. As an example, let's use a linked list. The base structure for a linked list might contain a pointer to the next item in the list. You could then write functions to add and delete nodes from the basic linked list.

Now, suppose you wanted to modify the linked = list node by adding a new field. You could define a new data structure type, perform a cut and paste to copy the old fields, and then add the new field. Deriving new functions from the old ones could be done in a similar manner. Although this technique enables you to "inherit" data structures, it can be difficult to maintain.

What happens if you have several levels of inheritance and you needed to make a change to your base data structure? You must modify each derived structure. A way around this is to use **#define**'s to specify each level of your data structures. This system allows you to have multiple levels of inheritance *and* ease of maintenance. The preprocessor will make sure that all of your data structures change when a base data structure has changed.

An Example

An example of this technique is presented in Listings 12.9, 12.10, and 12.11. LINKLIST.H (Listing 12.9) uses a macro to define the **LINKLIST_STRUCT** data type. Also defined are macros for type-casting derived data types to the **linkNode** type; these will ensure that the correct portions of the data structures are passed to the functions. Functions **AddLinkNode** and **DeleteLinkNode** are prototyped in LINKLIST.H and defined in LINKLIST.C (Lisiting 12.10).

EXAMPLE.C (Listing 12.11) is a short program that illustrates how to "inherit" the linked list. By using the LINKLIST_STRUCT macro, this definition can be changed in one place, LINKLIST.H, and the preprocessor will ensure that the change is propogated throughout the program. What is truly interesting, though, is that the linked = list data type can be extended without recompiling LINKLIST.C. The character array **name** is added by the example program to **my_struct**. Because they don't reference this data field, the previously defined functions **AddLinkNode** and **DeleteLinkNode** are never aware of its existence.

TIP: This technique takes advantage of a couple of ways of doing things that are specific to C. First, in C the calling functions are responsible for pushing and popping the parameters on and off the stack, so there is no need for the called function to know the true size and number of parameters. Second, by making sure that new fields are placed in the inherited data structures *after* the macro, the order of any fields declared in the ancestor data structure remains undisturbed. The called function does not need to be recompiled; it will continue to find the proper fields at the same offsets.

Object-oriented programming is changing the way many of us write code. This method will make it easier to inherit data structures as well as methods using straight C.

CODE DESCRIPTION

Overview

Program that illustrates the use of #define's to streamline reuse of data structures and functions by implementing a form of inheritance in straight C.

Listings Available

Listing	*Description*	*Used with*
LINKLIST.H	Contains the LINKLIST_STRUCT macro.	------
LINKLIST.C	Defines two functions which operate on a data. type derived from the LINKLIST_STRUCT macro.	------
EXAMPLE.C	Extends the data type derived from the LINKLIST_STRUCT macro, and uses the original data structures functions.	------

How to Compile/Assemble

Can be compiled and linked with any C/C++ compiler.

■ LISTING 12.9 LINKLIST.H

```
/*linklist.h*/

#define LINKLIST_STRUCT struct linkList *next
#define LINKNODE(X) ((linkNode) X)
#define LINKNODE_PTR(X)  ((linkNode *) &X)
#define NEXTNODE(X) ((void *)(X)->next)

typedef struct linkList{
LINKLIST_STRUCT;
} linkList, *linkNode;

void AddLinkNode(linkNode *head, linkNode element);

int DeleteLinkNode(linkNode *head, linkNode del_element);
```

■ LISTING 12.10 LINKLIST.C

```
/*linklist.c*/
#include <stdio.h>
#include <stdlib.h>
#include "linklist.h"

void AddLinkNode(linkNode *head, linkNode element)
{
    if (*head == NULL)
    {
        *head = element;
        element->next = NULL;
    }
    else
    {
        element->next = *head;
        *head = element;
    }
}

int DeleteLinknode(linkNode *head, linkNode del_element)
{
linkNode foo, last = NULL;

    foo = *head;
    while( foo && foo != del_element)
    {
        last = foo;
        foo = foo->next;
    }
    if (last == NULL)
       *head = foo->next;
    else if (foo)
       last->next = foo->next;
    else
        return -1;
```

```
    return 0;
}
```

■ LISTING 12.11 EXAMPLE.C

```
/*example.c*/
#include <stdio.h>
#include <stdlib.h>
#include "linklist.h"

typedef struct my_struct {
        LINKLIST_STRUCT;
        char name[40];
} my_struct, *my_ptr;

void main(void)
{

int i;
my_ptr tmp_node;
my_ptr head=NULL;

       for (i=0; i < 10; i++)
       {
         my_ptr node;
         node = calloc(1,sizeof(*node));
         sprintf(node->name, "TEST STRING %d", i);
         AddLinkNode(LINKNODE_PTR(head), LINKNODE(node));
       }
       tmp_node = head;
       while (tmp_node)
       {
        printf("%s\n", tmp_node->name);
        tmp_node = NEXTNODE(tmp_node);
       }
}
```

13

Dealing with Times and Dates

It's a shame we can't do for times and dates what the French did for linear measurement in the 18th century: Create one standard measurement base and then decimalize everything under the sun. I'd like to see a year consist of 100 days and a day consist of 100 shorter hours. (Any consultant who gets paid by the hour would certainly welcome *that.*)

Well, heck, this time we have the sun itself to consider, and a planet that spins and revolves at its own sweet rate. This makes time and date measurement fall out in a lot of highly inconvenient units that have spawned a whole subdiscipline of computing called calendrics.

We're only touching on the subject here, though it's a fascinating one. Want to make your system clock correct automatically for Daylight Saving Time? Donald Costello can tell you how. (Don't bother if you live in Arizona. We don't want another hour of sunlight in the summer; things might catch fire!) There is a trick to knowing whether or not midnight has passed according to DOS, and Jim Kyle will share it with you. Finally, if you ever really want to know how to detect the presence of Friday the 13ths, Donald Costello will return and lay it all out.

Me, I'd just as soon not know. Any day I wake up is a lucky one, and I'm more than happy to leave it at that.

Correct Your Clock for Daylight Saving Time

■ Donald Costello

Here's a clever technique to keep your PC's clock up to date.

Daylight Saving Time runs from the first Sunday in April to the last Sunday in October. The simplicity of this fact makes writing a program that adjusts the system time accordingly simple. Listing 13.1 (DLSCHECK. ASM) demonstrates this idea. On every powerup or system reboot the program DLSCHECK.COM reads the date and if necessary updates the DOS system clock to Daylight Saving Time.

If the date falls before April or after October, the program exits to DOS without taking any action. If the date falls after April and before October, DLSCHECK adjusts the clock by adding one hour's worth of ticks to the count of the timer ticks since midnight.

If the date falls in April, then we must do an additional check to determine if the date is before or after the first Sunday. Similarly, if the date falls in October, we must determine if it is before or after the last Sunday. A quick look at a calendar shows that the first Sunday in April must be on or after the 1st, and the last Sunday in October must always fall after the 25th. This means that the first day of Daylight Saving Time must fall on or after April 1 each year and the last day of daylight saving must fall on or after October 25 each year. For both April and October, if the day is before the "target" then we know that the switch has not occurred yet.

If the date is on or after the target, we have to check the day-of-the-week number to see if a Sunday has occurred on or after the target and before the present date. The DOS call for the date returns the day number in DL, and the day-of-the-week number in AL. If (DL – target – AL) is less than zero then the time switch has not yet occurred in the month. Note that the target is combined with the day-of-the-week number in AL before the subtraction is made. Since the switch in time is opposite in October from that in April, we have to swap AL and DL in October before we can use the compare.

The time is adjusted directly in the BIOS data segment at 40H so that the program will be independent of the system's hardware clock. The assembly instructions for the .COM version of the program are shown in the code description section:

TIP: The computer's hardware (battery) clock should *always* be set to standard time and DLSCHECK will adjust the internal clock used by DOS to adjust for Daylight Saving Time at each system startup. Just invoke it from your AUTOEXEC.BAT file.

NOTE: The program should only be run *once* during each session since an hour will be added to the system time each time the program is run if Daylight Saving Time happens to be in effect.

CODE DESCRIPTION

Overview

Short assembly language program which uses DOS date function to determine whether Daylight Saving Time is currently in force and adjusts the time accordingly. Directly accesses the BIOS data area at 0040:006Ch through 0040:006Eh.

Listings Available

Listing	*Description*	*Used with*
DSLCHECK.ASM	Assembly language code to be turned into .COM program.	------

How to Compile/Assemble

Can be assembled with any MASM or TASM compatible assembler. It is necessary to either run LINK and EXE2BIN or use TLINK with the /t option to create a .COM program.

■ LISTING 13.1 DSLCHECK.ASM

```
CSeg    segment
assume  cs:CSeg,ds:CSeg,es:nothing
        org     100h
Begin:  mov     ah,2ah   ; Get the system date.
        int     21h
; DH=Month; DL=Day; AL=Day-of-week (Sun=0 etc.).
        inc     al       ; For first Sun check.
        cmp     dh,4     ; Check for April.
        jl      Exit00   ; Standard time.
        je      AprCK    ; It's April, check Sun.
OcbCK:  cmp     dh,10    ; Check for October.
        jg      Exit00   ; Standard time.
        jl      Bump     ; Daylight saving.
        add     al,23    ; For last Sun check.
        xchg    dl,al    ; Swap compare for October.
AprCK:  cmp     dl,al    ; Last Sunday check.
        jl      Exit00   ; Standard time.
; Adjust for daylight saving time here.
Bump:   mov     ax,40h   ; Bump system time ahead
        mov     es,ax    ;  65543 counts (1 hour).
        cli              ; Do the deed without ticks.
        add     word ptr es:[6ch],7
        adc     word ptr es:[6eh],1
; Check for 24 hour rollover.
        cmp     word ptr es:[6eh],24
        jl      Exit00
        cmp     word ptr es:[6ch],168
        jb      Exit00
; Set the overflow and rollover the counts.
        mov     byte ptr es:[70h],1
```

```
        sub     word ptr es:[6ch],168
        mov     word ptr es:[6eh],0
Exit00: int     20h
CSeg    ends
        end     Begin
```

Coping with DOS Midnight Madness

■ Jim Kyle

Protect yourself from an unusual DOS bug.

There's a consistent belief among many, if not most, DOS users that the operating system contains a bug that results in failure to update the system calendar properly if the machine is in use when midnight rolls around.

While it's true that at least one version of DOS had a bug in its handling of the date (DOS simply refused to recognize the fact that midnight had happened), this was quickly fixed once recognized, and a cure for the problem has been made widely available on BBSs as CLKFIX.SYS. (This was probably DOS 3.2, which most people never used. If you use 3.2, it might pay to experiment and see.) What is generally referred to as "the midnight bug" is something totally different. It is not really a bug at all but is rather a mismatch between three subsystems: DOS, a device driver, and BIOS.

To see this second problem in action, leave a system running over a weekend or so, without touching the keyboard or running any program during that time. Then take a look at the date. You'll discover that it's a day behind; only one midnight was counted!

Here's the straight story: While the time of day is maintained by BIOS in RAM at locations 0040:006Ch through 0040:006Fh, the calendar itself is maintained within a device driver, CLOCK$. This means that BIOS and the driver have to work together to keep the calendar correct. When the BIOS detects a tick count that indicates midnight, it clears the tick-counter longint at 0040:006C-6F, and sets the midnight flag at 0040:0070 to 1.

When you ask DOS for either the time or the date, whether at the command-line prompt or from inside a program via DOS functions 2AH (get date) or 2CH (get time), DOS actually passes the request on to the CLOCK$ device driver. CLOCK$, in turn, normally asks BIOS to feed it the time by using function 00H of INT 1AH. When the BIOS returns the time, it also returns (in AL) the old value of the midnight flag, and has reset the flag itself to zero. The device driver then tests AL and, if AL is nonzero, updates the calendar to indicate that another day has gone by. This happens on any call to the device driver.

Since every call to the BIOS function clears the midnight flag, you can easily force a calendar error just by calling BIOS to see what time it is, rather than calling DOS. And since the device driver checks only for a nonzero value of the midnight flag (the BIOS does not use it as a counter, on the false assumption that nobody would leave a machine running over the weekend unattended), if two midnights pass by without any call to the device driver, only one day will be tallied on the calendar instead of the actual two days that passed.

The workaround is simple: Always make it a practice to get date and time data via the DOS functions rather than using BIOS, and never let the system go more than 24 hours without at least one call to one of the two DOS date/time functions. One way to ensure that this happens is to tie a TSR onto the timer tick interrupt, 1CH, to inspect the midnight flag at 0040:0070 and, if the flag is nonzero, force a call to DOS function 21H service 2AH to be made on the next INT 28H (when it will be safe to use DOS). Alternatively, you could do the same thing with a simple time-checking program that ran anytime you left the machine unattended, and thus avoid any TSR problems.

If you happen to be running a program written by someone else when midnight occurs, no precaution you can take will guarantee accuracy of the calendar. If that program used BIOS to get the time, it will have cleared the flag. The cure in this case is to ask DOS for the date immediately on leaving the program, and use the DATE command to fix the date if it's wrong.

Detecting Friday the 13ths

■ Donald Costello

Here's a fun programming technique for catching "bad luck" days.

For many people, Friday the 13th is an omen of bad luck. For them, a useful tool would be one that could predict the months that have a Friday the 13th for any given year. In this way they could plan in advance to work around these unlucky days. Besides, it gives us a good excuse to investigate a very interesting mathematical expression called Zeller's Congruence (see J. V. Uspensky and M. A. Heaslet, *Elementary Number Theory*, McGraw-Hill Book Company, Inc., New York, 1939, p. 206).

Zeller's congruence can be used to calculate the day of the week for any date in the Gregorian calendar. Using a simple syntax, the congruence is given by

```
Z=(INT((26*M-2)/10)
  +K
  +D
  +INT(D/4)
  +INT(C/4)
  -2*C
  +777) MOD  7
```

where

- Z is the day of the week number (Sunday = 0, Monday = 1, and so on)
- M is the month number, with January and February taken as months 11 and 12 of the preceding year; March is then number 1, April is number 2, . . . ,December is 10
- K is the day of the month
- C is the century
- D is the year in the century

The number 777, which is a multiple of 7 and therefore doesn't change the outcome, is added to prevent the sum from becoming negative.

To find out if a month contains a Friday the 13th for a given year substitute values for M, C, D, and K=13 into the above formula, and if Z is equal to 5, that month contains a Friday the 13th. The C program in Listing 13.2 (13TH.C) will list all the months in a given year that have a Friday the 13th.

The possibility of a year not having a Friday the 13th has been accounted for in 13TH.C. I suspect that this is not necessary since I have yet to find a year that does not have at least one month with a Friday the 13th. Since the Gregorian calendar repeats exactly every 400 years, a search through a 400-year span would be sufficient to find out if it is possible to have a super lucky year—that is, one without a Friday the 13th at all.

CODE DESCRIPTION

Overview

Program which checks a given year for Friday the 13ths. Uses a day of the week algorithm to determine if the 13th of each month is a Friday.

Listings Available

Listing	*Description*	*Used with*
13TH.C	Self-contained C program.	------

How to Compile/Assemble

Can be compiled and linked with any C/C++ compiler.

■ LISTING 13.2 13TH.C

```
#include <stdio.h>
#include <stdlib.h>

char *month[] = {"January",
                 "February",
                 "March",
                 "April",
                 "May",
                 "June",
                 "July",
                 "August",
                 "September",
                 "October",
                 "November",
                 "December"};

void main(void)
{
char buf[10];
int year;
int j;
int d,c,z;
int y;
```

```
int m;
int nflag=0;

puts("Enter the year: ");
gets(buf);
year = atoi(buf);
#define K 13
#define FRIDAY 5

//   Z=(INT((26*M-2)/10)+K+D+INT(D/4)+INT(C/4)-2*C+777) MOD 7
for (j = 1; j <= 12; j++)
{
    if (j < 3)
    {
       m = j +10;
       y = year -1;
    }
    else
    {
        m = j - 2;
        y = year;
    }
    d = y % 100;
    c = y / 100;
//    z = (((26*m-2)/10)+K+d+(d/4)+(c/4)-2*c + 777)%7;

    z = (26 * m - 2) /10;
    z = z + K;
    z = z + d;
    z = z + d/4;
    z = z + c/4;
    z = z - 2*c;
    z = z + 777;
    z = z % 7;

    if (z == FRIDAY)
    {
       puts(month[j-1]);
       nflag = 1;
    }
}
if (!nflag)
   puts("No months found with Friday the 13th\n");
}
```

14

Algorithms and Programming Methods

An algorithm is a recipe, basically. It's a way of doing something that produces predictable results. We've described algorithms elsewhere in this book; there's a dandy in the previous chapter that describes the operation of a self-optimizing data structure called a splay tree.

In this chapter we're dealing with algorithms and programming methods that aren't tied to a particular data structure or other constraint. The Soundex algorithm presented by Nicholas Wilt dates back to a time when computers could not even have been imagined—yes, Virginia, there were algorithms back when people had nothing more than pencil and paper and crude mechanical adding machines.

Kevin Dean's tutorial on implementing finite state machines (FSMs) is one of the best I've seen, and it comes with some very slick C++ code that makes highly effective use of multiple inheritance.

Kevin Weeks describes the process of installing simple virus protection. This isn't to say that the particular virus shield he describes is stunningly effective; what we want you to take away from the piece is an idea of how the virus/antivirus game is played. And Anthony Lander's description of how static members can be used to solve an interesting problem in library management gives you a flavor of the flexibility and power of C++.

The Indirect Membership Operator in C

■ Peter Aitken

Learn how to use indirect references to access C structures.

Like Pascal and the newest version of Microsoft BASIC, C has a user-defined data type called a structure or a **struct** for short. (Pascal and BASIC call it a *record*.) In C, a specific field or *member* of a structure is denoted by the membership operator "." (ASCII period). For example, consider a structure defined this way:

```
struct screencoords
  {
  int x;
  int y;
  } coords;
```

You can access its two members this way:

```
coord.x = 100;
coord.y = 200;
```

Things begin to get interesting when you declare a pointer to a structure, as follows:

```
struct screencoords *myptr;
```

Simply declaring a pointer does not, of course, point it to anything. We must give the pointer a referent with an explicit assignment statement:

```
myptr = &coord;  /* Make myptr equal to the address of coord */
```

Now we can access the structure with the pointer **myptr**. To do so, we must use the indirect membership operator, which is a dash followed by the "greater than" symbol: "->."

The following two assignment statements are equivalent to the statements shown earlier incorporating the membership operator:

```
myptr->x = 100;  /* Equivalent to coord.x = 100 */
myptr->y = 100;  /* Equivalent to coord.y = 100 */
```

In a function that declares a structure, there is almost always no need for the indirect membership operator, since we can always access structure members using the structure's name. It's when you pass structures to functions that the indirect membership operator is needed. Because C passes the *address* of a structure to a function rather than a separate copy of the structure itself, you must use -> when referencing structure members within the function, as shown in Listing 14.1

Always be aware of whether a structure is being referenced by its name or through a pointer—and use "." or "->" accordingly.

CODE DESCRIPTION

Overview

Simple program which demonstrates the use of indirect references to struct.

Listings Available

Listing	*Description*	*Used with*
INDEM.C	Simple example program.	------

How to Compile/Assemble

Can be compiled and linked with any C/C++ compiler.

■ LISTING 14.1 INDEM.C

```
struct screencoords
  {
  int     x;
  int     y;
  } coords;

void printcoords( struct screencoords *val );

main()
{
  coords.x = 100;
  coords.y = 200;

  printcoords( &coords );
}

void printcoords( struct screencoords *val )
{
  printf( "X coordinate = %d\n", val->x );
  printf( "Y coordinate = %d\n", val->y );
}
```

Bit Manipulation

■ Bryan Flamig

Here's a set of useful functions for setting, resetting, and toggling individual bits.

You've probably encountered cases in C programs where you've needed to set, reset, or toggle individual bits in a word. The formulas for doing this, while actually quite simple, are easy to forget. The three functions **setbit()**, **resetbit()**, and **togglebit()** presented here (Listing 14.2) show just how easy it is to do in C. All three take two arguments: a **word** value to modify, and a number (starting from 0) specifying the bit to be manipulated within that word. Bits are numbered from right to left.

The first function, **setbit()**, is the easiest. It forms a mask by taking a 1 bit and shifting it to the left **n** places, where **n** is a bit number from 0 to 15, from right to left. The mask thus contains all zeros except at the desired bit. The word to be modified is then ORed with this mask, resulting in bit **n** being set in the word without the other bits being affected.

Resetting a bit is a little harder. You form the mask as was done in **setbit()**, but then you take its inverse by performing a NOT operation on the mask. This creates a bit mask with all 1 bits, except at the desired bit. You then AND the word to be modified with the mask, thus resetting the bit.

Toggling a bit is the hardest to understand intuitively, but the formula is just as simple as setting a bit. The secret lies in the XOR (Exclusive OR) operation. Simply create a mask containing all zeros *except* at the bit in question, then XOR the word to be modified with this mask.

How does this latter function work? Recall the definition of XOR. It means "A or B but not both." The truth table for XOR is given in Table 14.1.

Notice that, in places where the mask bit is 0, the result is always the same as the original value of the word bit. In contrast, wherever the bit mask is 1, the result is always the inverse of the original word bit. Thus, by setting up our mask to have a 1 at the bit location to be toggled, we can toggle the corresponding bit in the word while leaving all other bits unaffected.

■ TABLE 14.1 Truth table for XOR

Word bit	Mask bit	Result
0	0	0
0	1	1
1	0	1
1	1	0

CODE DESCRIPTION

Overview

Short functions which clear or set individual bits in an unsigned int. Functions provided will clear, set, or toggle specific bits.

Listings Available

Listing	*Description*	*Used with*
BITSTUFF.C	Implementation of bit functions for inclusion in another C program.	------

How to Compile/Assemble

Can be compiled and linked with any C/C++ compiler.

■ **LISTING 14.2 BITSTUFF.C**

```
/* In the functions below, the bits are numbered from right */
/* to left, starting with 0. That is, the least significant */
/* bit is bit 0.    */

void setbit(unsigned *word, int n)
/* Sets bit in word */
{
  *word |= (1 << n);
}

void resetbit(unsigned *word, int n)
/* Clears bit in word */
{
  *word &= ~(1 << n);
}

void togglebit(unsigned *word, int n)
/* Toggles bit in word */
{
  *word ^= (1 << n);
}
```

C++ Static Members, Constructors, and Destructors

■ Anthony Lander

Learn how to get more out of C++'s key object-oriented features.

In a pure object-oriented language like Smalltalk, the programming environment takes care of allocating new object instances and deleting old ones. In C++, however, this is the programmer's responsibility; it is accomplished with the help of constructor and destructor methods. For the most part, this is looked on as a step in the wrong direction: Letting the system do everything Smalltalk-style virtually eliminates those awful pointer errors. But wait—if we're stuck doing the allocating and deallocating ourselves, perhaps we can somehow make it work in our favor.

For example, suppose you're writing a library book cataloguing system; and suppose further that you often have to report on the number of books stored in the system. The problem is keeping track of how many books are entered and deleted. One way would be to keep a list of all the books in the system, then ask the list how many books it contains. But what if we wanted to know how many science fiction books there were? We'd have to go through the list and count them all! There must be a better way.

Perhaps we could keep an **SFBooks** counter, and increment it each time we enter a new science fiction book. But then the first book's counter would say there was one book in the system, and the 10th book would say there were ten books in the system. What we really need is a way for class **Book** to know how many instances of itself currently exist; and more specifically, how many instances of **SFBooks** exist.

What we really need is some sort of variable that won't get allocated again each time we create a new instance. How about a static class member? Member variables declared as **static** in the class definition belong, in a sense, to the *class*, rather than to any particular object instance. In other words, each instance of **Book** will share the same **SFBooks** counter, and we could ask *any* book how many there were, and it would be able to tell us. That's certainly a step forward, but when do we increment **SFBooks**? How about in the constructor method? Each time we ask for a new SF book, it adds one to the **SFBooks** counter. The destructor method can decrement the counter each time we remove one. A class definition that demonstrates this is in Listing 14.3.

Static class member variables are a really good way to keep track of information pertaining to the whole class rather than individual instances. Constructors and destructors, furthermore, can be an excellent way to update static members as individual instances come and go.

CODE DESCRIPTION

Overview

This short section of C++ code implements a Book class which employs private static members to track the number of instances of the object.

Listings Available

Listing	*Description*	*Used with*
BOOKS.CPP	Contains the class implementation. No example code is provided.	------

How to Compile/Assemble

Can be compiled and linked with any C/C++ compiler.

■ LISTING 14.3 BOOKS.CPP

```
enum   _kindOfBook { SF, Fiction, Poetry };

//----------------------------------
class Book  {
   private:
      static int AllBooks,          // Total number of books
          SFBooks,           // Number of SF books
          FictionBooks,    // Number of Fiction books
          PoetryBooks;    // Number of Poetry books

      enum _kindOfBook Kind;     // what kind of book this is

   public:
      Book(enum _kindOfBook);
      ~Book(void);
      int numberOfBooks(void);
```

```
        int numberOfSFBooks(void);
        int numberOfFictionBooks(void);
        int numberOfPoetryBooks(void);
        int kind(void);     // what kind of book is this?
};

//----Book Kind-----
// Return what kind of book this is

int Book::kind(void)
{
  return Kind;
}

//---Book Constructor
// Build a new book of a particular kind.  Increment the
// appropriate counters

Book::Book(enum _kindOfBook kind)
{
   switch(kind)  {
       case SF:
          SFBooks ++;
          break;
       case Fiction:
          FictionBooks ++;
          break;
       case Poetry:
          PoetryBooks ++;
       default:
          // ERROR
          break;
    }
     Kind = kind;
   AllBooks ++;
}

//----Book Destructor------
//Destroy an instance of book; decrement the appropriate counter

Book::~Book(void)
{
   switch(Kind)  {
       case SF:
          SFBooks –;
          break;
       case Fiction:
          FictionBooks –;
          break;
       case Poetry:
          PoetryBooks –;
          break;
       default:
          // ERROR
          break;
```

```
   }
   AllBooks --;
}

//----Book numberOfBooks-----
// Return the total number of books in the system

int Book::numberOfBooks(void)
{
   return(AllBooks);
}

//----Book numberOfSFBooks------
int Book::numberOfSFBooks(void)
{
   return(SFBooks);
}

//----Book numberOfFictionBooks-----
int Book::numberOfFictionBooks(void)
{
   return(FictionBooks);
}

//----Book numberOfPoetryBooks-------
int Book::numberOfPoetryBooks(void)
{
   return(PoetryBooks);
}
```

Converting Binary Data to C Header Files

■ Michael Milligan

Here's a useful trick for recreating binary files.

While fighting a boot-sector virus that had invaded 200 or so of our PCs, I stumbled on a simple way to fix infected boot-sectors. After saving a clean boot-sector to a normal DOS file, I wrote a program, BINTOH, that converts the binary file into a C header (".H") file. (See Listing 14.4.) The generated header can then be included in another C program. The header file I created with BINTOH was a boot sector for a nonbootable diskette. I included it in a C program to write a clean boot sector—and the virus was history.

Here is a sample of the output created by BINTOH:

```
unsigned char bin_data[] = {
  '\xeb', '\x3c', '\x90', '\x44', '\x72', '\x2e',
  '\x4d', '\x52', '\x4d', '\x2e', '\x2e', '\x00',
  '\x02', '\x08', '\x01', '\x00', '\x02', '\x00',
    ...
  '\x00', '\x00', '\x00', '\x00', '\x00', '\x00',
  '\x55', '\xaa',
  };
```

This technique for creating a C header could be useful as a way of recreating screen images or any other binary files.

BINTOH expects two command line arguments: The first is the name of the binary file, the second is the name of the header file. The header file defines an array of **unsigned char** named **bin_data**. Of course, the header file can be edited to change the array name if necessary.

CODE DESCRIPTION

Overview

An example of translating a binary file into a format usable in a C header file. The program takes two parameters, a source (binary) file and a destination (.h) file.

Listings Available

Listing	*Description*	*Used with*
BINTOH.C	This program will read a file in binary mode and create a C header file containing the binary data.	------

How to Compile/Assemble

Can be compiled and linked with any C/C++ compiler.

■ LISTING 14.4 BINTOH.C

```
/*
  Program:              bin_to_h
  Author:               Dr. Michael Milligan
  Description:     This program will read a file in binary mode
                   and create a C header file containing the
                   binary data.
  To use:

  bin_to_h source dest

  where source is the name of a binary file to be
  converted, dest is the name of the header file created.

*/

#include <stdio.h>

#define LINE_1 "\t unsigned char bin_data[] = {"
#define LINE_LAST "\n\t};\n"
#define BUFSIZE 512
#define CRLF "\r\n"

void fatal( char * );

void main(int argc, char* argv[] )
{
```

```
        FILE *fin, *fout;
        char buf[BUFSIZE], *ch, xch;
        int i, nbytes, col=0;
        long totbytes = 0;

        if (argc != 3) fatal( "bin_to_h source dest\n");

        if ( !(fin  = fopen( argv[1], "rb" ) ) )
                fatal( "Error opening input file.\n") ;
        if ( !(fout = fopen( argv[2], "wb" ) ) )
                fatal( "Error opening output file.\n");

        fprintf( fout, LINE_1 );
        printf("bin_to_h converting...\n");

        while ( nbytes = fread( buf, 1, BUFSIZE, fin ) ) {
          for (i=0; i < nbytes; i++ ) {
               totbytes++;
               if ( !(col++ % 6))
                    fprintf( fout, CRLF "\t\t");
               fprintf( fout, "\'\\x" );
               fprintf( fout, "%02x", (unsigned char) buf[i] );
               fprintf( fout, "\', " );
          }
        }
        fprintf( fout, LINE_LAST );
        fclose( fin );
        fclose( fout );
        printf("\nTotal bytes processed: %ld\n", totbytes);
}

void fatal( char * error)
{
        fprintf( stderr, "%s", error );
        exit( 1 );
}
```

C Macros for Bit Manipulation

■ Alan Weiner

Here's a useful set of macros for manipulating bits.

Earlier in this chapter, Bryan Flamig proposed three functions to handle bit manipulations. Now we'll modify those functions by turning them into macros.

Macros are created with C's **#define** preprocessor keyword and are basically used to replace one text string with another. This is useful when defining constants, such as

```
#define BUFFER_LENGTH 255
```

The C compiler's preprocessor will replace occurrences of **BUFFER_LENGTH** with **255** throughout the file [except for inside comments and text strings delimited by quote marks (")]. The macro replacement string doesn't have to be a simple value, it can also be an expression. Macros with such expressions are called *function macros* because of their resemblance to normal function calls; they even can take arguments. However, as we will see, macros are often much more efficient than functions.

Each function macro contains the **#define** keyword, the name of the macro, an optional argument list, and the macro's definition, as in

```
#define isspace(x)     (x == ' ')
```

This defines a macro named **isspace,** which takes a single argument and calculates a value, the result of the expression (x == ' '). Macros differ from functions in a couple of key areas. The assembly code generated may be quite different, and there may also be "side effects" from the macro.

In a function, the assembly code to perform the function is generated once, and each time the function is called, code is generated that puts the arguments on the stack and calls the function. Macros on the other hand are *expanded* inline by the preprocessor. Each time the macro name appears in the body of the program, it is replaced by the definition's expression, with the arguments in the definition replaced by the arguments following the macro invocation. For example,

```
if (isspace(c)) {
printf("Yes, it is a space\n");
  }
```

is turned into

```
if ((c == ' ')) {
printf("Yes, it is a space\n");
  }
```

by the preprocessor. The macro invocation turns into the expression itself.

```
isspace(x)
{
       return(x == ' ');
}

use_func()
{
char   c;

    if (isspace(c))
       printf("Yes, it is a space");
}
```

■ **FIGURE 14.1a C code to define and use *isspace()* as a function**

```
_isspace proc near
        push    bp
        mov     bp,sp
        cmp     word ptr  [bp+4],32
        jne     @5
        mov     ax,1
        jmp     short @4
@5:     xor     ax,ax
@4:     pop     bp
        ret
_isspace endp
```

■ **FIGURE 14.1b Assembly code for the *isspace()* function**

Take a look at the accompanying figures. Figure 14.1a shows the C code for defining and using **isspace()** as a function. Figure 14.1b shows the assembly code generated for the function itself, and Figure 14.1c shows the assembly code generated for each call to the **isspace()** function. (The actual instructions will differ, depending on the processor—8088 instructions are shown.)

In Figure 14.2a, the C code involved in creating and using the **isspace** macro is used. Because macros are expanded inline, Figure 14.2b shows the assembly language equivalent of both calling and executing the **isspace** macro. In this case, two instructions are generated instead of 16. Quite a savings.

This example is slightly exaggerated, however. Because code for the actual function is generated only once, a second call to the **isspace()** function would result in adding only the seven instructions needed to invoke the function (Figure 14.1c), compared to two again for the macro version. While saving just a few instructions may not make a difference in most programs, if **isspace()** were to be called for every character in a large file, it would quickly add up to a noticeable increase in execution time.

On the other hand, if the macro were complex enough, it is possible that the generated code (as a macro) would end up longer than the code to call it as a function. In this case, although you would lose the tradeoff for size of code, you still might gain in execution time because calling and returning from functions are expensive in machine cycles. Experiment and see.

```
        mov     al,byte ptr [bp-1]
        cbw
        push    ax
        call    _isspace
        pop     cx
        or      ax,ax
        je      @7

        << call to printf() >>
@7:
```

■ **FIGURE 14.1c Assembly code generated to call *isspace()* as a function**

```
#define isspace(x)  (x == ' ')

use_macro()
{
char   c;

    if (isspace(c))
       printf("Yes, it is a space");
}
```

■ **FIGURE 14.2a C code to define and use *isspace* as a macro**

Arguments and Side Effects

Since the macro's definition is expanded as a string substitution, it is common (indeed recommended) to enclose its arguments within parentheses. This will prevent its meaning from being changed unintentionally. Compare

```
#define plusindent(x)    x + indent;
```

with

```
#define plusindent(x)    (x + indent)
```

when used in

```
z = 2 * plusindent(x)
```

This is an admittedly trivial function, but it makes a point. The first macro expands to

```
z = 2 * x + indent
```

while the second becomes

```
z = 2 * (x + indent)
```

Since multiplication is evaluated before addition, the expressions are not equal.

```
       cmp  byte ptr [bp-1],32
       jne  @2

       << call to printf() >>
@2:
```

■ **FIGURE 14.2b Assembly code generated when the *isspace* macro is invoked**

There is another interesting behavior involving *side effects*. Since the arguments are substitutcd as strings, as part of thc compilation proccss, it is possiblc to causc thc macro to expand into an erroneous expression:

```
#define squarearea(s)     (s * s)
a = squarearea(x++);
```

This expands into

```
a = (x++ * x++);
```

The side effect is that x is incremented *twice* when what was intended was

```
c = (x * x);
x++;
```

The point here is: Be careful when defining and invoking macros.

Now, taking a look at the three bit-manipulation functions from "Bit Manipulation," they can be changed into:

```
#define setbit(word, n)         (word |= (1 << n))
#define resetbit(word, n)    (word &= ~(1 << n))
#define togglebit(word, n)      (word ^= (1 << n))
```

Since each argument is used in the definition only once, there's no risk of side effects. Note that "word" no longer is a pointer. This means the call will be **setbit(foo, 7)** instead of **setbit(&foo, 7).** Additionally, using a macro permits the compiler to evaluate some expressions at compile time, saving your program's run time and code space. For example, **setbit(foo,15)** would be preprocessed into **foo |= (1<<15)**, allowing the compiler to precalculate the value **(1 << 15)**. Using macros requires some care, but they can improve the speed and size of compiled code.

TIP: Most C and C++ compilers have an option that tells the compiler to run only the preprocessor on your program. This intermediate code will still be valid C or C++ code, but will have all the header (.H and .HPP) included and all the macros will be evaluated and expanded. This gives you, the programmer, a chance to see how the preprocessor is translating your code.

A Simple Soundex Function in C

■ Nicholas Wilt

Learn how to put the simple but powerful Soundex algorithm to work.

When a spell-checker finds a misspelled word, it can usually help you find the correct spelling by "suggesting" words from its database. How can it decide which words are "similar" to the misspelled one? One way is the Soundex algorithm. The Soundex algorithm translates a character string into a prefix character and a 1–3 digit number. Words that are "similar" are assigned the same Soundex code. The Soundex code may be represented in C as a structure:

```
struct soundex  {
    char prefix;          /* Prefix character */
    unsigned int value;   /* Value */
};
```

Calculating the prefix character is easy: It's the first character in the word. Calculating the number is a little more complicated—you squash repeated letters ("ss" in "mission" gets counted as only one "s," for example) and assign a digit to each squashed letter. Similar-sounding letters such as C and K are assigned the same digit. Once three digits have been computed, the rest of the word is discarded. SOUNDEX.C (Listings 14.5 and 14.6) shows a C function that takes a string argument and stuffs a passback Soundex structure with the corresponding Soundex code. The function returns a nonzero value if it cannot compute the Soundex code.

CODE DESCRIPTION

Overview

An example program which demonstrates the use of the simplified Soundex algorithm described in the article. Syntax for using the program is: soundex <list>. For example,

```
soundex Greg Jon Gregg Jonathan Juan
```

will yield the following output:

```
Greg: G602
Jon: J5
Gregg: G602
Jonathan: J503
Juan: J5
Greg and Gregg sound similar
Jon and Juan sound similar
```

Listings Available

Listing	*Description*	*Used with*
SOUNDEX.H	Header file for use with SOUNDEX.C.	------
SOUNDEX.C	Contains the ret_soundex function and example program to demonstrate it.	------

How to Compile/Assemble

Can be compiled and linked with any C/C++ compiler.

■ LISTING 14.5 SOUNDEX.H

```
/* Header file for soundex package */

struct soundex {
  char prefix;
  unsigned int value;
};

int ret_soundex(struct soundex *sdx, char *s);
```

■ LISTING 14.6 SOUNDEX.C

```
#include <alloc.h>
#include <string.h>
#include <stdlib.h>
#include <stdio.h>
#include <ctype.h>
#include "soundex.h"

struct word {
  struct soundex sdx;
  char *s;
};

int ret_soundex(struct soundex *sdx, char *s)
{
  int numchars = 5;
  char r[8];
  char prev, *sc1, *sc2;
  static char winx[26] = {0, 1, 2, 3, 0, 1, 2, 0, 0, 2, 2, 4, 5,
                  5, 0, 1, 2, 6, 2, 3, 0, 1, 0, 2, 0, 2};

  if (s == NULL || *s == '\0') {          /* Return error if NULL */
    sdx->prefix = 0;
    sdx->value = 0;
    return(-1);
  }

  sdx->prefix = prev = toupper(*s); /* Set prefix */

  /* Set value */
  for (sc1 = s, sc2 = r; *sc1 && numchars--; sc1++)
    if (isalpha((int) *sc1) && (prev != *sc1))
      *sc2++ = winx[toupper((prev = *sc1)) - 'A'] + '0';
  *sc2 = r[4] = '\0';                       /* Terminate string */
  sdx->value = (unsigned) atoi(r);  /* Convert to int */
  return(0);
}

/* Compare routine for call to qsort in main */
int word_compare(const void *a, const void *b)
{
  int cmp;
```

```
  if (cmp = ((struct word *) a)->sdx.prefix - ((struct word *) b)->sdx.prefix)
    return(cmp);
  else
    return( ((struct word *) a)->sdx.value - ((struct word *) b)->sdx.value);
}

void main(int argc, char *argv[])
{
  int i, j;
  int numwords = argc - 1;
  struct word *words = malloc(numwords * sizeof(struct word));

  if (argc < 3) {
    printf("Usage: soundex words\n\t");
    printf("Program will report on similar-sounding words\n");
    exit(0);
  }
  for (i = 0; i < numwords; i++) {
    words[i].s = strdup(argv[i+1]);
    if (ret_soundex(&words[i].sdx, argv[i+1]))
      printf("Ignoring input string %s\n", argv[i+1]);
   printf("%s: %c%d\n", words[i].s, words[i].sdx.prefix, words[i].sdx.value);
  }
  for (i = 0; i < numwords; i++)
    for (j = i+1; j < numwords; j++)
      if ( (i != j) && (! word_compare(words+i, words+j)))
    printf("%s and %s sound similar\n", words[i].s, words[j].s);
}
```

15

Windows Programming

Regardless of what many in the press have been saying, the *real* Windows revolution hasn't happened yet. What we demand of a Windows-like environment can come to full fruition only when a genuine, 32-bit version of Windows comes along, as Microsoft is hinting will happen shortly with Windows NT (New Technology). Millions of older machines will never be able to run Windows acceptably; and for that market, DOS programming will always be the viable course.

But Windows is the future, whether Windows 3.x or its descendants. The current demand for Windows 3.x applications is hungry; the demand for Windows NT applications, finally making full use of our 386/486 machines, will be ravenous. Some people are skipping Windows 3.x entirely, holding that Windows 3.x is an interim product that won't last out the end of the century. (Which, after all, is barely seven years away—less far into the future than the PC AT is into the past . . .) My position is this: Whether or not you expect to release killer products for Windows 3.x, you should become familiar with its API and its underlying assumptions—because if you don't, when the rush to Windows NT begins, those other guys will trample you into the dust.

This chapter is a good mix of Windows items, including Eric Anderson's compact screen-saver application written using C and the SDK. But we're not just doling out buckets of code. The chapter contains some serious advice from Jeff Roberts on making DOS applications coexist peacefully with Windows, and ultimately converting code from DOS to Windows. Finally, David Stafford presents some "forbidden knowledge" in the area of creating a Windows shell that can act as a replacement Program Manager. Not for the faint-hearted, but if you're faint-hearted, well, this industry—not to mention Windows programming—isn't quite what you're looking for.

A Monitor Screen Saver for Windows

■ Eric Anderson

Build a Windows screen saver and learn some clever Windows programming tricks in the process.

Most windowing environments have some means for blanking the screen after some period of inactivity, usually with a wandering icon to indicate that the system is on and functional. This is particularly true of Microsoft Windows where version 3.1 came with several built-in screen savers. This feature presents *Monitor Saver*, a screen blanker for Microsoft Windows 3.x. Aside from being a brief but useful example of Windows SDK programming, Monitor Saver illustrates several uses of the Windows timer function **WM_TIMER()**.

Virtually all of the discussion in this feature centers on MS.C (see Listings 15.1 and 15.2), which contains the source code for the *Monitor Saver* program proper. Several other files are necessary to recompile and relink Monitor Saver, but most cannot be readily printed. All are available (along with the fully compiled and linked .EXE version) in the listings disk with this book. More on this later.

Monitor Saver in Motion

When Monitor Saver is executed it first checks for an existing instance of itself, since we don't want more than one copy to be running. If an existing instance is detected, the program displays a Windows error box informing the user that Monitor Saver is already active. This same message box is used a little later on if the program detects more than 16 active timers (the maximum allowed by Windows 3.0) and allows you to notify the end user of this with a message such as "Too many clocks or timers!" The Windows Clock program uses this same routine to check on the number of timers currently in use.

During instance initialization, to be as unobtrusive to the user as possible, the program is forced to a minimized active state by passing the **SW_SHOWMINNOACTIVE** parameter to the **ShowWindow()** function.

Setting the value of the Monitor Saver time delay is done by polling WIN.INI via a call to **GetProfileInt** for the following line:

```
[Monitor Saver] delay=X
```

Here, **X** equals a value from 1 to 99 minutes. If a "delay" line for Monitor Saver is not found in WIN.INI, the default delay time of 15 minutes (taken from constant **MAXMINUTES**) is used.

Once the correct delay time has been determined, the **WM_TIMER()** function takes control and polls the Windows message queue for the time of the last keyboard or mouse event. Each time a key is pressed or a mouse event occurs, the timer is reset to 0 and must begin counting up again. If and when the default delay time is reached, the screen blanking code in the **TIMER_QSEC** case takes control. To blank the screen, the code creates a window equal to the maximum displayable size and fills it with a black background using the **FillRect()** and **GetStockObject()** functions.

Making the Cursor Wander

A blank screen conserves screen phosphor, but it also looks just like a powered-down machine. To indicate that the system is active without displaying any image in a single place on the screen for any length of time, Monitor Saver makes the cursor wander around the screen. As with blanking the screen, the code to do this is found in the **TIMER_QSEC** case.

Windows allows you to create a custom cursor, and when the screen is blanked, the **SetCursor** function loads a replacement cursor that resembles the program's icon. The **SetTimer()** function starts a 5-second timer, the interval during which the cursor remains at the current cursor position. The **SetCursorPos()** function moves this custom cursor every five seconds to a random location on the screen. This loop will continue until a keyboard or mouse event occurs, at which time the original screen is restored.

A Problem and a Trick

A subtle problem that arose when Monitor Saver was being written was solved by a useful trick. If Monitor Saver were active in a window (rather than minimized as an icon) when timeout and screen blanking occurred, screen restore later occurred correctly. However, if Monitor Saver were minimized as an icon when it blanked the screen, Monitor Saver's icon would not redisplay upon restore. Only the white box and icon title would be there, as though Monitor Saver were in fact active in a window.

The heart of the problem is that Monitor Saver went from minimized to active behind the shield of its own full-screen child window. (The all-black window Monitor Saver uses to blank the screen is a child window.) Keep in mind that when timeout occurs, Monitor Saver becomes the foreground process, even if it was in the background before with another application active in the foreground. When Monitor Saver closes the full-screen black child window and restores the Windows desktop, it is active—but it was minimized when it blanked the screen. Accordingly, when Monitor Saver goes inactive and minimizes itself to an icon again, Windows assumes that Monitor Saver's icon is still there and does not restore the icon when it redraws the desktop.

The trick lies inside the **if(isicon)** statement, in the call to **SetClassWord()** that loads a "new" icon named **Restore**. **Restore** is physically distinct from the original icon pattern named **Ready**, but the two icons are visually identical. However, loading a new icon pattern forces Windows to redisplay the icon, which it does—even though the new icon is visually identical to the old one.

You can use a similar trick if you ever want to change the shape of an icon in response to a Windows event. For example, if a print-spooler is working in the background as an icon, it could use one icon pattern while printing and display a different icon pattern when all print jobs were completed.

Recreating the Utility

As mentioned earlier, in Windows development not all portions of a program can be reprinted as ASCII files. Many of the files listed above are binary files created using resource editors included with the Microsoft Windows SDK. To obtain all portions of

Monitor Saver you must use the listings with the listings diskette. The listings archive also contains the fully compiled .EXE form of Monitor Saver.

Monitor Saver has been tested with Microsoft C versions 5.1 and 6.0. Use the make file MS to build the .EXE file. Recompiling the code requires the Microsoft Windows SDK. Earlier versions of the SDK will not work, and Monitor Saver will not function with versions of Windows earlier than 3.0.

CODE DESCRIPTION

Overview

A complete utility that demonstrates how to build a Windows screen blanking program.

Listings Available

Listing	*Description*	*Used with*
MS.H	Header file for utility.	------
MS.C	Source code for program.	------

How to Compile/Assemble

Can be compiled and linked with any C/C++ Windows compiler. The following files are needed:

MS.H	The Monitor Saver header file (Listing 15.1).
MS.C	The full C source code (Listing 15.2).
MS.DEF	The Windows application definition file.
MS.RC	The Windows resource file.
MS.DLG	The Windows dialog definition file.
MS	The make file to build MS.EXE.
ACTIVE.CUR	The custom cursor pattern.
READY.ICO	The Monitor Saver icon pattern.
READY1.ICO	The alternate icon pattern.

■ LISTING 15.1 MS.H

```
/* ms.h Header file for Monitor Saver */
/* (c) 1990 Moon Valley Software      */
#define SET_TIMER     2
#define E_TEXT        100
#define OK_BUT        1
#define CANCEL        2
#define RESTORE_BUT   1
#define ABOUT         1
```

■ LISTING 15.2 MS.C

```
/**********************************************
     Monitor Saver For Microsoft Windows 3.0
```

```
 (c) Copyright 1990 By Moon Valley Software Inc.
***********************************************/

#include <windows.h>   /* Required for all Windows applications */
#include "ms.h"        /* Specific to this program */
#include <stdlib.h>    /* Needed for random */
#define TIMER_QSEC 1   /* Timer ID for 1/4 sec intervals */
#define TIMER_ICON 2   /* Timer for moving cursor on the screen */
#define T_SEC 250      /* 1/4 second interval timer */
#define MAXMINUTES 15  /* Default delay in minutes */

/******************* Global Variables ******************/

HANDLE hInst;                   /* Current instance */
RECT winrect;                   /* Client area */
WNDCLASS  wc;                   /* Window class */
HCURSOR savcurs,actcurs;        /* Handle to cursor */
HWND hWnd,prevwnd;              /* Handles to windows */
HDC hDC;                        /* Handle to device context */
PAINTSTRUCT pc;                 /* Paint client area */
int x=0,y=0,t_paint=0;          /* Window coordinates to paint */
                                /* Time and icon vars */
int maxmin=MAXMINUTES,minutes,restored=1,qsecs,isicon;
int xScreen, yScreen;           /* x and y window coordinates */
POINT oldpos,curpos;            /* Area of cursor location */
char szAppName[] = "Monitor Saver";

/* Forward Declarations */
long FAR PASCAL MainWndProc(HWND, unsigned, WORD, LONG);
BOOL InitApplication(HANDLE);
BOOL InitInstance(HANDLE, int);
BOOL FAR PASCAL About(HWND, unsigned, WORD, LONG);
BOOL FAR PASCAL Input(HWND, unsigned, WORD, LONG);
DWORD FAR PASCAL KeyHook(int, WORD, LONG);
FARPROC lpKeyHook, lpOldHook;

/***********************************************************
 FUNCTION: WinMain(HANDLE, HANDLE, LPSTR, int)
 PURPOSE: calls initialization function, processes message loop
***********************************************************/

int PASCAL WinMain(hInstance, hPrevInstance, lpCmdLine, nCmdShow)
HANDLE hInstance;          /* Current instance */
HANDLE hPrevInstance;      /* Previous instance */
LPSTR lpCmdLine;           /* Command line */
int nCmdShow;              /* Show window type Full or Iconic */
 {
   MSG msg;   /* Windows message  */
              /* Test for an existing instance */
              /* Only one instance is allowed  */
     if(hPrevInstance) {
       MessageBox(hWnd,"Monitor Saver Is Already Active!",
       szAppName,MB_ICONEXCLAMATION | MB_OK);
       return(FALSE);
     }
```

```
      if (!hPrevInstance)
        if  (!InitApplication(hInstance)) /* Init resources   */
            return (FALSE);           /* Exit if unable to init  */
      /* Perform initializations that apply to specific instance */
        if (!InitInstance(hInstance, nCmdShow))
        return (FALSE);
     while (GetMessage(&msg, NULL, NULL, NULL)) {
            /* Dispatch messages until WM_QUIT is received */
            TranslateMessage(&msg);
            DispatchMessage(&msg);
    }
     return (msg.wParam);  /* Returns value from PostQuitMessage */
}

/****************************************************************
  FUNCTION: InitApplication(HANDLE)
  PURPOSE: Initialize window data and registers window class
****************************************************************/

BOOL InitApplication(hInstance)
HANDLE hInstance;                   /* Current instance */
{
   wc.style = NULL;                 /* Class style(s) */
   wc.lpfnWndProc = MainWndProc;    /* Func to receive msg's */
                                    /*  for this class */
   wc.cbClsExtra = 0;               /* No per-class extra data */
   wc.cbWndExtra = 0;               /* No per-window data */
   wc.hInstance = hInstance;     /* App that owns window class */
   wc.hIcon = LoadIcon(hInstance,"Ready");
   wc.hCursor = NULL;                     /* Cursor to use */
   /* Bkground color */
   wc.hbrBackground = GetStockObject(WHITE_BRUSH);
   wc.lpszMenuName =  "MsMenu";     /* Menu name in rc file */
   wc.lpszClassName = szAppName;    /* Name used in call window */
   /* Register the windows class and return success/failure */
   return (RegisterClass(&wc));
}

/****************************************************************
 FUNCTION:  InitInstance(HANDLE, int)
 PURPOSE:  Saves instance handle and creates main window
****************************************************************/

BOOL InitInstance(hInstance, nCmdShow)
    HANDLE  hInstance;  /* Current instance */
    int     nCmdShow;   /* Param for first ShowWindow() call */
{
   HWND     hWnd;       /* Main win handle */
   hInst = hInstance;
   /* Save the instance handle in a static var */
    xScreen = GetSystemMetrics(SM_CXSCREEN);
   /* Get current sys. info */
   yScreen = GetSystemMetrics(SM_CYSCREEN);
    /* Cursor to use when screen is blank */
    actcurs = LoadCursor(hInstance,"Active");
    hWnd = CreateWindow(  /* Create main win for this instance */
```

```
        szAppName,        /* Registered class */
       "Monitor Saver",     /* Caption Bar Text */
        WS_OVERLAPPED | WS_CAPTION | WS_SYSMENU | WS_MINIMIZEBOX,
        CW_USEDEFAULT,        /* Initial x Pos */
        CW_USEDEFAULT,        /* Initial y Pos */
        165,                  /* Initial x size */
        37,                   /* Initial y size */
        NULL,                 /* Overlapped have no parent win */
        NULL,                 /* Use the window class menu */
        hInstance,            /* This instance owns the window */
        NULL);                /* Pointer not needed */
   if (!hWnd)                 /* If window could not be created */
     return (FALSE);          /* Fail */
                    /* Show window in minimized active state */
    ShowWindow(hWnd,SW_SHOWMINNOACTIVE);
    UpdateWindow(hWnd);  /* Sends WM_PAINT Message to window */
                         /* Only 16 timers total are permitted */
    while(!SetTimer(hWnd,TIMER_QSEC,T_SEC,NULL))
       if(IDCANCEL == MessageBox(hWnd,"Too Many Clocks Or Timers!",
          szAppName,MB_ICONEXCLAMATION | MB_RETRYCANCEL))
    return(FALSE);                 /* Fail */
    lpKeyHook = MakeProcInstance((FARPROC)KeyHook,hInst);
    /* catch all keyboard messages: */
    lpOldHook = SetWindowsHook(WH_KEYBOARD,lpKeyHook);
     return (TRUE); /* Return value from PostQuitMessage */
}

/*****************************************************************
 FUNCTION: MainWndProc(HWND, unsigned, WORD, LONG)
 PURPOSE:  Processes messages
*****************************************************************/

long FAR PASCAL MainWndProc(hWnd, message, wParam, lParam)
HWND hWnd;
unsigned message;
WORD wParam;
LONG lParam;
{
  FARPROC lpProcAbout,lpProcInput;
  DWORD savcol;

  switch (message) {
    case WM_CREATE:
         winrect.right = xScreen;
         winrect.bottom = yScreen;
                            /* Check win.ini for delay time */
         maxmin = GetProfileInt(szAppName,"delay",MAXMINUTES);
         break;
  case WM_COMMAND:
       switch(wParam) {
  case SET_TIMER:
       lpProcInput = MakeProcInstance(Input, hInst);
       DialogBox(hInst,"Input",hWnd,lpProcInput);
       FreeProcInstance(lpProcInput);
       break;
  case ABOUT:
```

```
        lpProcAbout = MakeProcInstance(About, hInst);
        DialogBox(hInst,"About",hWnd,lpProcAbout);
        FreeProcInstance(lpProcAbout);
        break;
        }
        break;
    case WM_KEYDOWN:
    case WM_SYSKEYDOWN:
    case WM_LBUTTONDOWN:
    case WM_RBUTTONDOWN:
        if(!restored) {
          hDC = GetWindowDC(hWnd); /* Get handle to device */
          FillRect(hDC,&winrect,GetStockObject(WHITE_BRUSH));
          ValidateRect(hWnd,NULL);
          ReleaseDC(hWnd,hDC);      /* Release the device context */
          if(isicon) {              /* If window was minimized */
            MoveWindow(hWnd, 0, 0, 165, 37,  1);
            ShowWindow(hWnd,SW_SHOWMINNOACTIVE); /* Minimize it */
            SetClassWord(hWnd,GCW_HICON,LoadIcon(hInst,"Restore"));
            UpdateWindow(hWnd);
         } else {
           MoveWindow(hWnd, 0, 0, 165, 37, 1);
           /* Show window */
           ShowWindow(prevwnd, SW_SHOWMINNOACTIVE);
           UpdateWindow(hWnd);                    /* Update it */
         }
       SetCursor(savcurs);         /* Restore cursor */
       restored = 1;         /* Show the screen as being restored */
       KillTimer(hWnd,TIMER_ICON);/* Re-set movement timer */
       minutes = qsecs = 0;
       SetActiveWindow(prevwnd);  /* Restore previous window */
       ShowWindow(hWnd,SW_HIDE);  /* Return focus to last App */
       /* Redisplay window from hidden: */
       ShowWindow(hWnd,SW_SHOWMINNOACTIVE);
       UpdateWindow(hWnd);         /* Update the window */
   }
   return (DefWindowProc(hWnd, message, wParam, lParam));
  case WM_TIMER:
        switch(wParam) {
  case TIMER_QSEC:
        GetCursorPos(&curpos);
         if(curpos.x == oldpos.x && curpos.y == oldpos.y) {
           qsecs++;    /* If cursor's not moved, add to counter */
         if(qsecs >= 240) {  /* If counter is more then 1 minute */
           minutes++;       /* Add one to minutes counter */
           qsecs = 0;
         }
  if(minutes >= maxmin) {        /* If minutes >= timeout limit? */
    if((curpos.x == oldpos.x && curpos.y == oldpos.y) && restored) {
      if((isicon = IsIconic(hWnd)))    /* Is it an icon? */
          OpenIcon(hWnd);              /* Restore icon */
          /* Make this window active */
          prevwnd = SetActiveWindow(hWnd);
          /* Make screen blanker win*/
          MoveWindow(hWnd,0,0,9900,9900,1);
          hDC = GetWindowDC(hWnd);       /* Get device context */
```

```
                    /* Fill the entire window with black */
          FillRect(hDC,&winrect,GetStockObject(BLACK_BRUSH));
          ValidateRect(hWnd,NULL);
          ReleaseDC(hWnd,hDC);
          savcurs = SetCursor(actcurs); /* Change cursor */
          restored = 0;   /* Display the screen as being blanked */
          /* Start 5 sec cursor timer: */
          SetTimer(hWnd,TIMER_ICON,5000,NULL);
          oldpos.x = curpos.x = x = 20 +
                     (rand() % (winrect.right - 64));
          oldpos.y = curpos.y = y = 50 +
                     (rand() % (winrect.bottom - 96));
          SetCursor(actcurs);  /* Change cursor to screen saver */
          SetCursorPos(x,y);       /* Draw cursor on screen */
          minutes = qsecs = 0;
          }
       }
   } else {
     if(!restored)
        SendMessage(hWnd,WM_RBUTTONDOWN,0,(DWORD)0);
        oldpos.x = curpos.x;
        oldpos.y = curpos.y;
        qsecs = minutes = 0;
        }
        break;
   case TIMER_ICON: /* Timer to place cursor at random locations */
        if(!IsIconic(hWnd)) {  /* If not minimized ... */
         oldpos.x = curpos.x = x = 20 +
                    (rand() % (winrect.right - 64));
         oldpos.y = curpos.y = y = 50 +
                    (rand() % (winrect.bottom - 96));
          SetCursor(actcurs); /* Change cursor to screen saver */
          SetCursorPos(x,y);  /* Draw cursor on screen */
        }
      break;
    }
   break;
   case WM_DESTROY:
        KillTimer(hWnd,TIMER_QSEC);
        /* Be SURE to unhook keyboard or Windows will CRASH with */
        /* next keystroke! */
        UnhookWindowsHook(WH_KEYBOARD,lpKeyHook);
        PostQuitMessage(0);
        break;
        default:
        return (DefWindowProc(hWnd, message, wParam, lParam));
     }
    return (0L);
}

/*****************
 The "About Box"
*****************/

BOOL FAR PASCAL About(hDlg, message, wParam, lParam)
HWND hDlg;
```

```
unsigned message;
WORD wParam;
LONG lParam;
{
int i;

switch (message) {
  case WM_INITDIALOG:
       return (TRUE);
  case WM_COMMAND:
       if (wParam == OK_BUT) {
           EndDialog(hDlg, TRUE);
           return (TRUE);
           }
           break;
      }
           return (FALSE);
}

/*********************************************
  Get Input From User To Adjust Delay Time.
*********************************************/

BOOL FAR PASCAL Input(hDlg, message, wParam, lParam)
HWND hDlg;
unsigned message;
WORD wParam;
LONG lParam;
{
int i;

switch (message) {
  case WM_INITDIALOG:
       SetFocus(hDlg);
       /* Place delay time minute field: */
       SetDlgItemInt(hDlg,E_TEXT,maxmin,0);
       return (TRUE);
 case WM_COMMAND:
      if (wParam == OK_BUT
          || wParam == CANCEL) {
      if(wParam == OK_BUT) {
         /* Get new delay value: */
         maxmin = GetDlgItemInt(hDlg,E_TEXT,&i,0);
         maxmin = (maxmin > 0)? maxmin : 1;
         }
         EndDialog(hDlg, TRUE);
         return (TRUE);
         }
       break;
     }
      return (FALSE);
}

/*************************************************************
FUNCTION: KeyHook
```

```
PURPOSE:  Captures keyboard messages to ensure screen will not
          blank prematurely.
*************************************************************/

DWORD FAR PASCAL KeyHook(iCode,wParam,lParam)
int iCode;
WORD wParam;
LONG lParam;
{
   if(iCode == HC_ACTION)
      /* If this is negative reset counter to zero: */
      if(HIWORD(lParam) & 0x8000)
         qsecs = minutes = 0;      /* Reset counters to 0 */
   /* Make sure to return this value! */
   return DefHookProc(iCode,wParam,lParam, &lpOldHook);
}
```

Ten Steps to Windows Coexistence

■ Jeff Roberts

Take your DOS text-mode applications halfway to Windows.

Microsoft Windows is complex—it mandates a whole new way of thinking. It requires a huge expense in time and training before you can even begin coding. Your existing DOS code probably will need major overhauls. You must purchase an entirely new set of development tools, which are quirky at best. The debuggers are horrible and the text editors are limited. You are not, in fact, in Kansas anymore.

"So why should I care about Windows at all?" you might ask. Well, you've heard only the bad news—the good news is that from a user's perspective, Windows is wonderful. It is beautiful to look at, and generally a pleasure to use. It simplifies resource management (with its font, printer, and device managers) and comes with a number of useful and even entertaining applications. But the most important reason to start looking at Windows is simply economic—users are buying it by the truckload, and there are still relatively few good Windows applications available.

But what if you work for a small company that can't afford to invest in Windows? Are you stuck with DOS and only DOS forever?

In a word, no. This article is in fact for you. We will cover the tricks necessary to make your normal DOS applications "Windows aware," that is, to make standard DOS applications that contain specific Windows support code. These tips won't replace Windows-specific applications (they aren't meant to). Rather, they provide a temporary solution to the "Windows learning curve" blues.

Supporting Windows with the Multiplex Interrupt

Windows provides DOS programs with an application program interface (API) through the multiplex interrupt. The multiplex interrupt, interrupt 02FH, is used by many programs to communicate with TSRs, device drivers, and other software with APIs. Multiple programs share the multiplex interrupt by identifying their calls with an ID number passed in the AH register. Windows itself uses the 016H ID number for its communication interface. WINOLDAP, the Windows extension that provides clipboard support to DOS applications, uses the 017H ID number.

TIP: For more information on the DOS multiplex interrupt, see Communicating with Your TSRs in Chapter 16.

The Windows API defines two types of messages: call-outs and call-ins. Call-outs are messages coming *out* from Windows. For example, when Windows is loading it broadcasts an INT 2FH/AX=01605H call. To receive these broadcasts, you must install an interrupt 02FH filter and watch AX for the values you are interested in. All call-out messages must be continued down the interrupt 02FH chain to ensure that all TSRs and device drivers act accordingly.

Call-ins are messages *in* to Windows from your code. Call-in messages are called just like the DOS interrupt 21H functions—just load up the registers and call interrupt 02FH. All useful call-out and call-in messages are described in the tips below.

Enhanced Mode Only!

As you have no doubt heard, Windows 3.x has three operating modes: Real, Standard, and Enhanced. It would have been nice to have use of the API in all three modes, but Microsoft has endowed only enhanced mode with the necessary hooks. DOS programs running under real and standard modes are limited to DOS services only. This isn't as big a problem as you might think—Windows is pokey enough on 286 machines to limit its widespread use. Rest assured that most Windows users will be using 80386-based (or better) machines running in enhanced mode. So, unless otherwise stated, these tips reflect Windows enhanced mode services only.

Where This Info Came From

Most of this information has been distilled from the Microsoft Windows Version 3.0 Device Driver Kit documentation. Although informative, there are only about 20 pages of interest to DOS programmers, so I really wouldn't recommend its purchase. The clipboard functions were described in the Windows 386 version 2.XX technical manuals, and are not described in any version 3.0 documentation that I've read. I have tested each of these currently unadvertised clipboard services with version 3.0, and all work as I have described them here.

Now, with all of that in mind, let me present ten tips to achieve "Windows awareness" in your DOS applications.

STEP 1: Have your application detect when it's running under Windows

Before using most of the API services, you must check to be sure an enhanced Windows API is running. This is accomplished by placing 01600H in AX and calling interrupt 02FH.

■ **TABLE 15.1 Identifying running version of Windows**

AL	Signifies
000h	An enhanced Windows API is NOT running
080h	An enhanced Windows API is NOT running
001h	Windows/386 version 2.XX is running
0FFh	Windows/386 version 2.XX is running
Else	AL = Major version number, AH = Minor version number

The return value indicates whether or not Windows is running in enhanced mode, and which version of Windows (if any) is in control. Possible return values are summarized in Table 15.1.

STEP 2: Release the current time slice for maximum performance

When running under the Windows multitasker, each DOS session is executed, one by one, for a brief period of time. By switching through these sessions very quickly, Windows gives the illusion that all of the applications are running concurrently. Each session's piece of time is called a time slice. The more applications executing, the shorter the time slices, and the slower Windows will appear.

There is a simple way to improve the performance of Windows multitasking. Since Windows can't tell what your code is doing, it distributes these time slices equally—even if one session is crunching hard, say, displaying the current federal budget deficit, and the other is simply waiting for a keystroke. Each session normally gets the same amount of processing time. However, if we were to modify the second program to tell Windows, in effect, "Hey, I'm not doing anything important, check with me again next slice," then Windows would favor the busier process and everything would get done faster—a lot faster.

This idleness notification is known as releasing your time slice. A program should release its time slice whenever it must wait for something: a keystroke, a slow printer, a hardware response, and so on. The general algorithm for releasing idle time is shown in Figure 15.1.

Algorithm:

```
WHILE (Idle)

    DO ReleaseTimeSlice;
Act on Non-Idleness;
```

Example:

```
while (!kbhit())
    ReleaseTimeSlice();
key = getch();
```

■ **FIGURE 15.1 Releasing time**

When implementing such an algorithm, you might want to add a flag to control the releasing of your idle time slice. You could then use this flag to prevent extra switching if you need optimum performance.

Interestingly, you can speed up your DOS session without hurting the others by increasing your background priority, as set in your PIF file. By releasing your slice when idle, you don't slow down the other sessions; by raising your background priority, you get maximum speed when you aren't idle.

The optimal priority boost is system dependent, but you can find a comfortable medium with a little testing: Load a benchmark program (I use Chips and Technology's MIPS program with an endless-loop batch file) in one session, and load your application in another. Now systematically change the background priority until you narrow in on the best setting.

Note: Implementing this call-in will improve more than just your enhanced Windows performance. OS/2 version 2.0 will support this service call, and other third-party multitaskers will surely follow.

To release the current time slice, simply load AX with 01680H and call interrupt 02FH. Worth the five bytes, eh?

STEP 3: Prevent task switches for critical code sections

The Windows 3.0 API supports two call-in services to mark the beginning and end of a critical section of code. Once you have called the Begin Critical Section call-in, no other task will be allowed to intervene until the End Critical Section call-in is processed. Critical pieces of code are fairly rare, and you should avoid using these functions whenever possible. However, when the need is there, so are these services.

Load AX with 01681H and call interrupt 02FH to begin a critical section. End the critical code section by loading 01682H into AX and again calling interrupt 02FH.

STEP 4: Use extended memory safely

Using extended memory is frightening enough in DOS, but under a Windows DOS session, the potential for spectacular crashes rises dramatically.

Extended memory should not be manipulated without using a memory manager (XMS, DPMI, or VCPI). Handling extended memory yourself, through BIOS calls, or with 32-bit registers (i.e., DS:ESI) is a sure way to spend long hours in the Technical Support Department. Stick to the exact descriptions for the memory management functions, don't assume anything, and debug thoroughly. The Windows Virtual Device Drivers create very complex memory structures and simulate much of what you interface to; one small overwrite will bring the entire system crumbling down.

The XMS (Extended Memory Specification) documentation can be found in the MSOPSYS CompuServe forum in a file called XMS.ARC. The DPMI (Dos Protected Mode Interface) documentation is available from Intel Technical Documents at 800-548-4725. The VCPI (Virtual Control Program Interface) documentation is available from Phar Lap Software at 617-661-1510.

STEP 5: Support the Windows clipboard

The clipboard is a common memory area where Windows applications can trade data. Information that is placed in the clipboard is "copied." Information retrieved from the clipboard is "pasted." Clipboard information exchange has long been one of Windows' nicest features, and now your DOS applications can support it too!

The DOS clipboard interface is managed by a program called WINOLDAP. WINOLDAP is automatically loaded into each created DOS session. By calling the appropriate WINOLDAP service, you can fully support the clipboard. So, logically, before any of these clipboard functions can be used, you must ensure that WINOLDAP is, in fact, resident.

To get WINOLDAP's version (and thereby check for residency), place 01700H into AX and call interrupt 02FH. If WINOLDAP is not loaded, 01700H will be returned in AX; otherwise, the major version number is placed in AL, and the minor version number in AH. You must check this function before calling any other of the clipboard services.

Three basic operations can be performed on the clipboard: read from it, write to it, and clear it. Accessing the clipboard is much like accessing a file: First you open the clipboard, then you operate (read, write, or empty) on it, and finally you close it.

The clipboard supports six different internal data formats, but most DOS applications usually only need to support the text format. The formats and their corresponding format numbers are

1: Text
2: BitMap
3: MetaPictFile
4: SYLK
5: DIF
6: TIFF

The SYLK and DIF formats contain spreadsheet data. Their format is described in the book, *File Formats for Popular PC Software,* by Jeff Walden, published by John Wiley & Sons. The TIFF (Tagged Image File Format) documentation is available on the Microsoft CompuServe forums. The BitMap and MetaPictFile data can be referenced using the structures presented in STRUCT.ASM (Listing 15.3).

By opening the clipboard, you prevent its contents from being changed while you are using it. To open the clipboard, place 01701H in AX and call interrupt 02FH. If AX equals zero on return, the clipboard is already open and you'll have to wait. Otherwise, the clipboard has been successfully opened and is ready for access.

Before you can read the clipboard data, you must first create a receive buffer big enough to hold it all. To determine the size of the necessary buffer, load 01704H into AX, the number of the format that you want to receive in DX, and then call interrupt 02FH. On return, DX:AX contains the size of the necessary receive buffer. If DX:AX is 0, there is no data of this format on the clipboard. For example, if you want the size of any text on the clipboard, load AX with 01704H, DX with 01H, and call interrupt 2FH.

Once you know the size of clipboard data, create a buffer the same size or larger. You can't get just a piece of the clipboard—it's all or nothing, and if your buffer isn't big enough, you're going to have one tough-to-find overwrite bug! After you have created the buffer, load 01705H into AX, the format number into DX, point ES:BX at your new buffer, and call interrupt 02FH. If an error occurs, AX will be set to zero on return; otherwise your buffer will be filled with clipboard data, ready for action! To recap, the exact steps to read clipboard data are these:

1. Open the clipboard.
2. Get the clipboard data size.
3. Create a large enough local buffer.
4. Call the read clipboard function to receive the data.
5. Close the clipboard.

Writing to the clipboard is even easier than reading it. To write a buffer of data to the clipboard, load 01703H in AX, set DX to the desired format number (1 through 6, as described above), point ES:BX to your buffer, set SI:CX to the length of this buffer, and call interrupt 02FH. If unsuccessful, AX will be zero on return; otherwise (when AX is nonzero) the data has been successfully written to the clipboard.

The final clipboard function is used to empty the clipboard. Emptying the clipboard is seldom necessary. The only normal use of this function is to free up memory in extremely tight RAM situations. But regardless of your motivation, to clear all clipboard data, load 01702H into AX, and execute interrupt 02FH. If successful, AX will be nonzero on return.

To close the clipboard, place 01708H in AX and call interrupt 02FH. If successful, AX will be nonzero on return. Keep the clipboard open for as little time as necessary: open, process, and then close. Don't, for example, open the clipboard when your program initializes, and close it only when the program exits.

STEP 6: Supply "ready-to-run" PIF files

PIF files are information files that allow Windows to execute DOS applications more efficiently. Don't leave this step to your user. You know your application better than anyone—you should create its PIF file.

Set your program to windowed display usage and background execution. These two options allow DOS applications to further emulate their native Windows counterparts. In the Advanced windows of the PIF editor, set the priority options to your tested values (see Step 3), and uncheck "Detect Idle Time." Since we will be informing Windows of all the idle moments (as described in Step 2), unchecking this option will speed up the multitasking slightly.

If, in standard DOS, your application uses a hot key to be activated, you will probably want to specify the same key at the "Application Shortcut Key" prompt. See Step 10 for further information on this setting.

STEP 7: Supply a custom icon

One of the most popular new features of Windows is its gorgeous display—keep it that way. Don't force your user to choose an ugly, standard icon. Supply product icons that stand out and are easily recognized. The idea here is to make the user want to click on your icon. Be sure to include two icons for your applications: one for color and one for monochrome displays.

There are several well-written shareware packages in the CompuServe MSWIN forum for icon creation. This is a fun step—don't deprive yourself!

STEP 8: Support Windows' Initialization and Exit in TSRs

In both enhanced and standard modes, Windows sends call-out messages as it loads and exits. TSRs and device drivers can watch for these call-outs and take special steps. Common actions that can be performed include disabling a known incompatible TSR, returning to real from V86 mode (like QEMM does), or return extra memory to the system (like SMARTDRV does).

When Windows loads, an interrupt 02FH is broadcast with 01605H in AX; zeros in ES, BX, DS, SI, and CX; the major Windows version in the upper byte of DI; and the minor version in the lower byte. Bit zero of DX signifies whether enhanced or standard mode is loading: 1 means standard, 0 means enhanced. On return, you will generally preserve all registers. In special circumstances, however, you can change some of these registers to enable unusual options.

For example, by setting CX to a nonzero value before chaining on, you force Windows to abort its loading. This feature can be used to limit the use of Windows while your TSR is loaded (this is useful when your TSR and Windows are utterly incompatible). Both the standard and enhanced Windows modes support this abort code.

In enhanced mode, there are several other special loading options, only a few of which are useful to DOS programmers. One option of possible use is a method of instructing Windows to load specified Windows device drivers. This feature saves the trouble of changing the SYSTEM.INI options. A network, for example, could use this feature to load special Windows support drivers when necessary. If this sort of device driver loading is of interest, then you should probably pick up the Microsoft Device Driver Kit. Pages D6 through D7 of the Virtual Device Adaptation Guide describe this complicated process.

A second handy feature of the enhanced Windows loader lies in the ability to create instance data. Due to both its complexity and utility, instance data is fully described in the next tip.

In both standard and enhanced modes, Windows broadcasts another call-out message as it exits. TSRs can then undo the changes they made when they received the Loading call-out (reallocate their memory, reenable their hot key, and so on). When Windows exits, interrupt 02FH is called with 01606H in AX. The zero bit of the DX register specifies whether Windows is exiting in enhanced or standard modes: 1 means standard mode, and 0 means enhanced mode.

Generally, you will not use any of the unusual features of these services. You will simply watch for the call-out, and execute any necessary tasks at that time.

STEP 9: Instantiate private TSR/device driver memory when appropriate

Normally, Windows "globalizes" all conventional memory owned by device drivers and TSRs. That is, each DOS session contains the same pieces of the physical TSR and device driver memory as all of the others. Usually, this system works well. You wouldn't want separate disk caches for every DOS session, would you?

There are, however, situations where separate copies of the TSR should be created for each DOS session. For example, without taking special steps, the same physical image of a command line recall utility that is loaded prior to Windows will appear in every DOS session. Entering a command in one of the DOS sessions will cause the command to appear in the recall list of all the other DOS sessions. Fortunately, Windows provides a way to privatize (or "instantiate") blocks of memory. When the Windows-Initialization call-out is received in an interrupt 02FH filter, changing the ES:BX vector to point to the **StartInfo** structure shown in STARTINF.ASM (Listing 15.4) allows any number of memory blocks to be instantiated.

The **siVersion** field contains the version of Windows that this structure is meant for—in this case, version 3.0. Before ES:BX is changed, you must place it in the **siNextsi** field. This allows multiple TSRs to instantiate their own private memory. The next two fields, **siDevice** and **siDeviceData**, are only used when Windows device drivers are loaded. Set them to zero when you are instantiating private data. Finally, the variable **siFirstInstance** must point to a list that defines the data areas to be instantiated. Each item in the list has the following structure:

```
struct InstanceItem
 InstanceAddr  dd ?
 InstanceSize  dw ?
ends
```

Any number of these **InstanceItem** structures can be contained in the list. The end of the list is marked by a zero in the **InstanceAddr** variable. For example, to instantiate 512 bytes of data at address 1234:7890h, set the **siFirstInstance** variable to point to the following data:

```
1234h:7890h ; The first InstanceAddr
0200h   '; The first InstanceSize
0000h:0000h ; Marks the end of the List
```

So, in the command line recall utility example, one could set the **InstanceAddr** variable to the address of the data segment and the **InstanceSize** variable to its length. Then, when Windows creates a new DOS session, it will allocate a new piece of resident data memory for the command recaller in each session.

To recap, the exact steps to instantiate private data are

1. Watch for the Windows-Initialization call-out in an interrupt 02FH filter (AX=01605h).
2. Once the call-out is received, create a **StartInfo** structure.
3. Set the **siNextsi** field to ES:BX.

4. Set ES:BX to the address of your StartInfo structure.
5. Set the **siFirstInstance** variable to the address of a list of **InstanceItem** structures.
6. Be sure to mark the end of the **InstanceItem** list with a zero in the **InstanceAddr** field.
7. Chain to the old interrupt 02Fh vector.

Instantiating private data is a complex task; it is suited primarily to assembly language applications (where you can very specifically set up your data areas to support instantiation). If a high-level language TSR must be private to each session, you should probably instantiate the program's entire occupied memory—the code space, the heap space, everything—which is not an especially efficient use of system memory. However, if your resident software must remain distinct for each DOS session, then you really have no other choice.

STEP 10: Support a nonresident mode in TSRs

When writing DOS mode pop-up TSR applications, it is a good idea to create a nonresident mode. Since most pop-up programs are essentially useless in a graphics mode, and swapping pop-up programs are, by their very nature, incompatible with Windows; offering a nonresident running mode allows your customers to continue using your programs, even in Windows.

With a command line option to load in a non-TSR mode, it is then a simple matter to create a PIF file that provides your users with basic Windows support. For your 386 users, you should specify the application short-cut key (set in the Advanced window of the PIF editor) to the same hot key that your TSR normally uses. This way, your users can access your application with the same hot key inside, or outside, Windows.

When you want to get really fancy, program your TSR to monitor Windows for loading and exiting, as explained in Tip 7. As Windows loads, release any resources that your TSR won't need (XMS or EMS memory, for example); disable hot key activation of your TSR (to prevent crashing in 386 mode); and, to really raise some eyebrows, open the WIN.INI file and add your PIF filename to the "LOAD=" command line. This last step causes Windows to load your application into memory, ready to be switched to with the press of the Windows short-cut key—your pop-up program can now be activated in DOS or Windows—all automatically!

Finally, on exit, restore any changes made in the WIN.INI file, reclaim your memory, and reactivate your TSR's hot key—your TSR will again work with straight DOS.

Make Your Applications Windows Aware!

The tips I've described here will allow most DOS-based programs to function nearly as well as simple Windows-specific applications. "Cheap and cheerful" is the key phrase here; most basic Windows features can be added with minimal coding.

Remember, these tips are not meant as an excuse for not learning real Windows programming. Windows-specific applications have possibilities that dwarf those outlined here. Start learning Windows programming—it's new and challenging.

TIP: For more information from this author on actually porting your DOS applications to Windows, see "Thirteen Tips for Windows Conversions" later in this chapter.

CODE DESCRIPTION

Overview

A complete utility which demonstrates how to build a Windows screen blanking program.

Listings Available

Listing	*Description*	*Used with*
STRUCT.ASM	Structures that can be used to access BitMap and MetaPictFile data.	------
STARTINF.ASM	Sample code that shows how to instantiate blocks of memory.	------

How to Compile/Assemble

Can be used with Microsoft or Borland assembler.

■ LISTING 15.3 STRUCT.ASM

```
; BitMap Structure
;
struct          bmap
bmType          dw    ?          ; Set to Zero
bmWidth         dw    ?          ; Width of bitmap (in pixels)
bmHeight        dw    ?          ; Height of bitmap in raster lines
bmWidthBytes    dw    ?          ; Bytes per raster line
bmPlanes        db    ?          ; # of color planes in bitmap
bmBitsPixel     db    ?          ; # of adjacent color bits in each pixel
bmBits          dq    ?          ; Ptr to the BitMapData variable's addr.
bmWidDim        dw    ?          ; Width of bitmap in 0.1 mm
bmHigDim        dw    ?          ; Height of bitmap in 0.1 mm
BitMapData      db    dup(?)     ; The bitmap data itself
ends

; MetaPictFile Structure
;
struct          MetaPFile
mfMM            dw    ?          ; Mapping mode
mfxExt          dw    ?          ; X Extent
mfyExt          dw    ?          ; Y Extent
mfData          db    dup(?)     ; The metafile itself
ends
```

■ LISTING 15.4 STARTINF.ASM

```
Struct          StartInfo
siVersion            db    3,0   ; Target Windows Version
siNextsi             dd    ?     ; Next StartInfo Address
siDevice             dd    0     ; Device Driver ASCIIZ string address
                                 ; (0=No driver)
siDeviceData         dd    0     ; Reference data address
siFirstInstance      dd    ?     ; Pointer to InstanceItem list
ends
```

Calling DOS Device Drivers from Windows

■ Nicholas Wilt

Here's a workaround for calling DOS device drivers.

If you're calling a DOS-resident device driver from Microsoft Windows, you may be in for more than you bargained for. It took me two solid weeks to track down a problem that can arise when a Windows application running in protected mode calls a DOS device driver.

In theory, DOS device drivers are available to Windows programs; the Windows program calls the device driver exactly as would a DOS program. The only difference is that when the Windows program sets DS:DX to point to the device driver's parameter structure, DS:DX contains a protected mode pointer. Since device drivers are always serviced in real mode, Windows has to catch the DOS call and translate DS:DX to a real-mode pointer (and possibly moving the parameter structure to memory accessible in real mode) before the device driver begins execution.

This mechanism breaks down if the device driver takes pointers inside its parameter structure. Windows only translates the pointer *to* the parameter structure—it doesn't do anything with the pointers *inside* the parameter structure. So if you pass a pointer inside the actual parameter structure from a Windows application to a device driver, the device driver gets a protected mode (read "garbage") pointer even though it is running in real mode.

The workaround is to use **GlobalDosAlloc**, a function in the Windows SDK. **GlobalDosAlloc** allocates memory that is accessible from both real and protected modes. Its **LONGWORD** return value contains two segments. Given these segments, you must then construct your own far pointers with zero offsets. One segment is a protected mode segment; use it to access the data from your Windows application. The other is a real mode segment; place this segment in the device driver's parameter structure.

Actually, the final solution to the problem is in the hands of device driver developers. If you write installable DOS device drivers, avoid having them take pointers inside their parameter structures. This scheme breaks down when you mix real and protected modes—so have mercy on those of us who must use your products!

Windows Cardfile Format

■ Wayne Yacco

Process Windows Cardfile data files in your own applications.

If you're using Microsoft Windows, the Cardfile accessory is a handy extra that costs you nothing. It's basically a free-form text database that's included with the environment's accessories. Besides its convenience, Cardfile is a fairly quick tool for storing short texts under a sorted index. The program graphically represents a standard 3x5 index card, and each card holds just about as much data (440 characters). It is also possible to place images from the Windows clipboard directly onto a card. There are plenty of applications, such as telephone and address lists, to which it is well suited.

Of course, there are limitations. Output is restricted to printing an image of each card. Windows will print it to a file, but there's no easy way to get a comma-delimited file that can be imported into other databases or mail merged. There's also no easy way to import data from another database or to extract data based on search criteria.

However, the Cardfile has a simple file structure that makes it easy if you want to program these functions yourself. In addition, Cardfile's format can be used to restore damaged files if they become corrupted by broken glass. (Well, what do you expect when Windows crashes?)

File Structure

Windows uses a partially inverted list for the Cardfile database. Information on each card's index line serves as the inverted key. This is stored as a sorted list of fixed-length index records at the head of the file. The balance of each card is stored as a variable-length record in an area that follows the last index. Figure 15.2 shows this layout.

Cardfile's three-byte ID is hex 4D 47 43 (ASCII MGC). The two-byte record count follows with bytes in low-byte, high-byte order. Each index record has a fixed 52-byte length which, if multiplied by the record count, gives the displacement (from the fifth byte of the file) to the end of the last index record.

Each index record starts with six bytes of hex zeros, which are apparently reserved. The reserved area is followed by a four-byte hex displacement from the first byte of the file to an associated record containing the text-and-graphics data. A lone byte of zeros precedes the index field. It appeared to have no function until I contacted Qili Zhang, developer of Prisma Software Group's YourWay, a Windows utility that includes a Cardfile-like database. According to Zhang, "Cardfile uses this byte as a flag to indicate changed records in memory." The index field is 40 bytes long. Index data is terminated by a byte of hex zeros if they are less than this fixed length. (The balance of the index field may contain garbage and, oddly enough, Cardfile has a data-dependent glitch that can prevent entry of the full 40 characters.) The index field is followed by a single byte of zeros that terminates the index record.

Data records have four fields: two bytes of hex graphic-field length, two bytes of hex text-field length, a variable-length graphic-data field, and a variable-length character-data field. Either, or both, data fields may be omitted if a zero length is specified in the appropriate field length field.

INDEX AREA

ID1 (3)	RECORD COUNT 1 (2)	RESERVED1 (6)	DISPLACEMENT1 (4)	FLAG1 (1)	INDEX1 (40)	STOP1 (1)
ID2	RC2	R2	D2	F2	I2	S2
ID3	RC3	R3	D3	F3	I3	S3
⋮						

DATA AREA

GRAPHIC COUNT1 (2)	TEXT COUNT1 (2)	GRAPHIC DATA1 (VARIABLE)	TEXT DATA1 (VARIABLE)
GC2	TC2	GD2	TD2
GC3	TC3	GD3	TD3
⋮			

■ **FIGURE 15.2 The Windows Cardfile Format**

Troubleshooting Your Windows App

■ George Shepherd

Learn the insider tips for writing reliable Windows programs.

Windows development consists of a labyrinth of poorly documented details that must be traversed just to show a window on the screen! For every reason that your program will work, there are several reasons why it won't work. And while the official documentation provided by Microsoft is certainly extensive, it's voluminous and unforgiving in its lack of organization. There is plenty of discussion regarding all of the functions and messages necessary to create your windows programs, but nowhere does it guide you through the details and nuances, many of which, if improperly applied, will cause your program to fail.

So, where do you turn when something goes wrong? What can you do when your window doesn't show, your combobox won't drop down, or your dialog box doesn't work? These are perplexing questions forced by all programmers who develop Windows applications with C, especially when starting out. Here are a few of these problems along with their solutions.

You just finished typing in your program. When you run it, the window doesn't show, or it doesn't look like you thought it would!

1. Is your window class properly registered? Every window in your application is inherited from a window class, which must have been previously registered with Windows. If Windows can't match the class of the window you're trying to create with a window class that has already been registered, the window won't be created.
2. Did you give your window an appropriate style during the call to **CreateWindow()**? Windows provides so much control during the creation of a window that sometimes it gets confusing. Using a style of **WS_OVERLAPPEDWINDOW** will bring up a plain vanilla window that is fine to use for your main window. Some styles simply will not work for your main window—**WS_CHILD** and **WS_POPUP** styles both require parent windows. Other styles work, but need tampering to get them to look right. Use a window style that is appropriate for the context.
3. Did you call **ShowWindow()** after you created the window? Simply creating a window will not get it displayed. To expose your window, you must either apply the **WS_VISIBLE** style when you call **CreateWindow()** or call **ShowWindow()** after you create it.
4. When you called **CreateWindow()**, did you give it reasonable size and position coordinates? If you use **CS_USEDEFAULT** as the size and position coordinates, Windows will automatically size your windows appropriately.

TIP: See VANILLA.C (Listing 15.5) for an example of creating a plain vanilla window.

You've made some attractive resources, but the application can't seem to find them.

1. Are you using the correct instance to locate your resource? Resources are objects like menus, icons, string tables, and bit maps that are used by your Windows application during its runtime. They are compiled into a . RES file and tacked onto the end of your program or DLL. These resources are accessed by resource management functions like **LoadResource()**, **LoadMenu()**, and **LoadIcon()** that require a "HANDLE to the instance containing the resources." If your resources aren't showing up, it's very possible that the wrong instance is being used. This confusion usually crops up when you want to grab a resource that is not bound to your program, as is the case when you are using a DLL containing resources. Remember, resources are accessed through module (program and library) instances. If you want to use the resources that you worked so hard to create, Windows needs to know where to find them.
2. Is the template name in the resource file the same as the argument you passed to the Resource Management function? Make sure both names match up.
3. Is the resource you are trying to access actually included in the program's resources? Be sure that your resource description is included in your resource file and that your resource file was completely compiled.

You can't get your dialog box to pop up.

1. A dialog box is just another resource. First check the problems common to all resources listed above.

2. Does your dialog box template use the attribute **WS_VISIBLE**? A dialog box will not appear automatically unless the **WS_VISIBLE** flag is used in the resource template. If the **WS_VISIBLE** flag is not used, then **ShowWindow()** must be used to display the window.

When you run your application, you get an Unrecoverable Application Error.
(Ahh . . . the ubiquitous UAE! A quick examination under Codeview or Turbo Debugger will probably reveal one of the following culprits causing this problem.)

1. Are you using an uninitialized pointer? Check to make sure your pointers are pointing to something.
   (a) If you have allocated memory using **GlobalAlloc()** or **LocalAlloc()**, did you get a valid handle back? The locking functions cannot return a valid pointer unless they are sent a valid handle.
   (b) Once you allocated memory using **GlobalAlloc()** or **LocalAlloc()**, did you lock the handle to get a valid pointer?
   (c) Is your global memory **DISCARDABLE**? If so, then perhaps Windows actually tossed it out. *Always* check your pointers to make sure they are not NULL.

TIP: See MEMSAMPL.C (Listing 15.6) for an example of proper memory allocation with error checking.

---

2. Did you set up your callback functions properly? Callback functions must fulfill three requirements before they can be used.
   (a) Is your callback function declared as **FAR**? This is required because Windows will be calling your function. Callback functions must be declared as **FAR** since they could be anywhere in memory.
   (b) Are all your callback functions exported in the .DEF file? Microsoft C generates special prologue and epilogue code for callback functions **EXPORT**ed in the .DEF file. Windows counts on this code being there. If it is not, your program will end up in the twilight zone when you try to use the callback function.
   (c) Did you create an "instance thunk" for your callback function by using **MakeProcInstance()**? In allowing several instances of the same program to be run simultaneously, Windows uses the same code for each instance, but gives each instance a different data segment. In this case, the address of a program's data segment is not known until runtime. To overcome this difficulty, Windows programming requires that you use **MakeProcInstance()** to bind callback functions to the data segment of their runtime instances.
3. Do your function parameters match up? If you try to call a function with the wrong number or type of parameters than the function expects, your program is history. If you prototype your functions consistently and are generous with your warning levels (/W3 or /W4 for Microsoft C), you will probably never see this problem.

4. Are you overwriting memory? Programming in C can be deadly because C provides no inherent way for you to check the bounds of your arrays. If your array runneth over, you will probably get a UAE.

Your combobox doesn't drop down.

1. Combo boxes are list boxes and edit boxes rolled into one. When the cursor is clicked on the arrow on the right side of the combo box, a list of items is supposed to drop down. If this isn't happening, check the template. The bottom half must be drawn at least as tall as the font you plan to use, and the combobox must be given the style **CBS_DROPDOWN**.

You have a variable inside a callback function that you're absolutely sure is initialized. However, whenever you use it, it contains some very bizarre value!

1. This is a very subtle predicament that exists by virtue of the Windows messaging architecture. The thing to remember here is that a callback procedure is not like your usual C function. When a standard C function gets called, it normally handles some data and returns. However, the job of a Windows callback function is usually to handle a single message at a time. Therefore, it gets called frequently (whenever a message is generated). Each time the function is called, all its automatic variables are recreated on the stack. The values you previously assigned to these variables have evaporated! If you need to retain a variable's value between messages, you can accomplish this by declaring the variable as static.

TIP: See CALLBACK.C (Listing 15.7) for an example of using static variables.

This is not an exhaustive list of challenges you can face while developing your Windows programs in C. However, they are common problems that can devour your development time if you have never seen them before. With practice, you will be able to spot them and solve them in no time.

CODE DESCRIPTION

Overview

Listings Available

Listing	*Description*	*Used with*
VANILLA.C	A function that demonstrates how to register, create and display a plain vanilla main window.	------
MEMSAMPL.C	A function that demonstrates allocating memory in Windows, checking for a pointer's validity before using it.	------
CALLBACK.C	A typical dialog box callback function demonstrating the use of static variables.	------

How to Compile/Assemble

Can be compiled and used inside your Windows program with any C/C++ Windows compiler.

■ LISTING 15.5 VANILLA.C

```
/*vanilla.c*/

#include <windows.h>
/*********************************************************
*
*  Call this function from WinMain,
*  sending it the instance of your program, the name
*  you would like for this class, a message handler, and the
*  command you want to use to show the window.
*
* Sample Call:
*  hWnd =
*   plainVanillaWindow( hInstance,
*                       szAppName,
*                       wndProc,
*                       nCmdShow );
*/

HWND plainVanillaWindow( HANDLE hInstance, /* Handle to     */
                                           /*  program      */
                                           /*  instance     */
                         LPSTR  className, /* Name by which */
                                           /*  this window  */
                                           /*  class will   */
                                           /*  be known...  */
                            /* Message handler...           */
                         LONG FAR PASCAL wndProc(HWND   hWnd,
                                                 unsigned msg,
                                                 WORD wParam,
                                                 LONG lParam),
                         int     nCmdShow ) /* How to show  */
                                            /* the window   */
{
  WNDCLASS wc;
  HWND     hWnd;

    /* Redraw vertically and horizontally... */
  wc.style         = CS_HREDRAW | CS_VREDRAW;
  wc.lpfnWndProc   = wndProc;   /* Deposit messages here...  */
  wc.cbClsExtra    = 0;         /* Extra...                  */
  wc.cbWndExtra    = 0;         /* Extra...                  */
  wc.hInstance     = hInstance; /* Program instance          */

    /* Use the default icon */
  wc.hIcon         = LoadIcon (NULL, IDI_APPLICATION);

    /* Use the arrow cursor...  */
```

```
  wc.hCursor      = LoadCursor (NULL, IDC_ARROW);

    /* Window has a white background */
  wc.hbrBackground= GetStockObject (WHITE_BRUSH);
  wc.lpszMenuName = NULL;       /* No menu for this window...*/
  wc.lpszClassName= className;  /* Name by which this class  */
                                /*  of window will be known. */

  RegisterClass ( &wc );  /* Try to register the class       */

  hWnd = CreateWindow( className,           /* window class */
                       "Plain Vanilla",     /* caption       */
                       WS_OVERLAPPEDWINDOW, /* window style.*/
                                  /* WS_OVERLAPPEDWINDOW */
                                  /* creates a regular   */
                                  /* resizeable window.  */
                       CW_USEDEFAULT,/* initial x position  */
                       CW_USEDEFAULT,/* initial y positon   */
                       CW_USEDEFAULT,/* initial x size      */
                       CW_USEDEFAULT,/* initial y size      */
                       NULL,         /* parent window handle*/
                       NULL,         /* window menu handle  */
                       hInstance,    /* program instance    */
                       NULL);        /* create parameters   */

  ShowWindow(hWnd, nCmdShow);       /* show the window       */
  UpdateWindow(hWnd);               /* send WM_PAINT message */

  return hWnd;

} /* plainVanillaWindow */
```

■ LISTING 15.6 MEMSAMPL.C

```
/*memsampl.c*/


BOOL allocMem( HWND hWnd )
{
  HANDLE hMem;  /* Windows is tricky- memory is not        */
                /*  allocated directly. You must allocate */
                /*  memory by using a handle. You lock    */
                /*  the handle to get a valid pointer.    */
  LPSTR  lpStr;

  /** First allocate the memory via a handle... **/
  hMem = GlobalAlloc( GMEM_MOVEABLE | GMEM_ZEROINIT, 81 );
  if ( hMem == NULL ) /* A NULL handle indicates error.   */
    return FALSE;

  /** Then try to lock it to get a valid pointer... **/
  lpStr = GlobalLock( hMem );
  if ( lpStr == NULL ) /* A NULL handle indicates error.  */
  {
    GlobalFree( hMem ); /* If it got this far, then a     */
```

```
                    /*  handle was allocated.        */
    return FALSE;     /*  Be sure to free it...        */
  }

  /* At this point, it is certain that the memory has     */
  /*  been allocated, so it can be used...                */
  wsprintf( lpStr,
            (LPSTR)"Hello, there. Memory allocated!" );
  MessageBox( hWnd, lpStr, NULL, MB_OK );

  GlobalUnlock( hMem );  /* Unlock the handle so it can   */
                         /*  be freed...                  */
  GlobalFree( hMem );    /* Free the handle...            */

  return TRUE;
} /* allocMem */
```

■ LISTING 15.7 CALLBACK.C

```
/*callback.c*/

BOOL FAR PASCAL About (HWND     hDlg,
              unsigned msg,
              WORD     wParam,
              LONG     lParam)
{
  static char staticStr[80]; /* This string will retain   */
                             /*  its value                */
         char autoStr[80];   /* This string will have a   */
                             /*  new value every message. */

  switch (msg)
  {
    case WM_INITDIALOG: /* message: initialize dialog box */
      sprintf( staticStr,
               "This string will retain its value." );
      sprintf( autoStr,
               "This string will lose its value after "
               "this message is processed..." );
      MessageBox( hDlg, staticStr, NULL, MB_OK );
      MessageBox( hDlg, autoStr, NULL, MB_OK );
      return (TRUE);

      case WM_COMMAND: /* message: received a command */
    if (wParam == IDOK)  /* "OK" box selected? */
    {
        /** Show the values of the strings. At this    */
        /*  point, many messages have been processed.  */
          MessageBox( hDlg,
                      staticStr,
                      "value of staticStr",
                      MB_OK );
          MessageBox( hDlg,
                      autoStr,
                      "value of autoStr",
```

```
                    MB_OK );
      EndDialog (hDlg, NULL); /* exit the dialog box */
      return (TRUE);
    }
    break;
    }
    return (FALSE); /* didn't process a message   */
} /** About **/
```

Thirteen Tips for DOS to Windows Conversion

■ Jeff Roberts

Learn how to master the art of converting DOS applications.

Most Windows programming guides do something I find inexplicable: They try to scare the hell out of you! Well, I'll be contrary: Windows programming is no more difficult than DOS programming. The first Windows program you write is a bit mystifying, but after that first one, I firmly believe you will find Windows applications easier, not harder to write. I'm now significantly more productive writing for Windows than I was for DOS. You will be too.

So, because the press on Windows programming is already destroying enough trees, and because it really isn't as difficult as you probably think, this feature will not focus on specific code, but rather on techniques and tips that you can use as you port your own DOS applications to Windows. So hold on—we'll be moving fast.

Use Windows, I Mean Use Windows!

It amazes me how many programmers aren't yet doing this. Windows isn't just a list of API calls, but also a standard way of interacting with the computer. If your application does things your own way (even if your way *is* better), it will die. This doesn't mean you have to sacrifice alternate methods of interaction; just make sure that they supplement, rather than replace, existing Windows conventions.

Both IBM and Microsoft have published guidelines that specifically outline these standard methods of interaction, but don't waste your time reading them—just use a few Windows applications. Note the order of the menu items, the default function key assignments, the button order in dialog boxes, and so on. Once you earn your Windows wings, these details will flow freely, but until then, take special care, or you could end up irritating the very people buying your program.

Choose Your Development Tools Carefully

Where Microsoft's SDK used to stand alone, now many alternatives exist—Borland C++, Zortech C++, Turbo Pascal for Windows, Visual Basic, Quick C for Windows, and others. All of these products are light years beyond the SDK, so really, any would be a good choice. I do, however, recommend giving special consideration to object-oriented languages.

OOP lends itself particularly well to Windows. Subclassing, the window life cycle, GDI objects, memory management, all drop effortlessly into the OOP paradigm. I have used OOP languages (TPW and C++) on several large projects and now find programming without their features impossible.

Once past the language decision, you should start looking for a resource manager. Specifically, resources are accelerators, bitmaps, cursors, dialog boxes, fonts, icons, menus, and strings. Maintaining and creating these resources is not an insignificant job. In fact, in small- to medium-sized projects, it may actually constitute the majority of the work; so finding a good manager is critical.

Once you have the tools to do the job itself, you then need to get the tools to make the job easier. One of the reasons I think programming is easier under Windows is that more people are using code libraries. Under DOS, most shops coded up everything themselves. Buoyed by Windows' DLLs and code-sharing capabilities, libraries are now the rule rather than the exception.

Libraries are even more powerful when combined with OOP languages. A few object-oriented libraries I can recommend are Borland's ObjectWindows Library, Blaise Computing's Win++, and TIER from Genesis Development.

OK. We've got our language, our tools, and a library or two ready to go. Now let's get down to the hard part: planning.

Determine Your Target Environments

Windows supports a huge range of hardware and, unlike DOS, can take full advantage of it. Therefore, choosing a minimum and a recommended configuration will strongly influence your coding. A minimum configuration is the least-featured machine configuration under which your application will load. That's not to say it will be a pleasure to use—just that it will be theoretically usable. The recommended configuration is your target machine; that is, the environment where your application runs *well*.

Currently, I specify a minimum configuration of a 286/12 with 1MB of RAM. My standard recommended configuration is a 386/16 with 2MB of RAM. These specifications work well for me, but yours may be completely different. After all, a game requires fewer resources than a CAD package.

Plan ahead in choosing your configurations! If you figure your product will take a year to complete, you can make a 386SX your minimum configuration, and enable 386-specific code generation in your compiler.

Prototype Your New User Interface

Under DOS, I never prototyped a single user interface—I used a hit-or-miss technique of interface design on my first Windows application. "Patients for Windows—A Medical Office Manager" was the name of my soon-to-be-renowned vertical market product. By the time the product was finished, I considered renaming it to "Patience for Windows—A Medical Office Disaster."

It was *bad*—there were operations that only worked with a mouse, operations that only worked with the keyboard, operations that only worked in a certain mode, and so on. Many of the problems stemmed from my basic ignorance of Windows applications (see Step 1), but the majority could have been avoided with just a bit of UI prototyping.

Good prototyping is somewhat of an art. You don't want to spend the entire development cycle in a dialog designer, but you also want to find any trouble spots before you've been coded into a corner. Also, you don't want to write a lot of code just for testing purposes. Therefore, an important feature of your resource manager should be the ability to test your menus and dialog boxes on the fly. This way, you can prototype much of your interface without having to recreate it once you have something acceptable.

Prototyping will also help you reconcile possible deadly differences between your old DOS and your new Windows interfaces. Deciding how and where to support your old key commands, how much the new dialogs should resemble the old dialogs, where gadgets like scroll bars and combo boxes would make your application easier to use, can all be resolved by basic prototyping. Too little change and your application will seem like a warmed-over port. Too much change and you might lose customer loyalty. Either way, say good-bye to upgrade dollars.

There are many complete prototyping packages available. Actor by The Whitewater Group, Smalltalk/V by Digitalk, ToolBook by Asymetrix, and KnowledgePro by Knowledge Garden are some of the more popular prototyping environments. However, I find that a good resource manager is 99% of what I need. If you can afford it, using these two types of tools together can virtually guarantee that your new interface will please old DOS and new Windows users alike.

Salvage Everything That Still Works!

Yes, improving old code is incredibly enticing, but once you're in there, revamping the interface, adding cool things like mouse support and device-independent printing, the temptation to modernize old (yet still functional) code is incredible. *Just Say No!* More conversion projects get botched on this temptation than any other.

Salvage everything possible. Plan on yanking your user interface code, but be prepared to justify rewriting anything else. The first thing I do on a big port job is determine the most prevalent interface routines. I then decide if they will work unchanged under Windows. If not, I try to write "shell" routines, that is, routines that take the existing parameters and map them to Windows compatible calls. That way, I spend a small amount of time tweaking the shell routines, rather than weeks converting each occurrence of the old routines.

Often, with a little cleverness, code that seems hopeless can still be reused. For example, I was contracted to convert a charting program to Windows. I had planned on a complete rewrite, but, by having the existing routines write to a passed memory address (rather than the video buffer) and then simply blitting the buffer to a window, my job was almost trivial. It's amazing how much work you can save by using your head before using your fingers.

Examine and Review Your Memory Management

Second to the user interface itself, Windows' memory management is the biggest complication in a conversion project. Once you're running in protected mode, a lot of the old tricks popular in DOS get thrown out the . . . er . . . window. Windows conveniently traps these memory usage problems by displaying the familiar Unrecoverable Application Error (UAE) message. Remember these memory subtips when converting to Windows:

1. Watch for failed **LocalAllocs**. If you dereference a null **GlobalAlloc**ed pointer, an exception error is immediately generated and you can fix the problem. However, dereferencing a null **LocalAlloc**ed pointer gives no such helpful exceptions—you will just merrily read or write from location DS:0! To avoid such evilness, use a short shell routine that always checks the return value—you will thank me later!
2. Consider a memory suballocation system. If your application does many allocations, a memory management system is a must. Under Windows, only 8192 selectors are available *systemwide*, and Windows itself uses a couple hundred. The more applications that are loaded, the greater the chance that you could empty the selector pool. A memory manager alleviates this problem by allocating several large chunks of memory versus many small ones.
3. Review your assembly source. One good source of memory problems in a conversion job lies in assembly modules. The first thing to search for are code segment overrides—almost all of these will have to go. Next, look for assumed absolute addresses like 0x40 for the BIOS data segment, 0x0 for the interrupt table, and 0xf000 for the BIOS code segment. None of these absolute address values will work correctly in protected mode. Under DOS, I often used ES as a temporary register for time-critical routines where I had run out of general purpose registers. Under Windows, this will usually crash the system.

   Look for any cases of segment math—that is, putting a segment value into a general purpose register, adding to it, and then moving the changed value back into a segment register. This will undoubtedly cause an exception. If you are using segment math to address a sub-64K memory block, you will have to change your routine. If you are using segment math to search through a huge (greater than 64K) chunk of memory, you must use the "magic" value of the offset of a Windows-exported function called **AHIncr**. Adding the offset of **AHIncr** to a selector will give you a selector exactly 65,536 bytes from your original selector. A code example that uses this strange practice to count the length of a huge zero-terminated string is shown in Figure 15.3.
4. Beware of reading past the edge of a segment. Under DOS, basic bugs like reading past the end of a segment are usually harmless. However, in protected mode, this too, causes exceptions.
5. Remove any writes to code segments. In DOS interrupt service routines, writing to your code segment is fairly common. However, under Windows, this is a no-no and will immediately cause an exception error.

Consider International Issues

Big software companies like Microsoft are now generating around 60% of their revenues overseas. Wouldn't everyone like to double their sales?

Most programmers are not yet taking advantage of Windows' international abilities. Take the extra time to add this support—even if you have no immediate plans for overseas

```
xor   dx,dx       ;Zero the upper word of the length
les   di,[StrPtr];Load the passed address
@Loop:
mov   cx,$FFFF ;Load a segment's worth
xor   al,al       ;Look for a terminating zero
repne scasb       ;Scan for the zero
je   @done        ;If found a zero, then we're done
scasb             ;Check the last byte of the segment
je   @done        ;If it was a zero, jump to done
inc   dx          ;Increment high word
mov   ax,es       ;Load the segment
add   ax,offset AHInc7r   ;Add the advance value
mov   es,ax       ;Save it back into ES
jmp   @Loop       ;And continue looking
@done:
not   cx          ;Flip the count
dec   cx
mov   ax,cx       ;Save the count (DX already holds high
```

■ **FIGURE 15.3 Use OF AHIncr to walk segments**

markets. Making a change like switching capitalization routines affects your entire application, forcing everything to be retested. Add it during the conversion, and you'll only have to do this testing once.

Remember, when adding international support:

1. Don't cramp your dialog boxes. Have you ever wondered why Microsoft's dialog boxes seem so big? They were planning for the international versions. Many languages (especially German) are much wordier than English, so if your dialog boxes are cramped, then you will have to expand or (worse yet) rearrange them. The magic number is 30%. Plan your displays such that if all text in the program grew 30%, everything would continue to be visible and usable.
2. Use the built-in language-aware string routines. Uppercasing and comparing strings in your application is a bit more tricky when you need to consider international alphabets. Fortunately, Windows has several simple routines for just this task. Use **AnsiUpper** and **AnsiLower** to replace your current uppercase and lowercase routines. Then use **lcmpstr** and **lcmpstri** to do your comparisons.
3. Put all (and I mean *all*) displayable text into string resources. If your language people have to delve into source code even once to change displayable text, then you haven't done your job properly. To keep development simple, I define all my strings normally, but keep them in a single string file. Then, when I'm nearing the end of the project, I move all the defined strings into the resource file, and use the original string source file as a shell to load the string resources.
4. Use Windows' file handling routines. If you call DOS directly, you run into problems with differences between OEM and ANSI character sets. If you must use DOS directly, be sure to use the **AnsiToOem** and **OemToAnsi** functions to insure that your filenames will be DOS compatible.

Form a Plan for Sharing the Processor

Windows is (mostly) a nonpreemptive operating platform. That is, for multitasking to work, all Windows applications must cooperate. There is, for example, nothing to prevent your application from demanding the entire machine for itself. Of course, such an application would be a great annoyance, but the point is that Windows itself doesn't do the task switching . . . you do!

Therefore, deciding when and where to share the processor is a crucial task when creating a successful Windows application. Sure, yielding while your application is idle works, but what about nonidle situations? A big spreadsheet can take minutes to recalculate. Where do you yield so as not to unduly slow the process?

To complicate matters, the **Yield** function doesn't always work! It is not an uncommon set of events that causes the **Yield** function to do nothing at all. So, one of the first functions to stick in your tool kit is the **GoodYield** function given in Listing 15.8.

Unfortunately, yielding is pretty application-specific, so my only advice is simply to do it as much as possible. Think about where you may hold the processor up: large file reads, long calculations, searching, and so on, and add breathing room. Forming a good yielding strategy now, before you begin the conversion, saves you the trouble of going back and finding the trouble spots later.

Output Issues

Windows output is not as easy as doing an INT 17 or writing to the LPTx devices in DOS. The process is, however, almost identical to the process used to display data on the screen, so you won't be learning everything from scratch. My favorite discussion of the printing process can be found in Jeffrey Richter's *Windows 3: A Developer's Guide.*

In addition to the output itself, you will also need to provide a way for the user to set up and choose a printer. A good description on creating a printer setup dialog box can be found in Tom Swan's "Shades of Windows" column in the Oct/Nov 1991 *PC TECHNIQUES.* Once you've added the printer setup code, allow your users to access it from both the File menu directly and from the File/Print dialog box through a setup button. This Burger King-esqe (do it your way) approach to program design is one of the extra touches your users will thank you for.

Hire People to Do What You Aren't Good At

Windows applications aren't just clever code any more. Icons, bitmaps, color schemes, dialogs, and music should all be created as meticulously as the code itself. There is a wonderful Windows paint program available that (ironically) has a completely horrible icon. It doesn't invite users to play with the program; rather, it turns them off!

So, don't allow your clever code to be judged this way—hire people to do the jobs that you aren't especially good at. Decent computer artists run around $50 per hour, and it's an unusual job that takes more than a couple of hours. Interface evaluators (people that tell you bright purple isn't a great background color) are very expensive and seem to live only in California. However, an interior decorator can often design acceptable color schemes inexpensively.

Musicians usually work on a per score rate, which can run from a couple of hundred to thousands of dollars. Try to find a piccc of music that you're already thinking of and have the musician do something similar. Getting a musician to produce something you'll find acceptable without any hints is as likely as Coke introducing a new caffeine-free programmer's soda.

Add Your Help System

Adding a good help system is one of the final steps in creating a polished Windows application. Since Windows includes a complete help application, you need only call it with your data file. You can create this data file with any word processor that supports the Rich Text Format (RTF). Word for Windows is one. To save time, use an RTF-compatible word processor to create your manual and it's a trivial job of simply inserting the standard help file boilerplate into the manual file.

Once you have created the data file, you need to add the support code in your application. This mainly consists of handling the standard Help submenu, but status quo now requires help access from inside every dialog box. This allows the user to access to your help system even when the menu bar is unavailable, as in a modal dialog box, for example.

The standard help system is one of my favorite features of Windows. It works well, users love it, and it's easy to implement. What more could a programmer ask for?

Debug, Debug, Debug . . .

Many Windows bugs are the result of the confusion of learning a new programming environment, but I believe most are the result of not debugging adequately. Here are a few hints to help find those hidden nasties.

1. The number one, absolute, most important Windows debugging tip is to install the debug version of Windows. The debug version of Windows is *not* automatically installed when you install the SDK. This is a fundamental misunderstanding in the use of SDK and is Microsoft's fault—they should install the debug version by default.

   The debug version of Windows traps many of the common errors made in Windows programming. Windows 3.1 will incorporate several of the debug version's parameter validation abilities, but it will still not catch the many bugs that can be found with the debug version. If you are programming for Windows 3.0 now, and you are not using the debug version of Windows, your application *will* have problems under Windows 3.1—install it immediately. If you do not own the SDK, you may purchase the debug version of Windows separately, from Microsoft.
2. Get a second monitor. Serious applications demand serious debugging. A single monitor setup simply does not cut it for Windows debugging. With monochrome card/monitor combinations dropping to under a hundred dollars (less when used), you should have no difficulty in justifying this kind of convenience.

   One annoying aspect of adding a debugging monochrome system is the loss of 32K of upper DOS memory. You can, however, regain most of this upper memory by including the range B100 to B7FF in your memory manager's command line

(INCLUDE=B100-B7FF, in QEMM, for example). You will also need to add the line "EMMEXCLUDE = B000 - B7FF" in your SYSTEM.INI file under the "386ENH" section. Recouping this video memory will not affect any debugger I have used, including Codeview, Turbo Debugger, and Periscope.

3. Use the monochrome segment as a status indicator. In DUMPMONO.C (Listing 15.9), a routine is shown that allows you to use the monochrome video segment to display text. The routine is completely reentrant, allowing you to display status information at any time. It is the easiest way I've found to view information in difficult-to-trap debugging situations.
4. Test in all targeted Windows modes. Your application is not bug-free until it is bug-free in every Windows mode you claim is appropriate. Just because your program operates correctly in Standard mode does not necessarily ensure proper operation in Enhanced mode. Test each mode on *all* of the appropriate processor types. For example, test Real mode on PCs, ATs, and 386s, test Standard mode on both ATs and 386s, and, finally, test Enhanced mode on a 386.
5. Try to test as much distinct hardware as possible. Windows supports an incredible number of hardware products and testing your application with everything is, of course, impossible. However, I've found that by testing a small range of intelligently chosen hardware, you can ensure your application's success in most environments. To uncover potential display glitches, be sure to test your program in both VGA and 1024x768 resolutions. To test your output routines, be sure to try both dot matrix and laser printer destinations. Test your application with third-party font managers such as Adobe Type Manager or Facelift. Test your application in various color modes; 16- and 256-color modes will usually suffice. Test under the multimedia version of Windows. Try to cover as many bases as possible.
6. Debug your memory usage. Due to the various types of Windows memory, debugging your application for memory leakage is not a trivial task. There are four potential areas of memory leakage, each with its own causes and effects:

   (A) The GDI and User local heaps. This type of leak is created by calling one of the many GDI handle-creation routines without also calling the appropriate handle-destruction routine. This type of leak is particularly insidious because it is almost invisible; and when these heaps run low, your application (and everybody else's) will behave unpredictably. Fortunately, tracking this memory is relatively easy and can be observed with several public domain utilities. For detailed information on tracking these system resources, see Paul Yao's article in the Sept/Oct 1991 issue of *Microsoft Systems Journal.*

   (B) The global heap. This type of leak is difficult to cause because Windows automatically frees global memory allocated by an application. To leak global memory, a DLL using special memory allocation flags would be at fault. This leak does not happen often, but when it does, it is difficult to track down. Display the amount of global memory available before and after your application executes to determine if you are the victim of this kind of leakage.

   (C) DPMI memory. Some Windows applications allocate memory with DPMI calls to get very specific placement of the allocated memory. Since DPMI is not necessarily

Windows-specific, Windows cannot automatically free allocated memory when your application terminates. Again, displaying the amount of DPMI memory before and after your application executes is the best way to ensure that no leakage is occurring.

7. Don't look for zebras. Not watching for zebras is more a state of mind than a specific technique. Watching for zebras refers to the habit of assuming the exotic before the basic. It means seeing hoof prints and thinking zebras rather than horses. Most Windows problems are basic and easily fixed, so don't assume the worst. Ninety nine times out of 100, a problem that gets you thinking, "Windows bug!" is just some goofy mistake *you* made. If you get stumped, walk away, have a Diet Jolt, get another opinion, but most important, think *horses*!

Finishing It—Installation Software

Installation software is how the user installs your program onto his machine. Under Windows, a professional installation routine is no longer optional—it is expected.

Fortunately, there are a number of means to facilitate your user's installation. The first method is to use the tools Windows provides for creating a standard installation program. Unfortunately, Microsoft chose to implement their standard setup in text mode only. That is, to use your installation procedure, the user would have to execute it from DOS! This type of setup program is used frequently and is easy to create. For more information on this type of installation, again, see Richter's wonderful book.

The second common route for installation procedures are third-party utilities. These are complete applications designed solely to expedite the installation of other applications. Popular examples of this type of utility are Install by Knowledge Dynamics, InstallSHIELD by The Stirling Group, and INSTALIT by HPI. These products all work well, and can accomplish almost anything your particular installation will require. This is usually the least expensive and easiest way to go.

Finally, you can write your own entire installation application. It is complex (in fact, sometimes as complex as your product itself), but once written, the same basic program can be used for all of your products. Since you own the source, you can modify it and jazz it up as much as you like. This approach is perhaps the most expensive, but by far the most flexible.

A Final Tip

Well, there they are: 13 cool and fruity tips for getting your DOS application running under Windows. Notice that the majority of the tips are advice on planning the project. That fact leads to my best tip for you: Plan and envision the final product *before* you start converting. The code-as-you-go method of product development is dead—fall into its jaws and you will never finish anything.

Once code is written and working, it takes on a life of its own. It fights for continued existence even when it's obvious that another approach will work better. Always plan ahead! Get an outliner, get a tape recorder, buy a diary . . . whatever works, but do get organized. Spend the majority of your time thinking, not typing. Good luck!

CODE DESCRIPTION

Overview

Two programming utilities to help in writing better Windows programs.

Listings Available

Listing	*Description*	*Used with*
GDYIELD.C	More effect version of the Windows supplied Yield function.	------
DUMPMONO.C	Utility to display text strings directly on a second (monochrome monitor).	------

How to Compile/Assemble

Can be compiled and linked with any C/C++ Windows compiler.

■ LISTING 15.8 GDYIELD.C

```
void GoodYield(void)
{
TMsg Msg;

    while (PeekMessage(Msg,0,0,0,PM_REMOVE))
      {
      TranslateMessage(Msg);
      DispatchMessage(Msg);
      }
}
```

■ LISTING 15.9 DUMPMONO.C

```
extern WORD _B000(void);
void DumpStr2Mono(char *str)
{
LPSTR *MonoScreen;
int i;
int len;

    len = strlen(str);
    mp = (LPSTR)MAKELONG(0,&_B000);
    for (i = 0; i < len; i++)
      *MonoScreen++ = str[i] || 0x7000; //set char & attrib
}
```

Rolling Your Own Windows Shell

■ David Stafford

Use these easy techniques to create a custom Windows shell.

Recently, I was writing a Windows application that could serve as the Windows shell, replacing the Program Manager. In the process I learned some things about writing shells for Windows, much of which is not documented anywhere and must be learned only from hard experience. The Windows shell is the first application to run when Windows is started. It has a variety of responsibilities including

1. Executing any programs listed after Windows on the DOS command line (e.g., WIN WINWORD)
2. Running any programs specified in the WIN.INI.
3. Providing a means of exiting Windows.

Generally speaking, the shell does a few more things than the three listed above, such as providing a means to execute other applications, associating data files with the appropriate programs, and reporting system statistics (free memory and system resources), but the listed three things are the minimum shell requirements.

Version 3 of Windows comes with three programs that can serve as the shell. Most people use Program Manager as their shell but there is also File Manager, and even the old MSDOS shell (a blast from Windows' past) is still available. Which shell to use is specified in the **Shell=** line of SYSTEM.INI.

First—Anybody Home?

The first thing your shell needs to know is that it is actually running as the Windows shell and not just as another application. On startup your program should call **GetNumTasks.** If the return value is 1, then your application is the only one running and must be the shell. Save this information for later. In particular, your program needs to know that it's the shell when the user attempts to close your application. At that time your program should perform a Windows shutdown (discussed later).

Windows Command Line and WinExec

Next, your program needs to execute the program (if any) listed on the Windows command line. The command line is made available as the **lpszCmdParam** argument to your **WinMain** function. Your program can pass this parameter directly to the **WinExec** API function call.

Be careful when using **WinExec.** Your program can pass **WinExec** a bogus file and it is very likely to crash Windows! Unfortunately, **WinExec** is terribly fragile, so if you want your shell to be robust you need to check to make sure you are telling **WinExec** to load and execute a real program. The easiest way to do this is to create a "wrapper" function for the call to **WinExec** that checks to see that the program name ends in a BAT, EXE, COM, or

PIF extension. If it passes this test, the wrapper can forward it on to **WinExec**. If not, the wrapper can return an error code.

This error checking can be complicated by the fact that the program may be specified without an extension. In that case you'll need to use **OpenFile** with the **OF_PARSE** flag to first find the file and get its exact name.

WIN.INI

Your shell also needs to execute the programs listed in the WIN.INI **Load**= and **Run**= lines. You can get these programs with the **GetProfileString** function call. There may be several different programs listed on each line, so you will have to parse them and load them one at a time.

How your shell interprets the semantic difference between the **Load=** and **Run=** usage is up to you. Program Manager interprets **Load=** as meaning the application should be started in an iconized state (passing **SW_SHOWMINIMIZED** as the **nCmdShow** parameter to **WinExec**). **Run=** means the application should be started as **SW_SHOWNORMAL**. If any programs are listed on the **Run=** line the Program Manager itself will start up iconized.

It's important to note that it's not simply good enough to just get the program name and execute it. The situation may be that the specified program requires a DLL that is located in its own directory and not on the system path. If you try to execute the program from another directory, Windows will not be able to find the DLL and the program will fail to load. If a path is included in the program name, you should change to the specified drive and directory before executing the program.

This behavior invites a handy trick that some clever Windows users have put to use for setting the current data directory when starting applications. If the application is on the path, it doesn't matter where it's executed from, but the shell has changed to the specified directory that contains the desired data files. For example

```
Load=C:\REPORTS\WRITE.EXE
```

The shell will first change to C:\REPORTS and then execute Write. The user can then conveniently load his data files from this "working" directory. Your shell should have this same behavior.

Multiple Instances

One of the things you need to decide how to handle is multiple instances of your shell. The user might legitimately want to work with more than one instance or perhaps has made some configuration changes and will want to reload the shell. You might simply disallow multiple instances by checking the **hPrevInst** argument to **WinMain.** If it isn't NULL, display a message box and quit.

If you are going to allow only one instance, a better method might be to terminate the previous one and let the user work with the second. To do this you will need to communicate with the previous instance in order to shut it down and (important!) to find out if the previous instance is running as the Windows shell. If so, then shut it down and assume the responsibility of the shell.

Establishing communication with the previous instance can be done in at least three ways: Use **FindWindow** to locate the shell's main window by its class; use **GetInstanceData** to pull the variables right out of the previous instance's data segment; or, if you want to get fancy, communicate via DDE. While the second approach is easier to code, I don't recommend it—it makes your code extremely version-dependent.

Saying Goodbye

If the user closes your application, you need to check to see if your program is the shell (saved the result from **GetNumTasks** earlier), and if so, you must exit Windows.

The actual exit procedure is a bit involved. Before Windows exits, each application gets a **WM_QUERYENDSESSION** message to give it a chance to shut down and save any open files. The application can also abort the exit by returning a value of **FALSE** (**TRUE** means it's OK to exit). Afterward, the applications get a **WM_ENDSESSION** message informing them that Windows really is exiting (which they cannot cancel).

The good news is that Windows will send and process these messages for you when you call the **ExitWindows** function. **ExitWindows** will not return unless an application responds to the **WM_QUERYENDSESSION** message with a return value of **FALSE**. This allows you to display a message box regarding the stubborn application.

There is an undocumented parameter to **ExitWindows**. If you pass 0x42 as the return code it will restart Windows (like the Setup program). Using documented features is dangerous, and your program may break under a future version of Windows, but sometimes there is no alternative. In this case, if you need to restart Windows there is no documented way to do it.

Reporting System Resources

The shells supplied with Windows include information regarding free memory and system resources in their "about" boxes. Getting the amount of free memory is easy—you can use the **GetFreeSpace** API call. However, determining the percentage of system resources available is not so easy. There is no documented way to do this, so we are reduced to using an undocumented method. The warning about using undocumented functions applies here as well.

As you already know, every DLL has a local heap and Windows itself is composed of many DLLs. Two of these DLLs are USER and GDI and their free space determines the amount of free system resources. No matter how much RAM you have, in Windows your system resources are limited to these two heaps. It's not at all uncommon to run out of system resources long before you run out of RAM.

TIP: Using the undocumented API call, **GetHeapSpaces**, you can determine two things for a given module: the total heap size for that module and the amount of that heap which is available. By calling this for both the USER and GDI modules and converting the values to percentages, you will then have the values needed to present free system resources. (Windows 3.0 simply reports the smaller of the two percentages; Windows 3.1 shows you both.) Listing 15.10 shows a small model assembly module that does this.

In Closing

Program Manager isn't the only way to run Windows. You may have specific needs that require a different approach (for security or compatibility with another GUI shell), or maybe you just have a better idea of how it should be done. In any case, the information here will help get you going. Good luck!

CODE DESCRIPTION

Overview

RESOURCE.ASM contains assembly source code of two functions **SystemsResources** and **PercentHeapFree**. **PercentHeapFree** returns the amount of heap space available in a given module. **SystemResources** returns the lower of the USER and GDI free space (as a percentage).

Listings Available

Listing	*Description*	*Used with*
RESOURCE.ASM	Contains both **SystemResources** and **HeapFree** functions.	------

How to Compile/Assemble

Can be assembled and linked with any C/C++ compiler using the following prototypes:

```
int pascal near SystemResources(void);
int pascal near PercentHeapFree(char far *Module)
```

■ LISTING 15.10 RESOURCE.ASM

```
        .286
        extrn GetHeapSpaces:far
        extrn GetModuleHandle:far

_TEXT   segment
        assume cs:_TEXT

;---------------------------------------
; int pascal near PercentHeapFree( char far *Module )
;   {
;   DWORD Heap;
;
;   Heap = GetHeapSpaces( GetModuleHandle( Module ) );
;
;   return( LOWORD( Heap ) / (HIWORD( Heap ) / 100) );
```

```
;   }
;-------------------------------
      public PercentHeapFree
PercentHeapFree proc near
      pop     cx    ;get return address
      pop     bx    ;get Module offset
      pop     ax    ;get Module seg
      push    cx    ;save return address

      push    ax    ;push Module
      push    bx
      call    GetModuleHandle
      push    ax
      call    GetHeapSpaces
      push    ax    ;save loword
      xchg    ax,dx
      mov     bx,100
      call    Divide
      xchg    ax,bx
      pop     ax    ;restore loword
Divide:  xor     dx,dx
      div     bx
      ret

;-------------------------------
; Gets the free system resources percentage.
;
; int pascal near SystemResources( void );
;-------------------------------

T_GDI    db 'GDI',0
T_USER db 'USER',0

      public SystemResources
SystemResources proc near
      push    cs
      push    offset T_GDI
      call    PercentHeapFree

      push    ax

      push    cs
      push    offset T_USER
      call    PercentHeapFree

      pop     bx

      cmp     ax,bx
      jbe     Done
      xchg    ax,bx
Done:       ret
      endp

_TEXT  ends
      end
```

16

TSR Programming

Much of what Windows was created to do was originally done using TSR (Terminate, Stay Resident) programs. The generic term for the concept is *context-switching*; that is, pressing a key and—wham!—being instantly inside another application.

TSRs were and are a messy business. DOS wasn't really designed with context-switching in mind, and at the core of it, most of the diciness in Windows 3.x falls to DOS's awkwardness when facing the challenge of multiple programs in memory. So you have to be aware that TSR programming is definitely pushing the DOS envelope, and if you don't do it *just* so, you'll have crashes and lots of other assorted weirdness to deal with.

On the other hand, a familiarity with TSR technology may allow you to exploit the "trailing edge" machines that will never run Windows but that are out there by the tens of millions.

In this chapter, TSR guru Kevin Dean explains how to calculate how much memory your TSRs have available to them, and also how to arrange communication among multiple TSRs, all resident in memory at the same time. Greg Chursenoff explains how to remove TSRs from memory, and how to prevent multiple instances of a single TSR from being loaded at the same time.

As one who couldn't have gotten as many books written in the 1980s as I did without Borland's seminal Sidekick TSR utility, I encourage you to become familiar with this stuff. Like any other technique in programming, you'd much rather have it and not need it than need it and not have it—and allow your closest competitor to make the sale.

Determining TSR Memory Usage in C

■ Kevin Dean

Make your TSRs calculate their own memory requirements at runtime.

Deciding how much memory to allocate to a TSR is a critical issue. On one hand, you need to be sure you have enough RAM to run the TSR; on the other hand, you want to leave as much memory as possible for DOS and the user. Allocating 16K simply to guarantee enough memory for a 12K TSR is a needless waste.

One way to determine the amount of memory used is to look at the map file produced by the linker when the TSR is linked. The map file shows the length of each program segment and thus how much memory the program is using. Although this approach works, it means that you have to go back to the source code, put this number into the call to the **keep()** function, and recompile. This process becomes especially tedious if you're in development and the size of the program is changing constantly. It could get even worse in high-level languages when the program has to do some dynamic memory allocation, which doesn't show up in the map file.

A better approach is to calculate the amount of memory the TSR requires at runtime and keep exactly that amount (plus some additional space for the stack and heap) before returning to DOS. There's a way to go about it. First, some background.

Microsoft's Segment-Ordering Convention

The Intel 8086 family of microprocessors keeps program code and data in separate areas of memory. These areas, or segments, can be up to 64K bytes long. Memory is seen as paragraphs of 16 bytes each. Memory addresses are written (in hexadecimal) as segment:offset pairs, where "segment" is the paragraph number and "offset" is the number of bytes from the beginning of that paragraph to the single byte in question. The offset can range from 0000h to FFFFh—that is, it can address up to a full 64K segment. For example, the first location in memory (at address 0) is addressed as 0000:0000h. The full memory address (the number of bytes from the beginning of memory) of a segment:offset pair is

```
((segment * 16) + offset)
```

Conversely, the number of paragraphs an address is from the beginning of memory can be given by:

```
(segment + (offset / 16))
```

Almost all DOS programs use what is called the Microsoft segment-ordering convention. This defines the memory layout of a program, in the following order:

- Segments of class CODE
- Segments of classes other than CODE but not part of DGROUP (Data Group)
- Segments that are part of DGROUP in the following order:

- Segments of classes other than STACK and BSS
- Segments of class BSS (uninitialized data)
- Segments of class STACK

Determining the amount of memory used by a TSR requires this order, which almost all compilers follow. When programming in assembly language, however, you have to do the segment ordering. Make sure the segments are ordered exactly as outlined above.

How Much Memory?

If you know where your program begins and ends, the amount of memory used is what lies between. Fortunately, DOS is more than happy to tell you where a program begins.

At the beginning of a program, DOS creates a 256-byte header called the Program Segment Prefix, or PSP. The PSP is aligned on a paragraph boundary—in other words, the offset portion of its segment:offset pair will always be 0000h. This allows the address of the PSP to be given as its segment alone, because the offset may safely be assumed to be 0.

The structure of the PSP is not important here, but its address is, because the start of the PSP is the beginning of memory used by any program and hence a TSR. DOS function 51H returns the PSP address in the BX register. The following assembly language code fetches the PSP address and returns it in the AX register:

```
_GetPSP PROC
mov     ah, 51H
int     21H
mov     ax, bx
ret
_GetPSP ENDP
```

This function can be implemented in most high-level languages as an external integer function, or by using other provided means of making DOS INT 21H calls.

Finding the End of a Program

Now that you've found the beginning of memory used by the program, what about the end? Unfortunately, DOS has no way of knowing just how much memory your program is going to need, so there is no corresponding DOS function to find the end of memory used. However, a few lines of assembly language will solve the problem. This is where the Microsoft segment-ordering convention enters the picture.

According to the Microsoft segment-ordering convention, the data segment comes after the code segment. If you know where the end of the data segment is, you could find the end of program code and data as well.

In assembler, the easiest way to find the end of program code and data is to create a pointer to the end of the data segment. One way to do this is by creating a label at the end of the data segment that you know will always be at the end of the program. Unless the program has only one module, however, you can never be sure that other modules won't define data for this segment and "bump" your label inward from the end of the segment.

Another and more reliable way to find the end of the data segment in an assembly language program is to create a separate segment altogether, and then make sure that it's at the end of all data, as shown in TSRMEM1.ASM (Listing 16.1).

The **_EODATA** (end of data) segment is placed after the **_BSS** (uninitialized data) segment but before the **_STACK** (stack) segment because we are more concerned with where the data used by the TSR ends; we may not want a stack as large as the default stack provided by the assembler or compiler. We may also choose to use the stack owned by the program the TSR is interrupting, but this is *not* a good idea since we don't know how much stack we can use without shooting off the edge of the owner's stack allocation and overwriting critical data. I'll come back to the matter of the stack shortly.

The **EndPrg** procedure simply loads the segment address represented by label **_EODATA** into AX and returns. Segment **_EODATA** is empty; because it is the last segment in the segment order, its address is the address of the very end of the code and data portion of the TSR. (Heap and stack are arbitrary allocations to which we can give as much RAM as we like, extending past the TSR's code and data requirements.)

If you're programming in a high-level language, the code in TSRMEM1.ASM should be added to the compiler's startup code, which is generally provided with the compiler. The startup code for Turbo C, for example, is in the file C0.ASM.

TSRMEM2.C (Listing 16.2) defines the size of its own stack to avoid taking a chance on a compiler default or application "hand-me-down" stack. The stack segment begins immediately after the **_EODATA** segment. The code guarantees that it will have a minimum stack size represented by the constant **MIN_STACK**, but beyond that the stack size is set by the parameter passed to **install_tsr()**. The heap size is also passed to **install_tsr**, but there is no guaranteed minimum heap size.

We now know where the program proper begins and where it ends, and how much extra space is needed for heap and stack. All that's left is to install the TSR and retain exactly the amount of memory it requires before returning to DOS. The algorithm is given in the following statement from TSRMEM2.C (Note that all values represent 16-byte *paragraphs*, not *bytes*):

```
keeplen = EODATA - PSP + heap + stack;
```

In essence, this is the last address in the program minus the first, plus extra space for the stack and heap. Although Turbo C is used for the example shown in TSRMEM2.C, it can be easily translated to another high-level language or to assembly.

The other function in TSRMEM2.C, **init_tsr()**, takes control when the TSR actually executes, usually in response to a hot key. (For the sake of brevity, I have not included hot-key monitoring code in the example; please understand that TSRMEM2.C does *not* represent a complete and operable skeleton TSR.) The **init_tsr()** function must save the address of the interrupted program's stack, install its own stack, perform its own tasks, and then restore the prior stack before returning control to the interrupted program. Function **run_tsr()** is what the TSR actually *does*; so, if the TSR is a pop-up editor, the editing code must reside in **run_tsr()**. Only the invocation of **run_tsr()** is shown in TSRMEM2.C; the implementation of the function is up to you.

What we have just developed is a very general algorithm for installing and initializing a TSR. It is portable to almost any high-level language. If possible, however, we would like to take advantage of some compiler-specific features and avoid assembly language altogether.

Compiler-Specific Features

Often, compiler vendors will provide library functions or macros that take care of some of these issues for you. My examples here are from Turbo C, but most major compilers contain similar features. Consult your compiler's documentation for further information.

In Turbo C, the variable **_psp** points to the Program Segment Prefix, so that takes care of knowing where the program begins. Finding the end, alas, is not quite so simple, even in Turbo C.

To find the end of the data segment, Turbo C provides the **sbrk(incr)** function, which adds **incr** bytes to the break value (the address of the first location beyond the end of the data segment) and returns a pointer to the old break value. To find the end of the data segment, we call **sbrk()** with **incr** equal to 0. (Passing 0 does not change the break value; hence the "old break value" returned by **sbrk()** is still the end of the data segment.)

However, the address returned by **sbrk()** does not necessarily point to a paragraph boundary, and we are allocating whole paragraphs of memory to our TSR. The statement **_eodata += 0xF;** adds 15 to the pointer **_eodata**, which will push the segment portion of the pointer to the next paragraph.

One special advantage in using the **sbrk()** function over the assembly code we developed earlier is that Turbo C's memory allocation functions automatically change the break value returned by **sbrk()** as memory is allocated and freed. This way, you will always know *exactly* how much memory is in use.

Turbo C has six memory models that provide different code and data segment sizes. Because the data segment or segments always fall after the code segment or segments, what we are concerned about is the size of the data segment. For near data models (maximum 64K data), all pointers are offsets only—that is, offsets from the DS register. For far data models (unlimited data), all pointers are stored as segment:offset pairs. The code in TSRMEM3.C (Listing 16.3) finds the amount of memory used by every memory model supported by Turbo C. The code for setting up the TSR stack is the same as the code developed in the previous section.

As Much as You Need

How much memory does a TSR need? As much as it uses—no more, no less. You can guess how much that is, or you can empower your TSRs to measure what they use themselves, and take only what they must have.

CODE DESCRIPTION

Overview

The program modules presented here are useful examples of how to: determine the amount of memory needed by a TSR, control how the TSR is stored in memory (so it can be freed), and use a private stack. They are intended for use inside another program, not as a stand-alone example.

Listings Available

Listing	*Description*	*Used with*
TSRMEM1.ASM	Forces Segment-ordering for the TSR program.	------
TSRMEM2.C	Demonstrates how to establish a TSR's private stack.	------
TSRMEM3.C	Demonstrates how to calculate the memory needs of a TSR.	------

How to Compile/Assemble

Can be compiled or assembled with any C/C++ compiler assembler. Some routines are specific to Borland C++ and Turbo C++, but are supported by other language vendors.

■ LISTING 16.1 TSRMEM1.ASM

```
_TEXT   SEGMENT BYTE PUBLIC 'CODE'
_TEXT   ENDS
_DATA   SEGMENT BYTE PUBLIC 'DATA'
_DATA   ENDS

; Class BSS is uninitialized data.
_BSS    SEGMENT BYTE PUBLIC 'BSS'
_BSS    ENDS

; This segment is empty since all we need is its
; paragraph number. By forcing it to align on a
; paragraph boundary, we safely skip any data that
; might be left in the last paragraph.
_EODATA SEGMENT PARA PUBLIC 'BSS'
_EODATA ENDS

_STACK  SEGMENT WORD PUBLIC 'STACK'
_STACK  ENDS

; Other segment declarations and grouping of
; segments other than those that are part of DGROUP.
. . .
; By the Microsoft segment ordering convention, the
; DGROUP group should always be at the end of the
; program.
DGROUP GROUP _DATA, ..., _BSS, _EODATA, _STACK, ...

_TEXT   SEGMENT
; Startup code, etc.
. . .
; Determine the segment address of next available
; paragraph.
; Segment address is returned in AX.
_EndPrg PROC
        mov     ax, _EODATA
        ret
```

```
_EndPrg ENDP
_TEXT   ENDS

; Other segment definitions.
        . . .
        END
```

■ LISTING 16.2 TSRMEM2.C

```
/* These variables define the stack segment and offset
to be used by the TSR. */
unsigned my_ss, my_sp;

/* Minimum number of paragraphs required for TSR's stack. */
#define MIN_STACK  0x40

/* Install a TSR.
Keep enough memory for the dynamic heap and stack.
The 'heap' and 'stack' parameters are the number of
paragraphs required by the heap and stack respectively. */
void install_tsr(unsigned heap, unsigned stack)
{
unsigned PSP, EODATA, keeplen;

/* Get beginning and end of program memory. */
PSP = GetPSP();
EODATA = EndPrg();

/* Make sure we have enough stack space. */
stack = max(MIN_STACK, stack);

/* Amount of memory required is (program size + heap + stack). */
keeplen = EODATA - PSP + heap + stack;

/* Stack comes after data segment and heap and grows
down in memory. */
my_ss = EODATA;
my_sp = (heap + stack) * 16;

/* keep(status, size) is a Turbo C function that keeps
'size' paragraphs in memory and exits to DOS with
status 'status'.  It uses DOS function 0x31. */
keep(0, keeplen);
}

/* Initialize TSR stack, run the TSR, restore
interrupted program's stack, and return control to
interrupted program. */
void init_tsr(void)
{
/* These must be static variables because local
variables are addressed from the stack, which we
will be changing. */
static unsigned old_ss, old_sp;
```

```
/* Save old stack frame.  _SS and _SP are Turbo C
pseudo-variables that directly address the SS and SP
registers. */
old_ss = _SS;
old_sp = _SP;

/* Set up the TSR stack.  disable() and enable() are
Turbo C pseudo-functions that disable and enable
interrupts.  The last thing we want is for an
interrupt to occur while we're changing the stack! */
disable();
_SS = my_ss;
_SP = my_sp;
enable();

/* run_tsr() is user-defined—implemented by the programmer. */
run_tsr();

/* Restore original program's stack. */
disable();
_SS = old_ss;
_SP = old_sp;
enable();
}
```

■ LISTING 16.3 TSRMEM3.C

```
#include <alloc.h>
#include <dos.h>
#include <stdlib.h>

/* Determine if we are using a large data model
(COMPACT, LARGE, or HUGE). The memory map for a
large data model differs from that for a small data
model in that the heap comes after, not before, the
stack. This code will compile and run for the
correct memory model. */
#if sizeof(void far *) == sizeof(void *)
#define LARGE_DATA
#endif

/* This is a Turbo C variable that determines the size
of the stack at startup. */
extern unsigned _stklen;

/* These variables define the stack segment and offset
to be used by the TSR. */
unsigned my_ss, my_sp;

/* Minimum number of paragraphs required for TSR's stack. */
#define MIN_STACK  0x40

/* Install a TSR. */
void install_tsr(unsigned heap, unsigned stack)
```

```
{
char *_eodata;
unsigned EODATA, keeplen;

/* In a large data model, the size of the stack cannot
be changed since it is "sandwiched" between the
global data segment and the heap.  To set the size
of the stack (which is initialized by the startup
code), use the following declaration somewhere in
your code:

unsigned _stklen = STACK_SIZE;

e.g. To allocate a 1k stack:
unsigned _stklen = 1024;

Changing _stklen itself will not change the size of
the stack and may have disastrous results, as it is
used by this routine. */
#if !defined(LARGE_DATA)
/* Make sure we have enough stack space. */
stack = max(MIN_STACK, stack);
#endif

/* Get end-of-data segment. If the end of the data
segment is not on a paragraph boundary, adding 15
(0xF) bytes will push it over to the next paragraph. */
_eodata = sbrk(0);
_eodata += 0xF;

/* Find the next paragraph available after the TSR.

FP_SEG() and FP_OFF() are Turbo C macros that
determine the segment and offset of a far pointer.
If the pointer is a near pointer, FP_SEG() casts it
to a far pointer and returns the value of the
appropriate segment register (DS). The paragraph
number is normalized by adding the number of
paragraphs included in the offset. */
EODATA = FP_SEG(_eodata) + (FP_OFF(_eodata) >> 4);

#if defined(LARGE_DATA)
/* Amount of memory required is (program size + heap). */
keeplen = EODATA - _psp + heap;

/* Use existing stack (i.e. stack that was set up by
the startup code). */
my_ss = _SS;
my_sp = _stklen;

#else

/* Amount of memory required is (program size + heap +
stack). */
```

```
keeplen = EODATA - _psp + heap + stack;

/* Stack comes after data segment and heap grows
down in memory. */
my_ss = _ss;
my_sp = ((EODATA -_ss) + heap + stack) * 16;
#endif

keep(0, keeplen);
}
```

Communicating with Your TSRs

■ Kevin Dean

Master the art of using the undocumented DOS multiplex interrupt.

TSR programs are downright useful critters. The numerous magazine and book articles devoted to them also indicate that they are popular programming projects. As you gain experience with TSRs and start pushing the TSR envelope, you'll encounter a new set of programming challenges:

1. How can you prevent a second, perhaps inadvertent, invocation of a TSR program from installing itself; that is, how can a TSR detect when it is already installed?
2. How can you make changes to the runtime parameters of a TSR program while it's installed?
3. How can you give non-TSR application programs access to the functions within the installed TSR?

In short, how do you communicate with an installed TSR?

There is one DOS TSR program that already performs many of these operations: the PRINT program. PRINT installs itself only once, the first time it is loaded. For every subsequent invocation, it detects itself in memory and simply passes new runtime parameters to the resident copy, rather than installing itself again. It is also possible for other programs to access the built-in print queueing functions. Let's examine how it works.

The Multiplex Interrupt

The mechanism used by the DOS PRINT program is the DOS multiplex interrupt, INT 2Fh. Like PRINT, this feature was introduced with DOS 2; however, for general programming usage, what is covered here will apply to DOS 3.x and greater. Despite its imposing name, the multiplex interrupt is one of the least publicized and least used features of general TSR programming. I've traced through many commercial TSR programs with a debugger and hardly any (outside of DOS) use this technique.

The DOS multiplex interrupt is so-called because it allows access to more than one TSR program through a single interrupt. Each TSR to be accessed must have its own handler for INT 2Fh. When the TSR installs itself, it retrieves a far pointer from location 0000:006Ch in lower memory. This is a pointer to the "current" INT 2Fh handler, and the new TSR saves it locally. It then stores a far pointer to its own INT 2Fh handler in the low memory location.

The procedure causes a linked chain of INT 2Fh handlers, starting with the last TSR installed. If an INT 2Fh call does not pertain to a particular TSR, the handler in that TSR passes control to its predecessor, using the locally stored pointer. This is very similar to the way multiple TSRs link themselves together on the keyboard interrupt, INT 09h.

With everyone linked together on the one INT 2Fh chain, you might be wondering how a calling application—including a second copy of the TSR itself—gets its message to the proper handler. The calling sequence for INT 2Fh holds the key for getting the message to the correct handler. You program each handler to respond to its own unique "multiplex ID number," which is loaded into the AH register before the INT 2Fh call. Each handler must check the value in AH, and pass control on to the next handler in the chain if AH does not hold its unique multiplexer ID.

Microsoft and IBM have reserved multiplex ID numbers in the range 00h through 0BFh (for example, DOS PRINT uses multiplex ID 01h, APPEND uses 0B7h). This leaves 64 values in the range 0C0h through 0FFh available for user-written TSR programs. Once a handler finds its ID number in AH, it must then check AL for a function code number. This number identifies the particular operation that the handler must perform.

Generally speaking, your TSR-based handlers can interpret this function number (as well as values passed in the other registers) in any way you see fit. The PRINT program interprets an AL value of 01h as a file submission operation, and expects DS:DX to point to a submission packet containing the name of the file to be printed. One special value in AL, however, is 00h. All multiplex interrupt handlers should interpret this as the "get installed state" function. On return from the interrupt for this function, AL should still contain 00h if there is no handler loaded for the ID given. This means that the TSR is not already installed and it is okay to install it.

If the TSR is already installed, its INT 2Fh handler should simply change AL from 00h to FFh, and return. This will inhibit the TSR program from installing itself a second time.

An INT 2Fh handler also might return other AL values in response to the function 00h call. For example, the *MS-DOS Encyclopedia* (Microsoft Press, ISBN 1-55615-174-8) states that PRINT returns AL set to 01h if it is "not installed, not okay to install." *Peter Norton's Programmers Guide to the IBM PC and PS/2* suggests that the INT 2Fh for a different TSR should return 01h in AL if it is using the same ID number as the caller. This idea requires information besides the ID number in AH to be passed between the caller and INT 2Fh, function 00h, handler; for example, a pointer to a unique "signature" code or string. Note, however, that this higher degree of complexity is not necessary if you're certain that your TSRs have unique multiplex numbers.

For any multiplex number (i.e., for any ID value in AH), DOS also reserves function codes (AL values) in the range 0F8h through 0FFh for its own use. Your TSR's INT 2Fh handler should immediately return from the interrupt if it receives a function code in this range.

Setting Up a Multiplex TSR

This programmer-defined function mechanism of INT 02Fh can satisfy all our communications requirements for TSR programs. Function 00h will tell us if the TSR is already installed. If necessary, we can assign another function code received by a new set of runtime parameters from a calling program. Still other function codes could invoke internal TSR functions on behalf of the calling program.

All we have to do now is set up our TSR to work with INT 2Fh. Let's review the necessary steps:

1. Add code to your TSR installation logic for retrieving the existing 2Fh pointer from lower memory, saving it locally, and saving your own handler's far pointer in lower memory.
2. Add an Interrupt Service Routine (ISR) for Int 2Fh to the body of your TSR program code. At minimum, this code should:
    a. Compare the entry value to the TSR's multiplex ID number, and if it doesn't match, make a far jump to the previously stored INT 2Fh handler.
    b. If the entry AL is 00h, reset it to 0FFh and return.
    c. Add logic to handle any other desired function code values in AL, using any and all registers that the caller may have set up. The overall data communications protocol is up to you.
3. Add code to the beginning of the main TSR program logic to retrieve and verify any command line parameters that you may use for setting up or altering the runtime parameters of the resident copy.
4. As part of your TSR installation, make an INT 2Fh call with AL set to 00h.
    a. If AL is returned still 00h, you can proceed with the regular TSR installation logic.
    b. If the TSR is already installed, you can make an INT 2Fh call to pass command line parameters to the resident copy, or simply to invoke TSR internal functions.

Some Gotchas

Once you realize the usefulness of the multiplex interrupt, setting things up is relatively simple and straightforward. Still, there are a few things to look out for, especially since you are working with TSRs, notoriously ornery beasties.

First, remember that when control is passed on to either the installed or previous handler, the state of the machine should continue to be almost exactly the same as when the caller invoked INT 2Fh. This means that no registers are changed (except for the flag register in comparing AH for the multiplex ID and **CS:IP** in the far jump), and nothing on the stack is changed. In this way, every "downstream" INT 2Fh handler sees the machine exactly like the first handler in the multiplex chain.

Second, to preserve the state of the machine, any variables used by the handler should be stored in the code segment. The CS register is the only "valid" register for the handler when it gets control; therefore, the code segment is the only place in which the local variables can be safely stored. If they were stored in a separate data segment, the interrupt

2Fh handler would first have to set up the DS register to point to that segment to access them. The PRINT program, for example, would be affected by the change in DS since it expects DS:DX to point to a submission packet and not to the data segment of some other multiplex handler.

Third, although a simple, user-defined INT 2Fh handler technically has control when invoked, it may not be properly set up as a TSR. This is because DOS still believes the PSP to be that of the calling program, rather than that of the TSR itself.

Last, extra thought must be given to a TSR that "uninstalls" itself. Part of the process of removing the TSR now involves removing it from the chain of INT 2Fh handlers. A TSR that uses the DOS multiplex interrupt can only uninstall itself if it is the first handler in the chain; that is, it was the last TSR installed. This is because only the first handler in the chain has no successor; there is no newer TSR out there in memory with a pointer to the soon-to-be-removed INT 2Fh handler.

TIP: See "Uninstall Your TSRs" later in this chapter for more information about removing a TSR from memory.

If Your TSR Doesn't Work on a 101-Key AT

■ Chuck Sommerville

Here's a clever patch to allow your TSRs to work correctly with 101-key keyboards.

Many TSR programs monitor the keyboard software interrupt (16H) to see if their hot key has been pressed. Most of these TSRs contain code at the beginning of their Interrupt 16H handler similar to the code shown here:

```
OLD_INT_16 DD 0     ; TSR install stores old INT 16H vector here
    ...
    ...
    ...
NEW_INT_16:         ; TSR install points INT 16H vector to here
    STI
    CMP     AH,00H         ; Request = 00H (get keystroke)?
    JE      CALL_BIOS      ; ..Yes, then CALL BIOS
                               ;   (and then back to us)
    JMP     CS:OLD_INT_16 ; ..No, just JMP to BIOS
                               ;   (it'll IRET to user)
CALL_BIOS:
    PUSHF       ; Simulate INT so BIOS's IRET returns to us
    CALL    CS:OLD_INT_16 ; Call BIOS INT 16H handler
            ; Now we're back...
    PUSHF                  ; Save any flags from the BIOS routine
    CMP     AX,CS:HOT_KEY ; Is it our hot key?
    JE      TSR_MAINLINE  ; ..Yes, go do the TSR's thing
    POPF                   ; ..No,  go back to user...
```

```
IRET
...
...
```

The TSR checks the Interrupt 16H function code in the AH register. If the function code is 00H (get keystroke), the TSR calls the "real" Interrupt 16H handler (the one in force when the TSR was loaded into memory). When the original INT 16H handler is returned, the program checks the keyboard scan code and the value of the character received to see if they represent the TSR's hot key. If the function code in AH turns out to be something other than 00H (such as the codes to check shift key status, set typematic rate, and so on), then the TSR does a long jump to the original handler to let the handler return to the user via **IRET**.

Few programmers are aware that, even if both 101-key keyboard and ROM BIOS 101-key keyboard supports are present, the INT 16H function 00H still provides a "filtered" get-keystroke service, in which only the keys present on an old 84-key keyboard are returned and the new extended keys (F11, F12, and so on) are ignored. This limitation exists to keep an old 84-key-aware application from being confused by extended keystrokes.

TIP: For more information about keyboard input, see Chapter 2.

An application can query the INT 16H services in a way that will determine the presence of BIOS-supported 101-key keyboards. If such a keyboard is present, the application may use the new INT 16H function 10H (get extended keystroke) service to get *all* possible keystrokes from the larger keyboard.

At least one application I have worked with does this extended keyboard I/O when it finds a supported 101-key keyboard: the Microsoft QuickC V2.1 programming environment. When I upgraded to an AT-class machine with a 101-key keyboard, several of my TSRs ceased to "pop up" when QuickC was running.

It was easy enough to add an additional test for AH = 10H after the test for 00H in the TSRs I had written, but I needed to find a way to enhance the TSRs for which I only had the .EXE file. Since the two INT 16H functions we now want to act on are 00H and 10H, testing for them is easy because they differ only in one bit. If you replace **CMP AH,00H** with **TEST AH,0EFH**, the flags will be set correctly regardless of whether 00H or 10H is in the AH register. (What we are saying to the program here is, "I want all the bits in AH to be zero, except bit 4, which is a don't-care.")

The machine code for **CMP AH,00H** is **80H FCH 00H**, and you can search the .EXE or .COM file for that three-byte sequence with DEBUG. Disassemble the machine code in the neighborhood of each search "hit." When you see code similar to listing presented earlier, just patch in the (fortunately also three-byte long) code for **TEST AH,0EFH**, which is **F6H C4H EFH**. The TSR then should work in both 84-key and 101-key environments.

TSR Debugging Tips

■ Bob Blumenfeld

Master the art of debugging TSRs by following these insider tips.

When you're debugging a TSR, fancy debuggers are of limited use. Stepping through code that locks out interrupts tends to hang the machine, while trying to step through a keyboard interrupt handler can be an exercise in futility and frustration.

It's more practical to selectively comment-out code. Work inward here. That is, first comment out a large block surrounding the suspect code. (Even if you wrote the code in assembler, you did code it using structured techniques, didn't you? No jumps into the middle of the block? A single exit point?) Compile/assemble and run. If the code doesn't fail, reactivate a subblock at the top or bottom of the block and try again. Continue this process until the code eventually fails again, at which point you know you've just reactivated the buggy code.

If you're lucky and skillful, you may be able to narrow down the suspects this way to just a few lines of code. Be careful, however, with commenting out interrupt lockouts and reenables. Do these only if you absolutely must, and then handle them like fragile bookends.

As you may have guessed from the above discussion, much TSR debugging is done by inference rather than from explicit knowledge of what's happening. So here are some rules of inference:

- The most common symptom of trouble is a locked keyboard. If even Ctrl+Alt+Del won't work, the code has probably either trashed the interrupt vectors, or else one of the interrupt handlers has failed to reenable interrupts.
- If the screen blanks or goes haywire, the code has trashed the interrupt vectors for certain.
- Random problems are often due to stack overflows. By default, interrupt handlers use the stack currently in use when they're invoked. If this happens to be DOS's stack, the stack may be too small for both DOS and your TSR. Since there's no way to detect a stack overflow, locations beyond the allocated end of the stack get wiped out. Anything can happen. The cure is to swap in your own stack on entry and swap it out on exit. Be careful, though, to protect against multiple stack-swapping. Increment a counter every time you enter and decrement it every time you exit; swap the stack in only on the first entry and out on the last exit.
- Always debug a new TSR in as vanilla an environment as you can, preferably one with no other TSRs. What you can see and modify is complicated enough. You hardly need someone else's invisible code playing some of the same games you are.
- To protect your hard disks from head crashes, it's a good idea to park their heads just prior to executing a suspicious or tricky piece of code. The algorithm for doing this is quite simple, as shown in Listing 16.4.

CODE DESCRIPTION

Overview

A C function to park the hard disk heads.

Listings Available

Listing	*Description*	*Used with*
PARK.C	Contains code for **ParkDisk.**	------

How to Compile/Assemble

Can be compiled and linked with any C/C++ compiler. Call using the following prototype:

```
void ParkDisk(void);
```

■ LISTING 16.4 PARK.C

```
/*------------------------------------------------------*/
/* Park_Disk:  Safety routine to park  the hard disk heads  */
/* prior to executing critical code that could hang the     */
/* machine and force a reboot.                              */
/*------------------------------------------------------*/

#include <dos.h>

#define BIOS_Disk_Interrupt_No 0x13

void ParkDisk(void)
{
int Disk_Ordinal;
union REGS regs;

  for(Disk_Ordinal = 0x0080; Disk_Ordinal < 0x0083; Disk_Ordinal++)
  {
    regs.h.ah = 0x08; /*Return drive parameters*/
    regs.x.dx = Disk_Ordinal;
    int86(BIOS_Disk_Interrupt_No, &regs, &regs);

/*------------------------------------------------------*/
/* If Carry set, early version of BIOS that cannot execute  */
/* Get Drive Parameters.                                    */
/*------------------------------------------------------*/

    if (! regs.x.cflag )
    {
/*------------------------------------------------------*/
/*  Bump "last usable cylinder" by one to get it off last   */
/*  cylinder.  Note:  This value is discontiguous in CX,    */
/*  hence the peculiar code.                                */
/*------------------------------------------------------*/
```

```
            regs.h.ch++;
            if (regs.h.ch == 0)
               regs.h.cl += 0x40;
            regs.x.dx = Disk_Ordinal;
            regs.x.ax = 0x0c01;  /*Seek to cylinder*/
            int86(BIOS_Disk_Interrupt_No,&regs,&regs);
         };
      };
   }
```

Uninstall Your TSRs

■ Greg Chursenoff

Here's a set of useful functions for controlling the Program Segment Prefix and releasing TSRs.

Clever TSRs can uninstall themselves, freeing up valuable memory and resolving hot-key conflicts. Once you understand the technique, your own TSRs can provide this handy feature. Three things must be accomplished to remove your TSR from memory.

First, if you reprogrammed any of the hardware you must restore its prior state. For example: If you modified the interrupt controller to enable an interrupt, you must remask the interrupt. If you reprogrammed the programmable timer to change the clock tick rate, you must restore it to its previous value.

Second, you must return any interrupt vectors to the values they contained before you intercepted them. If you hooked the keyboard interrupt to trap a hot key, the vector must be returned to its original handler. This step is the most critical part of the process of TSR removal. Before you restore the vector, you must be *absolutely* certain that another TSR hasn't been installed *after* your TSR, replacing your vector with one of its own. Compare the current vector to the value that you set it to. If it has changed, you cannot successfully remove your TSR because you have no way to tell the other TSR to chain the interrupt to the routine you intercepted—your TSR must refuse removal.

Finally, after you have successfully restored the hardware and interrupt vectors, you are ready to release the memory that your TSR occupies. This part is interesting because you must use undocumented DOS services. Let's review some DOS trivia before we get into the code itself.

DOS maintains an internal pointer that it uses to keep track of which program is currently executing; it points to the paragraph value of the current program segment prefix (PSP). Let's assume you have popped up your TSR over another program and instructed it to remove itself. The current program pointer no longer points to your TSR—it points to the PSP of the current program. This can be a problem because DOS has a safety mechanism; it will not allow a program to free memory it does not own. You must tell DOS that your TSR is the current program before it will honor your request to free memory.

UNTSR.C (Listing 16.5) presents three functions written in Turbo C inline assembly code that call the undocumented DOS services necessary for TSR removal. When you install your TSR, save the value of **_psp** for later use in the removal process. When removing your TSR, use **getpsp()** to get the current PSP and save it. Use **setpsp()** to set the current pointer to the value that you saved during installation. Then use **freemem()** to release the memory being occupied by your TSR's environment and PSP (two calls). You can find your environment by using the pointer DOS has provided at 0x2C of your PSP. Finally, use **setpsp()** again to restore the current PSP pointer and the removal process is complete!

The timing of these steps is also important. Deal with the hardware first. Turn off the interrupts when changing critical hardware or if you bypass DOS services to change interrupt vectors. Release the memory last. Exit from your TSR in your normal fashion, and *voila*! It will be as if your TSR had never been installed!

CODE DESCRIPTION

Overview

UNTSR.C contains three C functions that allow you to get and set the Program Segment Prefix and free memory to remove a TSR from memory.

Listings Available

Listing	*Description*	*Used with*
UNTSR.C	Utility functions for TSR programming.	------

How to Compile/Assemble

Can be compiled and linked with any C/C++ compiler.

■ LISTING 16.5 UNTSR.C

```
#pragma inline
#include <dos.h>

unsigned getpsp(void)            /* getpsp() returns segment */
{                                /* value of the current PSP */
  if (_osmajor < 3) _AH = 0x51;  /* pointer.  Service 0x62   */
  else _AH = 0x62;               /* is used preferentially,  */
  asm int 21h                    /* but is unavailable to    */
  _AX = _BX;                     /* versions before DOS 3.0  */
}

void setpsp(unsigned segment)    /* setpsp() sets DOS's      */
{                                /* current PSP pointer to   */
  _AH = 0x50;                    /* segment value passed.    */
  _BX = segment;
  asm int 21h
}

int freemem(unsigned segment)    /* freemem() frees memory   */
{                                /* beginning at the segment */
  _AH = 0x49;                    /* value passed.  Current   */
```

```
    _ES = segment;                 /* PSP pointer must aggree   */
    asm int 21h                    /* with owner of block to    */
    asm jc nok                     /* succeed.  Returns zero    */
    _AX = 0;                       /* if successful, DOS error */
  nok:                             /* code if unsuccessful.     */
    ;
  }
```

Prevent Reinstallation of TSRs

■ Greg Chursenoff

Use these utility functions to scan memory for an existing TSR.

Good commercial TSRs always check to see if they are already resident in memory before going through with their own installation. Otherwise multiple copies may be installed, wasting memory and performance, and possibly causing faulty operation. Here is a method you can use to determine if your TSR is already installed. There is an additional benefit—once your software knows where it is installed, a second copy executed from the DOS prompt can pass command line arguments to the resident copy before returning to DOS. This allows you to control your TSR from a hot key, the DOS prompt, or even a batch file!

The simplest way to tell if your TSR is installed would be to search all of memory for a signature that you put in your resident code. There is a better method that is both quick and elegant. It uses the interesting but undocumented DOS interrupt 0x21 function 0x52. This service returns a pointer (in ES:BX) to DOS's so-called list-of-lists. For DOS 2.1 and up, the word immediately preceding this list is a paragraph pointer to DOS's first memory control block (MCB).

DOS keeps track of memory using the MCBs. Each MCB is one paragraph (16 bytes) long and consists of a flag byte, an owner word, and a size word (the remainder is reserved but unused). The flag is set to 0x4D (M) for all blocks but the last, which is set to 0x5A (Z). The owner specifies the paragraph address of the owner's PSP. The size is given in paragraphs and excludes the MCB itself. The next MCB is always located at the first paragraph following the end of the current block. Each program (TSR or otherwise) starts out owning a block for its environment and another for its PSP, code, and data. Once you know the address of the PSP, you can access your code or data directly.

GETMCB1.C (Listing 16.6) shows Turbo C inline code for a function to get the address of the first MCB. The same function could be written in assembly language, or could be written using **intdosx()**, but it would be much longer and more complicated. This is exactly what inline code is for.

TSR.C (Listing 16.7) shows how to search memory for the signature you put into your program. Your signature can be any unique string stored as a static character array. The routine calculates the offset of your signature from the beginning of the PSP (256 bytes below the code segment), then compares the contents of that portion of each resident program to your signature. If your TSR is not installed, the routine will find only its reference copy of the signature and zero will be returned to your program. Otherwise, the paragraph address of the TSR's PSP is returned.

This routine is suitable for programs using the small memory model. The calculation would have to be modified for other memory models, particularly if the data segment is farther than 64K bytes from the beginning of the PSP. A simple alternative would be to poke the signature into your TSR's PSP at any offset after the first 0x5C bytes (up to 0xFF). It is safe for TSRs to use this area, since DOS needs only the initial part to terminate the TSR.

CODE DESCRIPTION

Overview

Two utility functions are presented here to illustrate how to scan memory for an existing TSR.

Listings Available

Listing	*Description*	*Used with*
GETMCB1.C	Returns address of first Memory Control Block.	------
TSR.C	Searches PSP's in memory for specific signature.	------

How to Compile/Assemble

Can be compiled and linked with any C/C++ compiler.

■ LISTING 16.6 GETMCB1.C

```
#pragma inline
unsigned getmcb1(void)
{
  _AH = 0x52;
  asm int 21h
  asm mov ax, es:[bx-2]
}
```

■ LISTING 16.7 TSR.C

```
#include <string.h>
#include <dos.h>

static char signature[] = "This is my signature.";

unsigned find_tsr_psp(void)

char i, ch, sig_size;
unsigned  mcb, owner, size, sig_addr, psp_addr = 0;

  sig_addr = 16 * (_DS - _CS) + 256 + (unsigned) &signature;
  sig_size = strlen(signature);
  mcb = getmcb1();
  do {
```

```
      ch = peekb(mcb, 0);
      owner = peek(mcb, 1);
      size = peek(mcb, 3);
      if (mcb == owner-1) {              /* examine only psp blocks */
        for(i=0; i<sig_size; i++) {
          if (peekb(owner, sig_addr+i) != signature[i]) break;
          if (i == sig_size-1) psp_addr = owner;    /* if last char */
        }
      }
      mcb += (size + 1);
    } while (ch == 'M' && !psp_addr);
    return(psp_addr != _psp ? psp_addr : 0);
}
```

Easier TSR Programs with C

■ Tony Rein

Here's a set of useful techniques for optimizing TSRs.

TSR programs should use as little RAM as possible and therefore are usually written in assembly language. Since writing in a higher-level language such as C is easier and less tedious than assembler, it would be nice to be able to write at least the installation portion in C, and save your tight, highly optimized assembler for the resident portion, where it really matters. But if you do this with Turbo C/C++ for example, Turbo C's startup code will end up being resident—thousands of bytes that your TSR almost certainly doesn't need. Here's how to get around that:

1. Assemble the file RESSEG.ASM (Listing 16.8).
2. Make sure everything you want to be resident is in a segment named in RESSEG.ASM.
3. In your C module, pass Borland C++'s **keep()** function (or the equivalent) the number of paragraphs (16-byte units) occupied by the resident code and data.
4. When you link, make sure RESSEG.OBJ is the *first* object file the linker sees, even before your compiler's startup modules. This will make sure the segments it defines are placed first in the .EXE file; and when DOS loads your program into memory, these segments will come right after the PSP. The **keep()** function leaves resident the number of paragraphs you pass, *starting at the PSP.*

ASM_CODE.ASM (Listing 16.9) and C_CODE.C (Listing 16.10) make an example program that does nothing but print a message and exit, leaving the contents of the .ASM file resident. You can modify this file to include your own assembly language TSR routines.

TIP: When modifying ASM_CODE.ASM for your own use, if you use the usual class names of **CODE**, **DATA**, and **STACK**, you won't be able to release the memory from your initialization routines. The linker will combine all segments of class **CODE** together, and all segments with class **DATA** together, and so on. In RESSEG.ASM, the .SEQ directive tells the linker to retain source-file order when it writes segment classes to the .EXE file. All segments in this file have the same class name (**RESIDENT**) so that the linker will keep them together in memory. You don't want your C module's (the installation code) segment kept together with your resident one.

Start_Address and **End_Res_Address** in C_CODE.C *must* be huge pointers to char, or the arithmetic to calculate **paras_to_reserve** won't work properly. The large or huge models will probably be the easiest to use for your version, since you'll almost certainly want to use library functions (**setvect()**, for example) to work with your resident data and functions, and you'll need far pointers to do that.

CODE DESCRIPTION

Overview

These three modules illustrate a mechanism for separating the initialization code for a TSR from the resident part. To keep your TSR small and fast, you will want to code the resident part in assembler. The initialization code, which might be more elaborate, can be coded in C.

Listings Available

Listing	*Description*	*Used with*
RESSEG.ASM	Describes the segment layout for freeing memory.	------
ASM_CODE.ASM	Modify this to contain your resident ASM code.	------
C_CODE.C	This is the initialization and startup code for your TSR.	------

How to Compile/Assemble

Can be compiled and linked with any C/C++ compiler which supports the **keep()** function (or its equivalent). Assemble RESSEG.ASM and ASM_CODE. Compile C_CODE.C and link the three modules together. Depending on your linker, you may need to specify RESEG.OBJ be linked first.

■ LISTING 16.8 RESSEG.ASM

```
; RESSEG.ASM

.SEQ

_RES_STACK      SEGMENT WORD STACK 'RESIDENT'
                ENDS

_RES_TEXT       SEGMENT BYTE PUBLIC 'RESIDENT'
                ENDS
```

```
_RES_DATA       SEGMENT PARA PUBLIC 'RESIDENT'
                ENDS

END
```

■ LISTING 16.9 ASM_CODE.ASM

```
;ASM_CODE.ASM

.SEQ

_RES_STACK      SEGMENT WORD STACK 'RESIDENT'
                db 20 dup ('STACK***')
Top_of_Stack  Label Byte
                ENDS

_RES_TEXT       SEGMENT BYTE PUBLIC 'RESIDENT'
                ENDS

_RES_DATA       SEGMENT PARA PUBLIC 'RESIDENT'
                PUBLIC _Message, _End_Resident_Stuff
_Message           db 'Message string', 0
_Space_filler   db 200H dup ('*')
_End_Resident_Stuff Label Byte
                ENDS


END
```

■ LISTING 16.10 C_CODE.C

```
/* C_CODE.C */


#include <dos.h>  /* for _psp, MK_FP(), and freemem() */
#include <stdio.h>

extern char Message;
extern char End_Resident_Stuff;

void main(void)
{
char huge * Start_Address, huge * End_Res_Address;
char far *cp;
unsigned int sg, paras_to_reserve;

/* Make a pointer from the address of 'Message':  */
cp = &Message;

puts("\n");
puts(cp);     /* Print 'Message' */

/*
```

```
 '_psp' is a global variable made available by Turbo C.
Use MK_FP() to make  a far pointer to offset 0x002C within
the PSP,   and cast it as a pointer  to unsigned int.
Dereference the pointer and assign the result to 'sg'.  'sg'
now holds the segment of this program's copy of the
environment.  Use 'freemem()' to release this, unless your
program needs the environment.
*/

 sg = *(unsigned int *)( MK_FP(_psp,0x002C) );
 freemem(sg);

 /* Point Start_Address at the beginning of the resident stuff   */
 /* (this will usually be at PSP:0000):                          */
 Start_Address = MK_FP(_psp, 0);

 /* Point End_Res_Address at the end of the resident stuff:      */
 End_Res_Address = &End_Resident_Stuff

 /* Find the difference between End and Start, and convert to     */
 /* paragraphs, rounding up if the number of bytes isn't a mul-   */
 /* tiple of 16:                                                  */
 paras_to_reserve = ((unsigned)(End_Res_Address - Start_Address)+15) / 16;

 /* Terminate: */
 keep(0, paras_to_reserve);
}
```

17

Working with DOS

Too many programmers look at DOS programming issues the way we earthlings tend to look at the moon: We've been there a few times, we walked around, took some pictures, and now we know everything about it, right?

Sheesh.

We get away with a lot of DOS ignorance because we *can*; DOS handles most everyday things transparently enough that we can use the standard runtime libraries in the standard language packages and not think much about it. It's mostly when you start getting a little exotic that you have to understand what DOS is actually doing Down There Somewhere.

DOS installable device drivers is a good example. Using them is easy; writing them is, well, a challenge. George Seaton lays out the ground rules in this chapter and provides a simple working model for a character driver. Paul Cilwa explains how to create a custom boot sector for diskettes, which isn't difficult—once you know how. Other authors will explain how to determine if a diskette is write-protected, how to pause a batch file using an installable device driver, and other DOS tidbits that are right handy to have when you need them.

Intercepting Critical Errors

■ Loren Heiny

Here's a clever trick for eliminating the bothersome "Abort, Retry, Fail" message.

Imagine that you're putting your finishing touches on your latest pride and joy, but there's just one problem: If you access one of the floppy drives in your program without a floppy in it, you get that darned "Abort, Retry, Fail" message—which does its very best to mess up your screen formatting.

Actually, it's fairly easy to get rid of this message. The "Abort, Retry, Fail" message is displayed by a routine called a *critical error handler* that is automatically accessed through interrupt vector 24h. You can modify this error handler routine to use your own display routines; however, since DOS is *not* reentrant, such code can be tricky. Another approach is simply to remove the message altogether by supplying an "empty" critical error handler that doesn't display anything to the screen. Just set the AX processor register to 0 and return. This is equivalent to pressing "I" for Ignore. In some cases, the Ignore option is not allowed. If this is the situation, returning 0 in AX will be treated as Fail. The **CritHandler** routines shown in CRITERR.C (Listing 17.1) do provide examples. To enable these routines, a call is made to **setvect()** near the beginning of your program to assign interrupt vector 24 hexadecimal to point to **CritHandler**:

```
setvect(0x24,CritHandler);
```

Of course, your code still needs to watch for file errors, but at least you won't get the "Abort, Retry, Fail" message again.

CODE DESCRIPTION

Overview

This is an interrupt 24h (Critical Error) handler routine which returns an "ignore" value to DOS.

Listings Available

Listing	*Description*	*Used with*
CRITERR.C	Disables Abort/Retry/Fail/Ignore messages on DOS Critical Errors.	------

How to Compile/Assemble

Can be compiled and linked with any C/C++ compiler.

■ LISTING 17.1 CRITERR.C

```
#include <dos.h>
void interrupt CritHandler();
```

```
void interrupt CritHandler(bp,di,si,ds,es,dx,cx,bx,ax,ip,cs,flgs)
{
  ax = 0;
}
```

Hiring a Driver

■ George Seaton

Create your own installable device driver for character devices.

Strange as it may seem, it is possible to live one's life without ever writing a single device driver. But, I ask you, can you say you've really *lived* without having done so?

The Nature of the Beast

As you probably know, device drivers are hardware-specific modules that pass data between hardware devices and the programs that use them. Drivers normally reside in files that have the extension SYS. You specify which drivers to load into memory by including one or more lines of the following format in your CONFIG.SYS file:

```
DEVICE=filename.SYS
```

DOS loads all the drivers from your CONFIG.SYS file into memory during the boot operation. It does this early in the process so that drivers can initialize their devices before anything—including COMMAND.COM—gets around to using them.

Device drivers come in two flavors: block and character. Block drivers handle devices like disks; that is, devices that move data in large chunks. These devices do not have "names;" instead, DOS uses a single letter in the range A through Z to address them.

Character devices generally move data one byte at a time. The keyboard, video, and printer drivers are in this category. These devices have names that you are already familiar with: CON, PRN, NUL, and so on.

Driver Innards

A device driver (particularly one for a character device) is not a particularly complicated beast. It has three main segments:

1. Driver header
2. Strategy routine
3. Interrupt routine

The interrupt routine usually includes a subroutine that sets up and initializes the device. DOS invokes the interrupt routine of a driver for an initialization pass when it first loads the driver into memory. The initialization logic can also take this opportunity to parse the "DEVICE=" command line from the CONFIG.SYS file, looking for any command line option switches. To facilitate this operation, DOS passes the driver a pointer to an in-memory copy of the text line from the CONFIG.SYS file.

I'll explain each major segment in more detail in the following paragraphs. The model for this exercise is a driver called PREFERS.SYS, and its assembler source appears in PREFERS.ASM (Listing 17.2). On examining the listing, you may be surprised to discover that this particular device drive doesn't actually drive a device. While it does "converse" with the video display and the keyboard, its main purpose is to set up the keyboard and video according to my own peculiar preferences. Since I currently use an AT clone with an EGA card and color monitor, these preferences include

1. Clearing (turning off) the NumLock state. (The BIOS sets it—turns it on—during the system reboot operation.)
2. Setting the EGA to the 43-line mode.
3. Turning off the EGA blink bit. (I use the high intensity background in my word processors to highlight selected text.)

Besides giving me an excuse to try my hand at writing a device driver, setting up my preferences in the driver lets me eliminate three small utility programs that I once invoked from my AUTOEXEC.BAT file. Not spectacular savings, but savings nevertheless. The lesson here is: You don't always need an actual "device" to have a driver.

Considering the way it's set up, PREFERS.SYS is a true DOS "character device" driver, having the assigned device name I_PREFER. When you dream up names for drivers, keep in mind that you must make it something truly unique. DOS simply refuses to deal with files that have the same eight-character names as a loaded character driver.

After reboot, programs can open and write to the I_PREFER device as though it were a text file. I_PREFER's driver logic expects to receive a single letter in the set ["N," "L," "B"]. You can send one of these characters to the device by doing a COPY CON I_PREFER from the DOS prompt, typing the character, and pressing Ctrl-Z. If, for example, you send an "L" to the I_PREFER device, the EGA should switch to or from 43-line mode, depending on its current state. (The initialization logic sets up my particular preferences; after that, the driver toggles the NumLock, EGA mode, and blink bit states.) BLINKTST.C (Listing 17.3) shows a small C program that exercises the "toggle blink bit" feature of the driver after installation.

The Driver Header

The header for a driver is an 18-byte data block. It must come first, and must be formatted as shown in lines 31-41 of PREFERS.ASM. DOS uses the first two words to point to the next device driver, if any, that it loads into memory. You initialize these words to 0FFFFh during the assembly step. If another device follows this one, DOS will fill in the offset and segment words while processing your CONFIG.SYS file. By so doing, DOS creates a linked chain of drivers in memory. If no other device follows, the two 0FFFFh words tell DOS that it has reached the end of the driver chain.

The word at offset +04h (line 34) is the Device Attribute Word. Bit 15 of this word specifies which class of driver this is: character or block. This specification tells DOS how to treat the device, and identifies the functions it must support. Table 17.1 lists the full set of device attribute bits and what they mean. Note that only bits 6, 11, 13, 14, and 15 apply to block devices; the other bits should be reset. For the simple character device created by my PREFERS.SYS file, only bit 15 really matters.

You set up the next two words (offsets +06 and +08; lines 37 and 38 in PREFERS.ASM) to hold the offsets of the Strategy and Interrupt routines within the driver. I'll get to these in just a moment.

The contents of the last eight-byte field in the header depend on the device class. For character devices, this is the eight-character device name. (You pad this with spaces if your name is shorter than eight characters.) For a replacement driver like ANSI.SYS, this field holds the standard device name: CON. (DOS loads the CONFIG.SYS drivers before its own built-in drivers. That way, when looking for the CON driver, it stops at ANSI.SYS (the first CON it finds), rather than using the built-in CON driver.) As seen in line 40 of PREFERS.ASM, I define my own device name (I_PREFER) for the PREFERS.SYS driver.

For block devices, DOS uses a single-letter identifier (A, B, C, and so on) for the device. In this case, you fill only the first byte of the name field, placing there the number of logical units supported by the physical device. The remaining seven bytes are reserved for DOS.

The Strategy Routine

When DOS wants to use a device, it first does a **FAR CALL** to the Strategy routine of the driver. It finds the offset of this routine at offset +06 of the header. When it calls the Strategy routine, DOS puts the address of the Request Header in the ES:BX register pair. (I'll discuss the Request Header and the actual request message later.)

■ TABLE 17.1 The device attribute word

Bit	Meaning
15	1 = Character Device; 0 = Block Device
14	1 = IOCTL Read/Write supported
13	1 = non-IBM format (for Block device) - or - 1 = Output Until Busy supported (Character device)
12	0...(Reserved)
11	1 = Open/Close Removable Media supported (DOS 3.0+)
10..7	0000...(Reserved)
6	1 = Generic IOCTL and Get/Set Logical Drive supported (DOS 3.2+)
5	0 (Reserved)
4	1 = Special CON output function supported
3	1 = This is current CLOCK device
2	1 = This is current NUL device
1	1 = This is current stdout device
0	1 = This is current stdin device

All the Strategy logic has to do is save these two words locally. (In PREFERS.ASM, the logic at label **STRAT** handles this task.) The Strategy routine can then execute a **RETF** (far return) instruction to go back to DOS.

The literature isn't clear about why DOS insists on this preliminary exchange of pleasantries before getting down to the business at hand. It would seem that the address of the Request Header could just as easily be passed during the subsequent call to the Interrupt routine, discussed next.

The Interrupt Routine

After handing off the Request Header address to the Strategy routine, DOS then calls the Interrupt routine. This is where the actual device driving occurs. The first thing normally done by an interrupt routine is to retrieve the Command Code from offset +2 of the Request Header. This tells the driver what function it should perform.

Tables 17.2 and 17.3 show the formats of the Request Headers from DOS, for the Initialization command and for the common Read/Write commands. Each table shows the corresponding Command Codes that the driver may receive. For the sake of brevity, I am showing only those Request Headers supporting these two common functions. The *MS-DOS Encyclopedia* (Microsoft Press, ISBN 1-55615-174-8) has the complete set of Request Header formats, for both character and block devices.

■ TABLE 17.2 Initialization request header

Offset (Byte)	Header Contents
+00H	Number of bytes in Request Header (byte)
+01H	{Don't Care}
+02H	Request Command Code (byte) 0 = Initialization
+03H	Returned Status {See NOTE 1}
+05H	Reserved by DOS (eight bytes)
+0DH	{Don't Care}
+0EH	Offset of initialization logic {See Note 2}
+10H	Segment of initialization logic
+12H	Offset of text after "DEVICE=" {See Note 3}
+14H	Segment of text after "DEVICE="
...	...

Notes:

1. The driver returns the status code to DOS, via the Request Header. (See Table 17.4)
2. The driver returns this data also. It points to the first location that DOS can reclaim from the "spent" initialization logic.
3. This is a far pointer to the text immediately after the "DEVICE=" line in the CONFIG.SYS file.

■ TABLE 17.3 Read/Write request header

Offset (Byte)	Header Contents	
+00H	Number of bytes in Request Header (byte)	
+01H	Unit Number request (byte) {Block device only}	
+02H	Request Command Code (byte)	
	3 = IOCTL Read	
	4 = Read	
	8 = Write	
	9 = Write with Verify	
	12 = IOCTL Write	
	14 = Output Until Busy	
+03H	Returned Status {See NOTE 1}	
+05H	Reserved by DOS (8 bytes)	
+0DH	Media Descriptor (byte)	
+0EH	Data Transfer Address (word:word)	
+12H	Byte or Sector count (word)	
+14H	Starting Sector Number (word)	{Block device only}
...	...	

Note:

The driver returns the status code to DOS, via the Request Header. (See Table 17.4)

For the PREFERS.SYS driver, we are only concerned about the Initialization and Write commands. As you'll see from the following paragraphs, the initialization logic does most of the work for this particular driver.

The Initialization Logic

DOS first calls a driver immediately after loading it into memory. When the call is made, DOS sets the Command Code (Request Header offset +2) to 0, for initialization. It also saves the segment and offset of the text line from the CONFIG.SYS line for this driver. As indicated above, this address points to the text immediately following the "DEVICE=" string. It is provided so that the initialization logic can parse the command line for option switches, like "/whatever."

In PREFERS.SYS, the initialization logic does its NumLock resetting and EGA setup, and then sends a message to the video screen, saying (in essence) "I'm here!" More complex drivers can devote their energies to such things as setting up interrupt response location or toggling device command lines.

Since initialization only happens once per reboot, there is no need to leave all that code sitting around in memory like so much deadwood. A driver can, therefore, send a pointer back to DOS to indicate the starting address of the now-completed and no longer necessary initialization logic. It does so by storing the segment and offset words back into the Request

Header, using the pointer that DOS originally sent to the driver Strategy routine. (Refer to the ending of PREFERS.ASM.)

When the driver itself executes its **FAR** return to DOS, DOS checks for the segment:offset data in the Request Header. If it finds an address, DOS reclaims the memory starting at that address, up to the end of the driver. (Obviously, you want to put your expendable initialization logic at the *end* of the driver—not at the beginning or in the middle!)

The Mainline Logic

As indicated above, the first task performed by the mainline logic of the Interrupt routine is to determine what function to perform. It does this by retrieving the Command Code from the Request Header, and then calling or jumping to the appropriate command-processing routine. You've already seen that a Command Code of zero sends the driver to its initialization logic.

For other command codes, the driver's dispatcher function vectors to the corresponding logic. (If the command is inappropriate, the driver returns an error code to DOS.) In PREFERS.SYS, only the "Write" and "Write With Verify" are legal; anything else returns an error code to DOS.

The Command Processors

The WRITE logic segment in PREFERS.SYS is an example of a command processor in a device driver. Since the command involves "output," the first order of business is to retrieve (from DOS) the output message that was sent to the driver. To do so, the logic uses the far pointer in words 0Eh through 11h of the Request Header. (Refer to Table 17.3.) For a real hardware device, this logic would then execute the necessary **OUT** instructions to transfer the message to the device. Here, however, you simply get the first character, convert it to uppercase, and call the appropriate subroutine for the command character retrieved from DOS.

In a driver for an asynchronous input device (such as a serial port), part of the mainline logic might be devoted to servicing the interrupts from the device and, if necessary, buffering the incoming data. (The initialization logic would have set up interrupt response addresses that point to the servicing logic in the driver.) Processing a "Read" command from DOS would then involve transferring the buffered data to the target location specified in the Request Header.

Errors Happen

While this little truism may not show up on a bumper sticker, a driver is obligated to let DOS know how things turn out in the device-driving game. The driver does so by writing a status word back into offset +03h of the original Request Header. The driver sets bit 15 of the word if it detected an error. In this case, the lower eight bits of the word are an error code. Table 17.4 lists the error codes that a driver may return to DOS.

If there was no error, but the driver is busy at the moment, it will set bit 9 of the status word. Finally, if things went just fine, the driver tells DOS that it is done by setting bit 8. From the PREFERS.SYS listing, you see that we return a status word of 0100h for a "Done, No Errors" return. For an unsupported Command Code, we return 8103h; "Done, With Error, Unknown Command."

Driver, Take Me Home

By now, you should have an understanding of what a device driver is, how it works, and what the "programming basics" are for creating one. You can even use a device driver for mythical devices (i.e., where no actual hardware device is involved) as PREFERS.SYS illustrates.

If you decide, therefore, to sit yourself down and write yourself a driver, you will probably want to check out Article 15 in Part C of Microsoft's reference tome *The MS-DOS Encyclopedia*. Besides being the official source for most (alas, not all) DOS functions, the encyclopedia has discussions on some of the more esoteric functions your device driver may be called on to perform.

Finally, I cannot, in good faith, take my leave without saying just a few words about programming and debugging your home-brew device drivers. The rather rigid structure of

■ TABLE 17.4 Driver error codes

Error Code	Meaning of Code
00H	Write-Protect Violation
01H	Unknown Unit
02H	Drive Not Ready
03H	Unknown Command
04H	CRC Error
05H	Bad Drive Request Structure Length
06H	Seek Error
07H	Unknown Media
08H	Sector Not Found
09H	No Printer Paper
0AH	Write Error
0BH	Read Error
0CH	General Device Failure
0DH	Reserved
0EH	Reserved
0FH	Invalid Disk Change (DOS 3.x)

Note:

These codes appear in bits 7..0 of the Returned Status word in the Request Header IF bit 15 is set.

the device driver usually dictates programming them in assembly language. As the PREFERS.SYS listing indicates, the source is set up with **ORG** sct to 0000h, rather than 0100h.

After fixing any syntax errors, you can then use the linker to create the .EXE file, and use the EXE2BIN program to convert it to binary (and rename it with the .SYS extension).

All that remains is to make a backup copy of your old CONFIG.SYS file adding the appropriate "DEVICE=" statement to your new CONFIG.SYS file and rebooting your PC. In a perfect universe, your new creation will display its "I'm here!" message during the reboot procedure, do whatever initialization you want it to do, and perform its other runtime functions flawlessly.

In a real world, things may not go so smoothly. And when things don't go smoothly with device drivers, you may not be able to get through the reboot procedure at all. It would be a good idea to keep a bootable DOS disk handy for just this situation. You can then return to your old CONFIG.SYS while you sort out what went wrong.

One approach to take is to program the driver in stages. In the first stage, just include the "interface" functions and basic function dispatcher, and leave out all the active initialization and command-processing code. This way, you can concentrate on any bugs associated with getting into and out of the driver itself. The *MS-DOS Encyclopedia* includes two driver templates written by the legendary Ray Duncan. They would be perfect starting points for your own driver development.

After convincing yourself that the driver does its administrative chores correctly, you can begin adding the working code, starting with the initialization routine. Depending on how many runtime commands your driver will handle (and how patient you are), you can add the command processors either singly or in groups.

Take it slow, make sure you have backups, and don't let the driver drive you—crazy!

CODE DESCRIPTION

Overview

A complete example of a DOS device driver program which "drives" specific parts of an AT system (EGA blink-bit, Num-Lock keyboard status, and 43/25-line vide mode).

Listings Available

Listing	*Description*	*Used with*
PREFERS.ASM	DOS device driver.	------
BLINKTST.C	Example program to manipulate driver.	------

How to Compile/Assemble

PREFERS.ASM can be assembled with a TASM compatible assembler program and linked with TLINK or LINK. Because of the particular structure or a DOS device driver, the result must then be converted to a .COM-type file with EXE2BIN. The final name should be changed to I_PREFER.SYS to reflect the program internal name.

BLINKTST.C can be compiled and linked with any C/C++ compiler.

■ LISTING 17.2 PREFERS.ASM

```
;                    P R E F E R S . S Y S
;       By George W. Seaton - Assemble with Borland's TASM
;
; This module is an example of a simple "character" device driver.
; It does not "drive" any particular device; instead, it sets up
; certain BIOS parameters for the video and keyboard, according
; to the user's personal preferences.  For the author's AT-clone
; with an EGA color video, these preferences include:
;
;  - Turning off the NumLock state.
;  - Setting the EGA video to 43-line mode.
;  - Turning OFF the video blink bit.
;
; After its initial installation, users can use the driver (i.e.,
; by writing to the device) to toggle these parameters.
;=================================================================
; Assembler setup commands
;=================================================================
CSEG   Segment byte public "CODE"
       Assume CS:CSEG,DS:CSEG,ES:CSEG
       Org 00H                 ;<============ NOTE!
PREFERS:
;=================================================================
;             D R I V E R   H E A D E R   B L O C K
;
; Bytes 0000h-0011h of the driver M-U-S-T be set up as follows:
;=================================================================
       DW     0FFFFh           ;+0: Offset of next Device (if any)
       DW     0FFFFh           ;+2: Segment of next Device (if any)
;--------------------------------
       DW     8000h            ;+4: Device Attribute Word
;                              (Bit 15 SET for "Character" device)
;--------------------------------
       DW     Offset STRAT     ;+6: Offset of "Strategy" routine
       DW     Offset INTRPT    ;+8: Offset of "Interrupt" routine
;--------------------------------
       DB     'I_PREFER'       ;+0Ah..+11h = Name of Driver
;                               (padded with spaces, as required)
;=================================================================
;                 S T R A T E G Y   R O U T I N E
;
; Called by DOS to save the pointer (in ES:BX) to the Device
; Driver Request Header.
;--------------------------------
STRAT:
       MOV     CS:[HDROFS],BX ;Save offset of Request Header
       MOV     CS:[HDRSEG],ES ;Save segment of Request Header
       RETF                   ;Return to DOS
;=================================================================
; Local Data Storage...
;--------------------------------
HEADER LABEL   DWORD           ;Allow for DD reference
```

```
HDROFS DW      0000           ;Segment storage
HDRSEG DW      0000           ;Offset storage
TOGGLE DB      01             ;Storage for current toggle states
;                              01 = EGA Blink Bit ON
;===============================================================
;            I N T E R R U P T   P R O C E D U R E
;
; Called by DOS to process a driver request, as defined in the
; Request Header.  The Request Header is found at the address
; previously passed to the Strategy Routine.
;
; Request Header format:
; +00 = NUMB     Number of bytes in Request Header (byte)
; +01 = UNIT     Unit Number of this request (byte) (BLOCK)
; +02 = CMMD     Request Command Code (byte)
; +03 = STAT     Returned Status (word)
; +05 = RESRVED  Reserved by DOS (eight bytes)
; +0D = MEDIA    Media Descriptor (byte)
; +0E = ADDR     Data Transfer Address (word:word)
; +12 = COUNT    Byte or sector count (word)
; +14 = SECT     Starting sector value (BLOCK DEVICE)
;===============================================================
;      I _ P R E F E R   I N T E R R U P T   L O G I C
;--------------------------------
INTRPT:
       PUSH     AX            ;Save the entry registers...
       PUSH     BX
       PUSH     CX
       PUSH     DX
       PUSH     ES
       PUSH     DI
       PUSH     SI
;--------------------------------
; Retrieve the address of the Request Header and get the CMMD.
;--------------------------------
       PUSH     CS
       POP      DS
       LES      BX,CS:[HEADER] ;ES:BX = [HDRSEG:HDROFS]
       MOV      AL,ES:[BX+02]  ;CMMD = HDRSEG:[HDROFS+2]
;--------------------------------
; If CMMD IS "Write" or "Write with Verify", go to the "WRITE"
; logic.
;--------------------------------
       CMP    AL,08h          ;If CMMD = "WRITE" then...
       JZ     WRITE           ;...WRITE
       CMP    AL,09h          ;If CMMD = "WRITEV" then...
       JZ     WRITE           ;...WRITE
;--------------------------------
; If CMMD IS "INIT," go to the Initialization logic.
;--------------------------------
       CMP    AL,00           ;If CMMD = "INIT" then...
       JMP    INIT            ;...INITIALIZE
;--------------------------------
       PAGE
;--------------------------------
```

```
; For any other CMMD, return an error code in the STATUS
; parameter and return to DOS.
;--------------------------------
BADRTN:
        MOV     Word Ptr ES:[BX+03],8103h
        JMP     RETURN          ;Return
        NOP
;--------------------------------
; Return through here when done
;--------------------------------
GUDRTN:
        MOV    Word Ptr ES:[BX+03],0100h
;--------------------------------
; Restore registers and return to DOS
;--------------------------------
RETURN:
        POP     SI              ;Restore the entry registers...
        POP     DI
        POP     ES
        POP     DX
        POP     CX
        POP     BX
        POP     AX
        RETF                    ;Return (Far)
;===============================================================
;                 W R I T E   P R O C E D U R E
;
; Retrieve the "output message" for the driver.  This should be
; one character, where...
;
; ... N or n toggles the NumLock state            (Initially OFF)
; ... L or l toggles the EGA 43-line mode          (Initially ON)
; ... B or b toggles the EGA video blink state    (Initially OFF)
;===============================================================
WRITE:
        LDS     SI,ES:[BX+0Eh] ;DS:SI = ADDR
        LODSB                   ;AL = DS:[SI] = [ADDR] = "x"
        PUSH    CS              ;Move CS...
        POP     DS              ;...into DS
;--------------------------------

; For [N,L,B]: Go to the appropriate "toggle" logic.
; (Otherwise, ignore the character.)
;--------------------------------
        AND     AL,5Fh          ;Make letter uppercase
        CMP     AL,4Eh          ;If (AL = 'N') then...
        JNE     NotNum
        CALL    NUMLCK          ;...CALL NUMLCK
        JMP     GUDRTN
NotNum:
        CMP     AL,4Ch          ;If (AL = 'L') then...
        JNE     NotLine
        CALL    EGA43           ;...CALL EGA43
        JMP     GUDRTN
NotLine:
```

```
        CMP     AL,42h          ;If (AL = 'B') then...
        JNE     BADRTN
        CALL    BLINK           ;...CALL BLINK
        JMP     GUDRTN
;==================================================================
        PAGE
;==================================================================
; NUMLCK: Toggles the NumLock State for the keyboard.
;----------------------------------
NUMLCK PROC NEAR
        PUSH AX                 ;Save the...
        PUSH ES                 ;...entry registers
        MOV  AX,0040h           ;Set DS to...
        MOV  ES,AX              ;...0040 (BIOS segment)
        MOV  AL,Byte Ptr ES:[0017h] ;Get the keyboard state
        TEST AL,20h             ;Test the NumLock bit
        JNZ  NumOFF             ;
NumON:
        OR   AL,20h             ;If OFF, turn it ON
        JMP  NumSet
NumOFF:
        AND  AL,0DFh            ;If ON, turn it OFF
NumSet:
        MOV  Byte Ptr ES:[0017h],AL ;Put it back
        POP  ES                 ;Restore the...
        POP  AX                 ;...entry registers
        RET                     ;Return to the caller
NUMLCK ENDP
;==================================================================
; BLINK: Toggles the EGA/VGA Blink Bit
;----------------------------------
BLINK  PROC NEAR
        PUSH AX                 ;Save the...
        PUSH BX
        PUSH DS                 ;...entry registers
        PUSH CS
        POP  DS
        MOV  AL,[TOGGLE]        ;Get the current toggle word
        TEST AL,01              ;Test the Blink state bit
        JNZ  BlkOff
BlkOn:
        MOV  BL,01              ;Turn ON if currently OFF
        OR   AL,01
        JMP  BlkSet
BlkOff:
        MOV  BL,00              ;Turn OFF if currently ON
        AND  AL,0FEh
BlkSet:
        MOV  [TOGGLE],AL
        MOV  AX,1003h
        INT  10h
        POP  DS                 ;Restore the...
        POP  BX
        POP  AX                 ;...entry registers
        RET
```

```
BLINK  ENDP
;==============================================================

; EGA43: Toggles the 43-line mode for the EGA video.
;        (Also, sets up a block cursor, "fixes" the EGA cursor
;         emulation, and selects the EGA BIOS "Print Screen"
;-------------------------------------

EGA43  PROC NEAR
       PUSH AX                  ;Save the...
       PUSH BX
       PUSH CX
       PUSH ES                  ;...entry registers
;-------------------------------------
; If the current BIOS screen lines count (less one) at 0040:0084
; is NOT 42, then go set up the 43-line mode.  Otherwise, restore
; the 25-line mode
;-------------------------------------
       MOV  AX,0040h            ;Set DS to...
       MOV  ES,AX               ;...0040 (BIOS segment)
       MOV  AL,Byte Ptr ES:[0084h] ;IF (0040:0084 <> 42) then...
       CMP  AL,42
       JNE  GoTo43              ;...GoTo43
;-------------------------------------
; Select the 8x14 font and adjust the screen lines (to 25).
;-------------------------------------
GoTo25:
       MOV  AX,1111h
       MOV  BL,00
       INT  10h
;-------------------------------------
; Turn the EGA cursor emulation logic back on and set up a block
; cursor.  Then return.
;-------------------------------------
       AND  Byte Ptr ES:[0087h],0FEh
       JMP  SetCur
;-------------------------------------
; Select the 8x8 character font and adjust the screen lines
;-------------------------------------
GoTo43:
       MOV  AX,1112h            ;Load the 8x8 font & recalculate
       MOV  BL,00               ;RAM block 0
       INT  10h                 ;BIOS Video Service
;-------------------------------------
; Select the alternate (EGA BIOS) Print Screen function
;-------------------------------------
       MOV  BL,20h
       MOV  AH,12h
       INT  10h
;-------------------------------------
; Turn off the buggy EGA cursor emulation and set up a block
; cursor.  Then return.
;-------------------------------------
       OR   Byte Ptr ES:[0087h],01
SetCur:
```

```
        MOV   CX,0007h          ;CH = Scan top; CL = Scan bottom
        MOV   AH,01             ;"Set Cursor Size"
        INT   10h
        POP   ES                ;Restore the...
        POP   CX
        POP   BX
        POP   AX                ;...entry registers
        RET
EGA43   ENDP
;================================================================
RUNSIZ EQU      $-PREFERS
       DB       (0100H-RUNSIZ) DUP(00)
;================================================================
;            I N I T I A L I Z A T I O N   L O G I C
;================================================================
; This logic is invoked when DOS installs the driver. (CMMD = 0).
; The initialization steps include:
;
;  1. Resetting the keyboard NumLock state.
;  2. Setting the EGA video into 43-line mode
;  3. Turning off the EGA blink bit
;  4. Displaying the "I'm here!" message on the video screen.
;
; When done, the logic tells DOS where the "expendable" part of
; the driver (the initialization logic itself) begins.  DOS will
; then release the memory AFTER that address for its own use.
;---------------------------------
INIT    LABEL   NEAR

        PUSH    AX              ;Save registers
        PUSH    BX              ;
        PUSH    CX              ;
        PUSH    DX              ;
        PUSH    ES              ;
;---------------------------------
; Call the mainline procedures to set the initial preferences.
;---------------------------------
        CALL    NUMLCK          ;Turn OFF the NumLock State
        CALL    EGA43           ;Turn ON the EGA 43-line mode
        CALL    BLINK           ;Turn OFF the EGA Blink bit
;---------------------------------
; Announce the installation of the driver.
;---------------------------------
        LEA     DX,IMHERE       ;DX = Offset(IMHERE)
        MOV     AH,09h          ;"Display string"
        INT     21h             ;DOS service
;---------------------------------
; Release the initialization logic and return.
;---------------------------------
        POP     ES              ;Restore the key entry registers
        POP     DX              ;
        POP     CX              ;
        POP     BX              ;
        LEA     AX,INIT         ;AX = Offset(INIT)
        MOV     Word Ptr ES:[BX+0Eh],AX ;"ADDR" = AX
```

```
        MOV     Word Ptr ES:[BX+10h],CS ;"ADDR+2" = CS
        POP     AX              ;Restore AX
        JMP     GUDRTN          ;Return
;==================================================================
IMHERE LABEL  NEAR
        DB      0Dh,0Ah,'PREFERS.SYS Preferences Driver Installed.'
        DB      0Dh,0Ah
        DB     'Write N, L, or B to I_Prefer to change',0Dh,0Ah,'$'
CSEG    ENDS
        END     PREFERS
```

■ LISTING 17.3 BLINKTST.C

```
/*blinktst.c*/
/*=================================================================
 Program to demonstrate the effect of the EGA Blink Bit,
  using the "I_PREFER" device (PREFERS.SYS).
===============================================================*/
#include <conio.h>
#include <stdio.h>

#define ESC 0x1b

void main(void)
{
char Toggle = 'b';  /*I_PREFER message to toggle blink bit*/
FILE *fileptr;      /*My preferences device is a "text" type*/

  clrscr();
  fileptr = fopen("I_PREFER","wt");   /*Open the preferences "device"*/
  setbuf(fileptr,NULL);
  textattr(0xCF);                     /*Bold white on red*/
  cprintf("Press [Esc] to quit; any other key to toggle the blink bit.\n");
  while (getch() != ESC)
    fputc(Toggle,fileptr); /*Command device to toggle blink bit*/
  fclose(fileptr);
}
```

Reading and Interpreting the DOS Allocation Table

■ Kenneth B. Gladden

Use the DOS allocation table to access a disk drive.

The DOS interrupt 21h functions 1Bh and 1Ch return allocation table information for a disk drive, including a pointer to the media ID byte. This ID byte allows you to tell what sort of media is present in a given drive.

Function 1Bh, which is supported by all versions of DOS, returns allocation information for the current default drive. Function 1Ch, introduced at DOS version 2.0, returns allocation information for a specified drive.

Before calling either of these functions, set registers to the following values:

```
AH = function number (1Bh or 1Ch)
DL = nn (function 1Ch only)
```

where nn=00 for the default drive, 01 for drive A, 02 for drive B, and so on.

The following values are returned by the two functions:

```
AL = Sectors per cluster, or FFh if error
CX = Bytes per sector
DX = Clusters per disk
DS:BX = Far pointer to media ID byte
```

Beginning with DOS Version 2.0, the DS:BX registers form a far pointer to a copy of the media ID byte, but in version 1 it actually points to a copy of the FAT in memory, the first byte of which contains the media ID.

The media ID byte provides certain essential information about the media currently installed in a given drive. This information is summarized in Table 17.5.

The disk's total capacity in bytes can be determined from the other information provided by the formula CX*AL*DX.

MEDIABYT.C (Listing 17.4) gets the allocation table information for the diskette in drive A from function 1Ch and displays the media byte and disk capacity information. The **intdosx()** function is a C runtime library function that executes DOS interrupt 21h which, unlike the **intdos()** function, also returns the segment registers, one of which is needed to obtain the segment address of the media ID byte. The segment address is then shifted left 16 bits and ORed with the offset address to create a far pointer to the media ID byte.

TIP: To determine the size of the disk in drive B:, substitute **sRegs.h.dl=2** just before the call to **intdosx**. To determine the size of the disk in the default (current drive) use **sRegs.h.dl= 0**.

■ TABLE 17.5 The DOS media ID codes

Code	Size	Description
FFH	3.5"	double-sided, 18 sectors - 1.44M or "other"
F8H	fixed disk	(any type)
F9H	5.25"	double-sided, 15 sectors - 1.2M (AL = 1)
	or 3.5"	double-sided, 9 sectors - 720K (AL = 2)
FCH	5.25"	single-sided, 9 sectors - 180K
FDH	5.25"	double-sided, 9 sectors - 360K
FEH	5.25"	single-sided, 8 sectors - 160K
FFH	5.25"	double-sided, 8 sectors - 320K

CODE DESCRIPTION

Overview

Utility program which displays the size of a diskette in a specific drive.

Listings Available

Listing	*Description*	*Used with*
MEDIABYT.C	Stand-alone C utility.	------

How to Compile/Assemble

Can be compiled and linked with any C/C++ compiler.

■ LISTING 17.4 MEDIABYT.C

```
/* MEDIABYT.C This is a program to determine what size diskette is in drive A:
by reading the media byte in the FAT via DOS Interrupt 21h Function 1Ch.
 */

#include <stdio.h>
#include <dos.h>

main()
{
    unsigned char far *fpMediaID;    /* Far pointer to media byte */
    union REGS sRegs;                /* Declare registers */
    struct SREGS sSregs;             /* Declare segment registers */

    sRegs.h.ah = 0x1C;       /* Set function to get drive data */
    sRegs.h.dl = 1;          /* Set drive id; 0=default, 1=A, etc. */
    intdosx(&sRegs, &sRegs, &sSregs);    /* Execute DOS interrupt */
    if (sRegs.h.al == 0xFF)
    {
    printf( "Invalid drive or critical error.");
    exit(2);
    }
/* Turn off checks for out of range pointers. (QuickC) */
#pragma check_pointer (off)
/* Pick up segment:offset address of media byte */
    fpMediaID = (unsigned char far *)
    ((((long)sSregs.ds) << 16) | sRegs.x.bx);
    printf( "\nMedia byte = %X\n", *fpMediaID); /* media byte */
    /* The media ID byte has the following meaning:
     *  0xF0    3.5"    double-sided, 18 sectors - 1.44M
     *                  or "other"
     *  0xF8    fixed disk
     *  0xF9    5.25"   double-sided, 15 sectors - 1.2M (AL = 1)
     *          or 3.5" double-sided,  9 sectors - 720K (AL = 2)
     *  0xFC    5.25"   single-sided,  9 sectors - 180K
     *  0xFD    5.25"   double-sided,  9 sectors - 360K
     *  0xFE    5.25"   single-sided,  8 sectors - 160K
     *  0xFF    5.25"   double-sided,  8 sectors - 320K
```

```
    */
#pragma check_pointer (on)

    printf ("Capacity = %ld bytes\n",
        (long)sRegs.x.cx*sRegs.h.al*sRegs.x.dx);
    return (0);
}
```

Tracing the DOS Device Driver Chain

■ Jim Mischel

Use undocumented DOS function 52h to find out where all your drivers are hiding.

Among the more interesting and useful of the undocumented DOS functions is function 52h of INT 21h. This function returns a pointer to a DOS internal structure popularly referred to as **invars** or DOS's "list of lists." The format of this structure is shown in Figure 17.1.

Three doubleword pointers in this structure are of particular interest when you are working with device drivers. The value at offset 08h from the start of the table points to the beginning of the CLOCK$ device driver. The value at offset 0Ch points to the beginning of the CON device driver and the pointer at offset 22h (for DOS versions 3.0 and later) or 17h (for DOS 2.X only) points to the NUL device driver, which is the first driver in the DOS device driver chain.

An MS-DOS device driver consists of three parts: a device header that provides information about the driver to MS-DOS, a strategy routine that sets the address of the MS-DOS request header prior to an actual request, and an interrupt routine that actually performs the required functions. The format of the device header is shown in Figure 17.2.

TIP: For more information about DOS device drivers, see Hiring a Driver, earlier in this chapter.

The device headers form a linked list of device drivers with the NUL device at the head of the list, followed by any user-loadable (i.e., **DEVICE=**) device drivers, followed by the standard device drivers that DOS loads automatically at boot time. The end of the list is indicated by a value of FFFFh in the offset portion of the next driver link. It is possible to create a program that walks down the device chain and examines the contents of each device header.

DDLST.C (Listing 17.5) is such a program. It obtains the address of the NUL device from the list of lists and proceeds down the list reporting what it finds. Figure 17.3 is a sample of the program's output when run on my system (DOS 4.01) with just the standard device drivers installed. User-installable device drivers would appear immediately after the NUL device.

Offset	Length	Description
-02h	2 bytes	Segment of first Memory Control Block
00h	4 bytes	Pointer to first Drive Parameter Block
04h	4 bytes	Pointer to first Device Control Block
08h	4 bytes	Pointer to CLOCK$ device driver
0Ch	4 bytes	Pointer to CON device driver
DOS Version 2.x		
10h	1 byte	Number of logical drives
11h	2 bytes	Maximum sector size on any block device
13h	4 bytes	Pointer to start of disk buffer chain
17h		Beginning of NUL device driver
DOS Version 3.0 and later		
10h	2 bytes	Maximum sector size on any block device
12h	4 bytes	Pointer to start of disk buffer chain (In V4.X this is a pointer to a pointer to the start of the disk buffer chain).
16h	4 bytes	Pointer to logical drive table
1Ah	4 bytes	Pointer to start of the DOS File Control Block chain
1Eh	2 bytes	Size of File Control Block table
20h	1 byte	Number of block devices
21h	1 byte	Number of logical drives (LASTDRIVE)
22h		Beginning of NUL device driver

FIGURE 17.1 "List of Lists" format

The code in DDLST.C may be grafted into applications that need to identify and perhaps manipulate device drivers at runtime. One simple example of such a scenario is an application that needs to temporarily disable the ANSI.SYS driver when it is found.

ANSI.SYS is loaded as a replacement CON device. The default CON device is still in the chain, but because ANSI.SYS is loaded after the original CON device, DOS finds it first when scanning the chain for a specific device name. By manipulating pointer values (and retaining the old values) a program could cut the replacement CON device out of the chain, and then restore the original pointer values before returning to DOS.

As DOS only walks the chain on opening a file or device, you would have to first close standard input and standard output (DOS file handles 0 and 1), cut the replacement CON device out of the chain, and then reopen standard input and output. On reopening, the standard CON device, rather than ANSI.SYS, would be attached to standard input and output. The ANSI.SYS CON driver is still in memory and can be reinserted by replacing the original pointer values and opening the handles 0 and 1 again.

Offset	Length	Description
00h	4 bytes	Pointer to next device driver header
04h	2 bytes	Device attribute word (see below)
06h	2 bytes	Pointer to device strategy routine
08h	2 bytes	Pointer to device interrupt routine
0Ah	8 bytes	Character Device: Device name Block Device: Number of units followed by 7 bytes of reserved space

Device Attribute Word

Bit 15	= 1 Character device
	= 0 Block device
Bit 14	= 1 IOCTL supported
Bit 13	= 1 non-IBM format (block devices)
	= 1 output until busy supported (character devices)
Bit 12	= Reserved
Bit 11	= 1 DOS 3.x functions supported
Bits 10-5	= Reserved
Bit 4	= 1 CON device supports INT 29h for fast screen output
Bit 3	= 1 current clock device
Bit 2	= 1 current NUL device
Bit 1	= 1 current standard output device
Bit 0	= 1 current standard input device

■ **FIGURE 17.2 Device header format**

```
invars at 02E5:0026
CLOCK$ device at 0070:01A4
CON device at 0070:016E

 seg:ofs  name    typ  strat intr  attr
02E5:0048 NUL       CHR  18DB  18E1  8004
0070:016E CON       CHR  062A  0635  8013
0070:0180 AUX       CHR  062A  063B  8000
0070:0192 PRN       CHR  062A  0658  A040
0070:01A4 CLOCK$    CHR  062A  067E  8008
0070:01B6    5      BLK  062A  0684  0842
0070:01CA COM1      CHR  062A  063B  8000
0070:01DC LPT1      CHR  062A  065E  A040
0070:01EE LPT2      CHR  062A  0666  A040
0070:0200 LPT3      CHR  062A  066E  A040
0070:0212 COM2      CHR  062A  0641  8000
0070:0224 COM3      CHR  062A  0647  8000
0070:0236 COM4      CHR  062A  064D  8000
```

■ **FIGURE 17.3 Sample DDLST output**

CODE DESCRIPTION

Overview

Program which traces the list of device drivers currently loaded in memory, displaying their names and other information.

Listings Available

Listing	*Description*	*Used with*
DDLST.C	Uses the DOS List of Lists to trace resident Device Drivers.	------

How to Compile/Assemble

Can be compiled and linked with any C/C++ compiler.

■ LISTING 17.5 DDLST.C

```
#include <stdio.h>
#include <dos.h>

#define DEVTYPE 0x8000  /* mask for "Device Type" bit */

struct dd_hdr {      /* device driver header structure */
    struct dd_hdr far *nxt_dev;
    unsigned attr;
    void near *strat;
    void near *intr;
    char devname[8];
};

struct invars {        /* abbreviated invars structure */
    char skip1[8];
    char far * clock;    /* pointer to CLOCK$ device */
    char far * con;   /* pointer to CON device */
    char skip2[7];
    /* location of NUL device in DOS 2.x */
    struct dd_hdr far *nuldev2;
    char skip3[7];
    /* location of NUL device in DOS 3.0 and later */
    struct dd_hdr far *nuldev3;
};

void main (void) {
    struct dd_hdr far *dev;
    struct invars far *InvarsPtr;

    if (_osmajor < 2) {
    puts ("This program requires DOS V 2.0 or later");
    return;
    }
```

```
    /* get address of "invars" in ES:BX */
    _AX = 0x5200;
    geninterrupt (0x21);

    /* create pointer from ES:BX */
    InvarsPtr = MK_FP (_ES, _BX);

    /* initialize dev to point to NUL device */
    dev = (struct dd_hdr far *)
       ((_osmajor >= 3) ? &InvarsPtr->nuldev3 :
              &InvarsPtr->nuldev2);

    printf ("\ninvars at %Fp\n", InvarsPtr);
    printf ("CLOCK$ device at %Fp\n", InvarsPtr->clock);
    printf ("CON device at %Fp\n", InvarsPtr->con);
    puts("\n seg:ofs    name   typ  strat intr  attr");

    while (FP_OFF (dev) != 0xffff) {
    /* Print driver starting address */
    printf ("%Fp ", dev);

    /* Print device name and type */
    if (dev->attr & DEVTYPE) {
        int x;    /* character device */
        for (x = 0; x < 8; x++)
       putchar (dev->devname[x]);
        printf (" CHR");
    }
    else       /* block device */
        printf ("   %-5d BLK", dev->devname[0]);

    printf ("  %Np  %Np  %04X\n",
           dev->strat, dev->intr, dev->attr);
    dev = dev->nxt_dev;   /* go for next device */
    }
}
```

Setting the DOS Prompt When Shelling to DOS

■ Jim Mischel

Use this clever trick to display a special message when shelling out to DOS.

When shelling out to DOS from within your program, it's often very desirable to let the user know how to get back into the program. Simply writing a message when first shelling out is insufficient—many people will either not see it or simply forget the instructions by the time they're ready to return to your program.

A better method, one used in WordPerfect and many other programs, is to set the **PROMPT** environment variable before shelling out to DOS. Since DOS displays the specified prompt after each command, your instructions to the user will always be available.

Turbo C provides functions **getenv()** and **putenv()** that facilitate working with DOS environment variables. Any changes made by **putenv()** remain in effect as long as the current program is in memory. Child processes, such as a new instance of COMMAND.COM, will inherit the modified environment. The parent environment, however, will not be affected by any changes you make with **putenv()**.

SHELLDOS.C (Listing 17.6) shells to DOS from your program and sets the PROMPT environment variable to provide instructions for returning. The values returned by **ShellToDOS()** are the same values returned by the Turbo C **spawnl()** function.

CODE DESCRIPTION

Overview

Program which demonstrates the use of environment information to modify the DOS prompt when spawning a new DOS shell.

Listings Available

Listing	*Description*	*Used with*
SHELLDOS.C	Stand-alone shell program.	------

How to Compile/Assemble

Can be compiled and linked with any C/C++ compiler.

■ LISTING 17.6 SHELLDOS.C

```
#define TESTING     /* comment if putting in library */
#include <process.h>
#include <stdlib.h>
#include <errno.h>

int ShellToDOS (char *Prompt) {
    char *Comspec = getenv ("COMSPEC");

    /* If no COMSPEC defined then report error and exit */
    if (Comspec == NULL) {
    errno = ENOENT;
    return -1;
    }
    if (putenv (Prompt)) {  /* Set the new PROMPT string */
    errno = ENOMEM;
    return -1;
    }
    /* Attempt to start the command processor. */
    return spawnl (P_WAIT, Comspec, NULL);
}
```

```
#ifdef TESTING
#include <stdio.h>
/* The message to be displayed at the DOS prompt */
static char *Message =
    "PROMPT=Type EXIT to return to program $_$P$G";

void main (void) {
    if (ShellToDOS (Message) == -1)
    perror ("ERROR executing DOS shell");
}
#endif
```

Nonobvious Uses for IF EXIST

■ Tim Farley

Use the IF EXIST command to easily access device drivers.

There are some nonobvious uses for **IF EXIST**, and they all hinge on one key fact: a "file" and a "character device" are the same thing as far as MS-DOS is concerned. Thus, we can use **IF EXIST** to test for the existence of certain devices on the system.

If a batch file needs to know if a given character device driver is installed before it can proceed, it can use **IF EXIST**. The LIM/EMS specification requires that all LIM/EMS drivers are named "EMMXXXX0." So, a batch file can test to see if an EMS driver is loaded this way:

```
IF EXIST EMMXXXX0 echo Yes there is an EMS driver loaded!
```

A word to the wise is in order here. Beware the case where a file by the same name might possibly exist, causing a "false positive." Fortunately, device names are often unusual and never have an extension, so this will rarely happen.

TIP: You can determine a driver's device name by doing a hex dump of the driver executable file. Look for the eight-byte string starting at the eleventh byte of the file. Some vendors, assuming that the device name will never be used, play games like putting lowercase or other "illegal" characters in this field—those drivers will not be accessible to **IF EXIST**. Also, block device drivers such as DRIVER.SYS, DMDRVR.SYS, RAM disk drivers, and so on, do not have "names" like character drivers, and are likewise inaccessible to **IF EXIST**. Table 17.6 contains a list of some popular drivers and what names to use to find them.

The built-in DOS device drivers (such as the drivers for COM1, LPT1, etc.) always exist, regardless of whether a real device is attached to them. So you can't use **IF EXIST LPT2** to test if a user has a second printer installed.

■ TABLE 17.6 Device drives and their names

Device Driver	Notes	Device Name
Any LIM/EMS driver		EMMXXXX0
Microsoft's HIMEM.SYS		XMSXXXX0
Microsoft's MOUSE.SYS	(1)	MS$MOUSE
PC-DOS's XMAEM.SYS		386XMAEM
Logitech's MOUSE.SYS	(1)	PC$MOUSE
Qualitas' 386MAX.SYS	(2)	386MAX$$
Qualitas' MOVE' EM		MOVE'EM$
Quarterdeck's EMS.SYS	(3)	EMSXXXX0
Quarterdeck's EMS2EXT.SYS	(3)	EXTXXXX0
Quarterdeck's QEXT.SYS	(3)	QEXTXXX0

NOTE (1): On the mouse drivers, naturally no device name is visible if the TSR version of the driver is loaded.

NOTE (2): Qualitas' LIM/EMS drivers support both the normal EMMXXXX0 name, plus their own name (for example, 386MAX$$).

NOTE (3): The three Quarterdeck drivers listed are all part of that company's QRAM package.

Devices always exist no matter what directory you reference them from. However, DOS won't skip checking the directory on a device, even though the test is meaningless. So you can use **IF EXIST** to see if a given directory exists:

```
IF NOT EXIST C:\INSTALL\NUL  MD C:\INSTALL
```

You can also test to see if a given drive exists by testing its root directory, like this:

```
IF NOT EXIST I:\NUL  ECHO There is no I: drive present!
```

Note that the "\" is mandatory here.

One rather unusual thing you can do with **IF EXIST** is test what DOS version is running. Support for COM3 and COM4 was not added to DOS until version 3.3. So, assuming you know the user is running MS-DOS or PC-DOS, the following can be used:

```
IF EXIST COM4  echo You are running DOS 3.3 or higher
```

All **IF EXIST** is doing is a DOS Find First call, so some of the above techniques are also applicable to normal programs having the ability to call Find First directly.

Writing a Custom Boot Sector

■ Paul S. Cilwa

Master the art of writing boot sector code.

If you have never forgotten to remove a data disk from the diskette drive before rebooting, then you have never seen the nonsystem disk message. The rest of us aren't so fortunate. We can even mark the evolution of our experience with PCs by how many seconds we remained puzzled by those words before we realized what the problem was, opened the diskette drive bay door, and pressed the "any" key.

That message may have been meaningful back in the earliest days of the PC, when machines contained a staggering 64K of RAM and no hard drive. Instead you had a fistful of diskettes, some formatted as system disks (meaning they including an image of the operating system) and some formatted as data disks (meaning they didn't). But now that virtually all of us boot from hard disks, the clarity of that message is less evident—and even worse for our nontechnical clients.

Looking for the Boot Sector

Whenever you boot your PC, the ROM BIOS checks to see if there is a disk in the first diskette drive. If there is, it loads the diskette's "boot sector" into memory and passes control to the short program it assumes is stored there. The reason for the "nonsystem disk" message when a data disk is left in a drive is that the boot program on MS-DOS data and system disks is identical. The boot program looks in the disk directory to see if any operating system files are present. If such files are present, the boot code loads them. If not, the infamous message is displayed.

To my mind there is enough difference between system and data disks to warrant their having different boot programs. The data disk boot program should display a more appropriate message to the hapless user—something on the order of "Oops! You've left a data disk in the diskette drive." Perhaps there could even be instructions there on what to do about it.

There is one more constraint: The boot sector—as with any sector of an MS-DOS formatted disk—is only 512 bytes long. The absolute limit on the size of our proposed boot program is, therefore, 512 bytes—and that *includes* data, such as the text of the message. No wonder the MS-DOS boot sector message is so cryptic!

The Boot Program

What, if anything, is special about a boot sector program? What can it do? What can it *not* do?

First, we can rely on the ROM BIOS having done all it needs to do prior to loading an operating system. The interrupt tables, for example, will have been initialized—but only for routines supplied by the ROM BIOS, of course. Interrupt 10h (video services) will be available, but interrupt 21h (DOS services) will not—DOS hasn't been loaded yet! High-level disk access will not be available, either, but that's OK; we only need the video services.

(Those of you who customarily bypass DOS and BIOS video services in favor of writing directly to the screen may wonder why on earth anyone would want to use the BIOS for the display of text. The answer is simple: The code involved in checking for the active display, setting attributes, sending text to the display, and so on, would not leave much room for the meaningful message we want to display!)

Another interesting aspect of this project is that the boot sector program is neither an .EXE nor a .COM file—it's more like ROMable code. An absolute linker, such as is used when writing an embedded system, would be nice to have here. But since I don't happen to have one, we'll have to make do with the following development cycle:

```
TASM boot
LINK boot;
EXE2BIN boot.exe boot.bin
```

Note that we're using Borland's assembler, but Microsoft's linker. Writing the code itself to the correct sector on a diskette is done with DEBUG, as I'll explain a little later.

Diskette Parameters

Running through the code from the beginning, we see that the first instruction is a **JMP** around the program's data. The first data item is the BIOS Parameter Block (BPB), which supplies DOS with information it needs in order to work correctly with the diskette.

The table is not identical for low and high density diskettes, nor is it the same for 5.25" and 3.5" diskettes. So when you put a boot program onto a diskette, you must be sure that the values in the BIOS Parameter Block are correct for that diskette. One way to do this is to assemble a different version of your boot program for each type of diskette that you use. Another is to write a program that reads the BIOS Parameter Block from a diskette and copies its information to the boot program before writing the composite boot sector back to the diskette. The data supplied in the sample program in BOOT.ASM (Listing 17.7) is appropriate for high-density, 5.25" diskettes. Change the BPB structure before writing the program to a different kind of diskette.

IBM, the Spoiler

There is an interesting anomaly regarding the OEM field of the BIOS Parameter Block. It is intended to identify the operating system under which the disk was formatted. However, PC-DOS version 4.0 requires that the characters "IBM" (the initials IBM followed by a space character) occupy the first four characters of the OEM field; otherwise DOS 4.0 refuses to recognize the diskette as a valid disk. So if you want to use some MS-DOS-formatted disks on a computer running PC-DOS 4.0, you have to forego the use of this field in the manner in which Microsoft intended. Since our boot sector program isn't really intended to represent any particular operating system, I have initialized the field with a string of hex digits that will enable the disk to operate under PC-DOS 4.0.

Following the BIOS Parameter Block I have placed some equates and the text for the messages. Note that these are not in a "data segment;" they are in our *only* segment—the code segment.

The **IDEAL** directive reveals that this program is intended to be assembled, not by MASM, but by Borland's TASM (Turbo Assembler). The only feature of IDEAL mode I am using here is the **SIZE** operator, which returns the actual length of my strings, rather than the useless value 1. We return to MASM mode to declare the **PrintString** proc in the traditional manner rather than using IDEAL mode's **PROC PrintString**.

Setting Things Up

The first thing we do at **ProgramSetup** is to initialize the stack. By setting SS:SP to 0000:0000h, we guarantee that the first **PUSH** will wrap around to 0000:FFFEh/0000:FFFFh—that is, 64K from the start of memory. This is not an arbitrary location, though it might seem to be, since we have all of the computer's memory to ourselves. But we do want the stack out of the way of the boot program itself, and 0000:FFFF is the highest address we can guarantee will be present in an IBM-compatible computer with an installed diskette drive. Remember, the first diskette-equipped models came with only 64K!

The **ProgramSetup** section of code is interesting for another reason. When writing a .COM program in assembler, we usually include an ORG 100h directive. This leaves a required 256 bytes of header in the .COM file the DOS Program Segment Prefix. But, as I mentioned, the boot sector program is *not* a .COM program. It is always loaded to an absolute address: 0000:7C00h. This address is not sacred to the 8086 family of chips themselves—any PC-compatible computer will load the boot sector program, whether it comes from a diskette or a hard disk, to that address. That is also the address to which control is transferred by the BIOS' bootstrap loader routine. And that brings us to the first quirk we must program around: the fact that the program really should be ORGed to 7C00h! But if we do that, we'll wind up with an enormous 30K .BIN file, of which we'll only want the last 512 bytes.

Fortunately, there is a trick that can be found in the first few bytes of the original MS-DOS boot sector program, following the BIOS Parameter Block. The values 07C0h and the offset of the first instruction following an **RETF** are pushed onto the stack. The **RETF** instruction is then executed, resulting in a far "return"—to the next instruction! And now the code segment register and the instruction pointer are set up appropriately for an ORG of 0. Also, having loaded the CS register with the desired value, we can copy it into DS as well.

Display Issues

The section labeled **Sky** actually clears the screen—to blue, if the display is a color monitor, and to black if monochrome. Different attributes are given to the bottom section of the screen, allowing for a company logo or some other highlighted element.

We then check to see whether the default display is set up for monochrome. If it is not, the section **ColorOOPS** builds a nice red box on our blue background, with various foreground attributes to emphasize different message lines. Otherwise the **MonochromeOOPS** section just puts up black letters on a white background box.

Finally we are ready to use **DisplayText**. Most of the work is done by the **PrintString** subroutine, a fairly conventional bit of assembly code. All we have to do here is set up the registers with the message, the message's length, and where on the screen it should go.

After the text has been displayed, we set the cursor to a convenient position—the next writes to the screen will be made by the next try at booting the machine, and you don't want any ugly overwriting of the message box at the center of the screen, nor text that starts one character after the last word of our message.

To end our boot program, we delay for a couple of seconds and then invoke the BIOS' bootstrap loader service. This way we do not need to make the user "press any key"; as soon as the diskette bay door is opened (or the latch released) the computer will reboot on its own.

Writing the Boot Sector

Now that we have our boot sector program, how do we get it onto a diskette? Well, assuming that the BIOS Parameter Block is appropriate for the target diskette, the easiest way is to use DOS DEBUG. The following commands will load BOOT.BIN and copy it onto the boot sector of the diskette in drive A:

```
n boot.bin
l
w 100 0 0 1
q
```

To write to the diskette in drive B:, change the "w" command to: w 100 1 0 1.

To test the boot program (given that the diskette is already in the A: drive) just press CTRL-ALT-DELETE. Be sure that each diskette contains parameter information appropriate to its type of disk! (360K, 1.2M, and so on)

Two Warnings

First, I've tried this program on about two dozen computers of various makes and models, and it performed flawlessly on all but one. That one had the same BIOS date and was of the same model as the computer next to it, where the program worked; I assume the BIOS or the video display card was flawed in some way. Second, remember that this boot sector program makes it impossible to load DOS into a diskette to which the custom boot program has been written without reformatting it. MS-DOS's SYS command was not written with custom boot programs in mind, and if you try to use it your computer will hang.

But who uses SYS for data diskettes, anyway? For folks who use a lot of data or backup disks, and sometimes forget to remove them from the diskette drive, putting this boot sector program on your diskettes may replace mild annoyance with good-natured sheepishness, and maybe make your day just a little more pleasant.

CODE DESCRIPTION

Overview

Program which writes a boot sector program for use on nonsystem disks to provide a user-friendly message when you are attempting to boot with the disk still in the drive.

Listings Available

Listing	*Description*	*Used with*
BOOT.ASM	Boot Sector Program.	------

How to Compile/Assemble

Assemble the program using a TASM-compatible assembler, link the .OBJ file, and convert to a .COM-style program by using EXE2BIN.
The program can then be loaded into a boot sector via the DEBUG utility. See article text for exact details.

■ LISTING 17.7 BOOT.ASM

```
                        ASSUME CS:_TEXT, DS:_TEXT, SS:_TEXT
_TEXT                   SEGMENT BYTE PUBLIC 'CODE'
                        ORG 0

ProgramStart:           jmp  ProgramSetup

BPB                     STRUC
OEM                     db   49h,42h,4Dh,20h,59h,55h,4Bh,21h
BytesPerSector          dw   512
SectorsPerCluster       db   1
ReservedSectors         dw   1
NumberOfFATs            db   2
NumberOfDirEntries      dw   224
TotalSectors            dw   2400
MediaDescriptor         db   0F9h
SectorsPerFAT           dw   7
SectorsPerTrack         dw   15
NumberOfHeads           dw   2
NumberOfHiddenSectors   dw   0
BPB                     ENDS

BIOS_Parameter_Block    BPB  <>

SkyAttribute            EQU  1Fh
CompanyAttribute        EQU  1Bh
OOPSAttribute           EQU  4Eh
MsgAttribute            EQU  4Fh
InstrucAttribute        EQU  4Bh
ShadowAttribute         EQU  0Bh

OOPS_Line1              db   'OOPS!'
```

```
OOPS_Line1_Row          EQU  6
OOPS_Line1_Col          EQU  37

OOPS_Line2              db   'You've accidentally left a data disk'
OOPS_Line2_Row          EQU  7
OOPS_Line2_Col          EQU  22

OOPS_Line3              db   'in diskette drive A: while booting.'
OOPS_Line3_Row          EQU  8
OOPS_Line3_Col          EQU  23

OOPS_Line4              db   'Please open the drive bay door!'
OOPS_Line4_Row          EQU  10
OOPS_Line4_Col          EQU  25

Company_Line1           db   'My Company, Inc.'
Company_Line1_Row       EQU  19
Company_Line1_Col       EQU  33

Company_Line2           db   'P.O. Box 100'
Company_Line2_Row       EQU  20
Company_Line2_Col       EQU  34

Company_Line3           db   'Mytown, USA 11111'
Company_Line3_Row       EQU  21
Company_Line3_Col       EQU  32

MonochromeMode  EQU     7


                IDEAL                         ; allow SIZE operator

ProgramSetup:   sti
                mov     ax,0                  ; initialize...
                mov     ss,ax                 ; stack...
                mov     sp,ax                 ; registers
                mov     ax,07C0h              ; trick to set...
                push    ax                    ; CS & IP...
                mov     ax,OFFSET CS_Loaded   ; to appropriate...
                push    ax                    ; values
                retf
                                              ; set DS = CS
CS_Loaded:      mov     ax,cs
                mov     ds,ax
Sky:            mov     ah,6                  ; Init window
                mov     al,0                  ; Blank entire window
                mov     bh,SkyAttribute       ; Attribute
                mov     cx,0                  ; Top, left = 0
                mov     dh,18                 ; bottom row
                mov     dl,79                 ; right column
                int     10h                   ; video services
                mov     bh,CompanyAttribute   ; New attribute
                mov     ch,19                 ; top row
                mov     dh,24                 ; bottom row
```

```
                int     10h                     ; video services
CheckDisplayMode:
                mov     ah,0Fh                  ; Get display mode
                int     10h                     ; video services
                cmp     al,MonochromeMode       ; if mono...
                je      MonochromeOOPS          ; jump
ColorOOPS:      mov     ah,6                    ; Init window
                mov     al,0                    ; Blank entire window
                mov     bh,OOPSAttribute        ; Attribute
                mov     ch,6                    ; Top row
                mov     cl,20                   ; Left column
                mov     dh,ch                   ; bottom row
                mov     dl,60                   ; right column
                int     10h                     ; video services
                mov     bh,MsgAttribute         ; Attribute
                mov     ch,7                    ; Top row
                mov     dh,9                    ; Bottom row
                int     10h                     ; video services
                mov     bh,InstrucAttribute     ; Attribute
                mov     ch,10                   ; Top row
                mov     dh,ch                   ; Bottom row
                int     10h                     ; video services
                mov     bh,ShadowAttribute      ; Attribute
                mov     ch,7                    ; Top row
                mov     cl,61                   ; Left column
                mov     dh,10                   ; Bottom row
                mov     dl,62                   ; Right column
                int     10h                     ; video services
                mov     ch,11                   ; Top row
                mov     cl,22                   ; Left column
                mov     dh,ch                   ; Bottom row
                mov     dl,62                   ; Right column
                int     10h                     ; video services
                jmp     DisplayText
MonochromeOOPS: mov     ah,6                    ; Init window
                mov     al,0                    ; Blank entire window
                mov     bh,070h                 ; Black on white
                mov     ch,6                    ; Top row
                mov     cl,20                   ; Left column
                mov     dh,10                   ; bottom row
                mov     dl,60                   ; right column
                int     10h                     ; video services
DisplayText:    mov     bp,OFFSET OOPS_Line1    ; Message
                mov     cx,SIZE OOPS_Line1      ; byte count
                mov     dh,OOPS_Line1_Row       ; row
                mov     dl,OOPS_Line1_Col       ; column
                call    PrintString             ; do it
                mov     bp,OFFSET OOPS_Line2    ; Message
                mov     cx,SIZE OOPS_Line2      ; byte count
                mov     dh,OOPS_Line2_Row       ; row
                mov     dl,OOPS_Line2_Col       ; column
                call    PrintString             ; do it
                mov     bp,OFFSET OOPS_Line3    ; Message
                mov     cx,SIZE OOPS_Line3      ; byte count
```

```
                mov     dh,OOPS_Line3_Row     ; row
                mov     dl,OOPS_Line3_Col     ; column
                call    PrintString           ; do it
                mov     bp,OFFSET OOPS_Line4  ; Message
                mov     cx,SIZE OOPS_Line4    ; byte count
                mov     dh,OOPS_Line4_Row     ; row
                mov     dl,OOPS_Line4_Col     ; column
                call    PrintString           ; do it
                mov     bp,OFFSET Company_Line1 ; Message
                mov     cx,SIZE Company_Line1   ; byte count
                mov     dh,Company_Line1_Row    ; row
                mov     dl,Company_Line1_Col    ; column
                call    PrintString             ; do it
                mov     bp,OFFSET Company_Line2 ; Message
                mov     cx,SIZE Company_Line2   ; byte count
                mov     dh,Company_Line2_Row    ; row
                mov     dl,Company_Line2_Col    ; column
                call    PrintString             ; do it
                mov     bp,OFFSET Company_Line3 ; Message
                mov     cx,SIZE Company_Line3   ; byte count
                mov     dh,Company_Line3_Row    ; row
                mov     dl,Company_Line3_Col    ; column
                call    PrintString             ; do it
SetCursorForReboot:
                mov     ah,2                  ; Set cursor
                mov     bh,0                  ; page 0
                mov     dh,22                 ; row
                mov     dl,0                  ; column
                int     10h                   ; video services
Delay2Seconds:  mov     ah,0                  ; Read the clock
                int     1Ah                   ; timer services
                add     dx,40                 ; add about 2 seconds
                mov     bx,dx                 ; save in BX
CheckDelay:     int     1Ah                   ; check the time again
                cmp     dx,bx                 ; 2 seconds yet?
                jne     CheckDelay            ; if not, try again
ProgramEnd:     int     25                    ; re-boot computer

                MASM                          ; return from IDEAL

PrintString     PROC
;
;   Input
;       ds:bp = pointer to string to be printed
;       dh = row
;       dl = column
;       cx = length of string
;

SetCursor:      mov     ah,2                  ; set cursor position
                mov     bh,0                  ; page 0
                int     10h                   ; video services
WriteText:      mov     ah,14                 ; write character
PrintNextChar:  mov     al,ds:[bp]            ; load char to write
```

```
                int     10h                 ; video services
                inc     bp                  ; next character
                loop    PrintNextChar       ; do again
                ret                         ; done
PrintString     ENDP

_TEXT           ENDS
                END     ProgramStart
```

Is That Disk Drive Write-Protected?

■ Evan Dygert

Use this clever technique to find out if a disk is write-protected.

The code in WRITEPRO.C (Listing 17.8) shows how to detect whether or not a diskette is write-protected. There is no DOS call to perform this function directly without receiving an "Abort, Retry, Ignore" message that disrupts your screen display and demands user intervention.

To determine whether or not a diskette is write-protected, you have to go beneath DOS to write directly to the disk. If the disk is write-protected, you will receive an error code on return, but the screen will not be disrupted. Unfortunately, if the diskette in question is *not* write-protected, you will also destroy any data at that location on the disk. The solution is to first read a sector to a buffer and then rewrite that same sector to disk using the absolute disk read and write interrupts (25h and 26h, respectively). The return code can then be tested to see whether the diskette is write-protected.

I wrote WRITEPRO.C intending it to be called from a batch file that will then use DOS BATCH "if errorlevel" to determine the error, as in TEST.BAT (Listing 17.9).

TIP: To have WRITEPRO check drive B: instead of A:, substitute **inregs.h.al = 0x01** just before the calls to **int86x**. To include this functionality in another application, change the name of **main** to something like **is_disk_write_p**, using the protoype:

```
int is_disk_write_p(void);
```

Modifying the code further would allow the function to take a variable for which disk drive you wanted to test.

CODE DESCRIPTION

Overview

Stand-alone program which tests whether a specific disk drive contains a write-protected diskette. Can be called with a BATCH program, or the program can be modified for use in another application.

Listings Available

Listing	*Description*	*Used with*
WRITEPRO.C	C code which tests the write-protected status of a diskette.	------
TEST.BAT	Illustrates the use of a batch file in conjunction with WRITEPRO.EXE.	------

How to Compile/Assemble

Can be compiled and linked with any C/C++ compiler.

■ LISTING 17.8 WRITEPRO.C

```
#include <stdio.h>
#include <dos.h>
#include <stdlib.h>

#define RETURN_OK               0
#define RETURN_WRITE_PROTECT    1
#define RETURN_OTHER            2

char far buffer[10000];
char far *pbuf = buffer;

void main(void);

void main(void)
{
    union REGS      inregs, outregs;
    struct SREGS    segregs;
    int             retries = 0;
    int             rc = RETURN_OK;

    // Read logical sector 1
    inregs.h.ah = 0x00;             // Just clear it out
    inregs.h.al = 0x00;             // Disk drive A:
    inregs.x.cx = 0x01;             // Number of sectors to read
    inregs.x.dx = 0x01;             // Logical sector 1 (FAT)
    inregs.x.bx = FP_OFF(pbuf);     // Offset of buffer
    segregs.ds  = FP_SEG(pbuf);     // Segment address of buffer
    int86x(0x25, &inregs, &outregs, &segregs);

    // If the carry flag is set, then there was an error
    if (outregs.x.cflag) {
           rc = RETURN_OTHER;
    } else {
    // Write logical sector 1
    inregs.h.ah = 0x00;           // Just clear it out
    inregs.h.al = 0x00;           // Disk drive A:
    inregs.x.cx = 0x01;           // Number of sectors to write
```

```
        inregs.x.dx = 0x01;            // Logical sector 1 (FAT)
        inregs.x.bx = FP_OFF(pbuf);    // Offset of buffer
        segregs.ds  = FP_SEG(pbuf);    // Segment address of buffer
        int86x(0x26, &inregs, &outregs, &segregs);

        // If the carry flag is set, then there was an error
        if (outregs.x.cflag) {
            // If ah = 3 then there was a write protect error
            if (outregs.h.ah == 3) {
          rc = RETURN_WRITE_PROTECT;
            } else {
          rc = RETURN_OTHER;
            }
        }
        }
        exit(rc);
    }
```

■ LISTING 17.9 TEST.BAT

```
@echo off
writepro
if errorlevel 2 goto other
if errorlevel 1 goto wprot
echo "No problem"
goto end
:other
echo "Other error"
goto end
:wprot
echo "Write protected"
goto end
:end
```

Pausing During Configuration

■ R. S. Fleischmann II

Use this utility to automatically pause your system during bootup.

Have you ever added a driver or otherwise modified your CONFIG.SYS file and been unable to read the error and information messages at bootup because they scroll by too fast? You have to hit Ctrl-NumLck at just the right moment to stop scrolling; and I have used machines that hang on that during booting.

PAUSE.SYS does just what you think it does. Install it in CONFIG.SYS as DEVICE=PAUSE.SYS anywhere that you want to stop configuration. During bootup, the screen will stop scrolling at that point; pressing almost any key restarts the process. When PAUSE.SYS ends, it returns all the memory it used to DOS and vanishes without a trace! It can be used as often as needed.

When DOS encounters a device during configuration, it reads it into memory and calls the device's Strategy routine. As a minimum, Strategy must save the address of a table of information supplied by DOS called the Request Header. DOS then calls the device's Interrupt routine with an Initialize command code in the Request Header. Interrupt calls Initialize, which does whatever setup is necessary and must end by returning the next available memory address to DOS.

Future calls to the device also call Strategy first. Then Interrupt is called with a code in the request header for some device function. The appropriate function is called by the Interrupt routine, usually by a table lookup method.

PAUSE.SYS is a very minimal device driver; its only service is initialization, which consists of displaying the message, waiting for a keypress, and uninstalling itself. Because it has no other services, the Interrupt routine itself is the initialization procedure. And, because the address it returns to DOS is that of the device itself and it clears the character bit in the attribute, DOS overwrites it with whatever comes next; no memory is wasted. You can produce PAUSE.SYS by assembling PAUSE.ASM (Listing 17.10), linking PAUSE.OBJ, and then converting it to the correct format with the command "EXE2BIN PAUSE.EXE PAUSE.SYS." Try it, you'll like it!

CODE DESCRIPTION

Overview

Assembly language device driver which pauses the action of CONFIG.SYS when loading drivers on boot.

Listings Available

Listing	*Description*	*Used with*
PAUSE.ASM	Source for the Device Driver.	------

How to Compile/Assemble

Assemble PAUSE.ASM with any TASM compatible assembler and link with TLINK or LINK. Then convert the file to binary image using EXE2BIN PAUSE.EXE PAUSE.SYS. Install into CONFIG.SYS by including the line:

```
device=PAUSE.SYS
```

■ LISTING 17.10 PAUSE.ASM

```
; PAUSE.SYS

; A device driver to show a message and wait for a
; keypress.  Use in CONFIG.SYS to pause during bootup so
; that messages can be read.  When acknowledged, it gives
; back the memory it used.

cseg     segment para public 'code'
PAUSE  proc far
       assume  cs:cseg, es:cseg, ds:cseg
               org     0

; Device header for DOS ------------------
```

```
header:

next_dev dd -1              ;only one device
attribute dw 8000h          ;character device
strategy dw dev_strategy    ;address of 1st call
interrupt dw dev_int        ;address of 2nd call
dev_name db 'PAUSE$  '      ;8 char device name

; Work space for the driver ----------------

rh_off   dw 0D0Ah        ;request header offset
rh_seg   dw 0D0Ah        ;request header segment

crlf     db 0Dh, 0Ah, 0Ah, '$'
msg1     db 0Dh, 0Ah
       db '    ** Press Enter to continue ***'
       db '$'

; The Strategy procedure -----------------

dev_strategy:                          ;save request header
       mov   cs:rh_off, bx   ; offset
       mov   cs:rh_seg, es   ; and segment
       ret

; The Interrupt procedure ----------------

dev_int:
       push ds               ;save registers
       push es
       push ax
       push bx
       push cx
       push dx
       push di
       push si


;display message

              mov     ah, 09h         ;display string
       push cs               ;ensure DS
       pop  ds               ;equals CS
       lea  dx, msg1         ;offset of message
              int     21h             ;call DOS to do it

;wait for response

              mov     ah, 0Ch         ;flush key buffer
              mov     al, 07h         ;and wait for key
              int     21h             ;call DOS

;flush buffer again
```

```
                mov     ah, 0Ch         ;flush key buffer
                mov     al, 0           ;just flush it
                int     21h             ;call DOS

;newlines
                mov     ah, 09h         ;display string
        lea  dx, crlf       ;offset of crlf
                int     21h             ;call DOS

;tell DOS that we're done

                mov bx, cs:rh_off   ;offset of req hdr
        mov  es, cs:rh_seg   ;segment of req hdr

                                        ;report done
        mov  word ptr es:[bx] + 3, 0100h

;give back memory used

        mov  word ptr es:[bx] + 14, offset header
        mov  word ptr es:[bx] + 16, cs
        mov  attribute, 0

                pop si              ;restore registers
        pop  di
        pop  dx
        pop  cx
        pop  bx
        pop  ax
        pop  es
        pop  ds
        ret                     ;that's all folks!

PAUSE     endp
cseg      ends
        end  header
```

18

System-Level Programming

When you come away from *Computer Science 106: Data Structures and Algorithms* your head is in the clouds with the sheer mathematical beauty of computing. Then you get a job at Acme Vertical Market Consulting, and the first thing they want you to do is make some piece of haywire code coexist peacefully with both DESQview and Novell NetWare.

Hey, you're a programmer, right?

Welcome to the Real World.

Programming is a lot of things and covers a lot of ground, not all of which they reveal in school. Mostly what they don't tell you about is how *messy* programming can get, messy in the sense that way down underneath everything is that cosmic junk drawer of contending minutiae called *the system*, which you must deeply understand to make certain things possible.

What we call "system programming" is not so much writing operating systems as crawling around in the cracks between the operating system, the CPU, BIOS, and peripherals. In the PC universe, there are a *lot* of such cracks. In this chapter, we're hoping to give you a taste for that sort of crack-crawling so that you can learn the skill of doing it on your own.

Peter Skye can tell you how to coexist with DESQview; it's really not that big a deal. Coexisting with NetWare is another matter; Chuck Cooper can tell you how to determine if NetWare is active and how to query a workstation address, but coexisting is still an inexact science. Good luck. Nicholas Wilt explains how to anticipate an 80x86 protection fault by testing selectors before using them in protected mode. And Kevin Dean explains how to configure .EXE files, with consideration for huge-model data.

Needless to say, the number of cracks to be explored in system-level work is near infinite. Have fun. But leave a trail of breadcrumbs behind you.

Rebooting from the Inside

■ Jeff Duntemann

Here's a trick to help you reboot your PC from within a program.

There are two distinct kinds of reboots. The cold reboot invokes the BIOS memory test mechanism, which takes time. This is the reboot you get when you power down the machine and power up again or (on some clones) press the Reset button on the front panel. The warm reboot skips the memory test and happens a lot more quickly. You get the warm reboot when you press Ctrl-Alt-Del.

Both kinds of reboot can be initiated from inside a program. It's done basically the same way in either case: by passing control to the long address stored in the ROM BIOS at FFFF:0000h. You select which of the two kinds of reboots by posting a 16-bit flag in low memory at 0040:0072h. The ROM BIOS code checks the value at this location. If the value is 1234h, the memory test is skipped and a warm reboot happens. If the value is anything *other* than 1234h, a cold reboot with full memory test happens.

A cold reboot with full memory test has an interesting side effect. It trashes *all* of memory, which might be important in secure situations when you don't want someone taking a snapshot of system memory to capture data left behind by major applications.

So it's as simple as this: Write 1234h to address 0040:0072h for a warm boot, and 0 to the same address for a cold boot, then jump to FFFF:0000h. The C implementation for rebooting is shown in REBOOT.C (Listing 18.1).

TIP: Although the program below could have used inline assembly to accomplish the far jump to address FFFF:0000h, a function variable was used instead. boot is defined as a pointer to a function which returns void. We can then assign the address of the function we want boot to point to, in this case, the BIOS routine to reboot. Depending on the settings, your compiler may complain that boot is not prototyped, but since the program is planning to reboot anyway, this doesn't matter much.

CODE DESCRIPTION

Overview

C function which will reboot the computer when called. Can be called with a parameter warm to control whether the machine performs a cold boot or warm boot.

Listings Available

Listing	*Description*	*Used with*
REBOOT.C	Reboot function.	------

How to Compile/Assemble

Can be compiled and linked with any C/C++ compiler. Use the following prototype:

```
void reboot(char warm);
```

■ LISTING 18.1 REBOOT.C

```
#include <dos.h>

#define WARM_BOOT 0x1234
#define COLD_BOOT 0x0000

void reboot(char warm)
{
int *boot_type;
void (far * boot)();   /*pointer to a void function*/

    boot_type = MK_FP(0x40,0x72);
   boot = MK_FP(0xFFFF,0x0);
    if (warm)
       *boot_type = WARM_BOOT;
    else
       *boot_type = COLD_BOOT;
    boot();
}
```

Storing Turbo C Far Pointers in Two Bytes

■ David Stafford

Learn how to master the art of using far pointers with Turbo C.

The far heap allocation routines in Turbo C++ always return a pointer that has an offset of 8. This applies to **malloc()**, **realloc()**, and **strdup()** in the large data models, and to **farmalloc()** in all models. If space is at a premium, you can take advantage of this little bit of trivia to halve the storage required to save a far pointer. The idea is to save only the segment portion of the address and store it in an unsigned integer. Whenever you need to get the far address, just use the **MK_FP** macro (from the C header file DOS.H) and supply the offset of 8.

A simplified before/after example (using the large memory model) is shown in FOURBYTE.C and TWOBYTE.C (Listings 18.2 and 18.3). The first function is the traditional method, which allocates four bytes to each far pointer. The second function does essentially the same thing, but uses only two bytes for each pointer.

Dereferencing a far pointer stored in two bytes becomes a little more complicated. Where before you would have used the far pointer directly, you must now supply the offset and then convert it to a far pointer with the **MK_FP** macro. For example:

```
puts( MK_FP( Names[ i ], 8 ) );
```

CODE DESCRIPTION

Overview

Two code fragments which illustrate the use of two-byte points to access far data.

Listings Available

Listing	*Description*	*Used with*
FOURBYTE.C	Uses normal, four-byte pointers to access **far** strings.	------
TWOBYTE.C	Uses special two-byte pointers to access **far** strings.	------

How to Compile/Assemble

Can be compiled with any C/C++ compiler.

■ LISTING 18.2 FOURBYTE.C

```
char far *Names[ 2000 ];        / * 8000 bytes of storage * /
int GetNames( FILE *InFile )
{
  char StrBuf[ 100 ];
  int Count = 0;

  while( fgets( StrBuf, 100, InFile ) != EOF ) {
    /* save the whole address (4 bytes) */
    Names[ Count++ ] = strdup( StrBuf );
  }
  return( Count );
}
```

■ LISTING 18.3 TWOBYTE.C

```
unsigned Names[ 2000] ;         / * 4000 bytes of storage * /
int GetNames( FILE *InFile )
{
  char StrBuf[ 100 ];
  int Count = 0;

  while( fgets( StrBuf, 100, InFile ) != EOF ) {
    /* Save only segment portion of the address (two bytes) * /
    Names[ Count++ ] = FP_SEG( strdup( StrBuf ) );
  }
  return( Count );
}
```

Reading the Instruction Pointer

■ Jeff Duntemann

Here's a useful tip to help you easily obtain the value of the instruction pointer.

Knowing the folklore can be important. It contains wisdom accumulated over the years by dint of much head banging by far better heads than our own. When I was first learning assembly language, I went nuts for several days trying to figure out how to read the instruction pointer register IP. (No 86-family opcode allows direct access to IP.) Finally, I gave up and called John Cockerham, who I heard had written a peculiar hack that somehow knew where it was executing. John hesitated not a moment:

```
CALL 0
POP AX
```

and you've got IP in AX. CALL 0 pushes the address of the next instruction on the stack and then branches to the next instruction. That next instruction, POP AX, cleans up the stack and comes away with IP, safe and sound. Intel won't tell you that. Write it in the margin of your blue card.

Configuring .EXE Files

■ Kevin Dean

Here's a trick for adding custom configuration information to your .EXE files.

In Chapter 3 of this book, a technique to modify global data in an .EXE file was described. The basic idea is to store a sentinel value to signal the location of the data in question. The program can then scan the file for the marker string and perform reads or writes on it as needed. While this technique works, there are several areas for improvements.

First of all, it requires that the file be searched on a character-by-character basis until the marker string is found. This can be a slow process. Second, as the author pointed out, there is no way to guarantee that the marker string is unique. It is conceivable for a program to contain (sheerly by coincidence) whatever string is chosen as part of its code sequence. Third and most important, the algorithm is not modular; all global data has to be stored in one structure and program maintenance becomes a nightmare.

While it is possible to maintain separate structures in each module with distinct marker strings for cach, this also means that the function has to search through the program for each marker, sacrificing speed for modularity. There is a solution, though. It is possible to rely on the structure of the .EXE file to locate the data within the file.

This trick relies on the fact that .EXE files are similar enough on disk to how they look in memory that we can find data which resides at a known offset. An .EXE file has three parts: a *header*, a *segment relocation table*, and the *load image* of the program. The segment relocation table and most of the .EXE header are not so important right now, but we'll come back to them shortly. What we are interested in is the load image. The load image is basically a fully linked image of what the program would look like if it were loaded at address 0000:0000h.

Of course, in normal DOS systems, an application program will not be loaded at the bottom of RAM, but somewhere higher up in memory. This is where the segment relocation table comes into play. The DOS loader mechanism uses this table to modify any direct segment references the program may make. Since all other references are relative, the rest of the program is inherently relocatable.

Executable code and initialized data are stored on disk inside the .EXE file. Stack, heap, and uninitialized data are stored only as start and end locations and are brought into being when DOS allocates memory to the loading program. By default, stack, heap, and uninitialized data (BSS segment) are placed in memory *after* the code and initialized data. The location of a specific piece of initialized data in the disk image is the same as the offset of the data within the memory image of the program plus the size of the .EXE header. If we can determine the size of an .EXE file's header (which fortunately also contains the length of the relocation table), we can easily calculate the data's position in the disk file:

```
disk_location = memory_location - program_start + disk_header_size
```

By taking into account the difference in header information, it is possible to do the same thing with .COM files. What we are missing, however, is the size (on the disk) of the executable's header. For .EXE files, the size of the header in paragraphs is stored at offset 08h in the disk file. For .COM files, the size of the header is always 16 paragraphs, or 256 bytes. (Remember the ORG 0100h that appears in the front of all .COM assembly files?).

One Limitation

This "brute force" method will work only with initialized data, that is data declared and initialized:

```
long initialized = 0;
long uninitialized;
void main(void)
{
long local_var;
...
```

In this case, the variable **initialized** would appear in the DATA segment (or something similarly named, depending on the exact compiler used), while space for **uninitialized** would be reserved in the BSS segment. It's a fine distinction, but one that bears repeating: **initialized** is actually stored on the disk in the .EXE file; **uninitialized** doesn't exist until the program is loaded into RAM. **local_var**, whether initialized or not, is stored on the stack and cannot be modified using this approach.

An Example

An example of how to modify global data is given in a function called **exemodify** in MODIFY.C (Listing 18.4 and 18.5). This function is called by the example program COUNT.C (Listing 18.6). **exemodify** itself takes a variable number of parameters, like **printf**, and uses **va_arg** and **va_start** to access the data given to it.

The first two parameters passed to the function are **progname** and **keepdt**. **progname** is a string that contains the name of the disk file to be modified. In DOS versions below 3.0, **exemodify** searches the DOS path for the program passed in **progname**. In DOS versions 3.0 and up, **exemodify** takes the program name from **_argv[0]**. If **keepdt** is true, then the original file date/time stamp is preserved.

The next parameters are pairs of offsets and values to be written to the file. The offsets are simply passed as the address of the global variable to be modified. **exemodify** determines whether the file mentioned is an .EXE or .COM file and calculates the exact file offset for the given memory address and writes the new value to it.

For a return value, **exemodify** returns the number of data items successfully modified (which may not be the same as the number of items passed) or -1 in case of error (such as file not found or invalid EXE file format). In the event of an error, the global variable **errno** is set to one of the following:

```
ENOENT   No such file or directory
EMFILE   Too many open files
EACCES   Permission denied
EINVACC     Invalid access code
EINVFMT     Invalid format
```

A Huge Problem

Some compilers treat huge model uninitialized data as if it were data initialized to 0. In other words, in huge model, uninitialized data is also written to the .EXE file. Since the compiler itself does not differentiate between initialized and uninitialized data in the huge model, neither can this program. Any changes written to what was intended to be the uninitialized data segment in the huge model will have unpredictable results.

CODE DESCRIPTION

Overview

This program modifies global variables in the initialized data segment of EXE or COM files. It cannot modify uninitialized global variables or local (nonstatic) variables.

Listings Available

Listing	*Description*	*Used with*
MODIFY.H	Header file for interfacing to MODIFY.C.	MODIFY.C
MODIFY.C	Source code for exemodify function.	------
COUNT.C	Example program on how to utilize exemodify.	------

How to Compile/Assemble

Can be compiled and linked with any C/C++ compiler.

■ LISTING 18.4 MODIFY.H

```
/*MODIFY.H - Header file for MODIFY.C.*/

struct exeheader
  {
  unsigned id;    /* EXE file id. */
  unsigned bytemod; /* Load module image size mod 512. */
  unsigned pages;   /* File size (including header) div 512. */
  unsigned reloc_items;  /* Number of relocation table items. */
  unsigned size;    /* Header size in 16-byte paragraphs. */
  unsigned minparagraphs;  /* Min number of paragraphs above program. */
  unsigned maxparagraphs;  /* Max number of paragraphs above program. */
  unsigned stackseg;  /* Displacement of stack segment. */
  unsigned spreg;   /* Initial SP register value. */
  int checksum;     /* Negative checksum (not used). */
  unsigned ipreg;   /* Initial IP register value. */
  unsigned codeseg; /* Displacement of code segment. */
  unsigned first_reloc;  /* First relocation item. */
  unsigned ovln;    /* Overlay number. */
  };

#define EXEH_SIZE  sizeof(struct exeheader)

/* EXE file signature. */
#define EXE_ID  0x5A4D

#if !defined(TRUE)
#define FALSE  0
#define TRUE   (!FALSE)
#endif

/* Function prototypes. */
int exemodify(const char *progname, int keepdt, ...);
```

■ LISTING 18.5 MODIFY.C

```
/* MODIFY.C - Modify global variables in EXE or COM file.
For Turbo C versions 2.0 and above.  This code is public domain. */

#include <dir.h>
```

```
#include <dos.h>
#include <errno.h>
#include <fcntl.h>
#include <io.h>
#include <stdarg.h>
#include <stdlib.h>
#include <string.h>
#include <modify.h>

/*
int exemodify(char *progname, int keepdt, [void *data1,
     unsigned n1, [void *data2, unsigned n2, [ ... ]]]
               NULL);
*/

int exemodify(const char *progname, int keepdt, ...)
{
char _progname[MAXPATH]; /* Program name. */
char ext[MAXEXT];      /* Program extension. */
struct exeheader exe;     /* EXE file header. */
char *pathptr;      /* Pointer to program path. */
int progfile;       /* Program file handle. */
int iscomfile;      /* TRUE if program is a COM file. */
long filelen;       /* Program file length. */
struct ftime dtstamp;     /* Program date/time stamp. */
va_list datalist;   /* List of data items to be written to file. */
char *data;       /* Pointer to current data item. */
unsigned n;       /* Size of current data item. */
long seeklen;       /* Seek length into program file. */
int retcode;        /* Function return code. */

if (_osmajor < 3)
  /* Search DOS PATH for program. */
  if ((pathptr = searchpath(progname)) != NULL)
    strcpy(_progname, pathptr);
  else
    _progname[0] = 0;
else
  /* Program name is 0th parameter in DOS versions 3.0 and up. */
  strcpy(_progname, _argv[0]);

/* Assume error. */
retcode = -1;
if (_progname[0])
  {
  if ((progfile = open(_progname, O_RDWR | O_BINARY)) != -1)
    {
     iscomfile = fnsplit(_progname, NULL, NULL, NULL, ext) & EXTENSION &&
!strnicmp(ext, ".COM", 4);
    if (!iscomfile && (read(progfile, &exe, EXEH_SIZE) != EXEH_SIZE || exe.id
!= EXE_ID))
      /* File is not a COM file and does not have a valid EXE file header. */
      errno = EINVFMT;
    else
```

```
      {
      /* Cannot write beyond end of file. */
      filelen = filelength(progfile);
      if (keepdt)
    /* Save date/time stamp. */
    getftime(progfile, &dtstamp);
      retcode = 0;
      va_start(datalist, keepdt);
      while ((data = va_arg(datalist, char *)) != NULL)
    {
    if (iscomfile)
      /* Seek length is data offset - PSP size. */
      seeklen = FP_OFF(data) - 256;
    else
      /* Seek length is (data segment - (PSP + PSP size) + EXE size) * 16 + data
offset. */
      seeklen = ((unsigned long)(FP_SEG(data) - (_psp + 16) + exe.size) << 4) +
(unsigned long)FP_OFF(data);
    n = va_arg(datalist, unsigned);
    if (seeklen + n <= filelen && lseek(progfile, seeklen, SEEK_SET) != -1L &&
write(progfile, data, n) == n)
      /* Seek and write was successful. */
      retcode++;
    }
      va_end(datalist);
      if (keepdt)
    /* Restore date/time stamp. */
    setftime(progfile, &dtstamp);
      }
    close(progfile);
    }
  }
else
  /* File not found. */
  errno = ENOENT;
return (retcode);
}
```

■ LISTING 18.6 COUNT.C

```
#include <stdio.h>
#include <modify.h>

int count = 0;
/***/
int main(void)
{
printf("Program has been called %d times.\n", ++count);
if (exemodify("COUNT.EXE", TRUE, &count, sizeof(count), NULL) == 1)
  printf("Datum count successfully modified.\n");
return (0);
}
```

Getting the IP Register in a Function

■ John Pack

Here's a simple assembly function for accessing the IP register.

We know that the value of the IP register is on top of the stack after a **CALL** instruction, so all that is needed is a procedure that does nothing but pop the IP value off the stack to a general-purpose register.

Because **POP** removes IP from the stack, you must then push the IP value *back* onto the stack before returning. Listing 18.7 contains GETIP.ASM. The IP is returned in AX.

CODE DESCRIPTION

Overview

Shows how to put the current Instruction Pointer value into a general-purpose register.

Listings Available

Listing	*Description*	*Used with*
GETIP.ASM	Returns the current Instruction Pointer.	------

How to Compile/Assemble

Can be linked with any C/C++ compiler using the following prototype:

```
int getIP(void);
```

■ **LISTING 18.7 GETIP.ASM**

```
_getIP PROC NEAR
       POP  AX ;Get IP value off stack
       PUSH AX ;Put IP back onto stack for return
       RET     ;Return, using IP value on stack
_getIP ENDP
```

Using 32-Bit Instructions in BASM

■ Jon Shemitz

Put 32-bit instructions to work right inside your Borland C++ programs.

The "built-in assembler" (BASM) is one of Borland C++'s most appealing features. The fact that it understands C++ declarations makes it much easier (and safer) to use than external procedures, which have to live in a separate .ASM file and require redeclaration of argument and global variable types. As if this weren't significant enough, the way BASM blocks can be freely embedded in C++ code has rendered the illegible and underpowered

INLINE statements nearly obsolete. (We're still stuck with **INLINE** for use in macros, at least with the current release of the compiler.)

The only other fly in the BASM ointment is that it doesn't support the 386/486 32-bit instructions. Obviously, in real mode we don't have much use for 32-bit addressing, but expressions that require multiplication and division of **long** values can be dramatically faster than when they call the runtime library's 32-bit subroutines. Similarly, just as a single **MOVSW** is twice as fast as an equivalent **MOVSB** instruction (assuming the data is word aligned) **REP MOVSD** is twice as fast as **REP MOVSW** for **DWORD-**aligned data.

Fortunately, (this time at least) "doesn't support" isn't the same as "can't do." Just like TASM, BASM allows you to freely mix data in with your code. A **db** declaration placed between two successive assembly statements will be placed right between the assembled opcodes. Since in real mode the 386/486 uses an instruction prefix byte to convert 16-bit opcodes like **MOVSW** to 32-bit ones like **MOVSD**, the only thing we have to do to use the 386/486 opcodes from BASM is to put the appropriate prefix byte in front of a normal 16-bit instruction.

One potential complication is that there are two different "32-bit" prefixes:

```
#define D32 )x66
#define A32 0x67
```

However, since most uses for 32-bit operations under DOS involve 32-bit math or **DWORD-**at-a-time string operations, you will almost always use **D32**. Where in TASM you would simply use **IMUL EBX** to perform a signed multiply of EAX and EBX with the 64-bit result in EDX:EAX, in BASM you would use the following:

```
asm DB D32
asm IMUL BX
```

Similarly, TASM's **REP MOVSD** and **REP STOSD** become (in BASM)

```
asm DB D32
asm REP MOVSW
asm DB D32
asm REP STOSW
```

Obviously, this isn't as easy as referring to EAX directly, but it's sure better than not being able to use the 32-bit instructions at all!

Coexisting with DESQview

■ Peter Skye

Here's a set of useful functions for working with the DESQview environment.

I work a lot with DESQview, which I like more than Windows, but that's not the point. With some effort I can write code that will recognize either platform and act accordingly.

They're quite similar, actually. Windows is both a multitasker and a graphical interface, while DESQview is a multitasker *without* a graphical interface. The multitasker sections have a lot in common, and you can always add a separate graphical interface to DESQview with DESQview/X.

TESTDESQ.C (Listing 18.8) contains some equivalent DESQview calls. Readers should find them worthwhile (especially since Stephen Davis left all calls out of his DESQview book); after all, there's an awful lot of copies of DESQview out there. The code is based on some assembler routines in the DESQview manual (in my manual, Appendix J).

I use the routines in TESTDESQ.C a lot; my benchmarks have found that background tasks can consume 75% of CPU time just waiting for input or some signal. For example, one of my DESQview tasks simply waits for the day of the week to change, then begins "New Day" processing. By testing the day of the week only once per time slice rather than for the *entire* time slice, the task is essentially never active, yet accomplishes its purpose.

For "Begin Critical" and "End Critical" code, replace the 0x1000 in TESTDESQ.C with 0x101B and 0x101C, respectively.

CODE DESCRIPTION

Overview

Function which tests for the presence of the DESQview multitasking environment. The function also shows how to hand back the remainder of a DESQview timeslice.

Listings Available

Listing	*Description*	*Used with*
TESTDESQ.C	Function determines the presence of DESQview.	------

How to Compile/Assemble

Can be compiled and linked with any C/C++ compiler. Can be called with the following prototype:

```
void testDesq(void);
```

■ LISTING 18.8 TESTDESQ.C

```
/*desqtest.c*/
#include <dos.h>
#include <stdlib.h>
#include <stdio.h>

#define TRUE 1
#define FALSE 0

union REGS regs;
char DESQview = FALSE;

void testDesq(void)
{
  /* See if DESQview is active. */
```

```
    regs.x.cx = 0x4445;  /* Put 'DESQ' into CX-DX so that */
    regs.x.dx = 0x5351;  /* DESQview will process this call. */
    regs.x.ax = 0x2B01;  /* DESQview uses DOS' set date function. */
    intdos(&regs,&regs);    /* This procedure does a DOS Interrupt 0x21. */

    /* If no 0xFF error code is returned, DESQview trapped and
      processed the interrupt before it could get to DOS. */
    if (regs.h.al != 0xFF)
    {
      printf("DESQview is running\n");
      /* BX contains DESQview version, for example "2.26". */
      printf("BH= %d\tBL= %d\t\n",regs.h.bh,regs.h.bl);
      printf("DESQview version is %d.%d\n",regs.h.bh,regs.h.bl);
      DESQview = TRUE;  /* Use this value at any later time. */
    }
    /* Discard the remainder of this time slice. */
    if (DESQview)
    {
    asm {
      db  0x50;         /* PUSH AX        ; Save whatever is currently
                                          ; in AX */
      dw  0xB80, 0x101A; /* MOV  AX,101Ah; Function: switch to
                                          ; DESQview's stack */
      db  0xCD, 0x15;   /* INT  15h       ; Make the call */
      db  0xB8          /* MOV  AX,1000h  ; Function: discard remaining*/
      dw  0x1000;       /*                ; time slice */
      db  0xCD, 0x15;   /* INT  15h       ; Make the call */
      db  0xB8          /* MOV  AX,1025h  ; Function: switch from*/
      dw  0x1025;       /*                ; DESQview's stack */
      db  0xCD, 0x15;   /* INT  15h       ; Make the call */
      db  0x58;         /* POP  AX        ; Restore AX */
     } /*end of asm */
    }
  }
```

Anticipating 80x86 Protection Faults

■ Nicholas Wilt

Learn how to run in protected mode and avoid protection faults.

When Intel introduced the 80286, they introduced with it a number of new instructions not available on the 8086. Many of these new instructions address shortcomings in the original instruction set. Others help to utilize the chip's protected mode. Most of these protected-mode instructions went unnoticed because protected-mode environments were almost unheard of at the time. Besides, they were generally of interest to operating systems programmers only. But some protected-mode instructions can be used in applications as well as in operating systems, and protected-mode environments are now so common that even an applications programmer can no longer afford to ignore them.

Two instructions introduced with the 80286, **VERR** (verify read) and **VERW** (verify write), help the programmer anticipate protection faults. Executing **VERR** or **VERW** sets

ZF (the zero flag) if the selector given can be read from (**VERR**) or written to (**VERW**). If ZF is zero after the instruction, using the selector will generate a protection fault. To make use of these two instructions, load the segment selector to be tested into some nonsegment register (say, AX) and run **VERR** or **VERW** on it. If ZF is set by the instruction, the pointer may be loaded into a segment register and used. Otherwise, the programmer can return an error or take other appropriate measures.

VERR and **VERW** can be used by any program running in protected mode, on any chip capable of running in protected mode. Probing an invalid selector with these instructions is perfectly safe; the tests do not generate protected mode violations, regardless of whether a test succeeds or fails. **VERR** and **VERW** do not protect from pointers with bad *offsets*, but the majority of invalid pointers have invalid selectors anyway. SMEMCPY.ASM (Listing 18.9) shows a C-callable memory copy routine that refuses to attempt the copy if one of the selectors is invalid. It could be modified to return an error state or jump to an error-handling routine, as appropriate.

CODE DESCRIPTION

Overview

Example of a "smart" copy routine which avoids protection faults by validating the points before attempting the copy. Runs in protected mode.

Listings Available

Listing	*Description*	*Used with*
SMEMCPY.ASM	Contains the replacement **memcpy** function.	------

How to Compile/Assemble

Can be assembled with any assembler which generates 80286 native code. Link to C/C++ programs via the following prototype:

```
void smemcpy(void *dest, void *src, unsigned numbytes);
```

■ LISTING 18.9 SMEMCPY.ASM

```
; smemcpy.asm: Smart memory copy routine
; Copyright (C) 1991 by Nicholas Wilt. All rights reserved.

.MODEL LARGE
.286P

.CODE

    PUBLIC  _smemcpy

_smemcpy    PROC
    push bp    ; Establish stack frame
    mov  bp,sp   ;
    push ds    ; Save registers
    push si    ;
```

```
    push di    ;
    mov  ax,[bp+8]  ; Get selector of dest pointer
    verw ax    ; Can we write to it?
    jnz  DoneCopy   ; Jump if no
    mov  es,ax   ; Otherwise put selector in ES
    mov  si,[bp+6]  ; Get offset portion of pointer
    mov  ax,[bp+12] ; Get selector of src pointer
    verr ax    ; Can we read from it?
    jnz  DoneCopy   ; Jump if no
    mov  ds,ax   ; Other
    mov  di,[bp+10] ; Get offset portion of pointer
    mov  cx,[bp+14] ; Get count
    rep  movsb   ; Do the copy (slowly, I know)
DoneCopy:
    pop  di    ; Restore registers
    pop  si    ;
    pop  ds    ;
    pop  bp    ; Restore stack frame
    ret        ; Return
_smemcpy   ENDP
    END
```

Pushing and Popping Parameters in C

■ Kevin Dean

Here's how to vary the number of C function parameters from call to call at runtime.

One of the beauties of the C language is that some functions, such as **printf()**, can take a variable number of parameters. These functions usually have little or no type checking on the number and types of parameters passed to them, but they share one thing in common with other C functions: The number of parameters passed to the function is fixed *at compile-time* at the point of each individual function call. Suppose, for example, that you had a function defined as follows:

```
void showElems(int n, ...);
```

Its purpose is to print the **n** integer elements passed to it, and it's called this way:

```
showElems(3, i, j, k);
```

The code comprising **showElems** would be bound *at compile-time* to display only those three elements, **i, j,** and **k**.

Now, suppose you wanted to write a function with a prototype like this:

```
showArray(int n, int a[]);
```

The purpose of the **showArray** function is to display the array **a[]** in the same format as **showElems()** did earlier. You would have to duplicate a lot of the code in **showElems()** to get the same effect. This might be very difficult if you don't happen to have the original source for **showElems().**

By exploiting a common feature of DOS C compilers, you can rewrite **showArray()** in terms of **showElems().** PUSHPOP.H (Listing 18.10), defines two functions, **va_push()** and **va_pop()**, that incorporate the Pascal calling convention. Functions incorporating the Pascal calling convention are expected to pop their parameters off the stack before returning to the caller.

The functions **va_push()** and **va_pop()** are redefined in PUSHPOP.H as macros that expand to call the functions with the correct parameters: **va_push()** takes a type argument (e.g., **int**) and a value of that type; **va_pop()** takes a type argument (e.g., **int**) and the number of elements of that type to pop off the stack.

PUSHPOP.ASM (Listing 18.11) is the actual code implementation of these two functions. As you can see, the function **va_push()** does *not* in fact pop its parameters off the stack; when it returns control it leaves them exactly where it pushed them onto the stack when it took control.

The function **va_pop()** pops more than just its own parameter off the stack: it pops off **stksize** bytes in all, **stksize** being the size of the parameters pushed using **va_push()** plus two bytes for the **stksize** parameter itself, by modifying the parameter to the **RET** assembly instruction. Self-modifying code like this has two important effects. One (obviously) is to make this technique non-ROMable. The other is that self-modifying code and caches do *not* get along very well, at least not on my machine. The far call to **flush_cache** is a quick way of flushing the instruction cache to prevent such problems.

TESTPP.C (Listing 18.12) is a simple program that uses the **showElems()** and **showArray()** functions discussed earlier. DOS C compilers push parameters on the stack in reverse order, so **showArray()** must push the array from the last element to the first to display it in the correct order. All it then has to do is call **showElems()** with the requisite number of fixed parameters (one, in this case).

It is not necessary for all elements pushed on the stack by **va_push()** to be the same type, as long as you make successive calls to **va_pop()** in the *reverse* order of that in which you called **va_push().**

A word of warning: By using these functions, you're throwing a lot of type checking and stack checking out the window. If you don't pop *exactly* the same number of parameters that you originally pushed, your instruction pointer is going to go wandering off to the twilight zone very quickly. This method certainly isn't portable to other platforms and should be used only with the greatest of care—but if used properly, it can offer your programs a degree of flexibility you may not have thought possible.

CODE DESCRIPTION

Overview

Example program which illustrates the use of va_push and va_pop to dynamically determine the number of arguments passed to a function at runtime.

Listings Available

Listing	*Description*	*Used with*
PUSHPOP.H	Header file for use with PUSHPOP.ASM.	TESTPP.C
PUSHPOP.ASM	Implements **va_push** and **va_pop.**	------
TESTPP.C	Example program which exercises **va_push** and **va_pop** functions.	------

How to Compile/Assemble

Can be compiled and linked with any C/C++ compiler and TASM-compatible assembler. Include PUSHPOP.ASM and TESTPP.C in the project or make file.

■ LISTING 18.10 PUSHPOP.H

```
#include <stddef.h>

#ifdef __cplusplus
extern "C" {
#endif

void pascal va_push(void);
void pascal va_pop(size_t stksize);

#ifdef __cplusplus
};
#endif

/* Convert va_push(void) to va_push(type value). */
#define va_push(type, value)  \
  ((*((void pascal (*)(type))va_push))(value))

/* Depth of stack popped is n * sizeof(type) + sizeof(size_t);
type    is word-aligned on stack and extra size_t is for
parameter to    va_pop() itself. */
#define va_pop(type, n)  \
  (va_pop((size_t)((sizeof(type) + 1) & 0xFFFE) *  \
          (size_t)(n) + (size_t)sizeof(size_t)))
```

■ LISTING 18.11 PUSHPOP.ASM

```
; This code requires Turbo Assembler Version 1.0 or greater.
; Assembly syntax:
;       TASM /ml /dMDL=<model> PUSHPOP
; where <model> is any one of TINY, SMALL, MEDIUM, COMPACT, LARGE,
; or HUGE (defaults to small model).

IFNDEF  MDL
        .MODEL  SMALL
ELSE
        .MODEL  MDL
ENDIF
```

```
        NOSMART
        .CODE
        PUBLIC  VA_PUSH, VA_POP

VA_PUSH         PROC
        ret                     ; Return leaving argument on stack.
VA_PUSH         ENDP

flush_cache     PROC FAR
        retf
flush_cache     ENDP

VA_POP          PROC
ARG     stksize : WORD
        push    bp
        mov     bp, sp
        mov     ax, stksize     ; Copy pop size to ret instruction.
        mov     word ptr cs:[retnum], ax
        pop     bp
        call    flush_cache     ; Flush the instruction cache.
        ret     0FFFFh          ; Pop size is dynamically changed.
        retnum  = $ - 2
VA_POP          ENDP
        END
```

■ LISTING 18.12 TESTPP.C

```
#include <stdarg.h>
#include <stdio.h>
#include "pushpop.h"

void showElems(int n, ...)
{
int i;
va_list elems;

for (i = 0, va_start(elems, n); i < n; i++)
  printf("%d ", va_arg(elems, int));
va_end(elems);
putchar('\n');
}

void showArray(int n, int a[])
{
int i;

for (i = n - 1; i >= 0; i—)
  va_push(int, a[i]);
showElems(n);
va_pop(int, n);
}

int main()
{
int a[] = { 1, 8, -6, 3, 9, 4, 2, -1 };
```

```
puts("Testing pushpop ...");
showElems(3, 6, 7, 9);
showArray(sizeof(a) / sizeof(int), a);
puts("Returned successfully ... pushpop OK.");
return (0);
}
```

Determining a NetWare Workstation Address

■ Chuck Cooper

Use this useful program provided to test your NetWare network.

Previously in this book, you've seen techniques demonstrated to configure an .EXE file that allows end users to customize an application. Although this approach works well in a single-user environment, it is not ideal for networks. Unless each user has their own copy of the executable program, the most recent changes will become the default values for everyone. On networks an external database using the internetwork address of a workstation as an index key is better suited for storing multiple setup configurations.

NETCHECK.C (Listing 18.13) illustrates how to determine if NetWare is currently active and, if so, how to get the internetwork address of a workstation using the Internetwork Packet Exchange (IPX) NetWare driver. The network/station address is stored as an array of 10 characters, **netnode_id[10]**. The first four bytes form the network address. The last six bytes constitute the station address. The network address is required to identify a workstation in case two or more networks are connected as an internetwork, and more than one network has a workstation with the same station address.

Although **netnode_id** is defined as a character array, this is not an ASCIIZ string with a null terminator: if you intend to use this variable in string functions you must define it as 11 characters and append a null to the end of the array.

Netnode_id can be used to identify uniquely a workstation, but this information cannot be directly displayed. The four byte network address is not stored in the same format as a long integer, and the six byte station address does not have a corresponding C data type. Consequently, the sample program simply prints out each byte as a hexadecimal number. This format permits the use of the NetWare "USERLIST /e" command to identify the user name and connection number associated with the workstation address.

Two Warnings

Also, a couple words of caution. First, the fact that IPX is active does not imply the computer is actually logged into a network. In addition to IPX, NET3 must be loaded into memory before a computer can communicate with a server. NET3 is the DOS 3.x version of this program; you will have another version if you are running a different version of DOS (NET4 for DOS 4.x, for example). If NET3 (or its equivalent) is not resident when **GetNSID()** is called, the first four bytes of **netnode_id** will all contain zeros. And the user must be logged into a server to access the network. If your application needs to know if the computer is logged in, you need to get the connection number as well.

Second, IPX was first introduced with NetWare version 2.11. Although most people have (or should have) upgraded from earlier versions, there may be some NetWare installations where this approach will not detect the presence of NetWare.

CODE DESCRIPTION

Overview

Program to test if netware is active and, if so, display the network and node address for this workstation using IPX calls in Turbo C++. This program can be modified for inclusion in your applications

Listings Available

Listing	*Description*	*Used with*
NETCHECK.C	Stand-alone example program.	------

How to Compile/Assemble

Can be compiled and linked with any C/C++ compiler.

■ LISTING 18.13 NETCHECK.C

```
/*netcheck.c*/
/*  Copyright (c) 1992 by Chuck Cooper.  This program may be used freely
as long as due credit is given. */

#include <dos.h>
#include <stdio.h>

void far (*ipx_addr)(void);
/* Far call entry address for IPX calls.
   The address is set in ipx_active.     */

int ipx_active(void)
{
 union  REGS  regs;
 struct SREGS sregs;

 regs.x.ax = 0x7A00;   /* determine far call entry address of IPX */
 int86x(0x2F,&regs,&regs,&sregs); /* 2Fh is DOS multiplex interrupt,
                                     which IPX takes over when loaded */
 if (regs.h.al == 0xFF)           /* if active IPX returns FF in
                                     al...so*/
   ipx_addr = MK_FP(sregs.es,regs.x.di);
                                  /* store far call IPX entry address */
                                  /* and return 1 if true, 0 if false */
 return(regs.h.al && 0xFF);
}


void GetNSId(unsigned char *nsid)
```

```
{
 _ES = FP_SEG(nsid);              /* set ES:SI to netnode_id */
 _SI = FP_OFF(nsid);
 _BX = 0x0009;                    /* IPX Get Internetwork Address */
 ipx_addr();                      /* call IPX entry address */
}

main()
{
  unsigned char netnode_id[10];  /* Network and node address for a
                                    workstation.  This array is unique
                                    for all workstations on a network
                                    and internetwork. */

 if (ipx_active())
  {
    printf("NetWare is active!\n");
    GetNSId(netnode_id);
    printf("\tNetwork id:     %02X%02X%02X%02X \n",
     (*(netnode_id))   & 0xFF,(*(netnode_id+1)) & 0xFF,
     (*(netnode_id+2)) & 0xFF,(*(netnode_id+3)) & 0xFF);
    printf("\tWorkstation id: %02X%02X%02X%02X%02X%02X",
     (*(netnode_id+4)) & 0xFF,(*(netnode_id+5)) & 0xFF,
     (*(netnode_id+6)) & 0xFF,(*(netnode_id+7)) & 0xFF,
     (*(netnode_id+8)) & 0xFF,(*(netnode_id+9)) & 0xFF);
  }
 else
  printf("NetWare is not active!\n");

 return(0);
}
```

19

Working with the BIOS

BIOS is DOS's little brother that doesn't get no respect. People complain when there's no BIOS support for something, but when there is, people complain that it's lousy. (Then they go off and write their own, which invariably turns out to be worse.)

As other elements of the system become exponentially more complex, the BIOS has remained relatively stable. Understanding it is fairly simple; it's a collection of machine-code subroutines with a crisply defined set of inputs and outputs. Dealing with the BIOS is mostly a question of documentation, which has always been fairly good. IBM set a positive example by printing the full assembly source of the PC BIOS in early days, and good books summarizing BIOS services have been with us for years.

The trick, when there is one, often comes down to interpreting what BIOS hands us back from one of its many services. Interpreting these values can tell you what generation of BIOS is out there, as Marty Franz explains. Is it a PC, XT, AT, or PS/2? In this chapter we'll tell you how to tell. Ron Aaron and Gordon Free suggest a unique use for the BIOS Interprocess Communication Area. Finally, John D. Porter imposes a C data structure on the entire BIOS data area, to allow easier access to its various nuggets of information.

PC Generations

■ Marty Franz

Here's a useful program for detecting what type of PC you are running on.

In theory, all PCs are compatible with one another, possessing common BIOS services, a common operating system, and a similar bus structure. But you and I know differently, don't we? The newer PC-compatible machines, including ATs and PS/2s, have more services to offer the application programmer. For example, on an AT or PS/2 you can control the keyboard's typematic rate and delay. There's also a real-time clock built into all ATs and PS/2s, a feature sorely lacking in the original PC. (Add-in clocks for the PC and XT are implemented in a multitude of nonstandard ways.) And PS/2s have the Micro Channel for add-in boards, instead of the earlier PC Bus.

Generation Gap

There are in fact three distinct generations of PC-compatible machines; the original PC and XT, the AT, and the PS/2. If your programs can identify the generation of PC they're running on, they can tap the particular powers of the machine at hand rather than settle for a least common denominator. Unfortunately, this is not a trivial task.

Originally, there was only the PC and its first clones, such as the Compaq Portable I. No standard method existed to identify the type of PC a program was running on. A variety of *ad hoc* methods, such as looking at the BIOS ROMs, was explored by programmers faced with the task of making products that ran on as many PCs as possible.

One of these ad hoc methods was unofficially adopted by nearly all PC makers. At location FFFFh in the ROM BIOS segment (F000h), an ID byte was burned into the ROM. The early values are shown in Table 19.1.

Some ID values, such as the 2DH and 9AH, are no longer in use except by those old Compaq machines. Others, such as FCH, have been adopted by newcomers such as the PS/2 Models 50 and 60. The result is that the ID byte alone no longer makes complete identification of a PC possible.

■ TABLE 19.1 Early PC IDs

ID Byte	Machine
0xff	Original IBM PC
0xfe	XT and first portable PC
0xfd	PCjr
0xfc	PC AT
0x2d	Compaq PC-equivalent
0x9a	Compaq XT-equivalent

Help from the BIOS

With the AT and PCjr, IBM provided a BIOS call to help clearly identify the PC. This is service C0H of interrupt 15H, called the Get Configuration Information service. Interrupt 15H was originally the cassette tape interface, but it has evolved over the years into a hodgepodge of functions. Using service C0H, you can glean more information about the type of PC a program is running on. To use it, set C0H in AH and call interrupt 15H. Here's what you'll get back:

If the machine is a PCjr or a PC with later ROMs, when the function completes, the carry flag will be set and 80H will be in AH.

If the machine is an early AT with a ROM BIOS date of 1/10/84, or an XT with a ROM BIOS date of 11/08/82 or later, the carry flag will be set and 86H will be in AH. You can tell which machine (XT or early AT) is in use by looking at the ROM ID byte in conjunction with this service. This value is used for many XT-compatible clone computers, such as those that have turbo motherboards. These are newer, faster versions of the XT with none of the AT features in it.

If the machine is a newer AT or a PS/2, you'll get back a pointer in the register pair ES:BX to an eight-byte work area. This work area contains a number of tidbits of information, as summarized in Table 19.2.

The model number will be the same number as the ROM ID at F000:FFFEh. In fact, this is a good way to check and see if the BIOS your program is talking to actually supports this service. The two bytes must be equal.

The submodel number is used to further identify machines that have the same model number. For example, model number FCH is used by IBM for all its 286-based products. These include not only the AT but also the newer PS/2 models 50 and 60 and the peculiar XT 286. Looking at the submodel number (0 for an AT, 4 and 5 for the PS/2s) tells you which machine it is.

The BIOS revision level can be used to further identify the machine. The first revision level of the BIOS will be numbered 00 and will continue upward. Usually, you won't see more than 02 or 03 stored in this byte.

To see what the combination of model and submodel bytes work out to, look at Table 19.3.

■ TABLE 19.2 PS/2 work area

Byte	Description
0	Byte count (should be 8, could be later)
1	Reserved
2	Model number
3	Submodel number
4	BIOS revision level
5	Feature byte (see below)
6	Reserved
7	Reserved

Where there is an N/A in Table 19.3, don't worry about what the submodel byte is. You can identify the machine without it. You chiefly need the submodel byte when the machine ID is FCH. The model byte identifies a 286 machine, but you don't know what it is beyond that. And if the submodel byte isn't 0-5, you can still safely assume you're running on an AT-class machine.

Checking the Features Byte

The features byte has additional information about the machine. The bits are encoded as shown in Table 19.4.

Exactly what these feature bits mean is beyond the scope of this article. Most ATs will have a feature byte of 70H, meaning that they are on a PC bus as opposed to a Micro Channel, they support a real-time clock, they have a keyboard interrupt of 09H, and they have a second interrupt controller chip.

Now let's put this information to work. The program WHATITIS.C (Listing 19.1) checks both the ROM ID byte and the Get Configuration Information BIOS service. It will then display information about the machine, trying to identify it as accurately as possible.

There are several things to notice in this program. First, we check the model ID returned by the BIOS call against the ROM ID at F000:FFFEh. If the two don't match, we assume that the machine type is unknown. After all, WHATITIS could've executed a null BIOS service and the configuration information returned would therefore be invalid.

The **model_table** structure is a machine-readable form of the model and submodel table shown earlier. It has a machine name string, a model number, and a submodel number for each of the model/submodel combinations shown. If there's a -1 in the submodel part of the entry, WHATITIS.C doesn't care what the submodel of that machine is, it can identify the submodel from the model byte alone. The function **model_name()** searches this table, given the model and submodel bytes.

The QuickC function **movedata()** is used to copy the configuration bytes into a local **char** array called **config**. This is done so we can easily look at them without declaring a **far**

■ TABLE 19.3 Model codes

Type	Model	Submodel
PC	0xff	N/A
PC XT	0xfe	N/A
PC XT	0xfb	N/A
PCjr	0xfd	N/A
AT	0xfc	0
AT or Compaq 286	0xfc	1
PC XT 286	0xfc	2
PC Convertible	0xf9	N/A
PS/2 Model 30	0xfa	N/A
PS/2 Model 50	0xfc	4
PS/2 Model 60	0xfc	5
PS/2 Model 80	0xf8	0

■ **TABLE 19.4 Feature settings**

Bit	Description
0	Reserved
1	Bus type: Micro Channel or PC Bus
2	Extended BIOS Data Area supported
3	External wait supported
4	Keyboard intercept is interrupt 0x09
5	Real-time clock present
6	Second interrupt chip present
7	DMA channel 3 used by hard-disk BIOS

pointer. We also use **movedata()** to copy the model ID byte from the ROM BIOS at F000:FFFEh. Since **movedata()** needs the destination segment and offset, we read our program's segment registers using QuickC's **segread()** function. This lets us use the value in **segregs.ds** as the destination segment.

Using the functions **pc_type()** and **pc_config()** in WHATITIS, and some customization, you can correctly identify the type of PC your program is running on. Being able to *know* what features are on the bus and at your program's disposal is infinitely better than making assumptions or a wild guess—and coming up empty-handed.

CODE DESCRIPTION

Overview

Complete, stand-alone program which examines the internal information stored in the PC on which it is running and reports what it finds to the screen.

Listings Available

Listing	*Description*	*Used with*
WHATITIS.C	Program which analyzes what kind of PC it is running.	------

How to Compile/Assemble

Can be compiled and linked with any C/C++ compiler. You must use the small or medium memory model for the program to work correctly.

■ **LISTING 19.1 WHATITIS.C**

```
/* WHATITIS.C:
(C) Copyright 1992 Marty Franz */


/* This module demonstrates functions that determine what
 type of PC, XT, AT, PCjr, etc. the machine is. */
#include <stdio.h>
#include <stdlib.h>
```

```
#include <dos.h>
#include <mem.h>


#define GET_CONFIG_INFO 0xc0      /* service */
#define MISC_INT 0x15     /* interrupt */

static union REGS inregs, outregs;
static struct SREGS segs;

struct model_entry
{
    char *name;
    int type;          /* these were unsigned before */
    int submodel;
};

#define N_MODELS 12
static struct model_entry model_table[N_MODELS] =
{
    {"PC",                 0xff, -1},
    {"PC XT",              0xfe, -1},
    {"PC XT",              0xfb, -1},
    {"PCjr",               0xfd, -1},
    {"AT",                 0xfc, 0},
    {"AT or Compaq 286",   0xfc, 1},
    {"PC XT 286",          0xfc, 2},
    {"PC Convertible",     0xf9, -1},
    {"PS/2 Model 30",      0xfa, -1},
    {"PS/2 Model 50",      0xfc, 4},
    {"PS/2 Model 60",      0xfc, 5},
    {"PS/2 Model 80",      0xf8, 0}
};

char *unknown = "Unknown";

int pc_type(void)
{
    /* This function returns the type of PC we're running on.
    It looks at the ROM ID byte in the BIOS.  We use it to
    check against the work area returned by the get
    configuration call. */

    unsigned id_byte;

    segread(&segs);
    movedata(0xf000, 0xfffe, segs.ss, (unsigned) &id_byte, 1);
    return id_byte & 0x00FF;
}

void features(unsigned b)
{
    /* Decode the feature byte returned from the get
    configuration service. */
```

```
    puts((b & 0x02) ? "Micro channel" : "PC bus");
    puts((b & 0x04) ? "EBDA allocated" :
      "No EBDA present");
    puts((b & 0x08) ? "External wait supported" :
      "No external wait");
    puts((b & 0x10) ?
              "Keyboard intercept called by Int 0x09" : "");
    puts((b & 0x20) ? "Real-time clock present" :
      "No real-time clock");
    puts((b & 0x40) ? "Second interrupt chip present" :
      "Second interrupt chip not present");
    puts((b & 0x80) ? "DMA channel 3 used by hard disk BIOS" :
      "DMA channel 3 not used by hard disk BIOS");
}

char *model_name(unsigned model, unsigned submodel)
{
    /* Return a string containing the model name given the model
    and submodel bytes.  A -1 in the structure means we don't
    care what the submodel is, the model byte is sufficient. */

    int i;

    for (i = 0; i < N_MODELS; i++)
    {
       if (model_table[i].type == model &&
         (model_table[i].submodel == -1 ||
         model_table[i].submodel == submodel))
         return (model_table[i].name);
    }
    return unknown;
}

void pc_config(void)
{
    /* This function reads the configuration in the BIOS.  It
    then displays additional information about the PC. */

    unsigned ds, model;
    char config[9];

    segread(&segs);
    ds = segs.ds;
    inregs.h.ah = GET_CONFIG_INFO;
    int86x(MISC_INT, &inregs, &outregs, &segs);
    movedata(segs.es, outregs.x.bx, ds, (unsigned) &config, 9);
    if (outregs.x.cflag)
    {
        if (outregs.h.ah == 0x80)
        {
           printf("PC or PCjr detected\n");
        }
        else if (outregs.h.ah == 0x86)
        {
           printf("XT BIOS 11/08/82 or AT BIOS 1/10/84\n");
```

```
            }
            else
            {
               printf("Carry flag set, unknown type of PC\n");
            }
         }
         else /* carry not set, data area filled in */
         {
            model = (unsigned)(config[2] & 0x00ff);
           if (model == pc_type() )
           {
              printf("Model: %s\n",
              model_name(model, config[3]));
              printf("Model type: %02x\n", model);
              printf("Submodel type: %d\n", config[3]);
              printf("BIOS revision level: %02d\n",
              config[4]);
              printf("Feature byte: %02x  These are:\n",
              config[5]);
              features(config[5]);
           }
           else
           {
              printf("Unknown type of PC\n");
           }
        }
}

void main(void)
{
     pc_config();
}
```

Tucking a Few Bytes Away

■ Ron Aaron and Gordon Free

Here's a trick for using the BIOS' interprocess communication area to store information.

There are many times when you'd like to report the value of a few bytes of information during execution of a program, but due to timing constraints, risk of reentrancy, or lack of screen real-estate, you can't use **printf** statements.

The BIOS provides 16 bytes of memory in low RAM at location 0000:04F0h for "interprocess communications." Very few applications make use of this memory—so why not put it to use as a data log? Inspection of the values can be done at any time from within a debugger or a memory-resident RAM viewer. One possible use would be to log the last 16 values received from a serial port.

The assembly language routine in LOG.ASM (Listing 19.2) allows easy insertion of a single byte value into the interprocess communication area while "scrolling" the previous values down to the next memory locations, in the manner of a FIFO queue.

On the other hand, if a single byte is sufficient, you can use the scratch register of the 16450 or 16550 UART chips. The I/O address of this register depends on which comm port you have; COM1's scratch register is at 03FFH. This has the advantage of being able to retain its value during a soft boot! One use would be to load the register with a unique byte on entry to each subroutine. Then if a hang occurs, it's a simple matter to determine the last routine entered.

One caution: The 16450 is not universally used for comm ports, especially in XT-class machines. The older 8250B UART does *not* contain the scratch register. Before you try to use the scratch register, you had better write and read back a distinctive value to make sure it is there!

CODE DESCRIPTION

Overview

Assembly language function which takes a single byte and stores it in the BIOS Inter-Process Communication area.

Listings Available

Listing	Description	Used with
LOG.ASM	Assembly language function to store a single byte in the BIOS area.	------

How to Compile/Assemble

Can be assembled with any TASM-compatible assembler and linked to a C/C++ program using the following prototype:

```
void LogByte(char cByteToLog);
```

■ LISTING 19.2 LOG.ASM

```
; ***

APPL_RAM        EQU     04F0h           ; starting BIOS ram address
RAM_SIZE        EQU     16              ; size of reserved area

LOG_TEXT        SEGMENT  WORD PUBLIC 'CODE'
               ASSUME        CS: LOG_TEXT
        public  _LogByte

; uses C calling convention as follows:
; void LogByte(char cByteToLog)

_LogByte        PROC    far
        push    bp
        mov     bp,sp
        push    ax              ; be polite and save all registers
        push    cx
        push    di
        push    si
```

```
        push    ds
        push    es
        std                          ; we're going to start at the back
                                     ; and work to the front
        xor        ax,ax               ; set ES and DS to segment 0
        mov        ds,ax
        mov     es,ax
        mov     di, APPL_RAM
        add     di, RAM_SIZE-1       ; es:di -> last byte in RAM
        mov     si, di
        dec     si                   ; ds:si -> next to last byte in RAM
        mov     cx, RAM_SIZE
        dec     cx
        rep     movsb                ; shift all bytes right one byte
        mov     al, [bp+6]           ; get byte (assumes large model)
        mov     [di], al             ; store it in first RAM location
        pop     es                   ; restore registers as they were
        pop     ds
        pop     si
        pop     di
        pop     cx
        pop     ax
        pop     bp
        ret
_LogByte        endp
LOG_TEXT        ENDS
END
```

Defining the BIOS as a Data Structure

■ John D. Porter

Here's a useful way to represent the BIOS for easy access by your programs.

Countless articles have appeared explaining how to access video memory directly, yet they all seem to ignore the other BIOS-maintained data areas. I've provided a listing of a header file called BIOSDATA.H (Listing 19.3). It defines a structure definition comprising all variables maintained by the ROM BIOS in low memory; these include the interrupt vector table, the keyboard buffer, video display parameters, and so on.

To use this information you must take note of several important points:

1. There is only one of these structures in a system, and its address is 0000:0000h.
2. Your compiler must conform to the packing alignment imposed by the BIOS, which is per byte.
3. The order and alignment of the fields is carved in stone for a specific version of BIOS.
4. Use of these variables should be considered NON-PORTABLE for MS-DOS systems; however, it is portable for IBM-PC (BIOS) compatible machines, regardless of operating system (mostly).

To deal efficiently with the first point, use the macro included at the end of the listing, which simplifies access to the members of the structure:

```
#define BD(F)  ((struct biosdata far *)0L)->F
```

An expression using this macro can be an *lvalue*, which means that it will be syntactically correct to assign values to the expression created by the macro. Great care should be used, though, when assigning directly to the BIOS data area.

TIP: Note that in the case of fields that are arrays, you can place the square brackets inside *or* outside the parentheses for BD:

```
BD(int_vect[0x21])
```

and

```
BD(int_vect)[0x21]
```

are equivalent.

To address the second point, a **#pragma** line appears at the top of the listing forcing packing on a byte boundary. Some compilers allot two bytes for single-byte data items to maintain even address boundaries. If you are using a C/C++ compiler that does not allow byte-alignment of data, you may need to restructure the data to properly access the data.

Regarding the third point, it is the programmer's responsibility to avoid rearranging any of these fields (although, of course, they may be renamed willy-nilly). To access some of these fields using symbolic names, we must first declare some data types:

Declaration	**Used for**
typedef unsigned char byte;	Accessing single-byte fields
typedef unsiged int word;	Accessing two-byte fields
typedef unsigned long dword;	Accessing four-byte fields
typedef void far *vfp;	Accessing 32-bit address fields

As for the fourth point, when accessing any system-specific data, the programmer is always taking a risk with nonportability. The interest in portability dictates using the Get and Set Interrupt Vector functions provided by DOS (Int 35h and 25h, respectively) instead of accessing a hard-coded memory location; but there are times when expediency takes priority over portability. But take note, several fields have names beginning with **res**; these are designated as reserved in the official IBM documentation. Other BIOSes (current and future) may make varying use of these bytes.

What BIOS Stores There

It's not just the interrupt vectors—ROM BIOS also uses this area to store information used by the video, disk, keyboard, communications, printer, and other input/output routines. For example, the port addresses for the machine's serial ports are stored in word-sized variables starting at 0040:0000h; parallel port addresses start at 0040:0008h. The "midnight" flag for the BIOS clock is kept at 0040:0070h. Bit number 7 at 0040:0071h is set to indicate that Ctrl-Break has been pressed at the keyboard.

For more detailed information about some of the more obscure and interesting data stored here, check the IBM BIOS Technical Reference Manual or a programmer's guide to DOS, which includes information on the BIOS *data area*, not just BIOS interrupts. (*The NEW Peter Norton Programmer's Guide to the IBM PC & PS/2*, Microsoft Press, ISBN 1-55615-131-4 is a standard example.)

Accessing the Equipment List

Included as an example of how to use the **biosdata** data structure is EQUIPLST.C (Listing 19.4), a brief program that checks the BIOS equipment list, located at 0040:0010h, and reports on information stored there. The format of the information stored there is shown in Table 19.5

CODE DESCRIPTION

Overview

A C header file for inclusion in programs. The structure defined in this header enables the programmer to access parts of the BIOS data fields using symbolic means. Also, an example program which uses this structure to access the BIOS Equipment List Word.

Listings Available

Listing	*Description*	*Used with*
BIOSDATA.H	Header file containing data structure description.	------
EQUIPLST.C	Uses BIOSDATA.H to obtain the BIOS Equipment List.	------

How to Compile/Assemble

Example can be compiled and linked with any C/C++ compiler. To use the header file in your own program, place the directive:

```
#include <biosdata.h>
```

at the beginning of your source file. Remember that pointers in the BIOS data area are far pointers.

■ LISTING 19.3 BIOSDATA.H

```
/*   BIOSDATA.H
 *   allows direct access to BIOS-maintained data in low ram.
 *   public domain; submitted by John Porter of BFS.
 */

#pragma pack(1)
```

■ **TABLE 19.5 Format of BIOS equipment list word**

Bits	Significance
0	Any disk drives present (1= Yes; 0 = No)
1	Math Co-Processor Present
2-3	For PC's: Amount of KB on MotherBoard; 00 = 16KB 01 = 32KB 10 = 48KB 11 = 64KB (Not Used on AT systems) On PS/2 systems, Bit 2 indicates presence of a pointing device (1= Yes; 0 = No)
4-5	Initial Video Mode 00 = Unknown 01 = 40 column color 10 = 80 column color 11 = 80 column monochrome
6-7	If Bit 0 is set, the number of diskette drives on the system, plus one. 00 = 1 diskette drive 01 = 2 diskette drives 10 = 3 diskette drives 11 = 4 diskette drives
8	Reserved
9-11	Number of RS-232 serial ports
12	Game Adapter present (0=No, 1 = Yes)
13	Reserved
14-15	Number of Printers installed

```
// define some simple types:
typedef unsigned char byte;
typedef unsigned int  word;
typedef unsigned long dword;
typedef void far *vfp;

struct biosdata {
     // the interrupt vector table:
  vfp int_vect[0x100];  // 00:00-30:FF

     // port addresses of each serial and parallel port:
  word serport[4];     // 40:00-40:07
  word ptrport[4];     // 40:08-40:0F

     // equipment list (same as returned by Int 11h):
  word eqlist;         // 40:10-40:11

     // status of POST; only pertinent for PC Convertibles.
  byte POSTstat;       // 40:12
```

```
   // usable RAM; 640 on a fully-loaded system.
word usableram;     // 40:13-40:14

byte res3[2];       // 40:15-40:16

   // keyboard buffer data:
word kbdstat;       // 40:17-40:18
byte altkeypad;     // 40:19
word kbdhead;       // 40:1A-40:1B
word kbdtail;       // 40:1C-40:1D
word kbdbuf[0x10];  // 40:1E-40:3D

   // floppy disk data:
byte recalstat;     // 40:3E
byte motorstat;     // 40:3F
byte motorcount;    // 40:40
byte floppyresult;  // 40:41
byte floppystat[7]; // 40:42-40:48

   // video parameters:
byte vidmode;       // 40:49
word rowlen;        // 40:4A-40:4B
word scrnsize;      // 40:4C-40:4D
word pageofs;       // 40:4E-40:4F
union { word w;
  struct { byte col, row; } b;
} cursloc[8];       // 40:50-40:5F
byte curscan2;      // 40:60
byte curscan1;      // 40:61
byte pageno;        // 40:62
word crtport;       // 40:63-40:64
byte crtportmode;   // 40:65       aka 3x8 Register setting
byte cgacoloreg;    // 40:66       aka 3x9 Register setting

   // cassette drive info:
byte tapectl[5];    // 40:67-40:6B

   // the master clock (soft):
dword masterclock;  // 40:6C-40:6F
byte midnight;      // 40:70

   // 'Control-Break Pressed' flag:
byte ctlbrk;        // 40:71

   // boot code
word bootflag;      // 40:72-40:73

   // hard disk data:
byte hdresult;      // 40:74
byte harddisks;     // 40:75
byte XThd;          // 40:76       NOTE: for PC-XT only
byte XThdport;      // 40:77         ditto

   // time-out values for all parallel and serial ports:
byte ptrtimout[4];  // 40:78-40:7B
```

```
byte auxtimout[4];  // 40:7C-40:7F

   // keyboard buffer:
word kbdbufstart;   // 40:80-40:81
word kbdbufend;     // 40:82-40:83

   // video parameters:
byte screenrows;    // 40:84
word charheight;    // 40:85-40:86
word vidstates;     // 40:87-40:88
word vidinfo;       // 40:89-40:8A

   // hard disk data:
byte mediacontrol;  // 40:8B
byte hdstat;        // 40:8C
byte hderror;       // 40:8D
byte hdint;         // 40:8E
byte res5_1;        // 40:8F
byte mediastate[2]; // 40:90-40:91
word res5_2;        // 40:92-40:93
byte cylinder[2];   // 40:94-40:95

   // keyboard status:
byte kbdflags;      // 40:96
byte ledflags;      // 40:97

   // User Wait data:
byte far *uwcfa;    // 40:98-40:9B address of Complete Flag
dword uwaitcount;   // 40:9C-40:9F
byte waitactive;    // 40:A0

byte res6[7];       // 40:A1-40:A7

   // pointer to a complex structure of video information:
void far *vidtbl;   // 40:A8-40:AB

byte res7[4];       // 40:AC-40:AF
byte res8[0x40];    // 40:B0-40:EF

   // Inter-application Communication Area:
byte ica[0x10];     // 40:F0-40:FF

   // status of print-screen operation:
byte int5stat;      // 50:00

byte res9[3];       // 50:01-50:03

   // used when a one-drive system mimics a two-drive system:
byte drivemimic;    // 50:04

byte resA[11];      // 50:05-50:0F

   /* the following basic... fields are only defined and
    * meaningful in machines with ROM BASIC (which is mainly
    * only true-blue IBM PCs):
```

```
     */
  word basicDS;              // 50:10-50:11
  void far *basiclockhdlr;   // 50:12-50:15
  void far *basicbrkhdlr;    // 50:16-50:19
  void far *basicdiskerrhdlr; // 50:1A-50:1D
};

// A macro to reference a field of this structure:
#define BD(F)  ((struct biosdata far *)0L)->F

/* An expression using this macro can be an lvalue, although
 *  great care should be used when assigning directly to the BIOS
 *  data area.
 */

/* Note that in the case of fields which are arrays, you can place
 * the square brackets inside OR outside the parens for BD:
 * BD(int_vect[0x21]) and BD(int_vect)[0x21]  are equivalent.
 */

/*   end of BIOSDATA.H
 */
```

■ LISTING 19.4 EQUIPLST.C

```
#include "biosdata.h"
#include <stdio.h>

void main(void)
{
     printf("Equipment List as Reported by BIOS\n\n");
     printf("Printers installed: %d\n",(BD(eqlist) & 0xC000) >> 14);
     printf("Game adapter:       %d\n",(BD(eqlist) & 0x1000) >> 12);
     printf("Number of RS-232 ports: %d\n",(BD(eqlist) & 0x0E00) >> 9);
     if (BD(eqlist) & 0x0001)
        printf("Number of diskette drives: %d\n",
           ((BD(eqlist) & 0x00C0) >> 6)+ 1);
     else
        printf("Number of diskette drives: 0\n");
     printf("Initial video mode: ");
     switch((BD(eqlist) & 0x0030) >> 4)
         {
         case 0 : printf("Unknown \n");
                  break;
         case 1 : printf("40 column color \n");
                  break;
         case 2 : printf("80 column color \n");
                  break;
         case 3 : printf("80 column mono \n");
                  break;
         }
     printf("Math Co-processor: %d\n", (BD(eqlist) & 0x0002) >> 1);
     printf("\n\nInt 21h vector: %p\n", BD(int_vect)[0x21]);

}
```

20

Code Optimization Techniques

Make it work. *Then* make it fast. This is the caution offered to overeager young hackers who want their code to burn a hole in the sky. The mirror image of that warning should also be offered to the excessively cautious, who are less noisy than the overeager but no less numerous: Make it work. *But don't stop there.*

Fast is important.

Fast is also difficult, and, worse, the conventional wisdom is often flawed. As Michael Abrash has pointed out in his various columns, much of what "everybody knows" about optimizing assembly code is simply wrong, and if followed blindly can make your code *slower* than it would be if left in its pristine, brute-force form.

The conventional wisdom fails for two major reasons: People often misunderstand the dynamics of the underlying system, including outrageously subtle things like the 80x86 prefetch queue. And people miss the fact that the Intel family of CPUs is a moving target—what makes the 8088 fly like a bat out of Manhattan can bring the 486 to its knees.

Not surprisingly, much of what we've got here comes from Michael Abrash, the Zen Master himself. Among other things, Michael explains the importance of aligning your data on word or doubleword boundaries, as well as the nature of the "sweet spot" in the stack, within which accesses are much faster than outside. Tim Farley later explains how this sweet spot can be moved around in a large stack frame.

I guess the bottom line on optimization is this: The more you learn about the system and the way it works, the better you'll be able to exploit the system's ability to run quickly. Learn everything you can, and if you don't then win the race, at least you won't be the guy coming in dead last.

Align Your Data!

■ Michael Abrash

Here's a trick to help you increase the performance of your assembly code.

You can as much as double the performance of code running on the 80286 simply by making sure all your word-sized data starts on word boundaries—that is, on even addresses. Why? Although the 80286 can read or write any word that starts at an even address with a single memory access, it must perform *two* memory accesses to read or write any word that starts at an *odd* address. Many compilers can align word-sized data; for example, the **-a** switch causes Turbo C to generate word-aligned word-sized data.

In assembler, the **ALIGN** directive is the key to data alignment. For instance:

```
ALIGN WORD      ;FORCE TO AN EVEN ADDRESS
DB    0         ;FORCE TO AN ODD ADDRESS
ALIGN WORD      ;FORCE TO AN EVEN ADDRESS
ARRAY     DW    100 DUP (?)
MOV  DI,SEG ARRAY
MOV  ES,DI
MOV  DI,OFFSET ARRAY      ;GUARANTEED TO BE EVEN
MOV  CX,100
SUB  AX,AX
CLD
REP  STOSW      ;FILL THE ARRAY WITH ZEROS
```

This code runs twice as fast on an 80286 as it would if the second **ALIGN WORD** were omitted.

As a general rule, all word-sized data in 80286-specific code should be word-aligned unless space is critically tight. (Word alignment does waste one byte about half the time, since the assembler inserts a **NOP** when necessary to force the location counter to an even address.) There's no point to aligning byte-sized data, which is always read or written with a single access. Word alignment of word-sized data also helps performance on the 80386, especially for DOS programs, which don't use 32-bit operands. For native-mode 80386 programs that do use 32-bit operands, doubleword alignment, via **ALIGN DWORD**, works best. Either way, data alignment is an effortless way to boost 80286 and 80386 performance considerably.

Negating 32-Bit Values in Assembler

■ Michael Abrash

Here's a quick and easy way to negate 32-bit values.

The 8086 assembly language is great at handling 8- and 16-bit values. For example, a single instruction can negate a 16-bit value (multiply a value by -1); the following negates the 16-bit value in AX:

```
neg ax
```

It's another story altogether with 32-bit values, which must be handled piecemeal by multiple instructions that work first with one 16-bit portion of each 32-bit value and then with the other 16-bit portion. While there are often surprisingly efficient ways to manipulate 32-bit values, those techniques are not necessarily apparent to the casual programmer. For instance, a programmer who understands two's-complement arithmetic might negate a 32-bit value in DX:AX as follows:

```
not dx
not ax
add ax,1
adc dx,0
```

That takes four instructions and ten bytes—not bad, but as it turns out, there's a better way:

```
not dx
neg ax
sbb dx,-1
```

It's certainly not an intuitive solution, but if you check it out you'll find that it does work—and at just three instructions and seven bytes, it's remarkably efficient.

Whenever you find yourself working with 32-bit values in assembler, take a moment to consider alternative approaches and see whether you can't find a better solution than the obvious one. You'll be surprised how often you'll be able to do just that.

Efficient Automatic Variables in C

■ Michael Abrash

Learn the "black art" of how automatic variables work with C compilers.

Have you ever wondered how your C compiler organizes its automatic variables? Probably not, but it's a question well worth asking. The order in which your compiler arranges the automatic variables for a given function determines which of those variables are located in the sweet part of the stack frame, where they can be accessed most efficiently.

The key is this: The 8088 can access automatic variables stored within 128 bytes of BP (the register that anchors the stack frame) with instructions that use just one displacement byte. All other automatic variables require instructions with two-byte displacements; such instructions are larger, and sometimes execute more slowly as well. Consequently, the fastest, most compact code results when as many automatic variables as possible are in the sweet portion of the stack frame, that is, within 128 bytes of BP.

How can you control the arrangement of automatic variables? There's no direct way, but if you can figure out the algorithm your compiler uses to allocate automatic variables, you may be able to select which variables lie closest to BP by the order in which the variables are declared. For example, Turbo C 2.0 allocates automatic variables in the order in which they're declared, with variables declared later placed closer to BP, so all of the following variables except **Array** are accessed with two-byte displacements:

```
int TestFunc() {
    int a,b,c,d,e,f,g,h;
    char Array[128];

        :
}
```

By contrast, all of the following variables except **Array** are accessed with one-byte displacements:

```
int TestFunc() {
    char Array[128];
    int a,b,c,d,e,f,g,h;

        :
}
```

Allocation rules for automatic variables vary from compiler to compiler; for example, Microsoft C 5.0 seems to allocate automatic variables grouped by data type. Check your own compiler by using CodeView, Turbo Debugger, or the like to examine your code.

TIP: Beware! Compilers often generate very different code when compiling programs to be used with a debugger. This is because the ordering and placement of highly optimized code can bear little relation to how it appears in the source file. Another method to examine code produced by your compiler is to compile your program to assembly language, if your compiler supports this feature (-S on Turbo and Borland compilers). There are also object module disassemblers available that support source name variables.

In functions with many automatic variables, judicious arrangement of automatic-variable declarations can cut code size significantly. It's often a good idea to put large data items such as arrays and sizable structures as far from BP as possible; one array in the sweet part of the stack frame can banish several dozen variables to the land of two-byte displacements. Of course, the variables best placed in the sweet part of the stack frame vary from function to function.

A final note: The issue of one- versus two-byte displacements also holds true for pointer-based access to structures larger than 128 bytes. In such structures, larger instructions are required to access the last-declared fields.

Bytes Are Best with the EGA and VGA Latches

■ Michael Abrash

Use bytes to speed up the performance of the EGA and VGA.

It's a solid rule of thumb that large data buffers are best processed a word, rather than a byte, at a time. However, there's at least one case in which that rule doesn't hold—when using the EGA and VGA latches. (I'll refer to both boards as the EVGA from here on.)

These latches are four eight-bit registers built into the EVGA, one for each of the adapter's four memory planes. Each latch is loaded with the data read from its corresponding plane during each display memory read operation. All, part, or none of the data in each latch can be written to the corresponding plane during each write. The four latches together hold 32 bits, so operations that use the latches can process an impressive 32 bits at a time.

The latches have many uses, including copying data from one area of display memory to another. The latches can only be used to copy data when the source and destination have the same byte alignment in display memory (that is, the coordinates of the upper-left corners, modulo 8, are the same). When this is the case, the latches allow you to copy data *four times as fast* as would otherwise be possible. Fortunately, all vertical scrolls—for example, scrolling bit-mapped text up or down—are aligned, so these frequently used operations can be performed with the latches. Better yet, **REP MOVS**, the fastest memory-accessing instruction of the 80x86 family, can be used to copy each line via the latches; in fact, a single **REP MOVS** can even scroll the entire screen with the help of the latches. (Either write mode one must be selected or the bit mask must be set to 0FFH to use the latches for scrolling, so that the EVGA will write the latches directly to display memory.)

There's a slight danger here, though. Normally, you'd want to use **REP MOVSW** to copy data a word at a time, because this instruction is twice as fast as using **REP MOVSB** to copy the same data a byte at a time. Don't do it when you're using the latches! Why? *The EVGA is an eight-bit device*, and each latch holds only eight bits. (Some VGAs are 16-bit devices bus-wise, but internally they're still eight-bit gadgets.)

When one repetition of **REP MOVSW** executes, the processor first reads a word—two bytes—and then writes a word. When a word is read from any address M on an eight-bit device such as the EVGA, the byte at address M is read, then the byte at address M+1 is read. The latches can hold only one byte each, so after **MOVSW** has read the word, the latches hold the last data read—the data from address M+1.

Now, **MOVSW** writes a word by performing two byte-sized writes to the EVGA. The latched data is written each time. Unfortunately, the data from address M+1 is written *both* times, when what we wanted was the data from M the first time and the data from M+1 the second time. The net result: Half of the source data is copied twice, and half of it isn't copied at all.

That's why you can't use word-sized instructions when you're copying by way of the EVGA latches. You can use word-sized instructions if you don't use the latches and you copy plane-by-plane instead, as is necessary for non-byte-aligned copying. Of course, there's a significant performance price to be paid—the latch-based approach accesses display memory only one-fourth as often as the plane-by-plane approach, so it's nearly four times as fast, even though byte-sized instructions must be used. The final word is this: Use the latches whenever you can—but use byte-sized instructions whenever you do.

Shorten Your Jumps on the 386

■ Michael Abrash

Here are some tricks for optimizing your 386 jump instructions.

One pleasant aspect of the 80386 is that conditional jump instructions, such as **JZ** and **JB**, can branch to any address in the current code segment. This is a marked improvement over the 8088 and 80286, which allow conditional jumps to branch a maximum of 127 bytes forward or 128 bytes backward. The difference is that, on the 386, a jump displacement—that is, a value built into the jump instruction that specifies the amount to be added to Instruction Pointer in order to branch relative to the byte after the jump instruction—may be eight, 16, or 32 bits. By contrast, an eight-bit displacement is the only choice on the 8088 and 286. An eight-bit displacement can reach only 127 bytes forward or 128 bytes backward; a 16-bit displacement can reach 32,767 bytes forward or 32,768 bytes backward, but a 32-bit displacement can reach about two *gigabytes* forward or backward.

Those larger 386 displacements (which are available only when you enable assembly of 386-specific code with the .386 directive) eliminate the awkward and slow jumps around jumps that crop up in 8088 code; for example,

```
    JNZ  YYY
    JMP  XXX
YYY:
    DB   128 DUP (?)
XXX:
```

However, larger conditional jump ranges have their price: Instructions that use them are bigger. An eight-bit displacement takes 1 byte, a 16-bit displacement takes two bytes, and a 32-bit displacement takes four bytes. There's more, though. The 386-specific conditional jump opcodes that use 16- and 32-bit displacements are a byte longer than the standard 8088 eight-bit-displacement jumps. So, where a standard jump is two bytes long, a 16-bit-displacement jump is for bytes, and a 32-bit-displacement jump is six bytes—and add yet another byte for an override prefix if you're using a 16-bit-displacement jump in a 32-bit segment or a 32-bit-displacement jump in a 16-bit segment.

Do you need to worry about all this? Sometimes. On backward jumps, the assembler automatically generates the shortest possible jump, and that's that. On forward jumps, however, the assembler doesn't know how far the jump will travel until after the instruction has been assembled, so it has to assume the worst and assemble the four- or six-byte version (depending on whether it's in a USE16 or USE32 segment) every time. Yes, the instruction works—but it's two or three times as large as the standard form, even if the jump travels only a few bytes. For example, in USE32 (native 32-bit) 386 code, this code

```
XXX:
    NOP
```

```
    JNZ  XXX
```

assembles to a two-byte instruction, but this

```
    JNZ  XXX
    NOP
XXX:
```

assembles to a six-byte instruction. What's to be done? The solution is a familiar one: Use the **SHORT** operator. Just as **JMP SHORT** saves one byte on forward jumps in 8088 code, **JZ SHORT** (and likewise for any conditional jump) saves two or four bytes on forward jumps. Thus

```
    JNZ  SHORT XXX
    NOP
XXX:
```

assembles to a standard two-byte (eight-bit-displacement) jump instruction, even when assembling in a USE32 segment when the 386 is in effect. Of course, the destination must be within 127 bytes forward or 128 bytes backward, just as on the 8088, but you can simply remove SHORT from any jump that turns out to span too many bytes.

Incidentally, **SHORT** can similarly save two or four bytes on forward unconditional jumps (performed with **JMP**) when assembling 386-specific code.

Moving the Stack Frame's "Sweet Spot"

■ Tim Farley

Use the "sweet spot" to greatly optimize your assembly code."

"Efficient Automatic Variables in C" earlier in this chapter discussed the use of BP as a stack frame pointer. The author pointed out that the 80x86 processors can access memory between [BP-128] and [BP+127] more efficiently than they can access other parts of the stack frame, due to the use of a signed single-byte offset in certain instructions. So, placing your automatic variables in C closer to BP allows them to be accessed more quickly and with less code.

This method allows only 128 bytes or fewer of local variables to be accessed most efficiently. The other 128 bytes of the "sweet spot" in the stack frame are virtually wasted. Of course, in high-level languages we have no control over this, because the compiler follows very strict rules in the allocation of stack frames. The area above BP in the stack segment is reserved for passed parameters, the return address, and so on. However, rarely will a subroutine have even close to 128 bytes of parameters. Plus, in many routines parameters are accessed only once or twice during the routine, while locals may be referenced constantly.

How can we make better use of the sweet spot? By moving it!

As long as you make sure BP gets put back when you exit, you can do anything you like with it inside your own routine. So why not subtract something from BP, thereby repointing BP right into the middle of your local variables? Then you can access some of them with positive BP offsets, and some with negative offsets. Up to the first 256 bytes of your local variables can then be accessed with single-byte signed offsets.

Of course, when we manipulate BP in this way, we lose fast access to the parameters being passed to our subroutine, since they are now outside of the "sweet spot." You may want to reserve this technique for routines that either have no parameters, or that pass the parameters in registers, or that have only a few parameters that are accessed only at the beginning of the routine (such as a pointer that is loaded into ES:DI, and is thereafter left in registers for the duration). In case, the **/THAT** parameter(s) can be loaded into registers before BP is adjusted.

The other main problem with this method is that it breaks most of the nice shortcuts our assemblers give us for precalculating stack frame offsets. In particular, the names you declare using the **LOCAL** and **ARG** pseudo-ops in many assemblers will become meaningless after BP has been altered. As mentioned above, we can work around the problem with **ARG** simply by being careful to access the passed arguments only before BP has been altered.

But there is no way I know of to make **LOCAL** computed offsets for local variables that are either negative or positive. Fortunately, another way out exists: Declare your locals in a **STRUC**, and use a few equates to glue things together. See XPROC.ASM (Listing 20.1) for the details of this technique.

Note: when declaring your locals using the method shown in XPROC, remember that the most efficiently accessed variables are those that occupy the *first* 256 bytes of the declared structure. If you have more than 256 bytes of local variables, you will want to declare the most frequently accessed variables first in the structure.

One final idea that could be used in conjunction with this technique: The BP-relative addressing modes allow you to use SI or DI as an additional offset. In taking advantage of this, we could locate the beginning of an array within the "sweet spot" of the stack, and use SI and DI to access elements *outside* the sweet spot. The instruction would still use a one-byte signed offset. This is just a matter of carefully placing your array declaration so it begins just inside the first 256 bytes of the **STRUC**.

CODE DESCRIPTION

Overview

Short assembly listing which demonstrates the technique of moving the stack frame to reference large amounts of local data with a single byte offset from the BP register. The function itself performs no useful task, returning local values in AX and BX, but could easily be modified to perform useful work.

Listings Available

Listing	*Description*	*Used with*
XPROC.ASM	Demonstration routine.	------

How to Compile/Assemble

Routines which utilize this method can be assembled with any TASM-compatible assembler and can be referenced in a normal manner from a C/C++ program.

■ LISTING 20.1 XPROC.ASM

```
; Copyright 1990, Tim Farley
; NOTE:  Don't use this technique unless you have more than 128
;        bytes of local variables!
xproc    PROC NEAR
; First, declare our local variables via a structure
xloc     STRUC
large1   dw   50 dup(?)            ; a large (100-byte) array
large2   dw   50 dup(?)            ; another one
word1    dw   ?                    ; a word
word2    dw   ?                    ; another word
xloc     ENDS

xlen     equ  SIZE xloc            ; size of our locals
xbpadj   equ  xlen-128             ; how far we will move sweet spot
xlocals equ   [bp-128]             ; use this to access locals
; Now, the actual code
         push bp              ; Standard prologue
         mov  bp,sp
         sub  sp,xlen         ; allocate space for locals
;Reference passed parameters declared with ARG here, before we    ;adjust  the
value of BP to move the sweet spot.
         sub  bp,xbpadj       ; move the sweet spot
; Example local references
         mov  si,xlocals.large1
         mov  ax,xlocals.word1
         mov  bx,xlocals.large2[di]
; Make sure to clean up stack
         add  bp,xbpadj       ; put bp back where we found it
;
; You can reference passed parameters declared with ARG again
; here if you need to alter them for return to the caller.
;
         mov  sp,bp       ; Standard epilogue
         pop  bp
         ret              ; Be sure to pop arguments if you need to
xproc    ENDP
```

Inline Assembly Methods with Turbo C++

■ Bryan Flamig

Turbo charge your C++ methods with inline assembly code.

Many assembly language programmers scoff at the idea of using high-level constructs such as objects, because they tend to create slow, bloated code. At the other extreme, many object-oriented programmers scoff at the idea of using assembly language, wondering why anyone would want to torment themselves by programming at such a low level.

Actually, both programming approaches have their strengths and, used together in the same project, produce good results. By doing so, you get both the speed and efficiency of assembly along with high-level expressibility of objects.

Nowhere is this easier to do than with Turbo C++, because it provides *inline assembly*—which means that you can insert assembly mnemonics right into your C++ code. For example, here's a Turbo C++ function containing inline assembly:

```
int twice(int i)
{
  // Load i into ax:
  asm mov ax, word ptr i
  // Double its result:
  asm shl ax, 1
  // And return the result:
  return _AX;
}
```

If you're familiar with Turbo C, you've probably used inline assembly like this for some of your time-critical functions. You'll now be able to harness even more power by using inline assembly in the member functions of your C++ objects.

Fast Screen Updates

One promising candidate for inline assembly is a class that represents a text mode screen driver. Such a driver could send characters directly to the screen refresh buffer. While this driver could be coded solely in C++, certain assembly language operations (such as repeated string moves) would allow you to greatly speed up screen updates.

I recently wanted to use inline assembly in such a class. But to my surprise, the Turbo C++ manuals don't explain how inline assembly works with member functions of objects. In particular, the biggest problem I had was determining how to access object data from inline assembly code.

To solve the problem, I used the -S option of the Turbo C++ compiler, which produces assembly language code instead of compiled object code. After viewing the assembly code produced for a simple C++ class, I found clues on how to code up the inline assembly. I'll use a similar approach in this article.

From C++ to Assembly

STAT.CPP (Listing 20.2) shows a simple statistician class. Objects from this class can input numbers and compute the total and the average of the numbers. Take a close look at the **input()** function, because we're going to examine the assembly code that is produced for it and then recode it using inline assembly.

In this example, the **input()** function is the only function that's not an inline function. It's important to keep straight that inline functions and inline assembly have nothing to do with one another. An *inline function* is simply a function for which the function body is inserted textually at the point of any calls to that function, much like a macro. *Inline assembly*, on the other hand, is assembly code that is inserted in the middle of high-level code.

You should also note that it's not possible to use inline assembly inside inline functions. Turbo C++ won't allow it. For that reason, we made **input()** non-inline so we could later modify it to use inline assembly.

INPUT.ASM (Listing 20.3) is the assembly language produced by the compiler using the -S option for **input()**. In this listing, I've annotated the output with comments so that you can see what the code is doing.

The **input()** routine can be split into five parts: creating a stack frame, saving important registers, accessing and modifying the data of the object, restoring the registers, and removing the stack frame.

In Turbo C++, each function has a standard mechanism that handles access to the hardware stack, called a *stack frame*. The stack frame is a convenient way to partition the parameters and local data on the stack. The stack frame is referenced with the BP register, and all parameters and local data are accessed using offsets from BP.

To understand the inner portion of the assembly code for **input()**, you must first understand how member functions work in C++. The trick with C++ member functions is that the data of the object, in this case **sum** and **n**, are accessed through a hidden pointer called **this**. If you were to translate **input()** to C, it would look like the code shown here:

```
void statistician_input(statistician *this, int i)
{
  this->sum += i; this->n++;
}
```

Note that **this** is always the first parameter, and that it always points to the object making the call. For instance, the call

```
mu.input(3);
```

is translated into

```
statistician_input(&mu,3);
```

But what does it mean to say that **this** points to the object making the call? What exactly is **this** pointing to? It turns out that **this** points to the first data member of the object. All of the other members of the object can be accessed by using the appropriate offset from the referent of **this**. For instance, Figure 20.1 shows the memory layout of a statistician object and how **this** can be used to access the members **sum** and **n**.

All parameters, including the **this** pointer, are passed on the stack. Figure 20.2 shows the layout of the stack during the call **mu.input(3)**, and how you can use the BP register to access the parameter **this** and the parameter **i**. Note that the stack layout shown presumes you're using the small memory model. In fact, the code given in INPUT.ASM is for the small model. In a later article we'll talk about using other memory models.

```
              object

  this >     |  sum  |

  this+2 >   |   n   |
```

■ **FIGURE 20.1 Memory Layout for an Object**

```
SP >            |    Caller's BP     |      < BP
                ||
    SP + 2      |  Return Address    |      BP + 2
                ||
    SP + 4      |    this (&mu)      |      BP + 4
                ||
    SP + 6      |       i (3)        |      BP + 6
```

■ **FIGURE 20.2 Stack Layout During input() Call**

In the small model, the **this** pointer is always at stack location BP+4. Since pointers in the small model are two bytes long, the next parameter (which would be the first visible parameter in the function call, in this case **i**), is at BP+6.

Given this information, you can almost guess how to access a data member of an object. First, use the **this** pointer as a base address. Then, using the appropriate offset from the address represented by **this**, access the data member itself.

One way to set up **this** as a base address is to store its value in the SI register, and then use SI as an index register. For instance, in the following code the first line points SI to the object by loading **this** into SI, and then the second line loads the value of **sum** into AX by using SI as a pointer:

```
mov si, word ptr [bp+4]
mov ax, [si]
```

Accessing **sum** is easy. Since it's the first member of the object, **this** points directly at it. To access the variable **n**, we must use an additional offset of 2 from **this**. In the following code, the first line (once again) loads **this** into SI, and the second line uses an offset of 2 from SI to load the value of **n** into AX:

```
mov si, word ptr [bp+4]
mov ax, [si+2]
```

You don't necessarily have to use the SI register to store the base address of the object. It turns out that you could use either the DI or the BX register as well. For instance, we could also write the code given above as follows, using BX instead of SI:

```
mov bx, word ptr [bp+4]
mov ax, [bx+2]
```

By now, you should understand how the middle portion of the assembly code for **input()** works. First, SI is loaded with the value of **this** by using the stack location BP+4, and then the **sum** and **n** variables are accessed using SI as a base. As shown below, the parameter **i** is accessed using the location BP+6. Then **sum** is added to **i**, and finally **n** is incremented:

```
mov    si,word ptr [bp+4]
mov    ax,word ptr [bp+6]
```

```
add    word ptr [si], ax
inc    word ptr [si+2]
```

(The full text of **input()** in INPUT.ASM contains the comments we can't fit here.)

From Assembly to Inline Assembly

Now that you see how **input()** can be coded in assembly, how do you turn it into inline assembly? This process is easy. Turbo C++ provides the **asm** keyword, which tells the compiler that an assembly instruction follows. For instance, we could add a line like the following right in the middle of a run of C++ code to load **this** into SI:

```
asm mov si, [bp+4]
```

Note that unlike other C++ statements, **asm** statements aren't normally terminated with a semicolon (although you can terminate them if you like). In addition, an **asm** statement must fit on one line. You can't wrap it to the next. Finally, a semicolon does not start a comment as in normal assembly language. To create comments, use either the /* ... */ C-style comments, or // C++-style comments.

If you have multiple **asm** statements, you can use a shorthand syntax by using a curly-bracket wrapper to enclose the **asm** statements. For example:

```
asm {
   mov si, [bp+4]
   mov ax, [si+2]
}
```

Using everything shown so far, the **input()** routine coded entirely in inline assembly is shown in INPUT.CPP (Listing 20.4).

There are several things to note about the function in INPUT.CPP. First, the stack frame referenced from the BP register is created automatically by the compiler, so we didn't have to include the code for it in our inline assembly. Second, you can use most of the registers without worrying about preserving their values. The only ones you need to be concerned with are CS, SS, SP, BP, and DS. The first four are managed by the compiler in the normal course of a C++ function call, so it's only the DS register you need to be concerned about.

Normally, you are also required to preserve the values of SI and DI in an assembly language routine that is to be linked in with Turbo C++ code. (That's because these registers are used when register optimization is enabled.) But when Turbo C++ sees SI and DI being used in inline assembly, it automatically adds the appropriate pushes and pops for SI and DI at the entry and exit to the function. (It also refrains from using register optimization in that function.) Therefore, we didn't have to worry about preserving the value of SI as the pure assembly language routine did.

Accessing Members by Name

While our inline assembly routine for **input()** (INPUT.CPP) is fairly simple, we can still improve on it. Note in the code how we had to know the offsets of the stack parameters and the data members. For instance, we had to know that the **this** parameter was located at an offset of 4 from the BP register, and that **n** was located at an offset of 2 from the start of the object data. Needless to say, it can become cumbersome and error-prone to code such offsets directly as literals.

Fortunately, Turbo C++ can come to the rescue. It turns out that you can reference these variables by their C++ names. This feature is what makes inline assembly so convenient and powerful. For example, here's how you can reference the **this** pointer by name:

```
mov   si, word ptr this
```

In the small memory model, Turbo C++ translates the name **this** to the text [bp+4]. In a similar fashion, we can access the parameter **i** by name as follows:

```
mov   ax, word ptr i
```

In this case, the name **i** is translated into the text [bp+6].

In my prior experience of using inline assembly with other Borland products, it didn't take me long to figure out how to access the parameters **this** and **i** by name. But what I couldn't figure out at first was how to access the object members **sum** and **n** by name.

The solution to this puzzle is hidden in the manuals. It turns out that Turbo C++ provides a way to reference the members of structures using the familiar dot operator. For instance, given the following structure

```
struct stat {
  int sum, n;
} my_data;
```

you can write inline assembly code like this:

```
mov ax, my_data.n
```

In this case, the code generated is equivalent to the following:

```
mov ax, ds:my_data+2
```

The member name **n**, when preceded by a dot, is converted into the value of the offset of **n** in the structure—in this case 2.

At this point in reading the manuals, a light went off in my head. Perhaps I could also access the members of objects the same way. After all, in Turbo C++, objects are nothing more than structures with functions attached. So, I read further in the manuals. I discovered you could write code like the following:

```
mov ax, [si].n
```

This involves some pretty peculiar syntax. Note how we're using SI as a base register and then following it with a dot and the member name **n**. This causes the offset of **n** to be added to SI. The code translates into the following:

```
mov ax, [si+2]
```

This is exactly what I was looking for! Now, I could code the **input()** routine in inline assembly and reference all of the member variables by name. The improved inline assembly version of **input()** is shown in INPUT2.CPP (Listing 20.5). The result is a very powerful combination of C++ and assembly language. You can get down to the details of assembly language, but still have the convenience of referencing parameters and object members by name.

CODE DESCRIPTION

Overview

An example program showing how to use inline assembly language in connection with C++ objects. STAT.C is a simple stand-alone program that averages three numbers. INPUT.ASM shows how you would implement the statistican::input method completely in assembly. INPUT.CPP shows how to implement this method without symbolic references to the high-level data structure. INPUT2.CPP uses symbolic references.

Listings Available

Listing	*Description*	*Used with*
STAT.CPP	Main program which calls **statistician::input**.	------
INPUT.ASM	**statistician::input** implemented in assembler.	------
INPUT.CPP	**statistician::input** implemented in in-line assembler.	------
INPUT2.CPP	**statistician::input** implemented in in-line assembler.	------

How to Compile/Assemble

Can be compiled and linked with any C/C++ compiler. To use the inline assembly versions, simply cut and paste them into the statistician::input method in STAT.CPP. These functions were designed for use in the Small Memory Model.

■ LISTING 20.2 STAT.CPP

```
// STAT.CPP.
// A sample statistician class in C++

#include <stdio.h>

class statistician {
private:
  int sum; // Running total
  int n;   // Number of inputs
public:
  statistician(void)  { sum = 0; n = 0; }
  void input(int i);
  int  total(void)    { return sum;     }
  float average(void) {
    return n ? float(sum)/float(n) : 0.0;
```

```
  }
};

void statistician::input(int i)
{
  sum += i;  // Add to sum
  n++;       // Count number of inputs
}

main()
{
  statistician mu;
  mu.input(1);  mu.input(2);  mu.input(3);
  printf("Sum is     : %d\n", mu.total());
  printf("Average is: %f\n", mu.average());
}
```

■ LISTING 20.3 INPUT.ASM

```
;  INPUT.ASM.
;  The input() method as pure assembly language

   push  bp                    ; Create stack frame
   mov   bp, sp
   push  si                    ; Must save si register
   mov   si, word ptr [bp+4]  ; Point to object data with si
   mov   ax, word ptr [bp+6]  ; Load AX with i
   add   word ptr [si],ax     ; sum += i
   inc   word ptr [si+2]      ; n++
   pop   si                    ; Restore si register
   pop   bp                    ; Remove the stack frame
   ret                         ; Return to caller
```

■ LISTING 20.4 INPUT.CPP

```
// INPUT.CPP.
// A first cut at an inline assembly input() method
void statistician::input(int i)
{
  asm {
    mov si, word ptr [bp+4]  // Point to object data with si
    mov ax, word ptr [bp+6]  // Load AX with i
    add word ptr [si], ax    // sum += i
    inc word ptr [si+2]      // n++
  }
}
```

■ LISTING 20.5 INPUT2.CPP

```
// INPUT2.CPP.
// inline assembly input() referencing C++ names
void statistician::input(int i)
{
  asm {
```

```
    mov si, word ptr this       // Point to object data with si
    mov ax, word ptr i          // Load AX with i
    add word ptr [si].sum, ax // sum += i
    inc word ptr [si].n         // n++
  }
}
```

Cut the Fat from Your TASM Executables

■ Ron Aaron

Streamline your executables with this useful programming trick.

Everyone knows that assembly language can be used to make the smallest .EXE files, right? But not everyone knows that there is a very simple way to ensure that your .EXE file is really as small as possible!

If you have static data areas that are not initialized (such as data-transfer buffers) you probably declare them as follows:

```
buffer  db 1024 DUP (?)
```

This is fine, but if you put this declaration in the data segment, and there is initialized data declared after it, you will have 1024 bytes of random data written to the .EXE file image—that is, 1024 bytes that don't need to be in the image!

The best solution is to put all uninitialized data in the **_BSS** segment. If you are using the simplified directives, put them in **UDATASEG**. TRIM.ASM (Listing 20.6) shows how to do this.

If you change the **UDATASEG** in TRIM.ASM to **DATASEG**, the .EXE file increases in size by 1K, exactly the size of the buffer! Note that in the small model you don't need to worry about the segment name; DS will access both **junk** and **buffer** in the example.

CODE DESCRIPTION

Overview

Brief assembly language listing to show the difference in the placement of uninitialized data. Placement in the default Data Segment causes an increase in the size of the .EXE file on disk.

Listings Available

Listing	*Description*	*Used with*
TRIM.ASM	Data defined in assembly for comparison between how default data and BSS segments are stored in .EXE files.	------

How to Compile/Assemble

Can be assembled with any TASM-compatible assembler.

■ LISTING 20.6 TRIM.ASM

```
IDEAL
MODEL SMALL

STACK 512

UDATASEG
buffer db 1024 dup (?) ; this will be put in the _BSS segment

DATASEG
junk    db 'junk'      ; this will be put in the _DATA segment

CODESEG

begin:
        mov ax, 4c00h  ; just bogus code; exits to DOS right away
        int 21h

END begin
```

Faster Block Moves

■ Alan Jay Weiner

Here's the information you'll need to greatly speed up block moves.

Many programmers are aware that they can greatly speed up block moves of data by using **movsw** instead of **movsb** insructions to handle two bytes of data at a time. This works very well when the number of bytes to be moved is even, although some kind of check needs to be made to account for the possibility of an odd number of bytes being moved. Something like the following is often suggested:

```
    cld
    shr   cx,1      ; Determine if CX is odd
    jae   even      ; Jump if CF = 0
    movsb           ; Move the odd byte
even:
    rep   movsw     ; Bytes left to move is even
```

Although basically very good, this approach has one drawback, and that's the **jae** instruction. Jumps on the Intel family of chips flush the instruction prefetch queue. This means that the execution of the next instruction must wait until it is retrieved all the way from memory, rather than the prefetch queue that resides on-chip.

By taking advantage of the fact that **movsw** does not affect the flags register, we can delay the check for the odd byte until after the move (and CX is 0). We can then use an **rcl** instruction to check the status of the Carry Flag, which will be set by the **shr** instruction if CX originally contains an odd value.

```
cld
shr   cx,1     ;Divide CX by 2
rep   movsw;Move the even number
rcl   cx,1     ;CX now contains CF
rep   movsb;Move the odd byte if needed
```

Optimal timing is another issue. A multi-byte transfer across odd-byte boundaries takes additonal bus-cycles. We have to make sure that the **movsw** operates on word-aligned data. Because block moves transfer data from DS:SI to ES:DI, if either SI or DI point to an odd address, additional bus cycles will be required with word-sized moves. It is possible to write a routine that also takes this possibility into account (Figure 20.3).

Faster Floating Point on the 80387

■ Jon Shemitz

Use this trick to speed up your floating point operations.

Recently, I tried speeding up an 8087 assembly language routine. It was already pretty tight, with all the intermediate values in the 8087 registers and all the control words in the CPU's registers. About the only thing left to try was the 287 extension that allows you to store the FPU's flags register directly to AX, instead of to main memory. I figured this would make a difference of only a percent or two at most, but it was worth a try.

TASM requires a **P287** directive before allowing the use of **FSTSW AX**. Surprisingly, a benchmark program showed the 287 version of the routine to be 12% faster than the 8087 version, while with one actual test data set, the whole program was 18% faster than the 8087 version! It just didn't seem possible that two memory references (writing the flags, then actually testing them) could be so slow, so I used a debugger to look at the actual object code.

The reason for the speed-up quickly proved quite obvious. In TASM's default 8087 mode, a line like **FMUL ST,ST** (which squares the "accumulator," the register at the top of the stack) actually generates two instructions:

```
9B     wait
D8 C8  fmul  st,st
```

That is, TASM inserts a **WAIT** instruction before every coprocessor instruction. This forces the CPU to wait until the coprocessor turns off the BUSY signal, so that it doesn't pass the 8087 a new instruction before the '87 is ready. The 286 (and later) processors have essentially built the **WAIT** instruction into hardware: They simply won't pass an instruction to the coprocessor while the BUSY signal is currently set. Thus, coprocessor instructions for the 287 and later don't need to be preceded by **WAIT**s, and the **P287** directive not only enables the expanded instruction set (including **FSTSW AX**) but also disables the **WAIT** insertion.

It's interesting to note that while a true-blue AT (8MHz 286/287) runs the routine just fine without the explicit **WAIT**s, it also doesn't run any faster without them. The perfor-

```
    cld

;check that we are moving at least one byte,
;since this routine may blindly move one byte
;to align SI

    jcxz _done   ;move count is zero, so exit

;force SI to even alignment

    mov  bx, cx  ;preserve bytes-to-move count
    mov  cx, si  ;get SI pointer
    and  cx, 1   ;get LSBit in SI
    sub  bx, cx  ;adjust bytes-to-move count
    rep  movsb   ;moves once if SI was odd
    mov  cx, bx  ;get adjusted bytes-to-move count

;move remainder of bytes as words, with a final
;byte move if necessary

    shr  cx, 1
    rep  movsw
    rcl  cx, 1
    rep  movsb

_done:
```

■ **FIGURE 20.3 Optimized Word-Sized Block Moves**

mance advantage appears when the **WAIT**-less code is run on an 386/387 combination. (Presumably a 486 and its built-in 487 would also be faster without the **WAIT**s.) It's unclear to me whether this is because the 387 is a lot faster than the 287 or a more subtle artifact of the 8MHz 286/287 running at bus speed while faster processors have to drag each instruction byte through an uncooperative bus. But it really doesn't matter; what's important is that the **WAIT**-less code will run as fast or faster is really all I need to know.

Is this worth taking advantage of? I think so. A 10% to 20% speed-up on a 386 is nothing to ignore, and if you're already going to the trouble of writing a coprocessor floating point routine by hand, you might as well go to the slight extra trouble of making two copies of the routine, assembling one for the 8087 and the other for the 287 and later, and calling the correct routine through a pointer. Borland languages, at least, provide a way to tell which FPU you have, if any (the **Test8087** and **_8087** variables in Pascal and C++, respectively), and it's certainly easy enough to set the pointer at program startup based on which FPU is actually there.

21

Debugging and Maintaining Code

I don't think there'd be much argument against my position that debugging is by far everyone's least-favorite aspect of programming. (No, there are programmers who actually *enjoy* documentation—I'm one of them.) Debugging means picking up after yourself; wiping up spills; carrying out corpses; scrubbing spilled paint from the cracks; and, of course, apologizing to yourself for not getting it right the first time.

It passes the time, but it's not fun.

There are some hard-won general principles for hunting down bugs, but no magic recipes, and nothing guaranteed to work every time in every situation. In this admittedly short chapter, we'll try to provide some general principles—and let you add the intuition and situational brilliance.

Michael Abrash has a lot to say in this chapter, mostly about the aggravated difficulties of assembly-level debugging. Eliminate the impossible, he says, and what's left *has* to be your bug. The trick (obviously) is eliminating the impossible—and Michael will help you learn that skill as well. Later, Michael shares some tips on doing remote debugging to keep down the wear and tear on your major development system. Finally, I'll step in myself and tell the story of a truly pathological bug it took me several *years* to understand.

Well, better late than never. Debugging can be like that.

Debugging the Tough Ones

■ Michael Abrash

Here's a set of debugging techniques by a master programmer you can't live without.

There's an old story about someone asking a sculptor how to make a sculpture. The sculptor replies, "Take a rock and chisel away everything that doesn't look like what you want to sculpt." That's assembly level debugging in a nutshell. Eliminate everything that can't possibly be the bug, and what's left *has* to be the bug, however improbable that may be.

Assembly Level Debugging

Programming is the lovely, logical process of turning an abstract concept into a concrete realization, bringing something new into the universe, alive and squalling. Assembly level debugging is what you need when the abstractions and structures of your programs break down (usually assembly language programs, but assembly level debugging is needed for particularly tough high-level language problems, too), when you need to look straight into the gruesome heart of the processor itself and deal with the endless minutiae of flags, registers, and machine language. And if you don't think that the full state of a computer as a program executes is more complicated than the source level state of a C or C++ program as *it* executes, brother, think again.

All debugging is frustrating, but assembly level debugging takes frustration to new heights. You have to reconstruct what your program does from ridiculously cryptic disassembled instructions in your debugger, all the while keeping an eye on a horde of registers with highly mnemonic and distinctive names like DX, DI, and DS. Worse, you can't remember *too* much of how your program works while reading the assembly level tea leaves, or you'll see only what you expect to see and not what's really there, and risk missing the bug altogether.

What's truly unique about assembly level debugging, however, is that only in assembly language can a program go wildly or subtly wrong *in any way during any instruction*, with effects that may be seen before another cycle passes, not for several gigacycles, or anywhere in between. High-level languages make most of the choices about programming the processor for you, and generally do so with great reliability, so only a sharply limited class of bugs can occur; this is not so with assembly language.

In assembly language, you can bet that someday you'll push two values but pop only one, thereby later (maybe much later) returning to the address you pushed on the stack rather than to the calling routine. That just ain't gonna happen in C, no matter how long you live. (You could get a similar bug by performing a far call to a near routine in C, though, which is why assembly level debugging is sometimes needed for high-level languages.)

Similarly, only in assembly language could you jump into the great unknown because you loaded a byte-sized jump index into BL and forgot to extend it to a word in BX. It's also unlikely that you'll accidentally alter the default data segment in C and thereby read and write the wrong part of memory altogether. Assembly language bugs are flat-out unmatched for their virulence, complexity, and sheer, mind-bending *variety*.

This feature can't give you a cut-and-dried way to find and fix those nasty bugs. Sorry, but bugs all look obvious once you find them, so showing you a few real-life bugs wouldn't teach you much. It's finding bugs that's hard, and that process is unique for every combination of person and bug, not to mention debugger. What I can do is give you an approach that should carry you through whatever the 8088 can throw at you.

How to Pan for Gold

Keep in mind, we're not talking about garden variety bugs here. We're not talking about the kind of bug where you don't get any output on the screen, so you go and look at your source code and find that not only did you forget to put the print string function number in AH, you also forgot to put the pointer to the string in DS:DX and in fact forgot the INT 21H DOS interrupt, too, for crying out loud.

We *might* be talking about the kind of bug where you left the "H" off the end of INT 21H, resulting in a call to the cassette interrupt (which is used for just about everything *except* cassette I/O these days). Sometimes a bug like that can only be found by watching the code execute. When you have all the registers set up properly and do an INT 21 and nothing appears on the screen, you may briefly conclude that DOS is broken. But eventually you will actually *look* at the disassembly and notice that you're actually executing INT 15H, and you will experience an epiphany in which you will not only know how to fix your bug but may also experience a strong desire to do something else for a living.

This, by the way, is why source-level debugging isn't suitable for the toughest bugs, even when you're working with assembly language source code; only the disassembled instructions themselves force you to see what the processor is really doing. If you were using source level assembly language debugging on the INT 21 bug, you'd see INT 21, exactly what you'd expect to see, when you need to see the disassembled INT 15H to jog your grey matter into recognizing the radix problem and wishing that people had 16 fingers.

Altered States

Reaching the point where you can have a flash of understanding is the object of the kind of debugging we're talking about. Assembly level debugging is tedious and incredibly detailed. You have to maintain a sort of mental timeline of the computer's state as you go, and the whole point is to catch the moment when that state deviates from the expected. The state of the 8088 is much too complex to keep in your head for more than a few dozen instructions, so it's absolutely essential that you reduce to a bare minimum the areas that you examine closely by narrowing down the possible places where the bug could be generated.

Then, and only then, can you bring together in your mind the various and sundry pieces of the execution of that part of your program in a moment of total comprehension and exclaim, "Oh, *right*, that should be *SN*, not *DN*," or "Heck, of *course* DX is wiped out by

MUL," or "Jeez, CX was zero when REP CMPSB executed, so *naturally* the flags didn't change," or "Gosh, I'd sure like to send a year's worth of toenail clippings to the folks who designed this processor!"

How to Narrow the Field

Eliminate the truly impossible. Sounds good, but how do you do it? One of my favorites is to use a debugger to step over subroutine calls one after another to determine which subroutine is causing a problem, then start the program again, step into that subroutine, and step over *its* subroutine calls in the same way. This allows you to zero in on the problem section of the code very quickly.

Many approaches are familiar from high-level languages, such as commenting out parts of a program to see if the bug is affected, putting in beeps or console output commands at checkpoints so you can see where the program hangs or what sequence of instructions it's executing.

The idea is to get irrefutable evidence that a certain part of the program isn't involved in the bug, or, better yet, that a certain part—the smaller the better—*is* involved, in which case you can confine all further debugging to that area. You can, of course, also watch the program execute line by line in a debugger. But for a big program you'll generally be happier using other techniques to zero in on the problem code, then watch each line in that area execute to identify the source of the problem.

Consider the example earlier in this article where two values were pushed but only one was popped, unbalancing the stack and causing an incorrect return at the end of the subroutine. The subroutine in which the double push occurred could be found almost immediately by stepping over one subroutine call after another until one failed to return, and repeating that at lower and lower levels until the errant subroutine was found.

Finding the bug would then be a simple matter of stepping through that subroutine to the end, noting with puzzlement that it didn't seem to do anything wrong, and then realizing it must be the **RET** at the end that's the problem. After all, you'd know for certain that the subroutine didn't return to the caller, and you'd just have found out that it didn't have any problem internally, so all that's left is the **RET**.

And, indeed, stepping through the **RET** would show that it returns to the wrong place altogether. Once you realized that the return address on the stack was wrong, you could check the stack pointer on entry and exit and see that they don't match, which would lead you to the actual bug—the mismatched pushes and pops. Once you know where to look and what to look for, the hard part is done.

Eliminate the Truly Impossible; What's Left Is Your Bug

If you can find a reproducible point at which the computer is in an erroneous state or about to hang, you're set. Just figure out exactly what's wrong at that point, then work backward by running the program to slightly preceding points until you find out how what's wrong got wrong—which is usually not too difficult (especially if you have a debugger that can show you a trace of the last few instructions). It's almost always much harder to figure out *where* to look for a bug than it is to pinpoint a bug once you know where to look.

In fact, your first step should always be to figure out how to reproduce the bug reliably, if possible. If you can't reproduce it on demand, how can you possibly go about methodically zeroing in on its source?

If you can identify a memory variable that changes to an incorrect state and you're using a debugger that takes advantage of the 386, like Turbo Debugger or Soft-ICE, you can find the bad line of code almost instantaneously. Just tell the debugger to stop when the variable is set to the incorrect value, and the debugger will use the hardware breakpoint capability of the 386 to trap the event in real time.

Waiting for the Lightning Bolt

Then there are those rare times when all the patient eliminating of the impossible that you can do fails to unearth a bug; there really *is* no part of your code that could cause the bug. This simply means that you don't know everything that's going on. For example, DOS, the BIOS, or an interrupt may be causing your problem, directly or indirectly. It happens, believe me. I once spent a morning figuring out that a widely used clone BIOS failed to preserve the same registers as the IBM BIOS during calls to the extended memory manipulation functions, and I encountered another clone BIOS that disabled nonmaskable interrupts during hard disk accesses and never reenabled them. Of course, since you don't know what else might be going on (or you would have checked it already), you're in a bit of a bind.

In such a case, you should think very, very hard about everything you've ever heard of that could produce the bug and talk to coworkers to see if they can think of anything. If you still come up blank, you should go away, do something else, and wait for the heavens to open and a lightning bolt to smite your brow and impart the needed information.

I am not kidding about this. (Well, maybe about the lightning bolt, but not the rest.) Your subconscious can often solve problems your conscious mind has hit a wall on, but you have to give it time and a bit of peace and quiet before it can do so. I once spent two days fruitlessly chasing a bug that once in a blue moon left a single garbage line at the bottom of an animated screen, then woke up from a dream with the correct answer fully formed in my head.

Unfortunately, there's no way to control subconscious debugging, but when all else fails, it can save the day. What you *can* do to help your subconscious work is (once again) to eliminate all the dead ends, so that you've narrowed the field of areas to think about to a manageable size. If your program crashes occasionally and you say to your subconscious, "Why is my program crashing?" it will rightfully respond with that uneasiness in the lower tract that is the nonverbal equivalent of "Because."

On the other hand, if you ask your subconscious, "Why is my program crashing when it leaves this one routine along this particular path?" you may get a response like, "Because you forgot to pop AX along that path, so you're returning to the interrupt table instead of your program." Or you may not, but it's worth a shot.

As an example, I once wrote a mouse handler that crashed once every five minutes or so, and then only when the Logitech mouse driver, not the Microsoft driver, was installed. My handler drew the mouse image and did some other housekeeping, but there was nothing in it that could conceivably cause a crash. I commented out calls from the mouse handler to one function after another, until finally the program ceased crashing. Unfortunately, it didn't matter exactly *which* functions I commented out; any of a number of functions did the trick. Finally, by doing nothing but allocating stack space in the handler and allocating more and more space until a crash occurred, I established that the key was the amount of stack space used.

This was a breakthrough, but it didn't turn up the bug. I put in code to check how much of my program's stack was in use at any time, and there was no question that my program's stack was big enough, and then some. My findings seemed to be that I was crashing the program by taking too much stack space, but that there was plenty of stack space. And there matters stayed for some time while I did other things.

Don't ask me why, but eventually it occurred to me that perhaps the too-small stack existed *outside* my program. I followed the vector for the DOS Read File function to the code in DOS that performed that function; from there I came at long last to the code for VDISK (DOS's RAM disk driver) just as I was considering retraining for a career in the exciting field of dental hygiene. Bingo.

VDISK, it seems, switches to an internal stack. That internal stack is in the neighborhood of 100 bytes in size, if memory serves. On a mouse interrupt, the Microsoft Mouse driver plus my code required about 96 bytes. The Logitech Mouse driver apparently pushes a few more values, because together with my code it took about 102 bytes, just barely managing to overwrite adjacent critical code.

The solution was nothing more complicated than switching to yet another internal stack in my mouse handler. Finding assembly level bugs is hard; fixing them is generally easy.

What are we to make of this particular tale? The key: I was correct when I concluded there were no bugs in my code; I *knew*, beyond a shadow of a doubt, that stack space was a problem and that I had allocated enough stack space in my program. Knowing that, I was forced to think along other lines that would normally reek of desperation, like DOS must be broken. DOS wasn't exactly broken, but a part of DOS (VDISK) did have a significant and undocumented limitation when interrupted. I can't tell you what prompted me to look at VDISK (no electrical intervention that I know of came from above on this one), but it almost certainly wouldn't have happened had I not methodically eliminated all other possibilities, chewed on the problem for a while, and given my subconscious time to do its stuff.

Time and Patience

When you get right down to it, your computer is capable of performing a limited set of actions, and you can look at exactly how each and every one is carried out. You're free to disassemble any code you care to, dump all the vectors, and poke wherever you please. In short, there's nothing your computer can hide from you, if you know where to look. Assembly level debugging is really nothing more than an iterative process of figuring out where to look—and time and patience are the keys.

Protect Your Loved Ones with TDREMOTE

■ Michael Abrash

Learn how to get the most out of TDREMOTE.

Turbo Debugger's remote mode (TDREMOTE) may seem a bit odd at first. With TDREMOTE, you download your program from your development computer to another computer via a serial link, and then run the program on the other computer, but you control debugging and view the debug status from your development computer.

This approach is in marked contrast to the remote debugging that some other debuggers offer. With TDREMOTE, the remote computer becomes a debugging terminal that allows your program to take over the keyboard and screen on your development system without interfering with the debugger. The download requirement of TD's remote mode can be a time-consuming nuisance, and because your development system is probably your fastest system, you may at times become impatient with the need to run applications on a slower remote computer while you are debugging. Nonetheless, TDREMOTE offers significant advantages.

One nice benefit: TDREMOTE requires only a small amount of memory on the remote computer. Since the application is actually running on this computer, TDREMOTE allows you to debug large applications that wouldn't fit into memory, along with all of TD, on a single computer. (However, TD386 can do even better in this regard, by taking advantage of the virtual mode of the 386 to give the application being debugged *all* of memory.)

Another, less obvious advantage of TDREMOTE is its ability to isolate your beloved development machine from the worst that a wayward application can do. Think about it: You usually edit, compile, and link an application you're developing on your favorite system. Then you run that application, which is practically *guaranteed* to contain potentially lethal bugs, on that very same computer that you love.

At the very least, an assembly language or C program run amok can (and in my case frequently does) hang the system, requiring a cold boot. And turning the computer off and back on is a major cause of wear and tear, especially for hard disks. (Don't speak to me about reset buttons; I've yet to encounter one that resets everything, including the video adapter and the keyboard.)

Runaway programs can also scramble the CMOS RAM, requiring that the system be set up again—and creating a major problem if you don't happen to have your system's disk type handy. It's also possible for an out-of-control program to mess up your hard disk, or even to misprogram hardware in such a way that it will actually damage equipment. (The latter isn't particularly common, but it is, for example, possible to misprogram a video adapter so that it blows a monochrome monitor. In fact, I've seen this happen.)

Finally, TDREMOTE allows you to plug adapters into another, less valuable computer when you're testing. That might not mean much to an end user. But it can save a developer, who has to test his or her software on, say, the ten leading graphics adapters, considerable abuse of the aforementioned highly prized development system. In fact, the ideal setup might be one in which a new, squeaky clean 486 machine is used to develop applications, while TDREMOTE is used to run those applications on a battered old 8-MHz AT that's configured as needed for each test. The AT might even have the cover left off to facilitate swapping of cards.

Trouble with BOUND

■ Jeff Duntemann

Watch out for the tricky BOUND instruction.

Three years ago, one version of my JDESK utility had this creative way of trashing the system: by triggering continuous Print Screen interrupts until I rebooted. I never figured out why. Now, being older and wiser, I think I know.

There's a *very* odd instruction called **BOUND** that was introduced to the x86 family with the 286. **BOUND** takes two operands: A signed integer value, and a pointer to a table containing two array bounds also represented as signed integers. When **BOUND** is executed, it checks to see if the integer value passed as the first operand falls within the two array bounds values in the table pointed to by the second operand.

If the integer is within the two bounds, nothing happens. However, if the integer value is outside the two bounds, an interrupt 5 is triggered. The INT 5 is hardcoded; there's nothing you can do to change it.

This in itself is bad; Intel reserved INT 5 for its own use but IBM flubbed things in 1981 by hardcoding INT 5 into the PC BIOS as the Print Screen handler. So if you intend to use the **BOUND** instruction even once, you also have to install a replacement INT 5 handler that shares the interrupt between **BOUND** and the Print Screen function.

It gets worse. **BOUND** pushes a return address on the stack while triggering INT 5, but that address is the address of the **BOUND** instruction itself, *not* the instruction following it! This means that if you execute a **BOUND** instruction that fails, it will call INT 5, execute whatever interrupt handler is attached to that vector, then return to the very same **BOUND** instruction, which will presumably fail once more and call INT 5 again...and again...and again.

Creating a whole new interrupt handler (and a shared one at that) is a lot of hassle just to check array bounds with a single instruction. I doubt **BOUND** gets a lot of use, and lord knows I've never used it. Nonetheless, if you ever get what seems to be an endless loop of print screen interrupts, you're probably executing a **BOUND** somewhere, perhaps somewhere where one doesn't exist.

The key is in a dicey practice most of us engaged in until very recently: manually calculating jump offsets in inline assembly statements. Do it wrong, and you can jump into the middle of a multi-byte instruction. If the byte at the target address happens to be 62H, you'll execute a **BOUND**, and whether or not it fails depends on whether the next several bytes constitute an index falling outside bounds in a table located at some random spot in memory.

I no longer have the errant version of JDESK, but I'm sure that's what tripped me up. Thank God for BASM and its like. Calculating jump offsets yourself is a little like bungee jumping. Do it right and get a thrill. Do it wrong and you're road kill.

No thanks. *You* do it. I'll watch.

22

The Craft of Programming

The difference between code that works and code that works *well* is the craft of programming. Using today's near-bulletproof tools, anyone can smear statements around on the screen until something works—sort of. Writing *good* code requires more than simple syntactic correctness. It requires attention to the details of configuring the compiler correctly; to specification and design; to the skill of making all the various tools you're using work together; and, of course, to the multitude of little gotchas that ride in on the back of every programming project more than a hundred lines long.

In other words, programming is more than just coding.

But of course, *you* knew that.

Many books have been written wholly on the craft of programming, and many more will appear in the next few years. We can't cover the subject thoroughly in a single chapter, but we've certainly got some solid information here that'll get you off to a good start on your next project.

Part of the craft of programming is keeping up with the newest generation of languages out there. Algol doesn't cut it anymore. Loren Heiny and Bryan Flamig explain how to compile your C programs under Turbo C++, in preparation for fully converting the code over. And I'll explain how to convert Turbo Pascal code to C++, which isn't actually necessary but may sometimes be desirable.

Jonathan Sachs gives us one of the slickest uses for DOS batch that I've seen in some time. Finally, Kevin Dean shows us how to develop finite state machines in C++.

Cleverness counts. So does foresight. And patience. And care. Whatever language you use, be a craftsman. (Or a craftswoman!) It pays off in the long haul.

Validate the File as Well as the User

■ Jeff Duntemann

Here are some useful tips to help you work with files.

You might hear about it on a tech support call from one of your customers: "I loaded a file into your KennelKlub program, and the machine went nuts!" That's impossible, of course. Your dog kennel management application checks every user response for legality, and no improper values can ever be accepted and written to the data file.

True, true—but hold on: What happens if something corrupts the data file *after* the application writes it to disk? Does the application check data for reasonableness as it loads the data from disk, or does it make the leap of faith that all data values are guaranteed legal and may be safely acted upon?

Consider your typical configurable vertical market database application. Within the header of the database file is a field count and descriptors for each field. You might well ask yourself what would happen if the application loaded a file with 0FFFFh in the count field. The user couldn't create such a file—but a power glitch, faulty disk controller, or modem line noise might. Will the application attempt to allocate 65,535 records and generate a heap error, or run out of stack space, or just vanish into limbo?

An essential part of any application that configures itself or allocates machine resources based on values in a data file is a routine to validate the data file as it is being read in from disk. This routine doesn't have to re-perform every last validation performed on user input—but it should check every field that has the potential to disrupt system operation. Even when pure safety issues are addressed, a "reasonableness" function on *every* part of the incoming database might help catch system-harmless but user-fatal data lapses, like 57-year-old dogs and 220,000-pound orders of Puppy Chow. Don't necessarily forbid the load, but certainly bring up a warning box pointing the user to the suspect data, with an opportunity to enter the correct or (at least) more probable values.

Users are the main causes of faulty data, but they are far from the *only* causes. Corrupted files can get you coming and going, so look both ways before placing your user in the hands of his or her data.

A Change Directory Command with a Memory

■ Jonathan Sachs

Use this director utility to easily move around your system.

Software development often requires that you work with two different subdirectories at once. When you're testing a program, for example, you may have to switch between a directory that holds your source and object files and another that holds your test data.

An elegant solution to the problem of quickly switching between two subdirectories is a CD (Change Directory) command with a memory—one that knows what directory it was last in, and can return there, on command. This article presents a DOS batch file to implement such a command. I call it SD, for "store directory."

If SD is called with a pathname parameter, it changes to the directory in the parameter. If not, SD changes back to the directory you were in the *last* time you ran it. (Be sure to run it the first time with a valid parameter; otherwise, it won't know what to do!)

Here is SD's algorithm:

```
Write the current directory's pathname to a file, X;
If there's a pathname parameter
    change to that directory;
Else
    change back to the previous directory;
Turn pathname in X into a CD command and store in a file, Y.
```

Suppose, for example, that we start out in a directory named \SOURCE. We enter the command SD \TEST.

SD does this:

```
Writes the pathname \SOURCE to the file, X;
Changes the directory to \TEST;
Derives a CD command (CD \SOURCE) from the directory name in
    file X and stores that command into file Y.
```

Later, we enter the command SD with no parameter. SD does this:

```
Writes \TEST to the file, X;
Executes the command in Y, thereby changing the directory
    back to \SOURCE;
Derives a CD command (CD \TEST) from the directory name in
    file X and stores that command into file Y.
```

If we continue to enter SD with no parameter, it will change back to \TEST, then back to \SOURCE, and so on.

SD.BAT (Listing 22.1) implements the SD command. SD.BAT requires a data file named SD.DAT, which we assume resides in C:\BAT, presumably the directory where batch files (including SD.BAT) are kept. You must change this path in SD.BAT to reflect the location of your batch files if you keep them somewhere else.

SD.DAT is an ASCII file that contains two lines:

```
echo.off<CR>
cd.
```

The <CR> represents a carriage return and the two periods represent ASCII spaces. Notice that the second line ends with a space, but *without* a carriage return. *This is essential* to SD's correct operation.

When SD is run, it turns echoing off and executes a CD command with no parameter. This displays the pathname of the current directory, which is redirected to a file named C:\BAT\LASTDIR.

Next, SD determines whether it has a parameter by comparing a null string ("") to its first parameter ("%1"). If the two are equal, there's no parameter.

If there *is* a parameter, SD changes to the specified directory, redirecting CD's display to NUL (that is, to nowhere). Then SD goes to the label **join**. At **join**, it creates a file named C:\BAT\SDX.BAT, which consists of SD.DAT and LASTDIR concatenated, producing text like this:

```
echo off<CR>
cd pathname<CR>
```

Here, **pathname** is the contents of LASTDIR. Finally, SD deletes LASTDIR, since that file is no longer needed.

If there is *not* a parameter, SD goes to the label **previous**. There it executes SDX.BAT, which changes the directory back to whatever it was before SD.BAT was last run. Then it falls through to the label **join**, where it creates a new version of SDX.BAT.

There are a couple of things that SD doesn't do:

- It doesn't behave reasonably if you enter no parameter the first time you run it.
- It doesn't change the current drive if you enter a drivename. For example, SD D:\X will make \X the current directory on drive D, but won't make drive D the current drive.

CODE DESCRIPTION

Overview

A change directory utility implemented as a batch file.

Listings Available

Listing	*Description*	*Used with*
SD.BAT	Batch file.	------

How to Compile/Assemble

Type SD at the command line.

■ LISTING 22.1 SD.BAT

```
echo off
  cd >c:\bat\lastdir
if ""=="%1" goto previous
  cd %1 >NUL
  goto join
:previous
  command /c c:\bat\sdx
:join
  copy c:\bat\sd.dat+c:\bat\lastdir c:\bat\sdx.bat >NUL
  del c:\bat\lastdir
echo on
```

MASM Simplified Segment Directives for .COM Files

■ Bill Pierpont

Master the art of using segment directives.

If you program in assembly language using Microsoft's MASM assembler, you know how much easier programming became when Microsoft introduced simplified segment directives with MASM version 5.0. One main reason for writing in assembly language is to create tiny, fast programs. This often means programs in .COM format. Unfortunately, Microsoft informs us, in no uncertain terms, that "The simplified segment directives cannot be used for programs written in the .COM format." Okay, so let's do it, anyway.

In the small model, the **.DATA**, **.CONST**, and **.DATA?** simplified directives result in segments that are all part of the group **DGROUP**. The **.CODE** directive generates a **_TEXT** segment that's not part of group **DGROUP**. The key to creating a .COM file format is to tell the assembler to make the **_TEXT** segment part of **DGROUP**. Refer to the example program in MAIN.ASM (Listing 22.2) to see the details.

First, make sure you do not use the **DOSSEG** directive (nor the /DOSSEG linker option). The **DOSSEG** directive causes the linker to increase the offset of the start of the code segment by 16 bytes in the small model, and you don't want this.

Next, specify the small model with the **.MODEL** directive. Then add the **_TEXT** segment to **DGROUP**. Now all your simplified segment directives will create segments within **DGROUP**, which is exactly what you want for a .COM file.

Make sure you do not use the **.STACK** directive. The **.STACK** directive is only used in .EXE files. Finally, the first line after the first **.CODE** directive must set the origin to 0100H. The DOS Program Segment Prefix is automatically loaded into memory below this location at runtime.

CODE DESCRIPTION

Overview

The program provided demonstrates how to set up and use segment directives.

Listings Available

Listing	*Description*	*Used with*
MAIN.ASM	Assembly listing that uses segment directives.	------

How to Compile/Assemble

Assemble with any TASM-compatible assembler and link. The linker may warn of the absence of a stack segment. This is okay to ignore since .COM files don't have stack segments. Then run EXE2BIN on the .EXE to convert it to a .COM:

```
EXE2BIN MAIN MAIN.COM
```

■ LISTING 22.2 MAIN.ASM

```
; Program MAIN.ASM
; Sample .COM program format in MASM 5.1 using
; simplified segment directives
; *** Do not use DOSSEG directive ***
    .MODEL small  ; *** Use small model ***
    DGROUP GROUP  _TEXT   ; *** Add _TEXT to DGROUP ***

; *** Do not use .STACK directive ***

    .DATA
msg db "Hello, World!", 13, 10, '$'

    .CODE
    ORG 0100H     ; *** Set origin to 0100H ***
main:
    mov dx, offset msg ; Display message
    mov ah, 09h
    int 21h
    mov ax, 4C00h   ; Exit for DOS 2.0 and above
    int 21h

    END main
```

Compiling C Programs with Turbo C++

■ Bryan Flamig

Here are some useful guidelines for compiling your C programs with a C++ compiler.

If you are running the new Turbo C++ compiler, you may be wondering: Can I compile my C programs without having to change them? Maybe. However, there are some important issues you'll need to be aware of in order to effectively use the C++ compiler with standard C code. A few problems arise because C++ is not exactly a strict superset of C. The biggest change is that you must make sure your C code contains function prototypes. When prototyping functions, it also important to completely prototype them. In C,

```
int foo()
```

means that function **foo** could takes any number of parameters. In C++, this means that **foo** take *no* parameters.

C++ has also added a number of keywords that are no longer for general use. **this**, **virtual**, **public**, **private**, **protected**, **operator**, **friend**, and **class** are all reserved words. **new** and **delete** are also new keywords, but with some special properties in that they refer to runtime functions.

The size of character constants is different. **sizeof(char)** returns 2 in C++ and 1 in C.

Repeat declarations are not allowed in C++. The following statements would be legal in C:

```
int x;
int x;
```

Some of the changes brought about by C++ will assist you in avoiding some bugs. For instance, array initialization is verified. The declaration **char a[4] = "12345"** would be caught and flagged by the compiler.

The type specifier for unsigned chars is more strongly enforced in C++. The linker will complain if you attempt to pass unsigned char values to a function with a declarations of parameters of type char.

You must specifically typecast a void pointer to another type when making an assignment in C++:

```
unsigned char *image; /* An unsigned char pointer */
image = malloc(1600); /* This line won't compile in C++ */
image = (unsigned char *) malloc(1600); /*This is valid C++*/
```

Structure tags are treated the same as type names in C++.

```
typedef int RECT; /* A type called RECT */
struct RECT { int wd, ht; }; /* This will cause a warning */
```

Constants are treated differently in C++. In C, constants use external linkage by default. Therefore you usually don't give constants a value in a header file. In C++, though, constants use static linkage by default. As a result, you cannot declare a constant without giving it a value unless you explicitly use the **extern** qualifier.

```
const int x;   /* Error: uninitialized constant */
const extern int x; /*Valid C++*/
const int x =5;   /*Also valid C++*/
```

C++ imposes constraints on the **goto** statement. In C, **goto** can force a jump to any location. In C++, **goto** cannot jump past a variable declaration.

Enumerated declarations inside a **struct** are hidden in C++:

```
struct toolbox
{ /* Defines a structure having an enumerated type */
  enum tools { hammer, saw, screwdriver; } t;
};

enum tools x; /* Uses the enumerated type to declare a variable */
/* Assigns the variable a value */

x = hammer;   /* This assignment is illegal in C++ */

x = toolbox::hammer; // Now legal in C++
```

Also, enumerated types can only be assigned one of their enumerators and not their equivalent **int** values, unless typecasting is used:

```
enum tools {hammer, saw, screwdriver};
/* Declaring an enumerated type */

tools x;

x = hammer;  /* A valid assignment in C and C++ */
x = 0; /* Same as x = hammer in C, but not legal in C++ */

x = (tools)0; /*awkward, but legal C++*/
```

C++ also enforces typesafe linkage to deal with the issue of overloaded functions. Overloaded functions in C++ are functions which have the same name in the source code, but take varying numbers and types of parameters. Different approaches are used to link to the correct function, but the most common is "name-mangling" where the name of the function is altered to reflect the number and type of parameters being passed to it. In order to get the C++ compiler to generate calls to a "normal" C function, it is necessary to notify it that the function being called has been compiled "externally." That is, the function will not follow the C++ naming convention. Examining the header files included with most popular C/C++ compilers reveals the following kind of construct:

```
#ifdef __cplusplus
extern "C" {
#endif
void standard_C_function(void);
#ifdef __cplusplus
}
#endif
```

When compiled with a C++ compiler, this is the equivalent of:

```
extern "C" {
void standard_C_function(void);
}
```

Calls to **standard_C_function** will then be made using the normal C naming and calling convention. This allows the programmer to use C functions with a C++ compiler. You can use the same mechanism to interface to your already existing code.

C++ for Pascal Programmers

■ Jeff Duntemann

C++ is closer to Pascal than C ever was. Now's the time to give it a shot.

People who know me know that I'm not a C fan. But C is not a lost cause; there's nothing wrong with it that a little discipline and structure wouldn't cure. For many years people have been telling me that Pascal and Modula-2 are losing the war against C, that C will triumph and wipe them both off the map. It's not quite that simple, though.

Remember that war is the world's greatest catalyst for change. In any battle between two adversaries, even though one might win, *both* are altered, for better or for worse. So while C has been out there winning converts, it has also been evolving. Much of this evolution has come about by absorbing features from other languages, much as the American culture has a way of absorbing everything that gets in its way without the quietest belch.

The last time I took a good look at C, it had become C++ 2.0. And by then it was pretty plain:

We'd won!

You don't have to tell the rabid C-hackers this, but C++ 2.0 is more like Pascal than it is like 1980-vintage C. The structure and the discipline are all there. Most of the old gonzo stuff is still there, too, but that's all right. They still sell creamed corn down at Safeway, but you don't actually have go down there and buy it.

Why Bother?

Why indeed? Turbo Pascal is a mighty damned potent language, thank you. It has all the classic features of a structured language (including objects), and all the platform-specific extensions you could ask for. If you're already in paradise, why visit purgatory?

Here's a handful of reasons that you may or may not find compelling:

- *C++ has more versatile object-oriented programming support than Turbo Pascal.* I'm a fan of multiple inheritance, which C++ has and Turbo Pascal does not. C++ destructors and constructors are considerably more powerful than those in Turbo Pascal, and C++ objects have more flexible control of object access rights.
- *Portability is becoming practical again.* The many diverse platforms are converging again, after growing apart for the past 15 years. The Xerox model of user interaction is rapidly becoming universal. Where it was once absurd to consider porting a Macintosh application to a text-mode PC under DOS, it is now a reasonable (if not easy) proposition to port a Macintosh application to Microsoft Windows 3.0. Or X/Windows under Unix. Or OS/2 Presentation Manager. C++ 2.0 (and its successors) is now or will soon be available for all these platforms. The situation can only improve.
- *There's a living in it.* This has always been true of C, if you had the intestinal fortitude. C++ is both an easier and a more difficult language to learn and use, depending on how deeply you choose to take it. I happen to think that C++ will ooze both upward, into the high-end scientific and systems programming arenas, and downward, into the COBOLesque read-a-file, write-a-record business applications that most of us have to write at one time or another to put food on the table. In a very real sense, C++ is what Ada should have been but will never be, and I can almost promise you that there will *always* be jobs there.

The View from a Height

Informally, a Turbo Pascal program consists of constant and variable definitions at the top, some subprogram definitions in the middle, and a main program **BEGIN..END** block at the bottom. One reason C++ is relatively easy for Turbo Pascal people to learn is that C++ programs are laid out in very much the same way: Definitions on top, subprograms in the middle, and the main program at the bottom.

Two complete programs (Listings 22.3 and 22.4) are given for comparison. Functionally, they do just about the same thing, which (for the sake of brevity) isn't very much. They're there to help you follow along on a short tour of the structure of C++, seen from a height.

The Main Program

There's no mistaking a C++ main program: It says **main** right on the label. The **main()** tag identifies a code block as being the main program, and the pair of curly brackets enclose the code block identified as **main**. In general, curly brackets in C++ serve the same function that the reserved words **BEGIN** and **END** do in Turbo Pascal.

The parentheses after the word **main** are vestigial; and although they must be present, you can ignore them for the time being. They are there because **main** is constructed *exactly* the same way a subprogram is constructed in C++. In a subprogram the parentheses would enclose parameters passed "in" to the subprogram. There is nothing to pass to **main** and so the parentheses go unused.

All subprograms in C++ are called "functions" whether they actually return a value or not. This is why you sometimes hear the main program referred to as "the **main** function."

The word **void** before the word **main** indicates that the **main** function does not return a value. The word **void** is the "no-op" of data types in C++; it's used to name a data type in situations where no data actually changes hands.

C++ Programs Are Not Named!

The actual word **main**, while not a reserved word in C++, is nevertheless important. The word **main** marks the point in a C++ program where execution begins.

Note that there is no statement at the top of the C++ program giving it a name. Neither is **main** the name of the program. All C++ programs contain a function named **main**. C++ programs are not named like their Pascal brethren.

Also notice that there is no closing punctuation after the final curly bracket. Turbo Pascal requires a period after the final **END**, but C++ is content that every opening curly bracket have a closing curly bracket.

Comments

C++ comments come in two flavors. One flavor is almost identical to Turbo Pascal's: Anything falling between the open-comment delimiter /* and the close-comment delimiter */ is a comment and is ignored by the compiler. The /* and */ delimiters correspond exactly to Pascal's **(*** and ***)**.

The other comment flavor is one long used in assembly language: A single symbol begins a comment, with the comment then running to the end of the current line. In C++ the symbol is //. Anything falling after the // symbol to the end of the line is ignored by the compiler.

Variable Definitions

In C++, variables are defined "backwards" from the method used in Pascal. The type of the defined variable is given *before* the variable's name, not after. In another departure from Pascal, no punctuation is used between type and name. Simply stating **int x;** defines a variable named **x** as an integer. All local variables must be defined inside a code block; that is, between the curly brackets defining the function body.

Function Definitions

Immediately before or after the **main** function are the definitions of other functions, which are the true subprograms of a C++ program. Subprograms are called functions in C++ whether or not they return a value; there is no C++ entity properly called a "procedure."

Function definitions consist of a header and a code block enclosed between curly brackets. Any code between the curly brackets is executed when the function is executed.

If a function has local variables, these variables must be defined *inside* the curly brackets. This is in contrast to Pascal, where variables are defined outside the **BEGIN..END** words enclosing subprogram code.

The C++ function header is very similar to a function header in Pascal. It names the function and defines the names, types, and order of parameters for the function. The header also specifies the type of the return value, if the function returns a value. If the function does *not* return a value, the reserved word **void** must be used in front of the function name.

Function parameters are declared just as variables are declared in C++: type first, then name. Where a function has multiple parameters, the parameters are separated by commas. (Pascal separates parameters with semicolons.)

By default, parameters are passed to a function by value; that is, a separate copy of the parameter is pushed onto the stack before the function is called. This is just as things are done in Pascal; unless preceded by the reserved word **VAR**, a Pascal parameter is a value parameter, passed by value into a subprogram.

C++ also has *reference parameters*, which are closely analogous to **VAR** parameters in Pascal. A reference parameter is not actually passed to the function. Instead, the *address* of the actual parameter is passed into the function, and changes made to the reference parameter within the function will alter the actual parameter existing outside the function. Again, this is exactly how **VAR** parameters work in Pascal.

Reference parameters are indicated by prefixing the parameter's identifier with the "&" symbol in the function header:

```
void swap(int &x, int &y);
{
  int temp; // Define local integer variable
  temp = x;  // Store x's value in temp
  x = y; // Copy y's value into x
  y = temp; // Copy x's value from temp to y
}
```

Each parameter must have its own type specifier and its own & symbol.

C++ Functions May Not Be Nested!

Note one *very* important difference between subprograms in C++ and Turbo Pascal. C++ functions may *not* be nested. In other words, you may not define a C++ function inside another C++ function. In Pascal, by contrast, functions and procedures may contain local functions and procedures. This is a serious deficiency of C++ that may be fixed in the future.

Function Prototypes

C++ imposes an additional requirement on the definition of functions: Before the function as a whole is defined, the function's full header—including all parameters—must be listed separately, just as it will later be used in defining the full body of the function. This lonely header is known as a *function prototype*. They serve very much the same purpose as the procedure and function headers in the interface portion of a Pascal unit.

It's a good idea to put the function prototypes together in a block at the top of your program.

Function Order

Unlike Pascal, C++ requires no special order for the definition of functions. In Pascal, you have to avoid forward references among procedures by taking some care to place procedures that are called by other procedures above the callers in the source code file.

C++ functions, by contrast, can be in any order. In C++, the compiler is alerted to the presence of all functions by the presence of the function prototypes, so Pascal-style subprogram ordering is unnecessary.

Header Files

You'll see something like this near the top of almost all C++ programs:

```
#include <stdio.h>
```

Most of the time there will be two or more such statements. The **#include** directive instructs the compiler to read source code from the file enclosed between the < and > symbols into the compilation as though it were part of the source file being compiled. This is very similar to the **$I** directive in Turbo Pascal, which instructs the compiler to read source code lines from the named file instead of the current source code file.

Files with a **.h** extension are called *header files*. Several are usually included with every commercial C++ compiler, including the ubiquitous STDIO.H. Pull one into an editor and look it over. (*Don't* change it!)

What you'll see, mostly, are declarations of constants, variables, and functions from the runtime library. Rather than complicate the compiler by predefining such frequently used items (as is done in Turbo Pascal), their declarations are instead put into a header file, and it's up to you the programmer to include that header file in your programs.

As you begin to write larger applications in C++, you'll eventually begin breaking programs into modules. Then you'll find that header files of your own creation are useful for ensuring that declarations of items used throughout your program will be defined identically for all modules.

Semicolons

Sad to say, there are semicolons in C++, as there are in Pascal. Worse, they serve an entirely different Prime Directive: Semicolons in C++ are statement *terminators*, rather than statement *separators*. Every statement in C++ must be terminated with a semicolon. This includes the last statement in a compound statement, where Pascal would let you get away without one.

Also, the statement immediately before an **else** reserved word needs a semicolon, exactly where all your Pascal instincts say to avoid one.

Placing a semicolon after a function header makes that function header a function prototype. When you actually define the full function, body and all, you *cannot* put a semicolon at the end of the header.

Plan on making a lot of semicolon mistakes. If it's any consolation, it's less painful than spilling hot tea in your lap.

Taking the Plunge

That's a quick summary of the anatomy of C++ programs, enough to get you to the stage where you can start banging the bugs out of your own efforts. Plan to spend considerable time with compiler documentation, puzzling out error messages. C++ is a big, complex language with plenty of subtleties.

There are two ways to proceed. The conservative way is to start small and begin writing simple C++ applications from scratch. This is like easing your way into a cold swimming pool an inch at a time. It takes forever, and the discomfort can get considerable along the way.

The gonzo path (which I took, natch) is to choose one of your own modest Turbo Pascal programs, and then beat it about the head and shoulders in the editor until it becomes a compilable C++ program. It's fun, and you will learn a great deal about C++ in a big hurry.

Here are some suggestions from my experience in learning C++. Follow them in order for best results:

1. Ditch the **PROGRAM** statement at the top of the file. Replace it with a **#include <stdio.h>** statement.
2. Convert all comments to C++ format. This can be done using a search-and-replace, changing { and (* to /*, and then } and *) to */.
3. Convert all instances of **BEGIN** to {, and all instances of **END** to }. Remove the period at the end of the file.
4. Un-nest any nested procedures and functions. Watch out for scoping conflicts, which can get ugly. This item gave me a *lot* of trouble, by the way. If you tend not to nest procedures in Turbo Pascal you'll get the conversion done a whole lot easier.
5. Convert your data definitions to C++ style. If your Pascal code contains objects, spend a little time studying C++ object syntax before wading in. Thankfully, converting from

Turbo Pascal objects to C++ objects is fairly straightforward. The reverse, however, is often impossible.

6. Move local variable definitions inside the function code block. If you had to move a good many local procedures out of a largish global procedure, consider moving some of the largish procedure's local variables out into globals. Remember that your formerly local procedures will now be global functions, and that they may be assuming that something belonging to the largish procedure is still within their scope.
7. Convert your function parameters to C++ style. Study your documentation before you begin. C++ parameter passing is straightforward.
8. Convert Pascal-style string handling to C-style string handling, which involves issues such as the length byte, string handling functions, and screen display mechanisms. Remember that you *cannot* use the assignment operator "=" to assign values to C++ strings; use the **strcpy()** and **strcat()** functions instead. There are a lot of string-handling functions in the runtime library. Study them.
9. Convert your Pascal control structures to their C++ forms. There is a C++ analog to every Pascal control structure. Remember that there's no **then** word in a C++ **if** statement! And watch out for **switch**—it's subtler than **CASE** by a nautical mile.
10. Try to find analogs for Turbo Pascal's library routines in your C++ compiler's libraries. The more complex your program, the tougher this will turn out to be, and the more likely you'll have to build something on the C++ side to handle what you took for granted in Turbo Pascal.

Actually, if you're using Turbo C++ you're in fairly good shape here. Both Turbo languages use the same BGI library, and many of the Turbo Pascal library routines have close analogs in the Turbo C++ library.

Rejoice! You're about a third of the way there. Bring up your compiler and turn it loose. The first few tries will leave you close to despair—but take it one boo-boo at a time, and after a while things will begin to gel.

Once you get your first program converted, haul out another . . . and repeat the process until it's easy.

CODE DESCRIPTION

Overview

Two complete programs which generate a hundred random values and sort them using a bubble sort. One program is in Turbo Pascal, the other is in C++. The intention is to show the similarity between two highly structured languages.

Listings Available

Listing	*Description*	*Used with*
BUBBLER.PAS	Pascal version of the Bubble-Up sort routine.	------
BUBBLER.CPP	C++ version of the same routine.	------

How to Compile/Assemble

The C++ program can be compiled and linked with any C++ compiler. The Pascal version can be compiled wih any Turbo Pascal-compatible Pascal compiler.

■ LISTING 22.3 BUBBLER.PAS

```
PROGRAM Bubbler;

CONST
  ARRAY_SIZE = 100;

TYPE
  IntArray = ARRAY[0..ARRAY_SIZE] OF INTEGER;

VAR
  I : Integer;
  TestArray : IntArray;

PROCEDURE Swap(VAR X : Integer; VAR Y : Integer);

VAR Temp : Integer;

BEGIN
  Temp := X;  { Store x's value in temp  }
  X := Y;     { Copy y's value into x    }
  Y := Temp;  { Copy x's value from temp into y }
END;


FUNCTION BubbleSort(VAR TargetArray : IntArray) : Integer;

VAR SortedFlag, PassFlag, I : Integer;

BEGIN
  SortedFlag := 1;
  REPEAT
    PassFlag := 1;
    FOR I := 0 TO ARRAY_SIZE DO
      IF (TargetArray[I] > TargetArray[I+1]) THEN
        BEGIN
          Swap(TargetArray[I],TargetArray[I+1]);
          SortedFlag := 0;
          PassFlag   := 0;
        END;
  UNTIL PassFlag = 1;
  BubbleSort := SortedFlag;
END;

PROCEDURE ShowArray(TargetArray : IntArray);

VAR I : Integer;
```

```
BEGIN
  FOR I := 0 TO ARRAY_SIZE DO
    BEGIN
      Write(TargetArray[I] : 3);
      IF ((I+1) MOD 20 = 0) THEN Writeln;
    END;
  Writeln;
END;

BEGIN
  FOR I := 0 TO ARRAY_SIZE DO
    TestArray[i] := Random(ARRAY_SIZE-1);
  Writeln('Here''s the unsorted array: ');
  ShowArray(TestArray);
  IF BubbleSort(TestArray) = 1
    THEN Writeln('That array was already sorted!')
  ELSE
    BEGIN
      Writeln;
      Writeln('The sort of the array is complete. Here it is:');
      ShowArray(TestArray);
    END;
END.
```

■ LISTING 22.4 BUBBLER.CPP

```
#include<stdlib.h>
#include<stdio.h>
#include<iostream.h>
#include<iomanip.h>

const int ARRAY_SIZE = 100;

void swap(int &x, int &y);
int  bubble_sort(int *target_array);
void show_array(int *target_array);

void swap(int &x, int &y)

{
  int temp;     // Define a local integer variable

  temp = x;     // Store x's value in temp
  x = y;        // Copy y's value into x
  y = temp;     // Copy x's value from temp into y
}

int  bubble_sort(int *target_array)

{
  int sorted_flag = 1;
  int i, pass_flag;

  do {
```

```
      pass_flag = 1;
      for (i=0; i < ARRAY_SIZE-1; i++)
        if (target_array[i] > target_array[i+1])
      {
        swap(target_array[i],target_array[i+1]);
        sorted_flag = 0;
        pass_flag   = 0;
      }
    } while (pass_flag == 0);
    return sorted_flag;
}

void show_array(int *target_array)
{
  int i,old_width;

  old_width = cout.width(5);
  for (i=0; i<ARRAY_SIZE; i++)
    {
      cout << setw(3) << target_array[i];
      if ((i+1) % 20 == 0) cout << '\n';
    }
  cout << '\n';
  cout.width(old_width);
}

void main()

{
  int i;
  int test_array[ARRAY_SIZE];  // Declare an array of 100 integers

  for (i=0; i<100; i++)
    test_array[i] = rand() % 100;
  cout << "Here's the unsorted array:" << "\n";
  show_array(test_array);
  if (bubble_sort(test_array))
    cout << "That array was already sorted!";
  else
    cout << "The sort of the array is complete.  Here it is: \n";
    show_array(test_array);
  cout << "\n";
}
```

Use an Assembler to Create Data Files

■ Ron Aaron

Mastering the art of creating data files with an assembler.

How many times have you had to make a data file for testing a new program? How many times have you written a small, one-time-only program just to generate such files?

Use your assembler to do the grunt work! It's easy and fast, and you don't have to write any code.

The example in DATAFILE.ASM (Listing 22.5) creates an indexed string data file by using facilities available in the assembler. The example uses Turbo Assembler because that's what I use, but it could be easily modified to work with Microsoft MASM or OPTASM. How long would it take you to create an indexed data file otherwise? TASM assembles this in just a few seconds!

TIP: The trick to using these records indexed in a C/C++ program is in the declaration:

```
LABEL Index BYTE
String1  DW offset String_1
```

By making the Index label PUBLIC, the strings can be accessed using array notation:

```
char extern *Index[];
```

Index[0] would then point to **String_1.**

CODE DESCRIPTION

Overview

Assembly language file which, when compiled and linked, turns into a non-executable data file containing indexed records for use with another program. This approach is useful for creating data in specific formats with a minimum of fuss.

Listings Available

Listing	*Description*	*Used with*
DATAFILE.ASM	Assembly file for producing binary data.	------

How to Compile/Assemble

To assemble, use TASM datafile. Link using the /t option for TLINK or use EXE2BIN to convert to a .COM-style file.

■ LISTING 22.5 DATAFILE.ASM

```
; DATAFILE.ASM  - Shows how to use TASM to make data files

ideal

model tiny
codeseg

   ORG 0h      ; offset of zero
```

```
begin:

;
; Declare your data here ...
;

File_Header DB 'DATAFILE! Using an assembler to make a data file'
            DB 26     ; Ctrl-Z

LABEL Index BYTE
String1  DW offset String_1
String2  DW offset String_2
String3  DW offset String_3
String4  DW offset String_4

LABEL Strings BYTE
String_1 DB 'The first string', 0
String_2 DB 'another one...', 0
String_3 DB 'Yet another string!',0
String_4 DB 'A BIG STRING', 13, 10
         DB 'Spread out over several', 13, 10
         DB 'lines.',0

   end   begin
```

Inline Assembly without an Assembler

■ Kevin Dean

Ease your way into assembly by using this programming technique.

Although I've been programming PCs for about five years, I still avoid assembly when I can, not because of the language itself but because of the insane headers and directives that assemblers (even TASM) require before I can even begin coding.

I write most of my stuff in C or C++, so Turbo C's inline assembly syntax is a godsend. The penalty I pay for the convenience of writing assembler routines with C function declarations and naming conventions is, of course, the overhead of having to pass the source through the compiler *and* assembler before getting an object file.

I explored Turbo C's language extensions to learn just how dirty my hands could get before having to go to raw assembly. For example, Turbo C can access the machine registers through the pseudo-variables **_AX**, **_BX**, and so on. Did you also know that

```
asm mov ax, es:[bx]
```

and

```
_AX = *(unsigned _es *)_BX;
```

are the same? It's amazing what you can do with the **_cs**, **_ds**, **_es**, **_seg**, and **_ss** pointer modifiers.

By far the most powerful (and dangerous) extension is the **__emit__()** function. With this function, you can insert literal bytes into your code like this:

```
__emit__(0xAC); /* lodsb */
```

ASM.H (Listing 22.6) defines a number of common assembler operations as __emit__() calls. To create others, use Turbo Debugger's interactive assembler in the CPU window to assemble the instructions you're interested in and record the opcodes generated in ASM.H.

Turbo C has a wealth of pseudo-functions defined in DOS.H. Some of them are **enable()**, **disable()**, **peek()**, **poke()**, **geninterrupt()**, and **MK_FP()**. Many of these are expanded inline to raw assembly language.

With a little thought and planning, it's possible to write entire functions in highly optimized, and often more readable, assembly without having to go to the assembler to generate the object file.

CODE DESCRIPTION

Overview

C/C++ header file which enables the programmer to insert machine code directly into the instruction stream. This allows you to place assembly-type instuctions directly in-line in a C/C++ program.

Listings Available

Listing	*Description*	*Used with*
ASM.H	Header file with assembly code **#defines**.	------

How to Compile/Assemble

Include in your C/C++ source program with #include "asm.h."
Can be compiled and linked with any C/C++ compiler.

■ LISTING 22.6 ASM.H

```
void __emit__();
#define pushAX()  __emit__(0x50)
#define pushBX()  __emit__(0x53)
#define pushCX()  __emit__(0x51)
#define pushDX()  __emit__(0x52)
#define pushSI()  __emit__(0x56)
#define pushDI()  __emit__(0x57)
#define pushBP()  __emit__(0x55)
#define pushSP()  __emit__(0x54)
#define pushDS()  __emit__(0x1E)
#define pushES()  __emit__(0x06)
#define pushSS()  __emit__(0x16)
```

```
#define pushCS()  __emit__(0x0E)
#define pushF()   __emit__(0x9C)

#define popAX()  __emit__(0x58)
#define popBX()  __emit__(0x5B)
#define popCX()  __emit__(0x59)
#define popDX()  __emit__(0x5A)
#define popSI()  __emit__(0x5E)
#define popDI()  __emit__(0x5F)
#define popBP()  __emit__(0x5D)
#define popSP()  __emit__(0x5C)
#define popDS()  __emit__(0x1F)
#define popES()  __emit__(0x07)
#define popSS()  __emit__(0x17)
#define popF()   __emit__(0x9D)

#define stosb()  __emit__(0xAA)
#define stosw()  __emit__(0xAB)
#define lodsb()  __emit__(0xAC)
#define lodsw()  __emit__(0xAD)
#define retn()   __emit__(0xC3)
#define retf()   __emit__(0xCB)
#define iret()   __emit__(0xCF)
```

Finite State Machines in C++

■ Kevin Dean

Learn the art of the state by developing a simple finite state machine application in C++.

Computer programs face choices all the time; a language would be almost useless without the if-then-else clause. The number of courses of action available to the program is finite, and the program should behave in exactly the same way for exactly the same input every time. There are many ways to formally model the behavior of a program or system, and one of these is the Finite State Machine (FSM) model.

A finite state machine is a model in which the states of the system are finite in number and for which the rules for moving from one state to another are finite and unambiguous. One or more states are defined as start states or entry points and one or more states are defined as end states or exit points.

Figure 22.1 is a simple FSM representing a badge reader, such as those found on parking lot gates. The states are represented as numbered circles and the state transition lines joining them move from one state to another in the directions shown. The transition rules are noted beside the transition lines; any line without an associated rule is an unconditional jump to the next state. The state transitions are all unidirectional: there is no way to move back up a FSM unless there is a state transition that does.

States B1 and BE are the start and end states respectively. The (V) beside state B3 indicates that it is a virtual state which may be overridden in a derived FSM; the default is to move unconditionally back to state B1.

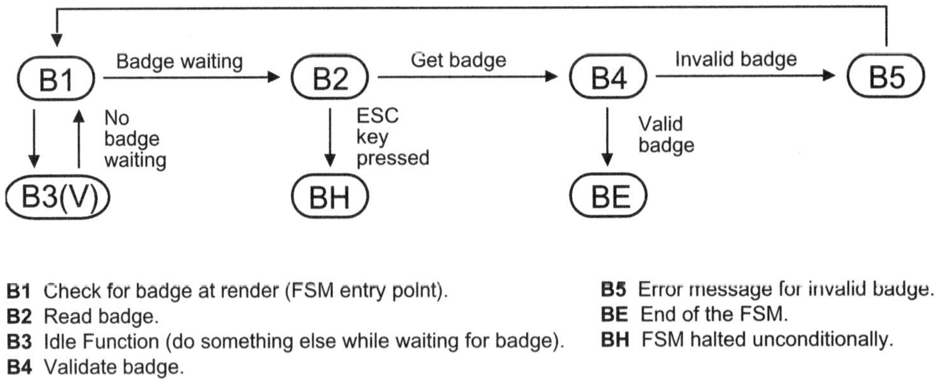

■ **Figure 22.1 Badge reader FSM**

Reality Check

Some time ago I designed an inventory control system for a lumber company in northern Ontario. Each arriving truck is identified at a gate with a badge reader, weighed in, and directed to a drop-off zone. While in the yard, the truck may optionally fill up at the company gas pump which is also controlled by a badge reader. On the way out, the truck is weighed and is later paid according to the difference in weight and the amount of gas it took.

In addition to inventory control, the company also wanted to control access to the employee parking lot with a badge reader. The inventory system and the parking lot had two things in common: They both required badge readers to control access and they both had gates to prevent access if the badge was invalid. These and other similarities in the system led to the desire for code reusability and to object-oriented programming, in this case to C++.

The next problem was how to model the system. A truck could be doing only one thing at a time and its transition from one state to another was rigidly defined ....

This Means Finite State Machines!

The best way to define each function of the system (truck unloading, parking access, etc.) was to define its components (badge reader, gate, weigh scale, gas pump, etc.) as FSM's. Maximum code reusability was thus achieved by combining the various components into a complete FSM for each function.

FSM.H (Listing 22.7) defines the classes that make up a FSM. Figure 22.2 shows the complete class hierarchy of a badge-controlled parking gate.

The primary design criteria for a C++ FSM class is that it be as extensible as the C++ language itself. This means two things:

- It should be possible to build larger FSM's from one or more base class FSM's (inheritance).
- It should be possible to redefine a state function in a derived class (polymorphism).

The FSM "stub" in Figure 22.2 satisfies both of these requirements. The **VirtualFSM** class contains all the information about the FSM that is currently running: where it starts and which base FSM and state is currently being executed. It also contains the definition of an abstract state (class **State**) and a transfer state for moving from one FSM to another (class **TransferState**). For the moment, we'll ignore the transfer state.

Most of the **VirtualFSM** member functions are simple management functions and should be self-explanatory. We'll come back to some of them later.

The **BaseFSM** class contains all the information specific to each FSM: namely, what the FSM should do when it ends. This feature is used by the **TransferState** class in large FSM's.

Finally, there is the FSM template itself. The template consolidates the **VirtualFSM** and **BaseFSM** classes and defines the class **FuncState** to control the state functions for the FSM. At first glance, it doesn't seem that the FSM template does much except define the **FuncState** class. The only member functions in the template simply pass control on to the **BaseFSM** class, so why not define **FuncState** itself as a template and leave out this extra layer?

The answer to this can be found in Figure 22.2. If we remove the **FSM<class T>** template, the class **BadgeGate** will then be derived directly from **BaseFSM**, **Badge**, and **Gate**. **Badge** and **Gate**, in turn, will be derived directly from **BaseFSM**, which makes **BaseFSM** both a direct and indirect base class of **BadgeGate**. This is illegal because a typecast from **BadgeGate** to **BaseFSM** is ambiguous: which of the three **BaseFSM**'s do we mean? The FSM template makes **BaseFSM** an indirect base class of all FSM's so we can cast first to the desired **FSM<T>** and then to **BaseFSM**.

The **FuncState** class, finally, is what manages the state functions. A state function is just that: A function representing the current state of the machine. Each **FuncState** holds a pointer to a void member function which can refer only to a function in the class **T** or an unambiguous base class of **T**; it cannot refer to a function in a class derived from **T**, which

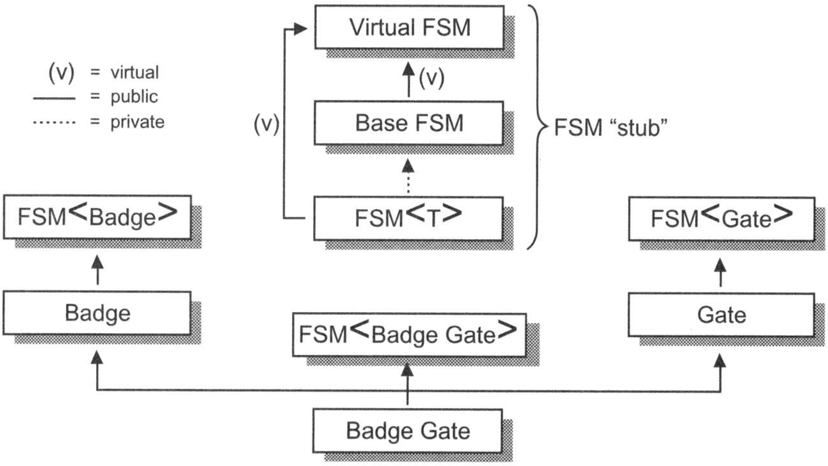

■ **Figure 22.2 Class hierarchy**

is why the **FuncState** definition is left to the FSM template and not to **VirtualFSM** or **BaseFSM**.

The **FuncState::exec()** function executes the current state. It is passed a pointer to the current base FSM which is (assumed to be) the base FSM closest to the matching class **T**, i.e. the instance of **BaseFSM** from which **FSM<T>** is derived. If not, the program will probably go out to lunch and never come back because this pointer in the state function will be hopelessly wrong. This indicates a problem in either the initialization of the FSM or in the definition of a **TransferState**.

BADGE.H and BADGE.CPP (Listings 22.8 and 22.9) define and implement the badge reader FSM in Figure 22.1. If you'd like to test the badge reader alone, define the macro **TEST_BADGE** to compile the **main()** function as well and run the program. The FSM halts unconditionally by calling **halt()** when the **ESC** key is pressed or ends normally by calling **endFSM()** when a valid four character badge is entered (the **isValid()** function returns true for all badges by default). The unconditional halt is part of the live implementation that allows maintenance staff to use a special badge to shut down a single reader without stopping the rest of the system.

Special Note: Ideally, the state functions themselves should be protected or private. What I think is an access bug in Borland C++ 3.0 won't allow these functions to be declared as anything except public so that they can be passed to the **FuncState** constructor, even though the **FuncState** object is a member of the class.

The current state of the machine is initialized by **VirtualFSM**'s constructor and is updated by successive calls to the **nextState()** functions. The **runState()** function returns true as long as **_curState** is not 0; the **runFSM()** function runs the FSM to completion, i.e. until the **runState()** function returns false.

The **FuncState** members of the **Badge** FSM (and others) are defined as static members of the class because they never change. This saves memory when there are many of the same type of FSM and speeds things up because the **nextState()** functions will refer to a fixed address, not to an offset from the this pointer. My naming convention for function states is to use the same name as the enclosed function with a leading underscore.

GATE.H and GATE.CPP (Listings 22.10 and 22.11) define and implement the parking gate FSM. The incoming and outgoing sensor pads are the left and right shift keys respectively.

An interesting point about the parking gate FSM is that it is split up into two FSMs, one of which doesn't terminate. If you ran this FSM alone with G1 as the entry point, it would never end. The virtual state G3 provides a hook into the FSM which we can use to end it or to transfer control to another FSM.

Putting It All Together

We now have two separate FSMs which we have to combine into the badge-controlled parking gate. This is accomplished in BADGGATE.H and BADGGATE.CPP (Listings 22.12 and 22.13). Note that there is no end state for the **BadgeGate** class, but this doesn't have to be the case.

First and foremost, the **BadgeGate** class is an FSM, so we have to derive it from **FSM<BadgeGate>** even though **FSM<T>** is a base class of the **Badge** and **Gate** classes. We now have several ambiguities to deal with:

1. There is more than one FuncState class defined in the FSM<T> base classes.
2. There is more than one FSM<T>::base() function.
3. There is more than one **FSM<T>::endFSM()** function.

We overcome these ambiguities by selecting the appropriate **FSM<T>** to which we are referring when using any of the above.

When constructing a FSM, we have to call the **VirtualFSM** constructor with a **BaseFSM** pointer and a start state that belongs to the same class. There is nothing to prevent us from initializing the **BadgeGate** FSM with **FSM<Badge>::base()** and **Badge::_checkForBadge** but that defeats the purpose of multiple inheritance: when the **Badge** FSM ends, it has nowhere to go. There is also nothing to prevent us from calling the constructor with **FSM<BadgeGate>::base()** and **Badge::_checkForBadge** but the assumption that **FuncState::exec()** makes about the **BaseFSM** pointer goes out the window, followed closely by the program.

Transfer States and Virtual Functions

Now that we've defined the FSM, we have to link all the components together. We do this with the **TransferState** class and by overriding some virtual functions.

The **TransferState** class transfers control to another part of the FSM and tells the new FSM where to return to when it finishes. Let's look at the **_checkReader** transfer state.

The first two parameters to the **TransferState** constructor tell the FSM where to go; the third parameter tells the new FSM where to return to when it ends. When the transfer state is run, the function **TransferState::exec()** is called to do the following:

1. Save the exit point or return address by calling the **saveEnd()** function of the destination **_transFSM** pointer.
2. Set the new state and base FSM by calling the **nextState()** function of the current FSM.

In this case, control is transferred to the _checkForBadge entry point of the Badge FSM. When the Badge FSM calls endFSM() (i.e. when a valid badge is entered), control will be returned to the _openIncoming state of the BadgeReader FSM.

Since transfer states refer to BaseFSM pointers that are different for each instance of the BadgeGate object, they are defined as nonstatic members of the class.

Virtual functions can cause trouble if not carefully defined, so let's look at them more closely.

The first virtual function, **isValid()**, is not a state function and so merits little attention except to note that a valid badge for this parking gate is one that starts with a 'P'.

The idle functions, **noBadge()** and **noOutgoing()**, are functions of the **BadgeGate** class but they are not, repeat *not*, state functions of the **BadgeGate** FSM. Let's look at the **noOutgoing()** function.

The **noOutgoing()** function transfers control to the **_checkReader** state, which is a member of the **BadgeGate** class. If we use the normal **nextState(State &)** function, the program will very likely hang because the **_curFSM** pointer is pointing to the **Gate** FSM (because **noOutgoing()** is a **Gate** state) and the **_checkReader** state belongs to the

BadgeReader class. We have to override the current FSM before transferring control to the new state by using the **nextState(State &, BaseFSM *)** function instead. If the next state is a Gate state, the normal **nextState(State &)** function may be used.

A Simple FSM Scheduler

FSMSCHED.CPP (Listing 22.14) is a C++ Turbo Vision framework for running FSMs in the background using the **idle()** function. When writing FSMs for something like this, it is important that no state of the FSM hold up the rest of the program.

TIP: For more information on Turbo Vision's **idle()** function, see the article "Turbo Vision's Idle Moments" by Kevin Dean in Chapter 6, User Interface Programming.

Where Can We Use FSMs?

While the badge-controlled parking gate is a good example of an FSM, it's not one that most of us run across except as drivers, so where else can we use FSMs?

Every program is a finite state machine where the current state of the program depends entirely on the input it has received to that point. An event-driven program like a Turbo Vision or Windows application is closest to the concept of the finite state machine: the current view is equivalent to the current state and the next view or state is determined by the next event that the current view receives.

While it's not practical or useful to model every program as a FSM, some modules (e.g. file transfer protocols like XModem) and programs (e.g. compilers) make more sense as FSMs. Almost any module with a large number of functions and where the next function to call is determined by the result of the current function can be better defined as a FSM.

CODE DESCRIPTION

Overview

A complete example of how to create and use finite state machines, implemented in C++.

Listings Available

Listing	*Description*	*Used with*
FSM.H	Defines Finite State Machine classes.	------
BADGE.H	Header file for Badge Reader Finite State Machine.	------
BADGE.CPP	Implementation of Badge Reader.	------
GATE.H	Header file for Gate Finite State Machine.	------
GATE.CPP	Implementation of Gate.	------
BADGGATE.H	Header file for combining Badge Reader and Gate.	------
BADGGATE.CPP	Implementation of Badge Reader and Gate Finite State Machine.	------
FSMSCHED.CPP	Example of running Finite State Machines in the background using Turbo Vision.	------

How to Compile/Assemble

Can be compiled and linked with any C++ compiler which supports templates. FSMSCHED.CPP makes use of Borland C++'s Turbo Vision library.

■ LISTING 22.7 FSM.H

```
/*
File     : fsm.h
Author   : Kevin Dean
Classes defined  : VirtualFSM, BaseFSM, FSM<class T>
This code is public domain.*/
#if !defined(_FSM_H)
#define _FSM_H
class BaseFSM;
// Virtual finite state machine (used as virtual base by BaseFSM).
class VirtualFSM {
  friend BaseFSM;
  protected:
  // State handler for FSM.
  class State {
    friend VirtualFSM;
    protected:
    State() { }
    ~State() { }
    // Run current state function.
    virtual void exec(BaseFSM * const fsm) = 0;
    };

  // FSM state transfer to base state.
  class TransferState : public State {
    BaseFSM * const _transFSM; // FSM to which to transfer control.
    State * const _transStart; // State at which to start new FSM.
    State * const _transEnd;   // State to which to return control.

    public:
    TransferState(BaseFSM * transFSM, State * transStart,
    State * transEnd) : State(), _transFSM(transFSM),
    _transStart(transStart), _transEnd(transEnd) { }
    ~TransferState() { }
    protected:
    // Run current state function.
    virtual void exec(BaseFSM * const fsm);
    };

  private:
  BaseFSM * _startFSM; // Initial finite state machine.
  State * _startState; // Initial state.
  BaseFSM * _curFSM;   // Current finite state machine.
  State * _curState;   // Current state.

  protected:
  // Protected constructor means class can only be base class.
```

```
VirtualFSM(BaseFSM * startFSM, State * startState) {
init(startFSM, startState);
}

// Set the initial FSM and state.
void init(BaseFSM * startFSM, State * startState) {
_startFSM = startFSM;
_startState = startFSM ? startState : 0;
restart();
}

// Set the next state.
void nextState(State & state) {
_curState = &state;
}

// Set the next state and current base FSM.
void nextState(State & state, BaseFSM * fsm) {
_curState = &state;
_curFSM = fsm;
}

public:
virtual ~VirtualFSM() { }

// Restart the FSM.
virtual void restart() {
_curFSM = _startFSM;
_curState = _startState;
}

// Call next state function if defined.
int runState() {
if (_curState)
  _curState->exec(_curFSM);
return (_curState != 0);
}

// Run the FSM to completion.
virtual void runFSM() {
while (runState());
}

// Halt the FSM regardless of the current state.
void halt() {
_curFSM = _startFSM;
_curState = 0;
}

// Determine if the FSM is running.
int running() {
return (_curState != 0);
}
};
```

```
// Base finite state machine (used only by FSM template).
class BaseFSM : virtual public VirtualFSM {
  friend void VirtualFSM::TransferState::exec(BaseFSM * const fsm);
  BaseFSM * _prevFSM;  // FSM from which control was transferred.
  State * _endState;   // State to which to transfer at end of FSM.
  protected:
  // Protected constructor means class can only be base class.
  BaseFSM() : VirtualFSM(0, 0), _prevFSM(0) { }
  virtual ~BaseFSM() { }
  private:
  // Save state to which to transfer at end (used by TransferState).
  void saveEnd(State * endState) {
  _prevFSM = _curFSM;
  _endState = endState;
  }

  protected:

  // End this FSM.
  void endFSM() {
  // If previous FSM exists, transfer control back to it.
  if (_prevFSM) {
    _curFSM = _prevFSM;
    _curState = _endState;
    _prevFSM = 0;
    }
  else
    // FSM ended normally.
    halt();
  }
  };

// Run current state function.
inline void VirtualFSM::TransferState::exec(BaseFSM * const fsm) {
BaseFSM * baseFSM;
State * state;

if (_transFSM) {
  _transFSM->saveEnd(_transEnd);
  baseFSM = _transFSM;
  state = _transStart;
  }
else {
  // No transfer FSM defined; bypass.
  baseFSM = fsm;
  state = _transEnd;
  }
// Set current state if new state defined else halt FSM.
if (state)
  fsm->nextState(*state, baseFSM);
else
  // Ended abnormally.
  fsm->halt();
}
```

```
// Finite state machine template.
template <class T>
class FSM : virtual public VirtualFSM, private BaseFSM {
  protected:

  // Simple FSM state function.
  class FuncState : public State {
    typedef
      void (T::* Func)();

    const Func _f;  // State function.
    public:
    FuncState(Func f) : State(), _f(f) { }
    ~FuncState() { }

    protected:
    // Run current state function.
    virtual void exec(BaseFSM * const fsm) {
    // Convert current FSM to T type.
    T * const t = (T * const)(FSM<T> * const)fsm;

    // Call associated member function.
    (t->*_f)();
    }
    };

  // Protected constructor means class can only be base class.
  FSM() : VirtualFSM(0, 0), BaseFSM() { }

  virtual ~FSM() { }
  // Return pointer to BaseFSM class.
  BaseFSM * base() {
  return ((BaseFSM * const)this);
  }

  // End this FSM.
  void endFSM() {
  // Class derived privately from BaseFSM; transfer control.
  BaseFSM::endFSM();
  }
  };
#endif
```

■ LISTING 22.8 BADGE.H

```
#include "fsm.h"

class Badge : public FSM<Badge> {
  char _badge[5];

  protected:
  // Determine if badge is valid.
```

```
virtual int isValid(const char * badge);

public:// *** See note 1.

// Check the reader for a badge.
void checkForBadge();

// Badge waiting at the reader.
void readBadge();

// No badge waiting at the reader.
virtual void noBadge();

// Test badge for validity.
void validateBadge();

// Badge was bad.
void badBadge();

protected:
static FuncState _checkForBadge;

private:
static FuncState _readBadge;
static FuncState _noBadge;
static FuncState _validateBadge;
static FuncState _badBadge;

public:
Badge() : VirtualFSM(base(), &_checkForBadge), FSM<Badge>() { }
~Badge() { }
};
```

■ LISTING 22.9 BADGE.CPP

```
#include <bios.h>
#include <iostream.h>
#include "badge.h"

FSM<Badge>::FuncState Badge::_checkForBadge(&Badge::checkForBadge);
FSM<Badge>::FuncState Badge::_readBadge(&Badge::readBadge);
FSM<Badge>::FuncState Badge::_noBadge(&Badge::noBadge);
FSM<Badge>::FuncState Badge::_validateBadge(&Badge::validateBadge);
FSM<Badge>::FuncState Badge::_badBadge(&Badge::badBadge);

// Determine if badge is valid.
int Badge::isValid(const char * badge) {
return (1);
}

// Check the reader for a badge.
void Badge::checkForBadge() {
```

```
nextState(bioskey(1) ? _readBadge : _noBadge);
}

// Badge waiting at the reader.
void Badge::readBadge() {
// Default next state is to validate badge.
nextState(_validateBadge);
for (int i = 0; i < 4; i++) {
  char c = bioskey(0) & 0xFF;
  // ESC key halts FSM.
  if (c == 0x1B) {
    i = 4;
    halt();
    }
  else {
    _badge[i] = c;
    cout << c;
    }
  }
_badge[4] = 0;
cout << endl;
}

// No badge waiting at the reader.
void Badge::noBadge() {
// Check again until badge is read.
nextState(_checkForBadge);
}

// Test badge for validity.
void Badge::validateBadge() {
if (isValid(_badge))
  // A valid badge means the end of this FSM.
  endFSM();
else
  nextState(_badBadge);
}

// Badge was bad.
void Badge::badBadge() {
cout << "Invalid badge." << endl;
nextState(_checkForBadge);
}

#if defined(TEST_BADGE)
int main() {
Badge b;

b.runFSM();
return (0);
}
#endif
```

■ LISTING 22.10 GATE.H

```
#include "fsm.h"

class Gate : public FSM<Gate> {
  int _timesOpen; // Number of times gate opened.

  // Open the gate.
  void openGate();

  // Close the gate.
  void closeGate();

  public: // *** See note 1.

  // Check for outgoing vehicle.
  void checkOutgoing();

  // Outgoing vehicle waiting.
  void outgoing();

  // No outgoing vehicle waiting.
  virtual void noOutgoing();

  // Wait for outgoing vehicle to clear gate.
  void outgoingWait();

  // Incoming vehicle waiting.
  void incoming();

  // Wait for incoming vehicle to clear gate.
  void incomingWait();

  protected:
  static FuncState _checkOutgoing;
  static FuncState _incoming;

  private:
  static FuncState _noOutgoing;
  static FuncState _outgoing;
  static FuncState _outgoingWait;
  static FuncState _incomingWait;

  public:
  Gate() : VirtualFSM(base(), &_checkOutgoing), FSM<Gate>(),
  _timesOpen(0) { }

  ~Gate() { }
  };
```

■ LISTING 22.11 GATE.CPP

```
#include <bios.h>
#include <iostream.h>
#include "gate.h"

FSM<Gate>::FuncState Gate::_checkOutgoing(&Gate::checkOutgoing);
FSM<Gate>::FuncState Gate::_incoming(&Gate::incoming);
FSM<Gate>::FuncState Gate::_outgoing(&Gate::outgoing);
FSM<Gate>::FuncState Gate::_noOutgoing(&Gate::noOutgoing);
FSM<Gate>::FuncState Gate::_outgoingWait(&Gate::outgoingWait);
FSM<Gate>::FuncState Gate::_incomingWait(&Gate::incomingWait);

// Open the gate.
void Gate::openGate() {
cout << '(' << ++_timesOpen << ")Gate is open ... proceed." << endl;
}

// Close the gate.
void Gate::closeGate() {
cout << "Gate is closed." << endl << endl;
}

// Check for outgoing vehicle.
void Gate::checkOutgoing() {
// Right shift is outgoing sensor pad.
nextState(bioskey(2) & 0x01 ? _outgoing : _noOutgoing);
}

// Outgoing vehicle waiting.
void Gate::outgoing() {
cout << "Outgoing vehicle." << endl;
openGate();
nextState(_outgoingWait);
}

// No outgoing vehicle waiting.
void Gate::noOutgoing() {
nextState(_checkOutgoing);
}

// Wait for outgoing vehicle to clear gate.
void Gate::outgoingWait() {
// Left shift is incoming sensor pad.
if (bioskey(2) & 0x02) {
  // Wait for vehicle to move off pad.
  while (bioskey(2) & 0x02);
  closeGate();
  nextState(_checkOutgoing);
  }
}

// Incoming vehicle waiting.
void Gate::incoming() {
```

```
cout << "Incoming vehicle." << endl;
openGate();
nextState(_incomingWait);
}

// Wait for incoming vehicle to clear gate.
void Gate::incomingWait() {
// Right shift is outgoing sensor pad.
if (bioskey(2) & 0x01) {
  // Wait for vehicle to move off pad.
  while (bioskey(2) & 0x01);
  closeGate();
  endFSM();
  }
}
```

■ LISTING 22.12 BADGGATE.H

```
#include "badge.h"
#include "gate.h"

class BadgeGate : public FSM<BadgeGate>, public Badge,
public Gate {
  protected:
  // Determine if badge is valid.
  virtual int isValid(const char * badge);

  public:// *** See note 1.

  // Prompt user for badge or outgoing vehicle.
  void promptUser();

  // No badge waiting at the reader.
  virtual void noBadge();

  // No outgoing vehicle waiting.
  virtual void noOutgoing();

  private:
  static FSM<BadgeGate>::FuncState _promptUser;
  TransferState _checkReader;
  TransferState _checkGate;
  TransferState _openIncoming;

  public:
  BadgeGate() : VirtualFSM(FSM<BadgeGate>::base(), &_promptUser),
  FSM<BadgeGate>(), Badge(), Gate(),
  _checkReader(FSM<Badge>::base(), &_checkForBadge, &_openIncoming),
  _checkGate(FSM<Gate>::base(), &_checkOutgoing, 0),
  _openIncoming(FSM<Gate>::base(), &_incoming, &_promptUser) { }

  ~BadgeGate() { }
  };
```

■ LISTING 22.13 BADGGATE.CPP

```
#include <iostream.h>
#include "baddgate.h"

FSM<BadgeGate>::FuncState
BadgeGate::_promptUser(&BadgeGate::promptUser);

// Determine if badge is valid.
int BadgeGate::isValid(const char * badge) {
return (badge[0] == 'P' || badge[0] == 'p');
}

// Prompt user for badge or outgoing vehicle.
void BadgeGate::promptUser() {
cout << "Scan badge or pass over outgoing sensor pad." << endl;
nextState(_checkReader);
}

// No badge waiting at the reader.
void BadgeGate::noBadge() {
nextState(_checkGate, FSM<BadgeGate>::base());
}

// No outgoing vehicle waiting.
void BadgeGate::noOutgoing() {
nextState(_checkReader, FSM<BadgeGate>::base());
}

int main() {
BadgeGate bg;

bg.runFSM();
return (0);
}
```

■ LISTING 22.14 FSMSCHED.CPP

```
#define Uses_TApplication
#define Uses_TNSCollection
#include <tv.h>
#include "fsm.h"

class FSMCollection : public TNSCollection {
  int _fsmIndex;
  public:
  FSMCollection() : TNSCollection(10, 5), _fsmIndex(0) { }

  // Remove the FSM that was last run.
  void removeFSM() {
  delete (VirtualFSM *)at(--_fsmIndex);
  atRemove(_fsmIndex);
  }
```

```
  // Return the current FSM and advance the index.
  VirtualFSM * curFSM() {
  if (_fsmIndex == count)
    _fsmIndex = 0;
  return (count ? (VirtualFSM *)at(_fsmIndex++) : 0);
  }
  };

class FSMScheduler : public TApplication {
  FSMCollection _fsmList;
  public:
  FSMScheduler();

  // Add an FSM to be run in the background.
  void insertFSM(VirtualFSM * fsm) {
  _fsmList.insert(fsm);
  }

  // Override idle() function to run scheduled FSM's.
  virtual void idle() {
  VirtualFSM * fsm;
  TApplication::idle();

  // Run FSM if any available and delete if it runs to completion.
  if ((fsm = _fsmList.curFSM()) != 0 && !fsm->runState())
    _fsmList.removeFSM();
  }
  };
```

Contributors

Jeff Duntemann has been in technical publishing since 1985, when he joined *PC Tech Journal* as Technical Editor. He created and edited Borland's *TURBO TECHNIX*, and is currently editor of *PC TECHNIQUES*, the programmers' magazine he founded with Keith Weiskamp. Jeff has written six books, including *Complete Turbo Pascal*, *Turbo Pascal Solutions*, and most recently *Assembly Language Step By Step*. Jeff lives in Scottsdale, AZ, with his wife, Carol, and Mr. Byte, a Bichon Frise who is older than the IBM PC, and (occasionally) crankier.

Keith Weiskamp is an accomplished writer, book developer, and publisher. He has authored and coauthored more than a dozen books on computers including *The Complete C++ Primer*, *Power Graphics Using Turbo C++*, *Object-Oriented Programming with Turbo C++*, and *Windows 3.1 Insider*. Keith is the publisher and cofounder of *PC TECHNIQUES* and president of the Coriolis Group. He lives in Scottsdale, AZ.

Martin O. Waldron is a writer, programmer, and computer consultant living in El Cerrito, CA. He is currently working with a company that develops automated customer service software. As technical editor of this book, Martin was responsible for adapting and fine-tuning the tools presented in the book. His major hobby is making beer.

Ron Aaron is currently a principal engineer at Traveling Software, where he tries to foment unrest while writing connectivity software. When not rabble-rousing, he enjoys reading, gardening, and raising his daughters. Ron can be reached on CompuServe at 71551,1767.

Michael Abrash writes high-performance graphics code for Microsoft. He is the author of *Zen of Assembly* and a contributor to *PC TECHNIQUES.*

Peter Aitken is on the faculty at Duke University Medical Center, where he uses PCs extensively in his research on the nervous system. He has been writing on microcomputer subjects for almost 10 years, with over 65 magazine articles and 13 books to his credit. Peter is a contributing editor at *PC TECHNIQUES.* Peter can be reached on CompuServe at 76367,136.

Eric D. Anderson is the president of Moon Valley Software, a software development and consulting firm in Phoenix, AZ, specializing in Windows programming.

Mike Bertrand teaches mathematics and programming at Madison Area Technical College, Madison, WI.

Bob Blumenfeld has been convincing computers to do what he wants them to since the early mainframe days of the mid-1960s. His impossible dream was always to have a computer of his own—now he does.

Michael Burton is a senior software engineer in the Advanced Technology Group at Key Tronic Corporation in Spokane, WA. He has been programming since 1967. Michael can be reached on CompuServe at 71211,70.

Scott Bussinger owns Professional Practice Systems, a vendor of practice management systems for optometric offices. Scott can bc rcachcd on CompuScrvc at 72247,2671.

Tom Campbell is the author of the *C Programmer's Guide to Windows* and *DOS File Formats* from Addison-Wesley and COMPUTE Book's *101 Tips for FoxPro for Windows*. He owns the South Bay Company and is currently at work on a new language.

Brian Cheetham is an independent consultant in Crofton, MD. His work includes using Windows "highroad" tools to develop Client /Server applications. He is interested in database design, as well as both DOS and Windows Programming.

Greg Chursenoff received his B.S. in Engineering at UCLA during the turbulent '60s. He worked at a variety of hardware and software design jobs during the '70s and '80s. He is now a consulting engineer in the Los Angeles area specializing in real-time embedded micro-controllers.

Paul S. Cilwa has been programming since 1978, having devoted his life to object-oriented programming for Microsoft Windows. He also writes humor and science fiction. Currently he resides in New Hampshire with his computer, 46-inch television set, and pictures of his four children.

David Clark has a Ph.D. in Chemistry and has been programming microcomputers since attending graduate school in the late 1970s. He works in the Diagnostics Division of Miles, Inc., where he develops test methods for automated blood chemistry analyzers. When not programming, David spends his time gardening or making furniture.

Chuck Cooper is the senior software engineer at Kallista, Inc., developing add-in products for Paradox users and developers. He has also worked on programs distributed by Borland International, Great Plains Software, Persoft, and others. His interests include relational database theory and object-oriented programming in C++, Turbo Pascal, and assembler.

Deborah Cooper has been programming in assembly language for the past ten years. Many of her utilities have been published in various computer journals. At the present time, she is in the process of writing a book about assembly programming techniques.

Russ Cooper is a freelance software engineer who writes embedded micro-controller firmware and PC application programs. Russ lives with his wife in Phoenix, AZ, where they enjoy flying, sailing, and judicious quantities of chocolate.

Donald Costello started his professional career as an experimental nuclear physicist. Over the last 30 years he has been slowly transformed into a computer programmer. Don is employed by IRT Corporation and is currently developing programs for automatic x-ray inspection equipment used to inspect automobile air bag inflators.

Michael Covington does research in Artificial Intelligence and computational linguistics at the University of Georgia. He is the author of *Natural Language Processing for Prolog Programmers* (forthcoming from Prentice-Hall), *Computer Science Study Keys* (Barron's Educational Series), several other books, and numerous articles covering computers, electronics, and astronomy.

Kevin Dean is a systems integrator with Application Solutions Inc., in Toronto, Canada. He specializes in serial communications and bar-code programming, mostly in C++. Kevin can be reached on CompuServe at 76336,3114.

Tom DePew has worked as a contract programmer and instructor in the Dallas, Texas, area for the past several years. He uses object-oriented programming techniques in his code, whether or not the language being used supports that methodology. He lives with his wife, Connie, and children, Tommy, Joseph, and Rebecca.

Evan H. Dygert is the owner of Dygert Consulting, Inc., which specializes in Microsoft Windows client server applications development.

Bruce Eckel is a member of the ANSI C++ committee and the owner of Revolution2, a C++ consulting firm. He is the author of *Using C++* (Osborne/McGraw Hill 1989) and *Computer Interfacing with Pascal & C* (1988, available from the author.)

Philip Erdelsky is an R&D engineer at Data/Ware Development Inc., in San Diego, CA. He was formerly an assistant professor of mathematics at the University of California at San Diego. He holds a Ph.D. in Mathematics from the California Institute of Technology.

Bob Falk is the President of Falk Data Systems and the editor in chief for Sofsource, Inc. He is the author of several software products including Easy Format and the Programmers Productivity Pack. Bob served on the Board of Directors of the Association of Shareware Professionals from 1990 to 1991.

Tim Farley is a software engineer for Magee Enterprises in Norcross, GA. He is the author of Magee's Network H.Q., a LAN workstation inventory utility. When not programming, he enjoys being involved in Atlanta's electronic BBS community, reading science fiction and comedy books, and competing in automobile road rallies.

Bryan Flamig is an independent software developer. He has authored and coauthored several books, including *The Complete C++ Primer* and *Turbo C++: A Self Teaching Guide*. Bryan can be reached on CompuServe at 73057,3172.

R.S. Fleischmann II received a B.S. in Chemical Engineering from Carnegie Mellon in 1959 and was employed in the commercial electronic power industry until his retirement in 1990. He has been building and programming computers, a natural outgrowth of his lifelong interest in electronics, since the late 1970s. He now teaches and consults in the PC field.

Marty Franz is a senior software engineer with Allen Test Products in Kalamazoo, MI. He is responsible for the design of automotive diagnostic systems on PCs and embedded processors. He is also a free-lance writer and contributing editor to *PC TECHNIQUES.*

Gordon Free graduated with an M.S. in Computer Science from the University of Illinois in 1984. He is currently a principal engineer at Traveling Software where he heads the Blackbird project. Gordon has been programming IBM PCs since 1982 and is often seen prying CPUs from their sockets to attach logic analyzers. When he's not tearing apart computers, Gordon enjoys photography, woodworking, and spending time with his wife and daughter.

Kenneth Gladden has been a daytime corporate drone since 1969, while moonlighting nights and weekends as a PC hacker since 1976. In addition, through his company, Kibbage Data Services, he is a value-added reseller and PC consultant. He can be reached on CompuServe at 72301,2627.

Brett Glass is a consultant and author residing in Palo Alto, CA.

Kim Hastings had been programming with C for five years. His work primarily consists of custom data acquisition programs with database and graphical output capabilities. His most recent projects have been written in C++ for the Windows 3.1 environment.

Loren Heiny is a software developer and author of numerous computer programming books including *Windows Graphics Programming with Borland C++*.

Dan Illowsky is a specialist in making programs run small and fast. He is a software magician at General Magic, a startup company in Mountain View, CA. Dan can be reached on Internet at Dan-Illowsky@genmagic.com.

Tab Julius is president of Penworks Corporation, a small software development company in New Hampshire. Previously he was the software manager and lead engineer for version 3.0 of Express Publisher, a popular desktop publishing program. When he's not slaving away, he's usually windsurfing or snowboarding somewhere, or eating chili peppers.

Jim Kyle has been an unabashed hacker since 1967 and a desktop-system programmer since 1981. He is Director of Research Projects at Automation Resources, Inc., and develops imaging software and programming tools when he's not writing books, magazine articles, or disassembling yet another operating system for fun. Jim can be reached on CompuServe as 76703,762.

Anthony Lander is an undergraduate student studying at the Carleton University School of Computer Science in Ottawa, Canada.

Marv Luse is founder and president of Autumn Hill Software. He has been involved in computing since the late '60s when he was a student at MIT. He is currently working on a book for Addison-Wesley titled *Graphic File Programming in C++* to be published in the spring of 1993.

Jack Mefford designs high performance in-circuit emulators for Applied Microsystems Corporation in Redmond, WA.

Dr. Michael Milligan is a professor of computer and information science at Front Range Community College. He also develops simulation models in the Wind Energy Laboratory. He lives in Colorado with his wife and two young daughters.

Jim Mischel is a technical editor for *PC TECHNIQUES* and the author of *Macro Magic with Turbo Assembler.*

Hugh Myers likes to think of himself as an ex-silversmith who finds cutting code easier than cleaning brushes.

Alan Nielsen works for Utah Power and Light as a Control Systems Analyst. His programming passion is the PC. When not programming, he can often be found in the refreshing Utah mountain air with his family, in the service of his religion, or pushing wood on a chess board.

Christopher Nelson is the president of S/Wizardry, Ltd., a computer consulting and software development company in Troy, NY. He writes the PC topics and Windows/NewWave columns for *Interact* and is a frequent contributor to *PC TECHNIQUES*. He can be reached on CompuServe at 70441,3321, and on Internet at nelsonc@cs.rpi.edu.

Dr. William G. Nettles, N5XLR/A, teaches physics and engineering at Mississippi College in Clinton, MS. He enjoys rose growing, traveling in the CIS, Bible studies, and his family. Currently he is studying Russian and is looking for scalable Cyrillic fonts for a Laserjet III.

John Pack was born in Sherman, TX, in 1951. He took a beginners' computer class at the local junior college in 1986. Before long, he had taken nearly every programming class available. He currently works in sales but does consulting and keeps busy with computers in one fashion or another. John's favorite languages are Pascal and assembly.

Bill Pierpoint enjoys hiking through the chaparral of the Santa Monica Mountains. When not hiking, he's tracking down software bugs as a consulting engineer at Computer Sciences Corporation.

Russell Preston received a B.S. degree in Systems Science in 1986. Using both VAXes and IBM PC clones, he has written software to collect and analyze data from SDI facility, remotely control test equipment, and control radar simulating hardware. He also has used C++ to create several Windows applications.

Tony Rein flies turboprops for a commuter airline and is learning how much money (and time) a house can take up. He has been playing with PCs for four years and is trying to start a one-person consulting firm (Oriole Computing). Tony can be reached on CompuServe at 76276,2662.

Jeff Roberts is a programmer at RAD Software, a Windows Programming house in Salt Lake City. He was the principal Windows programmer on Microsoft Golf and has contributed to many other products, including Norton Desktop for Windows, Quattro Pro, and RealSound for Windows.

Daev Roehr works for Borland International. He lives in the Santa Cruz Mountains with his wife and several peculiar cats. Powered by espresso, he dabbles with audio, video, electronics design, home renovation, and learning to spell his name.

Howard Rosenberg is president of Improve Yourself Software Company, a New Jersey firm that develops, in Turbo Pascal, both OOPS applications and automated testing software. He has a Ph.D. from Syracuse University, has taught at the college level, and is the author of the A La Carte menu program.

Rich Sadowsky is a software engineer for TurboPower Software in Colorado Springs, CO. Rich is the chief architect of TurboPower's Win/Sys Library product, and a frequent author on programming topics.

Bruce Schneiner has a B.S. in Physics and an M.S. in Computer Science. He is currently working as a consultant in computer and data security and can be reached at 730 Fair Oaks Dr., Oak Park, IL 60602.

George Seaton is the senior systems engineer with Sasec Inc., a Phoenix-based specialist in computer control systems support. And when he's not doing that, he's a technical editor for *PC TECHNIQUES* and a close, personal friend of Wynn E. Poohbah.

Jon Shemitz is a software craftsman who works at home in Santa Cruz, CA. He has a B.A. in Philosophy from Yale, and loves programming, cooking, gardening, desktop publishing, the beach, and his family. He has finally written enough that he's starting to enjoy writing itself, not just *having written*.

George Shepherd has been developing Windows and OS/2 Applications since 1989. He is currently a senior software engineer for NIRSystems in Silver Spring, MD., developing a software interface running under Windows NT for several of their Chemical Analyzers. George's CompuServe ID is 70023,1000.

Peter Skye was born in New York City in 1947 and holds a B.S. in Applied Mathematics and Computer Science from Washington University in St. Louis. He was an IBM Systems Engineer in the 1960s, a rock-and-roll disc jockey for five years in St. Louis, chief engineer for American Top 40 with Casey Kasem for 11 years in Hollywood, a rock-and-roll record producer, and a chief engineer for Capital Cities/American Broadcasting Corporation. He retired at age 38 in 1985.

Chuck Somerville, a programmer since 1976, writes software for mainframes, Pick Operating System minicomputers, and microcomputers, for Eastman Kodak's Dayton, Ohio, inkjet printer facility. He has also taught (Operating Systems, PC Assembly Language, C Programming, Introduction to MS-DOS, and Introduction to Data Processing) at a local college.

Tom Swan is the author of numerous books on computer programming, including *Turbo Pascal for Windows 3.0 Programming* published by Bantam. Tom is a regular columnist for *PC TECHNIQUES* and has written hundreds of articles for publications including *PC World* and *Borland Language Express*. In past years, Tom has worked as a contract programmer and consultant, and he recently developed the *World of ObjectWindows* video courses for Borland International. Tom and his wife, Anne, live in Pennsylvania and spend most of their free time traveling and sailing.

Nick Temple is currently a student at Jefferson Community College. He also works for Tek industries, where he can be reached at 5410 Pamela Drive, Louisville, KY. 40219-4037.

Kas Thomas is the author of the commercial data compression program PakWorks for MacIntosh. He is a consultant for high-speed compression utilities and can be reached via America Online at: MIRACLE3.

Leland Van Allen is an electronics engineer for Fairchild Space Company. He has written a family of filter designs in Turbo Pascal that he would be happy to share with anyone with similar interests. He can be reached at home (301) 681-5336, or work (301) 220-5664.

Terrence Vaughn started hacking computer hardware and software back when the 6502 was the big thing, later graduating to the 80x86 and embedded controllers. Writing occasionally for computer and electronics magazines, he works for a company specializing in high-reliability and weapons grade electronics.

Cye H. Waldman earned his Ph.D. from Princeton University in 1969. He has been a technical consultant for over 16 years, specializing in mathematical modeling of physical systems. His primary interests are radiative transfer and combustion. He is also interested in programming the numerical coprocessor and has developed several math libraries.

Kevin Weeks is a frequent contributor to programming magazines. He has been programming, primarily (and preferably) on microcomputers, since 1980, and has written programs ranging from the control system for a therapeutic bed to a multiuser, database query system using remote, hand-held, radio-linked terminals.

Alan Weiner is president of Technology 21, a loosely organized consulting group. He has been twiddling bits since the late 1960s and writing system-level software since the days of the 8080. Other interests include motorcycle touring, karate, and Annette. Alan can be reached on BIX as "aweiner" or at Technology 21 at (617) 893-7240.

Nicholas Wilt is a software engineer currently residing in Massachusetts. His interests include photorealistic computer graphics, 80x86 assembler, and C++ programming. He welcomes constructive feedback about his work and can be reached at 755 Middlesex Tpke., Billerica, MA 01821.

Shawn Wolf develops bar-code labeling software for General Data Company in Pittsburgh, PA. He is also the author of MOM, a shareware disk menu manager that is distributed by BBS's throughout the U.S. and Europe.

Allen Wyatt has been working with small computers for more than a dozen years and has worked in virtually all facets of programming. He has written 15 books related to computing, programming, and programming languages. He is the president of Discovery Computing, Inc., a microcomputer consulting and services corporation. In his spare time, he likes to spend time with his wife and children doing the things families do together.

Wayne Yacco is a formally trained information scientist, a former programmer, and consultant, who now devotes all his time to writing about computers.

Index

Page numbers in italic refer to code listings.

A

B

C

D

E

F

G

H

T

X

Y

Z